750
C+H

59-122 30

9-29-61

The Golden Age of American History

The
GOLDEN AGE
of AMERICAN
HISTORY

Selected and edited

with an introduction and notes by

FRANK FREIDEL

GEORGE BRAZILLER, INC.

NEW YORK 1959

For John D. Hicks

Contents

Introduction

by Frank Freidel

DURING THE MIDDLE YEARS OF THE NINETEENTH CENTURY, AMERICANS viewed with self-conscious pride the new expanse, wealth, and power of their nation. As befitted a prosperous and growing people, they produced their own talented array of men of letters who in novels, poetry, and essays developed American themes. Among the writers were a group of American historians who, writing sweeping narrative in a grand manner, celebrated the heritage of the United States. There were George Bancroft, William Hickling Prescott, Francis Parkman, and Henry Adams, whose great reputations are still remembered, and there were a number of others, some of whom made their names outside the field of history, as did Theodore Roosevelt and Woodrow Wilson. Altogether they so ably combined literary skill with scholarship that they justly obtained wide audiences and created a golden age of American historical writing.

Many of these historians, beginning with the first great trio—Prescott, Bancroft, and Parkman—undertook to write epic history on the model of the classic historians of Greece and Rome—Thucydides and Tacitus—and the more recent European historians. Almost all of them from Prescott to Roosevelt were admirers of Edward Gibbon's *Decline and Fall of the Roman Empire,* and indeed both Prescott and Henry Adams cited Gibbon's *Autobiography* as having given them an early impetus toward historical writing. Like the classical writers and Gibbon, they developed large themes on huge canvases, filled with heroes sometimes twice as large as life, who were engaged less often in the slow building of political, social, and economic institutions than in the flash and excitement of combat. The impression was sometimes not unlike that of the huge paintings of Peter Paul Rubens, Louis David, or Benjamin West.

These men produced readable history for large and appreciative audiences. Much of it at the present time is still readable, and worth reading. They were, as Samuel Eliot Morison has said of Prescott, masters of narrative, "which history essentially is, a fact which too many modern historians have forgotten." They regarded historical writing as a branch of letters, and careful though they might be in their research, they seldom neglected form and style. Prescott, as he prepared himself for a writing career, in 1821 outlined a course of study for himself:

"1. Principles of grammar, correct writing &c;

"2. Compendious history of North America;

"3. Fine prose-writers of English from Roger Ascham to the present day, principally with reference to their mode of writing,—not including historians, except as far as requisite for an acquaintance with style;

"4. Latin classics one hour a day."

Through the nineteenth century, an emphasis upon style was a hallmark of this group oi historians. Even one of the less successful writers of history viewed as literature, John Bach McMaster, tried to pattern his writing after the rolling sonorous phrases of Macaulay. Late in the century, when a group of professional historians were coming to emphasize history as a science rather than as an art, gentlemen-historians like Theodore Roosevelt protested vigorously. "It seems rather odd that it should be necessary to insist upon the fact that the essence of a book is to be readable," he wrote as a young man, "but most certainly the average scientific or historical writer needs to have this elementary proposition drilled into his brain." James Ford Rhodes, who even more than Roosevelt appreciated the necessity for diligent historical research, complained nevertheless in 1900:

"It seems to me that our scientific historians have done a good deal of good by their methods af teaching history, but in their eagerness to get at original material and make a comprehensive search, they have overlooked the importance of digesting materials, of accurate generalizations and method of expression. As Morse Stephens says, when he reads over a sentence of his that seems particularly good, he scratches it out and rewrites it, for fear someone will think he is aiming at fine writing."

Few of the writers of monographs had the opportunity or skill to write history that was literature; for the most part they were specialists who, writing for specialists, did not even notice that they had lost the broad audience of their nineteenth-century predecessors. They were content to leave popular historical writing to men who often lacked the literary as well as the scholarly standards of earlier generations. Yet between the technical monograph and the superficial potboiler there was a broad area in which historians combining modern standards of scholarship with vigorous style, built upon the old traditions. By the middle of the twentieth century, more sound, readable American history was being published than ever before.

The rise of the monograph had expanded the frontiers of historical knowledge; it had led to an exploration of many an economic or social area which had been *terra incognita* to the nineteenth century historians. It filled in with minute detail what had been hazy or ill-drawn lines on their maps. And with the zeal of explorers, many of the scientific historians in proclaiming their own discoveries had emphasized the errors in fact or interpretation, the shortcomings, and the omissions of the earlier writers. A pioneer generation of archaeologists and anthropologists hooted down Prescott's descriptions of the Aztec empire, only to have the modern generation find that Prescott, despite his outmoded early nineteenth-century judgments, was on the whole more accurate in his evaluations than his detractors. The works of Prescott and most of the others represented in this volume, with the notable exception of the polemicists on the outbreak of the Civil War and Woodrow Wilson writing on his own times, still merit being read both as history and literature.

The earlier group of nineteenth-century historians were genteel Bostonians, not dependent upon historical writing for their livelihood. They had sufficient funds to invest in extensive research, adequate leisure to engage in projects that consumed years of work, and an elite social circle that gave its approbation to their writings. Henry Adams, who, in some ways perpetuated their tradition in the closing years of the century, in 1872 wrote amusingly about them in a letter of advice to Henry Cabot Lodge:

"There is only one way to look at life, and that is the practical way. . . . The question is whether the historico-literary line is practically worth following, not whether it will amuse or improve you. Can you make it *pay?* either in money, reputation, or any other solid value. Now if you think for a moment of the most respectable and respected products of our town of Boston, I think you will see at once that this profession does pay. No one has done better and won more in any business or pursuit, than has been acquired by men like Prescott, Motley, Frank Parkman, Bancroft, and so on in historical writing; none of them men of extraordinary gifts, or who would have been likely to do very much in the world if they had chosen differently. What they did can be done by others."

Adams, as so often, was overcritical. There were few others, except for Adams himself, who could achieve as well as they; Adams was far too disparaging of his own nine-volume history. But Adams was right in one respect, the wonder was that Prescott and Parkman did anything in the world at all. Both of them were purblind and in ill health most of their adult years; in their comfortable financial circumstances they would have been excused by everyone if they had spent their lives idly as gentlemen of semi-invalided leisure.

William Hickling Prescott (1796-1859) when he was a junior at Harvard was a victim of student roistering. As he was leaving Commons Hall after dinner one day, he turned and was struck in the left eye by a large hard crust of bread. The appearance of the eye remained unchanged, but the sight in it was gone; a year and a half later, his right eye became so inflamed that he was threatened with total and permanent blindness. He recovered part of his sight, but for the remainder of his life suffered from attacks of acute rheumatism.

While all but a few intimates knew him only as a fine social companion, Prescott was quietly learning his craft and slowly writing a study of Ferdinand and Isabella. When finally in 1837 he arranged publication, he confessed his diffidence, remarking, "During the ten years I have been occupied with the work, few of my friends have heard me say as many words about it." Thus it was that Daniel Webster, who had known Prescott only in the drawing room, referred to him with surprise as a comet that suddenly burst upon the world.

It was no transitory flash, for Prescott immediately began to gather materials for even more ambitious studies. His background led him again toward a Spanish subject, and early in 1838 he concluded, "On reflection nothing in this field seems to me to offer such advantages for an American as the Conquest of Mexico by Cortés." For several years he employed manuscript researchers and copyists in Madrid, investing heavily in his materials. To his dismay when he was well embarked upon the project, he discovered that Washington Irving, who had recently finished a life of Columbus, was also planning to write on Cortés. Irving graciously relinquished the subject although, he later commented, "I, in a manner, gave him up my bread; for I depended upon the profit of it to recruit my waning finances."

Because of his defective sight, Prescott worked with a secretary who could read to him, and wrote with a noctograph or writing-case for the blind. Its parallel brass wires guided his ivory stylus as he wrote on a piece of carbon paper that made a barely legible impress on a sheet of white paper beneath. After he had gathered and weighed all his material, he would compose a whole chapter in his mind. His secretary once reminisced:

"Many of his best battle-scenes, he told me, he had composed while on horseback. His vivid imagination carried him back to the sixteenth century, and he almost felt himself a Castilian knight, charging with Cortés, Sandóval, and Alvarado on the Aztec foe. . . . When beginning to describe a battle, he would often, to rouse his military enthusiasm, as he said, hum to himself his favorite air, 'O give me but my Arab steed,'. . . . As the sheets were stricken off [on the noctograph], I deciphered them, and was ready to read them to him when he had finished the chapter. He was as cautious in correction as he was rapid in writing. Each word and sentence was carefully weighed, and subjected to the closest analysis. If found wanting in strength or beauty it was changed and turned until the exact expression required was found. . . . He hated fine writing, merely as fine writing. I have known him mercilessly to strike out several pages of beautiful imagery, which he believed on reflection had a tendency rather to weaken than enhance the effect he desired to produce."

Prescott gave as much pains to accuracy as he did to vividness. His reward when the *Conquest of Mexico* appeared in 1843 was the lavish praise of reviewers, and perhaps even more than this the tribute that a reader like Mrs. Henry Wadsworth Longfellow was moved to write in her journal, "Mr. Prescott seems to have seen it all with his own eyes as he makes his reader [see it]." Philip Hone noted in his diary, "Prescott has established his claim to rank as *the* historian of the United States." Before his death in 1859, Prescott was sometimes referred to as "the American Thucydides."

George Bancroft (1800-1891) made history as well as wrote it. He became such a personage that when he died in Washington, ripe with years, President Benjamin Harrison ordered the flags to fly at half-mast on all the public buildings in the city. Bancroft was born in Worcester, Massachusetts, the son of a Congregational minister of limited means and unbounded Calvinist and Federalist conviction. At sixteen he was graduated from Harvard; just before his twenty-first birthday he received his doctorate from Göttingen. The President of Harvard had sent Bancroft there to study theology in preparation for the Unitarian ministry, and this involved what in the end became more important, thorough training in the new German historical methods. Upon his return he did serve as a minister for a while; it left its mark permanently upon his writing in which he saw a favoring providence shaping the destiny of the American people. But he was not made for the pulpit, nor for the tutoring of Greek at Harvard, which he also tried. For four years he was headmaster of Round Hill School, patterned after a German gymnasium, but he tired of this also. He resigned in 1831 to enter upon the two vocations which thereafter absorbed his interest and efforts, politics and historical writing. In both he was a Jacksonian Democrat.

Bancroft's prominence began in 1834 when he attracted notoriety by running for the Massachusetts legislature on a workingmen's ticket, and fame by publishing the first volume of his *History of the United States*. The Democratic President Martin Van Buren appointed him Collector of the Port of Boston in 1837, and Bancroft in turn gave a customs house appointment to Nathaniel Hawthorne. Under President James K. Polk he served as Secretary of the Navy and established the Naval Academy at Annapolis, and in 1846 was appointed Minister to England. When Congress fatefully assembled in December, 1865, it was Bancroft who had written the statesmanlike message that President Andrew Johnson sent to them. It failed to stem the flood of Radical Republican anger against Johnson, but the Senate in 1867 ratified Johnson's appointment of Bancroft to be Minister to Berlin, where he remained into the second Grant administration in 1874.

During all these years Bancroft was collecting mountains of materials, laboriously entering data into bound notebooks, and publishing his enormously successful history volume by volume. Although the cliché is commonplace that every page of Bancroft's history voted for Jackson, his patriotic position stirred all readers regardless of their party affiliations. They might deplore his membership in the Democratic party, but they accepted him as the great historian of the United States. Bancroft was for his part so eager to be considered objective that he was rather bothered by an interchange in 1867 with the German historian Leopold von Ranke:

"One day when I met him . . . he gave an arch twinkle to his eyes and said 'Do you know what I say of you to my classes?' Of course I did not. 'And will you not be angry if I tell you?' And then he continued: 'I tell my hearers, that your history is the best book ever written from the democratic point of view. You are thoroughly consistent; adhere strictly to your method, carry it out in many directions but in all with fidelity, and are always true to it.' I am not certain if this is high praise; for ask yourself what books have been written from the democratic point of view? and then again consider if it is not rather a hard judgment to say that a book is written from a democratic point of view. I deny the charge; if there is democracy in the history it is not subjective, but objective as they say here, and so has necessarily its place in history and gives its colour as it should."

The scientific historians of the end of the nineteenth century and thereafter levelled more serious charges against Bancroft. They lamented that he rendered useless for their purposes the vast collection of documentary material upon which he based his writings since he seldom cited them fully in his footnotes, and seldom quoted them with scrupulous accuracy. His footnotes were sparse, and in several of the later volumes omitted entirely. "I see, sir, that you have many footnotes in your book," he commented to young John Bach McMaster. "That is a mistake. At the cost of great labor you have unearthed certain facts and you tell your readers where they may find them. Some of them will use them and give you no credit." As for Bancroft's habit of changing the language or tense of quotations, transposing them, and running together materials from different sources, these were devices commonplace among classic historians. At least he did not compose elaborate orations, as did they. Vexatious as these inaccuracies are to other historians, they seldom render invalid the general impression Bancroft sought to convey. Finally, critics have hooted at his purple style. An angry Southern reviewer during Reconstruction, with unconscious irony wrote: "Affected, stilted, pretentious, meretricious and hyperbolical, it sounds as if swaggering Thraso spoke it through a tragic mask." Bancroft was sensitive to such jibes, and in his final revision, from which come the selections reprinted, he removed adjectives with diligence. He never ceased to try to improve his work. When he was 82, he sent to one of the finest of the new historians, Justin Winsor, the request that if he or his collaborators "should find an error in my revision or in the as yet unrevised volumes, you will give me *swift* notice; for, brother, the time is short." Bancroft did in many ways improve as an historical writer throughout his long life, but his volumes, fine reading though they are today, bear the mark of the first half of the nineteenth century in their attitudes and assumptions.

Francis Parkman (1823-1893), more conservative in his attitudes, was brought up in the same romantic traditions as Bancroft, yet there ran though his writing echoes of newer voices of thought that set him apart from Prescott and Bancroft. A large part of his writing came in years after the Civil War; indeed only two of the dozen volumes of *France and England in North America* were published before 1865. Heroes dominated the pages of Parkman's books, as in those of earlier historians, but the Indians, despite his prejudice against inferior races, were living men. The great struggle between the French and the English lent itself to romance, but in Parkman's rendition there was scrupulous historical accuracy based on indefatigable research. His style was simple, swift-moving, and full of images. His writing has continued to be a model for those among later generations of historians who have sought to be readable.

Parkman, born into a well-to-do Boston family, went to Harvard, then briefly studied law. But his bad eyesight and chronic ill-health were deterrents against a career in the law, and the lure of the out-of-doors drew him in other directions. He wrote a friend in 1878:

"You ask why I conceived the purpose of writing the history of the French in America? The answer is very simple. In my youth I was fond of letters, and I also liked the forest, shooting, and the Indians. I frequented their camps, I roamed the woods with them, I went shooting, I journeyed on foot and in canoes. I passed my vacations in this way. Well, at an early day I saw that these two tastes, for books and for the forest, could be reconciled, could be made even mutually helpful, in the field of Franco-American history."

Thus it was that Parkman, leaving law school, intensified his visits to old battlefields and along one-time Indian trails in the East, and spent weeks gathering materials in libraries on Pontiac's conspiracy. In 1846, he engaged in the most strenuous of his adventures, travelling for weeks along the Oregon trail, living in an encampment of Sioux Indians, in their dignity and squalor. Parkman combined in his writings what he could learn from old books and manuscripts with what he himself had been able to see, hear, feel, and smell. First, in 1849 came *The Oregon Trail,* then two years later the first two volumes of his large history, *The Conspiracy of Pontiac.* He had married in 1850, had several children, and was happily engaged in his grand project. But he was plagued with arthritis, and in 1857-1858 lost first his only son and then his wife. He suffered such acute head pains that work became impossible, and for the next five years was in such great physical and mental ill-health that he could do little but devote himself to horticulture. In this he was so talented that in 1872 he served briefly as professor of horticulture at Harvard. As his health intermittently improved, he increased the time he spent on his writing. In 1883, he was well enough to take a six-day horseback ride into the White Mountains of New Hampshire. One after another he brought out his volumes. *Montcalm and Wolfe* was published in 1884, and *A Half-Century of Conflict,* which rounded out the series, appeared in 1892. The following year, aged seventy, he was planning a thorough revision of his entire history, but one day in the late autumn after a row on Jamaica Pond he suffered an acute attack of peritonitis, and three days later died. One can apply to Parkman himself the spirit of his tribute to the French explorer La Salle:

"He belonged not to the age of the knight-errant and the saint, but to the modern world of practical action. He was the hero not of a principle nor of a faith, but simply of a fixed idea and a determined purpose. As often happens with concentrated and energetic natures, his purpose was to him a passion and an inspiration; and he clung to it with a certain fanaticism of devotion. It was the offspring of an ambition vast and comprehensive, yet acting in the interest both of France and of civilization. . . . America owes him an enduring memory; for in this masculine figure she sees the pioneer who guided her to the possession of her richest heritage."

Henry Adams (1838-1918) was a young contemporary of Parkman and Bancroft, who combined their mastery of an effective style with a firm acceptance of the canons of modern scientific history. He was less carried away by narrative, less prone to focus on martial scenes and heroes, more insistent upon observing society and the growth of its institutions. To Adams, history was not so much story-telling as a science which might be made to yield useful generalizations.

Adams, who in his early childhood had known the impressive figure of his aged grandfather, ex-President John Quincy Adams, and who had served during the Civil War as secretary to his father, Charles Francis Adams, Minister to England, naturally aspired to an active political career. Disillusioned by the Washington of President Grant, he became an assistant professor at Harvard, where he taught a course in medieval history. He did not find it entirely enjoyable. "Between ourselves the instruction of boys is mean work," he once confided. In 1877, he moved to Washington and embarked upon his *History of the United States of America during the Administrations of Jefferson and Madison.* "The fragment I did," he wrote privately in 1899, "was merely an Introduction to our history during the Nineteenth Century and was intended only to serve the future historian with a fixed and documented starting-point. The real History that one would like to write, was to be built on it, and its merits or demerits, whatever they might be, could be seen only when the structure, of which it was to be the foundation, was raised."

It was indeed a foundation, as Adams had hoped, for the writing of history which would combine sound analysis with literary merit. The sale was disappointingly small compared with that of the works of Prescott, Bancroft, and Parkman—only three thousand sets during the first decade. But Adams's history had posed, and to a considerable degree answered, the challenge to modern historians. In his concluding volume, Adams had declared:

"Historians and readers maintained Old-World standards. No historian cared to hasten the coming of an epoch when man should study his own history in the same spirit and by the same methods with which he studied the formation of a crystal. Yet history has its scientific as well as its human side, and in American history the scientific interest was greater than the human. Elsewhere the student could study under better conditions the evolution of the individual, but nowhere could he study so well the evolution of a race. The interest of such a subject exceeded that of any other branch of science, for it brought mankind within sight of its own end."

Thus evolved historical writing in the United States during the nineteenth century. Very brief sketches of other writers represented in this volume precede the selections from their writings. Space limitations prevented including representative work of other major historians of the nineteenth century, especially Richard Hildreth, Hermann von Holst, and James Schouler. For further reading on the historians and their writings, see the notes at the end of the book. In the selections that follow, generally full sections or chapters appear, whatever their meanderings, in order to present accurately the flavor of the original. Footnotes, since they are for the most part bibliographical, have been eliminated; they may be consulted in the complete editions, cited in the back of this book. I hope these segments will tempt readers to turn to the full works, many of which have long been gathering dust on library shelves. Those that have been forgotten merit rediscovery.

WILLIAM HICKLING PRESCOTT

(1796-1859)

The conquest of Mexico was one of the earliest and most dramatic chapters of the epic unfolding in the New World. It was, commented William Hickling Prescott while he was writing his masterpiece, "as brilliant a subject, with adventures as daring and wonderful as ever occupied the pen of a historian." In his preface he wrote:

"Among the remarkable achievements of the Spaniards in the sixteenth century, there is no one more striking to the imagination than the conquest of Mexico. The subversion of a great empire by a handful of adventurers, taken with all its strange and picturesque accompaniments, has the air of romance rather than of sober history; and it is not easy to treat such a theme according to the severe rules prescribed by historical criticism. But, notwithstanding the seductions of the subject, I have conscientiously endeavored to distinguish fact from fiction, and to establish the narrative on as broad a basis as possible of contemporary evidence."

Prescott had sketched the broad setting in the conclusion of his Ferdinand and Isabella: *"Scarcely was Ferdinand's reign brought to a close before Magellan completed (1520) what the monarch had projected, the circumnavigation of the southern continent; the victorious banners of Cortés had already (1518) penetrated into the golden realms of Montezuma; and Pizarro, a very few years later, (1524), following up the lead of Balboa, embarked on the enterprise which ended in the downfall of the splendid dynasty of the Incas."*

The Conquest of Mexico *opens with rich descriptions of the splendor of Montezuma's empire, fiercely defended by Aztec warriors, and an analysis of its fatal weakness, the incessant levying upon subjugated tribes and warring against hostile ones to obtain thousands of victims for human sacrifice. "An enemy was never slain in battle, if there were a chance of taking him alive," Prescott pointed out. "To this circumstance the Spaniards repeatedly owed their preservation." Next the focus shifts to the ambitious and resourceful Hernando Cortés, landing on the shores of Mexico with an army of only five hundred. While the Aztecs from afar fearfully tried to forestall the advance of the "white god," Cortés skilfully fought, then formed alliances with, several of the tribes ripe for rebellion against the Aztec tyranny. He burned his ships to make retreat impossible, then slowly made his way into the interior to the capital, Tenochtitlán, the present-day Mexico City:*

The Conquest of Mexico

WITH THE FIRST FAINT STREAK OF DAWN, THE SPANISH GENERAL WAS UP, mustering his followers. They gathered, with beating hearts, under their respective banners, as the trumpet sent forth its spirit-stirring sounds across water and woodland, till they died away in distant echoes among the mountains. The sacred flames on the altars of numberless *teocallis,* dimly seen through the grey mists of morning, indicated the site of the capital, till temple, tower, and palace were fully revealed in the glorious illumination which the sun, as he rose above the eastern barrier, poured over the beautiful Valley. It was the eighth of November, 1519; a conspicuous day in history, as that on which the Europeans first set foot in the capital of the Western World.

Cortés with his little body of horse formed a sort of advanced guard to the army. Then came the Spanish infantry, who in a summer's campaign had acquired the discipline, and the weather-beaten aspect, of veterans. The baggage occupied the centre; and the rear was closed by the dark files of Tlascalan warriors. The whole number must have fallen short of seven thousand; of which less than four hundred were Spaniards.

For a short distance, the army kept along the narrow tongue of land that divides the Tezcucan from the Chalcan waters, when it entered on the great dike, which, with the exception of an angle near the commencement, stretches in a perfectly straight line across the salt floods of Tezcuco to the gates of the capital. It was the same causeway, or rather the basis of that, which still forms the great southern avenue of Mexico. The Spaniards had occasion more than ever to admire the mechanical science of the Aztecs, in the geometrical precision with which the work was executed, as well as the solidity of its construction. It was composed of huge stones well laid in cement; and wide enough, throughout its whole extent, for ten horsemen to ride abreast.

They saw, as they passed along, several large towns, resting on piles, and reaching far into the water,—a kind of architecture which found great favor with the Aztecs, being in imitation of that of their metropolis. The busy population obtained a good subsistence from the manufacture of salt,

From Prescott, *History of the Conquest of Mexico,* bk. 3, ch. 9; bk. 4, ch. 3; bk. 5, ch. 1, 3 (in part); bk. 6, ch. 6, 8 (in part).

which they extracted from the waters of the great lake. The duties on the traffic in this article were a considerable source of revenue to the crown.

Everywhere the Conquerors beheld the evidence of a crowded and thriving population, exceeding all they had yet seen. The temples and principal buildings of the cities were covered with a hard white stucco, which glistened like enamel in the level beams of the morning. The margin of the great basin was more thickly gemmed, than that of Chalco, with towns and hamlets. The water was darkened by swarms of canoes filled with Indians, who clambered up the sides of the causeway, and gazed with curious astonishment on the strangers. And here, also, they beheld those fairy islands of flowers, overshadowed occasionally by trees of considerable size, rising and falling with the gentle undulation of the billows. At the distance of half a league from the capital, they encountered a solid work or curtain of stone, which traversed the dike. It was twelve feet high, was strengthened by towers at the extremities, and in the centre was a battle-mented gate-way, which opened a passage to the troops. It was called the Fort of Xoloc, and became memorable in aftertimes as the position occupied by Cortés in the famous siege of Mexico.

Here they were met by several hundred Aztec chiefs, who came out to announce the approach of Montezuma, and to welcome the Spaniards to his capital. They were dressed in the fanciful gala costume of the country, with the *maxtlatl,* or cotton sash, around their loins, and a broad mantle of the same material, or of the brilliant feather-embroidery, flowing gracefully down their shoulders. On their necks and arms they displayed collars and bracelets of turquoise mosaic, with which delicate plumage was curiously mingled, while their ears, under-lips, and occasionally their noses, were garnished with pendants formed of precious stones, or crescents of fine gold. As each cacique made the usual formal salutation of the country separately to the general, the tedious ceremony delayed the march more than an hour. After this, the army experienced no further interruption till it reached a bridge near the gates of the city. It was built of wood, since replaced by one of stone, and was thrown across an opening of the dike, which furnished an outlet to the waters, when agitated by the winds, or swollen by a sudden influx in the rainy season. It was a draw-bridge; and the Spaniards, as they crossed it, felt how truly they were committing themselves to the mercy of Montezuma, who, by thus cutting off their communications with the country, might hold them prisoners in his capital.

In the midst of these unpleasant reflections, they beheld the glittering retinue of the emperor emerging from the great street which led then, as it still does, through the heart of the city. Amidst a crowd of Indian nobles, preceded by three officers of state, bearing golden wands, they saw the royal palanquin blazing with burnished gold. It was borne on the shoulders of nobles, and over it a canopy of gaudy feather-work, powdered with jewels, and fringed with silver, was supported by four attendants of the same rank. They were bare-footed, and walked with a slow, measured pace, and with eyes bent on the ground. When the train had come within a convenient distance, it halted, and Montezuma, descending from his litter, came forward leaning on the arms of the lords of Tezcuco and Iztapalapan, his nephew and brother, both of whom, as we have seen, had already been made known to the Spaniards. As the monarch advanced under the canopy, the obsequious attendants strewed the ground with cotton tapestry, that his imperial feet might not be contaminated by the rude soil. His subjects of high and low degree, who lined the sides of the causeway, bent forward with their eyes fastened on the ground as he passed, and some of the humbler class prostrated themselves before him. Such was the homage paid to the Indian despot, showing that the slavish forms of Oriental adulation were to be found among the rude inhabitants of the Western World.

Montezuma wore the girdle and ample square cloak, *tilmatli,* of his nation. It was made of the finest cotton, with the embroidered ends gathered in a knot round his neck. His feet were defended by sandals having soles of gold, and the leathern thongs which bound them to his ankles were embossed with the same metal. Both the cloak and sandals were sprinkled with pearls and precious stones, among which the emerald and the *chalchivitl*—a green stone of higher estimation than any other among the Aztecs—were conspicuous. On his head he wore no other ornament than a *panache* of plumes of the royal green which floated down his back, the badge of military, rather than of regal, rank.

He was at this time about forty years of age. His person was tall and thin, but not ill-made. His hair, which was black and straight, was not very long; to wear it short was considered unbecoming persons of rank. His beard was thin; his complexion somewhat paler than is often found in his dusky, or rather copper-colored race. His features, though serious in their expression, did not wear the look of melancholy, indeed, of dejection, which characterizes his portrait, and which may well have settled on them at a later period. He moved with dignity, and his whole demeanor, tempered by an expression of benignity not to have been anticipated from the reports circulated of his character, was worthy of a great prince.— Such is the portrait left to us of the celebrated Indian emperor, in this his first interview with the white men.

The army halted as he drew near. Cortés, dismounting, threw his reins to a page, and, supported by a few of the principal cavaliers, advanced to meet him. The interview must have been one of uncommon interest to both. In Montezuma, Cortés beheld the lord of the broad realms he had traversed, whose magnificence and power had been the burden of every tongue. In the Spaniard, on the other hand, the Aztec prince saw the strange being whose history seemed to be so mysteriously connected with his own; the predicted one of his oracles; whose achievements proclaimed him something more than human. But, whatever may have been the monarch's feelings, he so far suppressed them as to receive his guest with princely courtesy, and to express his satisfaction at personally seeing him in his capital. Cortés responded by the most profound expressions of respect, while he made ample acknowledgments for the substantial proofs which the emperor had given the Spaniards of his munificence. He then hung round Montezuma's neck a sparkling chain of colored crystal, accompanying this with a movement as if to embrace him, when he was restrained by the two Aztecs lords, shocked at the menaced profanation of the sacred person of their master. After the interchange of these civilities, Montezuma appointed his brother to conduct the Spaniards to their residence in the capital, and again entering his litter was borne off amidst prostrate crowds in the same state in which he had come. The Spaniards quickly followed, and with colors flying and music playing soon made their entrance into the southern quarter of Tenochtitlan.

Here, again, they found fresh cause for admiration in the grandeur of the city, and the superior style of its architecture. The dwellings of the poorer class were, indeed, chiefly of reeds and mud. But the great avenue through which they were now marching was lined with the houses of the nobles, who were encouraged by the emperor to make the capital their residence. They were built of a red porous stone drawn from quarries in the neighborhood, and, though they rarely rose to a second story, often covered a large space of ground. The flat roofs, *azoteas,* were protected by stone parapets, so that every house was a fortress. Sometimes these roofs resembled parterres of flowers, so thickly were they covered with them, but more frequently these were cultivated in broad terraced gardens, laid out between the edifices. Occasionally a great square or marketplace intervened, surrounded by its porticos of stone and stucco; or a pyramidal temple reared its colossal bulk, crowned with its tapering sanctuaries, and altars blazing with inextinguishable fires. The great street facing the southern causeway, unlike most others in the place, was wide, and extended some miles in nearly a straight line, as before noticed, through the centre of the city. A spectator standing at one end of it, as his eye ranged along the deep vista of temples, terraces, and gardens, might clearly discern the other, with the blue mountains in the distance, which, in the transparent atmosphere of the table-land, seemed almost in contact with the buildings.

But what most impressed the Spaniards was the throngs of people who swarmed through the streets and on the canals, filling every door-way and window, and clustering on the roofs of the buildings. "I well remember the spectacle," exclaims Bernal Diaz; "it seems now, after so many years, as present to my mind, as if it were but yesterday." But what must have been the sensations of the Aztecs themselves, as they looked on the portentous pageant! as they heard, now for the first time, the well-cemented pavement ring under the iron tramp of the horses,—the strange animals which fear had clothed in such supernatural terrors; as they gazed on the children of the East, revealing their celestial origin in their fair complexions; saw the bright falchions and bonnets of steel, a metal to them unknown, glancing like meteors in the sun, while sounds of unearthly music—at least, such as their rude instruments had never wakened—floated in the air! But every other emotion was lost in that of deadly hatred, when they beheld their detested enemy, the Tlascalan, stalking, in defiance, as it were, through their streets, and staring around with looks of ferocity and wonder, like some wild animal of the forest, who had strayed by chance from his native fastnesses into the haunts of civilization.

As they passed down the spacious street, the troops repeatedly traversed bridges suspended above canals, along which they saw the Indian barks gliding swifty with their little cargoes of fruits and vegetables for the markets of Tenochtitlan. At length, they halted before a broad area near the centre of the city, where rose the huge pyramidal pile dedicated to the patron war-god of the Aztecs, second only, in size, as well as sanctity, to the temple of Cholula, and covering the same ground now in part occupied by the great cathedral of Mexico.

Facing the western gate of the inclosure of the temple, stood a low range of stone buildings, spreading over a wide extent of ground, the palace of Axayacatl, Montezuma's father, built by that monarch about fifty years before. It was appropriated as the barracks of the Spaniards. The emperor himself was in the court-yard, waiting to receive them. Approaching Cortés, he took from a vase of flowers, borne by one of his slaves, a massy collar, in which the shell of a species of craw-fish, much prized by the Indians, was set in gold, and connected by heavy links of the same metal. From this chain depended eight ornaments, also of gold, made in resemblance of the same shell-fish, a span in length each, and of delicate workmanship; for the Aztec goldsmiths were confessed to have shown skill in their craft, not inferior to their brethren of Europe. Montezuma, as he hung the gorgeous collar round the general's neck said, "This palace belongs to you, Malinche," (the epithet by which he always addressed him,) "and your brethren. Rest after your fatigues, for you have much need to do so, and in a little while I will visit you again." So saying, he withdrew with his attendants, evincing, in this act, a delicate consideration not to have been expected in a barbarian.

Cortés' first care was to inspect his new quarters. The building, though spacious, was low, consisting of one floor, except, indeed, in the centre, where it rose to an additional story. The apartments were of great size, and afforded accommodations, according to the testimony of the Conquerors themselves, for the whole army! The hardy mountaineers of Tlascala were, probably, not very fastidious, and might easily find a shelter in the out-buildings, or under temporary awnings in the ample court-yards. The best apartments were hung with gay cotton draperies, the floors covered with mats or rushes. There were, also, low stools made of single pieces of wood elaborately carved, and in most of the apartments beds made of the palm-leaf, woven into a thick mat, with coverlets, and sometimes canopies of cotton. These mats were the only beds used by the natives, whether of high or low degree.

After a rapid survey of this gigantic pile, the general assigned his troops their respective quarters, and took as vigilant precautions for security, as if he had anticipated a siege, instead of a friendly entertainment. The place was encompassed by a stone wall of considerable thickness, with towers or heavy buttresses at intervals, affording a good means of defence. He planted his cannon so as to command the approaches, stationed his sentinels along the works, and, in short, enforced in every respect as strict military discipline as had been observed in any part of the march. He well knew the importance to his little band, at least for the present, of conciliating the good-will of the citizens; and, to avoid all possibility of collision, he prohibited any soldier from leaving his quarters without orders, under pain of death. Having taken these precautions, he allowed his men to partake of the bountiful collation which had been prepared for them.

They had been long enough in the country to become reconciled to, if not to relish, the peculiar cooking of the Aztecs. The appetite of the soldier is not often dainty, and on the present occasion it cannot be doubted that the Spaniards did full justice to the savory productions of the royal kitchen. During the meal they were served by numerous Mexican slaves, who were, indeed, distributed through the palace, anxious to do the bidding of the strangers. After the repast was concluded, and they had taken their *siesta,* not less important to a Spaniard than food itself, the presence of the emperor was again announced.

Montezuma was attended by a few of his principal nobles. He was received with much deference by Cortés; and, after the parties had taken their seats, a conversation commenced between them, through the aid of Doña Marina, while the cavaliers and Aztec chieftains stood around in respectful silence.

Montezuma made many inquiries concerning the country of the Spaniards, their sovereign, the nature of his government, and especially their own motives in visiting Anahuac. Cortés explained these motives by the desire to see so distinguished a monarch, and to declare to him the true Faith professed by the Christians. With rare discretion, he contented himself with dropping this hint, for the present, allowing it to ripen in the mind of the emperor, till a future conference. The latter asked, whether those white men, who in the preceding year had landed on the eastern shores of his empire, were their countrymen. He showed himself well informed of the proceedings of the Spaniards from their arrival in Tabasco to the present time, information of which had been regularly transmitted in the hieroglyphical paintings. He was curious, also, in regard to the rank of his visitors in their own country; inquiring, if they were the kinsmen of the sovereign. Cortés replied, they were kinsmen of one another, and subjects of their great monarch, who held them all in peculiar estimation. Before his departure, Montezuma made himself acquainted with the names of the principal cavaliers, and the position they occupied in the army.

At the conclusion of the interview, the Aztec prince commanded his attendants to bring forward the presents prepared for his guests. They consisted of cotton dresses, enough to supply every man, it is said, including the allies, with a suit! And he did not fail to add the usual accompaniment of gold chains and other ornaments, which he distributed in profusion among the Spaniards. He then withdrew with the same ceremony with which he had entered, leaving every one deeply impressed with his munificence and his affability so unlike what they had been taught to expect, by, what they now considered, an invention of the enemy.

That evening, the Spaniards celebrated their arrival in the Mexican capital by a general discharge of artillery. The thunders of the ordnance reverberating among the buildings and shaking them to their foundations, the stench of the sulphureous vapor that rolled in volumes above the walls of the encampment, reminding the inhabitants of the explosions of the great *volcan,* filled the hearts of the superstitious Aztecs with dismay. It proclaimed to them, that their city held in its bosom those dread beings whose path had been marked with desolation, and who could call down the thunderbolts to consume their enemies! It was doubtless the policy of Cortés to strengthen this superstitious feeling as far as possible, and to impress the natives, at the outset, with a salutary awe of the supernatural powers of the Spaniards.

On the following morning, the general requested permission to return the emperor's visit, by waiting on him in his palace. This was readily granted, and Montezuma sent his officers to conduct the Spaniards to his presence. Cortés dressed himself in his richest habit, and left the quarters attended by Alvarado, Sandoval, Velasquez and Ordaz, together with five or six of the common file.

The royal habitation was at no great distance. It stood on the ground, to the south-west of the cathedral, since covered in part by the *Casa del Estado,* the palace of the dukes of Monteleone, the descendants of Cortés. It was a vast, irregular pile of low stone buildings, like that garrisoned by the Spaniards. So spacious was it, indeed, that, as one of the Conquerors assures us, although he had visited it more than once, for the express purpose, he had been too much fatigued each time by wandering through the apartments ever to see the whole of it. It was built of the red porous stone of the country, *tetzontli,* was ornamented with marble, and on the façade over the principal entrance were sculptured the arms or device of Montezuma, an eagle bearing an ocelot in his talons.

In the courts through which the Spaniards passed, fountains of crystal water were playing, fed from the copious reservoir on the distant hill of Chapoltepec, and supplying in their turn more than a hundred baths in the interior of the palace. Crowds of Aztec nobles were sauntering up and down in these squares, and in the outer halls, loitering away their hours in attendance on the court. The apartments were of immense size, though not lofty. The ceilings were of various sorts of odoriferous wood ingeniously carved; the floors covered with mats of the palm-leaf. The walls were hung with cotton richly stained, with the skins of wild animals, or gorgeous draperies of feather-work wrought in imitation of birds, insects, and flowers, with the nice art and glowing radiance of colors that might compare with the tapestries of Flanders. Clouds of incense rolled up from censers, and diffused intoxicating odors through the apartments. The Spaniards might well have fancied themselves in the voluptuous precincts of an Eastern harem, instead of treading the halls of a wild barbaric chief in the Western World.

On reaching the hall of audience, the Mexican officers took off their sandals, and covered their gray attire with a mantle of *nequen,* a coarse stuff made of the fibres of the maguey, worn only by the poorest classes. This act of humiliation was imposed on all, except the members of his own family, who approached the sovereign. Thus bare-footed, with downcast eyes, and formal obeisance, they ushered the Spaniards into the royal presence.

They found Montezuma seated at the further end of a spacious saloon, and surrounded by a few of his favorite chiefs. He received them kindly, and very soon Cortés, without much ceremony, entered on the subject which was uppermost in his thoughts. He was fully aware of the importance of gaining the royal convert, whose example would have such an influence on the conversion of his people. The general, therefore, prepared to display the whole store of his theological science, with the most winning arts of rhetoric he could command, while the interpretation was conveyed through the silver tones of Marina, as inseparable from him, on these occasions, as his shadow.

He set forth, as clearly as he could, the ideas entertained by the Church in regard to the holy mysteries of the Trinity, the Incarnation, and the Atonement. From this he ascended to the origin of things, the creation of the world, the first pair, paradise, and the fall of man. He assured Montezuma, that the idols he worshipped were Satan under different forms. A sufficient proof of it was the bloody sacrifices they imposed, which he contrasted with the pure and simple rite of the mass. Their worship would sink him in perdition. It was to snatch his soul, and the souls of his people, from the flames of eternal fire by opening to them a purer faith, that the Christians had come to his land. And he earnestly besought him not to neglect the occasion, but to secure his salvation by embracing the Cross, the great sign of human redemption.

The eloquence of the preacher was wasted on the insensible heart of his royal auditor. It, doubtless, lost somewhat of its efficacy, strained through the imperfect interpretation of so recent a neophyte as the Indian damsel. But the doctrines were too abstruse in themselves to be comprehended at a glance by the rude intellect of a barbarian. And Montezuma may have, perhaps, thought it was not more monstrous to feed on the flesh of a fellow-creature, than on that of the Creator himself. He was, besides, steeped in the superstitions of his country from his cradle. He had been educated in the straitest sect of her religion; had been himself a priest before his election to the throne; and was now the head both of the religion and the state. Little probability was there that such a man would be open to argument or persuasion, even from the lips of a more practised polemic than the Spanish commander. How could he abjure the faith that was intertwined with the dearest affections of his heart, and the very elements of his being? How could he be false to the gods who had raised him to such prosperity and honors, and whose shrines were intrusted to his especial keeping?

He listened, however, with silent attention, until the general had concluded his homily. He then replied, that he knew the Spaniards had held this discourse wherever they had been. He doubted not their God was, as they said, a good being. His gods, also, were good to him. Yet what his visitor said of the creation of the world was like what he had been taught to believe. It was not worth while to discourse further of the matter. His ancestors, he said, were not the original proprietors of the land. They had occupied it but a few ages, and had been led there by a great Being, who, after giving them laws and ruling over the nation for a time, had withdrawn to the regions where the sun rises. He had declared, on his departure, that he or his descendants would again visit them and resume his empire. The wonderful deeds of the Spaniards, their fair complexions, and the quarter whence they came, all showed they were his descendants. If Montezuma has resisted their visit to his capital, it was because he had heard such accounts of their cruelties,—that they sent the lightning to consume his people, or crushed them to pieces under the hard feet of the ferocious animals on which they rode. He was now convinced that these were idle tales; that the Spaniards were kind and generous in their natures; they were mortals of a different race, indeed, from the Aztecs, wiser, and more valiant, —and for this he honored them.

"You, too," he added, with a smile, "have been told, perhaps, that I am a god, and dwell in palaces of gold and silver. But you see it is false. My houses, though large, are of stone and wood like those of others; and as to my body," he said, baring his tawny arm, "you see it is flesh and bone like yours. It is true, I have a great empire inherited from my ancestors; lands, and gold, and silver. But your sovereign beyond the waters is, I know, the rightful lord of all. I rule in his name. You, Malinche, are his ambassador; you and your brethren shall share these things with me. Rest now from your labors. You are here in your own dwellings, and every thing shall be provided for your subsistence. I will see that your wishes shall be obeyed in the same way as my own." As the monarch concluded these words, a few natural tears suffused his eyes, while the image of ancient independence, perhaps, flitted across his mind.

Cortés, while he encouraged the idea that his own sovereign was the great Being indicated by Montezuma, endeavored to comfort the monarch by the assurance that his master had no desire to interfere with his authority, otherwise than, out of pure concern for his welfare, to effect his conversion and that of his people to Christianity. Before the emperor dismissed his visitors he consulted his munificent spirit, as usual, by distributing rich stuffs and trinkets of gold among them, so that the poorest soldier, says Bernal Diaz, one of the party, received at least two heavy collars of the precious metal for his share. The iron hearts of the Spaniards were touched with the emotion displayed by Montezuma, as well as by his princely spirit of liberality. As they passed him, the cavaliers, with bonnet in hand, made him the most profound obeisance, and "on the way home," continues the same chronicler, "we could discourse of nothing but the gentle breeding and courtesy of the Indian monarch, and of the respect we entertained for him."

Speculations of a graver complexion must have pressed on the mind of the general, as he saw around him the evidences of a civilization, and consequently power, for which even the exaggerated reports of the natives— discredited from their apparent exaggeration—had not prepared him. In the pomp and burdensome ceremonial of the court, he saw that nice system of subordination and profound reverence for the monarch which characterize the semi-civilized empires of Asia. In the appearance of the capital, its massy, yet elegant architecture, its luxurious social accommodations, its activity in trade, he recognised the proofs of the intellectual progress, mechanical skill, and enlarged resources of an old and opulent community; while the swarms in the streets attested the existence of a population capable of turning these resources to the best account.

In the Aztec he beheld a being unlike either the rude republican Tlascalan, or the effeminate Cholulan; but combining the courage of the one with the cultivation of the other. He was in the heart of a great capital which seemed like an extensive fortification, with its dikes and its drawbridges, where every house might be easily converted into a castle. Its insular position removed it from the continent, from which, at the mere nod of the sovereign, all communication might be cut off, and the whole warlike population be at once precipitated on him and his handful of followers. What could superior science avail against such odds?

As to the subversion of Montezuma's empire, now that he had seen him in his capital, it must have seemed a more doubtful enterprise than ever. The recognition which the Aztec prince had made of the feudal supremacy, if I may so say, of the Spanish sovereign, was not to be taken too literally. Whatever show of deference he might be disposed to pay the latter, under the influence of his present—perhaps temporary—delusion, it was not to be supposed that he would so easily relinquish his actual power and possessions, or that his people would consent to it. Indeed, his sensitive apprehensions in regard to this very subject, on the coming of the Spaniards, were sufficient proof of the tenacity with which he clung to his authority. It is true that Cortés had a strong lever for future operations in the superstitious reverence felt for himself both by prince and people. It was undoubtedly his policy to maintain this sentiment unimpaired in both, as far as possible. But, before settling any plan of operations, it was necessary to make himself personally acquainted with the topography and local advantages of the capital, the character of its population, and the real nature and amount of its resources. With this view, he asked the emperor's permission to visit the principal public edifices.

* * *

The Spaniards had been now a week in Mexico. During this time, they had experienced the most friendly treatment from the emperor. But the mind of Cortés was far from easy. He felt that it was quite uncertain how long this amiable temper would last. A hundred circumstances might occur to change it. He might very naturally feel the maintenance of so large a body too burdensome on his treasury. The people of the capital might become dissatisfied at the presence of so numerous an armed force within their walls. Many causes of disgust might arise betwixt the soldiers and the citizens. Indeed, it was scarcely possible that a rude, licentious soldiery, like the Spaniards, could be long kept in subjection without active employment. The danger was even greater with the Tlascalans, a fierce race now brought into daily contact with the nation who held them in loathing and detestation. Rumors were already rife among the allies, whether well-founded or not, of murmurs among the Mexicans, accompanied by menaces of raising the bridges.

Even should the Spaniards be allowed to occupy their present quarters unmolested, it was not advancing the great object of the expedition. Cortés was not a whit nearer gaining the capital, so essential to his meditated subjugation of the country; and any day he might receive tidings that the Crown, or, what he most feared, the governor of Cuba, had sent a force of superior strength to wrest from him a conquest but half achieved. Disturbed by these anxious reflections, he resolved to extricate himself from his embarrassment by one bold stroke. But he first submitted the affair to a council of the officers in whom he most confided, desirous to divide with them the responsibility of the act, and, no doubt, to interest them more heartily in its execution, by making it in some measure the result of their combined judgments.

When the general had briefly stated the embarrassments of their position, the council was divided in opinion. All admitted the necessity of some instant action. One party were for retiring secretly from the city, and getting beyond the causeways before their march could be intercepted. Another advised that it should be done openly, with the knowledge of the emperor, of whose good-will they had had so many proofs. But both these measures seemed alike impolitic. A retreat under these circumstances, and so abruptly made, would have the air of a flight. It would be construed into distrust of themselves; and any thing like timidity on their part would be sure not only to bring on them the Mexicans, but the contempt of their allies, who would, doubtless, join in the general cry.

As to Montezuma, what reliance could they place on the protection of a prince so recently their enemy, and who, in his altered bearing, must have taken counsel of his fears, rather than his inclinations?

Even should they succeed in reaching the coast, their situation would be little better. It would be proclaiming to the world, that, after all their lofty vaunts, they were unequal to the enterprise. Their only hopes of their sovereign's favor, and of pardon for their irregular proceedings, were founded on success. Hitherto, they had only made the discovery of Mexico; to retreat would be to leave conquest and the fruits of it to another.—In short, to stay and to retreat seemed equally disastrous.

In this perplexity, Cortés proposed an expedient, which none but the most daring spirit, in the most desperate extremity, would have conceived. This was, to march to the royal palace, and bring Montezuma to the Spanish quarters, by fair means if they could persuade him, by force if necessary,— at all events, to get possession of his person. With such a pledge, the Spaniards would be secure from the assault of the Mexicans, afraid by acts of violence to compromise the safety of their prince. If he came by his own consent, they would be deprived of all apology for doing so. As long as the emperor remained among the Spaniards, it would be easy, by allowing him a show of sovereignty, to rule in his name, until they had taken measures for securing their safety, and the success of their enterprise. The idea of employing a sovereign as a tool for the government of his own kingdom, if a new one in the age of Cortés, is certainly not so in ours.

A plausible pretext for the seizure of the hospitable monarch—for the most barefaced action seeks to veil itself under some show of decency—was afforded by a circumstance of which Cortés had received intelligence at Cholula. He had left, as we have seen, a faithful officer, Juan de Escalante, with a hundred and fifty men in garrison at Vera Cruz, on his departure for the capital. He had not been long absent, when his lieutenant received a message from an Aztec chief named Quauhpopoca, governor of a district to the north of the Spanish settlement, declaring his desire to come in person and tender his allegiance to the Spanish authorities at Vera Cruz. He requested that four of the white men might be sent to protect him against certain unfriendly tribes through which his road lay. This was not an uncommon request, and excited no suspicion in Escalante. The four soldiers were sent; and on their arrival two of them were murdered by the false Aztec. The other two made their way back to the garrison.

The commander marched at once, with fifty of his men, and several thousand Indian allies, to take vengeance on the cacique. A pitched battle followed. The allies fled from the redoubted Mexicans. The few Spaniards stood firm, and with the aid of their fire-arms and the blessed Virgin, who was distinctly seen hovering over their ranks in the van, they made good the field against the enemy. It cost them dear, however; since seven or eight Christians were slain, and among them the gallant Escalante himself, who died of his injuries soon after his return to the fort. The Indian prisoners captured in the battle spoke of the whole proceedings as having taken place at the instigation of Montezuma.

One of the Spaniards fell into the hands of the natives, but soon after perished of his wounds. His head was cut off and sent to the Aztec emperor. It was uncommonly large and covered with hair; and, as Montezuma gazed on the ferocious features, rendered more horrible by death, he seemed to read in them the dark lineaments of the destined destroyers of his house. He turned from it with a shudder, and commanded that it should be taken from the city, and not offered at the shrine of any of his gods.

Although Cortés had received intelligence of this disaster at Cholula, he had concealed it within his own breast, or communicated it to very few only of his most trusty officers, from apprehension of the ill effect it might have on the spirits of the common soldiers.

The cavaliers whom Cortés now summoned to the council were men of the same mettle with their leader. Their bold, chivalrous spirits seemed to court danger for its own sake. If one or two, less adventurous, were startled by the proposal he made, they were soon overruled by the others, who, no doubt, considered that a desperate disease required as desperate a remedy.

That night, Cortés was heard pacing his apartment to and fro, like a man oppressed by thought, or agitated by strong emotion. He may have been ripening in his mind the daring scheme for the morrow. In the morning the soldiers heard mass as usual, and father Olmedo invoked the blessing of Heaven on their hazardous enterprise. Whatever might be the cause in which he was embarked, the heart of the Spaniard was cheered with the conviction that the Saints were on his side!

Having asked an audience from Montezuma, which was readily granted, the general made the necesary arrangements for his enterprise. The principal part of his force was drawn up in the court-yard, and he stationed a considerable detachment in the avenues leading to the palace, to check any attempt at rescue by the populace. He ordered twenty-five or thirty of the soldiers to drop in at the palace, as if by accident, in groups of three or four at a time, while the conference was going on with Montezuma. He selected five cavaliers, in whose courage and coolness he placed the most trust, to bear him company; Pedro de Alvarado, Gonzalo de Sandoval, Francisco de Lujo, Velasquez de Leon, and Alonso de Avila,—brilliant names in the annals of the Conquest. All were clad, as well as the common soldiers, in complete armor, a circumstance of too familiar occurrence to excite suspicion.

The little party were graciously received by the emperor, who soon, with the aid of the interpreters, became interested in a sportive conversation with the Spaniards, while he indulged his natural munificence by giving them presents of gold and jewels. He paid the Spanish general the particular compliment of offering him one of his daughters as his wife, an honor which the latter respectfully declined, on the ground that he was already accommodated with one in Cuba, and that his religion forbade a plurality.

When Cortés perceived that a sufficient number of his soldiers were assembled, he changed his playful manner, and with a serious tone briefly acquainted Montezuma with the treacherous proceedings in the *tierra caliente,* and the accusation of him as their author. The emperor listened to the charge with surprise; and disavowed the act, which he said could only have been imputed to him by his enemies. Cortés expressed his belief in his declaration, but added, that, to prove it true, it would be necessary to send for Quauhpopoca and his accomplices, that they might be examined and dealt with according to their deserts. To this Montezuma made no objection. Taking from his wrist, to which it was attached, a precious stone, the royal signet, on which was cut the figure of the War-god, he gave it to one of his nobles, with orders to show it to the Aztec governor, and require his instant presence in the capital, together with all those who had been accessory to the murder of the Spaniards. If he resisted, the officer was empowered to call in the aid of the neighboring towns, to enforce the mandate.

When the messenger had gone, Cortés assured the monarch that this prompt compliance with his request convinced him of his innocence. But it was important that his own sovereign should be equally convinced of it. Nothing would promote this so much as for Montezuma to transfer his residence to the palace occupied by the Spaniards, till on the arrival of Quauhpopoca the affair could be fully investigated. Such an act of condescension would, of itself, show a personal regard for the Spaniards, incompatible with the base conduct alleged against him, and would fully absolve him from all suspicion!

Montezuma listened to this proposal, and the flimsy reasoning with which it was covered, with looks of profound amazement. He became pale as death; but in a moment, his face flushed with resentment, as, with the pride of offended dignity, he exclaimed, "When was it ever heard that a great prince, like myself, voluntarily left his own palace to become a prisoner in the hands of strangers!"

Cortés assured him he would not go as a prisoner. He would experience nothing but respectful treatment from the Spaniards; would be surrounded by his own household, and hold intercourse with his people as usual. In short, it would be but a change of residence, from one of his palaces to another, a circumstance of frequent occurrence with him.—It was in vain. "If I should consent to such a degradation," he answered, "my subjects never would!" When further pressed, he offered to give up one of his sons and one of his daughters to remain as hostages with the Spaniards, so that he might be spared this disgrace.

Two hours passed in this fruitless discussion, till a high-mettled cavalier, Velasquez de Leon, impatient of the long delay, and seeing that the attempt, if not the deed, must ruin them, cried out, "Why do we waste words on this barbarian? We have gone too far to recede now. Let us seize him, and, if he resists, plunge our swords into his body!" The fierce tone and menacing gestures, with which this was uttered, alarmed the monarch, who inquired of Marina what the angry Spaniard said. The interpreter explained it in as gentle a manner as she could, beseeching him "to accompany the white men to their quarters, where he would be treated with all respect and kindness, while to refuse them would but expose himself to violence, perhaps to death." Marina, doubtless, spoke to her sovereign as she thought, and no one had better opportunity of knowing the truth than herself.

This last appeal shook the resolution of Montezuma. It was in vain that the unhappy prince looked around for sympathy or support. As his eyes wandered over the stern visages and iron forms of the Spaniards, he felt that his hour was indeed come; and, with a voice scarcely audible from emotion, he consented to accompany the strangers,—to quit the palace, whither he was never more to return. Had he possessed the spirit of the first Montezuma, he would have called his guards around him, and left his life-blood on the threshold, sooner than have been dragged a dishonored captive across it. But his courage sunk under circumstances. He felt he was the instrument of an irresistible Fate!

No sooner had the Spaniards got his consent, than orders were given for the royal litter. The nobles, who bore and attended it, could scarcely believe their senses, when they learned their master's purpose. But pride now came to Montezuma's aid, and, since he must go, he preferred that it should appear to be with his own free will. As the royal retinue, escorted by the Spaniards, marched through the street with downcast eyes and dejected mien, the people assembled in crowds, and a rumor ran among them, that the emperor was carried off by force to the quarters of the white men. A tumult would have soon arisen but for the intervention of Montezuma himself, who called out to the people to disperse, as he was visiting his friends of his own accord; thus sealing his ignominy by a declaration which deprived his subjects of the only excuse for resistance. On reaching the quarters, he sent out his nobles with similar assurances to the mob, and renewed orders to return to their homes.

He was received with ostentatious respect by the Spaniards, and selected the suite of apartments which best pleased him. They were soon furnished with fine cotton tapestries, feather-work, and all the elegancies of Indian upholstery. He was attended by such of his household as he chose, his wives and his pages, and was served with his usual pomp and luxury at his meals. He gave audience, as in his own palace, to his subjects, who were admitted to his presence, few, indeed, at a time, under the pretext of greater order and decorum. From the Spaniards themselves he met with a formal deference. No one, not even the general himself, approached him without doffing his casque, and rendering the obeisance due to his rank. Nor did they ever sit in his presence, without being invited by him to do so.

With all this studied ceremony and show of homage, there was one circumstance which too clearly proclaimed to his people that their sovereign was a prisoner. In the front of the palace a patrol of sixty men was established, and the same number in the rear. Twenty of each corps mounted guard at once, maintaining a careful watch, day and night. Another body, under command of Velasquez de Leon, was stationed in the royal antechamber. Cortés punished any departure from duty, or relaxation of vigilance, in these sentinels, with the utmost severity. He felt, as, indeed, every Spaniard must have felt, that the escape of the emperor now would be their ruin. Yet the task of this unintermitting watch sorely added to their fatigues. "Better this dog of a king should die," cried a soldier one day, "than that we should wear out our lives in this manner." The words were uttered in the hearing of Montezuma, who gathered something of their import, and the offender was severely chastised by order of the general. Such instances of disrespect, however, were very rare. Indeed, the amiable deportment of the monarch, who seemed to take pleasure in the society of his jailers, and who never allowed a favor or attention from the meanest soldier to go unrequited, inspired the Spaniards with as much attachment as they were capable of feeling—for a barbarian.

Things were in this posture, when the arrival of Quauhpopoca from the coast was announced. He was accompanied by his son and fifteen Aztec chiefs. He had travelled all the way, borne, as became his high rank, in a litter. On entering Montezuma's presence, he threw over his dress the coarse robe of *nequen,* and made the usual humiliating acts of obeisance. The poor parade of courtly ceremony was the more striking, when placed in contrast with the actual condition of the parties.

The Aztec governor was coldly received by his master, who referred the affair (had he the power to do otherwise?) to the examination of Cortés. It was, doubtless, conducted in a sufficiently summary manner. To the general's query, whether the cacique was the subject of Montezuma, he replied, "And what other sovereign could I serve?" implying that his sway was universal. He did not deny his share in the transaction, nor did he seek to shelter himself under the royal authority, till sentence of death was passed on him and his followers, when they all laid the blame of their proceedings on Montezuma. They were condemned to be burnt alive in the area before the palace. The funeral piles were made of heaps of arrows, javelins, and other weapons, drawn by the emperor's permission from the arsenals round the great *teocalli,* where they had been stored to supply means of defence in times of civic tumult or insurrection. By this politic precaution, Cortés proposed to remove a ready means of annoyance in case of hostilities with the citizens.

To crown the whole of these extraordinary proceedings, Cortés, while preparations for the execution were going on, entered the emperor's apartment, attended by a soldier bearing fetters in his hands. With a severe aspect, he charged the monarch with being the original contriver of the violence offered to the Spaniards, as was now proved by the declaration of his own instruments. Such a crime, which merited death in a subject, could not be atoned for, even by a sovereign, without some punishment. So saying, he ordered the soldier to fasten the fetters on Montezuma's ankles. He coolly waited till it was done; then, turning his back on the monarch, quitted the room.

Montezuma was speechless under the infliction of this last insult. He was like one struck down by a heavy blow, that deprives him of all his faculties. He offered no resistance. But, though he spoke not a word, low, ill-suppressed moans, from time to time, intimated the anguish of his spirit. His attendants, bathed in tears, offered him their consolations. They tenderly held his feet in their arms, and endeavored, by inserting their shawls and mantles, to relieve them from the pressure of the iron. But they could not reach the iron which had penetrated into his soul. He felt that he was no more a king.

Meanwhile, the execution of the dreadful doom was going forward in the court-yard. The whole Spanish force was under arms, to check any interruption that might be offered by the Mexicans. But none was attempted. The populace gazed in silent wonder, regarding it as the sentence of the emperor. The manner of the execution, too, excited less surprise, from their familiarity with similar spectacles, aggravated, indeed, by additional horrors, in their own diabolical sacrifices. The Aztec lord and his companions, bound hand and foot to the blazing piles, submitted without a cry or a complaint to their terrible fate. Passive fortitude is the virtue of the Indian warrior; and it was the glory of the Aztec, as of the other races on the North American continent, to show how the spirit of the brave man may triumph over torture and the agonies of death.

When the dismal tragedy was ended, Cortés reentered Montezuma's apartment. Kneeling down, he unclasped his shackles with his own hand, expressing at the same time his regret that so disagreeable a duty as that of subjecting him to such a punishment had been imposed on him. This last indignity had entirely crushed the spirit of Montezuma; and the monarch, whose frown, but a week since, would have made the nations of Anahuac tremble to their remotest borders, was now craven enough to thank his deliverer for his freedom, as for a great and unmerited boon!

Not long after, the Spanish general, conceiving that his royal captive was sufficiently humbled, expressed his willingness that he should return, if he inclined, to his own palace. Montezuma declined it; alleging, it is said, that his nobles had more than once importuned him to resent his injuries by taking arms against the Spaniards; and that, were he in the midst of them, it would be difficult to avoid it, or to save his capital from bloodshed and anarchy. The reason did honor to his heart, if it was the one which influenced him. It is probable that he did not care to trust his safety to those haughty and ferocious chieftains, who had witnessed the degradation of their master, and must despise his pusillanimity, as a thing unprecedented in an Aztec monarch. It is also said, that, when Marina conveyed to him the permission of Cortés, the other interpreter, Aguilar, gave him to understand the Spanish officers never would consent that he should avail himself of it.

Whatever were his reasons, it is certain that he declined the offer; and the general, in a well-feigned, or real ecstasy, embraced him, declaring, "that he loved him as a brother, and that every Spaniard would be zealously devoted to his interests, since he had shown himself so mindful of theirs!" Honeyed words, "which," says the shrewd old chronicler who was present, "Montezuma was wise enough to know the worth of."

The events recorded in this chapter are certainly some of the most extraordinary on the page of history. That a small body of men, like the Spaniards, should have entered the palace of a mighty prince, have seized his person in the midst of his vassals, have borne him off a captive to their quarters,—that they should have put to an ignominious death before his face his high officers, for executing, probably, his own commands, and have crowned the whole by putting the monarch in irons like a common malefactor,—that this should have been done, not to a drivelling dotard in the decay of his fortunes, but to a proud monarch in the plenitude of his power, in the very heart of his capital, surrounded by thousands and tens of thousands, who trembled at his nod, and would have poured out their blood like water in his defence,—that all this should have been done by a mere handful of adventurers, is a thing too extravagant, altogether too improbable, for the pages of romance! It is, nevertheless, literally true. Yet we shall not be prepared to acquiesce in the judgments of contemporaries who regarded these acts with admiration. We may well distrust any grounds on which it is attempted to justify the kidnapping of a friendly sovereign,—by those very persons, too, who were reaping the full benefit of his favors.

To view the matter differently, we must take the position of the Conquerors, and assume with them the original right of conquest. Regarded from this point of view, many difficulties vanish. If conquest were a duty, whatever was necessary to effect it was right also. Right and expedient become convertible terms. And it can hardly be denied, that the capture of the monarch was expedient, if the Spaniards would maintain their hold on the empire.

The execution of the Aztec governor suggests other considerations. If he were really guilty of the perfidious act imputed to him by Cortés, and if Montezuma disavowed it, the governor deserved death, and the general was justified by the law of nations in inflicting it. It is by no means so clear, however, why he should have involved so many in this sentence; most, perhaps all, of whom must have acted under his authority. The cruel manner of the death will less startle those who are familiar with the established penal codes in most civilized nations in the sixteenth century.

But, if the governor deserved death, what pretence was there for the outrage on the person of Montezuma? If the former was guilty, the latter surely was not. But, if the cacique only acted in obedience to orders, the responsibility was transferred to the sovereign who gave the orders. They could not both stand in the same category.

It is vain, however, to reason on the matter, on any abstract principles of right and wrong, or to suppose that the Conquerors troubled themselves with the refinements of casuistry. Their standard of right and wrong, in reference to the natives, was a very simple one. Despising them as an outlawed race, without God in the world, they, in common with their age, held it to be their "mission" (to borrow the cant phrase of our own day) to conquer and to convert. The measures they adopted certainly facilitated the first great work of conquest. By the execution of the caciques, they struck terror not only into the capital, but throughout the country. It proclaimed that not a hair of a Spaniard was to be touched with impunity! By rendering Montezuma contemptible in his own eyes and those of his subjects, Cortés deprived him of the support of his people, and forced him to lean on the arm of the stranger. It was a politic proceeding,—to which few men could have been equal, who had a touch of humanity in their natures.

A good criterion of the moral sense of the actors in these events is afforded by the reflections of Bernal Diaz, made some fifty years, it will be remembered, after the events themselves, when the fire of youth had become extinct, and the eye, glancing back through the vista of half a century, might be supposed to be unclouded by the passions and prejudices which throw their mist over the present. "Now that I am an old man," says the veteran, "I often entertain myself with calling to mind the heroical deeds of early days, till they are as fresh as the events of yesterday. I think of the seizure of the Indian monarch, his confinement in irons, and the execution

of his officers, till all these things seem actually passing before me. And, as
I ponder on our exploits, I feel that it was not of ourselves that we performed them, but that it was the providence of God which guided us. Much
food is there here for meditation!" There is so, indeed, and for a meditation
not unpleasing, as we reflect on the advance, in speculative morality, at
least, which the nineteenth century has made over the sixteenth. But should
not the consciousness of this teach us charity? Should it not make us the
more distrustful of applying the standard of the present to measure the
actions of the past?

*For six months Cortés ruled the Aztec empire through Montezuma, scour-
ing it for treasure. It was not the Aztecs but a rival expedition of Spaniards
who brought this interlude to an end. Cortés hurried to the coast, captured
their leader, and persuaded the men to join him. While he was gone, his
lieutenant Alvarado in Tenochtitlan, fearing insurrection, without warning
slaughtered six hundred or more unarmed Aztecs at a religious festival.
The populace of Tenochtitlan in wrath drove the Spaniards back to a palace
and besieged them there. The streets were empty when Cortés returned
with more than a thousand Spanish troops and a number of Indian allies,
but the Aztecs soon began a violent assault.*

    The palace of Axayacatl, in which the Spaniards were quartered, was,
as the reader may remember, a vast, irregular pile of stone buildings, having
but one floor, except in the centre, where another story was added, consisting of a suite of apartments which rose like turrets on the main building
of the edifice. A vast area stretched around, encompassed by a stone wall
of no great height. This was supported by towers or bulwarks at certain
intervals, which gave it some degree of strength, not, indeed, as compared
with European fortifications, but sufficient to resist the rude battering
enginery of the Indians. The parapet had been pierced here and there with
embrasures for the artillery, which consisted of thirteen guns; and smaller
apertures were made in other parts for the convenience of the arquebusiers.
The Spanish forces found accommodations within the great building; but
the numerous body of Tlascalan auxiliaries could have had no other shelter
than what was afforded by barracks or sheds hastily constructed for the
purpose in the spacious court-yard. Most of them, probably, bivouacked
under the open sky, in a climate milder than that to which they were accustomed among the rude hills of their native land. Thus crowded into a
small and compact compass, the whole army could be assembled at a
moment's notice; and, as the Spanish commander was careful to enforce
the strictest discipline and vigilance, it was scarcely possible that he could
be taken by surprise. No sooner, therefore, did the trumpet call to arms, as

the approach of the enemy was announced, than every soldier was at his post, the cavalry mounted, the artillery-men at their guns, and the archers and arquebusiers stationed so as to give the assailants a warm reception.

On they came, with the companies, or irregular masses, into which the multitude was divided, rushing forward each in its own dense column, with many a gay banner displayed, and many a bright gleam of light reflected from helmet, arrow, and spear-head, as they were tossed about in their disorderly array. As they drew near the inclosure, the Aztec set up a hideous yell, or rather that shrill whistle used in fight by the nations of Anahuac, which rose far above the sound of shell and atabal, and their other rude instruments of warlike melody. They followed this by a tempest of missiles,—stones, darts, and arrows,—which fell thick as rain on the besieged, while volleys of the same kind descended from the crowded terraces in the neighborhood.

The Spaniards waited until the foremost column had arrived within the best distance for giving effect to their fire, when a general discharge of artillery and arquebuses swept the ranks of the assailants, and mowed them down by hundreds. The Mexicans were familiar with the report of these formidable engines, as they had been harmlessly discharged on some holiday festival; but never till now had they witnessed their murderous power. They stood aghast for a moment, as with bewildered looks they staggered under the fury of the fire; but, soon rallying, the bold barbarians uttered a piercing cry, and rushed forward over the prostrate bodies of their comrades. A second and a third volley checked their career, and threw them into disorder, but still they pressed on, letting off clouds of arrows; while their comrades on the roofs of the houses took more deliberate aim at the combatants in the court-yard. The Mexicans were particularly expert in the use of the sling; and the stones which they hurled from their elevated positions on the heads of their enemies did even greater execution than the arrows. They glanced, indeed, from the mail-covered bodies of the cavaliers, and from those who were sheltered under the cotton panoply, or *escaupil*. But some of the soldiers, especially the veterans of Cortés, and many of their Indian allies, had but slight defences, and suffered greatly under this stony tempest.

The Aztecs, meanwhile, had advanced close under the walls of the intrenchment; their ranks broken and disordered, and their limbs mangled by the unintermitting fire of the Christians. But they still pressed on, under the very muzzle of the guns. They endeavored to scale the parapet, which, from its moderate height, was in itself a work of no great difficulty. But the moment they showed their heads above the rampart, they were shot down by the unerring marksmen within, or stretched on the ground by a blow of a Tlascalan *maquahuitl*. Nothing daunted, others soon appeared to take the place of the fallen, and strove, by raising themselves on the writhing bodies of their dying comrades, or by fixing their spears in the crevices of the wall, to surmount the barrier. But the attempt proved equally vain.

Defeated here, they tried to effect a breach in the parapet by battering it with heavy pieces of timber. The works were not constructed on those scientific principles by which one part is made to overlook and protect another. The besiegers, therefore, might operate at their pleasure, with but little molestation from the garrison within, whose guns could not be brought into a position to bear on them, and who could mount no part of their own works for their defence, without exposing their persons to the missiles of the whole besieging army. The parapet, however, proved too strong for the efforts of the assailants. In their despair they endeavored to set the Christian quarters on fire, shooting burning arrows into them, and climbing up so as to dart their firebrands through the embrasures. The principal edifice was of stone. But the temporary defences of the Indian allies, and other parts of the exterior works, were of wood. Several of these took fire, and the flame spread rapidly among the light, combustible materials. This was a disaster for which the besieged were wholly unprepared. They had little water, scarcely enough for their own consumption. They endeavored to extinguish the flames by heaping on earth. But in vain. Fortunately the great building was of materials which defied the destroying element. But the fire raged in some of the outworks, connected with the parapet, with a fury which could only be checked by throwing down a part of the wall itself, thus laying open a formidable breach. This, by the general's order, was speedily protected by a battery of heavy guns, and a file of arquebusiers, who kept up an incessant volley through the opening on the assailants.

The fight now raged with fury on both sides. The walls around the palace belched forth an unintermitting sheet of flame and smoke. The groans of the wounded and dying were lost in the fiercer battle-cries of the combatants, the roar of the artillery, the sharper rattle of the musketry, and the hissing sound of Indian missiles. It was the conflict of the European with the American; of civilized man with the barbarian; of the science of the one with the rude weapons and warfare of the other. And as the ancient walls of Tenochtitlan shook under the thunders of the artillery,—it announced that the white man, the destroyer, had set his foot within her precincts.

Night at length came, and drew her friendly mantle over the contest. The Aztec seldom fought by night. It brought little repose, however, to the Spaniards, in hourly expectation of an assault; and they found abundant occupation in restoring the breaches in their defences, and in repairing their battered armor. The beleaguering host lay on their arms through the night, giving token of their presence, now and then, by sending a stone or shaft over the battlements, or by a solitary cry of defiance from some warrior more determined than the rest, till all other sounds were lost in the vague, indistinct murmurs which float upon the air in the neighborhood of a vast assembly.

The ferocity shown by the Mexicans seems to have been a thing for which Cortés was wholly unprepared. His past experience, his uninterrupted career of victory with a much feebler force at his command, had led him to underrate the military efficiency, if not the valor, of the Indians. The apparent facility, with which the Mexicans had acquiesced in the outrages on their sovereign and themselves, had led him to hold their courage, in particular, too lightly. He could not believe the present assault to be any thing more than a temporary ebullition of the populace, which would soon waste itself by its own fury. And he proposed, on the following day, to sally out and inflict such chastisement on his foes as should bring them to their senses, and show who was master in the capital.

With early dawn, the Spaniards were up and under arms; but not before their enemies had given evidence of their hostility by the random missiles, which, from time to time, were sent into the inclosure. As the grey light of morning advanced, it showed the besieging army far from being diminished in numbers, filling up the great square and neighboring avenues in more dense array than on the preceding evening. Instead of a confused, disorderly rabble, it had the appearance of something like a regular force, with its battalions distributed under their respective banners, the devices of which showed a contribution from the principal cities and districts in the Valley. High above the rest was conspicuous the ancient standard of Mexico, with its well known cognizance, an eagle pouncing on an ocelot, emblazoned on a rich mantle of feather-work. Here and there priests might be seen mingling in the ranks of the besiegers, and, with frantic gestures, animating them to avenge their insulted deities.

The greater part of the enemy had little clothing save the *maxtlatl,* or sash round the loins. They were variously armed, with long spears tipped with copper, or flint, or sometimes merely pointed and hardened in the fire. Some were provided with slings, and others with darts having two or three points, with long strings attached to them, by which, when discharged, they could be torn away again from the body of the wounded. This was a formidable weapon, much dreaded by the Spaniards. Those of a higher order wielded the terrible *maquahuitl,* with its sharp and brittle blades of obsidian. Amidst the motley bands of warriors, were seen many whose showy dress and air of authority intimated persons of high military consequence. Their breasts were protected by plates of metal, over which was thrown the gay surcoat of feather-work. They wore casques resembling, in their form, the head of some wild and ferocious animal, crested with bristly hair, or overshadowed by tall and graceful plumes of many a brilliant color. Some few were decorated with the red fillet bound round the hair, having tufts of cotton attached to it, which denoted by their number that of the victories they had won, and their own preëminent rank among the warriors of the nation. The motley assembly plainly showed that priest, warrior, and citizen had all united to swell the tumult.

Before the sun had shot his beams into the Castilian quarters, the enemy were in motion, evidently preparing to renew the assault of the preceding day. The Spanish commander determined to anticipate them by a vigorous sortie, for which he had already made the necessary dispositions. A general discharge of ordnance and musketry sent death far and wide into the enemy's ranks, and, before they had time to recover from their confusion, the gates were thrown open, and Cortés, sallying out at the head of his cavalry, supported by a large body of infantry and several thousand Tlascalans, rode at full gallop against them. Taken thus by surprise, it was scarcely possible to offer much resistance. Those who did were trampled down under the horses' feet, cut to pieces with the broadswords, or pierced with the lances of the riders. The infantry followed up the blow, and the rout for the moment was general.

But the Aztecs fled only to take refuge behind a barricade, or strong work of timber and earth, which had been thrown across the great street through which they were pursued. Rallying on the other side, they made a gallant stand, and poured in turn a volley of their light weapons on the Spaniards, who, saluted with a storm of missiles at the same time, from the terraces of the houses, were checked in their career, and thrown into some disorder.

Cortés, thus impeded, ordered up a few pieces of heavy ordnance, which soon swept away the barricades, and cleared a passage for the army. But it had lost the momentum acquired in its rapid advance. The enemy had time to rally and to meet the Spaniards on more equal terms. They were attacked in flank, too, as they advanced, by fresh battalions, who swarmed in from the adjoining streets and lanes. The canals were alive with boats filled with warriors, who, with their formidable darts searched every crevice or weak place in the armor of proof, and made havoc on the unprotected bodies of the Tlascalans. By repeated and vigorous charges, the Spaniards succeeded in driving the Indians before them; though many, with a desperation which showed they loved vengeance better than life, sought to embarrass the movements of their horses by clinging to their legs, or, more successfully strove to pull the riders from their saddles. And woe to the unfortunate cavalier who was thus dismounted,—to be despatched by the brutal *maquahuitl*, or to be dragged on board a canoe to the bloody altar of sacrifice!

But the greatest annoyance which the Spaniards endured was from the missiles from the *azoteas*, consisting often of large stones, hurled with a force that would tumble the stoutest rider from his saddle. Galled in the extreme by these discharges, against which even their shields afforded no adequate protection, Cortés ordered fire to be set to the buildings. This was no very difficult matter, since, although chiefly of stone, they were filled with mats, cane-work, and other combustible materials, which were soon in a blaze. But the buildings stood separated from one another by canals and drawbridges, so that the flames did not easily communicate to the neighboring edifices. Hence, the labor of the Spaniards was incalculably increased, and their progress in the work of destruction—fortunately for the city—was comparatively slow. They did not relax their efforts, however, till several hundred houses had been consumed, and the miseries of a conflagration, in which the wretched inmates perished equally with the defenders, were added to the other horrors of the scene.

The day was now far spent. The Spaniards had been everywhere victorious. But the enemy, though driven back on every point, still kept the field. When broken by the furious charges of the cavalry, he soon rallied behind the temporary defences, which, at different intervals, had been thrown across the streets, and, facing about, renewed the fight with undiminished courage, till the sweeping away of the barriers by the cannon of the assailants left a free passage for the movements of their horse. Thus the action was a succession of rallying and retreating, in which both parties suffered much, although the loss inflicted on the Indians was probably tenfold greater than that of the Spaniards. But the Aztecs could better afford the loss of a hundred lives than their antagonists that of one. And, while the Spaniards showed an array broken, and obviously thinned in numbers, the Mexican army, swelled by the tributary levies which flowed in upon it from the neighboring streets, exhibited, with all its losses, no sign of diminution. At length, sated with carnage, and exhausted by toil and hunger, the Spanish commander drew off his men, and sounded a retreat.

On his way to his quarters, he beheld his friend, the secretary Duero, in a street adjoining, unhorsed, and hotly engaged with a body of Mexicans, against whom he was desperately defending himself with his poniard. Cortés, roused at the sight, shouted his war-cry, and, dashing into the midst of the enemy, scattered them like chaff by the fury of his onset; then, recovering his friend's horse, he enabled him to remount, and the two cavaliers, striking their spurs into their steeds burst through their opponents and joined the main body of the army. Such displays of generous gallantry were not uncommon in these engagements, which called forth more feats of personal adventure than battles with antagonists better skilled in the science of war. The chivalrous bearing of the general was emulated in full measure by Sandoval, De Leon, Olid, Alvarado, Ordaz, and his other brave companions, who won such glory under the eye of their leader, as prepared the way for the independent commands which afterwards placed provinces and kingdoms at their disposal.

The undaunted Aztecs hung on the rear of their retreating foes, annoying them at every step by fresh flights of stones and arrows; and, when the Spaniards had reëntered their fortress, the Indian host encamped around it, showing the same dogged resolution as on the preceding evening. Though true to their ancient habits of inaction during the night, they broke the stillness of the hour by insulting cries and menaces, which reached the ears of the besieged. "The gods have delivered you, at last, into our hands," they said; "Huitzilopotchli has long cried for his victims. The stone of sacrifice is ready. The knives are sharpened. The wild beasts in the palace are roaring for their offal. And the cages," they added, taunting the Tlascalans with their leanness, "are waiting for the false sons of Anahuac, who are to be fattened for the festival!" These dismal menaces, which sounded fearfully in the ears of the besieged, who understood too well their import, were mingled with piteous lamentations for their sovereign, whom they called on the Spaniards to deliver up to them.

Cortés suffered much from a severe wound which he had received in the hand in the late action. But the anguish of his mind must have been still greater, as he brooded over the dark prospect before him. He had mistaken the character of the Mexicans. Their long and patient endurance had been a violence to their natural temper, which, as their whole history proves, was arrogant and ferocious beyond that of most of the races of Anahuac. The restraint, which, in deference to their monarch, more than to their own fears, they had so long put on their natures, being once removed, their passions burst forth with accumulated violence. The Spaniards had encountered in the Tlascalan an open enemy, who had no grievance to complain of, no wrong to redress. He fought under the vague apprehension only of some coming evil to his country. But the Aztec, hitherto the proud lord of the land, was goaded by insult and injury, till he had reached that pitch of self-devotion, which made life cheap, in comparison with revenge. Armed thus with the energy of despair, the savage is almost a match for the civilized man; and a whole nation, moved to its depths by a common feeling, which swallows up all selfish considerations of personal interest and safety, becomes, whatever be its resources, like the earthquake and the tornado, the most formidable among the agencies of nature.

Considerations of this kind may have passed through the mind of Cortés, as he reflected on his own impotence to restrain the fury of the Mexicans, and resolved, in despite of his late supercilious treatment of Montezuma, to employ his authority to allay the tumult,—an authority so successfully exerted in behalf of Alvarado, at an earlier stage of the insurrection. He was the more confirmed in his purpose, on the following morning, when the assailants, redoubling their efforts, succeeded in scaling the works in one quarter, and effecting an entrance into the inclosure. It is true, they were met with so resolute a spirit, that not a man, of those who entered, was left alive. But, in the impetuosity of the assault, it seemed, for a few moments, as if the place was to be carried by storm.

Cortés now sent to the Aztec emperor to request his interposition with his subjects in behalf of the Spaniards. But Montezuma was not in the humor to comply. He had remained moodily in his quarters ever since the general's return. Disgusted with the treatment he had received, he had still further cause for mortification in finding himself the ally of those who were the open enemies of his nation. From his apartment he had beheld the tragical scenes in his capital, and seen another, the presumptive heir to his throne, taking the place which he should have occupied at the head of his warriors, and fighting the battles of his country. Distressed by his position, indignant at those who had placed him in it, he coldly answered, "What have I to do with Malinche? I do not wish to hear from him. I desire only to die. To what a state has my willingness to serve him reduced me!" When urged still further to comply by Olid and father Olmedo, he added, "It is of no use. They will neither believe me, nor the false words and promises of Malinche. You will never leave these walls alive." On being assured, however, that the Spaniards would willingly depart, if a way were opened to them by their enemies, he at length—moved, probably, more by a desire to spare the blood of his subjects, than of the Christians—consented to expostulate with his people.

In order to give the greater effect to his presence, he put on his imperial robes. The *tilmatli,* his mantle of white and blue, flowed over his shoulders, held together by its rich clasp of the green *chalchivitl.* The same precious gem, with emeralds of uncommon size, set in gold, profusely ornamented other parts of his dress. His feet were shod with the golden sandals, and his brows covered by the *copilli,* or Mexican diadem, resembling in form the pontifical tiara. Thus attired, and surrounded by a guard of Spaniards and several Aztec nobles, and preceded by the golden wand, the symbol of sovereignty, the Indian monarch ascended the central turret of the palace. His presence was instantly recognised by the people, and, as the royal retinue advanced along the battlements, a change, as if by magic, came over the scene. The clang of instruments, the fierce cries of the assailants, were hushed, and a deathlike stillness pervaded the whole assembly, so fiercely agitated, but a few moments before, by the wild tumult of war! Many prostrated themselves on the ground; others bent the knee; and all turned with eager expectation towards the monarch, whom they had been taught to reverence with slavish awe, and from whose countenance they had been wont to turn away as from the intolerable splendors of divinity! Montezuma saw his advantage; and, while he stood thus confronted with his awe-struck people, he seemed to recover all his former authority and confidence, as he felt himself to be still a king. With a calm voice, easily heard over the silent assembly, he is said by the Castilian writers to have thus addressed them.

"Why do I see my people here in arms against the palace of my fathers? Is it that you think your sovereign a prisoner, and wish to release him? If so, you have acted rightly. But you are mistaken. I am no prisoner. The strangers are my guests. I remain with them only from choice, and can leave them when I list. Have you come to drive them from the city? That is unnecessary. They will depart of their own accord if you will open a way for them. Return to your homes, then. Lay down your arms. Show your obedience to me who have a right to it. The white men shall go back to their own land; and all shall be well again within the walls of Tenochtitlan."

As Montezuma announced himself the friend of the detested strangers, a murmur ran through the multitude; a murmur of contempt for the pusillanimous prince who could show himself so insensible to the insults and injuries for which the nation was in arms! The swollen tide of their passions swept away all the barriers of ancient reverence, and, taking a new direction, descended on the head of the unfortunate monarch, so far degenerated from his warlike ancestors. "Base Aztec," they exclaimed "woman, coward, the white men have made you a woman,—fit only to weave and spin!" These bitter taunts were soon followed by still more hostile demonstrations. A chief, it is said, of high rank, bent a bow or brandished a javelin with an air of defiance against the emperor, when, in an instant, a cloud of stones and arrows descended on the spot where the royal train was gathered. The Spaniards appointed to protect his person had been thrown off their guard by the respectful deportment of the people during their lord's address. They now hastily interposed their bucklers. But it was too late. Montezuma was wounded by three of the missiles, one of which, a stone, fell with such violence on his head, near the temple, as brought him senseless to the ground. The Mexicans, shocked at their own sacrilegious act, experienced a sudden revulsion of feeling, and, setting up a dismal cry, dispersed panic-struck, in different directions. Not one of the multitudinous array remained in the great square before the palace!

The unhappy prince, meanwhile was borne by his attendants to his apartments below. On recovering from the insensibility caused by the blow, the wretchedness of his condition broke upon him. He had tasted the last bitterness of degradation. He had been reviled, rejected, by his people. The meanest of the rabble had raised their hands against him. He had nothing more to live for. It was in vain that Cortés and his officers endeavored to soothe the anguish of his spirit and fill him with better thoughts. He spoke not a word in answer. His wound, though dangerous, might still, with skilful treatment, not prove mortal. But Montezuma refused all the remedies prescribed for it. He tore off the bandages as often as they were applied, maintaining, all the while, the most determined silence. He sat with eyes dejected, brooding over his fallen fortunes, over the image of ancient majesty, and present humiliation. He had survived his honor. But a spark of his ancient spirit seemed to kindle in his bosom, as it was clear he did not mean to survive his disgrace.—From this painful scene the Spanish general and his followers were soon called away by the new dangers which menaced the garrison.

Within three days, on June 30, 1520, Montezuma died, breaking the last link between the Spaniards and the Aztecs. The bloody assaults against the besieged Spaniards continued relentlessly.

There was no longer any question as to the expediency of evacuating the capital. The only doubt was to the time of doing so, and the route. The Spanish commander called a council of officers to deliberate on these matters. It was his purpose to retreat on Tlascala, and in that capital to decide according to circumstances on his future operations. After some discussion, they agreed on the causeway of Tlacopan as the avenue by which to leave the city. It would, indeed, take them back by a circuitous route, considerably longer than either of those by which they had approached the capital. But, for that reason, it would be less likely to be guarded, as least suspected; and the causeway itself, being shorter than either of the other entrances, would sooner place the army in comparative security on the main land.

There was some difference of opinion in respect to the hour of departure. The day-time, it was argued by some, would be preferable, since it would enable them to see the nature and extent of their danger, and to provide against it. Darkness would be much more likely to embarrass their own movements than those of the enemy, who were familiar with the ground. A thousand impediments would occur in the night, which might prevent their acting in concert, or obeying, or even ascertaining, the orders of the commander. But, on the other hand, it was urged, that the night presented many obvious advantages in dealing with a foe who rarely carried his hostilities beyond the day. The late active operations of the Spaniards had thrown the Mexicans off their guard, and it was improbable they would anticipate so speedy a departure of their enemies. With celerity and caution, they might succeed, therefore, in making their escape from the town, possibly over the causeway, before their retreat should be discovered; and, could they once get beyond that pass of peril, they felt little apprehension for the rest.

These views were fortified it is said, by the counsels of a soldier named Botello, who professed the mysterious science of judicial astrology. He had gained credit with the army by some predictions which had been verified by the events; those lucky hits which make chance pass for calculation with the credulous multitude. This man recommended to his countrymen by all means to evacuate the place in the night, as the hour most propitious to them, although he should perish in it. The event proved the astrologer better acquainted with his own horoscope than with that of others.

It is possible Botello's predictions had some weight in determining the opinion of Cortés. Superstition was the feature of the age, and the Spanish general, as we have seen, had a full measure of its bigotry. Seasons of gloom, moreover, dispose the mind to a ready acquiescence in the marvellous. It is, however, quite as probable that he made use of the astrologer's opinion, finding it coincided with his own, to influence that of his men, and inspire them with higher confidence. At all events, it was decided to abandon the city that very night.

The general's first care was to provide for the safe transportation of the treasure. Many of the common soldiers had converted their share of the prize, as we have seen, into gold chains, collars, or other ornaments, which they easily carried about their persons. But the royal fifth, together with that of Cortés himself, and much of the rich booty of the principal cavaliers, had been converted into bars and wedges of solid gold and deposited in one of the strong apartments of the palace. Cortés delivered the share belonging to the Crown to the royal officers, assigning them one of the strongest horses, and a guard of Castilian soldiers, to transport it. Still, much of the treasure, belonging both to the Crown and to individuals, was necessarily abandoned, from the want of adequate means of conveyance. The metal lay scattered in shining heaps along the floor, exciting the cupidity of the soldiers. "Take what you will of it," said Cortés to his men. "Better you should have it, than these Mexican hounds. But be careful not to overload yourselves. He travels safest in the dark night who travels lightest." His own more wary followers took heed to his counsel, helping themselves to a few articles of least bulk, though, it might be, of greatest value. But the troops of Narvaez, pining for riches, of which they had heard so much, and hitherto seen so little, showed no such discretion. To them it seemed as if the very mines of Mexico were turned up before them, and, rushing on the treacherous spoil, they greedily loaded themselves with as much of it, not merely as they could accommodate about their persons, but as they could stow away in wallets, boxes, or any other mode of conveyance at their disposal.

Cortés next arranged the order of march. The van, composed of two hundred Spanish foot, he placed under the command of the valiant Gonzalo de Sandoval, supported by Diego de Ordaz, Francisco de Lujo, and about twenty other cavaliers. The rear-guard, constituting the strength of the infantry, was intrusted to Pedro de Alvarado, and Velasquez de Leon. The general himself took charge of the "battle," or centre, in which went the baggage, some of the heavy guns, most of which, however, remained in the rear, the treasure, and the prisoners. These consisted of a son and two daughters of Montezuma, Cacama, the deposed lord of Tezcuco, and several other nobles, whom Cortés retained as important pledges in his future negotiations with the enemy. The Tlascalans were distributed pretty equally among the three divisions; and Cortés had under his immediate command a hundred picked soldiers, his own veterans most attached to his service, who, with Christóval de Olid, Francisco de Morla, Alonso de Avila, and two or three other cavaliers, formed a select corps, to act wherever occasion might require.

The general had already superintended the construction of a portable bridge to be laid over the open canals in the causeway. This was given in charge to an officer named Magarino, with forty soldiers under his orders, all pledged to defend the passage to the last extremity. The bridge was to be taken up when the entire army had crossed one of the breaches, and transported to the next. There were three of these openings in the causeway, and most fortunate would it have been for the expedition, if the foresight of the commander had provided the same number of bridges. But the labor would have been great, and time was short.

At midnight the troops were under arms, in readiness for the march. Mass was performed by father Olmedo, who invoked the protection of the Almighty through the awful perils of the night. The gates were thrown open, and, on the first of July, 1520, the Spaniards for the last time sallied forth from the walls of the ancient fortress, the scene of so much suffering and such indomitable courage.

The night was cloudy, and a drizzling rain, which fell without intermission, added to the obscurity. The great square before the palace was deserted, as, indeed, it had been since the fall of Montezuma. Steadily, and as noiselessly as possible, the Spaniards held their way along the great street of Tlacopan, which so lately had resounded to the tumult of battle. All was now hushed in silence; and they were only reminded of the past by the occasional presence of some solitary corpse, or a dark heap of the slain, which too plainly told where the strife had been hottest. As they passed along the lanes and alleys which opened into the great street, or looked down the canals, whose polished surface gleamed with a sort of ebon lustre through the obscurity of night, they easily fancied that they discerned the shadowy forms of their foe lurking in ambush, and ready to spring on them. But it was only fancy; and the city slept undisturbed even by the prolonged echoes of the tramp of the horses, and the hoarse rumbling of the artillery and baggage trains. At length, a lighter space beyond the dusky line of buildings showed the van of the army that it was emerging on the open causeway. They might well have congratulated themselves on having thus escaped the dangers of an assault in the city itself, and that a brief time would place them in comparative safety on the opposite shore.—But the Mexicans were not all asleep.

As the Spaniards drew near the spot where the street opened on the causeway, and were preparing to lay the portable bridge across the uncovered breach, which now met their eyes, several Indian sentinels, who had been stationed at this, as at the other approaches to the city, took the alarm, and fled, rousing their countrymen by their cries. The priests, keeping their night watch on the summit of the *teocallis,* instantly caught the tidings and sounded their shells, while the huge drum in the desolate temple of the war-god sent forth those solemn tones, which, heard only in seasons of calamity, vibrated through every corner of the capital. The Spaniards saw that no time was to be lost. The bridge was brought forward and fitted with all possible expedition. Sandoval was the first to try its strength, and, riding across, was followed by his little body of chivalry, his infantry, and Tlascalan allies, who formed the first division of the army. Then came Cortés and his squadrons, with the baggage, ammunition wagons, and a part of the artillery. But before they had time to defile across the narrow passage, a gathering sound was heard, like that of a mighty forest agitated by the winds. It grew louder and louder, while on the dark waters of the lake was heard a splashing noise, as of many oars. Then came a few stones and arrows striking at random among the hurrying troops. They fell every moment faster and more furious, till they thickened into a terrible tempest, while the very heavens were rent with the yells and war-cries of myriads of combatants, who seemed all at once to be swarming over land and lake!

The Spaniards pushed steadily on through this arrowy sleet, though the barbarians, dashing their canoes against the sides of the causeway, clambered up and broke in upon their ranks. But the Christians, anxious only to make their escape, declined all combat except for self-preservation. The cavaliers, spurring forward their steeds, shook off their assailants, and rode over their prostrate bodies, while the men on foot with their good swords or the butts of their pieces drove them headlong again down the sides of the dike.

But the advance of several thousand men, marching, probably, on a front of not more than fifteen or twenty abreast, necessarily required much time, and the leading files had already reached the second breach in the causeway before those in the rear had entirely traversed the first. Here they halted; as they had no means of effecting a passage, smarting all the while under unintermitting volleys from the enemy, who were clustered thick on the waters around this second opening. Sorely distressed, the van-guard sent repeated messages to the rear to demand the portable bridge. At length the last of the army had crossed, and Magarino and his sturdy followers endeavored to raise the ponderous framework. But it stuck fast in the sides of the dike. In vain they strained every nerve. The weight of so many men and horses, and above all of the heavy artillery, had wedged the timbers so firmly in the stones and earth, that it was beyond their power to dislodge them. Still they labored amidst a torrent of missiles, until, many of them slain, and all wounded, they were obliged to abandon the attempt.

The tidings soon spread from man to man, and no sooner was their dreadful import comprehended, than a cry of despair arose, which for a moment drowned all the noise of conflict. All means of retreat were cut off. Scarcely hope was left. The only hope was in such desperate exertions as each could make for himself. Order and subordination were at an end. Intense danger produced intense selfishness. Each thought only of his own life. Pressing forward, he trampled down the weak and the wounded, heedless whether it were friend or foe. The leading files, urged on by the rear, were crowded on the brink of the gulf. Sandoval, Ordaz, and the other cavaliers dashed into the water. Some succeeded in swimming their horses across. Others failed, and some, who reached the opposite bank, being overturned in the ascent, rolled headlong with their steeds into the lake. The infantry followed pellmell, heaped promiscuously on one another, frequently pierced by the shafts, or struck down by the war-clubs of the

Aztecs; while many an unfortunate victim was dragged half-stunned on board their canoes, to be reserved for a protracted, but more dreadful death.

The carnage raged fearfully along the length of the causeway. Its shadowy bulk presented a mark of sufficient distinctness for the enemy's missiles, which often prostrated their own countrymen in the blind fury of the tempest. Those nearest the dike, running their canoes alongside, with a force that shattered them to pieces, leaped on the land, and grappled with the Christians, until both came rolling down the side of the causeway together. But the Aztec fell among his friends, while his antagonist was borne away in triumph to the sacrifice. The struggle was long and deadly. The Mexicans were recognised by their white cotton tunics, which showed faint through the darkness. Above the combatants rose a wild and discordant clamor, in which horrid shouts of vengeance were mingled with groans of agony, with invocations of the saints and the blessed Virgin, and with the screams of women; for there were several women, both natives and Spaniards, who had accompanied the Christian camp. Among these, one named María de Estrada is particularly noticed for the courage she displayed, battling with broadsword and target like the stanchest of the warriors.

The opening in the causeway, meanwhile, was filled up with the wreck of matter which had been forced into it, ammunition-wagons, heavy guns, bales of rich stuffs scattered over the waters, chests of solid ingots, and bodies of men and horses, till over this dismal ruin a passage was gradually formed, by which those in the rear were enabled to clamber to the other side. Cortés, it is said, found a place that was fordable, where, halting, with the water up to his saddle-girths, he endeavored to check the confusion, and lead his followers by a safer path to the opposite bank. But his voice was lost in the wild uproar, and finally, hurrying on with the tide, he pressed forwards with a few trusty cavaliers, who remained near his person, to the van; but not before he had seen his favorite page, Juan de Salazar, struck down, a corpse, by his side. Here he found Sandoval and his companions, halting before the third and last breach, endeavoring to cheer on their followers to surmount it. But their resolution faltered. It was wide and deep; though the passage was not so closely beset by the enemy as the preceding ones. The cavaliers again set the example by plunging into the water. Horse and foot followed as they could, some swimming, others with dying grasp clinging to the manes and tails of the struggling animals. Those fared best, as the general had predicted, who travelled lightest; and many were the unfortunate wretches, who, weighed down by the fatal gold which they loved so well, were buried with it in the salt floods of the lake. Cortés, with his gallant comrades, Olid, Morla, Sandoval, and some few others, still kept in the advance, leading his broken remnant off the fatal causeway. The din of battle lessened in the distance; when the rumor reached them, that the rearguard would be wholly overwhelmed without speedy relief. It seemed almost an act of desperation; but the generous hearts of the Spanish cavaliers did not stop to calculate danger, when the cry for succour reached them. Turning their horses' bridles, they galloped back to the theatre of action, worked their way through the press, swam the canal, and placed themselves in the thick of the *mêlée* on the opposite bank.

The first grey of the morning was now coming over the waters. It showed the hideous confusion of the scene which had been shrouded in the obscurity of night. The dark masses of combatants, stretching along the dike, were seen struggling for mastery, until the very causeway on which they stood appeared to tremble, and reel to and fro, as if shaken by an earthquake; while the bosom of the lake, as far as the eye could reach, was darkened by canoes crowded with warriors, whose spears and bludgeons, armed with blades of "volcanic glass," gleamed in the morning light.

The cavaliers found Alvarado unhorsed, and defending himself with a poor handful of followers against an overwhelming tide of the enemy. His good steed, which had borne him through many a hard fight, had fallen under him. He was himself wounded in several places, and was striving in vain to rally his scattered column, which was driven to the verge of the canal by the fury of the enemy, then in possession of the whole rear of the causeway, where they were reinforced every hour by fresh combatants from the city. The artillery in the earlier part of the engagement had not been idle, and its iron shower, sweeping along the dike, had mowed down the assailants by hundreds. But nothing could resist their impetuosity. The front ranks, pushed on by those behind, were at length forced up to the pieces, and, pouring over them like a torrent, overthrew men and guns in one general ruin. The resolute charge of the Spanish cavaliers, who had now arrived, created a temporary check, and gave time for their countrymen to make a feeble rally. But they were speedily borne down by the returning flood. Cortés and his companions were compelled to plunge again into the lake,—though all did not escape. Alvarado stood on the brink for a moment, hesitating what to do. Unhorsed as he was, to throw himself into the water, in the face of the hostile canoes that now swarmed around the opening, afforded but a desperate chance of safety. He had but a second for thought. He was a man of powerful frame, and despair gave him unnatural energy. Setting his long lance firmly on the wreck which strewed the bottom of the lake, he sprung forward with all his might, and cleared the wide gap at a leap! Aztecs and Tlascalans gazed in stupid amazement, exclaiming, as they beheld the incredible feat, "This is truly the *Tonatiuh,*— the child of the Sun!"—The breadth of the opening is not given. But it was so great, that the valorous captain Diaz, who well remembered the place, says the leap was impossible to any man. Other contemporaries, however, do not discredit the story. It was, beyond doubt, matter of popular belief at the time; it is to this day familiarly known to every inhabitant of the capital; and the name of the *Salto de Alvarado,* "Alvarado's Leap," given to the spot, still commemorates an exploit which rivalled those of the demi-gods of Grecian fable.

Cortés and his companions now rode forward to the front, where the troops, in a loose, disorderly manner, were marching off the fatal causeway. A few only of the enemy hung on their rear, or annoyed them by occasional flights of arrows from the lake. The attention of the Aztecs was diverted to the rich spoil that strewed the battle-ground; fortunately for the Spaniards, who, had their enemy pursued with the same ferocity with which he had fought, would, in their crippled condition, have been cut off, probably, to a man. But little molested, therefore, they were allowed to defile through the adjacent village, or suburbs, it might be called, of Popotla.

The Spanish commander there dismounted from his jaded steed, and, sitting down on the steps of an Indian temple, gazed mournfully on the broken files as they passed before him. What a spectacle did they present! The cavalry, most of them dismounted, were mingled with the infantry, who dragged their feeble limbs along with difficulty; their shattered mail and tattered garments dripping with the salt ooze, showing through their rents many a bruise and ghastly wound; their bright arms soiled, their proud crests and banners gone, the baggage, artillery, all, in short, that constitutes the pride and panoply of glorious war, for ever lost. Cortés, as he looked wistfully on their thinned and disordered ranks, sought in vain for many a familiar face, and missed more than one dear companion who had stood side by side with him through all the perils of the Conquest. Though accustomed to control his emotions, or, at least, to conceal them, the sight was too much for him. He covered his face with his hands, and the tears, which trickled down, revealed too plainly the anguish of his soul.

He found some consolation, however, in the sight of several of the cavaliers on whom he most relied. Alvarado, Sandoval, Olid, Ordaz, Avila, were yet safe. He had the inexpressible satisfaction, also, of learning the safety of the Indian interpreter, Marina, so dear to him, and so important to the army. She had been committed, with a daughter of a Tlascalan chief, to several of that nation. She was fortunately placed in the van, and her faithful escort had carried her securely through all the dangers of the night. Aguilar, the other interpreter, had also escaped. And it was with no less satisfaction, that Cortés learned the safety of the ship-builder, Martin Lopez. The general's solicitude for the fate of this man, so indispensable, as he proved, to the success of his subsequent operations, showed, that, amidst all his affliction, his indomitable spirit was looking forward to the hour of vengeance. . . .

Cortés retreated to Tlaxcala, where slowly gathering new supplies and allies, he began reconquering the periphery of the Aztec empire, moving slowly toward Tenochtitlán. In May, 1521, he began a three-month siege of the city.

Famine was now gradually working its way into the heart of the beleaguered city. It seemed certain, that, with this strict blockade, the
crowded population must in the end be driven to capitulate, though no
arm should be raised against them. But it required time; and the Spaniards,
though constant and enduring by nature, began to be impatient of hardships
scarcely inferior to those experienced by the besieged. In some respects their
condition was even worse, exposed, as they were, to the cold, drenching
rains, which fell with little intermission, rendering their situation dreary
and disastrous in the extreme.

In this state of things, there were many who would willingly have
shortened their sufferings, and taken the chance of carrying the place by
a *coup de main*. Others thought it would be best to get possession of the
great market of Tlatelolco, which, from its situation in the north-western
part of the city, might afford the means of communication with the camps
of both Alvarado and Sandoval. This place, encompassed by spacious
porticos, would furnish accommodations for a numerous host; and, once
established in the capital, the Spaniards would be in a position to follow
up the blow with far more effect than at a distance.

These arguments were pressed by several of the officers, particularly by
Alderete, the royal treasurer, a person of much consideration, not only
from his rank, but from the capacity and zeal he had shown in the service.
In deference to their wishes, Cortés summoned a council of war, and laid
the matter before it. The treasurer's views were espoused by most of the
high-mettled cavaliers, who looked with eagerness to any change of their
present forlorn and wearisome life; and Cortés, thinking it, probably, more
prudent to adopt the less expedient course, than to enforce a cold and reluctant obedience to his own opinion, suffered himself to be overruled.

A day was fixed for the assault, which was to be made simultaneously
by the two divisions under Alvarado and the commander-in-chief. Sandoval
was instructed to draw off the greater part of his forces from the northern
causeway, and to unite himself with Alvarado, while seventy picked soldiers
were to be detached to the support of Cortés.

On the appointed morning, the two armies, after the usual celebration
of mass, advanced along their respective causeways against the city. They
were supported, in addition to the brigantines, by a numerous fleet of
Indian boats, which were to force a passage up the canals, and by a countless multitude of allies, whose very numbers served in the end to embarrass
their operations. After clearing the suburbs, three avenues presented themselves, which all terminated in the square of Tlatelolco. The principal one,
being of much greater width than the other two, might rather be called a
causeway than a street, since it was flanked by deep canals on either side.
Cortés divided his force into three bodies. One of them he placed under
Alderete, with orders to occupy the principal street. A second he gave in
charge to Andres de Tapia and Jorge de Alvarado; the former a cavalier

of courage and capacity, the latter, a younger brother of Don Pedro, and possessed of the intrepid spirit which belonged to that chivalrous family. These were to penetrate by one of the parallel streets, while the general himself, at the head of the third division, was to occupy the other. A small body of cavalry, with two or three fieldpieces, was stationed as a reserve in front of the great street of Tacuba, which was designated as the rallying point for the different divisions.

Cortés gave the most positive instructions to his captains, not to advance a step without securing the means of retreat, by carefully filling up the ditches, and the openings in the causeway. The neglect of this precaution by Alvarado, in an assault which he had made on the city but a few days before, had been attended with such serious consequences to his army, that Cortés rode over, himself, to his officer's quarters, for the purpose of publicly reprimanding him for his disobedience of orders. On his arrival at the camp, however, he found that his offending captain had conducted the affair with so much gallantry, that the intended reprimand—though well deserved— subsided into a mild rebuke.

The arrangements being completed, the three divisions marched at once up the several streets. Cortés, dismounting, took the van of his own squadron, at the head of his infantry. The Mexicans fell back as he advanced, making less resistance than usual. The Spaniards pushed on, carrying one barricade after another, and carefully filling up the gaps with rubbish, so as to secure themselves a footing. The canoes supported the attack, by moving along the canals, and grappling with those of the enemy; while numbers of the nimble-footed Tlascalans, scaling the terraces, passed on from one house to another, where they were connected, hurling the defenders into the streets below. The enemy, taken apparently by surprise, seemed incapable of withstanding for a moment the fury of the assault; and the victorious Christians, cheered on by the shouts of triumph which arose from their companions in the adjoining streets, were only the more eager to be first at the destined goal.

Indeed, the facility of his success led the general to suspect that he might be advancing too fast; that it might be a device of the enemy to draw them into the heart of the city, and then surround or attack them in the rear. He had some misgivings, moreover, lest his too ardent officers, in the heat of the chase, should, notwithstanding his commands, have overlooked the necessary precaution of filling up the breaches. He, accordingly, brought his squadron to a halt, prepared to baffle any insidious movement of his adversary. Meanwhile he received more than one message from Alderete, informing him that he had nearly gained the market. This only increased the general's apprehension, that, in the rapidity of his advance, he might have neglect to secure the ground. He determined to trust no eyes but his own, and, taking a small body of troops, proceeded at once to reconnoitre the route followed by the treasurer.

He had not proceeded far along the great street, or causeway, when his progress was arrested by an opening ten or twelve paces wide, and filled with water, at least two fathoms deep, by which a communication was formed between the canals on the opposite sides. A feeble attempt had been made to stop the gap with the rubbish of the causeway, but in too careless a manner to be of the least service; and a few straggling stones and pieces of timber only showed that the work had been abandoned almost as soon as begun. To add to his consternation, the general observed that the sides of the causeway in this neighborhood had been pared off, and, as was evident, very recently. He saw in all this the artifice of the cunning enemy; and had little doubt that his hot-headed officer had rushed into a snare deliberately laid for him. Deeply alarmed, he set about repairing the mischief as fast as possible, by ordering his men to fill up the yawning chasm.

But they had scarcely begun their labors, when the hoarse echoes of conflict in the distance were succeeded by a hideous sound of mingled yells and war-whoops, that seemed to rend the very heavens. This was followed by a rushing noise, as of the tread of thronging multitudes, showing that the tide of battle was turned back from its former course, and was rolling on towards the spot where Cortés and his little band of cavaliers were planted.

His conjecture proved too true. Alderete had followed the retreating Aztecs with an eagerness which increased with every step of his advance. He had carried the barricades, which had defended the breach, without much difficulty, and, as he swept on, gave orders that the opening should be stopped. But the blood of the high-spirited cavaliers was warmed by the chase, and no one cared to be detained by the ignoble occupation of filling up the ditches, while he could gather laurels so easily in the fight; and they all pressed on, exhorting and cheering one another with the assurance of being the first to reach the square of Tlatelolco. In this way they suffered themselves to be decoyed into the heart of the city; when suddenly the horn of Guatemozin—the sacred symbol, heard only in seasons of extraordinary peril—sent forth a long and piercing note from the summit of a neighboring *teocalli*. In an instant, the flying Aztecs, as if maddened by the blast, wheeled about, and turned on their pursuers. At the same time, countless swarms of warriors from the adjoining streets and lanes poured in upon the flanks of the assailants, filling the air with the fierce, unearthly cries which had reached the ears of Cortés, and drowning, for a moment, the wild dissonance which reigned in the other quarters of the capital.

The army, taken by surprise, and shaken by the fury of the assault, were thrown into the utmost disorder. Friends and foes, white men and Indians, were mingled together in one promiscuous mass. Spears, swords, and warclubs were brandished together in the air. Blows fell at random. In their eagerness to escape, they trod down one another. Blinded by the missiles, which now rained on them from the *azoteas,* they staggered on, scarcely knowing in what direction, or fell, struck down by hands which they could not see. On they came like a rushing torrent sweeping along some steep declivity, and rolling in one confused tide towards the open breach, on the further side of which stood Cortés and his companions, horror-struck at the sight of the approaching ruin. The foremost files soon plunged into the gulf, treading one another under the flood, some striving ineffectually to swim, others, with more success, to clamber over the heaps of their suffocated comrades. Many, as they attempted to scale the opposite sides of the slippery dike, fell into the water, or were hurried off by the warriors in the canoes, who added to the horrors of the rout by the fresh storm of darts and javelins, which they poured on the fugitives.

Cortés, meanwhile, with his brave followers, kept his station undaunted on the other side of the breach. "I had made up my mind," he says, "to die, rather than desert my poor followers in their extremity!" With out-stretched hands he endeavored to rescue as many as he could from the watery grave, and from the more appalling fate of captivity. He as vainly tried to restore something like presence of mind and order among the distracted fugitives. His person was too well known to the Aztecs, and his position now made him a conspicuous mark for their weapons. Darts, stones, and arrows fell around him thick as hail, but glanced harmless from his steel helmet and armor of proof. At length a cry of "Malinche," "Malinche," arose among the enemy; and six of their number, strong and athletic warriors, rushing on him at once, made a violent effort to drag him on board their boat. In the struggle he received a severe wound in the leg, which, for the time, disabled it. There seemed to be no hope for him; when a faithful follower, Christóval de Olea, perceiving his general's extremity, threw himself on the Aztecs, and with a blow cut off the arm of one savage, and then plunged his sword in the body of another. He was quickly supported by a comrade named Lerma, and by a Tlascalan chief, who, fighting over the prostrate body of Cortés, despatched three more of the assailants, though the heroic Olea paid dearly for his self-devotion, as he fell mortally wounded by the side of his general.

The report soon spread among the soldiers, that their commander was taken; and Quiñones, the captain of his guard, with several others, pouring in to the rescue, succeeded in disentangling Cortés from the grasp of his enemies who were struggling with him in the water, and, raising him in their arms, placed him again on the causeway. One of his pages, meanwhile, had advanced some way through the press, leading a horse for his master to mount. But the youth received a wound in the throat from a javelin, which prevented him from effecting his object. Another of his attendants was more successful. It was Guzman, his chamberlain; but, as he held the bridle, while Cortés was assisted into the saddle, he was snatched away by the Aztecs, and, with the swiftness of thought, hurried off by their canoes. The general still lingered, unwilling to leave the spot, while his presence could be of the least service. But the faithful Quiñones, taking his horse by the bridle, turned his head from the breach, exclaiming, at the same time, that "his master's life was too important to the army to be thrown away there."

Yet it was no easy matter to force a passage through the press. The surface of the causeway, cut up by the feet of men and horses, was knee-deep in mud, and in some parts was so much broken, that the water from the canals flowed over it. The crowded mass, in their efforts to extricate themselves from their perilous position, staggered to and fro like a drunken man. Those on the flanks were often forced by the lateral pressure of their comrades down the slippery sides of the dike, where they were picked up by the canoes of the enemy, whose shouts of triumph proclaimed the savage joy with which they gathered in every new victim for the sacrifice. Two cavaliers, riding by the general's side, lost their footing, and rolled down the declivity into the water. One was taken and his horse killed. The other was happy enough to escape. The valiant ensign, Corral, had a similar piece of good fortune. He slipped into the canal, and the enemy felt sure of their prize, when he again succeeded in recovering the causeway with the tattered banner of Castile still flying above his head. The barbarians set up a cry of disappointed rage, as they lost possession of a trophy, to which the people of Anahuac attached, as we have seen, the highest importance, hardly inferior in their eyes to the capture of the commander-in-chief himself.

Cortés at length succeeded in regaining the firm ground, and reaching the open place before the great street of Tacuba. Here, under a sharp fire of the artillery, he rallied his broken squadrons, and, charging at the head of the little body of horse, which, not having been brought into action, were still fresh, he beat off the enemy. He then commanded the retreat of the two other divisions. The scattered forces again united; and the general, sending forward his Indian confederates, took the rear with a chosen body of cavalry to cover the retreat of the army, which was effected with but little additional loss.

Andres de Tapia was despatched to the western causeway to acquaint Alvarado and Sandoval with the failure of the enterprise. Meanwhile the two captains had penetrated far into the city. Cheered by the triumphant shouts of their countrymen in the adjacent streets, they had pushed on with extraordinary vigor, that they might not be outstripped in the race of glory. They had almost reached the market-place, which lay nearer to their quarters than to the general's, when they heard the blast from the dread horn of Guatemozin, followed by the overpowering yell of the barbarians, which had so startled the ears of Cortés; till at length the sounds of the receding conflict died away in the distance. The two captains now understood that the day must have gone hard with their countrymen. They soon had further proof of it, when the victorious Aztecs, returning from the pursuit of Cortés, joined their forces to those engaged with Sandoval and Alvarado, and fell on them with redoubled fury. At the same time they rolled on the ground

two or three of the bloody heads of the Spaniards, shouting the name of
"Malinche." The captains, struck with horror at the spectacle,—though
they gave little credit to the words of the enemy,—instantly ordered a retreat. Indeed, it was not in their power to maintain their ground against the
furious assaults of the besieged, who poured on them, swarm after swarm,
with a desperation, of which, says one who was there, "although it seems as
if it were now present to my eyes, I can give but a faint idea to the reader,
God alone could have brought us off safe from the perils of that day."
The fierce barbarians followed up the Spaniards to their very intrenchments.
But here they were met, first by the cross fire of the brigantines, which,
dashing through the palisades planted to obstruct their movements, completely enfiladed the causeway, and next by that of the small battery erected
in front of the camp, which, under the management of a skilful engineer,
named Medrano, swept the whole length of the defile. Thus galled in front
and on flank, the shattered columns of the Aztecs were compelled to give
way and take shelter under the defences of the city.

The greatest anxiety now prevailed in the camp, regarding the fate of
Cortés; for Tapia had been detained on the road by scattered parties of the
enemy, whom Guatemozin had stationed there to interrupt the communications between the camps. He arrived, at length, however, though bleeding
from several wounds. His intelligence, while it reassured the Spaniards
as to the general's personal safety, was not calculated to allay their uneasiness in other respects.

Sandoval, in particular, was desirous to acquaint himself with the actual
state of things, and the further intentions of Cortés. Suffering as he was
from three wounds, which he had received in that day's fight, he resolved
to visit in person the quarters of the commander-in-chief. It was mid-day,—
for the busy scenes of the morning had occupied but a few hours,—when
Sandoval remounted the good steed, on whose strength and speed he knew
he could rely. It was a noble animal, well-known throughout the army, and
worthy of its gallant rider, whom it had carried safe through all the long
marches and bloody battles of the conquest. On the way he fell in with
Guatemozin's scouts, who gave him chase, and showered around him volleys
of missiles, which fortunately found no vulnerable point in his own harness,
or that of his well-barbed charger.

On arriving at the camp, he found the troops there much worn and
dispirited by the disaster of the morning. They had good reason to be so.
Besides the killed, and a long file of wounded, sixty-two Spaniards, with
a multitude of allies, had fallen alive into the hands of the enemy,—an
enemy who was never known to spare a captive. The loss of two field-pieces
and seven horses crowned their own disgrace and the triumphs of the Aztecs.
This loss, so insignificant in European warfare, was a great one here, where
both horses and artillery, the most powerful arms of war against the barbarians, were not to be procured without the greatest cost and difficulty.

Cortés, it was observed, had borne himself throughout this trying day with his usual intrepidity and coolness. The only time he was seen to falter was when the Mexicans threw down before him the heads of several Spaniards, shouting, at the same time, "Sandoval," "Tonatiuh," the well-known epithet of Alvarado. At the sight of the gory trophies, he grew deadly pale,—but, in a moment recovering his usual confidence, he endeavored to cheer up the drooping spirits of his followers. It was with a cheerful countenance, that he now received his lieutenant; but a shade of sadness was visible through this outward composure, showing how the catastrophe of the *puente cuidada,* "the sorrowful bridge," as he mournfully called it, lay heavy at his heart.

To the cavalier's anxious inquiries, as to the cause of the disaster, he replied: "It is for my sins, that it has befallen me, son Sandoval"; for such was the affectionate epithet with which Cortés often addressed his best-beloved and trusty officer. He then explained to him the immediate cause, in the negligence of the treasurer. Further conversation followed, in which the general declared his purpose to forego active hostilities for a few days. "You must take my place," he continued, "for I am too much crippled at present to discharge my duties. You must watch over the safety of the camps. Give especial heed to Alvarado's. He is a gallant soldier, I know it well; but I doubt the Mexican hounds may, some hour, take him at disadvantage." These few words showed the general's own estimate of his two lieutenants; both equally brave and chivalrous; but the one uniting with these qualities the circumspection so essential to success in perilous enterprises, in which the other was signally deficient. The future conqueror of Guatemala had to gather wisdom, as usual, from the bitter fruits of his own errors. It was under the training of Cortés that he learned to be a soldier.— The general, having concluded his instructions, affectionately embraced his lieutenant, and dismissed him to his quarters.

It was late in the afternoon when he reached them; but the sun was still lingering above the western hills, and poured his beams wide over the Valley, lighting up the old towers and temples of Tenochtitlan with a mellow radiance, that little harmonized with the dark scenes of strife, in which the city had so lately been involved. The tranquillity of the hour, however, was, on a sudden, broken by the strange sounds of the great drum in the temple of the war-god,—sounds which recalled the *noche triste,* with all its terrible images, to the minds of the Spaniards, for that was the only occasion on which they had ever heard them. They intimated some solemn act of religion within the unhallowed precincts of the *teocalli*; and the soldiers, startled by the mournful vibrations, which might be heard for leagues across the Valley, turned their eyes to the quarter whence they proceeded. They there beheld a long procession winding up the huge sides of the pyramid; for the camp of Alvarado was pitched scarcely a mile from the city, and objects are distinctly visible, at a great distance, in the transparent atmosphere of the table-land.

As the long file of priests and warriors reached the flat summit of the *teocalli,* the Spaniards saw the figures of several men stripped to their waists, some of whom, by the whiteness of their skins, they recognised as their own countrymen. They were the victims for sacrifice. Their heads were gaudily decorated with coronals of plumes, and they carried fans in their hands. They were urged along by blows, and compelled to take part in the dances in honor of the Aztec war-god. The unfortunate captives, then stripped of their sad finery, were stretched, one after another, on the great stone of sacrifice. On its convex surface, their breasts heaved up conveniently for the diabolical purpose of the priestly executioner, who cut asunder the ribs by a strong blow with his sharp razor of *itztli,* and, thrusting his hand into the wound, tore away the heart, which, hot and reeking, was deposited on the golden censer before the idol. The body of the slaughtered victim was then hurled down the steep stairs of the pyramid, which, it may be re-membered, were placed at the same angle of the pile, one flight below an-other; and the mutilated remains were gathered up by the savages beneath, who soon prepared with them the cannibal repast which completed the work of abomination!

We may imagine with what sensations the stupefied Spaniards must have gazed on this horrid spectacle, so near that they could almost recognise the persons of their unfortunate friends, see the struggles and writhing of their bodies, hear—or fancy that they heard—their screams of agony! yet so far removed, that they could render them no assistance. Their limbs trembled beneath them, as they thought what might one day be their own fate; and the bravest among them, who had hitherto gone to battle, as careless and light-hearted, as to the banquet or the ball-room, were unable, from this time forward, to encounter their ferocious enemy without a sickening feel-ing, much akin to fear, coming over them.

Such was not the effect produced by this spectacle on the Mexican forces, gathered at the end of the causeway. Like vultures maddened by the smell of distant carrion, they set up a piercing cry, and, as they shouted that "such should be the fate of all their enemies," swept along in one fierce torrent over the dike. But the Spaniards were not to be taken by surprise; and, before the barbarian horde had come within their lines, they opened such a deadly fire from their battery of heavy guns, supported by the musketry and crossbows, that the assailants were compelled to fall back slowly, but fearfully mangled, to their former position.

The five following days passed away in a state of inaction, except, indeed, so far as was necessary to repel the *sorties,* made from time to time, by the militia of the capital. The Mexicans, elated with their success, meanwhile, abandoned themselves to jubilee; singing, dancing, and feasting on the mangled relics of their wretched victims. Guatemozin sent several heads of the Spaniards, as well as of the horses, round the country, calling on his old vassals to forsake the banners of the white men, unless they would share the doom of the enemies of Mexico. The priests now cheered the

young monarch and the people with the declaration, that the dread Huitzilo-
pochtli, their offended deity, appeased by the sacrifices offered up on his
altars, would again take the Aztecs under his protection, and deliver their
enemies, before the expiration of eight days, into their hands.

This comfortable prediction, confidently believed by the Mexicans, was
thundered in the ears of the besieging army in tones of exultation and defiance. However it may have been contemned by the Spaniards, it had a
very different effect on their allies. The latter had begun to be disgusted with
a service so full of peril and suffering, and already protracted far beyond
the usual term of Indian hostilities. They had less confidence than before
in the Spaniards. Experience had shown that they were neither invincible
nor immortal, and their recent reverses made them even distrust the ability
of the Christians to reduce the Aztec metropolis. They recalled to mind the
ominous words of Xicotencatl, that "so sacrilegious a war could come to no
good for the people of Anahuac." They felt that their arm was raised against
the gods of their country. The prediction of the oracle fell heavy on their
hearts. They had little doubt of its fulfilment, and were only eager to turn
away the bolt from their own heads by a timely secession from the cause.

They took advantage, therefore, of the friendly cover of night to steal
away from their quarters. Company after company deserted in this manner,
taking the direction of their respective homes. Those belonging to the great
towns of the Valley, whose allegiance was the most recent, were the first
to cast it off. Their example was followed by the older confederates, the
militia of Cholula, Tepeaca, Tezcuco, and even the faithful Tlascala. There
were, it is true, some exceptions to these, and, among them, Ixtlilxochitl, the
young lord of Tezcuco, and Chichemecatl, the valiant Tlascalan chieftain,
who, with a few of their immediate followers, still remained true to the
banner under which they had enlisted. But their number was insignificant.—
The Spaniards beheld with dismay the mighty array, on which they relied
for support, thus silently melting away before the breath of superstition.
Cortés alone maintained a cheerful countenance. He treated the prediction
with contempt, as an invention of the priests, and sent his messengers after
the retreating squadrons, beseeching them to postpone their departure, or
at least to halt on the road, till the time, which would soon elapse, should
show the falsehood of the prophecy.

The affairs of the Spaniards, at this crisis, must be confessed to have
worn a gloomy aspect. Deserted by their allies, with their ammunition nearly
exhausted, cut off from the customary supplies from the neighborhood,
harassed by unintermitting vigils and fatigues, smarting under wounds, of
which every man in the army had his share, with an unfriendly country in
their rear, and a mortal foe in front, they might well be excused for faltering
in their enterprise. They found abundant occupation by day in foraging the
country, and in maintaining their position on the causeways against the
enemy, now made doubly daring by success, and by the promises of their

priests; while at night their slumbers were disturbed by the beat of the melancholy drum, the sounds of which, booming far over the waters, tolled the knell of their murdered comrades. Night after night fresh victims were led up to the great altar of sacrifice; and, while the city blazed with the illumination of a thousand bonfires on the terraced roofs of the dwellings, and in the areas of the temples, the dismal pageant, showing through the fiery glare like the work of the ministers of hell, was distinctly visible from the camp below. One of the last of the sufferers was Guzman, the unfortunate chamberlain of Cortés, who lingered in captivity eighteen days before he met his doom.

Yet in this hour of trial the Spaniards did not falter. Had they faltered, they might have learned a lesson of fortitude from some of their own wives, who continued with them in the camp, and who displayed a heroism, on this occasion, of which history has preserved several examples. One of these, protected by her husband's armor, would frequently mount guard in his place, when he was wearied. Another, hastily putting on a soldier's *escaupil,* and seizing a sword and lance, was seen, on one occasion, to rally their retreating countrymen, and led them back against the enemy. Cortés would have persuaded these Amazonian dames to remain at Tlascala; but they proudly replied, "It was the duty of Castilian wives not to abandon their husbands in danger, but to share it with them,—and die with them, if necessary." And well did they do their duty.

Amidst all the distresses and multiplied embarrassments of their situation, the Spaniards still remained true to their purpose. They relaxed in no degree the severity of the blockade. Their camps still occupied the only avenues to the city; and their batteries, sweeping the long defiles at every fresh assault of the Aztecs, mowed down hundreds of the assailants. Their brigantines still rode on the waters, cutting off the communication with the shore. It is true, indeed, the loss of the auxiliary canoes left a passage open for the occasional introduction of supplies to the capital. But the whole amount of these supplies was small; and its crowded population, while exulting in their temporary advantage, and the delusive assurances of their priests, were beginning to sink under the withering grasp of an enemy within, more terrible than the one which lay before their gates.

For several weeks the Spaniards rested, then resumed their systematic destruction of Tenochtitlán. By mid-August, the half-starved Aztecs had been driven back into a small northwest corner of the city and the end was near.

It was the memorable 13th of August, 1521, the day of St. Hypolito,— from this circumstance selected as the patron saint of modern Mexico,—

that Cortés led his warlike array for the last time across the black and
blasted environs which lay around the Indian capital. On entering the Aztec
precincts, he paused, willing to afford its wretched inmates one more chance
of escape, before striking the fatal blow. He obtained an interview with
some of the principal chiefs, and expostulated with them on the conduct of
their prince. "He surely will not," said the general, "see you all perish, when
he can so easily save you." He then urged them to prevail on Guatemozin
to hold a conference with him, repeating the assurances of his personal
safety.

The messengers went on their mission, and soon returned with the
cihuacoatl at their head, a magistrate of high authority among the Mexicans.
He said, with a melancholy air, in which his own disappointment was visible,
that "Guatemozin was ready to die where he was, but would hold no interview with the Spanish commander"; adding, in a tone of resignation, "it is
for you to work your pleasure." "Go, then," replied the stern Conqueror,
"and prepare your countrymen for death. Their hour is come."

He still postponed the assault for several hours. But the impatience of
his troops at this delay was heightened by the rumor, that Guatemozin and
his nobles were preparing to escape with their effects in the *piraguas* and
canoes which were moored on the margin of the lake. Convinced of the
fruitlessness and impolicy of further procrastination, Cortés made his final
dispositions for the attack, and took his own station on an *azotea,* which
commanded the theatre of operations.

When the assailants came into presence of the enemy, they found them
huddled together in the utmost confusion, all ages and sexes, in masses
so dense that they nearly forced one another over the brink of the causeways
into the water below. Some had climbed on the terraces, others feebly supported themselves against the walls of the buildings. Their squalid and
tattered garments gave a wildness to their appearance, which still further
heightened the ferocity of their expression, as they glared on their enemy
with eyes in which hate was mingled with despair. When the Spaniards had
approached within bowshot, the Aztecs let off a flight of impotent missiles,
showing, to the last, the resolute spirit, though they had lost the strength,
of their better days. The fatal signal was then given by the discharge of an
arquebuse,—speedily followed by peals of heavy ordnance, the rattle of
fire-arms, and the hellish shouts of the confederates, as they sprang upon
their victims. It is unnecessary to stain the page with a repetition of the
horrors of the preceding day. Some of the wretched Aztecs threw themselves
into the water, and were picked up by the canoes. Others sunk and were
suffocated in the canals. The number of these became so great, that a bridge
was made of their dead bodies, over which the assailants could climb to the
opposite banks. Others again, especially the women, begged for mercy,
which, as the chroniclers assure us, was everywhere granted by the

Spaniards, and, contrary to the instructions and entreaties of Cortés, everywhere refused by the confederates.

While this work of butchery was going on, numbers were observed pushing off in the barks that lined the shore, and making the best of their way across the lake. They were constantly intercepted by the brigantines, which broke through the flimsy array of boats; sending off their volleys to the right and left, as the crews of the latter hotly assailed them. The battle raged as fiercely on the lake as on the land. Many of the Indian vessels were shattered and overturned. Some few, however, under cover of the smoke, which rolled darkly over the waters, succeeded in clearing themselves of the turmoil, and were fast nearing the opposite shore.

Sandoval had particularly charged his captains to keep an eye on the movements of any vessel in which it was at all probable that Guatemozin might be concealed. At this crisis, three or four of the largest *piraguas* were seen skimming over the water, and making their way rapidly across the lake. A captain, named Garci Holguin, who had command of one of the best sailers in the fleet, instantly gave them chase. The wind was favorable, and, every moment, he gained on the fugitives, who pulled their oars with a vigor that despair alone could have given. But it was in vain; and, after a short race, Holguin, coming alongside of one of the *piraguas,* which, whether from its appearance, or from information he had received, he conjectured might bear the Indian emperor, ordered his men to level their crossbows at the boat. But, before they could discharge them, a cry arose from those in it, that their lord was on board. At the same moment, a young warrior, armed with buckler and *maquahuitl,* rose up, as if to beat off the assailants. But, as the Spanish captain ordered his men not to shoot, he dropped his weapons, and exclaimed, "I am Guatemozin; lead me to Malinche, I am his prisoner; but let no harm come to my wife and my followers."

Holguin assured him, that his wishes should be respected, and assisted him to get on board the brigantine, followed by his wife and attendants. These were twenty in number, consisting of Coanaco, the deposed lord of Tezcuco, the lord of Tlacopan, and several other caciques and dignitaries, whose rank, probably, had secured them some exemption from the general calamities of the siege. When the captives were seated on the deck of his vessel, Holguin requested the Aztec prince to put an end to the combat by commanding his people in the other canoes to surrender. But, with a dejected air, he replied, "It is not necessary. They will fight no longer, when they see that their prince is taken." He spoke truth. The news of Guatemozin's capture spread rapidly through the fleet, and on shore, where the Mexicans were still engaged in conflict with their enemies. It ceased, however, at once. They made no further resistance; and those on the water quickly followed the brigantines, which conveyed their captive monarch to land. It seemed as if the fight had been maintained thus long, the better to divert the enemy's attention, and cover their master's retreat.

Meanwhile Sandoval, on receiving tidings of the capture, brought his own brigantine alongside of Holguin's, and demanded the royal prisoner to be surrendered to him. But his captain claimed him as his prize. A dispute arose between the parties, each anxious to have the glory of the deed, and perhaps the privilege of commemorating it on his escutcheon. The controversy continued so long that it reached the ears of Cortés, who, in his station on the *azotea,* had learned, with no little satisfaction, the capture of his enemy. He instantly sent orders to his wrangling officers, to bring Guatemozin before him, that he might adjust the difference between them. He charged them, at the same time, to treat their prisoner with respect. He then made preparations for the interview; caused the terrace to be carpeted with crimson cloth and matting, and a table to be spread with provisions, of which the unhappy Aztecs stood so much in need. His lovely Indian mistress, Doña Marina, was present to act as interpreter. She had stood by his side through all the troubled scenes of the Conquest, and she was there now to witness its triumphant termination.

Guatemozin, on landing, was escorted by a company of infantry to the presence of the Spanish commander. He mounted the *azotea* with a calm and steady step, and was easily to be distinguished from his attendant nobles, though his full, dark eye was no longer lighted up with its accustomed fire, and his features wore an expression of passive resignation, that told little of the fierce and fiery spirit that burned within. His head was large, his limbs well proportioned, his complexion fairer than those of his bronze-colored nation, and his whole deportment singularly mild and engaging.

Cortés came forward with a dignified and studied courtesy to receive him. The Aztec monarch probably knew the person of his conqueror, for he first broke silence by saying; "I have done all that I could, to defend myself and my people. I am now reduced to this state. You will deal with me, Malinche, as you list." Then, laying his hand on the hilt of a poniard, stuck in the general's belt, he added, with vehemence, "Better despatch me with this, and rid me of life at once." Cortés was filled with admiration at the proud bearing of the young barbarian, showing in his reverses a spirit worthy of an ancient Roman. "Fear not," he replied, "you shall be treated with all honor. You have defended your capital like a brave warrior. A Spaniard knows how to respect valor even in an enemy." He then inquired of him, where he had left the princess, his wife; and, being informed that she still remained under protection of a Spanish guard on board the brigantine, the general sent to have her escorted to his presence.

She was the youngest daughter of Montezuma, and was hardly yet on the verge of womanhood. On the accession of her cousin, Guatemozin, to the throne, she had been wedded to him as his lawful wife. She is celebrated by her contemporaries for her personal charms; and the beautiful princess, Tecuichpo, is still commemorated by the Spaniards, since from her, by a subsequent marriage, are descended some of the illustrious families of their own nation. She was kindly received by Cortés, who showed her the respectful attentions suited to her rank. Her birth, no doubt, gave her an additional interest in his eyes, and he may have felt some touch of compunction, as he gazed on the daughter of the unfortunate Montezuma. He invited his royal captives to partake of the refreshments, which their exhausted condition rendered so necessary. Meanwhile the Spanish commander made his dispositions for the night, ordering Sandoval to escort the prisoners to Cojohuacan, whither he proposed, himself, immediately to follow. The other captains, Olid and Alvarado, were to draw off their forces to their respective quarters. It was impossible for them to continue in the capital, where the poisonous effluvia from the unburied carcasses loaded the air with infection. A small guard only was stationed to keep order in the wasted suburbs.—It was the hour of vespers when Guatemozin surrendered, and the siege might be considered as then concluded. The evening set in dark, and the rain began to fall, before the several parties had evacuated the city.

During the night, a tremendous tempest, such as the Spaniards had rarely witnessed, and such as is known only within the tropics, burst over the Mexican Valley. The thunder, reverberating from the rocky amphitheatre of hills, bellowed over the waste of waters, and shook the *teocallis* and crazy tenements of Tenochtitlan—the few that yet survived—to their foundations. The lightning seemed to cleave asunder the vault of heaven, as its vivid flashes wrapped the whole scene in a ghastly glare, for a moment, to be again swallowed up in darkness. The war of elements was in unison with the fortunes of the ruined city. It seemed as if the deities of Anahuac, scared from their ancient abodes, were borne along shrieking and howling in the blast, as they abandoned the fallen capital to its fate!

On the day following the surrender, Guatemozin requested the Spanish commander to allow the Mexicans to leave the city, and to pass unmolested into the open country. To this Cortés readily assented, as, indeed, without it he could take no steps for purifying the capital. He gave his orders, accordingly, for the evacuation of the place, commanding that no one, Spaniard or confederate, should offer violence to the Aztecs, or in any way obstruct their departure. The whole number of these is variously estimated at from thirty to seventy thousand, beside women and children, who had survived the sword, pestilence, and famine. It is certain they were three days in defiling along the several causeways,—a mournful train; husbands and wives, parents and children, the sick and the wounded, leaning on one another for support, as they feebly tottered along, squalid, and but half covered with rags, that disclosed at every step hideous gashes, some recently received, others festering from long neglect, and carrying with them an atmosphere of contagion. Their wasted forms and famine-stricken faces told the whole history of the siege; and, as the straggling files gained the opposite shore, they were observed to pause from time to time, as if to take one more look at the spot so lately crowned by the imperial city, once their pleasant home, and endeared to them by many a glorious recollection.

On the departure of the inhabitants, measures were immediately taken to purify the place, by means of numerous fires kept burning day and night, especially in the infected quarter of Tlatelolco, and by collecting the heaps of dead, which lay mouldering in the streets, and consigning them to the earth.—Of the whole number, who perished in the course of the siege, it is impossible to form any probable computation. The accounts range widely from one hundred and twenty thousand, the lowest estimate, to two hundred and forty thousand. The number of the Spaniards who fell was comparatively small, but that of the allies must have been large, if the historian of Tezcuco is correct in asserting, that thirty thousand perished of his own countrymen alone. That the number of those destroyed within the city was immense cannot be doubted, when we consider, that, besides its own redundant population, it was thronged with that of the neighboring towns, who, distrusting their strength to resist the enemy, sought protection within its walls.

The booty found there—that is, the treasures of gold and jewels, the only booty of much value in the eyes of the Spaniards—fell far below their expectations. It did not exceed, according to the general's statement, a hundred and thirty thousand *castellanos* of gold, including the sovereign's share, which, indeed, taking into account many articles of curious and costly workmanship, voluntarily relinquished by the army, greatly exceeded his legitimate fifth. Yet the Aztecs must have been in possession of a much larger treasure, if it were only the wreck of that recovered from the Spaniards on the night of the memorable flight from Mexico. Some of the spoil may have been sent away from the capital; some spent in preparations for defence, and more of it buried in the earth, or sunk in the water of the lake. Their menaces were not without a meaning. They had, at least, the satisfaction of disappointing the avarice of their enemies.

Cortés had no further occasion for the presence of his Indian allies. He assembled the chiefs of the different squadrons, thanked them for their services, noticed their valor in flattering terms, and, after distributing presents among them, with the assurance that his master, the Emperor, would recompense their fidelity yet more largely, dismissed them to their own homes. They carried off a liberal share of the spoils, of which they had plundered the dwellings,—not of a kind to excite the cupidity of the Spaniards,—and returned in triumph, short-sighted triumph! at the success of their expedition, and the downfall of the Aztec dynasty.

Great, also, was the satisfaction of the Spaniards at this brilliant termination of their long and laborious campaign. They were, indeed, disappointed at the small amount of treasure found in the conquered city. But the soldier is usually too much absorbed in the present to give much heed to the future; and, though their discontent showed itself afterwards in a more clamorous form, they now thought only of their triumph, and abandoned themselves to jubilee. Cortés celebrated the event by a banquet, as sumptuous as circumstances would permit, to which all the cavaliers and officers were invited. Loud and long was their revelry, which was carried to such an excess, as provoked the animadversion of father Olmedo, who intimated that this was not the fitting way to testify their sense of the favors shown them by the Almighty. Cortés admitted the justice of the rebuke, but craved some indulgence for a soldier's license in the hour of victory. The following day was appointed for the commemoration of their successes in a more suitable manner.

A procession of the whole army was then formed with father Olmedo at its head. The soiled and tattered banners of Castile, which had waved over many a field of battle, now threw their shadows on the peaceful array of the soldiery, as they slowly moved along, rehearsing the litany, and displaying the image of the Virgin and the blessed symbol of man's redemption. The reverend father pronounced a discourse, in which he briefly reminded the troops of their great cause for thankfulness to Providence for conducting them safe through their long and perilous pilgrimage; and, dwelling on the responsibility incurred by their present position, he besought them not to abuse the rights of conquest, but to treat the unfortunate Indians with humanity. The sacrament was then administered to the commander-in-chief and the principal cavaliers, and the services concluded with a solemn thanksgiving to the God of battles, who had enabled them to carry the banner of the Cross triumphant over this barbaric empire.

Thus, after a siege of nearly three months' duration, unmatched in history for the constancy and courage of the besieged, seldom surpassed for the severity of its sufferings, fell the renowned capital of the Aztecs. Unmatched, it may be truly said, for constancy and courage, when we recollect that the door of capitulation on the most honorable terms was left open to them throughout the whole blockade, and that, sternly rejecting every proposal of their enemy, they, to a man, preferred to die rather than surrender. More than three centuries had elapsed, since the Aztecs, a poor and wandering tribe from the far North-west had come on the plateau. There they built their miserable collection of huts on the spot— as tradition tells us—prescribed by the oracle. Their conquests, at first confined to their immediate neighborhood, gradually covered the Valley, then, crossing the mountains, swept over the broad extent of the table-land, descended its precipitous sides, and rolled onwards to the Mexican Gulf, and the distant confines of Central America. Their wretched capital, meanwhile, keeping pace with the enlargement of territory, had grown into a flourishing city, filled with buildings, monuments of art, and a numerous population, that gave it the first rank among the capitals of the Western World. At this crisis, came over another race from the remote East, strangers like themselves, whose coming had also been predicted by the oracle, and, appearing on the plateau, assailed them in the very zenith of their prosperity, and blotted them out from the map of nations for ever! The whole story has the air of fable, rather than of history! a legend of romance,—a tale of the genii!

Yet we cannot regret the fall of an empire, which did so little to promote the happiness of its subjects, or the real interests of humanity. Notwithstanding the lustre thrown over its latter days by the glorious defence of its capital, by the mild munificence of Montezuma, by the dauntless heroism of Guatemozin, the Aztecs were emphatically a fierce and brutal race, little calculated, in their best aspects, to excite our sympathy and regard. Their civilization, such as it was, was not their own, but reflected, perhaps imperfectly, from a race whom they had succeeded in the land. It was, in respect to the Aztecs, a generous graft on a vicious stock, and could have brought no fruit to perfection. They ruled over their wide domains with a sword, instead of a sceptre. They did nothing to ameliorate the condition, or in any way promote the progress, of their vassals. Their vassals were serfs, used only to minister to their pleasure, held in awe by armed garrisons, ground to the dust by imposts in peace, by military conscriptions in war. They did not, like the Romans, whom they resembled in the nature of their conquests, extend the rights of citizenship to the conquered. They did not amalgamate them into one great nation, with common rights and interests. They held them as aliens,—even those, who in the Valley were gathered round the very walls of the capital. The Aztec metropolis, the heart of the monarchy, had not a sympathy, not a pulsation, in common with the rest of the body politic. It was a stranger in its own land.

The Aztecs not only did not advance the condition of their vassals, but, morally speaking, they did much to degrade it. How can a nation, where human sacrifices prevail, and especially when combined with cannibalism, further the march of civilization? How can the interests of humanity be consulted, where man is levelled to the rank of the brutes that perish? The influence of the Aztecs introduced their gloomy superstition into lands before unacquainted with it, or where, at least, it was not established in any great strength. The example of the capital was contagious. As the latter increased in opulence, the religious celebrations were conducted with still more terrible magnificence; in the same manner, as the gladiatorial shows of the Romans increased in pomp with the increasing splendor of the capital. Men became familiar with scenes of horror and the most loathsome abominations. Women and children—the whole nation became familiar with, and assisted at them. The heart was hardened, the manners were made ferocious, the feeble light of civilization, transmitted from a milder race, was growing fainter and fainter, as thousands and thousands of miserable victims, throughout the empire, were yearly fattened in its cages, sacrificed on its altars, dressed and served at its banquets! The whole land was converted into a vast human shambles! The empire of the Aztecs did not fall before its time.

Whether these unparalleled outrages furnish a sufficient plea to the Spaniards for their invasion, whether, with the Protestant, we are content to find a warrant for it in the natural rights and demands of civilization, or, with the Roman Catholic, in the good pleasure of the Pope,—on the one or other of which grounds, the conquests by most Christian nations in the East and the West have been defended,—it is unnecessary to discuss, as it has already been considered in a former Chapter. It is more material to inquire, whether, assuming the right, the conquest of Mexico was conducted with a proper regard to the claims of humanity. And here we must admit, that, with all allowance for the ferocity of the age and the laxity of its principles, there are passages which every Spaniard, who cherishes the fame of his countrymen, would be glad to see expunged from their history; passages not to be vindicated on the score of self-defence, or of necessity of any kind, and which must forever leave a dark spot on the annals of the Conquest. And yet, taken as a whole, the invasion, up to the capture of the capital, was conducted on principles less revolting to humanity, than most, perhaps than any, of the other conquests of the Castilian crown in the New World.

It may seem slight praise to say, that the followers of Cortés used no blood-hounds to hunt down their wretched victims, as in some other parts of the Continent, nor exterminated a peaceful and submissive population in mere wantonness of cruelty, as in the Islands. Yet it is something, that they were not so far infected by the spirit of the age, and that their swords were rarely stained with blood, unless it was indispensable to the success of their enterprise. Even in the last siege of the capital, the sufferings of the Aztecs, terrible as they were, do not imply any unusual cruelty in the victors; they were not greater than those inflicted on their own countrymen at home, in many a memorable instance, by the most polished nations, not merely of ancient times, but of our own. They were the inevitable consequences which follow from war, when, instead of being confined to its legitimate field, it is brought home to the hearthstone, to the peaceful community of the city,—its burghers untrained to arms, its women and children yet more defenceless. In the present instance, indeed, the sufferings of the besieged were in a great degree to be charged on themselves,—on their patriotic, but desperate, self-devotion. It was not the desire, as certainly it was not the interest, of the Spaniards, to destroy the capital, or its inhabitants. When any of these fell into their hands, they were kindly entertained, their wants supplied, and every means taken to infuse into them a spirit of conciliation; and this, too, it should be remembered, in despite of the dreadful doom to which they consigned their Christian captives. The gates of a fair capitulation were kept open, though unavailingly, to the last hour.

The right of conquest necessarily implies that of using whatever force may be necessary for overcoming resistance to the assertion of that right. For the Spaniards to have done otherwise than they did would have been to abandon the siege, and, with it, the conquest of the country. To have suffered the inhabitants, with their high-spirited monarch, to escape, would but have prolonged the miseries of war by transferring it to another and more inaccessible quarter. They literally, as far as the success of the expedition was concerned, had no choice. If our imagination is struck with the amount of suffering in this, and in similar scenes of the Conquest, it should be borne in mind, that it is a natural result of the great masses of men engaged in the conflict. The amount of suffering does not of itself show the amount of cruelty which caused it; and it is but justice to the Conquerors of Mexico to say, that the very brilliancy and importance of their exploits have given a melancholy celebrity to their misdeeds, and thrown them into somewhat bolder relief than strictly belongs to them.— It is proper that thus much should be stated, not to excuse their excesses, but that we may be enabled to make a more impartial estimate of their conduct, as compared with that of other nations under similar circumstances, and that we may not visit them with peculiar obloquy for evils which necessarily flow from the condition of war. I have not drawn a veil over these evils; for the historian should not shrink from depicting, in their true colors, the atrocities of a condition, over which success is apt to throw a false halo of glory, but which, bursting asunder the strong bonds of human fellowship, purchases its triumphs by arming the hand of man against his brother, makes a savage of the civilized, and kindles the fires of hell in the bosom of the savage.

Whatever may be thought of the Conquest in a moral view, regarded as a military achievement it must fill us with astonishment. That a handful of adventurers, indifferently armed and equipped, should have landed on the shores of a powerful empire inhabited by a fierce and warlike race, and, in defiance of the reiterated prohibitions of its sovereign, have forced their way into the interior;—that they should have done this, without knowledge of the language or of the land, without chart or compass to guide them, without any idea of the difficulties they were to encounter, totally uncertain whether the next step might bring them on a hostile nation, or on a desert, feeling their way along in the dark, as it were;—that, though nearly overwhelmed by their first encounter with the inhabitants, they should have still pressed on to the capital of the empire, and, having reached it, thrown themselves unhesitatingly into the midst of their enemies;—that, so far from being daunted by the extraordinary spectacle there exhibited

of power and civilization, they should have been but the more confirmed in
their original design;—that they should have seized the monarch, have
executed his ministers before the eyes of his subjects, and, when driven
forth with ruin from the gates, have gathered their scattered wreck together, and, after a system of operations, pursued with consummate policy
and daring, have succeeded in overturning the capital, and establishing
their sway over the country;—that all this should have been so effected by
a mere handful of indigent adventurers, is a fact little short of the miracu-
lous,—too startling for the probabilities demanded by fiction, and without
a parallel in the pages of history.

Yet this must not be understood too literally; for it would be unjust to
the Aztecs themselves, at least to their military prowess, to regard the
Conquest as directly achieved by the Spaniards alone. This would indeed
be to arm the latter with the charmed shield of Ruggiero, and the magic
lance of Astolfo, overturning its hundreds at a touch. The Indian empire
was in a manner conquered by Indians. The first terrible encounter of the
Spaniards with the Tlascalans, which had nearly proved their ruin, did in
fact insure their success. It secured to them a strong native support, on
which to retreat in the hour of trouble, and round which they could rally
the kindred races of the land for one great and overwhelming assault. The
Aztec monarchy fell by the hands of its own subjects, under the direction
of European sagacity and science. Had it been united, it might have bidden
defiance to the invaders. As it was, the capital was dissevered from the rest
of the country, and the bolt, which might have passed off comparatively
harmless, had the empire been cemented by a common principle of loyalty
and patriotism, now found its way into every crack and crevice of the ill-
compacted fabric, and buried it in its own ruins.—Its fate may serve as a
striking proof, that a government, which does not rest on the sympathies
of its subjects, cannot long abide; that human institutions, when not connected with human prosperity and progress, must fall,—if not before the
increasing light of civilization, by the hand of violence; by violence from
within, if not from without. And who shall lament their fall?

GEORGE BANCROFT

(1800-1891)

It was almost a century after the Spanish had founded their empire in the Western hemisphere before the British began establishing the chain of colonies which in time became the United States. From the perspective of the age of Jackson, the evolution of the American nation seemed a splendid theme for the historian. George Bancroft, publishing his first volume in 1834, announced, "I have formed the design of writing a History of the United States from the Discovery of the American Continent to the present time. . . . I am impressed more strongly than ever with a sense of the grandeur and vastness of the subject." Bancroft's former teacher, Edward Everett, reading the first volume within twenty-four hours of receiving it, wrote: "I am afraid to tell you how much I like it; not for fear you will suspect my honesty; but for fear that, in thus writing to you, under the excitement of the recent perusal of the book, and with my mind labouring with all the noble ideas and warm feelings it has awakened, I may say more, than, at a cooler moment, I can stand to. Of that I must take my chance; and for the present, I must tell you, that I think you have written a Work which will last while the memory of America lasts; and which will instantly take its place among the classics of our language. It is full of learning, information, common sense, and philosophy; full of taste and eloquence; full of life and power. You give us not wretched pasteboard men; not a sort of chronological table, with the dates written out at length, after the manner of most historians:—but you give us real, individual, living men and women, with their passions, interests, and peculiarities." A generation of American readers agreed, as over the next half-century Bancroft brought out eleven more volumes, carrying his narrative only to the inauguration of Washington.

Bancroft saw a divine shaping of American destinies, from the founding of the individual colonies through the successful culmination of the struggle for independence, and beyond to his own day. He wrote in his preface in 1834, "It is the object of the present work to explain how the change in the condition of our land has been brought about; and, as the fortunes of a nation are not under the control of blind destiny, to follow the steps by which a favoring Providence, calling our institutions into being, has conducted the country to its present happiness and glory." As an old man in 1882, making a final revision of his history, he allowed these words to remain, "because the intervening years have justified their expression of confidence in the progress of our republic."

Founding the English Colonies

ENGLAND PLANTS A NEW NATION IN VIRGINIA

"I SHALL YET LIVE TO SEE VIRGINIA AN ENGLISH NATION," WROTE RALEIGH to Sir Robert Cecil shortly before the accession of James I. When the period for success had arrived, changes in European politics and society had moulded the forms of colonization. The Reformation had broken the harmony of religious opinion, and differences in the church began to constitute the basis of political parties. After the East Indies had been reached by doubling the southern promontory of Africa, the great commerce of the world was carried upon the ocean. The art of printing had been perfected and diffused; and the press spread intelligence and multiplied the facilities of instruction. The feudal institutions were undermined by the current of time and events. Productive industry had built up the fortunes and extended the influence of the middle classes, while habits of indolence and expense had impaired the estates and diminished the power of the nobility. These changes produced corresponding results in the institutions which were to rise in America.

A revolution had equally occurred in the objects for which voyages were undertaken. Columbus sought a new passage to the East Indies. The passion for gold next became the prevailing motive. Then islands and countries near the equator were made the tropical gardens of Europeans. At last the higher design was matured: to plant permanent Christian colonies; to establish for the oppressed and the enterprising places of refuge and abode; to found states in a temperate clime, with all the elements of independent existence.

In the imperfect condition of industry, a redundant population had grown up in England even before the peace with Spain, which threw out of employment the gallant men who had served under Elizabeth by sea and land, and left them no option but to engage as mercenaries in the quarrels of strangers, or incur the hazards of "seeking a New World." The minds of many persons of intelligence and rank were directed to Virginia. The brave and ingenious Gosnold, who had himself witnessed the fertility of the western soil, after long solicitations, prevailed with Edward Maria

From Bancroft, *History of the United States of America* (The Author's Last Revision, 6 vols., 1883), vol. 1, p. 1, ch. 6, 12.

Wingfield, a merchant of the west of England, Robert Hunt, a clergyman of fortitude and modest worth, and Captain John Smith, an adventurer of indomitable perseverance, to risk their hopes of fortune in an expedition. For more than a year this little company revolved their project. Nor had the assigns of Raleigh become indifferent to "western planting," which the most distinguished of them all, "industrious Hakluyt," still promoted by his personal exertions, his weight of character, and his invincible zeal. Possessed of whatever information could be derived from foreign sources and a correspondence with eminent navigators of his times, and anxiously watching the progress of Englishmen in the west, his extensive knowledge made him a counsellor in colonial enterprise.

With these are to be named George Popham, a kinsman of the chief justice, and Raleigh Gilbert. They and "certain knights, gentlemen, merchants, and other adventurers of the city of London and elsewhere," and "of the cities of Bristol and Exeter, and of the town of Plymouth and other places in the west," applied to James I. for "his license to deduce a colony into Virginia." The king, alike from vanity, the wish to promote the commerce of Great Britain, and the ambition of acquiring new dominions, entered heartily into the great design. From the "coast of Virginia and America" he selected a territory of ten degrees of latitude, reaching from the thirty-fourth to the forty-fifth parallel, and into the backwoods without bound. For the purposes of colonization, he divided the almost limitless region equally between the two rival companies of London and of the West. The London company were to lead forth the "FIRST COLONY OF VIRGINIA" to lands south of the thirty-eighth degree; and north of the forty-first parallel the Western company was to plant what the king called "THE SECOND COLONY OF VIRGINIA." The three intermediate degrees were reserved for the eventual competition of the two companies, except that each was to possess the soil extending fifty miles north and south of its first settlement. The conditions of tenure were homage and rent; the rent was no other than one fifth of the net produce of gold and silver, and one fifteenth of copper. The right of coining money was conceded. The natives, it was hoped, would receive Christianity and the arts of civilized life. The general superintendence was confided to a council in England; the local administration of each colony to a resident council. The members of the superior council in England were appointed exclusively by the king, and were to hold office at his good pleasure. Their authority extended to both colonies, which jointly took the name of VIRGINIA. Each of the two was to have its own resident council, of which the members were from time to time to be ordained and removed according to the instructions of the king. To the king, moreover, was reserved supreme legislative authority over the several colonies, extending to their general condition and the most minute regulation of their affairs. A duty of five per cent, to be levied within their precincts, on the traffic of strangers not owing obeisance to the British crown, was, for one-and-twenty years, to be wholly employed for the benefit of the several plantations; at the end of that time was to be taken for the king. To the emigrants it was promised that they and their children should continue to be Englishmen.

The charter for colonizing the great central territory of the North American continent, which was to be the chosen abode of liberty, gave to the mercantile corporation nothing but a wilderness, with the right of peopling and defending it. By an extension of the prerogative, which was in itself illegal, the monarch assumed absolute legislative as well as executive powers. The emigrants were subjected to the ordinances of a commercial corporation, in which they could not act as members; to the dominion of a domestic council, in appointing which they had no voice; to the control of a superior council in England; and, finally, to the arbitrary legislation of the sovereign. The first "treasurer" or governor of the London company, to whom fell the chief management of its affairs, was Sir Thomas Smythe, a merchant zealous for extending the commerce of his country, and equally zealous for asserting the authority of the corporation.

The summer was spent in preparations for planting the first colony, for which the king found a grateful occupation in framing a code of laws. The superior council in England was permitted to name the colonial council, which was independent of the emigrants, and had power to elect or remove its president, to remove any of its members, and to supply its own vacancies. Not an element of popular liberty or control was introduced. Religion was established according to the doctrine and rites of the church within the realm; and no emigrant might avow dissent, or affect the superstitions of the church of Rome, or withdraw his allegiance from King James. Lands were to descend according to the laws of England. Not only murder, manslaughter, and adultery, but dangerous tumults and seditions, were punishable by death, at the discretion of the magistrate, restricted only by the trial by jury. All civil causes, requiring corporal punishment, fine, or imprisonment, might be summarily determined by the president and council, who possessed legislative authority in cases not affecting life or limb. Kindness to the savages was enjoined, with the use of all proper means for their conversion. It was further ordered that the industry and commerce of the several colonies should, for five years at least, be conducted in a joint stock.

The council of the English company added instructions to the emigrants to search for navigable rivers, and, if any of them had two branches, to ascend that which tended most toward the north-west to its sources, and seek for some stream running the contrary way toward the South sea. Then, on the nineteenth day of December, in the year of our Lord one thousand six hundred and six, one hundred and nine years after the discovery of the American continent by Cabot, forty-one years from the settlement of Florida, the squadron of three vessels, the largest not exceeding one hun-

dred tons' burden, with the favor of all England, stretched their sails for
"the dear strand of Virginia, earth's only paradise." Michael Drayton, the
patriot poet "of Albion's glorious isle," cheered them on, saying:

Go, and in regions far such heroes bring ye forth
    As those from whom we came; and plant our name
Under that star not known unto our north.

Yet the enterprise was ill concerted. Of the one hundred and five on the
list of emigrants, there were but twelve laborers, and few mechanics. They
were going to a wilderness, in which, as yet, not a house was standing; and
there were forty-eight gentlemen to four carpenters. Neither were there any
men with families.

Newport, who commanded the ships, was acquainted with the old passage, and sailed by way of the Canaries and the West India islands. As
he turned to the north, a severe storm, in April, 1607, carried his fleet
beyond the settlement of Raleigh, into the magnificent bay of the Chesapeake. The headlands received and retain the names of Cape Henry and
Cape Charles, from the sons of King James; the deep water for anchorage,
"putting the emigrants in good Comfort," gave a name to the northern
Point; and within the capes a country opened, which appeared to "claim
the prerogative over the most pleasant places in the world." "Heaven and
earth seemed never to have agreed better to frame a place for man's com-
modious and delightful habitation." A noble river was soon entered, which
was named from the monarch; and, after a search of seventeen days, during
which the comers encountered the hostility of one savage tribe, and at
Hampton smoked the calumet of peace with another, on the thirteenth of
May they reached a peninsula about fifty miles above the mouth of the
stream, where the water near the shore was so very deep that the ships
were moored to trees. Here the council, except Smith, who for no reason
unless it were jealousy of his superior energy was for nearly a month kept
out of his seat, took the oath of office, and the majority elected Edward
Maria Wingfield president for the coming year. Contrary to the earnest and
persistent advice of Bartholomew Gosnold, the peninsula was selected for
the site of the colony, and took the names of Jamestown.

While the men toiled in felling trees to make room for their tents, and
in gathering freight for the two ships which were soon to return to England,
Newport, Smith, and twenty others ascended the river, with a perfect resolution not to return till they should have found its head and a passage
through the mountains to the western ocean. Trading on their way with
the riparian tribes, they were soon arrested by the falls of the river, below
which they were hospitably entertained by the great chief of the country.
They examined the cataract to find a mode of passing around it, but "the
water falleth so rudely and with such violence not any boat could possibly
pass them." The next day in idle admiration they gazed upon the scene,

while Newport erected a cross with the inscription, "James the king, 1607," and proclaimed him to have most right unto the river. They were again at Jamestown on the twenty-seventh of May.

During their absence the Indians had shown a hostile disposition. Captain Newport set things in order, made peace with one of the neighboring chiefs, and completed the palisado around the fort. On the twenty-first of June, in a church which consisted only of a sail spread from tree to tree to keep off the midsummer sun, with rails for walls and logs for benches, the communion was administered, and on the next day he embarked for England, leaving behind him a colony of one hundred and four persons, reported to be "in good health and comfort."

Meantime the adventurers of the west of England had wholly disconnected themselves from the London company by obtaining for the superintendence of their affairs a separate council resident in the kingdom, and had completed their arrangements for the colonization of the northern part of Virginia.

Five months after the departure of the southern colony, one hundred and twenty passengers sailed as planters from Plymouth in the Mary and John, with Raleigh Gilbert for its captain, and in the Gift of God, a fly boat commanded by a kinsman of the chief justice, George Popham, who was "well strickened in years and infirm, yet willing to die in acting something that might be serviceable to God and honorable to his country." The corps with which they went forth, to plant the English monarchy and the English church in that part of Virginia which lay north of the forty-first parallel, was more numerous and more carefully chosen than that of their rivals.

After a voyage of two months, in the afternoon of the last day of July, they stood in for the shore, and found shelter under Monhegan island. Their first discovery was that the fishermen of France and Spain had been there before them. They had not ridden at anchor two hours when a party of Indians in a Spanish shallop came to them from the shore and rowed about them; and the next day returned in a Biscay boat with women, bringing beaver-skins to exchange for knives and beads. In the following days the emigrants explored the coast and islands, and on the sixteenth of August both ships entered the Kennebec.

On the nineteenth all the members of this "second colony of Virginia" went on shore, made choice of the Sabine peninsula, near the mouth of that river, for the site of their fort, and "had a sermon delivered unto them by their preacher." After the sermon they listened to the reading of the commission of George Popham, their president, and of the laws appointed for them by King James. Five men were sworn assistants. Without delay, most of the company, under the oversight of the president, labored hard on a fort which they named St. George, a storehouse, fifty rude cabins for their own shelter, and a church. The shipwrights set about the building of

a small pinnace, the chief shipwright being one Digby, the first constructor
of sea-going craft in that region. Meantime Gilbert coasted toward the west,
judged the land to be exceeding fertile, and brought back the news of the
beauty of Casco bay with its hundreds of isles. When, at the invitation of
the mighty Indian chief who ruled on the Penobscot, Gilbert would have
visited that river, he was driven back by foul weather and cross winds. Remaining faithfully in the colony, in December he sent back his ship under
another commander, who bore letters announcing to the chief justice the
forwardness of the plantation, and importuning supplies for the coming
year. A letter from President Popham informed King James that his praises
and his virtues had been proclaimed to the natives; that the country produced fruits resembling spices, as well as timber of pine; and that it lay
hard by the great highway to China over the southern ocean.

The winter proved to be intensely cold; no mines were discovered; the
natives, at first most friendly, grew restless; the storehouse caught fire and
a part of the provisions of the colony was consumed; the president found
his grave on American soil, "the only one of the company that died there."
To the despair of the planters, the ship which revisited the settlement with
supplies brought news of the death of the chief justice, who had been the
stay of the enterprise, and Gilbert, who had succeeded to the command at
St. George, had, by the decease of his brother, become heir to an estate
in England which required his presence. So, notwithstanding all things were
in good forwardness, the fur trade with the Indians prosperous, and a store
of sarsaparilla gathered, "all former hopes were frozen to death," and
nothing was thought of but to quit the place. Wherefore in the ship which
had lately arrived, and in the Virginia, their own new pinnace, they all set
sail for England. So ended "the second colony of Virginia." The colonists
"did coyne many excuses" for their going back; but the Western company
was dissatisfied; Gorges esteemed it a weakness to be frightened at a blast.
Three years had elapsed since the French had hutted themselves at Port
Royal; and the ships which carried the English from the Kennebec were on
the ocean at the same time with the outward-bound squadron of those who
in that summer built Quebec.

The first colony of Virginia was suffering under far more disastrous
trials. Scarcely had Newport, in June, 1607, weighed anchor for home than
the English whom he left behind stood face to face with misery. They were
few in numbers, ignorant of the methods of industry, without any elements
of union, and surrounded by distrustful and hostile natives.

The air which they breathed was unwholesome with the exhalations from
steaming marshes; their drink was the brackish water of the river; their food
was a scant daily allowance of porridge made of barley which had been
spoiled on the long voyage from England. They had no houses to cover
them; their tents were rotten. They were weakened by continual labor at
the defences in the extremity of the heat; and they watched by turns every

third night, lying on the cold bare ground, what weather soever came. It made the heart bleed to hear the pitiful murmurings and outcries of sick men without relief, night and day, for six weeks; and sometimes three or four died in a night. Fifty men, one half of the colony, perished before autumn; among them Bartholomew Gosnold, a man of rare merit, worthy of perpetual memory in the plantation.

Incessant broils heightened the confusion. The only efficient member of the government was Smith, who went up and down the river trading with the natives for corn, which brought relief to the colony. Wingfield, the president, gave offence by caring too much for his own comfort; and, being wholly inefficient, was, on the tenth of September, by general consent, deposed. The faint-hearted man, so he records of himself, offered a hundred pounds toward fetching home the emigrants if the plan of a colony should be given over. The office of president fell to John Ratcliffe from his place in the council, but he proved a passionate man, without capacity to rule himself, and still less to rule others. Of the only three remaining councillors, one was deposed, and afterward shot to death for mutiny; another was an invalid, and there was no one left to guide in action but Smith, whose buoyant spirit alone inspired confidence. In boyhood, such is his own narrative, he had sought for the opportunity of "setting out on brave adventures;" and, though not yet thirty years of age, he was already famed for various service in foreign wars. On regaining England, his mind was wholly mastered by the general enthusiasm for planting states in America; and now the infant commonwealth of Virginia depended for its life on his firmness. For the time he was the cape merchant or treasurer, as well as the only active councillor. His first thought was to complete the building of Jamestown, and, setting the example of diligent labor, he pushed on the construction of houses with success. He next renewed trade with the natives, and was most successful in his expedition for the purchase of corn. On the approach of winter, when he had defeated a proposal to let the pinnace go for England, and when the fear of famine was removed by good supplies from the Indian harvest of maize and by the abundance of game, he began the exploration of the country. Ascending the Chickahominy as far as it was navigable in a barge, he then, with two red men as guides and two of his own company, proceeded twelve miles further; but, while with one Indian he went on shore to examine the nature of the soil and the bendings of the stream, his two companions were killed, and he himself was surrounded in the wilderness by so many warriors that he cast himself upon their mercy.

The leader of his captors was Opechancanough, a brother and subordinate of Powhatan, the great chieftain of all the neighborhood. He knew the rank of the prisoner, "used him with kindness," and sent his letters to the English fort; and from the villages on the Chickahominy the Virginia councillor was escorted through Indian towns to an audience with Powhatan, who chanced to be on what is now York river. The "emperor," studded with ornaments, and clad in raccoon skins, showed a grave and majestical countenance as he welcomed him with good words and "great platters of sundrie" food, and gave assurance of friendship. After a few days, which Smith diligently used in inquiries respecting the country, especially the waters to the north-west, he was, early in January, 1608, sent home, attended by four men, of whom two were laden with maize.

The first printed "Newes from Virginia" spread abroad these adventures of Smith; and they made known to English readers the name of Pocahontas, the daughter of Powhatan, a child "of tenne," or more probably of twelve "years old, who not only for feature, countenance, and expression, much exceeded any of the rest of his people, but for wit and spirit was the only nonpareil of the country." The captivity of the bold explorer became a benefit to the colony; for he not only observed with care the country between the James and the Potomac and gained some knowledge of the language and manners of the natives, but he established a peaceful intercourse between the English and the tribes of Powhatan. The child, to whom in later days he attributed his rescue from death, visited the fort with companions, bringing baskets of corn.

Restored to Jamestown after an absence of but four weeks, Smith found the colony reduced to forty men; and of these, the strongest were preparing to escape with the pinnace. This attempt at desertion he repressed at the hazard of his life.

Meantime the council in England, having received an increase of its numbers and its powers, determined to send out recruits and supplies; and Newport had hardly returned from his first voyage before he was again despatched with one hundred and twenty emigrants. Yet the joy in Virginia on their arrival in April was of short continuance; for the new comers were chiefly gentlemen and goldsmiths, who soon persuaded themselves that they had discovered grains of gold in a glittering soil which abounded near Jamestown; and "there was now no talk, no hope, no work, but dig gold, wash gold, refine gold, load gold." Martin, one of the council, promised himself honors in England as the discoverer of a mine; and Newport believed himself rich, as in April he embarked for England with a freight of worthless earth.

Disgusted at the follies which he vainly opposed, Smith undertook the perilous and honorable task of exploring the bay of the Chesapeake, and the rivers which it receives. Two voyages, in an open boat, with a few companions, over whom his superior courage, rather than his station as a magistrate, gave him authority, occupied him about three months of the summer. With slender means, but with persistency and skill, he surveyed the bay to the Susquehanna, and left only the borders of that remote river to remain for some years longer the fabled dwelling-place of a giant progeny. He was the first to publish to the English the power of the Mohawks, "who dwelt upon a great water, and had many boats, and many men," and, as it seemed to the feebler Algonkin tribes, "made war upon all the world;" in the Chesapeake he encountered a fleet of their canoes. The Patapsco was discovered and explored, and Smith probably entered the harbor of Baltimore. The Potomac especially invited curiosity; and he ascended to its lower falls. Nor did he merely examine the rivers and inlets. He penerated the territories, and laid the foundation for beneficial intercourse with the native tribes. The map which he prepared and sent to the company in London delineates correctly the great outlines of nature. The expedition was worthy of the romantic age of American history; he had entered upon it in the beginning of June, and had pursued the discovery with inflexible constancy, except for three days in July, when at Jamestown Ratcliffe, for his pride and cruelty, was deposed. The government would then have devolved on Smith; but he substituted for the time "his good friend Matthew Scrivener," a new councillor, who had come over but a few months before.

On the tenth of September, 1608, three days after his return from his discoveries, Smith was formally constituted president of the council. Order and industry began to be established, when Newport entered the river with about seventy new emigrants, of whom two were women.

The London company had grown exceedingly impatient at receiving no returns for its outlays. Of themselves they were helpless in counsel, without rational plans, looking vaguely for a mine of gold, or a short route to India, and listening too favorably to the advice of Newport. By their orders a great company proceeded to York river to go through the senseless ceremony of crowning Powhatan as emperor of that country. A boat in five parts was sent over from England, to be borne above the falls, in the hope of reaching the waters which flow to the South sea, or by some chance of finding a mine of gold. For several weeks the store of provisions and the labor of one hundred and twenty of the best men that could be chosen were wasted in examining James river above the falls.

A few Germans and Poles were sent over to make pitch, tar, soap ashes, and glass, when the colony could not yet raise provisions enough for its support. "When you send again," Smith was obliged to reply, "I entreat you rather send but thirty carpenters, husbandmen, gardeners, fishermen, blacksmiths, masons, and diggers up of trees' roots, well provided, than a thousand of such as we have."

The charge of the voyage of Newport was more than two thousand pounds; unless the ships should return full freighted with commodities, corresponding in value to the costs of the adventure, the colonists were threatened with being "left in Virginia as banished men." "We have not received the value of one hundred pounds," answered Smith. "From toiling to satisfy the desire of present profit, we can scarce ever recover ourselves from one supply to another. These causes stand in the way of laying in

Virginia a proper foundation; as yet, you must not look for any profitable returning."

After the long delayed departure of the ships, the first care of Smith was to obtain supplies for the colony from the Indians. In the spring of 1610 he introduced the culture of maize, which was taught by two savages, and thirty or forty acres were "digged and planted." Authority was employed to enforce industry; he who would not work might not eat, and six hours in the day were spent in toil. The gentlemen learned the use of the axe, and became excellent wood-cutters. Jamestown assumed the appearance of a regular place of abode. It is worthy of remembrance that Smith proposed to plant a town near the falls of the river, where the city of Richmond now stands. Eight months of good order under his rule gave to the colony a period of peace and industry, of order and health. The quiet of his administration was disturbed in its last days by the arrival of seven ships with emigrants, sent out from England under new auspices, so that they for the moment formed an element of anarchy. Smith maintained his authority until his year of office was over; and, under special arrangements, a little longer, until he was accidentally disabled by wounds which the medical skill of the colony could not relieve. He then delegated his office to Percy and embarked for England, never to see the Chesapeake again.

Captain John Smith united the strongest spirit of adventure with eminent powers of action. Full of courage and self-possession, he was fertile in expedients, and prompt in execution. He had a just idea of the public good, and clearly discerned that it was not the true interest of England to seek in Virginia for gold and sudden wealth. "Nothing," said he, "is to be expected thence but by labor;" and as a public officer he excelled in its direction. The historians of Virginia have with common consent looked to him as the preserver of their commonwealth in its infancy; and there is hardly room to doubt that, but for his vigor, industry, and resolution, it would have been deserted like the Virginia of the north, and with better excuse. Of government under the forms of civil liberty he had no adequate comprehension; but his administration was the most wise, provident, and just of any one known to the colony under its first charter. It was his weakness to be apt to boast. As a writer, he deals in exaggeration and romance, but in a less degree than the foreign historians who served as his models; his reports and his maps are a proof of his resolute energy, his keenness of observation, and his truthfulness of statement. His official report to the company is replete with wise remarks and just reproof. He was public spirited, brave, and constantly employed, and, with scanty means, did more toward the discovery of the country than all others of his time.

After the desertion of the northern part of Virginia, intercourse was kept up with that part of the country by vessels annually employed in the fisheries and the trade in furs; and it may be that once at least, perhaps oftener, some part of a ship's company remained during the winter on the coast. John Smith, on his return to England, still asserted, with unwearied importunity and firmness of conviction, that colonization was the true policy of England; and, in April, 1614, sailed with two ships for the region that had been appropriated for the second colony of Virginia. This private adventure of "four merchants of London and himself" was very successful. The freights were profitable, the health of the mariners did not suffer, and the voyage was accomplished in less than seven months. While the sailors were busy with their hooks and lines, Smith examined the shore from the Penobscot to Cape Cod, prepared of the coast a map—the first which gives its outline intelligibly well; and he named the country New England—a title which Prince Charles confirmed; though the French could boast, with truth, that New France had been colonized before New England obtained a name; that Port Royal was older than Plymouth, Quebec than Boston.

Encouraged by commercial success, Smith, in the next year, in the employment of Sir Ferdinando Gorges and of friends in London who were members of the Western company, endeavored to establish a colony, though but of sixteen men, for the occupation of New England. The attempt was made unsuccessful by violent storms.

Again renewing his enterprise, Smith was captured by French pirates. His ship having been taken away, he escaped alone, in an open boat, from the harbor of Rochelle. The severest privations in a new settlement would have been less wearisome than the labors which his zeal now prompted him to undertake. Having published a map and description of New England, he spent many months in visiting the merchants and gentry of the west: he proposed to the cities mercantile profits, to be realized in short and safe voyages; to the noblemen vast domains; to men of small means he drew a lively picture of the rapid advancement of fortune by colonial industry, of the abundance of game, the delights of unrestrained liberty, the pleasures to be derived from "angling and crossing the sweet air from isle to isle over the silent streams of a calm sea." His private fortunes never recovered from his disastrous capture by the French; but his zeal for the interests of the nation redounded to his honor; and he retired from American history with the rank of Admiral of New England for life.

THE PILGRIMS

Our narrative leads us to the manor-house of Scrooby, in Nottinghamshire, where William Brewster, who had been educated at Cambridge, had been employed in public affairs by an English secretary of state, and had taken part in an embassy to the Netherlands, resided as successor to his father in a small office under the queen. He furthered religion by procuring good preachers to all places thereabouts, charging himself most commonly deepest, and sometimes above his means. The tyranny of the bishops against godly preachers and people, in silencing the one and persecuting the other, led him and many more of those times to look further into particulars, and to see the burden of many anti-Christian corruptions which both he and they endeavored to cast off.

The age of the queen and the chance of favor to Puritans from her successor conspired to check persecution. The Independents had, it is true, been nearly exterminated; but the non-conforming clergy, after forty years of molestation, had increased, and taken deeper root in the nation. Their followers constituted a powerful political party, inquired into the nature of government, in parliament opposed monopolies, restrained the royal prerogative, and demanded a reform of ecclesiastical abuses. Popular liberty, which used to animate its friends by appeals to the examples of ancient republics, now listened to a voice from the grave of Wycliffe, from the vigils of Calvin. Victorious over her foreign enemies, Elizabeth never could crush the religious party of which she held the increase dangerous to the state. In the latter years of her reign her popularity declined, and after her death "in four days she was forgotten." The accession of King James, on the third day of April, 1603, would, it was hoped, introduce a milder system; for he had called the church of Scotland "the sincerest kirk of the world;" and had censured the service of England as "an evil said mass."

The pupil of Buchanan was not destitute of shrewdness nor unskilled in rhetoric. He aimed at the reputation of a "most learned clerk," and so successfully that Bacon pronounced him incomparable for learning among kings; and Sully, who knew him well, esteemed him the wisest fool in Europe. At the mature age of thirty-six, the imbecile man, afflicted with an ungainly frame and a timorous nature, escaped from austere supervision in Scotland to freedom of self-indulgence in the English court. His will, like his passions, was feeble, so that he could never carry out a wise resolution; and, in his love of ease, he had no fixed principles of conduct or belief. Moreover, cowardice, which was the core of his character, led him to be false; and he could vindicate deception and cunning as worthy of a king; but he was an awkward liar rather than a crafty dissembler. On his way to a country where the institution of a parliament existed, he desired "to get rid of it," being persuaded that its privileges were not an ancient undoubted right and inheritance, but were derived solely from grace and favor. His experience in Scotland had persuaded him that Presbyterian government in the church would, in a monarchy, bring forth perpetual rebellions; and while he denied the divine institution of bishops, and cared not for the profits the church might reap from them, he believed they would prove useful instruments to turn a monarchy with a parliament into absolute dominion.

The English hierarchy had feared in their new sovereign the approach of a "Scottish mist;" but the borders of Scotland were hardly passed before James began to identify the interests of the English church with those of his prerogative. "No bishop, no king," was a maxim often in his mouth, at the moment when Archbishop Whitgift could not conceal his disappointment and disquiet of mind, that the Puritans were too numerous to be borne down. While James was in his progress to London, more than seven hundred of them presented a petition for a redress of ecclesiastical grievances; and a decent respect for the party in which he had been bred, joined to a desire of displaying his talents for theological debate, induced him to appoint a conference at Hampton court.

The conference, held in January, 1604, was distinguished on the part of the king by a strenuous vindication of the church of England. Refusing to discuss the question of its power in things indifferent, he substituted authority for argument, and, where he could not produce conviction, demanded obedience. "I will have none of that liberty as to ceremonies; I will have one doctrine, one discipline, one religion in substance and in ceremony. Never speak more to that point, how far you are bound to obey."

The Puritans desired permission occasionally to assemble, and at their meetings to have the liberty of free discussions; but the king interrupted their petition: "You are aiming at a Scot's presbytery, which agrees with monarchy as well as God and the devil. Then Jack and Tom and Will and Dick shall meet, and at their pleasure censure me and my council, and all our proceedings. Then Will shall stand up and say, It must be thus; then Dick shall reply and say, Nay, marry, but we will have it thus; and, therefore, here I must once more reiterate my former speech, and say, The king forbids." Turning to the bishops, he avowed his belief that the hierarchy was the firmest supporter of the throne. Of the Puritans, he added: "I will make them conform, or I will harry them out of the land, or else worse," "only hang them; that's all."

On the last day of the conference, the king defended the necessity of subscription, concluding that, "if any would not be quiet and show their obedience, they were worthy to be hanged." He approved the high commission and inquisitorial oaths, despotic authority and its instruments. A few alterations in the Book of Common Prayer were the only reforms which the conference effected. It was determined that a time should be set, within which all should conform, or be removed. He had insulted the Puritans with vulgar rudeness and indecorous jests, and had talked much Latin; a part of the time in the presence of the nobility of Scotland and England. "Your majesty speaks by the special assistance of God's spirit," said the aged Whitgift, just six weeks before his death. Bishop Bancroft, on his knees, exclaimed that his heart melted for joy, "because God had given England such a king as, since Christ's time, has not been;" and, in a foolish letter, James boasted that "he had soundly peppered off the Puritans."

In the parliament which assembled in 1604, the party for the reform of the church asserted their liberties with such tenacity and vigor that King James began to hate them as embittering royalty itself. "I had rather live like a hermit in the forest," he writes, "than be a king over such a people as the pack of Puritans are that overrule the lower house." "The will of man or angel cannot devise a pleasing answer to their propositions, except I should pull the crown not only from my own head, but also from the head of all those that shall succeed unto me, and lay it down at their feet." At the opening of the session, he had offered "to meet the Catholics in the midway;" while he added that "the sect of Puritans is insufferable in any well-governed commonwealth." At the next session of parliament he declared the Roman Catholics to be faithful subjects, but the Puritans worthy of fire for their opinions. Against the latter he inveighed bitterly in council, saying "that the revolt in the Low Countries began for matters of religion, and so did all the troubles in Scotland; that his mother and he, from their cradles, had been haunted with a Puritan devil, which he feared would not leave him to his grave; and that he would hazard his crown but he would supress those malicious spirits."

The convocation of the clergy were very ready to decree against obstinate Puritans excommunication and all its consequences. Bancroft, the successor of Whitgift, required conformity with unrelenting rigor; King James issued a proclamation of equal severity; and it is asserted, perhaps with exaggeration, yet by those who had opportunities of judging rightly, that in the year 1604 alone three hundred Puritan ministers were silenced, imprisoned, or exiled. The oppressed resisted the surplice, not as a mere vestment, but as the symbol of a priest, ordained by a bishop, imposed upon a church, and teaching by authority. The clergy proceeded with a consistent disregard of the national liberties. The importation of foreign books was impeded, and a severe censorship of the press was exercised by the bishops. The convocation of 1606, in a series of canons, asserted the superiority of the king to the parliament and the laws, and admitted no exception to the duty of passive obedience. The English separatists and non-conformists became the sole protectors of the system which gave to England its distinguishing glory. "The stern and exasperated Puritans," writes Hallam, "were the depositaries of the sacred fire of liberty." "So absolute was the authority of the crown," said Hume, "that the precious spark of liberty had been kindled and was preserved by the Puritans alone; and it was to this sect that the English owe the whole freedom of their constitution." The lines of the contending parties were sharply drawn. Immediate success was obtained by the established authority; but the contest was to be transmitted to another continent. The interests of human freedom were at issue on the contest.

In the year of this convocation, "a poor people" in the north of England, in towns and villages of Nottinghamshire, Lincolnshire, and the borders of Yorkshire, in and near Scrooby, had "become enlightened by the word of God." "Presently they were both scoffed and scorned by the profane multitude; and their ministers, urged by the yoke of subscription," were, by the increase of troubles, led "to see further," that not only "the beggarly ceremonies were monuments of idolatry," but "that the lordly power of the prelates ought not to be submitted to." Many of them, therefore, "whose hearts the Lord had touched with heavenly zeal for his truth," resolved, "whatever it might cost them, to shake off the anti-Christian bondage, and, as the Lord's free people, to join themselves by a covenant into a church estate in the followship of the gospel."

"The gospel is every man's right; and it is not to be endured that any one should be kept therefrom. But the evangel is an open doctrine; it is bound to no place, and moves along freely under heaven, like the star, which ran in the sky to show the wizards from the east where Christ was born. Do not dispute with the prince for place. Let the community choose their own pastor, and support him out of their own estates. If the prince will not suffer it, let the pastor flee into another land, and let those go with him who will, as Christ teaches." Such was the counsel of Luther, on reading "the twelve articles" of the insurgent peasants of Suabia. What Luther advised, what Calvin planned, was carried into effect by this rural community of Englishmen.

The reformed church chose for one of their ministers John Robinson, "a man not easily to be paralleled," "of a most learned, polished, and modest spirit." Their ruling elder was William Brewster, who "was their special stay and help." They were beset and watched night and day by the agents of prelacy. For about a year they kept their meetings every sabbath in one place or another; exercising the worship of God among themselves, notwithstanding all the diligence and malice of their adversaries, till the peaceful members of "the poor persecuted flock of Christ," despairing of rest in England, resolved to go into Holland, "where, they heard, was freedom of religion for all men."

The departure from England was effected with much suffering and hazard. The first attempt, in 1607, was prevented; but the magistrates checked the ferocity of the subordinate officers; and, after a month's arrest of the whole company, seven only of the principal men were detained a little longer in prison.

The next spring the design was renewed. An unfrequented heath in Lincolnshire, near the mouth of the Humber, was the place of secret meeting. Just as a boat was bearing a part of the emigrants to their ship, a company of horsemen appeared in pursuit, and seized on the helpless women and children who had not yet adventured on the surf. "Pitiful it was to see the heavy case of these poor women in distress; what weeping and crying on every side." But, when they were apprehended, it seemed impossible to punish and imprison wives and children for no other crime than that they would not part from their husbands and fathers. They could not be sent home, for "they had no homes to go to;" so that, at last, the magistrates were "glad to be rid of them on any terms," "though, in the mean time, they, poor souls, endured misery enough." Such was the flight of Robinson and Brewster and their followers from the land of their fathers.

Their arrival in Amsterdam, in 1608, was but the beginning of their wanderings. "They knew they were PILGRIMS, and looked not much on those things, but lifted up their eyes to Heaven, their dearest country, and quieted their spirits." In 1609, removing to Leyden, "they saw poverty coming on them like an armed man;" but, being "careful to keep their word, and painful and diligent in their callings," they attained "a comfortable condition, grew in the gifts and grace of the spirit of God, and lived together in peace and love and holiness." "Never," said the magistrates of the city, "never did we have any suit or accusation against any of them;" and, but for fear of offence to King James, they would have met with public favor. "Many came there from different parts of England, so as they grew a great congregation." "Such was the humble zeal and fervent love of this people toward God and his ways, and their single-heartedness and sincere affection one toward another," that they seemed to come surpassingly near "the primitive pattern of the first churches." A clear and well-written apology of their discipline was published by Robinson, who, in the controversy on free-will, as the champion of orthodoxy, "began to be terrible to the Arminians," and disputed in the university with such power that, as his friends assert, "the truth had a famous victory."

The career of maritime discovery had, meantime, been pursued with intrepidity and rewarded with success. The voyages of Gosnold, Waymouth, Smith, and Hudson; the enterprise of Raleigh, Delaware, and Gorges; the compilations of Eden, Willes, and Hakluyt—had filled the commercial world with wonder; Calvinists of the French church had sought, though vainly, to plant themselves in Brazil, in Carolina, and, with De Monts, in Acadia; while weighty reasons, often and seriously discussed, inclined the pilgrims to change their abode. They had been bred to the pursuits of husbandry, and in Holland they were compelled to learn mechanical trades; Brewster became a teacher of English and a printer; Bradford, who had been educated as a farmer, learned the art of dyeing silk. The Dutch language never became pleasantly familiar to them, and the Dutch manners still less so. They lived but as men in exile. Many of their English friends would not come to them, or departed from them weeping. "Their continual labors, with other crosses and sorrows, left them in danger to scatter or sink." "Their children, sharing their parents' burdens, bowed under the weight, and were becoming decrepit in early youth." Conscious of ability to act a higher part in the great drama of humanity, they, after ten years, were moved by "a hope and inward zeal of advancing the gospel of the kingdom of Christ in the remote parts of the New World; yea, though they should be but as stepping-stones unto others for performing so great a work."

"Upon their talk of removing, sundry of the Dutch would have them go under them, and made them large offers;" but an inborn love for the English nation and for their mother tongue led them to the generous purpose of recovering the protection of England by enlarging her dominions. They were "restless" with the desire to remove to "the most northern parts of Virginia," hoping, under the general government of that province, "to live in a distinct body by themselves." To obtain the consent of the London company, John Carver, with Robert Cushman, in 1617, repaired to England. They took with them "seven articles," from the members of the church at Leyden, to be submitted to the council in England for Virginia. These articles discussed the relations which, as separatists in religion, they bore to their prince; and they adopted the theory which the admonitions of Luther and a century of persecution had developed as the common rule of plebeian sectaries on the continent of Europe. They expressed their concurrence in the creed of the Anglican church, and a desire of spiritual communion with its members. Toward the king and all civil authority derived from him, including the civil authority of bishops, they promised, as they would have done to Nero and the Roman pontifex, "obedience in all things, active if the thing commanded be not against God's word, or passive if it be." They denied all power to ecclesiastical bodies, unless it were given by the temporal magistrate. They pledged themselves to honor their superiors, and to preserve unity of spirit in peace with all men. "Divers selecte gentlemen of the council for Virginia were well satisfied with their statement, and resolved to set forward their desire." The London company listened very willingly to their proposal, so that their agents "found God going along with them;" and, through the influence of "Sir Edwin Sandys, a religious gentleman then living," a patent might at once have been taken, had not the envoys desired first to consult "the multitude" at Leyden.

On the fifteenth of December, 1617, the pilgrims transmitted their formal request, signed by the hands of the greatest part of the congregation. "We are well weaned," added Robinson and Brewster, "from the delicate milk of our mother country, and inured to the difficulties of a strange land; the people are industrious and frugal. We are knit together as a body in a most sacred covenant of the Lord, of the violation whereof we make great conscience, and by virtue whereof we hold ourselves straitly tied to all care of each other's good, and of the whole. It is not with us as with men whom small things can discourage."

The messengers of the pilgrims, satisfied with their reception by the Virginia company, petitioned the king for liberty of religion, to be confirmed under the king's broad seal. But here they encountered insurmountable difficulties. Of all men in the government of that day, Lord Bacon had given the most attention to colonial enterprise. The settlements of the Scotch in Ireland enjoyed his particular favor. To him, as "to the encourager, pattern, and perfecter of all vertuous endeavors," Strachey at this time dedicated his "Historie of Travaile into Virginia"; to him John Smith, in his "povertie," turned for encouragement of colonizing New England, as to "a chief patron of his country and the greatest favorer of all good designs." To him Sir George Villiers, the favorite of James, addressed himself for advice, and received instructions how to govern himself in office.

The great master of speculative wisdom knew too little of religion to inculcate freedom of conscience. He saw that the established church, which he cherished as the eye of England, was not without blemish; that the wrongs of the Puritans could neither be dissembled nor excused; that the silencing of ministers, for the sake of enforcing the ceremonies, was, in the scarcity of good preachers, a punishment that lighted on the people; and he esteemed controversy "the wind by which truth is winnowed." But Bacon was formed for contemplative life, not for action; his will was feeble, and yet, having an incessant yearning for vain distinction and display, he became a craven courtier and an intolerant statesman. "Discipline by bishops," said he, "is fittest for monarchy of all others. The tenets of separatists and sectaries are full of schism, and inconsistent with monarchy. The king will beware of Anabaptists, Brownists, and others of their kinds; a little connivency sets them on fire. For the discipline of the church in colonies, it will be necessary that it agree with that which is settled in England, else it will make a schism and a rent in Christ's coat, which must be seamless; and, to that purpose, it will be fit that by the king's supreme power in causes ecclesiastical, within all his dominions, they be subordinate under some bishop and bishoprick of this realm. This caution is to be observed, that if any transplant themselves into plantations abroad, who are known schismatics, outlaws, or criminal persons, they be sent for back upon the first notice."

These maxims prevailed at the council-board, when the envoys from the independent church at Leyden preferred their requests. "Who shall make your ministers?" it was asked of them; and the avowal of their principle, that ordination requires no bishop, threatened to spoil all. To advance the dominions of England, King James esteemed "a good and honest motion; and fishing was an honest trade, the apostles' own calling;" yet he referred the suit to the prelates of Canterbury and London. Even while the negotiations were pending, a royal declaration constrained the Puritans of Lancashire to conform or leave the kingdom; and nothing more could be obtained for the wilds of America than an informal promise of neglect. On this the community relied, being advised not to entangle themselves with the bishops. "If there should afterward be a purpose to wrong us," thus they communed with themselves, "though we had a seal as broad as the house-floor, there would be means enough found to recall or reverse it. We must rest herein on God's providence."

Better hopes seemed to dawn when, in 1619, the London company for Virginia elected for their treasurer Sir Edwin Sandys, who from the first had befriended the pilgrims. Under his presidency, so writes one of their number, the members of the company in their open court "demanded our ends of going; which being related, they said the thing was of God, and granted a large patent." As it was taken in the name of one who failed to accompany the expedition, the patent was never of any service. And, besides, the pilgrims, after investing all their own means, had not sufficient capital to execute their schemes.

In this extremity, Robinson looked for aid to the Dutch. He and his people and their friends, to the number of four hundred families, professed themselves well inclined to emigrate to the country on the Hudson, and to plant there a new commonwealth under the command of the stadholder and the states general. The West India company was willing to transport them without charge, and to furnish them with cattle; but when its directors petitioned the states general to promise protection to the enterprise against all violence from other potentates, the request was found to be in conflict with the policy of the Dutch republic, and was refused.

The members of the church of Leyden, ceasing "to meddle with the Dutch, or to depend too much on the Virginia company," now trusted to their own resources and the aid of private friends. The fisheries had commended American expeditions to English merchants; and the agents from Leyden were able to form a partnership between their employers and men of business in London. The services of each emigrant were rated as a capital of ten pounds, and belonged to the company; all profits were to be reserved till the end of seven years, when the whole amount, and all houses and land, gardens and fields, were to be divided among the share-holders according to their respective interests. The London merchant, who risked one hundred pounds, would receive for his money tenfold as much as the penniless laborer for his services. This arrangement threatened a seven years' check to the pecuniary prosperity of the community; yet, as it did not interfere with civil rights or religion, it was accepted.

And now, in July, 1620, the English at Leyden, trusting in God and in themselves, made ready for their departure. The ships which they had provided—the Speedwell, of sixty tons, the Mayflower, of one hundred and eighty tons—could hold but a minority of the congregation; and Robinson was therefore detained at Leyden, while Brewster, the governing elder, who was an able teacher, conducted "such of the youngest and strongest as freely offered themselves." A solemn fast was held. "Let us seek of God," said they, "a right way for us, and for our little ones, and for all our substance." Anticipating the sublime lessons of liberty that would grow out of their religious tenets, Robinson gave them a farewell, saying:

"I charge you, before God and his blessed angels, that you follow me no farther than you have seen me follow the Lord Jesus Christ. The Lord has more truth yet to break forth out of his holy word. I cannot sufficiently bewail the condition of the reformed churches, who are come to a period in religion, and will go at present no farther than the instruments of their reformation. Luther and Calvin were great and shining lights in their times, yet they penetrated not into the whole counsel of God. I beseech you, remember it—'tis an article of your church covenant—that you be ready to receive whatever truth shall be made known to you from the written word of God."

"When the ship was ready to carry us away," writes Edward Winslow, "the brethren that stayed at Leyden, having again solemnly sought the Lord with us and for us, feasted us that were to go, at our pastor's house, being large; where we refreshed ourselves, after tears, with singing of psalms, making joyful melody in our hearts, as well as with the voice, there being many of the congregation very expert in music; and, indeed, it was the sweetest melody that ever mine ears heard. After this they accompanied us to Delft-Haven, where we went to embark, and then feasted us again; and, after prayer, performed by our pastor, when a flood of tears was poured out, they accompanied us to the ship, but were not able to speak one to another for the abundance of sorrow to part. But we only, going aboard, gave them a volley of small shot and three pieces of ordnance; and so, lifting up our hands to each other, and our hearts for each other to the Lord our God, we departed."

In August the Mayflower and the Speedwell left Southampton for America. But as they were twice compelled to put back by the dismay of the captain of the Speedwell, at Plymouth "they agreed to dismiss her, and those who were willing returned to London, though this was very grievous and discouraging." Having thus winnowed their numbers, the little band, not of resolute men only, but wives, some far gone in pregnancy, children, infants, a floating village of one hundred and two souls, went on board the single ship, which was hired only to convey them across the Atlantic; and, on the sixth day of September, 1620, thirteen years after the first colonization of Virginia, they set sail for a new world.

Had New England been colonized immediately on the discovery of the American continent, the old English institutions would have been planted with the Roman Catholic hierarchy; had the settlement been made under Elizabeth, it would have been before activity of the popular mind in religion had awakened a corresponding activity in politics. The pilgrims were Englishmen, Protestants, exiles for conscience, men disciplined by misfortune, cultivated by opportunities of wide observation, and equal in rank as in rights.

The eastern coast of the United States abounds in convenient harbors, bays, and rivers. The pilgrims, having selected for their settlement the country on the Hudson, the best position on the whole coast, were conducted to the least fertile part of Massachusetts. After a boisterous voyage of sixty-three days, during which one person had died and one was born, they espied land; and, in two days more, on the ninth of November, cast anchor in the first harbor within Cape Cod. On the eleventh, before they landed, they formed themselves into a body politic by this voluntary compact:

"In the name of God, amen; we, whose names are underwritten, the loyal subjects of our dread sovereign King James, having undertaken, for the glory of God, and advancement of the Christian faith, and honor of our king and country, a voyage to plant the first colony in the northern parts of Virginia, do, by these presents, solemnly and mutually, in the presence of God and one of another, covenant and combine ourselves together into a civil body politic, for our better ordering and preservation and further-ance of the ends aforesaid; and, by virtue thereof, to enact, constitute, and frame such just and equal laws, ordinances, acts, constitutions, and offices, from time to time, as shall be thought most convenient for the general good of the colony. Unto which we promise all due submission and obedi-ence."

This instrument was signed by the whole body of men, forty-one in num-ber, who, with their families, constituted the one hundred and two, the whole colony, "the proper democracy," that arrived in New England. In the cabin of the Mayflower humanity recovered its rights, and instituted gov-ernment on the basis of "equal laws" enacted by all the people for "the general good." John Carver was immediately and unanimously chosen governor for the year.

Men who emigrate, even in well-inhabited districts, pray that their jour-ney may not be in winter. Wasted by the rough voyage, scantily supplied with provisions, the Engish fugitives found themselves, in the last days of the year, on a bleak and barren coast, in a severe climate, with the ocean on one side and the wildernes on the other. The nearest French settlement was at Port Royal; it was five hundred miles to the English plantation at Virginia. As they attempted to disembark, the water was found so shallow that they were forced to wade; and, in the freezing weather, this sowed the seeds of consumption. The bitterness of mortal disease was their welcome to the inhospitable shore.

The spot for the settlement remained to be chosen. The shallop was unshipped, and it was a real disaster to find that it needed repairs. The carpenter made slow work, so that sixteen or seventeen days elapsed before it was ready for service. But Standish and Bradford and others, impatient of the delay, determined to explore the country by land. "In regard to the danger," the expedition "was rather permitted than approved." Much hard-ship was endured; but no beneficial discoveries could be made in the deep sands near Paomet creek. The first expedition in the shallop was likewise unsuccessful; "some of the people that died that winter took the original of their death" in the enterprise; "for it snowed and did blow all the day and night, and froze withal." The men who were set on shore "were tired with marching up and down the steep hills and deep valleys, which lay half a foot thick with snow." A heap of maize was discovered; and further search led to a burial-place of the Indians; but they found "no more corn, nor any-thing else but graves."

On the sixth, the shallop was again sent out, with Carver, Bradford, Winslow, Standish, and others, and eight or ten seamen. The spray of the sea froze as it fell on them, and made their clothes like coats of iron. That day they reached Billingsgate point, half way to the bottom of the bay of Cape Cod, on the western shore of Wellfleet harbor. The next morning the party divided; those on land find a burial-place, graves, and four or five deserted wigwams, but neither people nor any place inviting a settlement. Before night they all met by the sea-side, and encamped near Namskeket, or Great Meadow creek.

On the eighth day they rose at five; their morning prayers were finished, when, as the day dawned, a war-whoop and a flight of arrows announced an attack from Indians. They were of the tribe of the Nausites, who knew the English as kidnappers; but the encounter was without further result. Again the boat's crew give thanks to God, and steer their bark along the coast for the distance of fifteen leagues. But no convenient harbor is discovered. The pilot, who had been in those regions before, gives assurance of a good one, which may be reached before night; and they follow his guidance. After some hours' sailing, a storm of snow and rain begins; the sea swells; the rudder breaks; the boat must now be steered with oars; the storm increases; night is at hand; to reach the harbor before dark, as much sail as possible is borne; the mast breaks into three pieces; the sail falls overboard; but the tide is favorable. The pilot, in dismay, would have run the boat on shore in a cove full of breakers. "About with her," exclaimed a sailor, "or we are cast away." They get her about immediately; and, passing over the surf, they enter a fair sound, and shelter themselves under the lee of a small rise of land. It becomes dark, and the rain beats furiously. After great difficulty, they kindle a fire on shore.

The light of the morning of the ninth showed them to be on a small island within the entrance of a harbor. The day was spent in rest and repairs. The next day was the "Christian sabbath," and the pilgrims kept it sacredly, though every consideration demanded haste.

On Monday, the eleventh of December, old style, on the day of the winter solstice, the exploring party of the forefathers land at Plymouth. That day is kept as the origin of New England.

The spot, when examined, promised them a home, and on the fifteenth the Mayflower was safely moored in its harbor. In memory of the hospitalities which the company had received at the last English port from which they had sailed, this oldest New England colony took the name of Plymouth. The system of civil government had been established by common agreement; the church had been organized before it left Leyden. As the pilgrims landed, their institutions were already perfected. Democratic liberty and independent Christian worship started into being.

On the ninth of January, 1621, they began to build—a difficult task for men of whom one half were wasting away with consumptions and lung-fevers. For the sake of haste, it was agreed that every man should build his own house; but, though the winter was unwontedly mild, frost and foul weather were great hindrances; they could seldom work half of the week; and tenements rose slowly in the intervals between storms of sleet and snow.

A few years before, a pestilence had swept away the neighboring tribes. Yet when, in February, a body of Indians from abroad was discovered hovering near, though disappearing when pursued, the colony was organized for defence, with Miles Standish as its captain. But dangers from the natives were not at hand.

One day in March, Samoset, an Indian who had learned a little English of the fishermen at Penobscot, entered the town, and, passing to the rendezvous, exclaimed in English: "Welcome, Englishmen." He was the envoy of Massassoit himself, "the greatest commander of the country," sachem of the tribe possessing the land north of Narragansett bay, and between the rivers of Providence and Taunton. After some little negotiation, in which an Indian, who had been carried to England, acted as an interpreter, the chieftain came in person to visit the pilgrims. With their wives and children they amounted to more than fifty. He was received with due ceremonies, and a treaty of friendship was completed in few and unequivocal terms. Both parties promised to abstain from mutual injuries, and to deliver up offenders; the colonists were to receive assistance, if attacked; to render it, if Massassoit should be attacked unjustly. The treaty included the confederates of the sachem; it is the oldest act of diplomacy recorded in New England; was concluded in a day; and was sacredly kept for more than half a century. Massassoit neeeded the alliance, for the powerful Narragansetts were his enemies; his tribe desired an interchange of commodities; while the emigrants obtained peace, security, and a profitable commerce.

On the third of March, a south wind had brought warm and fair weather. "The birds sang in the woods most pleasantly." But spring had far advanced before the mortality grew less. It was afterward remarked, with modest gratitude, that, of the survivors, very many lived to an extreme old age. A shelter, not less than comfort, had been wanting; the living had been scarce able to bury the dead; the well too few to take care of the sick. At the season of greatest distress there were but seven able to render assistance. Carver, the governor, at his first landing, lost a son; by his care for the common good, he shortened his own days; and his wife, broken-hearted, followed him in death. Brewster was the life and stay of the plantation; but, he being its ruling elder, William Bradford, its historian, was chosen Carver's successor. The record of misery was kept by the graves of the governor and half the company.

After sickness abated, privation and want remained to be encountered. Yet, when in April the Mayflower was despatched for England, not one returned in her, while just before autumn new emigrants arrived. In July, an embassy from the little colony to Massassoit, their ally, performed through the forests and on foot, confirmed the treaty of amity, and prepared the way for a trade in furs.

The influence of the English over the aborigines was rapidly extended. A sachem, who menaced their safety, was compelled to sue for mercy; and, in September, nine chiefs subscribed an instrument of submission to King James. The bay of Massachusetts and harbor of Boston were explored. The supply of bread was scanty; but, at their rejoicing together after the harvest, the colonists had great plenty of wild fowl and venison, so that they feasted Massassoit with some ninety of his men.

Canonicus, the sachem of the Narragansetts, whose territory had escaped the ravages of the pestilence, at first desired to treat of peace; in 1622, a bundle of arrows, wrapped in the skin of a rattlesnake, was his message of hostility. But, when Bradford sent back the skin stuffed with powder and shot, his courage quailed, and he sued for amity.

The returns from agriculture were uncertain so long as the system of common property prevailed. After the harvest of 1623, there was no general want of food; in the spring of that year, each family planted for itself; and parcels of land, in proportion to numbers, were assigned for tillage, though not for inheritance. This arrangement produced contented labor and universal industry; "even women and children now went into the field to work." In the spring of 1624, every person obtained a little land in perpetual fee, and neat cattle were introduced. Before many harvests, so much corn was raised that the Indians, preferring the chase to tillage, looked to the men of Plymouth for their supply.

The fur trade was an object of envy; and Thomas Weston, who had been active among the London adventurers in establishing the colony, desired to engross its profits. In 1622, a patent for land near Weymouth, the first plantation in Boston harbor, was easily obtained; and sixty men were sent over. Helpless at their arrival, they intruded themselves, for most of the summer, upon the unrequited hospitality of the people of Plymouth. In their own plantation, they were soon reduced to necessity by their want of thrift and injustice toward the Indians; and a plot was formed for their destruction. But Massassoit revealed the design to his allies; and the planters at Weymouth were saved by the wisdom of the older colony and the intrepid gallantry of Standish. It was "his capital exploit." Some of the rescued men went to Plymouth; some sailed for England. One short year saw the beginning and decay of Weston's adventure.

The partnership of the Plymouth men with English merchants proved oppressive; for it kept from them their pastor. Robinson and the rest of his church at Leyden were longing to rejoin their brethren; the adventurers in England refused to provide them a passage, and attempted, with but short success, to force upon the colony a clergyman more friendly to the established church. Offended by opposition, and discouraged at the small returns from their investments, they became ready to prey upon their associates in America. A ship was despatched to rival them in their business; goods, which were sent for their supply, were sold to them at an advance of seventy per cent. The curse of usury, which always falls so heavily upon new settlements, did not spare them; for, being left without help from the partners, they were obliged to borrow money at fifty per cent and at thirty per cent interest. At last the emigrants purchased the entire rights of the English adventurers; and the common property was equitably divided. For a six years' monopoly of trade, eight of the most enterprising men assumed all the engagements of the colony; so that the cultivators of the soil became really freeholders; neither debts nor rent-day troubled them.

Hardly were they planted in America when their enterprise took a wide range; before Massachusetts was settled, they had acquired rights at Cape Ann, as well as an extensive domain on the Kennebec; and they were the first of the English to estabish a post on the Connecticut. But the progress of population was very slow; and at the end of ten years the colony contained no more than three hundred souls. Robinson died at Leyden; his heart was in America, where his memory will never die. The remainder of his people, and with them his wife and children, came over, so soon as means could be provided to defray the costs.

The frame of civil government in the old colony was of the utmost simplicity. A governor was chosen by general suffrage, whose power, always subordinate to the common will, was, at the desire of Bradford, in 1624, restricted by a council of five, and, in 1633, of seven, assistants. In the council, the governor had but a double vote. There could be no law or imposition without consent of the freemen. For more than eighteen years "the whole body of the male inhabitants" constituted the legislature; the state was governed, like a town, as a strict democracy; and the people were frequently convened to decide on executive not less than on judicial questions. At length, in 1639, after the increase of population, and its diffusion over a wider territory, each town sent its committee to a general court.

The men of Plymouth exercised self-government without the sanction of a royal charter, which it was ever impossible for them to obtain; it was, therefore, in themselves that their institutions found the guarantee for stability. The never hesitated to punish small offences; it was only after some scruples that they inflicted capital punishment. Their doubts being once removed, they exercised the same authority as the charter governments. Death was, by subsequent laws, made the penalty for several crimes, but was never inflicted except for murder. House-breaking and highway robbery were offences unknown in their courts, and too little apprehended to be made subjects of severe legislation.

"To enjoy religious liberty was the known end of the first comers' great adventure into this remote wilderness;" and they desired no increase but from the friends of their communion. Yet their residence in Holland had

made them acquainted with various forms of Christianity; a wide experience
had emancipated them from bigotry; and they were never betrayed into the
excesses of religious persecution, though they sometimes permitted a disproportion between punishment and crime. In 1645, a majority of the house
of delegates were in favor of an act to "allow and maintain full and free
toleration to all men that would preserve the civil peace and submit unto
government; and there was no limitation or exception against Turk, Jew,
Papist, Arian, Socinian, Nicolaitan, Familist, or any other;" but the governor refused to put the question, and so stifled the law.

It is as guides and pioneers that the fathers of the old colony merit gratitude. Through scenes of gloom and misery they showed the way to an
asylum for those who would go to the wilderness for the liberty of conscience. Accustomed "in their native land to a plain country life and the
innocent trade of husbandry," they set the example of colonizing New
England with freeholders, and formed the mould for the civil and religious
character of its institutions. They enjoyed, in anticipation, the fame which
their successors would award to them. "Out of small beginnings," said
Bradford, "great things have been produced; and, as one small candle may
light a thousand, so the light here kindled hath shone to many, yea, in
some sort to our whole nation." "Let it not be grievous to you"—such
was the consolation offered from England to the pilgrims in the season of
their greatest sufferings—"let it not be grievous to you that you have been
instruments to break the ice for others. The honor shall be yours to the
world's end." "Yea, the memory of the adventurers to this plantation shall
never die."

BROOKS ADAMS

(1848-1927)

Writing as a gentleman-historian in the latter part of the nineteenth century, Brooks Adams was even more iconoclastic than his brother Henry. In the Emancipation of Massachusetts *he reacted sharply against the ancestor worship of most earlier historians of New England to attack vigorously the Puritan oligarchy of the seventeenth century. The book, he explained to Henry Cabot Lodge, "is not an attempt to break down the Puritans or to abuse the clergy, but to follow out the action of the human mind as we do the human body. I believe they are one and subject to the same laws. . . . The story I look on as only an illustration of a law."*

Few historians would agree today that that brilliant clerical father and son, Increase and Cotton Mather, helped fan the witchcraft excitement into flames in order to strengthen their waning power in the colony. But Adams's indignant pages are a trenchant, and basically accurate, account of a shocking episode.

Witchcraft in Massachusetts

AT THE CLOSE OF THE SIXTEENTH CENTURY THE BELIEF IN WITCHCRAFT was widespread, and among the more ignorant well-nigh universal. The superstition was, moreover, fostered by the clergy, who, in adopting this policy, were undoubtedly actuated by mixed motives. Their credulity probably made them for the most part sincere in the unbounded confidence they professed in the possibility of compacts between the devil and mankind; but, nevertheless, there is abundant evidence in their writings of their having been keenly alive to the fact that men horror-stricken at the sight of the destruction of their wives and children by magic would grovel in the submission of abject terror at the feet of the priest who promised to deliver them.

The elders began the agitation by sending out a paper of proposals for collecting stories of apparitions and witchcrafts, and in obedience to their wish Increase Mather published his "Illustrious Providences" in 1683–4. Two chapters of this book were devoted to sorceries, and the reverend author took occasion to intimate his opinion that those who might doubt the truth of his relations were probably themselves either heretics or wizards. This movement of the clergy seems to have highly inflamed the popular imagination, yet no immediate disaster followed; and the nervous exaltation did not become deadly until 1688. In the autumn of that year four children of a Boston mason named Goodwin began to mimic the symptoms they had so often heard described; the father, who was a pious man, called in the ministers of Boston and Charlestown, who fasted and prayed, and succeeded in delivering the youngest, who was five. Meanwhile, one of the daughters had "cried out upon" an unfortunate Irish washerwoman, with whom she had quarrelled. Cotton Mather was now in his element. He took the eldest girl home with him and tried a great number of interesting experiments as to the relative power of Satan and the Lord; among others he gravely relates how when the sufferer was tormented elsewhere he would carry her struggling to his own study, into which entering, she stood immediately upon her feet, and cried out, "They are gone! They are gone! They say they cannot—God won't let 'em come here."

It is not credible that an educated and a sane man could ever have

From Adams, *The Emancipation of Massachusetts* (1887), ch. 7 (in part).

honestly believed in the absurd stuff which he produced as evidence of the supernatural; his description of the impudence of the children is amazing.

"They were divers times very near burning or drowning of themselves, but . . . by their own pittiful and seasonable cries for help still procured their deliverance: which made me consider, whether the little ones had not their angels, in the plain sense of our Saviour's intimation. . . . And sometimes, tho' but seldome, they were kept from eating their meals, by having their teeth sett when they carried any thing to their mouthes."

And it was upon such evidence that the washerwoman was hanged. There is an instant in the battle as the ranks are wavering, when the calmness of the officers will avert the rout; and as to have held their soldiers then is deemed their highest honor, so to have been found wanting is their indelible disgrace; the people stood poised upon the panic's brink, their pastors lashed them in.

Cotton Mather forthwith published a terrific account of the ghostly crisis, mixed with denunciations of the Sadducee or Atheist who disbelieved; and to the book was added a preface, written by the four other clergymen who had assisted with their prayers, the character of which may be judged by a single extract. "The following account will afford to him that shall read with observation, a further clear confirmation, that, there is both a God, and a devil, and witchcraft: that there is no outward affliction, but what God may, (and sometimes doth) permit Satan to trouble his people withal." Not content with this, Mather goaded his congregation into frenzy from the pulpit. "Consider also, the misery of them whom witchcraft may be let loose upon. What is it to fall into the hands of devils? . . . O what a direful thing is it, to be prickt with pins, and stab'd with knives all over, and to be fill'd all over with broken bones? 'Tis impossible to reckon up the varieties of miseries which those monsters inflict where they can have a blow. No less than death, and that a languishing and a terrible death will satisfie the rage of those formidable dragons." The pest was sure to spread in a credulous community, fed by their natural leaders with this morbid poison, and it next broke out in Salem village in February, 1691–2. A number of girls had become intensely excited by the stories they had heard, and two of them, who belonged to the family of the clergyman, were seized with the usual symptoms. Of Mr. Parris it is enough to say that he began the investigation with a frightful relish. Other ministers were called in, and prayer-meetings lasting all day were held, with the result of throwing the patients into convulsions. Then the name of the witch was asked, and the girls were importuned to make her known. They refused at first, but soon the pressure became too strong, and the accusations began. Among the earliest to be arrested and examined was Goodwife Cory. Mr. Noyes, teacher of Salem, began with prayer, and when she was brought in the sufferers "did vehemently accuse her of afflicting them, by biting, pinching, strangling, &c., and they said, they did in their fits see her likeness coming to them, and bringing a book for them to sign." By April the number of informers and of the suspected had greatly increased and the prisons began to fill. Mr. Parris behaved like a madman; not only did he preach inflammatory sermons, but he conducted the examinations, and his questions were such that the evidence was in truth nothing but what he put in the mouths of the witnesses; yet he seems to have been guilty of a darker crime, for there is reason to suppose he garbled the testimony it was his sacred duty to truly record. And in all this he appears to have had the approval and the aid of Mr. Noyes. Such was the crisis when Sir William Phips landed on the 14th of May, 1692; he was the Mathers' tool, and the result could have been foretold. Uneducated and credulous, he was as clay in the hands of his creators; and his first executive act was to cause the miserable prisoners to be fettered. Jonathan Cory has described what befell his wife: "Next morning the jaylor put irons on her legs (having received such a command) the weight of them was about eight pounds; these irons and her other afflictions, soon brought her into convulsion fits, so that I thought she would have died that night."

At the beginning of June the governor, by an arbitrary act, created a court to try the witches, and at its head put William Stoughton. Even now it is impossible to read the proceedings of this sanguinary tribunal without a shudder, and it has left a stain upon the judiciary of Massachusetts that can never be effaced.

Two weeks later the opinion of the elders was asked, as it had been of old, and they recommended the "speedy and vigorous prosecutions of such as have rendered themselves obnoxious," nor did their advice fall upon unwilling ears. Stoughton was already at work, and certain death awaited all who were dragged before that cruel and bloodthirsty bigot; even when the jury acquitted, the court refused to receive the verdict. The accounts given of the legal proceedings seem monstrous. The preliminary examinations were conducted amid such "hideous clamours and screechings," that frequently the voice of the defendant was drowned, and if a defence was attempted at a trial, the victim was browbeaten and mocked by the bench.

The ghastly climax was reached in the case of George Burroughs, who had been the clergyman at Wells. At his trial the evidence could hardly be heard by reason of the fits of the sufferers. "The chief judge asked the prisoner, who he thought hindered these witnesses from giving their testimonies? and he answered, he supposed it was the devil. That honourable person then replied, How comes the devil so loath to have any testimony born against you? Which cast him into very great confusion." Presently the informers saw the ghosts of his two dead wives, whom they charged him with having murdered, stand before him "crying for vengeance;" yet though much appalled, he steadily denied that they were there. He also roused his judges' ire by asserting that "there neither are, nor ever were, witches."

He and those to die with him were carried through the streets of Salem in a cart. As he climbed the ladder he called God to witness he was innocent, and his words were so pathetic that the people sobbed aloud, and it seemed as though he might be rescued even as he stood beneath the tree. Then when at last he swung above them, Cotton Mather rode among the throng and told them of his guilt, and how the fiend could come to them as an angel of light, and so the work went on. They cut him down and dragged him by his halter to a shallow hole among the rocks, and threw him in, and there they lay together with the rigid hand of the wizard Burroughs still pointing upward through his thin shroud of earth.

By October it seemed as though the bonds of society were dissolving; nineteen persons had been hanged, one had been pressed to death, and eight lay condemned; a number had fled, but their property had been seized and they were beggars; the prisons were choked, while more than two hundred were accused and in momentary fear of arrest; even two dogs had been killed. The plague propagated itself; for the only hope for those cried out upon was to confess their guilt and turn informers. Thus no one was safe. Mr. Willard, pastor of the Old South, who began to falter, was threatened; the wife of Mr. Hale, pastor of Beverly, who had been one of the great leaders of the prosecutions, was denounced; Lady Phips herself was named. But the race who peopled New England had a mental vigor which even the theocracy could not subdue, and Massachusetts had among her sons liberal and enlightened men, whose voice was heard, even in the madness of the terror. Of these, the two Brattles, Robert Calef, and John Leverett were the foremost; and they served their mother well, though the debt of gratitude and honor which she owes them she has never yet repaid.

On the 8th, four days before the meeting of the legislature, and probably at the first moment it could be done with safety, Thomas Brattle wrote an admirable letter, in which he exposed the folly and wickedness of the delusion with all the energy the temper of the time would bear; had he miscalculated, his error of judgment would probably have cost him his life. At the meeting of the General Court the illegal and blood-stained commission came to an end, and as the reaction slowly and surely set in, Phips began to feel alarm lest he should be called to account in England; accordingly, he tried to throw the blame on Stoughton: "When I returned, I found people much dissatisfied at the proceedings of the court; . . . The deputy-governor, [Stoughton] notwithstanding, persisted vigorously in the same method. . . . When I put an end to the court, there was at least fifty persons in prison, in great misery by reason of the extreme cold and their poverty. . . . I permitted a special superior court to be held at Salem, . . . on the third day of January, the lieutenant-governor being chief judge. . . . All . . . were cleared, saving three. . . . The deputy-governor signed a warrant for their speedy execution, and also of five others who were condemned at the former court. . . . But . . . I sent a reprieve; . . . the lieutenant-governor upon this occasion was enraged and filled with passionate anger, and refused to sit upon the bench at a superior court, at that time held at Charlestown; and, indeed, hath from the beginning hurried on these matters with great precipitancy, and by his warrant hath caused the estates, goods, and chattels of the executed to be seized and disposed of without my knowledge or consent." Some months earlier, also, just before the meeting of the legislature, he had called on Cotton Mather to defend him against the condemnation he had even then begun to feel, and the elder had responded with a volume which remains as a memorial of him and his compeers. He gave thanks for the blood that had already flowed, and prayed to God for more. "They were some of the gracious words, inserted in the advice, which many of the neighbouring ministers, did this summer humbly lay before our honourable judges: 'We cannot but with all thankfulness, acknowledge the success which the merciful God has given unto the sedulous and assiduous endeavours of our honourable rulers, to detect the abominable witchcrafts which have been committed in the country; humbly praying that the discovery of those mysterious and mischievous wickednesses, may be perfected.' If in the midst of the many dissatisfactions among us, the publication of these trials, may promote such a pious thankfulness unto God, for justice being so far, executed among us, I shall rejoyce that God is glorified; and pray that no wrong steps of ours may ever sully any of his glorious works."

"These witches . . . have met in hellish randezvouszes. . . . In these hellish meetings, these monsters have associated themselves to do no less a thing than to destroy the kingdom of our Lord Jesus Christ, in these parts of the world. . . . We are truly come into a day, which by being well managed might be very glorious, for the exterminating of those, accursed things, . . . But if we make this day quarrelsome, . . . Alas, O Lord, my flesh trembles for fear of thee, and I am afraid of thy judgments."

While reading such words the streets of Salem rise before the eyes, with the cart dragging Martha Cory to the gallows while she protests her innocence, and there, at her journey's end, at the gibbet's foot, stands the Rev. Nicholas Noyes, pointing to the dangling corpses, and saying: "What a sad thing it is to see eight firebrands of hell hanging there."

The sequence of cause and effect is sufficiently obvious. Although at a moment when the panic had got beyond control, even the most ultra of the clergy had been forced by their own danger to counsel moderation, the conservatives were by no means ready to abandon their potent allies from the lower world; the power they gave was too alluring. " 'Tis a strange passage recorded by Mr. Clark, in the life of his father, That the people of his parish refusing to be reclaimed from their Sabbath breaking, by all the zealous testimonies which that good man bore against it; at last [one night] . . . there was heard a great noise, with rattling of chains, up and

down the town, and an horrid scent of brimstone. . . . Upon which the
guilty consciences of the wretches, told them, the devil was come to fetch
them away; and it so terrify'd them, that an eminent reformation follow'd
the sermons which that man of God preached thereupon." They therefore
saw the constant acquittals, the abandonment of prosecutions, and the
growth of incredulity with regret. The next year Cotton Mather laid bare
the workings of their minds with cynical frankness. "The devils have with
most horrendous operations broke in upon our neighbourhood, and God
has at such a rate overruled all the fury and malice of those devils, that . . .
the souls of many, especially of the rising generation, have been thereby
waken'd unto some acquaintance with religion; our young people who
belonged unto the praying meetings, of both sexes, apart would ordinarily
spend whole nights by the whole weeks together in prayers and psalms upon
these occasions; . . . and some scores of other young people, who were
strangers to real piety, were now struck with the lively demonstrations of
hell . . . before their eyes. . . . In the whole—the devil got just nothing, but
God got praises, Christ got subjects, the Holy Spirit got temples, the church
got addition, and the souls of men got everlasting benefits."

Mather prided himself on what he had done. "I am not so vain as to say
that any wisdom or virtue of mine did contribute unto this good order of
things; but I am so just as to say, I did not hinder this good." Men with such
beliefs, and lured onward by such temptations, were incapable of letting the
tremendous power superstition gave them slip from their grasp without an
effort on their own behalf; and accordingly it was not long before the
Mathers were once more at work. On the 10th of September, 1693, or
about nine months after the last spasms at Salem, and when the belief in
enchantments was fast falling into disrepute, a girl named Margaret Rule
was taken with the accustomed symptoms in Boston. Forthwith these two
godly divines repaired to her bedside, and this is what took place:—

Then Mr. M——father and son came up, and others with them, in the
whole were about thirty or forty persons, they being sat, the father on a
stool, and the son upon the bedside by her, the son began to question her:
Margaret Rule, how do you do? Then a pause without any answer.
Question. What. Do there a great many witches sit upon you? *Answer.*
Yes.
Question. Do you not know that there is a hard master?
Then she was in a fit. He laid his hand upon her face and nose, but,
as he said, without perceiving breath; then he brush'd her on the face with
his glove, and rubb'd her stomach (her breast not being covered with the
bed clothes) and bid others do so too, and said it eased her, then she revived.
Q. Don't you know there is a hard master? *A.* Yes.
Reply. Don't serve that hard master, you know who.
Q. Do you believe? Then again she was in a fit, and he again rub'd her

breast &c. . . . He wrought his fingers before her eyes and asked her if she saw the witches? *A*. No. . . .

Q. Who is it that afflicts you? *A*. I know not, there is a great many of them. . . .

Q. You have seen the black man, hant you? *A*. No.

Reply. I hope you never shall.

Q. You have had a book offered you, hant you? *A*. No.

Q. The brushing of you gives you ease, don't it? *A*. Yes. She turn'd her-selfe, and a little groan'd.

Q. Now the witches scratch you, and pinch you, and bite you, don't they? *A*. Yes. Then he put his hand upon her breast and belly, viz. on the clothes over her, and felt a living thing, as he said; which moved the father also to feel, and some others.

Q. Don't you feel the live thing in the bed? *A*. No. . . .

Q. Shall we go to pray . . . spelling the word. *A*. Yes. The father went to prayer for perhaps half an hour, chiefly against the power of the devil and witchcraft, and that God would bring out the afflicters. . . . After prayer he [the son] proceeded.

Q. You did not hear when we were at prayer did you? *A*. Yes.

Q. You don't hear always? you don't hear sometimes past a word or two, do you? *A*. No. Then turning him about said, this is just another Mercy Short. . . .

Q. What does she eat or drink? *A*. Not eat at all; but drink rum.

To sanctify to the godly the ravings of this drunken and abandoned wench was a solemn joy to the heart of this servant of Christ, who gave his life to "unwearied cares and pains, to rescue the miserable from the lions and bears of hell," therefore he prepared another tract. But his hour was well-nigh come. Though it was impossible that retribution should be meted out to him for his crimes, at least he did not escape unscathed, for Calef and the Brattles, who had long been on his father's track and his, now seized him by the throat. He knew well they had been with him in the chamber of Margaret Rule, that they had gathered all the evidence; and so when Calef sent him a challenge to stand forth and defend himself, he shuffled and equivocated.

At length a rumor spread abroad that a volume was to be published exposing the whole black history, and then the priest began to cower. His Diary is full of his prayers and lamentations. "The book is printed, and the impression is this week arrived here. . . . I set myself to humble myself before the Lord under these humbling and wondrous dispensations, and obtain the pardon of my sins, that have rendered me worthy of such dispensations. . . .

"28d. 10 m. Saturday.—The Lord has permitted Satan to raise an extraordinary storm upon my father and myself. All the rage of Satan against the holy churches of the Lord falls upon us. First Calf's book, and then Coleman's, do set the people in a mighty ferment. All the adversaries of the churches lay their heads together, as if, by blasting of us, they hoped utterly to blow up all. The Lord fills my soul with consolations, inexpressible consolations, when I think on my conformity to my Lord Jesus Christ in the injuries and reproaches that are cast upon me. . . .

"5d. 2m. Saturday [1701].—I find the enemies of the churches are set with an implacable enmity against myself; and one vile fool, namely, R. Calf, is employed by them to go on with more of his filthy scribbles to hurt my precious opportunities of glorifying my Lord Jesus Christ. I had need be much in prayer unto my glorious Lord that he would preserve his poor servant from the malice of this evil generation, and of that vile man particularly."

"More Wonders of the Invisible World" appeared in 1700, and such was the terror the clergy still inspired it is said it had to be sent to London to be printed, and when it was published no bookseller in Boston dared to offer it in his shop. Yet though it was burnt in the college yard by the order of Increase Mather, it was widely read, and dealt the deathblow to the witchcraft superstition of New England. It did more than this: it may be said to mark an era in the intellectual development of Massachusetts, for it shook to its centre that moral despotism which the pastors still kept almost unimpaired over the minds of their congregations, by demonstrating to the people the necessity of thinking for themselves. But what the fate of its authors would have been had the priests still ruled may be guessed by the onslaught made on them by those who sat at the Mathers' feet. "Spit on, Calf; thou shalt be but like the viper on Pauls hand, easily shaken off, and without any damage to the servant of the Lord."

FRANCIS PARKMAN

(1823-1893)

*Well into the second half of the eighteenth century, the English colonists
lived in the shadow of war or fear of war—of sudden attacks from Indians
and behind the Indians the relentless pressure of the French, for decades
struggling intermittently with the English for the control of the North
American continent. When Francis Parkman was a boy in the Jackson
period, the American Revolution had overshadowed but not erased family
stories of the wars against the French and the Indians. Much of the terrain
over which Parkman hunted and fished still looked the same; he once saw
the part-Indian grandson of one of the children kidnapped during the
Deerfield massacre of 1704. While he was still an undergraduate at Harvard
he conceived the idea of writing a part of what became the monumental*
France and England in North America. *Many years later he wrote:*

*"Before the end of my sophomore year my various schemes had crystal-
lized into a plan of writing a story of what was then known as the 'Old
French War'—that is, the War that ended in the conquest of Canada—for
here, as it seemed to me, the forest drama was more stirring and the forest
stage more thronged with appropriate actors than in any other passage of
our history. It was not until some years later that I enlarged the plan to
include the whole course of the American conflict between France and England, or, in other words, the history of the American forest; for this was the
light in which I regarded it."*

*Most of Parkman's many volumes focussed upon the French explorers,
missionaries, settlers, and soldiers. In his accounts of the wars, he tried to
take his readers "within the French lines," but did so without disguising
his sympathies with the English colonists. In these chapters from* A Half-
Century of Conflict *and* Montcalm and Wolfe, *Parkman was writing from
the viewpoint of the colonials. Near the beginning of* A Half-Century of
Conflict *Parkman described the precarious life on the New England frontier,
and the attack upon Deerfield early in Queen Anne's War (The War of the
Spanish Succession) which broke out in 1702.*

France and England in the New World

FOR UNTOLD AGES MAINE HAD BEEN ONE UNBROKEN FOREST, AND IT WAS so still. Only along the rocky seaboard or on the lower waters of one or two great rivers a few rough settlements had gnawed slight indentations into this wilderness of woods, and a little farther inland some dismal clearing around a blockhouse or stockade let in the sunlight to a soil that had lain in shadow time out of mind. This waste of savage vegetation survives, in some part, to this day, with the same prodigality of vital force, the same struggle for existence and mutual havoc that mark all organized beings, from men to mushrooms. Young seedlings in millions spring every summer from the black mould, rich with the decay of those that had preceded them, crowding, choking, and killing each other, perishing by their very abundance; all but a scattered few, stronger than the rest, or more fortunate in position, which survive by blighting those about them. They in turn, as they grow, interlock their boughs, and repeat in a season or two the same process of mutual suffocation. The forest is full of lean saplings dead or dying with vainly stretching towards the light. Not one infant tree in a thousand lives to maturity; yet these survivors form an innumerable host, pressed together in struggling confusion, squeezed out of symmetry and robbed of normal development, as men are said to be in the level sameness of democratic society. Seen from above, their mingled tops spread in a sea of verdure basking in light; seen from below, all is shadow, through which spots of timid sunshine steal down among legions of lank, mossy trunks, toadstools and rank ferns, protruding roots, matted bushes, and rotting carcases of fallen trees. A generation ago one might find here and there the rugged trunk of some great pine lifting its verdant spire above the undistinguished myriads of the forest. The woods of Maine had their aristocracy; but the axe of the woodman has laid them low, and these lords of the wilderness are seen no more.

The life and light of this grim solitude were in its countless streams and lakes, from little brooks stealing clear and cold under the alders, full of the small fry of trout, to the mighty arteries of the Penobscot and the Kennebec; from the great reservoir of Moosehead to a thousand nameless ponds shining in the hollow places of the forest.

From Parkman, *A Half-Century of Conflict* (2 vols., 1884), vol. 1, ch. 3, 4 (in part); and *Montcalm and Wolfe* (2 vols., 1892), vol. 1, ch. 5, 7.

It had and still has its beast of prey,—wolves, savage, cowardly, and mean; bears, gentle and mild compared to their grisly relatives of the Far West, vegetarians when they can do no better, and not without something grotesque and quaint in manners and behavior; sometimes, though rarely, the strong and sullen wolverine; frequently the lynx; and now and then the fierce and agile cougar.

The human denizens of this wilderness were no less fierce, and far more dangerous. These were the various tribes and sub-tribes of the Abenakis, whose villages were on the Saco, the Kennebec, the Penobscot, and the other great watercourses. Most of them had been converted by the Jesuits, and, as we have seen already, some had been persuaded to remove to Canada, like the converted Iroquois of Caughnawaga. The rest remained in their native haunts, where, under the direction of their missionaries, they could be used to keep the English settlements in check.

We know how busily they plied their tomahawks in William and Mary's War, and what havoc they made among the scattered settlements of the border. Another war with France was declared on the 4th of May, 1702, on which the Abenakis again assumed a threatening attitude. In June of the next year Dudley, Governor of Massachusetts, called the chiefs of the various bands to a council at Casco. Here presently appeared the Norridgewocks from the Kennebec, the Penobscots and Androscoggins from the rivers that bear their names, the Penacooks from the Merrimac, and the Pequawkets from the Saco, all well armed, and daubed with ceremonial paint. The principal among them, gathered under a large tent, were addressed by Dudley in a conciliatory speech. Their orator replied that they wanted nothing but peace, and that their thoughts were as far from war as the sun was from the earth,—words which they duly confirmed by a belt of wampum. Presents were distributed among them and received with apparent satisfaction, while two of their principal chiefs, known as Captain Samuel and Captain Bomazeen, declared that several French missionaries had lately come among them to excite them against the English, but that they were "firm as mountains," and would remain so "as long as the sun and moon endured." They ended the meeting with dancing, singing, and whoops of joy, followed by a volley of musketry, answered by another from the English. It was discovered, however, that the Indians had loaded their guns with ball, intending, as the English believed, to murder Dudley and his attendants, if they could have done so without danger to their chiefs, whom the Governor had prudently kept about him. It was afterwards found, if we may believe a highly respectable member of the party, that two hundred French and Indians were on their way, "resolved to seize the Governor, Council, and gentlemen, and then to sacrifice the inhabitants at pleasure;" but when they arrived, the English officials had been gone three days.

The French Governor, Vaudreuil, says that about this time some of the

Abenakis were killed or maltreated by Englishmen. It may have been so; desperadoes, drunk or sober, were not rare along the frontier: but Vaudreuil gives no particulars, and the only English outrage that appears on record at the time was the act of a gang of vagabonds who plundered the house of the younger Saint-Castin, where the town of Castine now stands. He was Abenaki by his mother; but he was absent when the attack took place, and the marauders seem to have shed no blood. Nevertheless, within six weeks after the Treaty of Casco, every unprotected farm-house in Maine was in a blaze.

The settlements of Maine, confined to the southwestern corner of what is now the State of Maine, extended along the coast in a feeble and broken line from Kittery to Casco. Ten years of murderous warfare had almost ruined them. East of the village of Wells little was left except one or two forts and the so-called "garrisons," which were private houses pierced with loopholes and having an upper story projecting over the lower, so that the defenders could fire down on assailants battering the door or piling fagots against the walls. A few were fenced with palisades, as was the case with the house of Joseph Storer, at the east end of Wells, where an overwhelming force of French and Indians had been gallantly repulsed in the summer of 1692. These fortified houses were, however, very rarely attacked, except by surprise and treachery. In case of alarm such of the inhabitants as found time took refuge in them with their families, and left their dwellings to the flames; for the first thought of the settler was to put his women and children beyond reach of the scalping-knife. There were several of these asylums in different parts of Wells; and without them the place must have been abandoned. In the little settlement of York, farther westward, there were five of them, which had saved a part of the inhabitants when the rest were surprised and massacred.

Wells was a long, straggling settlement, consisting at the beginning of William and Mary's War of about eighty houses and log-cabins, strung at intervals along the north side of the rough track, known as the King's Road, which ran parallel to the sea. Behind the houses were rude, half-cleared pastures, and behind these again, the primeval forest. The cultivated land was on the south side of the road, in front of the houses, and beyond it spread great salt-marshes, bordering the sea and haunted by innumerable game-birds.

The settlements of Maine were a dependency of Massachusetts,—a position that did not please their inhabitants, but which they accepted because they needed the help of their Puritan neighbors, from whom they differed widely both in their qualities and in their faults. The Indian wars that checked their growth had kept them in a condition more than half barbarous. They were a hard-working and hard-drinking race; for though tea and coffee were scarcely known, the land flowed with New England rum, which was ranked among the necessaries of life. The better sort could read and write in a bungling way; but many were wholly illiterate, and it was not till long after Queen Anne's War that the remoter settlements established schools, taught by poor students from Harvard or less competent instructors, and held at first in private houses or under sheds. The church at Wells had been burned by the Indians; and though the settlers were beggared by the war, they voted in town meeting to build another. The new temple, begun in 1699, was a plain wooden structure thirty feet square. For want of money the windows long remained unglazed, the walls without plaster, and the floor without seats; yet services were duly held here under direction of the minister, Samuel Emery, to whom they paid £45 a year, half in provincial currency, and half in farm produce and firewood.

In spite of these efforts to maintain public worship, they were far from being a religious community; nor were they a peaceful one. Gossip and scandal ran riot; social jealousies abounded; and under what seemed entire democratic equality, the lazy, drunken, and shiftless envied the industrious and thrifty. Wells was infested, moreover, by several "frightfully turbulent women," as the chronicle styles them, from whose rabid tongues the minister himself did not always escape; and once, in its earlier days, the town had been indicted for not providing a ducking-stool to correct these breeders of discord.

Judicial officers were sometimes informally chosen by popular vote, and sometimes appointed by the Governor of Massachusetts from among the inhabitants. As they knew no law, they gave judgment according to their own ideas of justice, and their sentences were oftener wanting in wisdom than in severity. Until after 1700 the county courts met by beat of drum at some of the primitive inns or taverns with which the frontier abounded.

At Wells and other outlying and endangered hamlets life was still exceedingly rude. The log-cabins of the least thrifty were no better furnished than Indian wigwams. The house of Edmond Littlefield, reputed the richest man in Wells, consisted of two bedrooms and a kitchen, which last served a great variety of uses, and was supplied with a table, a pewter pot, a frying-pan, and a skillet; but no chairs, cups, saucers, knives, forks, or spoons. In each of the two bedrooms there was a bed, a blanket, and a chest. Another village notable—Ensign John Barrett—was better provided, being the possessor of two beds, two chests and a box, four pewter dishes, four earthen pots, two iron pots, seven trays, two buckets, some pieces of wooden-ware, a skillet, and a frying-pan. In the inventory of the patriarchal Francis Littlefield, who died in 1712, we find the exceptional items of one looking-glass, two old chairs, and two old books. Such of the family as had no bed slept on hay or straw, and no provision for the toilet is recorded.

On the 10th of August, 1703, these rugged borderers were about their usual callings, unconscious of danger,—the women at their household work, the men in the fields or on the more distant saltmarshes. The wife of Thomas Wells had reached the time of her confinement, and her husband had gone for a nurse. Some miles east of Wells's cabin lived Stephen Harding,—hunter, blacksmith, and tavern-keeper, a sturdy, good-natured man, who loved the woods, and whose frequent hunting trips sometimes led him nearly to the White Mountains. Distant gunshots were heard from the westward, and his quick eye presently discovered Indians approaching, on which he told his frightened wife to go with their infant to a certain oak-tree beyond the creek while he waited to learn whether the strangers were friends or foes.

That morning several parties of Indians had stolen out of the dismal woods behind the houses and farms of Wells, and approached different dwellings of the far-extended settlement at about the same time. They entered the cabin of Thomas Wells, where his wife lay in the pains of child-birth, and murdered her and her two small children. At the same time they killed Joseph Sayer, a neighbor of Wells, with all his family.

Meanwhile Stephen Harding, having sent his wife and child to a safe distance, returned to his blacksmith's shop, and, seeing nobody, gave a defiant whoop; on which four Indians sprang at him from the bushes. He escaped through a back-door of the shop, eluded his pursuers, and found his wife and child in a cornfield, where the woman had fainted with fright. They spent the night in the woods, and on the next day, after a circuit of nine miles, reached the palisaded house of Joseph Storer.

They found the inmates in distress and agitation. Storer's daughter Mary, a girl of eighteen, was missing. The Indians had caught her, and afterwards carried her prisoner to Canada. Samuel Hill and his family were captured, and the younger children butchered. But it is useless to record the names and fate of the sufferers. Thirty-nine in all, chiefly women and children, were killed or carried off, and then the Indians disappeared as quickly and silently as they had come, leaving many of the houses in flames.

This raid upon Wells was only part of a combined attack on all the settlements from that place to Casco. Those eastward of Wells had been, as we have seen, abandoned in the last war, excepting the forts and fortified houses; but the inhabitants, reassured, no doubt, by the Treaty of Casco, had begun to return. On this same day, the 10th of August, they were startled from their security. A band of Indians mixed with Frenchmen fell upon the settlements about the stone fort near the Falls of the Saco, killed eleven persons, captured twenty-four, and vainly attacked the fort itself. Others surprised the settlers at a place called Spurwink, and killed or captured twenty-two. Others, again, destroyed the huts of the fishermen at Cape Porpoise, and attacked the fortified house at Winter Harbor, the inmates of which, after a brave resistance, were forced to capitulate. The settlers at Scarborough were also in a fortified house, where they made a long and obstinate defence till help at last arrived. Nine families were settled at Purpooduck Point, near the present city of Portland. They had no place of refuge, and the men, being, no doubt, fishermen, were all absent, when the

Indians burst into the hamlet, butchered twenty-five women and children, and carried off eight.

The fort at Casco, or Falmouth, was held by Major March, with thirty-six men. He had no thought of danger, when three well-known chiefs from Norridgewock appeared with a white flag, and asked for an interview. As they seemed to be alone and unarmed, he went to meet them, followed by two or three soldiers and accompanied by two old men named Phippeny and Kent, inhabitants of the place. They had hardly reached the spot when the three chiefs drew hatchets from under a kind of mantle which they wore and sprang upon them, while other Indians, ambushed near by, leaped up and joined in the attack. The two old men were killed at once; but March, who was noted for strength and agility, wrenched a hatchet from one of his assailants, and kept them all at bay till Sergeant Hook came to his aid with a file of men and drove them off.

They soon reappeared, burned the deserted cabins in the neighborhood, and beset the garrison in numbers that continually increased, till in a few days the entire force that had been busied in ravaging the scattered settlements was gathered around the place. It consisted of about five hundred Indians of several tribes, and a few Frenchmen under an officer named Beaubassin. Being elated with past successes, they laid siege to the fort, sheltering themselves under a steep bank by the water-side and burrowing their way towards the rampart. March could not dislodge them, and they continued their approaches till the third day, when Captain Southack, with the Massachusetts armed vessel known as the "Province Galley," sailed into the harbor, recaptured three small vessels that the Indians had taken along the coast, and destroyed a great number of their canoes, on which they gave up their enterprise and disappeared.

Such was the beginning of Queen Anne's War. These attacks were due less to the Abenakis than to the French who set them on. "Monsieur de Vaudreuil," writes the Jesuit historian Charlevoix, "formed a party of these savages, to whom he joined some Frenchmen under the direction of the Sieur de Beaubassin, when they effected some ravages of no great consequence; they killed, however, about three hundred men." This last statement is doubly incorrect. The whole number of persons killed and carried off during the August attacks did not much exceed one hundred and sixty; and these were of both sexes and all ages, from octogenarians to new-born infants. The able-bodied men among them were few, as most of the attacks were made upon unprotected houses in the absence of the head of the family; and the only fortified place captured was the garrison-house at Winter Harbor, which surrendered on terms of capitulation. The instruments of this ignoble warfare and the revolting atrocities that accompanied it, were all, or nearly all, converted Indians of the missions. Charlevoix has no word of disapproval for it, and seems to regard its partial success as a gratifying one so far as it went.

One of the objects was, no doubt, to check the progress of the English settlements; but, pursues Charlevoix, "the essential point was to commit the Abenakis in such a manner that they could not draw back." This object was constantly kept in view. The French claimed at this time that the territory of Acadia reached as far westward as the Kennebec, which therefore formed, in their view, the boundary between the rival nations, and they trusted in the Abenakis to defend this assumed line of demarcation. But the Abenakis sorely needed English guns, knives, hatchets, and kettles, and nothing but the utmost vigilance could prevent them from coming to terms with those who could supply their necessities. Hence the policy of the French authorities on the frontier of New England was the opposite of their policy on the frontier of New York. They left the latter undisturbed, lest by attacking the Dutch and English settlers they should stir up the Five Nations to attack Canada; while, on the other hand, they constantly spurred the Abenakis against New England, in order to avert the dreaded event of their making peace with her.

The attack on Wells, Casco, and the intervening settlements was followed by murders and depredations that lasted through the autumn and extended along two hundred miles of frontier. Thirty Indians attacked the village of Hampton, killed the widow Mussey, a famous Quakeress, and then fled to escape pursuit. At Black Point nineteen men going to their work in the meadows were ambushed by two hundred Indians, and all but one were shot or captured. The fort was next attacked. It was garrisoned by eight men under Lieutenant Wyatt, who stood their ground for some time, and then escaped by means of a sloop in the harbor. At York the wife and children of Arthur Brandon were killed, and the Widow Parsons and her daughter carried off. At Berwick the Indians attacked the fortified house of Andrew Neal, but were repulsed with the loss of nine killed and many wounded, for which they revenged themselves by burning alive Joseph Ring, a prisoner whom they had taken. Early in February a small party of them hovered about the fortified house of Joseph Bradley at Haverhill, till, seeing the gate open and nobody on the watch, they rushed in. The woman of the house was boiling soap, and in her desperation she snatched up the kettle and threw the contents over them with such effect that one of them, it is said, was scalded to death. The man who should have been on the watch was killed, and several persons were captured, including the woman. It was the second time that she had been a prisoner in Indian hands. Half starved and bearing a heavy load, she followed her captors in their hasty retreat towards Canada. After a time she was safely delivered of an infant in the midst of the winter forest; but the child pined for want of sustenance, and the Indians hastened its death by throwing hot coals into its mouth when it cried. The astonishing vitality of the woman carried her to the end of the frightful journey. A Frenchman bought her from the Indians, and she was finally ransomed by her husband.

By far the most dangerous and harassing attacks were those of small parties skulking under the edge of the forest, or lying hidden for days together, watching their opportunity to murder unawares, and vanishing when they had done so. Against such an enemy there was no defence. The Massachusetts Government sent a troop of horse to Portsmouth, and another to Wells. These had the advantage of rapid movement in case of alarm along the roads and forest-paths from settlement to settlement; but once in the woods, their horses were worse than useless, and they could only fight on foot. Fighting, however, was rarely possible; for on reaching the scene of action they found nothing but mangled corpses and burning houses.

The best defence was to take the offensive. In September Governor Dudley sent three hundred and sixty men to the upper Saco, the haunt of the Pequawket tribe; but the place was deserted. Major, now Colonel, March soon after repeated the attempt, killing six Indians and capturing as many more. The General Court offered £40 for every Indian scalp, and one Captain Tyng, in consequence, surprised an Indian village in midwinter and brought back five of these disgusting trophies. In the spring of 1704 word came from Albany that a band of French Indians had built a fort and planted corn at Co-os meadows, high up the river Connecticut. On this, one Caleb Lyman with five friendly Indians, probably Mohegans, set out from Northampton, and after a long march through the forest, surprised, under cover of a thunderstorm, a wigwam containing nine warriors, —bound, no doubt, against the frontier. They killed seven of them; and this was all that was done at present in the way of reprisal or prevention.

The murders and burnings along the borders were destined to continue with little variety and little interruption during ten years. It was a repetition of what the pedantic Cotton Mather calls *Decennium luctuosum,* or the "woful decade" of William and Mary's War. The wonder is that the outlying settlements were not abandoned. These ghastly, insidious, and ever-present dangers demanded a more obstinate courage than the hottest battle in the open field.

One curious frontier incident may be mentioned here, though it did not happen till towards the end of the war. In spite of poverty, danger, and tribulation, marrying and giving in marriage did not cease among the sturdy borderers; and on a day in September there was a notable wedding feast at the palisaded house of John Wheelwright, one of the chief men of Wells. Elisha Plaisted was to espouse Wheelwright's daughter Hannah, and many guests were assembled, some from Portsmouth, and even beyond it. Probably most of them came in sail-boats; for the way by land was full of peril, especially on the road from York, which ran through dense woods, where Indians often waylaid the traveller. The bridegroom's father was present with the rest. It was a concourse of men in homespun, and women and girls in such improvised finery as their poor resources could supply; possibly, in default of better, some wore nightgowns, more or less disguised, over their daily dress, as happened on similar occasions half a century later among the frontiersmen of west Virginia. After an evening of rough merriment and gymnastic dancing, the guests lay down to sleep under the roof of their host or in adjacent barns and sheds. When morning came, and they were preparing to depart, it was found that two horses were missing; and not doubting that they had strayed away, three young men, Sergeant Tucker, Joshua Downing, and Isaac Cole, went to find them. In a few minutes several gunshots were heard. The three young men did not return. Downing and Cole were killed, and Tucker was wounded and made prisoner.

Believing that, as usual, the attack came from some small scalping party, Elisha Plaisted and eight or ten more threw themselves on the horses that stood saddled before the house, and galloped across the fields in the direction of the firing; while others ran to cut off the enemy's retreat. A volley was presently heard, and several of the party were seen running back towards the house. Elisha Plaisted and his companions had fallen into an ambuscade of two hundred Indians. One or more of them were shot, and the unfortunate bridegroom was captured. The distress of his young wife, who was but eighteen, may be imagined.

Two companies of armed men in the pay of Massachusetts were then in Wells, and some of them had come to the wedding. Seventy marksmen went to meet the Indians, who ensconced themselves in the edge of the forest, whence they could not be dislodged. There was some desultory firing, and one of the combatants was killed on each side, after which the whites gave up the attack, and Lieutenant Banks went forward with a flag of truce, in the hope of ransoming the prisoners. He was met by six chiefs, among whom were two noted Indians of his acquaintance, Bomazeen and Captain Nathaniel. They well knew that the living Plaisted was worth more than his scalp; and though they would not come to terms at once, they promised to meet the English at Richmond's Island in a few days and give up both him and Tucker on payment of a sufficient ransom. The flag of truce was respected, and Banks came back safe, bringing a hasty note to the elder Plaisted from his captive son. This note now lies before me, and it runs thus, in the dutiful formality of the olden time:

Sir,—I am in the hands of a great many Indians, with which there is six captains. They say that what they will have for me is 50 pounds, and thirty pounds for Tucker, my fellow prisoner, in good goods, as broadcloth, some provisions, some tobacco pipes, Pomisstone [pumice-stone], stockings, and a little of all things. If you will, come to Richmond's Island in 5 days at farthest, for here is 200 Indians, and they belong to Canada.

If you do not come in 5 days, you will not see me, for Captain Nathaniel the Indian will not stay no longer, for the Canada Indians is not willing for to sell me. Pray, Sir, don't fail, for they have given me one day, for the days were but 4 at first. Give my kind love to my dear wife. This from your dutiful son till death,

ELISHA PLAISTED.

The alarm being spread and a sufficient number of men mustered, they set out to attack the enemy and recover the prisoners by force; but not an Indian could be found.

Bomazeen and Captain Nathaniel were true to the rendezvous; in due time Elisha Plaisted was ransomed and restored to his bride.

* * *

About midwinter the Governor of Canada sent another large war-party against the New England border. The object of attack was an unoffending hamlet, that from its position could never be a menace to the French, and the destruction of which could profit them nothing. The aim of the enterprise was not military, but political. "I have sent no war-party towards Albany," writes Vaudreuil, "because we must do nothing that might cause a rupture between us and the Iroquois; but we must keep things astir in the direction of Boston, or else the Abenakis will declare for the English." In short, the object was fully to commit these savages to hostility against New England, and convince them at the same time that the French would back their quarrel.

The party consisted, according to French accounts, of fifty Canadians and two hundred Abenakis and Caughnawagas,—the latter of whom, while trading constantly with Albany, were rarely averse to a raid against Massachusetts or New Hampshire. The command was given to the younger Hertel de Rouville, who was accompanied by four of his brothers. They began their march in the depth of winter, journeyed nearly three hundred miles on snowshoes through the forest, and approached their destination on the afternoon of the 28th of February, 1704. It was the village of Deerfield,—which then formed the extreme northwestern frontier of Massachusetts, its feeble neighbor, the infant settlement of Northfield, a little higher up the Connecticut, having been abandoned during the last war. Rouville halted his followers at a place now called Petty's Plain, two miles from the village; and here, under the shelter of a pine forest, they all lay hidden, shivering with cold,—for they dared not make fires,—and hungry as wolves, for their provisions were spent. Though their numbers, by the lowest account, were nearly equal to the whole population of Deerfield,—men, women, and children,—they had no thought of an open attack, but trusted to darkness and surprise for an easy victory.

Deerfield stood on a plateau above the river meadows, and the houses— forty-one in all—were chiefly along the road towards the villages of Hadley and Hatfield, a few miles distant. In the middle of the place, on a rising ground called Meeting-house Hill, was a small square wooden meeting-house. This, with about fifteen private houses, besides barns and sheds, was enclosed by a fence of palisades eight feet high, flanked by "mounts," or block-houses, at two or more of the corners. The four sides of this palisaded enclosure, which was called the fort, measured in all no less than two hundred and two rods, and within it lived some of the principal inhabitants of the village, of which it formed the centre or citadel. Chief among its inmates was John Williams, the minister, a man of character and education, who, after graduating at Harvard, had come to Deerfield when it was still suffering under the ruinous effects of King Philip's War, and entered on his ministry with a salary of sixty pounds in depreciated New England currency, payable, not in money, but in wheat, Indian-corn, and pork. His parishioners built him a house, he married, and had now eight children, one of whom was absent with friends at Hadley. His next neighbor was Benoni Stebbins, sergeant in the county militia, who lived a few rods from the meeting-house. About fifty yards distant, and near the northwest angle of the enclosure, stood the house of Ensign John Sheldon, a framed building, one of the largest in the village, and, like that of Stebbins, made bullet-proof by a layer of bricks between the outer and inner sheathing, while its small windows and its projecting upper story also helped to make it defensible.

The space enclosed by the palisade, though much too large for effective defence, served in time of alarm as an asylum for the inhabitants outside, whose houses were scattered,—some on the north towards the hidden enemy, and some on the south towards Hadley and Hatfield. Among those on the south side was that of the militia captain, Jonathan Wells, which had a palisade of its own, and, like the so-called fort, served as an asylum for the neighbors.

These private fortified houses were sometimes built by the owners alone, though more often they were the joint work of the owners and of the inhabitants, to whose safety they contributed. The palisade fence that enclosed the central part of the village was made under a vote of the town, each inhabitant being required to do his share; and as they were greatly impoverished by the last war, the General Court of the province remitted for a time a part of their taxes in consideration of a work which aided the general defence.

Down to the Peace of Ryswick the neighborhood had been constantly infested by scalping-parties, and once the village had been attacked by a considerable force of French and Indians, who were beaten off. Of late there had been warnings of fresh disturbance. Lord Cornbury, Governor of New York, wrote that he had heard through spies that Deerfield was again to be attacked, and a message to the same effect same from Peter Schuyler, who had received intimations of the danger from Mohawks lately on a visit to their Caughnawaga relatives. During the autumn the alarm was so great that the people took refuge within the palisades, and the houses of the enclosure were crowded with them; but the panic had now subsided, and many, though not all, had returned to their homes. They were reassured by the presence of twenty volunteers from the villages below, who, on application from the minister, Williams, the General Court had sent as a garrison to Deerfield, where they were lodged in the houses of the villagers. On the night when Hertel de Rouville and his band lay hidden among the pines there were in all the settlement a little less than three hundred souls, of whom two hundred and sixty-eight were inhabitants, twenty were yeomen soldiers of the garrison, two were visitors from Hatfield, and three were negro slaves. They were of all ages,—from the Widow Allison, in her eighty-fifth year, to the infant son of Deacon French, aged four weeks.

Heavy snows had lately fallen and buried the clearings, the meadow, and the frozen river to the depth of full three feet. On the northwestern side the drifts were piled nearly to the top of the palisade fence, so that it was no longer an obstruction to an active enemy.

As the afternoon waned, the sights and sounds of the little border hamlet were, no doubt, like those of any other rustic New England village at the end of a winter day,—an ox-sledge creaking on the frosty snow as it brought in the last load of firewood, boys in homespun snowballing each other in the village street, farmers feeding their horses and cattle in the barns, a matron drawing a pail of water with the help of one of those long well-sweeps still used in some remote districts, or a girl bringing a pail of milk from the cow-shed. In the houses, where one room served as kitchen, dining-room, and parlor, the housewife cooked the evening meal, children sat at their bowls of mush and milk, and the men of the family, their day's work over, gathered about the fire, while perhaps some village coquette sat in the corner with fingers busy at the spinning-wheel, and ears intent on the stammered wooings of her rustic lover. Deerfield kept early hours, and it is likely that by nine o'clock all were in their beds. There was a patrol inside the palisade, but there was little discipline among these extemporized soldiers; the watchers grew careless as the frosty night went on; and it is said that towards morning they, like the villagers, betook themselves to their beds.

Rouville and his men, savage with hunger, lay shivering under the pines till about two hours before dawn; then, leaving their packs and their snow-shoes behind, they moved cautiously towards their prey. There was a crust on the snow strong enough to bear their weight, though not to prevent a rustling noise as it crunched under the feet of so many men. It is said that from time to time Rouville commanded a halt, in order that the sentinels, if such there were, might mistake the distant sound for rising and falling gusts of wind. In any case, no alarm was given till they had mounted the palisade and dropped silently into the unconscious village. Then with one accord they screeched the war-whoop, and assailed the doors of the houses with axes and hatchets. The hideous din startled the minister, Williams, from his sleep. Half-wakened, he sprang out of bed, and saw dimly a crowd of savages bursting through the shattered door. He shouted to two soldiers who were lodged in the house; and then, with more valor than discretion, snatched a pistol that hung at the head of the bed, cocked it, and snapped it at the breast of the foremost Indian, who proved to be a Caughnawaga chief. It missed fire, or Williams would, no doubt, have been killed on the spot. Amid the screams of his terrified children, three of the party seized him and bound him fast; for they came well provided with cords, since prisoners had a market value. Nevertheless in the first fury of their attack they dragged to the door and murdered two of the children and a negro woman called Parthena, who was probably their nurse. In an upper room lodged a young man named Stoddard, who had time to snatch a cloak, throw himself out of the window, climb the palisade, and escape in the darkness. Half-naked as he was, he made his way over the snow to Hatfield, binding his bare feet with strips torn from the cloak.

They kept Williams shivering in his shirt for an hour while a frightful uproar of yells, shrieks, and gunshots sounded from without. At length they permitted him, his wife, and five remaining children to dress themselves. Meanwhile the Indians and their allies burst into most of the houses, killed such of the men as resisted, butchered some of the women and children, and seized and bound the rest. Some of the villagers escaped in the confusion, like Stoddard, and either fled half dead with cold towards Hatfield, or sought refuge in the fortified house of Jonathan Wells.

The house of Stebbins, the minister's next neighbor, had not been attacked so soon as the rest, and the inmates had a little time for preparation. They consisted of Stebbins himself, with his wife and five children, David Hoyt, Joseph Catlin, Benjamin Church, a namesake of the old Indian fighter of Philip's War, and three other men,—probably refugees who had brought their wives and families within the palisaded enclosure for safety. Thus the house contained seven men, four or five women, and a considerable number of children. Though the walls were bullet-proof, it was not built for defence. The men, however, were well supplied with guns, powder, and lead, and they seem to have found some means of barricading the windows. When the enemy tried to break in, they drove them back with loss. On this, the French and Indians gathered in great numbers before the house, showered bullets upon it, and tried to set it on fire. They were again repulsed, with the loss of several killed and wounded; among the former a Caughnawaga chief, and among the latter a French officer. Still the firing continued. If the assailants had made a resolute assault, the defenders must have been overpowered; but to risk lives in open attack was contrary to every maxim of forest warfare. The women in the house behaved with great courage, and moulded bullets, which the men shot at the enemy. Stebbins was killed outright, and Church was wounded, as was also the wife of David Hoyt. At length most of the French and Indians, disgusted with the obstinacy of the defence, turned their attention to other quarters; though some kept up their fire under cover of the meeting-house and another building within easy range of gunshot.

This building was the house of Ensign John Sheldon, already mentioned. The Indians had had some difficulty in mastering it; for the door being of thick oak plank, studded with nails of wrought iron and well barred, they could not break it open. After a time, however, they hacked a hole in it, through which they fired and killed Mrs. Sheldon as she sat on the edge of a bed in a lower room. Her husband, a man of great resolution, seems to have been absent. Their son John, with Hannah his wife, jumped from an upper chamber window. The young woman sprained her ankle in the fall, and lay helpless, but begged her husband to run to Hatfield for aid, which he did, while she remained a prisoner. The Indians soon got in at a back door, seized Mercy Sheldon, a little girl of two years, and dashed out her brains on the door-stone. Her two brothers and her sister Mary, a girl of sixteen, were captured. The house was used for a short time as a depot for prisoners, and here also was brought the French officer wounded in the attack on the Stebbins house. A family tradition relates that as he lay in great torment he begged for water, and that it was brought him by one of the prisoners, Mrs. John Catlin, whose husband, son, and infant grandson had been killed, and who, nevertheless, did all in her power to relieve the sufferings of the wounded man. Probably it was in recognition of this charity that when the other prisoners were led away, Mrs. Catlin was left behind. She died of grief a few weeks later.

The sun was scarcely an hour high when the miserable drove of captives was conducted across the river to the foot of a mountain or high hill. Williams and his family were soon compelled to follow, and his house was set on fire. As they led him off he saw that other houses within the palisade were burning, and that all were in the power of the enemy except that of his neighbor Stebbins, where the gallant defenders still kept their assailants at bay. Having collected all their prisoners, the main body of the French and Indians began to withdraw towards the pine forest, where they had left their packs and snow-shoes, and to prepare for a retreat before the country should be roused, first murdering in cold blood Marah Carter, a little girl of five years, whom they probably thought unequal to the march. Several parties, however, still lingered in the village, firing on the Stebbins house, killing cattle, hogs, and sheep, and gathering such plunder as the place afforded.

Early in the attack, and while it was yet dark, the light of burning houses, reflected from the fields of snow, had been seen at Hatfield, Hadley, and Northampton. The alarm was sounded through the slumbering hamlets, and parties of men mounted on farm-horses, with saddles or without, hastened to the rescue, not doubting that the fires were kindled by Indians. When the sun was about two hours high, between thirty and forty of them were gathered at the fortified house of Jonathan Wells, at the southern end of the village. The houses of this neighborhood were still standing, and seem not to have been attacked; the stubborn defence of the Stebbins house having apparently prevented the enemy from pushing much beyond the palisaded enclosure. The house of Wells was full of refugee families. A few Deerfield men here joined the horsemen from the lower towns, as also did four or five of the yeoman soldiers who had escaped the fate of most of their comrades. The horsemen left their horses within Wells's fence; he himself took the lead, and the whole party rushed in together at the southern gate of the palisaded enclosure, drove out the plunderers, and retook a part of their plunder. The assailants of the Stebbins house, after firing at it for three hours, were put to flight, and those of its male occupants who were still alive joined their countrymen, while the women and children ran back for harborage to the house of Wells.

Wells and his men, now upwards of fifty, drove the flying enemy more than a mile across the river meadows, and ran in headlong pursuit over the crusted snow, killing a considerable number. In the eagerness of the chase many threw off their overcoats, and even their jackets. Wells saw the danger, and vainly called on them to stop. Their blood was up, and most of them were young and inexperienced.

Meanwhile the firing at the village had been heard by Rouville's main body, who had already begun their retreat northward. They turned back to support their comrades, and hid themselves under the bank of the river till the pursuers drew near, when they gave them a close volley and rushed upon them with the war-whoop. Some of the English were shot down, and the rest driven back. There was no panic. "We retreated," says Wells, "facing about and firing." When they reached the palisade they made a final stand, covering by their fire such of their comrades as had fallen within range of musket-shot, and thus saving them from the scalping-knife. The French did not try to dislodge them. Nine of them had been killed, several were wounded, and one was captured.

The number of English carried off prisoners was one hundred and eleven, and the number killed was according to one list forty-seven, and according to another fifty-three, the latter including some who were smothered in the cellars of their burning houses. The names, and in most cases the ages, of both captives and slain are preserved. Those who escaped with life and freedom were, by the best account, one hundred and thirty-seven. An official tabular statement, drawn up on the spot, sets the number of houses burned at seventeen. The house of the town clerk, Thomas French, escaped, as before mentioned, and the town records, with other papers in his charge, were saved. The meeting-house also was left standing. The house of Sheldon was hastily set on fire by the French and Indians when their rear was driven out of the village by Wells and his men; but the fire was extinguished, and "the Old Indian House," as it was called, stood till the year 1849. Its door, deeply scarred with hatchets, and with a hole cut near the middle, is still preserved in the Memorial Hall at Deerfield.

Vaudreuil wrote to the minister, Ponchartrain, that the French lost two or three killed, and twenty or twenty-one wounded, Rouville himself being among the latter. This cannot include the Indians, since there is proof that the enemy left behind a considerable number of their dead. Wherever resistance was possible, it had been of the most prompt and determined character.

Long before noon the French and Indians were on their northward march with their train of captives. More armed men came up from the settlements below, and by midnight about eighty were gathered at the ruined village. Couriers had been sent to rouse the country, and before evening of the next day (the 1st of March) the force at Deerfield was increased to two hundred and fifty; but a thaw and a warm rain had set in, and as few of the men had snow-shoes, pursuit was out of the question. Even could the agile savages and their allies have been overtaken, the probable consequence would have been the murdering of the captives to prevent their escape.

In spite of the foul blow dealt upon it, Deerfield was not abandoned. Such of its men as were left were taken as soldiers into the pay of the province, while the women and children were sent to the villages below. A small garrison was also stationed at the spot, under command of Captain Jonathan Wells, and thus the village held its ground till the storm of war should pass over.

We have seen that the minister, Williams, with his wife and family were led from their burning house across the river to the foot of the mountain, where the crowd of terrified and disconsolate captives—friends, neighbors, and relatives—were already gathered. Here they presently saw the fight in the meadow, and were told that if their countrymen attempted a rescue, they should all be put to death. "After this," writes Williams, "we went up the mountain, and saw the smoke of the fires in town, and beheld the awful desolation of Deerfield; and before we marched any farther they killed a sucking child of the English."

The French and Indians marched that afternoon only four or five miles,— to Greenfield meadows,—where they stopped to encamp, dug away the snow, laid spruce-boughs on the ground for beds, and bound fast such of the prisoners as seemed able to escape. The Indians then held a carousal on some liquor they had found in the village, and in their drunken rage murdered a negro man belonging to Williams. In spite of their precautions, Joseph Alexander, one of the prisoners, escaped during the night, at which they were greatly incensed; and Rouville ordered Williams to tell his companions in misfortune that if any more of them ran off, the rest should be burned alive.

The prisoners were the property of those who had taken them. Williams had two masters; one of the three who had seized him having been shot in the attack on the house of Stebbins. His principal owner was a surly fellow who would not let him speak to the other prisoners; but as he was presently chosen to guard the rear, the minister was left in the hands of his other master, who allowed him to walk beside his wife and help her on the way. Having borne a child a few weeks before, she was in no condition for such a march, and felt that her hour was near. Williams speaks of her in the strongest terms of affection. She made no complaint, and accepted her fate with resignation. "We discoursed," he says, "of the happiness of those who had God for a father and friend, as also that it was our reasonable duty quietly to submit to his will." Her thoughts were for her remaining children, whom she commended to her husband's care. Their intercourse was short. The Indian who had gone to the rear of the train soon returned, separated them, ordered Williams to the front, "and so made me take a last farewell of my dear wife, the desire of my eyes and companion in many mercies and afflictions." They came soon after to Green River, a stream then about knee-deep, and so swift that the water had not frozen. After wading it with difficulty, they climbed a snow-covered hill beyond. The minister, with strength almost spent, was permitted to rest a few moments at the top; and as the other prisoners passed by in turn, he questioned each for news of his wife. He was not left long in suspense. She had fallen from weakness in fording the stream, but gained her feet again, and, drenched in the icy current, struggled to the farther bank, when the savage who owned her, finding that she could not climb the hill, killed her with one stroke of his hatchet. Her body was left on the snow till a few of her townsmen, who had followed the trail, found it a day or two after, carried it back to Deerfield, and buried it in the churchyard.

On the next day the Indians killed an infant and a little girl of eleven years; on the day following, Friday, they tomahawked a woman, and on Saturday four others. This apparent cruelty was in fact a kind of mercy. The victims could not keep up with the party, and the death-blow saved them from a lonely and lingering death from cold and starvation. Some of the children, when spent with the march, were carried on the backs of their owners,—partly, perhaps, through kindness, and partly because every child had its price.

On the fourth day of the march they came to the mouth of West River, which enters the Connecticut a little above the present town of Brattleboro'. Some of the Indians were discontented with the distribution of the captives, alleging that others had got more than their share; on which the whole troop were mustered together, and some changes of ownership were agreed upon. At this place, dog-trains and sledges had been left, and these served to carry their wounded, as well as some of the captive children. Williams was stripped of the better part of his clothes, and others given him instead, so full of vermin that they were a torment to him through all the journey. The march now continued with pitiless speed up the frozen Connecticut, where the recent thaw had covered the ice with slush and water ankle-deep.

On Sunday they made a halt, and the minister was permitted to preach a sermon from the text, "Hear, all people, and behold my sorrow: my virgins and my young men are gone into captivity." Then amid the ice, the snow, the forest, and the savages, his forlorn flock joined their voices in a psalm. On Monday, guns were heard from the rear, and the Indians and their allies, in great alarm, bound their prisoners fast, and prepared for battle. It proved, however, that the guns had been fired at wild geese by some of their own number; on which they recovered their spirits, fired a volley for joy, and boasted that the English could not overtake them. More women fainted by the way and died under the hatchet,—some with pious resignation, some with despairing apathy, some with a desperate joy.

Two hundred miles of wilderness still lay between them and the Canadian settlements. It was a waste without a house or even a wigwam; except here and there the bark shed of some savage hunter. At the mouth of White River, the party divided into small bands,—no doubt in order to subsist by hunting, for provisions were fast failing. The Williams family were separated. Stephen was carried up the Connecticut; Samuel and Eunice, with two younger children, were carried off in various directions; while the wretched father, along with two small children of one of his parishioners, was compelled to follow his Indian masters up the valley of White River. One of the children—a little girl—was killed on the next morning by her Caughnawaga owner, who was unable to carry her. On the next Sunday, the minister was left in camp with one Indian and the surviving child,—a boy of nine,—while the rest of the party were hunting. "My spirit," he says, "was almost overwhelmed within me." But he found comfort in the text, "Leave thy fatherless children, I will preserve them alive." Nor was his hope deceived. His youngest surviving child,—a boy of four,—though harshly treated by his owners, was carried on their shoulders or dragged on a sledge to the end of the journey. His youngest daughter—seven years old—was treated with great kindness throughout. Samuel and Eunice suffered much from hunger, but were dragged on sledges when too faint to walk. Stephen nearly starved to death; but after eight months in the forest, he safely reached Chambly with his Indian masters.

Of the whole band of captives, only about half ever again saw friends and home. Seventeen broke down on the way and were killed; while David Hoyt and Jacob Hix died of starvation at Co-os meadows, on the upper Connecticut. During the entire march, no woman seems to have been subjected to violence; and this holds true, with rare exceptions, in all the Indian wars of New England. This remarkable forbearance towards female prisoners, so different from the practice of many Western tribes, was probably due to a form of superstition, aided perhaps by the influence of the missionaries. It is to be observed, however, that the heathen savages of King Philip's War, who had never seen a Jesuit, were no less forbearing in this respect.

The hunters of Williams's party killed five moose, the flesh of which, smoked and dried, was carried on their backs and that of the prisoner, whom they had provided with snow-shoes. Thus burdened, the minister toiled on, following his masters along the frozen current of White River till, crossing the snowy backs of the Green Mountains, they struck the headwaters of the stream then called French River, now the Winooski, or Onion. Being in great fear of a thaw, they pushed on with double speed. Williams was not used to snow-shoes, and they gave him those painful cramps of the legs and ankles called in Canada *mal à la raquette*. One morning at dawn, he was waked by his chief master and ordered to get up, say his prayers, and eat his breakfast, for they must make a long march that day. The minister was in despair. "After prayer," he says, "I arose from my knees; but my feet were so tender, swollen, bruised, and full of pain that I could scarce stand upon them without holding on the wigwam. And when the Indians said, 'You must run to-day,' I answered I could not run. My master, pointing to his hatchet, said to me, 'Then I must dash out your brains and take your scalp.' " The Indian proved better than his word, and Williams was suffered to struggle on as he could. "God wonderfully supported me," he writes, "and my strength was restored and renewed to admiration." He thinks that he walked that day forty miles on the snow. Following the Winooski to its mouth, the party reached Lake Champlain a little north of the present city of Burlington. Here the swollen feet of the prisoner were tortured by the rough ice, till snow began to fall and cover it with a soft carpet. Bending under his load, and powdered by the falling flakes, he toiled on till, at noon of a Saturday, lean, tired, and ragged, he and his masters reached the French outpost of Chambly, twelve or fifteen miles from Montreal.

Here the unhappy wayfarer was treated with great kindness both by the officers of the fort and by the inhabitants, one of the chief among whom lodged him in his house and welcomed him to his table. After a short stay at Chambly, Williams and his masters set out in a canoe for Sorel. On the way a Frenchwoman came down to the bank of the river and invited the party to her house, telling the minister that she herself had once been a prisoner among the Indians, and knew how to feel for him. She seated him at a table, spread a table-cloth, and placed food before him, while the Indians, to their great indignation, were supplied with a meal in the chimney-corner. Similar kindness was shown by the inhabitants along the way till the party reached their destination, the Abenaki village of St. Francis, to which his masters belonged. Here there was a fort, in which lived two Jesuits, directors of the mission, and here Williams found several English children, captured the summer before during the raid on the settlements of Maine, and already transformed into little Indians both in dress and behavior. . . .

In Montcalm and Wolfe, *Parkman described the final great struggle between France and England for domination in the New World. The "Old French War" or French and Indian War of 1756-1763 (called the Seven Years War in Europe) came to an end with the British defeat of the French on the Plains of Abraham before Quebec. The following selection concerns its origins in 1754 when a young Virginia officer, George Washington, attacked the French near the forks of the Ohio River in an "obscure skirmish that began the war that set the world on fire."*

Towards the end of spring the vanguard of the expedition sent by Duquesne to occupy the Ohio landed at Presquisle, where Erie now stands. This route to the Ohio, far better than that which Céloron had followed, was a new discovery to the French; and Duquesne calls the harbor "the finest in nature." Here they built a fort of squared chestnut logs, and when it was finished they cut a road of several leagues through the woods to Rivière aux Bœufs, now French Creek. At the farther end of this road they began another wooden fort and called it Fort Le Bœuf. Thence, when the water was high, they could descend French Creek to the Alleghany, and follow that stream to the main current of the Ohio.

It was heavy work to carry the cumbrous load of baggage across the portages. Much of it is said to have been superfluous, consisting of velvets, silks, and other useless and costly articles, sold to the King at enormous prices as necessaries of the expedition. The weight of the task fell on the Canadians, who worked with cheerful hardihood, and did their part to admiration. Marin, commander of the expedition, a gruff, choleric old man of sixty-three, but full of force and capacity, spared himself so little that he was struck down with dysentery, and, refusing to be sent home to Montreal, was before long in a dying state. His place was taken by Péan, of whose private character there is little good to be said, but whose conduct as an officer was such that Duquesne calls him a prodigy of talents, resources, and zeal. The subalterns deserve no such praise. They disliked the service, and made no secret of their discontent. Rumors of it filled Montreal; and Duquesne wrote to Marin: "I am surprised that you have not told me of this change. Take note of the sullen and discouraged faces about you. This sort are worse than useless. Rid yourself of them at once; send them to Montreal, that I may make an example of them." Péan wrote at the end of September that Marin was in extremity; and the Governor, disturbed and alarmed, for he knew the value of the sturdy old officer, looked anxiously for a successor. He chose another veteran, Legardeur de Saint-Pierre, who had just returned from a journey of exploration towards the Rocky Mountains, and whom Duquesne now ordered to the Ohio.

Meanwhile the effects of the expedition had already justified it. At first the Indians of the Ohio had shown a bold front. One of them, a chief

whom the English called the Half-King, came to Fort Le Bœuf and ordered
the French to leave the country; but was received by Marin with such
contemptuous haughtiness that he went home shedding tears of rage and
mortification. The Western tribes were daunted. The Miamis, but yesterday
fast friends of the English, made humble submission to the French, and
offered them two English scalps to signalize their repentance; while the
Sacs, Pottawattamies, and Ojibwas were loud in professions of devotion.
Even the Iroquois, Delawares, and Shawanoes on the Alleghany had come
to the French camp and offered their help in carrying the baggage. It
needed but perseverance and success in the enterprise to win over every
tribe from the mountains to the Mississippi. To accomplish this and to
curb the English, Duquesne had planned a third fort, at the junction of
French Creek with the Alleghany, or at some point lower down; then,
leaving the three posts well garrisoned, Péan was to descend the Ohio with
the whole remaining force, impose terror on the wavering tribes, and complete their conversion. Both plans were thwarted; the fort was not built,
nor did Péan descend the Ohio. Fevers, lung diseases, and scurvy made
such deadly havoc among troops and Canadians, that the dying Marin saw
with bitterness that his work must be left half done. Three hundred of the
best men were kept to garrison Forts Presquisle and Le Bœuf; and then,
as winter approached, the rest were sent back to Montreal. When they arrived, the Governor was shocked at their altered looks. "I reviewed them,
and could not help being touched by the pitiable state to which fatigues and
exposures had reduced them. Past all doubt, if these emaciated figures had
gone down the Ohio as intended, the river would have been strewn with
corpses, and the evil-disposed savages would not have failed to attack the
survivors, seeing that they were but spectres."

Legardeur de Saint-Pierre arrived at the end of autumn, and made his
quarters at Fort Le Bœuf. The surrounding forests had dropped their
leaves, and in gray and patient desolation bided the coming winter. Chill
rains drizzled over the gloomy "clearing," and drenched the palisades and
log-built barracks, raw from the axe. Buried in the wilderness, the military
exiles resigned themselves as they might to months of monotonous solitude;
when, just after sunset on the eleventh of December, a tall youth came
out of the forest on horseback, attended by a companion much older and
rougher than himself, and followed by several Indians and four or five
white men with packhorses. Officers from the fort went out to meet the
strangers; and, wading through mud and sodden snow, they entered at the
gate. On the next day the young leader of the party, with the help of an
interpreter, for he spoke no French, had an interview with the commandant, and gave him a letter from Governor Dinwiddie. Saint-Pierre and
the officer next in rank, who knew a little English, took it to another room
to study it at their ease; and in it, all unconsciously, they read a name
destined to stand one of the noblest in the annals of mankind; for it intro-

duced Major George Washington, Adjutant-General of the Virginia militia.

Dinwiddie, jealously watchful of French aggression, had learned through traders and Indians that a strong detachment from Canada had entered the territories of the King of England, and built forts on Lake Erie and on a branch of the Ohio. He wrote to challenge the invasion and summon the invaders to withdraw; and he could find none so fit to bear his message as a young man of twenty-one. It was this rough Scotchman who launched Washington on his illustrious career.

Washington set out for the trading station of the Ohio Company on Will's Creek; and thence, at the middle of November, struck into the wilderness with Christopher Gist as a guide, Vanbraam, a Dutchman, as French interpreter, Davison, a trader, as Indian interpreter, and four woodsmen as servants. They went to the forks of the Ohio, and then down the river to Logstown, the Chiningué of Céloron de Bienville. There Washington had various parleys with the Indians; and thence, after vexatious delays, he continued his journey towards Fort Le Bœuf, accompanied by the friendly chief called the Half-King and by three of his tribesmen. For several days they followed the traders' path, pelted with unceasing rain and snow, and came at last to the old Indian town of Venango, where French Creek enters the Alleghany. Here there was an English trading-house; but the French had seized it, raised their flag over it, and turned it into a military outpost. Joncaire was in command, with two subalterns; and nothing could exceed their civility. They invited the strangers to supper; and, says Washington, "the wine, as they dosed themselves pretty plentifully with it, soon banished the restraint which at first appeared in their conversation, and gave a license to their tongues to reveal their sentiments more freely. They told me that it was their absolute design to take possession of the Ohio, and, by G—, they would do it; for that although they were sensible the English could raise two men for their one, yet they knew their motions were too slow and dilatory to prevent any undertaking of theirs."

With all their civility, the French officers did their best to entice away Washington's Indians; and it was with extreme difficulty that he could persuade them to go with him. Through marshes and swamps, forests choked with snow, and drenched with incessant rain, they toiled on for four days more, till the wooden walls of Fort Le Bœuf appeared at last, surrounded by fields studded thick with stumps, and half-encircled by the chill current of French Creek, along the banks of which lay more than two hundred canoes, ready to carry troops in the spring. Washington describes Legardeur de Saint-Pierre as "an elderly gentleman with much the air of a soldier." The letter sent him by Dinwiddie expressed astonishment that his troops should build forts upon lands "so notoriously known to be the property of the Crown of Great Britain." "I must desire you," continued the letter, "to acquaint me by whose authority and instructions you have lately marched from Canada with an armed force, and invaded the

King of Great Britain's territories. It becomes my duty to require your peaceable departure; and that you would forbear prosecuting a purpose so interruptive of the harmony and good understanding which His Majesty is desirous to continue and cultivate with the Most Christian King. I persuade myself you will receive and entertain Major Washington with the candor and politeness natural to your nation; and it will give me the greatest satisfaction if you return him with an answer suitable to my wishes for a very long and lasting peace between us."

Saint-Pierre took three days to frame the answer. In it he said that he should send Dinwiddie's letter to the Marquis Duquesne and wait his orders; and that meanwhile he should remain at his post, according to the commands of his general. "I made it my particular care," so the letter closed, "to receive Mr. Washington with a distinction suitable to your dignity as well as his own quality and great merit." No form of courtesy had, in fact, been wanting. "He appeared to be extremely complaisant," says Washington, "though he was exerting every artifice to set our Indians at variance with us. I saw that every stratagem was practised to win the Half-King to their interest." Neither gifts nor brandy were spared; and it was only by the utmost pains that Washington could prevent his red allies from staying at the fort, conquered by French blandishments.

After leaving Venango on his return, he found the horses so weak that, to arrive the sooner, he left them and their drivers in charge of Vanbraam and pushed forward on foot, accompanied by Gist alone. Each was wrapped to the throat in an Indian "matchcoat," with a gun in his hand and a pack at his back. Passing an old Indian hamlet called Murdering Town, they had an adventure which threatened to make good the name. A French Indian, whom they met in the forest, fired at them, pretending that his gun had gone off by chance. They caught him, and Gist would have killed him; but Washington interposed, and they let him go. Then, to escape pursuit from his tribesmen, they walked all night and all the next day. This brought them to the banks of the Alleghany. They hoped to have found it dead frozen; but it was all alive and turbulent, filled with ice sweeping down the current. They made a raft, shoved out into the stream, and were soon caught helplessly in the drifting ice. Washington, pushing hard with his setting-pole, was jerked into the freezing river; but caught a log of the raft, and dragged himself out. By no efforts could they reach the farther bank, or regain that which they had left; but they were driven against an island, where they landed, and left the raft to its fate. The night was excessively cold, and Gist's feet and hands were badly frost-bitten. In the morning, the ice had set, and the river was a solid floor. They crossed it, and succeeded in reaching the house of the trader Fraser, on the Monongahela. It was the middle of January when Washington arrived at Williamsburg and made his report to Dinwiddie.

Robert Dinwiddie was lieutenant-governor of Virginia, in place of the titular governor, Lord Albemarle, whose post was a sinecure. He had been clerk in a government office in the West Indies; then surveyor of customs in the "Old Dominion,"—a position in which he made himself cordially disliked; and when he rose to the governorship he carried his unpopularity with him. Yet Virginia and all the British colonies owed him much; for, though past sixty, he was the most watchful sentinel against French aggression and its most strenuous opponent. Scarcely had Marin's vanguard appeared at Presquisle, when Dinwiddie warned the Home Government of the danger, and urged, what he had before urged in vain on the Virginian Assembly, the immediate building of forts on the Ohio. There came in reply a letter, signed by the King, authorizing him to build the forts at the cost of the Colony, and to repel force by force in case he was molested or obstructed. Moreover, the King wrote, "If you shall find that any number of persons shall presume to erect any fort or forts within the limits of our province of Virginia, you are first to require of them peaceably to depart; and if, notwithstanding your admonitions, they do still endeavor to carry out any such unlawful and unjustifiable designs, we do hereby strictly charge and command you to drive them off by force of arms."

The order was easily given; but to obey it needed men and money, and for these Dinwiddie was dependent on his Assembly, or House of Burgesses. He convoked them for the first of November, sending Washington at the same time with the summons to Saint-Pierre. The burgesses met. Dinwiddie exposed the danger, and asked for means to meet it. They seemed more than willing to comply; but debates presently arose concerning the fee of a pistole, which the Governor had demanded on each patent of land issued by him. The amount was trifling, but the principle was doubtful. The aristocratic republic of Virginia was intensely jealous of the slightest encroachment on its rights by the Crown or its representative. The Governor defended the fee. The burgesses replied that "subjects cannot be deprived of the least part of their property without their consent," declared the fee unlawful, and called on Dinwiddie to confess it to be so. He still defended it. They saw in his demand for supplies a means of bringing him to terms, and refused to grant money unless he would recede from his position. Dinwiddie rebuked them for "disregarding the designs of the French, and disputing the rights of the Crown;" and he "prorogued them in some anger."

Thus he was unable to obey the instructions of the King. As a temporary resource, he ventured to order a draft of two hundred men from the militia. Washington was to have command, with the trader, William Trent, as his lieutenant. His orders were to push with all speed to the forks of the Ohio, and there build a fort; "but in case any attempts are made to obstruct the works by any persons whatsoever, to restrain all such offenders, and, in case of resistance, to make prisoners of, or kill and destroy them." The Governor next sent messengers to the Catawbas, Cherokees, Chickasaws, and Iroquois of the Ohio, inviting them to take up the hatchet against the

French, "who, under pretence of embracing you, mean to squeeze you to death." Then he wrote urgent letters to the governors of Pennsylvania, the Carolinas, Maryland, and New Jersey, begging for contingents of men, to be at Wills Creek in March at the latest. But nothing could be done without money; and trusting for a change of heart on the part of the burgesses, he summoned them to meet again on the fourteenth of February. "If they come in good temper," he wrote to Lord Fairfax, a nobleman settled in the colony, "I hope they will lay a fund to qualify me to send four or five hundred men more to the Ohio, which, with the assistance of our neighboring colonies, may make some figure."

The session began. Again, somewhat oddly, yet forcibly, the Governor set before the Assembly the peril of the situation, and begged them to postpone less pressing questions to the exigency of the hour. This time they listened; and voted ten thousand pounds in Virginia currency to defend the frontier. The grant was frugal, and they jealously placed its expenditure in the hands of a committee of their own. Dinwiddie, writing to the Lords of Trade, pleads necessity as his excuse for submitting to their terms. "I am sorry," he says, "to find them too much in a republican way of thinking." What vexed him still more was their sending an agent to England to complain against him on the irrepressible question of the pistole fee; and he writes to his London friend, the merchant Hanbury: "I have had a great deal of trouble from the factious disputes and violent heats of a most impudent, troublesome party here in regard to that silly fee of a pistole. Surely every thinking man will make a distinction between a fee and a tax. Poor people! I pity their ignorance and narrow, ill-natured spirits. But, my friend, consider that I could by no means give up this fee without affronting the Board of Trade and the Council here who established it." His thoughts were not all of this harassing nature, and he ends his letter with the following petition: "Now, sir, as His Majesty is pleased to make me a military officer, please send for Scott, my tailor, to make me a proper suit of regimentals, to be here by His Majesty's birthday. I do not much like gayety in dress, but I conceive this necessary. I do not much care for lace on the coat, but a neat embroidered button-hole; though you do not deal that way, I know you have a good taste, that I may show my friend's fancy in that suit of clothes; a good laced hat and two pair stockings, one silk, the other fine thread."

If the Governor and his English sometimes provoke a smile, he deserves admiration for the energy with which he opposed the public enemy, under circumstances the most discouraging. He invited the Indians to meet him in council at Winchester, and, as bait to attract them, coupled the message with a promise of gifts. He sent circulars from the King to the neighboring governors, calling for supplies, and wrote letter upon letter to rouse them to effort. He wrote also to the more distant governors, Delancey of New York, and Shirley of Massachusetts, begging them to make what he called a "faint" against Canada, to prevent the French from sending so large a force to the Ohio. It was to the nearer colonies, from New Jersey to South Carolina, that he looked for direct aid; and their several governors were all more or less active to procure it; but as most of them had some standing dispute with their assemblies, they could get nothing except on terms with which they would not, and sometimes could not, comply. As the lands invaded by the French belonged to one of the two rival claimants, Virginia and Pennsylvania, the other colonies had no mind to vote money to defend them. Pennsylvania herself refused to move. Hamilton, her governor, could do nothing against the placid obstinacy of the Quaker non-combatants and the stolid obstinacy of the German farmers who chiefly made up his Assembly. North Carolina alone answered the appeal, and gave money enough to raise three or four hundred men. Two independent companies maintained by the King in New York, and one in South Carolina, had received orders from England to march to the scene of action; and in these, with the scanty levies of his own and the adjacent province, lay Dinwiddie's only hope. With men abundant and willing, there were no means to put them into the field, and no commander whom they would all obey.

From the brick house at Williamsburg pompously called the Governor's Palace, Dinwiddie despatched letters, orders, couriers, to hasten the tardy reinforcements of North Carolina and New York, and push on the raw soldiers of the Old Dominion, who now numbered three hundred men. They were called the Virginia regiment; and Joshua Fry, an English gentleman, bred at Oxford, was made their colonel, with Washington as next in command. Fry was at Alexandria with half the so-called regiment, trying to get it into marching order; Washington, with the other half, had pushed forward to the Ohio Company's storehouse at Wills Creek, which was to form a base of operations. His men were poor whites, brave, but hard to discipline; without tents, ill armed, and ragged as Falstaff's recruits. Besides these, a band of backwoodsmen under Captain Trent had crossed the mountains in February to build a fort at the forks of the Ohio, where Pittsburg now stands,—a spot which Washington had examined when on his way to Fort Le Bœuf, and which he had reported as the best for the purpose. The hope was that Trent would fortify himself before the arrival of the French, and that Washington and Fry would join him in time to secure the position. Trent had begun the fort; but for some unexplained reason had gone back to Wills Creek, leaving Ensign Ward with forty men at work upon it. Their labors were suddenly interrupted. On the seventeenth of April a swarm of bateaux and canoes came down the Alleghany, bringing, according to Ward, more than a thousand Frenchmen, though in reality not much above five hundred, who landed, planted cannon against the incipient stockade, and summoned the ensign to surrender, on pain of what might ensue. He complied, and was allowed to depart with his men. Retracing his steps over the mountains, he reported his mishap to Washington; while the French demolished his unfinished fort, began a much larger and better one, and named it Fort Duquesne.

They had acted with their usual promptness. Their Governor, a practised soldier, knew the value of celerity, and had set his troops in motion with the first opening of spring. He had no refractory assembly to hamper him; no lack of money, for the King supplied it; and all Canada must march at his bidding. Thus, while Dinwiddie was still toiling to muster his raw recruits, Duquesne's lieutenant, Contrecœur, successor of Saint-Pierre, had landed at Presquisle with a much greater force, in part regulars, and in part Canadians.

Dinwiddie was deeply vexed when a message from Washington told him how his plans were blighted; and he spoke his mind to his friend Hanbury: "If our Assembly had voted the money in November which they did in February, it's more than probable the fort would have been built and garrisoned before the French had approached; but these things cannot be done without money. As there was none in our treasury, I have advanced my own to forward the expedition; and if the independent companies from New York come soon, I am in hopes the eyes of the other colonies will be opened; and if they grant a proper supply of men, I hope we shall be able to dislodge the French or build a fort on that river. I congratulate you on the increase of your family. My wife and two girls join in our most sincere respects to good Mrs. Hanbury."

The seizure of a king's fort by planting cannon against it and threatening it with destruction was in his eyes a beginning of hostilities on the part of the French; and henceforth both he and Washington acted much as if war had been declared. From their station at Wills Creek, the distance by the traders' path to Fort Duquesne was about a hundred and forty miles. Midway was a branch of the Monongahela called Redstone Creek, at the mouth of which the Ohio Company had built another storehouse. Dinwiddie ordered all the forces to cross the mountains and assemble at this point, until they should be strong enough to advance against the French. The movement was critical in presence of an enemy as superior in discipline as he was in numbers, while the natural obstacles were great. A road for cannon and wagons must be cut through a dense forest and over two ranges of high mountains, besides countless hills and streams. Washington set all his force to the work, and they spent a fortnight in making twenty miles. Towards the end of May, however, Dinwiddie learned that he had crossed the main ridge of the Alleghanies, and was encamped with a hundred and fifty men near the parallel ridge of Laurel Hill, at a place called the Great Meadows. Trent's backwoodsmen had gone off in disgust; Fry, with the rest of the regiment, was still far behind; and Washington was daily expecting an attack. Close upon this, a piece of good news, or what seemed such, came over the mountains and gladdened the heart of the Governor.

He heard that a French detachment had tried to surprise Washington, and that he had killed or captured the whole. The facts were as follows.

Washington was on the Youghiogany, a branch of the Monongahela, exploring it in hopes that it might prove navigable, when a messenger came to him from his old comrade, the Half-King, who was on the way to join him. The message was to the effect that the French had marched from their fort, and meant to attack the first English they should meet. A report came soon after that they were already at the ford of the Youghiogany, eighteen miles distant. Washington at once repaired to the Great Meadows, a level tract of grass and bushes, bordered by wooded hills, and traversed in one part by a gully, which with a little labor the men turned into an entrenchment, at the same time cutting away the bushes and clearing what the young commander called "a charming field for an encounter." Parties were sent out to scour the woods, but they found no enemy. Two days passed; when, on the morning of the twenty-seventh, Christopher Gist, who had lately made a settlement on the farther side of Laurel Hill, twelve or thirteen miles distant, came to the camp with news that fifty French-men had been at his house towards noon of the day before, and would have destroyed everything but for the intervention of two Indians whom he had left in charge during his absence. Washington sent seventy-five men to look for the party; but the search was vain, the French having hidden themselves so well as to escape any eye but that of an Indian. In the eve-ning a runner came from the Half-King, who was encamped with a few warriors some miles distant. He had sent to tell Washington that he had found the tracks of two men, and traced them towards a dark glen in the forest, where in his belief all the French were lurking.

Washington seems not to have hesitated a moment. Fearing a stratagem to surprise his camp, he left his main force to guard it, and at ten o'clock set out for the Half-King's wigwams at the head of forty men. The night was rainy, and the forest, to use his own words, "as black as pitch." "The path," he continues, "was hardly wide enough for one man; we often lost it, and could not find it again for fifteen or twenty minutes, and we often tumbled over each other in the dark." Seven of his men were lost in the woods and left behind. The rest groped their way all night, and reached the Indian camp at sunrise. A council was held with the Half-King, and he and his warriors agreed to join in striking the French. Two of them led the way. The tracks of the two French scouts seen the day before were again found, and, marching in single file, the party pushed through the forest into the rocky hollow where the French were supposed to be con-cealed. They were there in fact; and they snatched their guns the moment they saw the English. Washington gave the word to fire. A short fight ensued. Coulon de Jumonville, an ensign in command, was killed, with nine others; twenty-two were captured, and none escaped but a Canadian who had fled at the beginning of the fray. After it was over, the prisoners told Washington that the party had been sent to bring him a summons from Contrecœur, the commandant at Fort Duquesne.

Five days before, Contrecœur had sent Jumonville to scour the country as far as the dividing ridge of the Alleghanies. Under him were another officer, three cadets, a volunteer, an interpreter, and twenty-eight men. He was provided with a written summons, to be delivered to any English he might find. It required them to withdraw from the domain of the King of France, and threatened compulsion by force of arms in case of refusal. But before delivering the summons Jumonville was ordered to send two couriers back with all speed to Fort Duquesne to inform the commandant that he had found the English, and to acquaint him when he intended to communicate with them. It is difficult to imagine any object for such an order except that of enabling Contrecœur to send to the spot whatever force might be needed to attack the English on their refusal to withdraw. Jumonville had sent the two couriers, and had hidden himself, apparently to wait the result. He lurked nearly two days within five miles of Washington's camp, sent out scouts to reconnoitre it, but gave no notice of his presence; played to perfection the part of a skulking enemy, and brought destruction on himself by conduct which can only be ascribed to a sinister motive on the one hand, or to extreme folly on the other. French deserters told Washington that the party came as spies, and were to show the summons only if threatened by a superior force. This last assertion is confirmed by the French officer Pouchot, who says that Jumonville, seeing himself the weaker party, tried to show the letter he had brought.

French writers say that, on first seeing the English, Jumonville's interpreter called out that he had something to say to them; but Washington, who was at the head of his men, affirms this to be absolutely false. The French say further that Jumonville was killed in the act of reading the summons. This is also denied by Washington, and rests only on the assertion of the Canadian who ran off at the outset, and on the alleged assertion of Indians who, if present at all, which is unlikely, escaped like the Canadian before the fray began. Druillon, an officer with Jumonville, wrote two letters to Dinwiddie after his capture, to claim the privileges of the bearer of a summons; but while bringing forward every other circumstance in favor of the claim, he does not pretend that the summons was read or shown either before or during the action. The French account of the conduct of Washington's Indians is no less erroneous. "This murder," says a chronicler of the time, "produced on the minds of the savages an effect very different from that which the cruel Washington had promised himself. They have a horror of crime; and they were so indignant at that which had just been perpetrated before their eyes, that they abandoned him, and offered themselves to us in order to take vengeance." Instead of doing this, they boasted of their part in the fight, scalped all the dead Frenchmen, sent one scalp to the Delawares as an invitation to take up

the hatchet for the English, and distributed the rest among the various
Ohio tribes to the same end.

Coolness of judgment, a profound sense of public duty, and a strong
self-control, were even then the characteristics of Washington; but he was
scarcely twenty-two, was full of military ardor, and was vehement and
fiery by nature. Yet it is far from certain that, even when age and experience had ripened him, he would have forborne to act as he did, for there
was every reason for believing that the designs of the French were hostile;
and though by passively waiting the event he would have thrown upon
them the responsibility of striking the first blow, he would have exposed
his small party to capture or destruction by giving them time to gain reinforcements from Fort Duquesne. It was inevitable that the killing of
Jumonville should be greeted in France by an outcry of real or assumed
horror; but the Chevalier de Lévis, second in command to Montcalm, probably expresses the true opinion of Frenchmen best fitted to judge when he
calls it "a pretended assassination." Judge it as we may, this obscure
skirmish began the war that set the world on fire.

Washington returned to the camp at the Great Meadows; and, expecting
soon to be attacked, sent for reinforcements to Colonel Fry, who was lying
dangerously ill at Wills Creek. Then he set his men to work at an entrenchment, which he named Fort Necessity, and which must have been of the
slightest, as they finished it within three days. The Half-King now joined
him, along with the female potentate known as Queen Alequippa, and some
thirty Indian families. A few days after, Gist came from Wills Creek with
news that Fry was dead. Washington succeeded to the command of the
regiment, the remaining three companies of which presently appeared and
joined their comrades, raising the whole number to three hundred. Next
arrived the independent company from South Carolina; and the Great
Meadows became an animated scene, with the wigwams of the Indians, the
camp-sheds of the rough Virginians, the cattle grazing on the tall grass or
drinking at the lazy brook that traversed it; the surrounding heights and
forests; and over all, four miles away, the lofty green ridge of Laurel Hill.

The presence of the company of regulars was a doubtful advantage.
Captain Mackay, its commander, holding his commission from the King,
thought himself above any officer commissioned by the Governor. There
was great courtesy between him and Washington; but Mackay would take
no orders, nor even the countersign, from the colonel of volunteers. Nor
would his men work, except for an additional shilling a day. To give this
was impossible, both from want of money, and from the discontent it would
have bred in the Virginians, who worked for nothing besides their daily
pay of eightpence. Washington, already a leader of men, possessed himself
in a patience extremely difficult to his passionate temper; but the position
was untenable, and the presence of the military drones demoralized his
soldiers. Therefore, leaving Mackay at the Meadows, he advanced towards
Gist's settlement, cutting a wagon road as he went.

On reaching the settlement the camp was formed and an entrenchment thrown up. Deserters had brought news that strong reinforcements were expected at Fort Duquesne, and friendly Indians repeatedly warned Washington that he would soon be attacked by overwhelming numbers. Forty Indians from the Ohio came to the camp, and several days were spent in councils with them; but they proved for the most part to be spies of the French. The Half-King stood fast by the English, and sent out three of his young warriors as scouts. Reports of attack thickened. Mackay and his men were sent for, and they arrived on the twenty-eighth of June. A council of war was held at Gist's house; and as the camp was commanded by neighboring heights, it was resolved to fall back. The horses were so few that the Virginians had to carry much of the baggage on their backs, and drag nine swivels over the broken and rocky road. The regulars, though they also were raised in the provinces, refused to give the slightest help. Toiling on for two days, they reached the Great Meadows on the first of July. The position, though perhaps the best in the neighborhood, was very unfavorable, and Washington would have retreated farther, but for the condition of his men. They were spent with fatigue, and there was no choice but to stay and fight.

Strong reinforcements had been sent to Fort Duquesne in the spring, and the garrison now consisted of about fourteen hundred men. When news of the death of Jumonville reached Montreal, Coulon de Villiers, brother of the slain officer, was sent to the spot with a body of Indians from all the tribes in the colony. He made such speed that at eight o'clock on the morning of the twenty-sixth of June he reached the fort with his motley following. Here he found that five hundred Frenchmen and a few Ohio Indians were on the point of marching against the English, under Chevalier Le Mercier; but in view of his seniority in rank and his relationship to Jumonville, the command was now transferred to Villiers. Hereupon, the march was postponed; the newly-arrived warriors were called to council, and Contrecœur thus harangued them: "The English have murdered my children; my heart is sick; to-morrow I shall send my French soldiers to take revenge. And now, men of the Saut St. Louis, men of the Lake of Two Mountains, Hurons, Abenakis, Iroquois of La Présentation, Nipissings, Algonquins, and Ottawas,—I invite you all by this belt of wampum to join your French father and help him to crush the assassins. Take this hatchet, and with it two barrels of wine for a feast." Both hatchet and wine were cheerfully accepted. Then Contrecœur turned to the Delawares, who were also present: "By these four strings of wampum I invite you, if you are true children of Onontio, to follow the example of your brethren;" and with some hesitation they also took up the hatchet.

The next day was spent by the Indians in making moccasins for the march, and by the French in preparing for an expedition on a larger scale than had been at first intended. Contrecœur, Villiers, Le Mercier, and Longueuil, after deliberating together, drew up a paper to the effect that "it was fitting (*convenable*) to march against the English with the greatest possible number of French and savages, in order to avenge ourselves and chastise them for having violated the most sacred laws of civilized nations;" that, though their conduct justified the French in disregarding the existing treaty of peace, yet, after thoroughly punishing them, and compelling them to withdraw from the domain of the King, they should be told that, in pursuance of his royal orders, the French looked on them as friends. But it was further agreed that should the English have withdrawn to their own side of the mountains, "they should be followed to their settlements to destroy them and treat them as enemies, till that nation should give ample satisfaction and completely change its conduct."

The party set out on the next morning, paddled their canoes up the Monongahela, encamped, heard Mass; and on the thirtieth reached the deserted storehouse of the Ohio Company at the mouth of Redstone Creek. It was a building of solid logs, well loopholed for musketry. To please the Indians by asking their advice, Villiers called all the chiefs to council; which, being concluded to their satisfaction, he left a sergeant's guard at the storehouse to watch the canoes, and began his march through the forest. The path was so rough that at the first halt the chaplain declared he could go no farther, and turned back for the storehouse, though not till he had absolved the whole company in a body. Thus lightened of their sins, they journeyed on, constantly sending out scouts. On the second of July they reached the abandoned camp of Washington at Gist's settlement; and here they bivouacked, tired, and drenched all night by rain. At daybreak they marched again, and passed through the gorge of Laurel Hill. It rained without ceasing; but Villiers pushed his way through the dripping forest to see the place, half a mile from the road, where his brother had been killed, and where several bodies still lay unburied. They had learned from a deserter the position of the enemy, and Villiers filled the woods in front with a swarm of Indian scouts. The crisis was near. He formed his men in column, and ordered every officer to his place.

Washington's men had had a full day at Fort Necessity; but they spent it less in resting from their fatigue than in strengthening their rampart with logs. The fort was a simple square enclosure, with a trench said by a French writer to be only knee deep. On the south, and partly on the west, there was an exterior embankment, which seems to have been made, like a rifle-pit, with the ditch inside. The Virginians had but little ammunition, and no bread whatever, living chiefly on fresh beef. They knew the approach of the French, who were reported to Washington as nine hundred strong, besides Indians. Towards eleven o'clock a wounded sentinel came in with news that they were close at hand; and they presently appeared at the edge of the woods, yelling, and firing from such a distance that their shot fell harmless. Washington drew up his men on the meadow before the fort, thinking, he says, that the enemy, being greatly superior in force, would attack at once; and choosing for some reason to meet them on the open plain. But Villiers had other views. "We approached the English," he writes, "as near as possible, without uselessly exposing the lives of the King's subjects;" and he and his followers made their way through the forest till they came opposite the fort, where they stationed themselves on two densely wooded hills, adjacent, though separated by a small brook. One of these was about a hundred paces from the English, and the other about sixty. Their position was such that the French and Indians, well sheltered by trees and bushes, and with the advantage of higher ground, could cross their fire upon the fort and enfilade a part of it. Washington had meanwhile drawn his followers within the entrenchment; and the firing now began on both sides. Rain fell all day. The raw earth of the embankment was turned to soft mud, and the men in the ditch of the outwork stood to the knee in water. The swivels brought back from the camp at Gist's farm were mounted on the rampart; but the gunners were so ill protected that the pieces were almost silenced by the French musketry. The fight lasted nine hours. At times the fire on both sides was nearly quenched by the showers, and the bedrenched combatants could do little but gaze at each other through a gray veil of mist and rain. Towards night, however, the fusillade revived, and became sharp again until dark. At eight o'clock the French called out to propose a parley.

Villiers thus gives his reasons for these overtures. "As we had been wet all day by the rain, as the soldiers were very tired, as the savages said that they would leave us the next morning, and as there was a report that drums and the firing of cannon had been heard in the distance, I proposed to M. Le Mercier to offer the English a conference." He says further that ammunition was falling short, and that he thought the enemy might sally in a body and attack him. The English, on their side, were in a worse plight. They were half starved, their powder was nearly spent, their guns were foul, and among them all they had but two screw-rods to clean them. In spite of his desperate position, Washington declined the parley, thinking it a pretext to introduce a spy; but when the French repeated their proposal and requested that he would send an officer to them, he could hesitate no longer. There were but two men with him who knew French, Ensign Peyroney, who was disabled by a wound, and the Dutchman, Captain Vanbraam. To him the unpalatable errand was assigned. After a long absence he returned with articles of capitulation offered by Villiers; and while the officers gathered about him in the rain, he read and interpreted the paper by the glimmer of a sputtering candle kept alight with difficulty. Objection was made to some of the terms, and they were changed. Vanbraam, however, apparently anxious to get the capitulation signed and the affair ended, mistranslated several passages, and rendered the words *l'assassinat du Sieur de Jumonville* as *the death of the Sieur de Jumonville*. As thus understood, the articles were signed about midnight. They provided that the English should march out with drums beating and the honors of war, carrying with them one of their swivels and all their other property; that they should be protected against insult from French or Indians; that the prisoners taken in the affair of Jumonville should be set free; and that two officers should remain as hostages for their safe return to Fort Duquesne. The hostages chosen were Vanbraam and a brave but eccentric Scotchman, Robert Stobo, an acquaintance of the novelist Smollett, said to be the original of his Lismahago.

Washington reports that twelve of the Virginians were killed on the spot, and forty-three wounded, while of the casualties in Mackay's company no returns appear. Villiers reports his own loss at only twenty in all. The numbers engaged are uncertain. The six companies of the Virginia regiment counted three hundred and five men and officers, and Mackay's company one hundred; but many were on the sick list, and some had deserted. About three hundred and fifty may have taken part in the fight. On the side of the French, Villiers says that the detachment as originally formed consisted of five hundred white men. These were increased after his arrival at Fort Duquesne, and one of the party reports that seven hundred marched on the expedition. The number of Indians joining them is not given; but as nine tribes and communities contributed to it, and as two barrels of wine were required to give the warriors a parting feast, it must have been considerable. White men and red, it seems clear that the French force was more than twice that of the English, while they were better posted and better sheltered, keeping all day under cover, and never showing themselves on the open meadow. There were no Indians with Washington. Even the Half-King held aloof; though, being of caustic turn, he did not spare his comments on the fight, telling Conrad Weiser, the provincial interpreter, that the French behaved like cowards, and the English like fools.

In the early morning the fort was abandoned and the retreat began. The Indians had killed all the horses and cattle, and Washington's men were so burdened with the sick and wounded, whom they were obliged to carry on their backs, that most of the baggage was perforce left behind. Even then they could march but a few miles, and then encamped to wait for wagons. The Indians increased the confusion by plundering, and threatening an attack. They knocked to pieces the medicine-chest, thus causing great distress to the wounded, two of whom they murdered and scalped. For a time there was danger of panic; but order was restored, and the wretched march began along the forest road that led over the Alleghanies, fifty-two miles to the station at Wills Creek. Whatever may have been the feelings of Washington, he has left no record of them. His immense fortitude was doomed to severer trials in the future; yet perhaps this miserable morning was the darkest of his life. He was deeply moved by sights of suffering; and all around him were wounded men borne along in torture, and weary men staggering under the living load. His pride was humbled, and his young ambition seemed blasted in the bud. It was the fourth of July. He could not foresee that he was to make that day forever glorious to a new-born nation hailing him as its father.

The defeat at Fort Necessity was doubly disastrous to the English, since it was a new step and a long one towards the ruin of their interest with the Indians; and when, in the next year, the smouldering war broke into flame, nearly all the western tribes drew their scalping-knives for France.

Villiers went back exultant to Fort Duquesne, burning on his way the buildings of Gist's settlement and the storehouse at Redstone Creek. Not an English flag now waved beyond the Alleghanies.

In the winter of 1754-1755, the British sent troops to America under General Edward Braddock. In the spring, Braddock with British and colonial forces made his way westward to try to dislodge the reinforced French from Fort Duquesne. Present-day historians would disagree with a few of the reasons Parkman gives for Braddock's failure. The French and Indians attacked in fairly open woodland rather than thick underbrush as Parkman says, and the officers seem to have been more to blame for the debacle than were the enlisted men.

"I have the pleasure to acquaint you that General Braddock came to my house last Sunday night," writes Dinwiddie, at the end of February, to Governor Dobbs of North Carolina. Braddock had landed at Hampton from the ship "Centurion," along with young Commodore Keppel, who commanded the American squadron. "I am mighty glad," again writes Dinwiddie, "that the General is arrived, which I hope will give me some ease; for these twelve months past I have been a perfect slave." He conceived golden opinions of his guest. "He is, I think, a very fine officer, and a sensible, considerate gentleman. He and I live in great harmony."

Had he known him better, he might have praised him less. William Shirley, son of the Governor of Massachusetts, was Braddock's secretary; and after an acquaintance of some months wrote to his friend Governor Morris: "We have a general most judiciously chosen for being disqualified for the service he is employed in in almost every respect. He may be brave for aught I know, and he is honest in pecuniary matters." The astute Franklin, who also had good opportunity of knowing him, says: "This general was, I think, a brave man, and might probably have made a good figure in some European war. But he had too much self-confidence; too high an opinion of the validity of regular troops; too mean a one of both Americans and Indians." Horace Walpole, in his function of gathering and immortalizing the gossip of his time, has left a sharply drawn sketch of Braddock in two letters to Sir Horace Mann, written in the summer of this year: "I love to give you an idea of our characters as they rise upon the stage of history. Braddock is a very Iroquois in disposition. He had a sister who, having gamed away all her little fortune at Bath, hanged herself with a truly English deliberation, leaving only a note upon the table with those lines: 'To die is landing on some silent shore,' etc. When Braddock was told of it, he only said: 'Poor Fanny! I always thought she would play till she would be forced to *tuck herself up.*' " Under the name of Miss Sylvia S——, Goldsmith, in his life of Nash, tells the story of this unhappy woman. She was a rash but warm-hearted creature, reduced to penury and dependence, not so much by a passion for cards as by her lavish generosity to a lover ruined by his own follies, and with whom her relations are said to have been entirely innocent. Walpole continues: "But a more ridiculous story of Braddock, and which is recorded in heroics by Fielding in his *Covent Garden Tragedy*, was an amorous discussion he had formerly with a Mrs. Upton, who kept him. He had gone the greatest lengths with her pin-money, and was still craving. One day, that he was very pressing, she pulled out her purse and showed him that she had but twelve or fourteen shillings left. He twitched it from her: 'Let me see that.' Tied up at the other end he found five guineas. He took them, tossed the empty purse in her face, saying: 'Did you mean to cheat me?' and never went near her more. Now you are acquainted with General Braddock."

"He once had a duel with Colonel Gumley, Lady Bath's brother, who had been his great friend. As they were going to engage, Gumley, who had good-humor and wit (Braddock had the latter), said: 'Braddock, you are a poor dog! Here, take my purse; if you kill me, you will be forced to run away, and then you will not have a shilling to support you.' Braddock refused the purse, insisted on the duel, was disarmed, and would not even ask his life. However, with all his brutality, he has lately been governor of Gibraltar, where he made himself adored, and where scarce any governor was endured before."

Another story is told of him by an accomplished actress of the time, George Anne Bellamy, whom Braddock had known from girlhood, and with whom his present relations seem to have been those of an elderly adviser and friend. "As we were walking in the Park one day, we heard a poor fellow was to be chastised; when I requested the General to beg off the offender. Upon his application to the general officer, whose name was Dury, he asked Braddock how long since he had divested himself of the brutality and insolence of his manners? To which the other replied: 'You never knew me insolent to my inferiors. It is only to such rude men as yourself that I behave with the spirit which I think they deserve.' "

Braddock made a visit to the actress on the evening before he left London for America. "Before we parted," she says, "the General told me that he should never see me more; for he was going with a handful of men to conquer whole nations; and to do this they must cut their way through unknown woods. He produced a map of the country, saying at the same time: 'Dear Pop, we are sent like sacrifices to the altar,' "—a strange presentiment for a man of his sturdy temper.

Whatever were his feelings, he feared nothing, and his fidelity and honor in the discharge of public trusts were never questioned. "Desperate in his fortune, brutal in his behavior, obstinate in his sentiments," again writes Walpole, "he was still intrepid and capable." He was a veteran in years and in service, having entered the Coldstream Guards as ensign in 1710.

The transports bringing the two regiments from Ireland all arrived safely at Hampton, and were ordered to proceed up the Potomac to Alexandria, where a camp was to be formed. Thither, towards the end of March, went Braddock himself, along with Keppel and Dinwiddie, in the Governor's coach; while his aide-de-camp, Orme, his secretary, Shirley, and the servants of the party followed on horseback. Braddock had sent for the elder Shirley and other provincial governors to meet him in council; and on the fourteenth of April they assembled in a tent of the newly formed encampment. Here was Dinwiddie, who thought his troubles at an end, and saw in the redcoated soldiery the near fruition of his hopes. Here, too, was his friend and ally, Dobbs of North Carolina; with Morris of Pennsylvania, fresh from Assembly quarrels; Sharpe of Maryland, who, having once been a soldier, had been made a sort of provisional commander-in-chief before the arrival of Braddock; and the ambitious Delancey of New York, who had lately led the opposition against the Governor of that province, and now filled the office himself,—a position that needed all his manifold adroitness. But, next to Braddock, the most noteworthy man present was Shirley, governor of Massachusetts. There was a fountain of youth in this old lawyer. A few years before, when he was boundary commissioner in Paris, he had had the indiscretion to marry a young Catholic French girl, the daughter of his landlord; and now, when more than sixty years old, he thirsted for military honors, and delighted in contriving operations of war. He was one of a very few in the colonies who at this time entertained the idea of expelling the French from the continent. He held that Carthage must be destroyed; and, in spite of his Parisian marriage, was the foremost advocate of the root-and-branch policy. He and Lawrence, governor of Nova Scotia, had concerted an attack on the French fort of Beauséjour; and, jointly with others in New England, he had planned the capture of Crown Point, the key of Lake Champlain. By these two strokes and by fortifying the portage between the Kennebec and the Chaudière, he thought that the northern colonies would be saved from invasion, and placed in a position to become themselves invaders. Then, by driving the enemy from Niagara, securing that important pass, and thus cutting off the communication between Canada and her interior dependencies, all the French posts in the West would die of inanition. In order to commend these schemes to the Home Government, he had painted in gloomy colors the dangers that beset the British colonies. Our Indians, he said, will all desert us if we submit to French encroachment. Some of the provinces are full of negro slaves, ready to rise against their masters, and of Roman Catholics, Jacobites, indented servants, and other dangerous persons, who would aid the French in raising a servile insurrection. Pennsylvania is in the hands of Quakers, who will not fight, and of Germans, who are likely enough to join the enemy. The Dutch of Albany would do anything to save their trade. A strong force of French regulars might occupy that place without resistance, then descend the Hudson, and, with the help of a naval force, capture New York and cut the British colonies asunder.

The plans against Crown Point and Beauséjour had already found the approval of the Home Government and the energetic support of all the New England colonies. Preparation for them was in full activity; and it was with great difficulty that Shirley had disengaged himself from these cares to attend the council at Alexandria. He and Dinwiddie stood in the front of opposition to French designs. As they both defended the royal prerogative and were strong advocates of taxation by Parliament, they have found scant justice from American writers. Yet the British colonies owed them a debt of gratitude, and the American States owe it still.

Braddock, laid his instructions before the Council, and Shirley found them entirely to his mind; while the General, on his part, fully approved the schemes of the Governor. The plan of the campaign was settled. The French were to be attacked at four points at once. The two British regiments lately arrived were to advance on Fort Duquesne; two new regiments, known as Shirley's and Pepperell's, just raised in the provinces, and taken into the King's pay, were to reduce Niagara; a body of provincials from New England, New York, and New Jersey was to seize Crown Point; and another body of New England men to capture Beauséjour and bring Acadia to complete subjection. Braddock himself was to lead the expedition against Fort Duquesne. He asked Shirley, who, though a soldier only in theory, had held the rank of colonel since the last war, to charge himself with that against Niagara; and Shirley eagerly assented. The movement on Crown Point was intrusted to Colonel William Johnson, by reason of his influence over the Indians and his reputation for energy, capacity, and faithfulness. Lastly, the Acadian enterprise was assigned to Lieutenant-Colonel Monckton, a regular officer of merit.

To strike this fourfold blow in time of peace was a scheme worthy of Newcastle and of Cumberland. The pretext was that the positions to be attacked were all on British soil; that in occupying them the French had been guilty of invasion; and that to expel the invaders would be an act of self-defence. Yet in regard to two of these positions, the French, if they had no other right, might at least claim one of prescription. Crown Point had been twenty-four years in their undisturbed possession, while it was three quarters of a century since they first occupied Niagara; and, though New York claimed the ground, no serious attempt had been made to dislodge them.

Other matters now engaged the Council. Braddock, in accordance with his instructions, asked the governors to urge upon their several assemblies the establishment of a general fund for the service of the campaign; but the governors were all of opinion that the assemblies would refuse,—each being resolved to keep the control of its money in its own hands; and all present, with one voice, advised that the colonies should be compelled by Act of Parliament to contribute in due proportion to the support of the war. Braddock next asked if, in the judgment of the Council, it would not be well to send Colonel Johnson with full powers to treat with the Five Nations, who had been driven to the verge of an outbreak by the misconduct of the Dutch Indian commissioners at Albany. The measure was cordially approved, as was also another suggestion of the General, that vessels should be built at Oswego to command Lake Ontario. The Council then dissolved.

Shirley hastened back to New England, burdened with the preparation for three expeditions and the command of one of them. Johnson, who had been in the camp, though not in the Council, went back to Albany, provided with a commission as sole superintendent of Indian affairs, and charged, besides, with the enterprise against Crown Point; while an express was despatched to Monckton at Halifax, with orders to set at once to his work of capturing Beauséjour.

In regard to Braddock's part of the campaign, there had been a serious error. If, instead of landing in Virginia and moving on Fort Duquesne by the long and circuitous route of Wills Creek, the two regiments had disembarked at Philadelphia and marched westward, the way would have been shortened, and would have lain through one of the richest and most populous districts on the continent, filled with supplies of every kind. In Virginia, on the other hand, and in the adjoining province of Maryland, wagons, horses, and forage were scarce. The enemies of the Administration ascribed this blunder to the influence of the Quaker merchant, John Hanbury, whom the Duke of Newcastle had consulted as a person familiar with American affairs. Hanbury, who was a prominent stockholder in the Ohio Company, and who traded largely in Virginia, saw it for his interest that the troops should pass that way; and is said to have brought the Duke to this opinion. A writer of the time thinks that if they had landed in Pennsylvania, forty thousand pounds would have been saved in money, and six weeks in time.

Not only were supplies scarce, but the people showed such unwillingness to furnish them, and such apathy in aiding the expedition, that even Washington was provoked to declare that "they ought to be chastised." Many of them thought that the alarm about French encroachment was a device of designing politicians; and they did not awake to a full consciousness of the peril till it was forced upon them by a deluge of calamities, produced by the purblind folly of their own representatives, who, instead of frankly promoting the expedition, displayed a perverse and exasperating narrowness which chafed Braddock to fury. He praises the New England colonies, and echoes Dinwiddie's declaration that they have shown a "fine martial spirit," and he commends Virginia as having done far better than her neighbors; but for Pennsylvania he finds no words to express his wrath. He knew nothing of the intestine war between proprietaries and people, and hence could see no palliation for a conduct which threatened to ruin both the expedition and the colony. Everything depended on speed, and speed was impossible; for stores and provisions were not ready, though notice to furnish them had been given months before. The quartermaster-general, Sir John Sinclair, "stormed like a lion rampant," but with small effect. Contracts broken or disavowed, want of horses, want of wagons, want of forage, want of wholesome food, or sufficient food of any kind, caused such delay that the report of it reached England, and drew from Walpole the comment that Braddock was in no hurry to be scalped. In reality he was maddened with impatience and vexation.

A powerful ally presently came to his aid in the shape of Benjamin Franklin, then postmaster-general of Pennsylvania. That sagacious personage,—the sublime of common-sense, about equal in his instincts and motives of character to the respectable average of the New England that produced him, but gifted with a versatile power of brain rarely matched on earth,— was then divided between his strong desire to repel a danger of which he saw the imminence, and his equally strong antagonism to the selfish claims of the Penns, proprietaries of Pennsylvania. This last motive had determined his attitude towards their representative, the Governor, and led him into an opposition as injurious to the military good name of the province as it was favorable to its political longings. In the present case there was no such conflict of inclinations; he could help Braddock without hurting Pennsylvania. He and his son had visited the camp, and found the General waiting restlessly for the report of the agents whom he had sent to collect wagons. "I stayed with him," says Franklin, "several days, and dined with him daily. When I was about to depart, the returns of wagons to be obtained were brought in, by which it appeared that they amounted only to twenty-five, and not all of these were in serviceable condition." On this the General and his officers declared that the expedition was at an end, and denounced the Ministry for sending them into a country void of the means of transportation. Franklin remarked that it was a pity they had not landed in Pennsylvania, where almost every farmer had his wagon. Braddock caught eagerly at his words, and begged that he would use his influence to enable the troops to move. Franklin went back to Pennsylvania, issued an address to the farmers appealing to their interest and their fears, and in a fortnight procured a hundred and fifty wagons, with a large number of horses. Braddock, grateful to his benefactor, and enraged at everybody else, pronounced him "Almost the only instance of ability and honesty I have known in these provinces." More wagons and more horses gradually arrived, and at the eleventh hour the march began.

On the tenth of May Braddock reached Wills Creek, where the whole force was now gathered, having marched thither by detachments along the banks of the Potomac. This old trading-station of the Ohio Company had been transformed into a military post and named Fort Cumberland. During the past winter the independent companies which had failed Washington in his need had been at work here to prepare a base of operations for Braddock. Their axes had been of more avail than their muskets. A broad wound had been cut in the bosom of the forest, and the murdered oaks and chestnuts turned into ramparts, barracks, and magazines. Fort Cumberland was an enclosure of logs set upright in the ground, pierced with loopholes, and armed with ten small cannon. It stood on a rising ground near the point where Wills Creek joined the Potomac, and the forest girded it like a mighty hedge, or rather like a paling of gaunt brown stems upholding a canopy of green. All around spread illimitable woods, wrapping hill, valley, and mountain. The spot was an oasis in a desert of leaves,—if the name oasis can be given to anything so rude and harsh. In this rugged area, or "clearing," all Braddock's force was now assembled, amounting, regulars, provincials, and sailors, to about twenty-two hundred men. The two regiments, Halket's and Dunbar's, had been completed by enlistment in Virginia to seven hundred men each. Of Virginians there were nine companies of fifty men, who found no favor in the eyes of Braddock or his officers. To Ensign Allen of Halket's regiment was assigned the duty of "making them as much like soldiers as possible,"—that is, of drilling them like regulars. The General had little hope of them, and informed Sir Thomas Robinson that "their slothful and languid disposition renders them very unfit for military service,"—a point on which he lived to change his mind. Thirty sailors, whom Commodore Keppel had lent him, were more to his liking, and were in fact of value in many ways. He had now about six hundred baggage-horses, besides those of the artillery, all weakening daily on the diet of leaves; for no grass was to be found. There was great show of discipline, and little real order. Braddock's executive capacity seems to have been moderate, and his dogged, imperious temper, rasped by disappointments, was in constant irritation. "He looks upon the country, I believe," writes Washington, "as void of honor or honesty. We have frequent disputes on this head, which are maintained with warmth on both sides, especially on his, as he is incapable of arguing without it, or giving up any point he asserts, be it ever so incompatible with reason or common sense." Braddock's secretary, the younger Shirley, writing to his friend Governor Morris, spoke thus irreverently of his chief: "As the King said of a neighboring governor of yours [*Sharpe*], when proposed for the command of the American forces about a twelvemonth ago, and recommended as a very honest man, though not remarkably able, 'a little more ability and a little less honesty upon the present occasion might serve our turn better.' It is a joke to suppose that secondary officers can make amends for the defects of the first; the mainspring must be the mover. As to the others, I don't think we have much to boast; some are insolent and ignorant, others capable, but rather aiming at showing their own abilities than making a proper use of them. I have a very great love for my friend Orme, and think it uncommonly fortunate for our leader that he is under the influence of so honest and capable a man; but I wish for the sake of the public he had some more experience of business, particularly in America. I am greatly disgusted at seeing an expedition (as it is called), so ill-concerted originally in England, so improperly conducted since in America."

Captain Robert Orme, of whom Shirley speaks, was aide-de-camp to Braddock, and author of a copious and excellent Journal of the expedition, now in the British Museum. His portrait, painted at full length by Sir Joshua Reynolds, hangs in the National Gallery at London. He stands by his horse, a gallant young figure, with a face pale, yet rather handsome, booted to the knee, his scarlet coat, ample waistcoat, and small three-cornered hat all heavy with gold lace. The General had two other aides-de-camp, Captain Roger Morris and Colonel George Washington, whom he had invited, in terms that do him honor, to become one of his military family.

It has been said that Braddock despised not only provincials, but Indians. Nevertheless he took some pains to secure their aid, and complained that Indian affairs had been so ill conducted by the provinces that it was hard to gain their confidence. This was true; the tribes had been alienated by gross neglect. Had they been protected from injustice and soothed by attentions and presents, the Five Nations, Delawares, and Shawanoes would have been retained as friends. But their complaints had been slighted, and every gift begrudged. The trader Croghan brought, however, about fifty warriors, with as many women and children, to the camp at Fort Cumberland. They were objects of great curiosity to the soldiers, who gazed with astonishment on their faces, painted red, yellow, and black, their ears slit and hung with pendants, and their heads close shaved, except the feathered scalp-lock at the crown. "In the day," says an officer, "they are in our camp, and in the night they go into their own, where they dance and make a most horrible noise." Braddock received them several times in his tent, ordered the guard to salute them, made them speeches, caused cannon to be fired and drums and fifes to play in their honor, regaled them with rum, and gave them a bullock for a feast; whereupon, being much pleased, they danced a war-dance, described by one spectator as "droll and odd, showing how they scalp and fight;" after which, says another, "they set up the most horrid song or cry that ever I heard." These warriors, with a few others, promised the General to join him on the march; but he apparently grew tired of them, for a famous chief, called Scarroyaddy, afterwards complained: "He looked upon us as dogs, and would never hear anything that we said to him." Only eight of them remained with him to the end.

Another ally appeared at the camp. This was a personage long known in Western fireside story as Captain Jack, the Black Hunter, or the Black Rifle. It was said of him that, having been a settler on the farthest frontier, in the Valley of the Juniata, he returned one evening to his cabin and found it burned to the ground by Indians, and the bodies of his wife and children lying among the ruins. He vowed undying vengeance, raised a band of kindred spirits, dressed and painted like Indians, and became the scourge of the red man and the champion of the white. But he and his wild crew, useful as they might have been, shocked Braddock's sense of military fitness; and he received them so coldly that they left him.

It was the tenth of June before the army was well on its march. Three hundred axemen led the way, to cut and clear the road; and the long train of packhorses, wagons, and cannon toiled on behind, over the stumps, roots, and stones of the narrow track, the regulars and provincials marching in the forest close on either side. Squads of men were thrown out on the flanks, and scouts ranged the woods to guard against surprise; for, with all his scorn of Indians and Canadians, Braddock did not neglect reasonable precautions. Thus, foot by foot, they advanced into the waste of lonely mountains that divided the streams flowing to the Atlantic from those flowing to the Gulf of Mexico,—a realm of forests ancient as the world. The road was but twelve feet wide, and the line of march often extended four miles. It was like a thin, long party-colored snake, red, blue, and brown, trailing slowly through the depth of leaves, creeping round inaccessible heights, crawling over ridges, moving always in dampness and shadow, by rivulets and waterfalls, crags and chasms, gorges and shaggy steeps. In glimpses only, through jagged boughs and flickering leaves, did this wild primeval world reveal itself, with its dark green mountains, flecked with the morning mist, and its distant summits pencilled in dreamy blue. The army passed the main Alleghany, Meadow Mountain, and Great Savage Mountain, and traversed the funereal pine-forest afterwards called the Shades of Death. No attempt was made to interrupt their march, though the commandant of Fort Duquesne had sent out parties for that purpose. A few French and Indians hovered about them, now and then scalping a straggler or inscribing filthy insults on trees; while others fell upon the border settlements which the advance of the troops had left defenceless.

Here they were more successful, butchering about thirty persons, chiefly women and children.

It was the eighteenth of June before the army reached a place called the Little Meadows, less than thirty miles from Fort Cumberland. Fever and dysentery among the men, and the weakness and worthlessness of many of the horses, joined to the extreme difficulty of the road, so retarded them that they could move scarcely more than three miles a day. Braddock consulted with Washington, who advised him to leave the heavy baggage to follow as it could, and push forward with a body of chosen troops. This counsel was given in view of a report that five hundred regulars were on the way to reinforce Fort Duquesne. It was adopted. Colonel Dunbar was left to command the rear division, whose powers of movement were now reduced to the lowest point. The advance corps, consisting of about twelve hundred soldiers, besides officers and drivers, began its march on the nineteenth with such artillery as was thought indispensable, thirty wagons, and a large number of packhorses. "The prospect," writes Washington to his brother, "conveyed infinite delight to my mind, though I was excessively ill at the time. But this prospect was soon clouded, and my hopes brought very low indeed when I found that, instead of pushing on with vigor without regarding a little rough road, they were halting to level every mole-hill, and to erect bridges over every brook, by which means we were four days in getting twelve miles." It was not till the seventh of July that they neared the mouth of Turtle Creek, a stream entering the Monongahela about eight miles from the French fort. The way was direct and short, but would lead them through a difficult country and a defile so perilous that Braddock resolved to ford the Monongahela to avoid this danger, and then ford it again to reach his destination.

Fort Duquesne stood on the point of land where the Alleghany and the Monongahela join to form the Ohio, and where now stands Pittsburg, with its swarming population, its restless industries, the clang of its forges, and its chimneys vomiting foul smoke into the face of heaven. At that early day a white flag fluttering over a cluster of palisades and embankments betokened the first intrusion of civilized men upon a scene which, a few months before, breathed the repose of a virgin wilderness, voiceless but for the lapping of waves upon the pebbles, or the note of some lonely bird. But now the sleep of ages was broken, and bugle and drum told the astonished forest that its doom was pronounced and its days numbered. The fort was a compact little work, solidly built and strong, compared with others on the continent. It was a square of four bastions, with the water close on two sides, and the other two protected by ravelins, ditch, glacis, and covered way. The ramparts on these sides were of squared logs, filled in with earth, and ten feet or more thick. The two water sides were enclosed by a massive stockade of upright logs, twelve feet high, mortised together and loopholed. The armament consisted of a number of small cannon

mounted on the bastions. A gate and drawbridge on the east side gave access
to the area within, which was surrounded by barracks for the soldiers, officers' quarters, the lodgings of the commandant, a guardhouse, and a storehouse, all built partly of logs and partly of boards. There were no case-
mates, and the place was commanded by a high woody hill beyond the
Monongahela. The forest had been cleared away to the distance of more
than a musket shot from the ramparts, and the stumps were hacked level
with the ground. Here, just outside the ditch, bark cabins had been built
for such of the troops and Canadians as could not find room within; and
the rest of the open space was covered with Indian corn and other crops.

The garrison consisted of a few companies of the regular troops stationed
permanently in the colony, and to these were added a considerable number
of Canadians. Contrecœur still hell the command. Under him were three
other captains, Beaujeu, Dumas, and Ligneris. Besides the troops and
Canadians, eight hundred Indian warriors, mustered from far and near, had
built their wigwams and camp-sheds on the open ground, or under the edge
of the neighboring woods,—very little to the advantage of the young corn.
Some were baptized savages settled in Canada,—Caughnawagas from Saut
St. Louis, Abenakis from St. Francis, and Hurons from Lorette, whose chief
bore the name of Anastase, in honor of that Father of the Church. The
rest were unmitigated heathen,—Pottawattamies and Ojibwas from the
northern lakes under Charles Langlade, the same bold partisan who had
led them, three years before, to attack the Miamis at Pickawillany; Shawanoes and Mingoes from the Ohio; and Ottawas from Detroit, commanded,
it is said, by that most redoubtable of savages, Pontiac. The law of the
survival of the fittest had wrought on this heterogeneous crew through
countless generations; and with the primitive Indian, the fittest was the
hardiest, fiercest, most adroit, and most wily. Baptized and heathen alike,
they had just enjoyed a diversion greatly to their taste. A young Pennsylvanian named James Smith, a spirited and intelligent boy of eighteen,
had been waylaid by three Indians on the western borders of the province
and led captive to the fort. When the party came to the edge of the clearing,
his captors, who had shot and scalped his companion, raised the scalp-yell;
whereupon a din of responsive whoops and firing of guns rose from all
the Indian camps, and their inmates swarmed out like bees, while the
French in the fort short off muskets and cannon to honor the occasion. The
unfortunate boy, the object of this obstreperous rejoicing, presently saw a
multitude of savages, naked, hideously bedaubed with red, blue, black,
and brown, and armed with sticks or clubs, ranging themselves in two long
parallel lines, between which he was told that he must run, the faster the
better, as they would beat him all the way. He ran with his best speed, under
a shower of blows, and had nearly reached the end of the course, when
he was knocked down. He tried to rise, but was blinded by a handful of sand
thrown into his face; and then they beat him till he swooned. On coming

to his senses he found himself in the fort, with the surgeon opening a vein in his arm and a crowd of French and Indians looking on. In a few days he was able to walk with the help of a stick; and, coming out from his quarters one morning, he saw a memorable scene.

Three days before, an Indian had brought the report that the English were approaching; and the Chevalier de la Perade was sent out to reconnoitre. He returned on the next day, the seventh, with news that they were not far distant. On the eighth the brothers Normanville went out, and found that they were within six leagues of the fort. The French were in great excitement and alarm; but Contrecœur at length took a resolution, which seems to have been inspired by Beaujeu. It was determined to meet the enemy on the march, and ambuscade them if possible at the crossing of the Monongahela, or some other favorable spot. Beaujeu proposed the plan to the Indians, and offered them the war-hatchet; but they would not take it. "Do you want to die, my father, and sacrifice us besides?" That night they held a council, and in the morning again refused to go. Beaujeu did not despair. "I am determined," he exclaimed, "to meet the English. What! will you let your father go alone?" The greater part caught fire at his words, promised to follow him, and put on their war-paint. Beaujeu received the communion, then dressed himself like a savage, and joined the clamorous throng. Open barrels of gunpowder and bullets were set before the gate of the fort, and James Smith, painfully climbing the rampart with the help of his stick, looked down on the warrior rabble as, huddling together, wild with excitement, they scooped up the contents to fill their powder-horns and pouches. Then, band after band, they filed off along the forest track that led to the ford of the Monongahela. They numbered six hundred and thirty-seven; and with them went thirty-six French officers and cadets, seventy-two regular soldiers, and a hundred and forty-six Canadians, or about nine hundred in all. At eight o'clock the tumult was over. The broad clearing lay lonely and still, and Contrecœur, with what was left of his garrison, waited in suspense for the issue.

It was near one o'clock when Braddock crossed the Monongahela for the second time. If the French made a stand anywhere, it would be, he thought, at the fording-place; but Lieutenant-Colonel Gage, whom he sent across with a strong advance-party, found no enemy, and quietly took possession of the farther shore. Then the main body followed. To impose on the imagination of the French scouts, who were doubtless on the watch, the movement was made with studied regularity and order. The sun was cloudless, and the men were inspirited by the prospect of near triumph. Washington afterwards spoke with admiration of the spectacle. The music, the banners, the mounted officers, the troop of light cavalry, the naval detachment, the red-coated regulars, the blue-coated Virginians, the wagons and tumbrils, cannons, howitzers, and coehorns, the train of packhorses, and the droves of cattle, passed in long procession through the rippling shallows, and slowly entered the bordering forest. Here, when all were over, a short halt was ordered for rest and refreshment.

Why had not Beaujeu defended the ford? This was his intention in the morning; but he had been met by obstacles, the nature of which is not wholly clear. His Indians, it seems, had proved refractory. Three hundred of them left him, went off in another direction, and did not rejoin him till the English had crossed the river. Hence perhaps it was that, having left Fort Duquesne at eight o'clock, he spent half the day in marching seven miles, and was more than a mile from the fording-place when the British reached the eastern shore. The delay, from whatever cause arising, cost him the opportunity of laying an ambush either at the ford or in the gullies and ravines that channelled the forest through which Braddock was now on the point of marching.

Not far from the bank of the river, and close by the British line of march, there was a clearing and a deserted house that had once belonged to the trader Fraser. Washington remembered it well. It was here that he found rest and shelter on the winter journey homeward from his mission to Fort Le Bœuf. He was in no less need of rest at this moment; for recent fever had so weakened him that he could hardly sit his horse. From Fraser's house to Fort Duquesne the distance was eight miles by a rough path, along which the troops were now beginning to move after their halt. It ran inland for a little; then curved to the left, and followed a course parallel to the river along the base of a line of steep hills that here bordered the valley. These and all the country were buried in dense and heavy forest, choked with bushes and the carcases of fallen trees. Braddock has been charged with marching blindly into an ambuscade; but it was not so. There was no ambuscade; and had there been one, he would have found it. It is true that he did not reconnoitre the woods very far in advance of the head of the column; yet, with this exception, he made elaborate dispositions to prevent surprise. Several guides, with six Virginian light horsemen, led the way. Then, a musket-shot behind, came the vanguard; then three hundred soldiers under Gage; then a large body of axemen, under Sir John Sinclair, to open the road; then two cannon with tumbrils and tool-wagons; and lastly the rear-guard, closing the line, while flanking-parties ranged the woods on both sides. This was the advance-column. The main body followed with little or no interval. The artillery and wagons moved along the road, and the troops filed through the woods close on either hand. Numerous flanking-parties were thrown out a hundred yards and more to right and left; while, in the space between them and the marching column, the pack horses and cattle, with their drivers, made their way painfully among the trees and thickets; since, had they been allowed to follow the road, the line of march would have been too long for mutual support. A body of regulars and provincials brought up the rear.

Gage, with his advance-column, had just passed a wide and bushy ravine that crossed their path, and the van of the main column was on the point of entering it, when the guides and light horsemen in the front suddenly fell back; and the engineer, Gordon, then engaged in marking out the road, saw a man, dressed like an Indian, but wearing the gorget of an officer, bounding forward along the path. He stopped when he discovered the head of the column, turned, and waved his hat. The forest behind was swarming with French and savages. At the signal of the officer, who was probably Beaujeu, they yelled the warwhoop, spread themselves to right and left, and opened a sharp fire under cover of the trees. Gage's column wheeled deliberately into line, and fired several volleys with great steadiness against the now invisible assailants. Few of them were hurt; the trees caught the shot, but the noise was deafening under the dense arches of the forest. The greater part of the Canadians, to borrow the words of Dumas, "fled shamefully, crying 'Sauve qui peut!' " Volley followed volley, and at the third Beaujeu dropped dead. Gage's two cannon were now brought to bear, on which the Indians, like the Canadians, gave way in confusion, but did not, like them, abandon the field. The close scarlet ranks of the English were plainly to be seen through the trees and the smoke; they were moving forward, cheering lustily, and shouting "God save the King!" Dumas, now chief in command, thought that all was lost. "I advanced," he says, "with the assurance that comes from despair, exciting by voice and gesture the few soldiers that remained. The fire of my platoon was so sharp that the enemy seemed astonished." The Indians, encouraged, began to rally. The French officers who commanded them showed admirable courage and address; and while Dumas and Ligneris, with the regulars and what was left of the Canadians, held the ground in front, the savage warriors, screeching their war-cries, swarmed through the forest along both flanks, of the English, hid behind trees, bushes, and fallen trunks, or crouched in gullies and ravines, and opened a deadly fire on the helpless soldiery, who, themselves completely visible, could see no enemy, and wasted volley after volley on the impassive trees. The most destructive fire came from a hill on the English right, where the Indians lay in multitudes, firing from their lurking-places on the living target below. But the invisible death was everywhere, in front, flank, and rear. The British cheer was heard no more. The troops broke their ranks and huddled together in a bewildered mass, shrinking from the bullets that cut them down by scores.

When Braddock heard the firing in the front, he pushed forward with the main body to the support of Gage, leaving four hundred men in the rear, under Sir Peter Halket, to guard the baggage. At the moment of his arrival Gage's soldiers had abandoned their two cannon, and were falling back to escape the concentrated fire of the Indians. Meeting the advancing troops, they tried to find cover behind them. This threw the whole into confusion. The men of the two regiments became mixed together; and in a short time the entire force, except the Virginians and the troops left with Halket, were massed in several dense bodies within a small space of ground, facing some one way and some another, and all alike exposed without shelter to the bullets that pelted them like hail. Both men and officers were new to this blind and frightful warfare of the savage in his native woods. To charge the Indians in their hiding-places would have been useless. They would have eluded pursuit with the agility of wildcats, and swarmed back, like angry hornets, the moment that it ceased. The Virginians alone were equal to the emergency. Fighting behind trees like the Indians themselves, they might have held the enemy in check till order could be restored, had not Braddock, furious at a proceeding that shocked all his ideas of courage and discipline, ordered them, with oaths, to form into line. A body of them under Captain Waggoner made a dash for a fallen tree lying in the woods, far out towards the lurking-places of the Indians, and, crouching behind the huge trunk, opened fire; but the regulars, seeing the smoke among the bushes, mistook their best friends for the enemy, shot at them from behind, killed many, and forced the rest to return. A few of the regulars also tried in their clumsy way to fight behind trees; but Braddock beat them with his sword, and compelled them to stand with the rest, an open mark for the Indians. The panic increased; the soldiers crowded together, and the bullets spent themselves in a mass of human bodies. Commands, entreaties, and threats were lost upon them. "We would fight," some of them answered, "if we could see anybody to fight with." Nothing was visible but puffs of smoke. Officers and men who had stood all the afternoon under fire afterwards declared that they could not be sure they had seen a single Indian. Braddock ordered Lieutenant-Colonel Burton to attack the hill where the puffs of smoke were thickest, and the bullets most deadly. With infinite difficulty that brave officer induced a hundred men to follow him; but he was soon disabled by a wound, and they all faced about. The artillerymen stood for some time by their guns, which did great damage to the trees and little to the enemy. The mob of soldiers, stupefied with terror, stood panting, their foreheads beaded with sweat, loading and firing mechanically, sometimes into the air, sometimes among their own comrades, many of whom they killed. The ground, strewn with dead and wounded men, the bounding of maddened horses, the clatter and roar of musketry and cannon, mixed with the spiteful report of rifles and the yells that rose from the indefatigable throats of six hundred unseen savages, formed a chaos of anguish and terror scarcely paralleled even in Indian war. "I cannot describe the horrors of that scene," one of Braddock's officers wrote three weeks after; "no pen could do it. The yell of the Indians is fresh on my ear, and the terrific sound will haunt me till the hour of my dissolution."

Braddock showed a furious intrepidity. Mounted on horseback, he dashed to and fro, storming like a madman. Four horses were shot under him, and he mounted a fifth. Washington seconded his chief with equal courage; he too no doubt using strong language, for he did not measure words when the fit was on him. He escaped as by miracle. Two horses were killed under him, and four bullets tore his clothes. The conduct of the British officers was above praise. Nothing could surpass their undaunted self-devotion; and in their vain attempts to lead on the men, the havoc among them was frightful. Sir Peter Halket was shot dead. His son, a lieutenant in his regiment, stooping to raise the body of his father, was shot dead in turn. Young Shirley, Braddock's secretary, was pierced through the brain. Orme and Morris, his aides-de-camp, Sinclair, the quartermaster-general, Gates and Gage, both afterwards conspicuous on opposite sides in the War of the Revolution, and Gladwin, who, eight years later, defended Detroit against Pontiac, were all wounded. Of eighty-six officers, sixty-three were killed or disabled; while out of thirteen hundred and seventy-three non-commissioned officers and privates, only four hundred and fifty-nine came off unharmed.

Braddock saw that all was lost. To save the wreck of his force from annihilation, he at last commanded a retreat; and as he and such of his officers as were left strove to withdraw the half-frenzied crew in some semblance of order, a bullet struck him down. The gallant bulldog fell from his horse, shot through the arm into the lungs. It is said, though on evidence of no weight, that the bullet came from one of his own men. Be this as it may, there he lay among the bushes, bleeding, gasping, unable even to curse. He demanded to be left where he was. Captain Stewart and another provincial bore him between them to the rear.

It was about this time that the mob of soldiers, having been three hours under fire, and having spent their ammunition, broke away in a blind frenzy, rushed back towards the ford, "and when," says Washington, "we endeavored to rally them, it was with as much success as if we had attempted to stop the wild bears of the mountains." They dashed across, helter-skelter, plunging through the water to the farther bank, leaving wounded comrades, cannon, baggage, the military chest, and the General's papers, a prey to the Indians. About fifty of these followed to the edge of the river. Dumas and Ligneris, who had now only about twenty Frenchmen with them, made no attempt to pursue, and went back to the fort, because, says Contrecœur, so many of the Canadians had "retired at the first fire." The field, abandoned to the savages, was a pandemonium of pillage and murder.

James Smith, the young prisoner at Fort Duquesne, had passed a day of suspense, waiting the result. "In the afternoon I again observed a great noise and commotion in the fort, and, though at that time I could not understand French, I found it was the voice of joy and triumph, and feared that they had received what I called bad news. I had observed some of the old-country soldiers speak Dutch; as I spoke Dutch, I went to one of them and asked him what was the news. He told me that a runner had just arrived who said that Braddock would certainly be defeated; that the Indians and French had surrounded him, and were concealed behind trees and in gullies, and kept a constant fire upon the English; and that they saw the English falling in heaps; and if they did not take the river, which was the only gap, and make their escape, there would not be one man left alive before sundown. Some time after this, I heard a number of scalp-halloos, and saw a company of Indians and French coming in. I observed they had a great number of bloody scalps, grenadiers' caps, British canteens, bayonets, etc., with them. They brought the news that Braddock was defeated. After that another company came in, which appeared to be about one hundred, and chiefly Indians; and it seemed to me that almost every one of this company was carrying scalps. After this came another company with a number of wagon-horses, and also a great many scalps. Those that were coming in and those that had arrived kept a constant firing of small arms, and also the great guns in the fort, which were accompanied with the most hideous shouts and yells from all quarters, so that it appeared to me as though the infernal regions had broke loose.

"About sundown I beheld a small party coming in with about a dozen prisoners, stripped naked, with their hands tied behind their backs and their faces and part of their bodies blacked; these prisoners they burned to death on the bank of Alleghany River, opposite the fort. I stood on the fort wall until I beheld them begin to burn one of these men; they had him tied to a stake, and kept touching him with firebrands, red-hot irons, etc., and he screaming in a most doleful manner, the Indians in the meantime yelling like infernal spirits. As this scene appeared too shocking for me to behold, I retired to my lodging, both sore and sorry. When I came into my lodgings I saw Russel's *Seven Sermons,* which they had brought from the field of battle, which a Frenchman made a present of to me."

The loss of the French was slight, but fell chiefly on the officers, three of whom were killed, and four wounded. Of the regular soldiers, all but four escaped untouched. The Canadians suffered still less, in proportion to their numbers, only five of them being hurt. The Indians, who won the victory, bore the principal loss. Of those from Canada, twenty-seven were killed and wounded; while the casualties among the Western tribes are not reported. All of these last went off the next morning with their plunder and scalps, leaving Contrecœur in great anxiety lest the remnant of Braddock's troops, reinforced by the division under Dunbar, should attack him again. His doubts would have vanished had he known the condition of his defeated enemy.

In the pain and languor of a mortal wound, Braddock showed unflinching resolution. His bearers stopped with him at a favorable spot beyond the Monongahela; and here he hoped to maintain his position till the arrival of Dunbar. By the efforts of the officers about a hundred men were collected around him; but to keep them there was impossible. Within an hour they abandoned him, and fled like the rest. Gage, however, succeeded in rallying about eighty beyond the other fording-place; and Washington, on an order from Braddock, spurred his jaded horse towards the camp of Dunbar to demand wagons, provisions, and hospital stores.

Fright overcame fatigue. The fugitives toiled on all night, pursued by spectres of horror and despair; hearing still the war-whoops and the shrieks; possessed with the one thought of escape from this wilderness of death. In the morning some order was restored. Braddock was placed on a horse; then, the pain being insufferable, he was carried on a litter, Captain Orme having bribed the carriers by the promise of a guinea and a bottle of rum apiece. Early in the succeeding night, such as had not fainted on the way reached the deserted farm of Gist. Here they met wagons and provisions, with a detachment of soldiers sent by Dunbar, whose camp was six miles farther on; and Braddock ordered them to go to the relief of the stragglers left behind.

At noon of that day a number of wagoners and packhorse-drivers had come to Dunbar's camp with wild tidings of rout and ruin. More fugitives followed; and soon after a wounded officer was brought in upon a sheet. The drums beat to arms. The camp was in commotion, and many soldiers and teamsters took to flight, in spite of the sentinels, who tried in vain to stop them. There was a still more disgraceful scene on the next day, after Braddock, with the wreck of his force, had arrived. Orders were given to destroy such of the wagons, stores, and ammunition as could not be carried back at once to Fort Cumberland. Whether Dunbar or the dying General gave these orders is not clear; but it is certain that they were executed with shameful alacrity. More than a hundred wagons were burned; cannons, coehorns, and shells were burst or buried; barrels of gunpowder were staved, and the contents thrown into a brook; provisions were scattered through the woods and swamps. Then the whole command began its retreat over the mountains to Fort Cumberland, sixty-miles distant. This proceeding, for which, in view of the condition of Braddock, Dunbar must be held answerable, excited the utmost indignation among the colonists. If he could not advance, they thought, he might at least have fortified himself and held his ground till the provinces could send him help; thus covering the frontier, and holding French war-parties in check.

Braddock's last moment was near. Orme, who, though himself severely wounded, was with him till his death, told Franklin that he was totally silent all the first day, and at night said only, "Who would have thought it?" that all the next day he was again silent, till at last he muttered, "We shall better know how to deal with them another time," and died a few minutes after. He had nevertheless found breath to give orders at Gist's for the succor of the men who had dropped on the road. It is said, too, that in his last hours "he could not bear the sight of a red coat," but murmured praises of "the blues," or Virginians, and said that he hoped he should live to reward them. He died at about eight o'clock in the evening of Sunday, the thirteenth. Dunbar had begun his retreat that morning, and was then encamped near the Great Meadows. On Monday the dead commander was buried in the road; and men, horses, and wagons passed over his grave, effacing every sign of it, lest the Indians should find and mutilate the body.

Colonel James Innes, commanding at Fort Cumberland, where a crowd of invalids with soldiers' wives and other women had been left when the expedition marched, heard of the defeat, only two days after it happened, from a wagoner who had fled from the field on horseback. He at once sent a note of six lines to Lord Fairfax: "I have this moment received the most melancholy news of the defeat of our troops, the General killed, and numbers of our officers; our whole artillery taken. In short, the account I have received is so very bad, that as, please God, I intend to make a stand here, 'tis highly necessary to raise the militia everywhere to defend the frontiers." A boy whom he sent out on horseback met more fugitives, and came back on the fourteenth with reports as vague and disheartening as the first. Innes sent them to Dinwiddie. Some days after, Dunbar and his train arrived in miserable disorder, and Fort Cumberland was turned into a hospital for the shattered fragments of a routed and ruined army.

On the sixteenth a letter was brought in haste to one Buchanan at Carlisle, on the Pennsylvanian frontier:—

SIR,—I thought it proper to let you know that I was in the battle where we were defeated. And we had about eleven hundred and fifty private men, besides officers and others. And we were attacked the ninth day about twelve o'clock, and held till about three in the afternoon, and then we were forced to retreat, when I suppose we might bring off about three hundred whole men, besides a vast many wounded. Most of our officers were either wounded or killed; General Braddock is wounded, but I hope not mortal; and Sir John Sinclair and many others, but I hope not mortal. All the train is cut off in a manner. Sir Peter Halket and his son, Captain Polson, Captain Gethen, Captain Rose, Captain Tatten killed, and many others. Captain Ord of the train is wounded, but I hope not mortal. We lost all our artillery entirely, and everything else.

To Mr. John Smith and Buchannon, and give it to the next post, and let him show this to Mr. George Gibson in Lancaster, and Mr. Bingham, at the sign of the Ship, and you'll oblige,

Yours to command,

JOHN CAMPBELL, *Messenger.*

The evil tidings quickly reached Philadelphia, where such confidence had prevailed that certain over-zealous persons had begun to collect money for fireworks to celebrate the victory. Two of these, brother physicians named Bond, came to Franklin and asked him to subscribe; but the sage looked doubtful. "Why, the devil!" said one of them, "you surely don't suppose the fort will not be taken?" He reminded them that war is always uncertain; and the subscription was deferred. The Governor laid the news of the disaster before his Council, telling them at the same time that his opponents in the Assembly would not believe it, and had insulted him in the street for giving it currency.

Dinwiddie remained tranquil at Williamsburg, sure that all would go well. The brief note of Innes, forwarded by Lord Fairfax, first disturbed his dream of triumph; but on second thought he took comfort. "I am willing to think that account was from a deserter who, in a great panic, represented what his fears suggested. I wait with impatience for another express from Fort Cumberland, which I expect will greatly contradict the former." The news got abroad, and the slaves showed signs of excitement. "The villany of the negroes on any emergency is what I always feared," continues the Governor. "An example of one or two at first may prevent these creatures entering into combinations and wicked designs." And he wrote to Lord Halifax: "The negro slaves have been very audacious on the news of defeat on the Ohio. These poor creatures imagine the French will give them their freedom. We have too many here; but I hope we shall be able to keep them in proper subjection." Suspense grew intolerable. "It's monstrous they should be so tardy and dilatory in sending down any farther account." He sent Major Colin Campbell for news; when, a day or two later, a courier brought him two letters, one from Orme, and the other from Washington, both written at Fort Cumberland on the eighteenth. The letter of Orme began thus: "My dear Governor, I am so extremely ill in bed with the wound I have received that I am under the necessity of employing my friend Captain Dobson as my scribe." Then he told the wretched story of defeat and humiliation. "The officers were absolutely sacrificed by their unparalleled good behavior; advancing before their men sometimes in bodies, and sometimes separately, hoping by such an example to engage the soldiers to follow them; but to no purpose. Poor Shirley was shot through the head, Captain Morris very much wounded. Mr. Washington had two horses shot under him, and his clothes shot through in several places; behaving the whole time with the greatest courage and resolution."

Washington wrote more briefly, saying that, as Orme was giving a full account of the affair, it was needless for him to repeat it. Like many others in the fight, he greatly underrated the force of the enemy, which he placed at three hundred, or about a third of the actual number,—a natural error, as most of the assailants were invisible. "Our poor Virginians behaved like men, and died like soldiers; for I believe that out of three companies that were there that day, scarce thirty were left alive. Captain Peronney and all his officers down to a corporal were killed. Captain Polson shared almost as hard a fate, for only one of his escaped. In short, the dastardly behavior of the English soldiers exposed all those who were inclined to do their duty to almost certain death. It is imagined (I believe with great justice, too) that two thirds of both killed and wounded received their shots from our own cowardly dogs of soldiers, who gathered themselves into a body, contrary to orders, ten and twelve deep, would then level, fire, and shoot down the men before them."

To Orme, Dinwiddie replied: "I read your letter with tears in my eyes; but it gave me much pleasure to see your name at the bottom, and more so when I observed by the postscript that your wound is not dangerous. But pray, dear sir, is it not possible by a second attempt to retrieve the great loss we have sustained? I presume the General's chariot is at the fort. In it you may come here, and my house is heartily at your command. Pray take care of your valuable health; keep your spirits up, and I doubt not of your recovery. My wife and girls join me in most sincere respects and joy at your being so well, and I always am, with great truth, dear friend, your affectionate humble servant."

To Washington he is less effusive, though he had known him much longer. He begins, it is true, "Dear Washington," and congratulates him on his escape; but soon grows formal, and asks: "Pray, sir, with the number of them remaining, is there no possibility of doing something on the other side of the mountains before the winter months? Surely you must mistake. Colonel Dunbar will not march to winter-quarters in the middle of summer, and leave the frontiers exposed to the invasions of the enemy! No; he is a better officer, and I have a different opinion of him. I sincerely wish you health and happiness, and am, with great respect, sir, your obedient, humble servant."

Washington's letter had contained the astonishing announcement that Dunbar meant to abandon the frontier and march to Philadelphia. Dinwiddie, much disturbed, at once wrote to that officer, though without betraying any knowledge of his intention. "Sir, the melancholy account of the defeat of our forces gave me a sensible and real concern"—on which he enlarges for a while; then suddenly changes style: "Dear Colonel, is there no method left to retrieve the dishonor done to the British arms? As you now command all the forces that remain, are you not able, after a proper refreshment of your men, to make a second attempt? You have four months now to come of the best weather of the year for such an expedition. What a fine field for honor will Colonel Dunbar have to confirm and establish his character as a brave officer." Then, after suggesting plans of operation, and entering into much detail, the fervid Governor concludes: "It gives me great pleasure that under our great loss and misfortunes the command devolves on an officer of so great military judgment and established character. With my sincere respect and hearty wishes for success to all your proceedings, I am, worthy sir, your most obedient, humble servant."

Exhortation and flattery were lost on Dunbar. Dinwiddie received from him in reply a short, dry note, dated on the first of August, and acquainting him that he should march for Philadelphia on the second. This, in fact, he did, leaving the fort to be defended by invalids and a few Virginians. "I acknowledge," says Dinwiddie, "I was not brought up to arms; but I think common sense would have prevailed not to leave the frontiers exposed after having opened a road over the mountains to the Ohio, by which the enemy can the more easily invade us. . . . Your great colonel," he writes to Orme, "is gone to a peaceful colony, and left our frontiers open. . . . The whole conduct of Colonel Dunbar appears to me monstrous. . . . To march off all the regulars, and leave the fort and frontiers to be defended by four hundred sick and wounded, and the poor remains of our provincial forces, appears to me absurd."

He found some comfort from the burgesses, who gave him forty thousand pounds, and would, he thinks, have given a hundred thousand if another attempt against Fort Duquesne had been set afoot. Shirley, too, whom the death of Braddock had made commander-in-chief, approved the Governor's plan of renewing offensive operations, and instructed Dunbar to that effect; ordering him, however, should they prove impracticable, to march for Albany in aid of the Niagara expedition. The order found him safe in Philadelphia. Here he lingered for a while; then marched to join the northern army, moving at a pace which made it certain that he could not arrive in time to be of the least use.

Thus the frontier was left unguarded; and soon, as Dinwiddie had foreseen, there burst upon it a storm of blood and fire.

GEORGE BANCROFT

(1800-1891)

Long before the successful conclusion of the wars against France, the seeds of discontent had taken firm root in the English colonies. In the years after 1763 the old grievances grew; new ones sprang up, and misunderstandings burgeoned into major crises. Most of the controversies centered on the two questions: To what extent were the colonists entitled to govern themselves? Conversely, in what degree were they obliged to submit to British authority? The popular slogan, "No taxation without representation," came in practice to mean to patriot extremists like Samuel Adams, no British taxation whatever. At the same time extremists in England were ready in practice to strip the colonists of their rights of self-government. This was the mighty principle involved in a trivial tax on tea, and explains why on the night of December 16, 1773, a hundred and fifty of Adams's followers, crudely masquerading as Indians, boarded three East India company ships and threw their cargoes of tea into Boston harbor. The British retaliated firmly, precipitating the final crisis which set off the American Revolution.

The American Revolution

THE CRISIS

THE MINISTRY, OVERRULING THE LINGERING SCRUPLES OF DARTMOUTH
and Lord North, decided that there existed a rebellion which required
coercion. Inquiries were made, with the object of enabling the king to
proceed in "England against the ringleaders," and inflict on them immediate
and exemplary punishment. But, after laborious examinations before the
privy council, and the close attention of Thurlow and Wedderburn, it appeared that British law and the British constitution set bounds to the anger
of the government, which gave the first evidence of its weakness by ac-
knowledging a want of power to wreak its will.

During the delay attending an appeal to parliament, the secretary of
state would speak with the French minister of nothing but harmony; and he
said to the representative of Spain: "Never was the union between Versailles, Madrid, and London so solid; I see nothing that can shake it." Yet the
old distrust lurked under the pretended confidence.

One day in February 1774, while the government feared no formidable
opposition, Charles James Fox, then of the treasury board, censured Lord
North for want of decision and courage. "Greatly incensed at his presumption," the king wrote: "That young man has so thoroughly cast off every
principle of common honor and honesty that he must become as contemptible as he is odious." Dismissed from office, and connected with no party,
he was left free to follow his own generous impulses, and "to discover
powers for regular debate, which neither his friends had hoped nor his
enemies foreboded." Disinterested observers already predicted that he would
one day be classed among the greatest statesmen of his country.

The cause of liberty obtained in him a friend who was independent of
party allegiance and traditions, just when the passion for ruling America
by the central authority was producing anarchy in the colonies. In South
Carolina, whose sons esteemed themselves disfranchised on their own
soil by the appointment of strangers to every office, the governor had for
four years negatived every tax bill, in the hope of controlling the appro-

From Bancroft, *History of the United States of America* (The Author's Last Revision, 6 vols., 1883), vol. 3, ep. 2, ch. 36; vol. 4, ep. 3, ch. 1, 10; vol. 5, ep. 4, ch. 12,
13, ep. 5, ch. 5.

priations. In North Carolina the law establishing courts of justice had expired; in the conflict of claims of power between the governor and the legislature every new law on the subject was negatived, and there were no courts of any kind in the province. The most orderly and the best governed part of Carolina was the self-organized republic of Watauga, beyond the mountains, where the settlements were extending along the Holston, as well as south of the Nollichucky.

An intrepid population, heedless of proclamations, was pouring westward through all the gates of the Alleghanies; seating themselves on the New River and the Greenbrier, on the branches of the Monongahela, or even making their way to the Mississippi; accepting from nature their title-deeds to the unoccupied wilderness. Connecticut kept in mind that its charter bounded its territory by the Pacific; and had already taken courage to claim lands westward to the Mississippi, "seven or eight hundred miles in extent of the finest country and happiest climate on the globe. In fifty years," said they, pleasing themselves with visions of the happiness of their posterity and "the glory of this New World," "our people will be more than half over this tract, extensive as it is; in less than one century the whole may become even well cultivated. If the coming period bears due proportion to that from the first landing of poor distressed fugitives at Plymouth, nothing that we can in the utmost stretch of imagination fancy of the state of this country at an equally future period, can exceed what it will then be. A commerce will and must arise, independent of everything external, and superior to anything ever known in Europe, or of which a European can have an adequate idea." The commerce of Philadelphia and New York had outgrown the laws of trade; and the revenue officers, weary of attempts to enforce them, received what duties were paid almost as a favor.

The New England people who dwelt on each side of the Green Mountains repelled the jurisdiction which the royal government of New York would have enforced even at the risk of bloodshed, and administered their own affairs by means of permanent committees.

The people of Massachusetts knew that "they had passed the river and cut away the bridge." In March, voting the judges of the superior court ample salaries from the colonial treasury, they called upon them to refuse the corrupting donative from the crown. Four of them yielded; Oliver, the chief justice, alone refused; the house, therefore, impeached him before the council, and declared him suspended till the issue of the impeachment. They began to familiarize the public mind to the thought of armed resistance, by ordering some small purchases of powder on account of the colony to be stored in a building of its own, and by directing the purchase of twelve pieces of cannon. "Don't put off the boat till you know where you will land," advised the timid. "We must put off the boat," cried Boston patriots, "even though we do not know where we shall land." "Put off the boat; God will bring us into a safe harbor," said Hawley of Northampton. "Anarchy itself," repeated one to another, "is better than tyranny."

The proposal for a general congress was deferred to the next June; but the committees of correspondence were to prepare the way for it. A circular letter explained why Massachusetts had been under the necessity of proceeding so far of itself, and entreated for its future guidance the benefit of the councils of the whole country. Hancock, on the fifth of March, spoke to a crowded audience in Boston: "Permit me to suggest a general congress of deputies from the several houses of assembly on the continent as the most effectual method of establishing a union for the security of our rights and liberties." "Remember," he continued, "from whom you sprang. Not only pray, but act; if necessary, fight, and even die, for the prosperity of our Jerusalem;" and, as he pointed out Samuel Adams, the vast multitude seemed to promise that in all succeeding times the great patriot's name, and with him "the roll of fellow-patriots, should grace the annals of history."

Samuel Adams prepared the last instructions of Massachusetts to Franklin. "It will be in vain," such were his solemn words officially pronounced, "for any to expect that the people of this country will now be contented with a partial and temporary relief; or that they will be amused by court promises, while they see not the least relaxation of grievances. By means of a brisk correspondence among the several towns in this province they have wonderfully animated and enlightened each other. They are united in sentiments, and their opposition to unconstitutional measures of government is become systematical. Colony begins to communicate freely with colony. There is a common affection among them; and shortly the whole continent will be as united in sentiment and in their measures of opposition to tyranny as the inhabitants of this province. Their old good-will and affection for the parent country are not totally lost; if she returns to her former moderation and good humor, their affection will revive. They wish for nothing more than a permanent union with her upon the condition of equal liberty. This is all they have been contending for; and nothing short of this will or ought to satisfy them."

Such was the ultimatum of America, sent by one illustrious son of Boston for the guidance of another. But the sense of the English people was manifestly with the ministers, who were persuaded that there was no middle way, and that the American continent would not interpose to shield Boston from the necessity of submission.

On the seventh of March, Dartmouth and North, grievously lamenting their want of greater executive power, and the consequent necessity of laying their measures before parliament, presented to the two houses a message from the king. "Nothing," said Lord North, "can be done to reestablish peace without additional powers." "The question now brought to issue," said Rice, on moving the address which was to pledge parliament to the exertion of every means in its power, "is whether the colonies are or are not the colonies of Great Britain." Nugent, now Lord Clare, entreated that there might be no divided counsels. "On the repeal of the stamp act," said Dowdeswell, "all America was quiet; but in the following year you would go in pursuit of a pepper-corn; you would collect from pepper-corn to pepper-corn; you would establish taxes as tests of obedience. Unravel the whole conduct of America; you will find out the fault is at home." "The dependence of the colonies is a part of the constitution," said Pownall, the former governor of Massachusetts. "I hope, for the sake of this country, for the sake of America, for the sake of general liberty, that this address will go with a unanimous vote."

Edmund Burke only taunted the ministry with their wavering policy. Lord George Germain derived all the American disturbance from the repeal of the stamp-tax. Conway pleaded for unanimity. "I speak," said William Burke, "as an Englishman; we applaud ourselves for the struggle we have had for our constitution; the colonists are our fellow-subjects; they will not lose theirs without a struggle." Barré thought the subject had been discussed with good temper, and refused to make any opposition. "The leading question," said Wedderburn, who bore the principle part in the debate, "is the dependence or independence of America." The address was adopted without a division.

In letters which arrived the next day from America, calumny, with its hundred tongues, exaggerated the turbulence of the people, and invented wild tales of violence; so that the king believed there was, in Boston, a regular committee for tarring and feathering; and that they were next, to use his own words, to "pitch and feather" Hutchinson himself. The press roused the national pride, till the zeal of the English people for maintaining English supremacy became equal to the passions of the ministry. Even the merchants and manufacturers were made to believe that their command of the American market depended on the enforcement of British authority.

It was, therefore, to a parliament and people as unanimous as when in Grenville's day they sanctioned the stamp act, that Lord North, on the fourteenth of March, opened the first branch of his American plan by a measure for the instant punishment of Boston. Its port was to be closed against all commerce until it should have indemnified the East India company, and until the king should be satisfied that for the future it would obey the laws. All branches of the government, all political parties, alike those who denied and those who asserted the right to tax, members of parliament, peers, merchants, all ranks and degrees of people, were invited to proceed steadily in the one course of maintaining the authority of Great Britain. Yet it was noticed that Lord North spoke of the indispensable necessity for vigorous measures with an unusual air of languor. This appeal was successful. Of the Rockingham party, Cavendish approved the measure, which was but a corollary from their own declaratory act. "After having weighed the noble lord's proposition well," said even Barré, "I cannot help giving it my hearty and determinate affirmative. I like it, adopt and embrace it for its moderation." "There is no good plan," urged Fox, "except the repeal of the taxes forms a part of it." "The proposition does not fully answer my expectations," said John Calvert; "seize the opportunity, and take away their charter."

On the eighteenth, Lord North, by unanimous consent, presented to the house the Boston port bill. To its second reading, George Bynge was the only one who cried no. "This bill," said Rose Fuller, in the debate, on the twenty-third, "shuts up one of the ports of the greatest commerce and consequence in the English dominions in America. The North Americans will look upon it as a foolish act of oppression. You cannot carry this bill into execution but by a military force." "If a military force is necessary," replied Lord North, "I shall not hesitate a moment to enforce a due obedience to the laws of this country." Fox would have softened the bill by opening the port on the payment of indemnity to the East India company; and he took care that his motion should appear on the journal. "Obedience," replied Lord North, "not indemnification, will be the test of the Bostonians." "The offence of the Americans is flagitious," said Van. "The town of Boston ought to be knocked about their ears and destroyed. You will never meet with proper obedience to the laws of this country until you have destroyed that nest of locusts." The clause to which Fox had objected was adopted without any division, and with but one or two negatives.

The current, within doors and without, set strongly against America. It was only for the acquittal of their own honor and the discharge of their own consciences that, two days later, on the third reading, Dowdeswell and Edmund Burke, unsupported by their former friends, spoke very strongly against a bill which punished the innocent with the guilty, condemned both without an opportunity of defence, deprived the laborer and the sailor of bread, injured English creditors by destroying the trade out of which the debts due them were to be discharged, and ultimately oppressed the English manufacturer. "You will draw a foreign force upon you," said Burke; "I will not say where that will end, but think, I conjure you, of the consequences." "The resolves at Boston," said Gray Cooper, "are a direct issue against the declaratory act;" and half the Rockingham party went with him. Rose Fuller opposed the bill, unless the tax on tea were repealed. Pownall was convinced that the time was not proper for a repeal of the duty on tea. "This is the crisis," said Lord North, who had by degrees assumed a style of authority and decision. "The contest ought to be determined. To repeal the tea duty or any measure would stamp us with timidity." "The present bill," observed Johnstone, late governor of West Florida, "must produce a confederacy, and will end in a general revolt." But it passed without a division, and very unfairly went to the lords as the unanimous voice of the commons. The king sneered at "the feebleness and futility of the opposition."

In the midst of the general anger, a book was circulating in England, on the interest of Great Britain in regard to the colonies, and the only means

of living in peace and harmony with them, which judged the past and estimated the future with calmness and sagacity. Its author, Josiah Tucker,
dean of Gloucester, a most loyal churchman, an apostle of free trade, saw
clearly that the reduction of Canada had put an end to the sovereignty of
the mother country; that it is in the very nature of all colonies, and of the
Americans more than others, to aspire after independence. He would not
suffer things to go on as they had lately done, for that would only make the
colonies more headstrong; nor attempt to persuade them to send over
deputies or representatives to sit in parliament, for that scheme could only
end in furnishing a justification to the mother country for making war
against them; nor have recourse to arms, for the event was uncertain, and
England, if successful, could still never treat America as an enslaved people,
or govern them against their own inclinations. There remained but one
wise solution; and it was to declare the American colonies to be a free and
independent people.

"If we separate from the colonies," it was objected, "we shall lose their
trade." "Why so?" answered Tucker. "The colonies will trade even with
their bitterest enemies in the hottest of a war, provided they shall find it
their interest so to do. The question before us will turn on this single point:
Can the colonists, in a general way, trade with any other European state
to greater advantage than they can with Great Britain? If they cannot, we
shall retain their custom;" and he demonstrated that England was for
America the best market and the best storehouse; that the prodigious increase of British trade was due, not to prohibition, but to the suppression
of monopolies and exclusive companies for foreign trade; to the repeal of
taxes on raw materials; to the improvements, inventions, and discoveries
for the abridgment of labor; to roads, canals, and better postal arrangements. The measure would not decrease shipping and navigation, or dimin-
ish the breed of sailors.

But, "if we give up the colonies," it was pretended, "the French will take
immediate possession of them." "The Americans," resumed Tucker, "cannot brook our government; will they glory in being numbered among the
slaves of the grand monarch?" "Will you leave the church of England in
America to suffer persecution?" asked the churchmen. "Declare North
America independent," replied Tucker, "and all their fears of ecclesiastical
authority will vanish away; a bishop will be no longer looked upon as a
monster, but as a man; and an episcopate may then take place." No minister, he confessed, would dare, as things were then circumstanced, to do
so much good to his country; neither would their opponents wish to see it
done; and "yet," he added, "measures evidently right will prevail at last."

A love of liberty revealed the same truth to John Cartwright. The young
enthusiast was persuaded that humanity, as well as the individual man,
obtains knowledge, wisdom, and virtue progressively, so that its latter days
will be more wise, peaceable, and pious than the earlier periods of its ex-

istence. He was destined to pass his life in efforts to purify the British constitution, which, as he believed, had within itself the seeds of immortality. With the fervid language of sincerity, he advocated the freedom of his American kindred, and proclaimed American independence to be England's interest and glory.

Thus spoke the forerunners of free trade and reforms. But the infatuated people turned from them to indulge unsparingly in ridicule and illiberal jests on the Bostonians, whom the hand of power was extended to chastise and subdue. At the meeting of the commons on the twenty-eighth, Lord North asked leave to bring in a bill for regulating the government of the province of Massachusetts Bay. On this occasion Lord George Germain showed anxiety to take a lead. "I wish," said he, "to see the council of that country on the same footing as that of other colonies. Put an end to their town-meetings. I would not have men of a mercantile cast every day collecting themselves together and debating about political matters. I would have them follow their occupations as merchants, and not consider themselves as ministers of that country. I would wish that all corporate powers might be given to certain people in every town, in the same manner that corporations are formed here. Their juries require regulation. I would wish to bring the constitution of America as similar to our own as possible; to see the council of that country similar to a house of lords in this; to see chancery suits determined by a court of chancery. At present their assembly is a downright clog; their council thwart and oppose the security and welfare of that government. You have no government, no governor; the whole are the proceedings of a tumultuous and riotous rabble, who ought, if they had the least prudence, to follow their mercantile employment, and not trouble themselves with politics and government, which they do not understand. Some gentlemen say: 'Oh, don't break their charter; don't take away rights granted them by the predecessors of the crown.' Whoever wishes to preserve such charters, I wish him no worse than to govern such subjects. By a manly perseverance, things may be restored from anarchy and confusion to peace, quietude, and obedience."

"I thank the noble lord," said Lord North, "for every one of the propositions he has held out; they are worthy of a great mind; I see their propriety, and wish to adopt them;" and the house directed North, Thurlow, and Wedderburn to prepare and bring in a bill accordingly.

On the twenty-ninth of March the Boston port bill underwent in the house of lords a fuller and fairer discussion. Rockingham, supported by the duke of Richmond, resisted it with firmness. "Nothing can justify the ministers hereafter," said Temple, "except the town of Boston proving in an actual state of rebellion." The good Lord Dartmouth called what passed in Boston commotion, not open rebellion. Lord Mansfield, a man "in the cool decline of life," acquainted only with the occupations of peace, a civil magistrate, covered with ermine that should have no stain of blood, with eyes broad open to the consequences, rose to take the guidance of the house out of the hands of the faltering minister. "What passed in Boston," said he, "is the last overt act of high treason, proceeding from our over-lenity and want of foresight. It is, however, the luckiest event that could befall this country; for all may now be recovered. Compensation to the East India company I regard as no object of the bill. The sword is drawn, and you must throw away the scabbard. Pass this act, and you will have passed the Rubicon. The Americans will then know that we shall temporize no longer; if it passes with tolerable unanimity, Boston will submit, and all will end in victory without carnage." In vain did Camden meet the question fully; in vain did Shelburne prove the tranquil and loyal condition in which he had left the colonies on giving up their administration. There was no division in the house of lords; and its journal, like that of the commons, declares that the Boston port bill passed unanimously.

The king in person made haste to give it his approval. To bring Boston on its knees and terrify the rest of America by enforcing the act, Gage, the military commander-in-chief for all North America, received the commission of civil governor of Massachusetts as swiftly as official forms would permit; and, in April, was sent over with four regiments, which he had reported would be sufficient to enforce submission. He was ordered to shut the port of Boston; and, having as a part of his instructions the opinion of Thurlow and Wedderburn, that acts of high treason had been committed there, he was directed to bring the ringleaders to condign punishment. Foremost among these, Samuel Adams was marked out for sacrifice as the chief of the revolution. "He is the most elegant writer, the most sagacious politician, and celebrated patriot, perhaps, of any who have figured in the last ten years," is the contemporary record of John Adams. "I cannot sufficiently respect his integrity and abilities," said Clymer, of Pennsylvania; "all good Americans should erect a statue to him in their hearts." Even where his conduct had been questioned, time proved that he had been right, and many in England "esteemed him the first politician in the world." He saw that "the rigorous measures of the British administration would the sooner bring to pass" the first wish of his heart, "the entire separation and independence of the colonies, which Providence would erect into a mighty empire." Indefatigable in seeking for Massachusetts the countenance of her sister colonies, he had no anxiety for himself, no doubt of the ultimate triumph of freedom; but, as he thought of the calamities that hung over Boston, he raised the prayer "that God would prepare that people for the event by inspiring them with wisdom and fortitude."

"We have enlisted in the cause of our country," said its committee of correspondence, "and are resolved at all adventures to promote its welfare; should we succeed, our names will be held up by future generations with that unfeigned plaudit with which we recount the great deeds of our ancestors." Boston had now no option but to make good its entire independence, or to approach the throne as a penitent, and promise for the future passive "obedience" to British "laws" in all cases whatsoever. In the palace there were no misgivings. "With ten thousand regulars," said the creatures of the ministry, "we can march through the continent."

The act closing the port of Boston did not necessarily provoke a civil war. It was otherwise with the second. The opinion of Lord Mansfield had been obtained in favor of altering the charter of Massachusetts; and the king learned "with supreme satisfaction" that, on the fifteenth of April, a bill to regulate the government of the province of Massachusetts Bay had been read for the first time in the house of commons. Without any hearing or even notice to that province, parliament was to change its charter and its government. Its institution of town-meetings was the most perfect system of local self-government that the world had ever known; the king's measure abolished them, except for the choice of town officers, or on the special permission of the governor. The council had been annually chosen in a convention of the outgoing council and the house of representatives, and men had in this manner been selected more truly loyal than the councillors of any one of the royal colonies; the clause in the charter establishing this method of election was abrogated. The power of appointing and removing sheriffs was conferred on the executive; and the trial by jury was changed into a snare, by intrusting the returning of juries to dependent sheriffs. Lord North placed himself in conflict with institutions sanctioned by royal charters, rooted in custom, confirmed by possession through successive generations, endeared by the just and fondest faith, and infolded in the affections and life of the people.

Against the bill Conway spoke with firmness. The administration, he said, would take away juries from Boston; though Preston, in the midst of an exasperated town, had been acquitted. They sent the sword, but no olive branch. The bill at its different stages in the house of commons was combated by Dowdeswell, Pownall, Sir George Saville, Conway, Burke, Fox, Barré, and most elaborately by Dunning; yet it passed the commons by a vote of more than three to one. Though vehemently opposed in the house of lords, it was carried by a still greater majority, but not without an elaborate protest. The king did not dream that by that act, which, as he writes, gave him "infinite satisfaction," all power of command in Massachusetts had, from that day forth, gone out from him, and that there his word would never more be obeyed.

The immediate repeal of the tax on tea and its preamble remained the only possible avenue to conciliation. On the nineteenth of April this repeal was moved by Rose Fuller in concert with the opposition. The subject in its connections was the gravest that could engage attention, involving the prosperity of England, the tranquillity of the British empire, the principles of colonization, and the liberties of mankind. But Cornwall, speaking for the ministers, stated the question to be simply "whether the whole of

British authority over America should be taken away." On this occasion Edmund Burke pronounced an oration such as had never been heard in the British parliament. His boundless stores of knowledge came obedient at his command; and his thoughts and arguments, the facts which he cited, and his glowing appeals, fell naturally into their places; so that his long and elaborate speech was one harmonious and unbroken emanation from his mind. He first demonstrated that the repeal of the tax would be productive of unmixed good; he then surveyed comprehensively the whole series of the parliamentary proceedings with regard to America, in their causes and their consequences. After exhausting the subject, he entreated parliament to "reason not at all," but to "oppose the ancient policy and practice on the empire, as a rampart against the speculations of innovators on both sides of the question."

"Again and again," such was his entreaty, "revert to your old principles; seek peace and ensue it; leave America, if she has taxable matter, to tax herself. Be content to bind America by laws of trade; you have always done it; let this be your reason for binding their trade. Do not burden them by taxes; you were not used to do so from the beginning. Let this be your reason for not taxing. These are the arguments of states and kingdoms. Leave the rest to the schools. The several provincial legislatures ought all to be subordinate to the parliament of Great Britain. She, as from the throne of heaven, superintends and guides and controls them all. To coerce, to restrain, and to aid, her powers must be boundless."

During the long debate, the young and fiery Lord Carmarthen had repeated what so many had said before him: "The Americans are our children, and how can they revolt against their parent? If they are not free in their present state, England is not free, because Manchester and other considerable places are not represented." "So, then," retorted Burke, "because some towns in England are not represented, America is to have no representative at all. Is it because the natural resistance of things and the various mutations of time hinder our government, or any scheme of government, from being any more than a sort of approximation to the right, is it therefore that the colonies are to recede from it infinitely? When this child of ours wishes to assimilate to its parent, are we to give them our weakness for their strength, our opprobrium for their glory? and the slough of slavery which we are not able to work off, to serve them for their freedom?"

The words fell from him as burning oracles; while he spoke for the rights of America, he seemed to prepare the way for renovating the constitution of England. Yet it was not so. Though more than half a century had intervened, Burke would not be wiser than the whigs of the days of King William. It was enough for him if the aristocracy applauded. He did not believe in the dawn of a new light, in the coming on of a new order, though a new order of things was at the door, and a new light had broken. He would not turn to see, nor bend to learn, if the political system of Somers and Walpole and the Pelhams was to pass away; if it were so, he himself was determined not to know it, but "rather to be the last of that race of men." As Dante sums up the civilization of the middle age so that its departed spirit still lives in his immortal verse, Burke idealizes as he portrays the lineaments of that old whig aristocracy which in its day achieved mighty things for liberty and for England. He that will study under its best aspect the enlightened character of England in the first half of the eighteenth century, the wonderful intermixture of privilege and prerogative, of aristocratic power and popular liberty, of a free press and a secret house of commons, of an established church and a toleration of Protestant sects, of a fixed adherence to prescription and liberal tendencies in administration, must give his days and nights to the writings of Edmund Burke. But time never keeps company with the mourners; it flies from the memories of the expiring past, though clad in the brightest colors of imagination; it leaves those who stand still to their despair, and hurries onward to fresh fields of action and scenes forever new.

Resuming the debate, Fox said, earnestly: "If you persist in your right to tax the Americans, you will force them into open rebellion." On the other hand, Lord North asked that his measures might be sustained with firmness and resolution; and then, said he, "there is no doubt but peace and quietude will soon be restored." "We are now in great difficulties," said Dowdeswell, speaking for all who adhered to Lord Rockingham; "let us do justice before it is too late." But it was too late. Even Burke's motive had been "to refute the charges against that party with which he had all along acted." After his splendid eloquence, no more divided with him than forty-nine, just the number that had divided against the stamp act, while on the other side stood nearly four times as many. The repeal of the tea-tax was never to be obtained so long as the authority of parliament was publicly rejected or opposed.

On the day on which the house of commons was voting not to repeal the duty on tea, the people of New York sent back the tea-ship which had arrived but the day before; and eighteen chests of tea, found on board of another vessel, were hoisted on deck and emptied into "the slip."

A third penal measure, which had been questioned by Dartmouth and recommended by the king, transferred the place of trial of any magistrates, revenue officers, or soldiers, indicted for murder or other capital offence in Massachusetts Bay, to Nova Scotia or Great Britain. As Lord North brought forward this wholesale bill of indemnity to the governor and soldiers, if they should trample upon the people of Boston and be charged with murder, it was noticed that he trembled and faltered at every word, showing that he was the vassal of a stronger will than his own, and vainly struggled to wrestle down the feelings which his nature refused to disavow. "If the people of America," said Van, "oppose the measures of government that are now sent, I would do as was done of old in the time of the ancient

Britons: I would burn and set fire to all their woods, and leave their country open. If we are likely to lose it, I think it better lost by our own soldiers than wrested from us by our rebellious children." "The bill is meant to enslave America," said Sawbridge, with only forty to listen to him. "I execrate the present measure," cried Barré; "you have had one meeting of the colonies in congress; you may soon have another. The Americans will not abandon their principles; for, if they submit, they are slaves."

The bill passed the commons by a vote of more than four to one. But evil comes intermixed with good: the ill is evanescent, the good endures. The British government inflamed the passions of the English people against America, and courted their sympathy; as a consequence, the secrecy of the debates in parliament came to an end; and this great change in the political relation of the legislature to public opinion was the irrevocable concession of a tory government, seeking strength from popular excitement.

A fourth measure legalized the quartering of troops within the town of Boston. The fifth professed to regulate the affairs of the province of Quebec. The nation, which would not so much as legally recognise the existence of a Catholic in Ireland, from political considerations sanctioned on the St. Lawrence "the free exercise of the religion of the church of Rome, and confirmed to its clergy their accustomed dues and rights," with the tithes as fixed in 1672 by the edict of Louis XIV. But the act did not stop there. In disregard of the charters and rights of Massachusetts, Connecticut, New York, and Virginia, it extended the boundaries of the new government of Quebec to the Ohio and the Mississippi, and over the region which included, besides Canada, the area of the present states of Ohio, Michigan, Indiana, Illinois, and Wisconsin; and, moreover, it decreed for this great part of a continent an unmixed arbitrary rule. The establishment of colonies on principles of liberty is "the peculiar and appropriated glory of England," rendering her venerable throughout all time in the history of the world. The office of peopling a continent with free and happy commonwealths was renounced. The Quebec bill, which quickly passed the house of lords without an adverse petition or a protest, and was borne through the commons by the zeal of the ministry and the influence of the king, left the people who were to colonize the most fertile territory in the world without the writ of habeas corpus to protect the rights of persons, and without a share of power in any one branch of the government. "The Quebec constitution," said Thurlow, in the house of commons, "is the only proper constitution for colonies; it ought to have been given to them all, when first planted; and it is what all now ought to be reduced to."

In this manner Great Britain, allured by a phantom of absolute authority over colonies, made war on human freedom. The liberties of Poland had been sequestered, and its territory began to be parcelled out among the usurpers. The aristocratic privileges of Sweden had been swept away by treachery and usurpation. The free towns of Germany, which had preserved in that empire the example of republics, were "like so many dying sparks that go out one after another." Venice and Genoa had stifled the spirit of independence in their prodigal luxury. Holland was ruinously divided against itself. In Great Britain, the house of commons had become so venal that it might be asked whether a body so chosen and so influenced was fit to legislate even within the realm. If it shall succeed in establishing by force of arms its "boundless" authority over America, where shall humanity find an asylum! But this decay of the old forms of liberty was the forerunner of a new creation. The knell of the ages of servitude and inequality was rung; those of equality and brotherhood were to come in.

As the fleets and armies of England went forth to consolidate arbitrary power, the sound of war everywhere else on the earth died away. Kings sat still in awe, and nations turned to watch the issue.

AMERICA SUSTAINS THE TOWN OF BOSTON

The hour of the American revolution was come. The people of the continent obeyed one general impulse, as the earth in spring listens to the command of nature and without the appearance of effort bursts into life. The movement was quickened, even when it was most resisted; and its fiercest adversaries worked with the most effect for its fulfilment. Standing in manifold relations with the governments, the culture, and the experience of the past, the Americans seized as their peculiar inheritance the traditions of liberty. Beyond any other nation, they had made trial of the possible forms of popular representation, and respected individual conscience and thought. The resources of the country in agriculture and commerce, forests and fisheries, mines and materials for manufactures, were so diversified and complete that their development could neither be guided nor circumscribed by a government beyond the ocean. The numbers, purity, culture, industry, and daring of its inhabitants proclaimed the existence of a people rich in creative energy, and ripe for institutions of their own.

They refused to acknowledge even to themselves the hope that was swelling within them, and yet in their political aspirations they deduced from universal principles a bill of rights, as old as creation and as wide as humanity. The idea of freedom had always revealed itself at least to a few of the wise whose prophetic instincts were quickened by love of their kind, and its growth can be traced in the tendency of the ages. In America, it was the breath of life to the people. For the first time it found a region and a race where it could be professed with the earnestness of an indwelling conviction, and be defended with the enthusiasm that had marked no wars but those for religion. When all Europe slumbered over questions of liberty, a band of exiles, keeping watch by night, heard the glad tidings which promised the political regeneration of the world. A revolution, unexpected in the moment of its coming, but prepared by glorious forerunners, grew naturally and necessarily out of the series of past events by the formative principle of a living belief. And why should man organize resistance to the grand design of Providence! Why should not the consent of the ancestral land and the gratulations of every other call the young nation to its place among the powers of the earth? Britain was the mighty mother who bred men capable of laying the foundation of so noble an empire, and she alone could have trained them up. She had excelled all the world as the founder of colonies. The condition which entitled them to independence was now fulfilled. Their vigorous vitality refused conformity to foreign laws and external rule. They could take no other way to perfection than by the unconstrained development of that which was within them. They were not only able to govern themselves, they alone were able to do so; subordination visibly repressed their energies. Only by self-direction could they at all times employ their collective and individual faculties in the fullest extent of their ever-increasing intelligence. Could not the illustrious nation, which had gained no distinction in war, in literature, or in science, comparable to that of having wisely founded distant settlements on a system of liberty, willingly perfect its beneficent work, now when no more was required than the acknowledgment that its offspring was come of age? Why must the ripening of lineal virtue be struck at, as rebellion in the lawful sons? Why is their unwavering attachment to the essential principle of their existence to be persecuted as treason, rather than viewed with delight as the crowning glory of the country from which they sprung? If the institutions of Britain were so deeply fixed in its usages and opinions that their deviations from justice could not as yet be rectified; if the old continent was pining under systems of authority not fit to be borne, and not ripe for amendment, why should not a people be heartened to build a commonwealth in the wilderness, where alone it was offered a home?

So reasoned a few in Britain, who were jeered at "as visionary enthusiasts." Parliament had asserted an absolute lordship over the colonies in all cases whatsoever, and, fretting itself into a frenzy at the denial of its unlimited dominion, was destroying its recognised authority by its eagerness for more. The majority of the ministers, including the most active and resolute, were bent on the immediate employment of force. Lord North, recoiling from civil war, exercised no control over his colleagues, leaving the government to be conducted by the several departments. As a consequence, the king became the only point of administrative union. In him an approving conscience had no misgiving as to his duty. His heart knew no relenting; his will never wavered. Though America were to be drenched in blood and its towns reduced to ashes, though its people were to be driven to struggle for total independence, though he himself should find it necessary to bid high for hosts of mercenaries from the Scheldt to Moscow, and in quest of savage allies go tapping at every wigwam from Lake Huron to the

Gulf of Mexico, he was resolved to coerce the thirteen colonies into submission.

On the tenth of May 1774, which was the day of the accession of Louis XVI, the act closing the port of Boston, transferring the board of customs to Marblehead, and the seat of government to Salem, reached the devoted town. The king was confident that the slow torture which was to be applied to its inhabitants would constrain them to cry out for mercy and promise unconditional obedience. Success in resistance could come only from an American union, which was not to be hoped for, unless Boston should offer herself as a willing sacrifice. The mechanics and merchants and laborers, altogether scarcely so many as thirty-five hundred able-bodied men, knew that they were acting not for a province of America, but for freedom itself. They were inspired by the thought that the Providence which rules the world demanded of them heroic self-denial as the champions of humanity, and they never doubted the fellow-feeling of the continent.

As soon as the act was received, the Boston committee of correspondence, by the hand of Joseph Warren, invited eight neighboring towns to a conference "on the critical state of public affairs." On the twelfth, at noon, Metcalf Bowler, the speaker of the assembly of Rhode Island, came before them with the cheering news that, in answer to a recent circular letter from the body over which he presided, all the thirteen governments had pledged themselves to union. Punctually, at the hour of three in the afternoon of that day, the committees of Dorchester, Roxbury, Brookline, Newton, Cambridge, Charlestown, Lynn, and Lexington, joined them in Faneuil Hall, the cradle of American liberty, where for ten years the freemen of the town had debated the question of justifiable resistance. The lowly men who now met there were most of them accustomed to feed their own cattle, to fold their own sheep, to guide their own ploughs; all were trained to public life in the little democracies of their towns; some of them were captains in the militia and officers of the church according to the discipline of Congregationalists; nearly all of them communicants, under a public covenant with God. They grew in greatness as their sphere enlarged. Their virtues burst the confines of village life. They felt themselves to be citizens not of little municipalities, but of the whole world of mankind. In the dark hour, light broke upon them from their own truth and courage. Placing Samuel Adams at their head, and guided by a report prepared by Joseph Warren of Boston, Thomas Gardner of Cambridge, and others, they agreed unanimously on the injustice and cruelty of the act, by which parliament, without competent jurisdiction and contrary as well to natural right as to the laws of all civilized states, had, without a hearing, set apart, accused, tried, and condemned the town of Boston. The delegates from the eight towns were reminded by those of Boston that that port could recover its trade by paying for the tea which had been thrown overboard; but they held it unworthy even to notice the offer, promising on their part to join "their suffering brethren in every measure of relief."

The meeting knew that a declaration of independence would have alienated their sister colonies, nor had they as yet found out that independence was the desire of their own hearts. To suggest nothing till a congress could be convened would have seemed to them like abandoning the town to bleed away its life. The king had expected to starve its people into submission; in their circular letter to the committees of the other colonies they proposed, as a counter action, a general cessation of trade with Britain. "Now," they added, "is the time when all should be united in opposition to this violation of the liberties of all. The single question is, whether you consider Boston as suffering in the common cause, and sensibly feel and resent the injury and affront offered to her? We cannot believe otherwise; assuring you that, not in the least intimidated by this inhuman treatment, we are still determined to maintain to the utmost of our abilities the rights of America."

The next day, while Gage was sailing into the harbor, Samuel Adams presided over a very numerous town-meeting, at which many were present who had hitherto kept aloof. The thought of republican Rome, in its purest age, animated their consultations. The port act was read, and in bold debate was pronounced repugnant to law, religion, and common sense. At the same time those, who from loss of employment were to be the first to encounter want, were remembered with tender compassion, and measures were put in train to comfort them. Then the inhabitants, by the hand of Samuel Adams, made their appeal "to all the sister colonies, inviting a universal suspension of exports and imports, promising to suffer for America with a becoming fortitude, confessing that singly they might find their trial too severe, and entreating not to be left to struggle alone, when the very being of every colony, considered as a free people, depended upon the event."

On the seventeenth, Gage, who had remained four days with Hutchinson at Castle William, landed at Long Wharf, amid salutes from ships and batteries. Received by the council and civil officers, he was escorted by the Boston cadets, whom Hancock commanded, to the state-house, where the council presented a loyal address, and his commission was proclaimed with three volleys of musketry and as many cheers. He then partook of a public dinner in Faneuil Hall, at which he proposed "the prosperity of the town of Boston." His toast in honor of Hutchinson "was received with a general hiss." Yet many favored a compromise, and put forward a subscription to pay for the tea. On the eighteenth, Jonathan Amory very strongly urged that measure in town-meeting, but it was rejected by the common voice. There still lingered a hope of relief through the intercession of Gage; but he was fit neither to reconcile nor to subdue. By his mild temper and love of society he gained the good-will of his boon companions and escaped personal enmities; but in earnest business he inspired neither confidence nor fear. He was so poor in spirit and so weak of will, so dull in his perceptions and so unsettled in his opinions, that he was sure to vacillate between words of concession and merciless severity. He had promised the king that with four regiments he would play the "lion," and troops beyond his requisition were hourly expected; but he stood too much in dread of the leading patriots of Boston to attempt their arrest.

The people of Massachusetts were almost exclusively of English origin; beyond any other colony, they loved the land of their ancestors; for that reason were they more sensitive to its tyranny. Taxing them without their consent was robbing them of their birthright; they scorned the British parliament as "a junto of the servants of the crown, rather than the representatives of England." Not disguising to themselves their danger, but confident of victory, they were resolved to stand together as brothers for a life of liberty.

The merchants of Newburyport were the first who agreed to suspend all commerce with Britain and Ireland. Salem, the place marked out as the new seat of government, in a very full town-meeting and after unimpassioned debates, decided almost unanimously to stop trade not with Britain only, but even with the West Indies. If in Boston a few still proposed to purchase a relaxation of the blockade by "a subscription to pay for the tea," the majority were beset by no temptation so strong as that of routing at once the insignificant number of troops who had come to overawe them. But Samuel Adams, while he compared their spirit to that of Sparta or Rome, inculcated "patience as the characteristic of a patriot;" and the people, having sent forth their cry to the continent, waited self-possessed for voices of consolation.

New York anticipated the prayer of Boston. Its people who had received the port act directly from England, felt the wrong to that town as a wound to themselves, and even the lukewarm kindled with resentment. From the epoch of the stamp act, their Sons of Liberty, styled by the royalists "the Presbyterian junto," had kept up a committee of correspondence. Yet Sears, Macdougall, and Lamb, still its principal members, represented the mechanics of the city more than its merchants; and they never enjoyed the confidence of the great landed proprietors, who by the tenure of estates in New York formed a recognised aristocracy. To unite the province, a more comprehensive combination was required. The old committee, while they accepted the questionable policy of an immediate suspension of commerce with Britain, proposed a general congress of deputies from all the colonies. These recommendations they forwarded through Connecticut to Boston, with entreaties to that town to stand firm; and, in full confidence of approval, they sent them to Philadelphia, and through Philadelphia to every colony at the south.

The inception of the continental congress of 1774 was the last achievement of the Sons of Liberty of New York. On the evening of the sixteenth of May they convoked the inhabitants of their city. A sense of the impending

change tempered passionate rashness. Some who were in a secret understanding with officers of the crown sought to evade all decisive measures;
the merchants were averse to headlong engagements for suspending trade;
the gentry feared lest the men who on all former occasions had led the
multitude should preserve the control in the day which was felt to be near
at hand, when an independent people would shape the permanent institutions of a continent. Under a conservative influence, the motion prevailed
to supersede the old committee of correspondence by a new one of fifty,
and its members were selected by open nomination. The choice included
men from all classes. Nearly a third part were of those who followed the
British standard to the last; others were lukewarm, unsteady, and blind to
the nearness of revolution; others again were enthusiastic Sons of Liberty.
The friends to government claimed that the majority was inflexibly loyal;
the control fell into the hands of men who still aimed at reconciling a
continued dependence on England with the just freedom of the colonies.

The port act was rapidly circulated through the country. In some places
it was printed upon paper with a black border, and cried about the streets
as a barbarous murder; in others, it was burnt in the presence of a crowd
of the people. On the seventeenth, the representatives of Connecticut made
a declaration of rights. "Let us play the man," said they, "for the cause of
our country; and trust the event to Him who orders all events for the best
good of his people." On the same day, the freemen of the town of Providence, unsolicited from abroad and after full discussion, voted to promote "a
congress of the representatives of all the North American colonies." Declaring "personal liberty an essential part of the natural rights of mankind," they
expressed the wish to prohibit the importation of negro slaves, and to set
free all negroes born in the colony.

On the nineteenth, the city and county of New York inaugurated their
new committee with the formality of public approval. Two parties appeared
in array: on the one side, men of property; on the other, tradesmen and
mechanics. Foreboding a revolution, they seemed to contend in advance
whether their future government should be formed upon the basis of property or on purely popular principles. The mass of the people were ready
to found a new social order in which they would rule; but on that day they
chose to follow the wealthier class if it would but make with them a common cause; and the nomination of the committee was accepted, even with
the addition of Isaac Low as its chairman, who was more of a loyalist than
a patriot.

In Philadelphia, where Wedderburn and Hutchinson had been burnt in
effigy, the letter from the New York Sons of Liberty had been received, and
when, on the nineteenth, the messenger from Boston arrived with despatches, he found Charles Thomson, Thomas Mifflin, Joseph Reed, and
others preparing to call a public meeting on the evening of the next day.

On the morning of the twentieth, the king gave in person his assent to the act which made the British commander-in-chief in America, his army, and the civil officers, no longer amenable to American courts of justice; and to the act which mutilated the charter of Massachusetts, and destroyed the freedom of its town-meetings. "The law," wrote Garnier, "the extremely intelligent" French chargé, "must either lead to the complete reduction of the colonies, or clear the way for their independence." "I wish from the bottom of my heart," said the duke of Richmond, during a debate in the house of lords, "that the Americans may resist, and get the better of the forces sent against them." Four years later, Fox observed: "The alteration of the government of Massachusetts was certainly a most capital mistake, because it gave the whole continent reason to think that their government was liable to be subverted at our pleasure and rendered entirely despotic. From thence all were taught to consider the town of Boston as suffering in the common cause."

While the king, in the presence of parliament, was accepting the laws which began a civil war, in Philadelphia the Presbyterians, true to their traditions, held it right to resist tyranny; "the Germans, who composed a large part of the inhabitants of the province were all on the side of liberty;" the merchants refused to sacrifice their trade; the Quakers in any event scrupled to use arms; a numerous class, like Reed, cherished the most passionate desire for a reconciliation with the mother country. The cause of America needed intrepid counsellors; but the great central state fell under the influence of Dickinson. His claims to public respect were indisputable. He was honored for spotless morals, eloquence, and good service in the colonial legislature. His writings had endeared him to America as a sincere friend of liberty. Residing at a country seat which overlooked Philadelphia and the Delaware river, he delighted in study and repose, and wanted boldness of will. "He had an excellent heart, and the cause of his country lay near it;" "he loved the people of Boston with the tenderness of a brother;" yet he was more jealous of their zeal than touched by their sorrows. "They will have time enough to die," were his words on that morning. "Let them give the other provinces opportunity to think and resolve. If they expect to drag them by their own violence into mad measures, they will be left to perish by themselves, despised by their enemies, and almost detested by their friends." Having matured his scheme in solitude, he received at dinner Thomson, Mifflin, and Reed, who, for the sake of his public co-operation, acquiesced in his delays.

In the evening, about three hundred of the principal citizens of Philadelphia assembled in the long room of the City Tavern. The letter from the Sons of Liberty of New York was read aloud, as well as the letters from Boston. Two measures were thus brought under discussion: that of New York for a congress, that of Boston for an immediate cessation of trade. The latter proposition was received with loud and general murmurs. Dickinson, having conciliated the wavering merchants by expressing himself strongly against it, was heard with applause as he spoke for a general congress. He insisted, however, on a preliminary petition to his friend John Penn, the proprietary governor, to call together the legislature of the colony. This request every one knew would be refused. But then, reasoned Mifflin and the ardent politicians, a committee of correspondence, after the model of Boston, must, in consequence of the refusal, be named for the several counties in the province. Delegates will then be appointed to a general congress; "and, when the colonies are once united in councils, what may they not effect?" At an early hour Dickinson retired from the meeting, of which the spirit far exceeded his own; but even the most zealous acknowledged the necessity of deferring to his advice. Accepting, therefore, moderation and prudence as their watchwords, they did little more than resolve that Boston was suffering in the general cause; and they appointed a committee of intercolonial correspondence, with Dickinson as its chief.

On the next day, the committee, at a meeting from which Dickinson stayed away, in a letter to Boston drafted mainly by William Smith, embodied the system which, for the coming year, was to control the counsels of America. It proposed a general congress of deputies from the different colonies, who, in firm but dutiful terms, should make to the king a petition of their rights. This, it was believed, would be granted through the influence of the wise and good in the mother country; and the most sanguine predicted that the very idea of a general congress would compel a change in the policy of Great Britain.

In like manner, the fifty-one who now represented the city and county of New York adopted from their predecessors the plan of a continental congress, and to that body they referred all questions relating to commerce, thus postponing the proposal for an immediate suspension of trade, but committing themselves irrevocably to union and resistance. At the same time, they invited every county in the colony to make choice of a committee.

The messenger, on his return with the letters from Philadelphia and New York, found the people of Connecticut anxious for a congress, even if it should not at once embrace the colonies south of the Potomac; and their committee wisely entreated Massachusetts to fix the place and time for its meeting.

At Boston, the agents and supporters of the British ministers strove to bend the firmness of its people by holding up to the tradesmen the grim picture of misery and want; while Hutchinson promised to obtain in England a restoration of trade, if the town would but pay the first cost of the tea. Before his departure, one hundred and twenty-three merchants and others of Boston addressed him, "lamenting the loss of so good a governor," confessing the propriety of indemnifying the East India company, and appealing to his most benevolent disposition to procure by his representations some speedy relief; but at a full meeting of the merchants and traders the address was disclaimed. Thirty-three citizens of Marblehead, who signed a similar paper, brought upon themselves the public reprobation of their townsmen. Twenty-four lawyers, including judges of admiralty and attorneys of the crown, subscribed an extravagant panegyric of Hutchinson's general character and conduct; but those who for learning and integrity most adorned their profession, withheld their names.

On the other hand, the necessity of a response to the courage of the people, the hearty adhesion of the town of Providence, and the cheering letter from the old committee of New York, animated a majority of the merchants of Boston, and through their example those of the province, to an engagement to cease all importations from England. Confidence prevailed that their brethren, at least as far south as Philadelphia, would embrace the same mode of peaceful resistance. The letter from that city was received with impatience. But Samuel Adams suppressed all murmurs. "I am fully of the Farmer's sentiments," said he; "violence and submission would at this time be equally fatal;" but he exerted himself the more to promote the immediate suspension of commerce.

The legislature of Massachusetts, on the last Wednesday of May, organized the government for the year by the usual election of councillors; of these, the governor negatived thirteen, among them James Bowdoin, Samuel Dexter, William Phillips, and John Adams, than whom the province could not show purer or abler men. The desire of the assembly that he would appoint a fast was refused; "for," said he to Dartmouth, "the request was only to give an opportunity for sedition to flow from the pulpit." On Saturday, the twenty-eighth, Samuel Adams was on the point of proposing a general congress, when the assembly was unexpectedly prorogued, to meet after ten days at Salem.

The people of Boston, then the most flourishing commercial town on the continent, never regretted their being the principal object of ministerial vengeance. "We shall suffer in a good cause," said the thousands who depended on their daily labor for bread; "the righteous Being, who takes care of the ravens that cry unto him, will provide for us and ours."

Hearts glowed warmly on the banks of the Patapsco. That admirable site for commerce—whose river-side and hill-tops are now covered with stately warehouses, mansions, and monuments, whose bay sparkles round the prows of the swiftest barks, whose wharfs invite the wealth of the West Indies and South America, and whose happy enterprise, availing itself of its nearness to the west, sends across the mountains its iron pathway of many arms—had for a century been tenanted only by straggling cottages. But its convenient proximity to the border counties of Pennsylvania and Virginia had been observed by Scotch-Irish Presbyterians and others; and within a few years they had created the town of Baltimore, which already was the chief emporium within the Chesapeake bay. When the messages from the old committee of New York, from Philadelphia, and from Boston, reached its inhabitants, they could not "see the least grounds

for expecting relief from a petition and remonstrance." Calling to mind
the contempt with which for ten years their petitions had been thrust aside,
they were "convinced that something more sensible than supplications
would best serve their purpose."

After consultation with the men of Annapolis, who promptly resolved
to stop all trade with Great Britain, the inhabitants of the city and county
of Baltimore advocated suspending commerce with Great Britain and the
West Indies, chose deputies to a colonial convention, recommended a continental congress, appointed a numerous committee of correspondence, and
sent cheering words to their "friends" at Boston. "The Supreme Disposer
of all events," said they, "will terminate this severe trial of your patience
in a happy confirmation of American freedom." For this spirited conduct,
Baltimore was applauded as the model; and its example kindled new life
in New York.

On the twenty-eighth, the assembly of New Hampshire, though still
desiring to promote harmony with the parent land, began its organization
for resisting encroachments on American rights.

Three days later, the people of New Jersey declared for a suspension
of trade and a congress, and claimed "to be fellow-sufferers with Boston
in the cause of liberty."

For South Carolina, the character of its labor forbade all thought of
rivalling British skill in manufactures. Its wealthy inhabitants, shunning the
occupations of city life, loved to reside in hospitable elegance on their large
and productive estates. Its annual exports to the northern provinces were
of small account, while to Great Britain they exceeded two millions of
dollars in value. Enriched by this commerce, its people cherished a warm
affection for the mother country, and delighted in sending their sons
"home," as England was called, for their education. The harbor of Charleston was almost unguarded, except by the sand-bar at its entrance. The
Creeks and Cherokees on the frontier, against whom the English government had once been solicited by South Carolina herself to send over a
body of troops as a protection, were still numerous and warlike. The negro
slaves, who in the country near the ocean very far outnumbered the free,
were so many hostages for the allegiance of their masters. The trade of
Charleston was in the hands of British factors, some of whom speculated
already on the coming confiscations of the rice-swamps and indigo-fields
of "many a bonnie rebel." The upland country was numerously peopled
by loyal men who felt no grievances. And yet the planters refused to take
counsel of their interests or their danger. "Boston," said they, "is but the
first victim at the altar of tyranny." Reduced to the dilemma either to hold
their liberties as tenants at will of the British house of commons, or to
prepare for resistance, their choice was never in doubt. "The whole continent," they said, "must be animated with one great soul, and all Americans
must resolve to stand by one another even unto death. Should they fail, the

constitution of the mother country itself would lose its excellence." They knew the imminent ruin which they risked; but they "remembered that the happiness of many generations and many millions depended on their spirit and constancy."

The burgesses of Virginia sat as usual in May. The extension of the province to the west and north-west was their great ambition, which the governor, greedy of a large possession of land and of fees for conniving at the acquisitions of others, selfishly seconded in flagrant disregard of his instructions. To Lady Dunmore, who had just arrived, the assembly voted a congratulatory address, and its members invited her to a ball. The thought of revolution was not harbored; but they none the less held it their duty to resist the systematic plan of parliamentary despotism; and, without waiting for an appeal from Boston, they resolved on its deliverance. First among them as an orator stood Patrick Henry. But eloquence was his least merit: he was revered as the ideal of a patriot of Rome in its austerest age. At the approach of danger his language gained the boldness of prophecy. He was borne up by the strong support of Richard Henry Lee and Washington. It chanced that George Mason was then at Williamsburg, a man of strong and true affections; learned in constitutional law; a profound reasoner; honest and fearless in council; shunning the way of ambition from sorrow at the death of his wife for whom he never ceased to mourn; but earnestly mindful of his country, as became one whose chastened spirit looked beyond the interests of the moment. After deliberation with these associates, Jefferson prepared the resolution which, on the twenty-fourth, at the instance of Robert Carter Nicholas, the house of burgesses adopted. In the name of Virginia it recommended to their fellow-citizens that the day on which the Boston port act was to take effect should be set apart "as a day of fasting and prayer, devoutly to implore the divine interposition for averting the dreadful calamity which threatened destruction to their civil rights, and the evils of a civil war; and to give to the American people one heart and one mind firmly to oppose, by all just and proper means, every injury to American rights." The resolve, which bound only the members themselves, was distributed by express through their respective counties as a general invitation to the people. Especially Washington sent the notice to his constituents; and Mason charged his little household of sons and daughters to keep the day strictly, and attend church clad in mourning.

On the morning which followed the adoption of this measure Dunmore dissolved the house. The burgesses immediately repaired to the Raleigh tavern, about one hundred paces from the capitol; and with Peyton Randolph, their late speaker, in the chair, voted that the attack on Massachusetts was an attack on all the colonies, to be opposed by the united wisdom of all. In conformity with this declaration, they advised for future time an annual continental congress. They named Peyton Randolph, with others, a committee of correspondence to invite a general concurrence in this design. As yet social relations were not imbittered. Washington, of whom Dunmore sought information respecting western affairs, continued his visits at the governor's house; the ball in honor of Lady Dunmore was well attended. Not till the offices of courtesy and of patriotism were fulfilled did most of the burgesses return home, leaving their committee on duty.

On the afternoon of Sunday, the twenty-ninth, the letters from Boston reached Williamsburg. So important did they appear that the next morning, at ten o'clock, the committee, having called to their aid Washington and all other burgesses who were still in town, inaugurated a revolution. Being but twenty-five in number, they refused to assume the responsibility of definite measures of resistance; but, as the province was without a legislature, they summoned a convention of delegates to be elected by the several counties, and to meet at the capitol on the first day of the ensuing August.

The rescue of freedom even at the cost of a civil war, a convention of the people for the regulation of their own internal affairs, an annual congress of all the colonies for the perpetual assertion of common rights, were the policy of Virginia. When the report of her measures reached England, the startled ministers called to mind how often she had been the model for other colonies. Her influence continued undiminished; and her system was promptly adopted by the people of North Carolina.

"Lord North had no expectation that we should be thus sustained," said Samuel Adams; "he trusted that Boston would be left to fall alone." In three weeks after the receipt of the port act, less time than was taken by the unanimous British parliament for its enactment, the continent, as "one great commonwealth," made the cause of Boston its own.

TO LEXINGTON AND CONCORD, AND BACK TO BOSTON

Gage, who had under his command about three thousand effective men, was informed by his spies of military stores, pitiful in their amount, collected by provincial committees at Worcester and Concord; and he resolved on striking a blow, as the king desired. On the afternoon of the day on which the provincial congress of Massachusetts adjourned he took the light infantry and grenadiers off duty, and secretly prepared an expedition to destroy the colony's stores at Concord. The attempt had for several weeks been expected; and signals were concerted to announce the first movement of troops for the country. Samuel Adams and Hancock, who had not yet left Lexington for Philadelphia, received a timely message from Warren, and, in consequence, the committee of safety removed a part of the public stores and secreted the cannon.

On Tuesday, the eighteenth of April, ten or more British sergeants in disguise dispersed themselves through Cambridge and farther west to intercept all communication. In the following night the grenadiers and light infantry, not less than eight hundred in number, the flower of the army at Boston, commanded by Lieutenant-Colonel Smith, crossed in the boats of the transport ships from the foot of the common to East Cambridge. There they received a day's provisions; and near midnight, after wading through wet marshes that are now covered by a stately city, they took the road through West Cambridge to Concord.

Gage directed that no one else should leave the town; but Warren had, at ten o'clock, despatched William Dawes through Roxbury, and Paul Revere by way of Charlestown, to Lexington.

Revere stopped only to engage a friend to raise the concerted signals, and two friends rowed him across Charles river five minutes before the sentinels received the order to prevent it. All was still, as suited the hour. The Somerset man-of-war was winding with the young flood; the waning moon just peered above a clear horizon; while, from a couple of lanterns in the tower of the North church, the beacon streamed to the neighboring towns as fast as light could travel.

A little beyond Charlestown neck, Revere was intercepted by two British officers on horseback; but, being well mounted, he turned suddenly, and escaped by the road to Medford. Of that town, he waked the captain of the minute-men, and continued to rouse almost every house on the way to Lexington. The troops had not advanced far when the firing of guns and ringing of bells announced that their expedition had been heralded; and Smith sent back for a re-enforcement.

In the earliest moments of the nineteenth of April the message from Warren reached Adams and Hancock, who at once divined the object of the expedition. Revere, therefore, and Dawes, joined by Samuel Prescott, "a high Son of Liberty" from Concord, rode forward, calling up the inhabitants as they passed along, till in Lincoln they fell upon a party of British officers. Revere and Dawes were seized and taken back to Lexington, where they were released; but Prescott leaped over a low stone wall, and galloped on for Concord.

There, at about two hours after midnight, a peal from the bell of the meeting-house brought together the inhabitants of the place, young and old, with their firelocks, ready to make good the resolute words of their town debates. Among the most alert was William Emerson, the minister, with gun in hand, his powder-horn and pouch of balls slung over his shoulder. By his sermons and his prayers his flock learned to hold the defence of their liberties a part of their covenant with God; his presence with arms strengthened their sense of duty.

From daybreak to sunrise, the summons ran from house to house through Acton. Express messengers and the call of minute-men spread widely the alarm. How children trembled as they were scared out of sleep by the cries! how women, with heaving breasts, bravely seconded their husbands!

how the countrymen, forced suddenly to arm, without guides or counsellors, took instant counsel of their courage! The mighty chorus of voices rose from the scattered farm-houses, and, as it were, from the ashes of the dead. Come forth, champions of liberty; now free your country; protect your sons and daughters, your wives and homesteads; rescue the houses of the God of your fathers, the franchises handed down from your ancestors. Now all is at stake; the battle is for all.

Lexington, in 1775, may have had seven hundred inhabitants; their minister was the learned and fervent Jonas Clark, the bold inditer of patriotic state papers, that may yet be read on their town records. In December 1772, they had instructed their representative to demand "a radical and lasting redress of their grievances, for not through their neglect should the people be enslaved." A year later, they spurned the use of tea. In 1774, at various town-meetings, they voted "to increase their stock of ammunition," "to encourage military discipline, and to put themselves in a posture of defence against their enemies." In December they distributed to "the train band and alarm list" arms and ammunition, and resolved to "supply the training soldiers with bayonets."

At two in the morning, under the eye of the minister, and of Hancock and Adams, Lexington common was alive with the minute-men; and not with them only, but with the old men, who were exempts, except in case of immediate danger to the town. The roll was called, and, of militia and alarm men, about one hundred and thirty answered to their names. The captain, John Parker, ordered every one to load with powder and ball, but to take care not to be the first to fire. Messengers, sent to look for the British regulars, reported that there were no signs of their approach. A watch was therefore set, and the company dismissed with orders to come together at beat of drum. Some went to their own homes; some to the tavern, near the south-east corner of the common. Samuel Adams and Hancock, whose seizure was believed to be intended, were persuaded to retire toward Woburn.

The last stars were vanishing from night, when the foremost party, led by Pitcairn, a major of marines, was discovered, advancing quickly and in silence. Alarm guns were fired, and the drums beat, not a call to village husbandmen only, but the reveille to humanity. Less than seventy, perhaps less than sixty, obeyed the summons, and, in sight of half as many boys and unarmed men, were paraded in two ranks, a few rods north of the meeting-house.

How often in that building had they, with renewed professions of their faith, looked up to God as the stay of their fathers and the protector of their privileges! How often on that green, hard by the burial-place of their forefathers, had they pledged themselves to each other to combat manfully for their birthright inheritance of liberty! There they now stood side by side, under the provincial banner, with arms in their hands, silent and fearless, willing to shed their blood for their rights, scrupulous not to begin civil war. The ground on which they trod was the altar of freedom, and they were to furnish the victims.

The British van, hearing the drum and the alarm guns, halted to load; the remaining companies came up; and, at half an hour before sunrise, the advance party hurried forward at double quick time, almost upon a run, closely followed by the grenadiers. Pitcairn rode in front, and, when within five or six rods of the minute-men, cried out: "Disperse, ye villains! ye rebels, disperse! lay down your arms! why don't you lay down your arms and disperse?" The main part of the countrymen stood motionless in the ranks, witnesses against aggression; too few to resist, too brave to fly. At this, Pitcairn discharged a pistol, and with a loud voice cried, "Fire!" The order was followed first by a few guns, which did no execution, and then by a close and deadly discharge of musketry.

In the disparity of numbers, Parker ordered his men to disperse. Then, and not till then, did a few of them, on their own impulse, return the British fire. These random shots of fugitives or dying men did no harm, except that Pitcairn's horse was perhaps grazed, and a private of the tenth light infantry was touched slightly in the leg.

Jonas Parker, the strongest and best wrestler in Lexington, had promised never to run from British troops; and he kept his vow. A wound brought him on his knees. Having discharged his gun, he was preparing to load it again, when he was stabbed by a bayonet, and lay on the post which he took at the morning's drum-beat. So fell Isaac Muzzey, and so died the aged Robert Munroe, who in 1758 had been an ensign at Louisburg. Jonathan Harrington, junior, was struck in front of his own house on the north of the common. His wife was at the window as he fell. With blood gushing from his breast, he rose in her sight, tottered, fell again, then crawled on hands and knees toward his dwelling; she ran to meet him, but only reached him as he expired on their threshold. Caleb Harrington, who had gone into the meeting-house for powder, was shot as he came out. Samuel Hadley and John Brown were pursued, and killed after they had left the green. Asahel Porter, of Woburn, who had been taken prisoner by the British on the march, endeavoring to escape, was shot within a few rods of the common. Seven men of Lexington were killed, nine wounded; a quarter part of all who stood in arms on the green.

Day came in all the beauty of an early spring. The trees were budding; the grass growing rankly a full month before its time; the blue bird and the robin gladdening the genial season, and calling forth the beams of the sun which on that morning shone with the warmth of summer; but distress and horror gathered over the inhabitants of the peaceful town. There on the green lay in death the gray-haired and the young; the grassy field was red "with the innocent blood of their brethren slain," crying unto God for vengeance from the ground.

These are the village heroes, who were more than of noble blood, proving by their spirit that they were of a race divine. They gave their lives in testimony to the rights of mankind, bequeathing to their country an assurance of success in the mighty struggle which they began. The expanding millions of their countrymen renew and multiply their praise from generation to generation. They fulfilled their duty not from an accidental impulse of the moment; their action was the ripened fruit of Providence and of time. The light that led them on was combined of rays from the whole history of the race; from the traditions of the Hebrews in the gray of the world's morning; from the heroes and sages of republican Greece and Rome; from the example of Him who died on the cross for the life of humanity; from the religious creed which proclaimed the divine presence in man, and on this truth, as in a life-boat, floated the liberties of nations over the dark flood of the middle ages; from the customs of the Germans transmitted out of their forests to the councils of Saxon England; from the burning faith and courage of Martin Luther; from trust in the inevitable universality of God's sovereignty as taught by Paul of Tarsus and Augustine, through Calvin and the divines of New England; from the avenging fierceness of the Puritans, who dashed the mitre on the ruins of the throne; from the bold dissent and creative self-assertion of the earliest emigrants to Massachusetts; from the statesmen who made, and the philosophers who expounded, the revolution of England; from the liberal spirit and analyzing inquisitiveness of the eighteenth century; from the crowd of witnesses of all the ages to the reality and the rightfulness of human freedom. All the centuries bowed themselves from the recesses of the past to cheer in their sacrifice the lowly men who proved themselves worthy of their forerunners, and whose children rise up and call them blessed.

Heedless of his own danger, Samuel Adams, with the voice of a prophet, exclaimed: "Oh, what a glorious morning is this!" for he saw his country's independence hastening on, and, like Columbus in the tempest, knew that the storm bore him more swiftly toward the undiscovered world.

The British troops drew up on the village green, fired a volley, huzzaed thrice by way of triumph, and, after a halt of less than thirty minutes, marched on for Concord. There, in the morning hours, children and women fled for shelter to the hills and the woods, and men were hiding what was left of cannon and military stores.

The minute-men and militia formed on the usual parade, over which the congregation of the town for near a century and a half had passed to public worship, the freemen to every town-meeting, and lately the patriot members of the povincial congress twice a day to their little senate house. Near that spot Winthrop, the father of Massachusetts, had given counsel; and Eliot, the apostle of the Indians, had spoken words of benignity and wisdom. The people of Concord, of whom about two hundred appeared in arms on that day, derived their energy from their sense of the divine power. This looking to God as their sovereign brought the fathers to their pleasant valley; this controlled the loyalty of the sons; and this has made the name of Concord venerable throughout the world.

The alarm company of the place rallied near the liberty-pole on the hill, to the right of the Lexington road, in the front of the meeting-house. They went to the perilous duties of the day "with seriousness and acknowledgment of God," as though they were to engage in acts of worship. The minute company of Lincoln, and a few men from Acton, pressed in at an early hour; but the British, as they approached, were seen to be four times as numerous as the Americans. The latter therefore retreated, first to an eminence eighty rods farther north, then across Concord river, by the North Bridge, till just beyond it, by a back road, they gained high ground, about a mile from the centre of the town. There they waited for aid.

About seven o'clock, under brilliant sunshine, the British marched with rapid step into Concord; the light infantry along the hills, and the grenadiers in the lower road. Left in undisputed possession of the hamlet, they made search for stores. To this end, one small party was sent to the South Bridge over Concord river; and, of six companies under Captain Laurie, three, comprising a hundred soldiers or more, were stationed as a guard at the North Bridge, while three others advanced two miles farther, to the residence of Barrett, the highest military officer of the neighborhood, where arms, it was thought, had been concealed. But they found there nothing to destroy except some carriages for cannon. His wife, at their demand, gave them refreshment, but refused pay, saying: "We are commanded to feed our enemy, if he hunger."

At daybreak the minute-men of Acton crowded at the drum-beat to the house of Isaac Davis, their captain, who "made haste to be ready." Just thirty years old, the father of four little ones, stately in his person, a man of few words, earnest even to solemnity, he parted from his wife, saying: "Take good care of the children;" and, while she gazed after him with resignation, he led off his company.

Between nine and ten the number of Americans on the rising ground above Concord bridge had increased to more than four hundred. Of these, there were twenty-five minute-men from Bedford, with Jonathan Wilson for their captain; others were from Westford, among them Thaxter, a preacher; others from Littleton, from Carlisle, and from Chelmsford. The Acton company came last, and formed on the right. The whole was a gathering not so much of officers and soldiers as of brothers and equals, of whom every one was a man well known in his village, observed in the meeting-house on Sundays, familiar at town-meetings, and respected as a freeholder or a freeholder's son.

Near the base of the hill Concord river flows languidly in a winding channel, and was approached by a causeway over the wet ground of its left bank. The by-road from the hill on which the Americans had rallied ran southerly till it met the causeway at right angles. The Americans saw before them, within gunshot, British troops holding possession of their bridge, and in the distance a still larger number occupying their town, which, from the rising smoke, seemed to have been set on fire.

In Concord itself, Pitcairn had fretted and fumed with oaths and curses at the tavern-keeper for shutting against him the doors of the inn, and exulted over the discovery of two twenty-four pounders in the tavern yard, as though they reimbursed the expedition. These were spiked; sixty barrels of flour were broken in pieces, but so imperfectly that afterward half the flour was saved; five hundred pounds of ball were thrown into a mill-pond. The liberty-pole and several carriages for artillery were burned, and the court-house took fire, though the fire was put out. Private dwellings were rifled, but this slight waste of public stores was all the advantage for which Gage precipitated a civil war.

The Americans had as yet received only uncertain rumors of the morning's events at Lexington. At the sight of fire in the village, the impulse seized them "to march into the town for its defence." But were they not subjects of the British king? Had not the troops come out in obedience to acknowledged authorities? Was resistance practicable? Was it justifiable? By whom could it be authorized? No union had been formed, no independence proclaimed, no war declared. The husbandmen and mechanics who then stood on the hillock by Concord river were called on to act, and their action would be war or peace, submission or independence. Had they doubted, they must have despaired. Prudent statesmanship would have asked for time to ponder. Wise philosophy would have lost from hesitation the glory of opening a new era on mankind. The train-bands at Concord acted, and God was with them.

"I never heard from any person the least expression of a wish for a separation," Franklin, not long before, had said to Chatham. In October 1774, Washington wrote: "No such thing as independence is desired by any thinking man in America." "Before the nineteenth of April 1775," relates Jefferson, "I never heard a whisper of a disposition to separate from Great Britain." Just thirty-seven days had passed since John Adams published in Boston: "That there are any who pant after independence, is the greatest slander on the province."

The American revolution grew out of the soul of the people, and was an inevitable result of a living affection for freedom, which set in motion harmonious effort as certainly as the beating of the heart sends warmth and color through the system. The rustic heroes of that hour obeyed the simplest, the highest, and the surest instincts, of which the seminal principle existed in all their countrymen. From necessity they were impelled toward independence and self-direction; this day revealed the plastic will which was to attract the elements of a nation to a centre, and by an innate force to shape its constitution.

The officers, meeting in front of their men, spoke a few words with one another, and went back to their places. Barrett, the colonel, on horseback in the rear, then gave the order to advance, but not to fire unless attacked. The calm features of Isaac Davis, of Acton, became changed; the town schoolmaster of Concord, who was present, could never afterward find words strong enough to express how deeply his face reddened at the word of command. "I have not a man that is afraid to go," said Davis, looking at the men of Acton; and, drawing his sword, he cried: "March!" His company, being on the right, led the way toward the bridge, he himself at their head, and by his side Major John Buttrick, of Concord, with John Robinson, of Westford, lieutenant-colonel in Prescott's regiment, but on this day a volunteer without command.

These three men walked together in front, followed by minute-men and militia, in double file, trailing arms. They went down the hillock, entered the by-road, came to its angle with the main road, and there turned into the causeway that led straight to the bridge. The British began to take up the planks; to prevent it, the Americans quickened their step. At this, the British fired one or two shots up the river; then another, by which Luther Blanchard and Jonas Brown were wounded. A volley followed, and Isaac Davis and Abner Hosmer fell dead. Three hours before, Davis had bid his wife farewell. That afternoon he was carried home and laid in her bedroom. His countenance was pleasant in death. The bodies of two others of his company, who were slain that day, were brought to her house, and the three were followed to the village graveyard by a concourse of the neighbors from miles around. Heaven gave her length of days in the land which his self-devotion assisted to redeem. She lived to see her country reach the Gulf of Mexico and the Pacific; when it was grown great in numbers, wealth, and power, the United States in congress bethought themselves to pay honors to her husband's martyrdom, and comfort her under the double burden of sorrow and of more than ninety years.

As the British fired, Emerson, who was looking on from an upper window in his house near the bridge, was for one moment uneasy lest the fire should not be returned. It was only for a moment; Buttrick, leaping into the air, and at the same time partially turning round, cried aloud: "Fire, fellow-soldiers! for God's sake, fire!" and the cry, "fire, fire, fire," ran from lip to lip. Two of the British fell; several were wounded. In two minutes all was hushed. The British retreated in disorder toward their main body; the countrymen were left in possession of the bridge. This is the world renowned BATTLE OF CONCORD; more eventful than Agincourt or Blenheim.

The Americans stood astonished at what they had done. They made no pursuit and did no further harm, except that one wounded soldier, attempting to rise as if to escape, was struck on the head by a young man with a hatchet. The party at Barrett's might have been cut off, but was not molested. As the Sudbury company, commanded by the brave Nixon, passed near the

South Bridge, Josiah Haynes, then eighty years of age, deacon of the Sudbury church, urged an attack on the British party stationed there; his advice was rejected by his fellow-soldiers as premature, but the company in which he served proved among the most alert during the rest of the day.

In the town of Concord, Smith, for half an hour, showed by marches and countermarches his uncertainty of purpose. At last, about noon, he left the town, to retreat the way he came, along the hilly road that wound through forests and thickets. The minute-men and militia, who had taken part in the fight, ran over the hills opposite the battle-field into the east quarter of the town, crossed the pasture known as the "Great Fields," and placed themselves in ambush a little to the eastward of the village, near the junction of the Bedford road. There they were re-enforced by men from all around, and at that point the chase of the English began.

Among the foremost were the minute-men of Reading, led by John Brooks, and accompanied by Foster, the minister of Littleton, as a volunteer. The company of Billerica, whose inhabitants, in their just indignation at Nesbit and his soldiers, had openly resolved to "use a different style from that of petition and complaint," came down from the north, while the East Sudbury company appeared on the south. A little below the Bedford road at Merriam's corner the British faced about; but, after a sharp encounter, in which several of them were killed, they resumed their retreat.

At the high land in Lincoln the old road bent toward the north, just where great trees on the west and thickets on the east offered cover to the pursuers. The men from Woburn came up in great numbers, and well armed. Along these defiles fell eight of the British. Here Pitcairn for safety was forced to quit his horse, which was taken with his pistols in their holsters. A little farther on, Jonathan Wilson, captain of the Bedford minute-men, too zealous to keep on his guard, was killed by a flanking party. At another defile in Lincoln, the minute-men of Lexington, commanded by John Parker, renewed the fight. Every piece of wood, every rock by the wayside, served as a lurking-place. Scarce ten of the Americans were at any time seen together; yet the hills seemed to the British to swarm with "rebels," as if they had dropped from the clouds, and "the road was lined" by an unintermitted fire from behind stone walls and trees.

At first the invaders moved in order; as they drew near Lexington, their flanking parties became ineffective from weariness; the wounded were scarce able to get forward. In the west of Lexington, as the British were rising Fiske's hill, a sharp contest ensued. It was at the eastern foot of the same hill that James Hayward, of Acton, encountered a regular, and both at the same moment fired; the regular dropped dead; Hayward was mortally wounded. A little farther on fell the octogenarian, Josiah Haynes, who had kept pace with the swiftest in the pursuit.

The British troops, "greatly exhausted and fatigued, and having expended almost all their ammunition," began to run rather than retreat in order.

The officers vainly attempted to stop their flight. "They were driven before the Americans like sheep." At last, about two in the afternoon, after they had hurried through the middle of the town, about a mile below the field of the morning's bloodshed, the officers made their way to the front, and by menaces of death began to form them under a very heavy fire.

At that moment Lord Percy came in sight with the first brigade, consisting of Welsh fusileers, the fourth, the forty-seventh, and the thirty-eighth regiments, in all about twelve hundred men, with two field-pieces. Insolent as usual, they marched out of Boston to the tune of Yankee Doodle; but they grew alarmed at finding every house on the road deserted. They met not one person to give them tidings of the party whom they were sent to rescue; and now that they had made the junction, they could think only of their own safety.

While the cannon kept the Americans at bay, Percy formed his detachment into a square, enclosing the fugitives, who lay down for rest on the ground, "their tongues hanging out of their mouths like those of dogs after a chase."

After the junction of the fugitives with Percy, the troops under his command amounted to fully two thirds of the British army in Boston; and yet they must fly before the Americans speedily and fleetly, or be overwhelmed. Two wagons, sent out to them with supplies, were waylaid and captured by Payson, the minister of Chelsea. From far and wide minute-men were gathering. The men of Dedham, even the old men, received their minister's blessing and went forth, in such numbers that scarce one male between sixteen and seventy was left at home. That morning William Prescott mustered his regiment; and, though Pepperell was so remote that he could not be in season for the pursuit, he hastened down with five companies of guards. Before noon a messenger rode at full speed into Worcester, crying, "To arms!" A fresh horse was brought, and the tidings went on, while the minute-men of that town, after joining hurriedly on the common in a fervent prayer from their minister, kept on the march till they reached Cambridge.

Aware of his perilous position, Percy, resting but half an hour, renewed the retreat. The light infantry marched in front, the grenadiers next, while the first brigade, which furnished the very strong flanking parties, brought up the rear. They were exposed to a fire on each side, in front, and from behind. The Americans, who were good marksmen, would lie down concealed to load their guns at one place, and discharge them at another, running from front to flank, and from flank to rear. Rage and revenge and shame at their flight led the regulars to plunder houses by the wayside, to destroy in wantonness windows and furniture, to set fire to barns and houses.

Beyond Lexington the troops were attacked by men chiefly from Essex and the lower towns. The fire from the rebels slackened till they approached West Cambridge, where Joseph Warren and William Heath, both of the committee of safety, the latter a provincial general officer, gave for a moment some appearance of organization to the pursuit, and the fight grew sharper and more determined. Here the company from Danvers, which made a breastwork of a pile of shingles, lost eight men, caught between the enemy's flank guard and main body. Here, too, a musket-ball grazed the hair of Joseph Warren, whose heart beat to arms, so that he was ever in the place of greatest danger. The British became more and more "exasperated," and indulged themselves in savage cruelty. In one house they found two aged, helpless, unarmed men, and butchered them both without mercy, stabbing them, breaking their skulls, and dashing out their brains. Hannah Adams, wife of Deacon Joseph Adams, of Cambridge, lay in child-bed with a babe of a week old, but was forced to crawl with her infant in her arms and almost naked to a corn-shed, while the soldiers set her house on fire. At Cambridge, an idiot, perched on a fence to gaze at the British army, was wantonly shot at and killed. Of the Americans, there were never more than four hundred together at any one time; but, as some grew tired or used up their ammunition, others took their places; and, though there was not much concert or discipline, and no attack with masses, the pursuit never flagged.

Below West Cambridge the militia from Dorchester, Roxbury, and Brookline came up. Of these, Isaac Gardner, of the latter place, one on whom the colony rested many hopes, fell about a mile west of Harvard college. The field-pieces began to lose their terror, so that the Americans pressed upon the rear of the fugitives, whose retreat was as rapid as it possibly could be. A little after sunset the survivors escaped across Charlestown neck.

The troops of Percy had marched thirty miles in ten hours; the party of Smith, in six hours, had retreated twenty miles; the guns of the ships-of-war and the menace to burn the town of Charlestown saved them from annoyance during their rest on Bunker Hill, and while they were ferried across Charles river.

On that day forty-nine Americans were killed, thirty-four wounded, and five missing. The loss of the British in killed, wounded, and missing, was two hundred and seventy-three. Among the wounded were many officers; Smith was hurt severely. Many more were disabled by fatigue.

All the following night the men of Massachusetts streamed in from scores of miles around, old men as well as young. They had scarce a semblance of artillery or warlike stores, no powder, nor organization, nor provisions; but there they were, thousands with brave hearts, determined to rescue the liberties of their country. "The night preceding the outrages at Lexington there were not fifty people in the whole colony that ever expected any blood would be shed in the contest;" the night after, the king's governor and the king's army found themselves closely beleaguered in Boston.

"The next news from England must be conciliatory, or the connection between us ends," said Warren. "This month," so William Emerson of Concord, late chaplain to the provincial congress, chronicled in a blank leaf of his almanac, "is remarkable for the greatest events of the present age." "From the nineteenth of April 1775," said Clark, of Lexington, on its first anniversary, "will be dated the liberty of the American world."

Great Britain would not submit to the colonists' demands, and sent additional troops to punish the rebels. The Continental Congress, acting as a de facto government, appointed General George Washington to command the Continental Army. He was not a great tactician, but did manage despite defeats and vicissitudes to keep an army in the field. As the grim war unfolded, patriots increasingly felt that there was no valid reason for continuing a pretended tie with England. On July 4, 1776 the Continental Congress passed in its final form a Declaration of Independence. But independence had to be won as well as asserted, and in the summer of 1777 the British put into operation a large-scale plan of operations to crush the rebellion.

THE ADVANCE OF BURGOYNE FROM CANADA

"This campaign will end the war," was the opinion given by Riedesel; and through Lord Suffolk he solicited the continued favor of the British king, who was in his eyes "the adoration of all the universe." Flushed with expectations of glory, Carleton employed the unusually mild winter in preparations. On the last day of April he gave audience to the deputies of the Six Nations, and accepted their services with thanks and gifts. Other large bodies of Indians were engaged, under leaders of their own approval. "Wretched colonies!" said Riedesel, "if these wild souls are indulged in war."

To secure the Mohawks to the British side, Joseph Brant urged them to abandon their old abode for lands more remote from American settlements. To counteract his authority, Gates, near the end of May, thus spoke to a council of warriors of the Six Nations:

"The United States are now one people; suffer not any evil spirit to lead you into war. Brothers of the Mohawks, you will be no more a people from the time you quit your ancient habitations; if there is any wretch so bad as to think of prevailing upon you to leave the sweet stream so beloved by your forefathers, he is your bitterest enemy. Before many moons pass away, the pride of England will be laid low; then how happy will it make you to reflect that you have preserved the neutrality so earnestly recommended to you from the beginning of the war! Brothers of the Six Nations, the Americans well know your great fame and power as warriors; the only reason why they did not ask your help against the cruelty of the king was, that they thought it ungenerous to desire you to suffer in a quarrel in which you had no concern. Brothers, treasure all I have now said in your hearts; for the day will come when you will hold my memory in veneration for the good advice contained in this speech."

The settlers in the land which this year took the name of Vermont refused by a great majority to come under the jurisdiction of New York; on the fifteenth of January 1777, their convention declared the independence of their state. At Windsor, on the second of June, they appointed a committee to prepare a constitution; and they hoped to be received into the American union. But, as New York opposed, congress, by an uncertain majority against a determined minority, disclaimed the intention of recognising Vermont as a separate state.

Gates charged Saint-Clair to "call lustily for aid of all kinds, for no general ever lost by surplus numbers or overpreparation;" and he then repaired to Philadelphia, to intrigue for his reinstatement.

On the twelfth, Saint-Clair, the best of the brigadiers then in the North, reached Ticonderoga. Five days later Schuyler visited his army. Mount Defiance, which overhangs the outlet of Lake George and was the "key of the position," was left unoccupied. From the old French intrenchments to the southeastern works on the Vermont side the wretchedly planned and unfinished defences extended more than two miles and a half; and from end to end of the straggling lines and misplaced block-houses there was no spot which could be held against a superior force. The British could reach the place by the lake more swiftly than the Americans through the forest. A necessity for evacuating the post might arise; but Schuyler shrunk from giving definite instructions, and, returning to Albany, busied himself with forwarding to Ticonderoga supplies for a long siege.

On the sixth of May, Buryogne arrived at Quebec. Carleton received with amazement despatches censuring his conduct in the last campaign, and ordering him, for "the speedy quelling of the rebellion," to make over to an inferior officer the command of the Canadian army as soon as it should cross the boundary of the province of Quebec. Answering with passionate recrimination the just reproaches of Germain and of his adviser Lord Amherst, he at once yielded up the chief military authority, and, as civil governor, paid a haughty but unquestioning obedience to the requisitions of Burgoyne. Contracts were made for fifteen hundred horses and five hundred carts; a thousand Canadians, reluctant and prone to desertion, were called out as road-makers and wagoners; and six weeks' supplies for the army were crowded forward upon the one line of communication by the Sorel. Burgoyne had very nearly all the force which he had represented as sufficient. His officers were well chosen, especially Phillips and Riedesel as major-generals and the Highlander Fraser as an acting brigadier. A diversion, from which great consequences were expected, was to proceed by way of Lake Ontario to the Mohawk river. Sir William Howe was notified that Burgoyne had orders to force a junction with his army.

On the fifteenth of June, Burgoyne advanced from St. John's, as he thought, to easy victories and high promotion. Officers' wives attended their husbands, promising themselves an agreeable trip. On the twentieth some of the Indians, shedding the first blood, brought in ten scalps and as many prisoners. The next day, at the camp near the river Bouquet, a little north of Crown Point, Burgoyne, the applauded writer of plays for the stage, gathering round him the chief officers of his army in their gala uniforms, met in congress about four hundred Iroquois, Algonkin, and Ottawa savages, and thus appealed to what he called "their wild honor":

"Warriors, you are free; go forth in might of your valor and your cause; strike at the common enemies of Great Britain and America, disturbers of public order, peace, and happiness, destroyers of commerce, parricides of the state. The circle round you, the chiefs of his majesty's European forces, and of those of the princes, his allies, esteem you as brothers in the war; emulous in glory and in friendship, we will reciprocally give and receive examples. Be it our task to regulate your passions when they overbear. I positively forbid bloodshed, when you are not opposed in arms. Aged men, women, children, and prisoners must be held sacred from the knife and the hatchet, even in the time of actual conflict. You shall receive compensation for the prisoners you take, but you shall be called to account for scalps. Your customs have affixed an idea of honor to such badges of victory: you shall be allowed to take the scalps of the dead, when killed by your fire in fair opposition; but on no pretence are they to be taken from the wounded or even dying. Should the enemy, on their part, dare to countenance acts of barbarity toward those who may fall into their hands, it shall be yours to retaliate."

An old Iroquois chief replied: "When you speak, we hear the voice of our great father beyond the great lake. We have been tried and tempted by the Bostonians; but we loved our father, and our hatchets have been sharpened upon our affections. In proof of sincerity, our whole villages, able to go to war, are come forth. The old and infirm, our infants and wives, alone remain at home. With one common assent we promise a constant obedience to all you have ordered and all you shall order; and may the Father of days give you many, and success."

Having feasted the Indians according to their custom, Burgoyne published his speech, which reflected his instructions. Edmund Burke, who had learned that the natural ferocity of those tribes far exceeded the ferocity of all barbarians mentioned in history, pronounced that they were not fit allies for the king in a war with his people; that Englishmen should never confirm their evil habits by fleshing them in the slaughter of British colonists. In the house of commons Fox censured the king for suffering them in his camp, when it was well known that "brutality, murder, and destruction were ever inseparable from Indian warriors." When Suffolk, before the lords, contended that it was perfectly justifiable to use all the means which God and nature had put into their hands, Chatham called down "the most decisive indignation at these abominable principles and this more abominable avowal of them."

In a proclamation issued at Crown Point, Burgoyne, claiming to speak "in consciousness of Christianity and the honor of soldiership," enforced his persuasions to the Americans by menaces like these: "Let not people consider their distance from my camp; I have but to give stretch to the Indian forces under my direction, and they amount to thousands, to over-take the hardened enemies of Great Britain. If the frenzy of hostility should remain, I trust I shall stand acquitted in the eyes of God and man in executing the vengeance of the state against the wilful outcasts."

On the last day of June, Burgoyne declared in general orders: "This army must not retreat;" while Saint-Clair wrote to Schuyler: "Should the enemy attack us, they will go back faster than they came." On the first of July the invading army moved up the lake. As they encamped at evening before Ticonderoga and Mount Independence, the rank and file, exclusive of Indians, numbered three thousand seven hundred and twenty-four British, three thousand and sixteen Germans, two hundred and fifty provincials, besides four hundred and seventy-three skilful artillerists, with an excessive supply of artillery. On the third, one of Saint-Clair's aids promised Washington "the total defeat of the enemy." On that day Riedesel was studying how to invest Mount Independence. On the fourth, Phillips seized the mills near the outlet of Lake George, and hemmed in Ticonderoga on that side. In the following night a party of infantry, following the intimation of Lieutenant Twiss of the engineers, took possession of Mount Defiance. In one day more, batteries from that hill would play on both forts, and Riedesel complete the investment of Mount Independence. "We must away," said Saint-Clair; his council of war were all of the same mind, and the retreat must be made the very next night. The garrison, according to his low esti-mate, consisted of thirty-three hundred men, of whom two thirds were effec-tive, but with scarcely more than one bayonet to every tenth soldier. One regiment, the invalids, and such stores as there was time to lade, were sent in boats up the lake to Whitehall, while the great body of the troops, under Saint-Clair, took the new road through the wilderness to Hubbardton.

They left ample stores of ammunition, flour, salt meat, and herds of oxen, more than seventy cannon, and a large number of tents. Burgoyne, who came up in the fleet, sent Fraser with twenty companies of English grena-diers, followed by Riedesel's infantry and reserve corps, in pursuit of the army of Saint-Clair; and, as soon as the channel between Ticonderoga and Mount Independence could be cleared, the fleet, bearing Burgoyne and the rest of his forces, chased after the detachment which had escaped by water. The Americans, burning three of their vessels, abandoned two others and the fort at Whitehall. Everything which they brought from Ticonderoga was destroyed, or fell a prey to their pursuers.

On the same day Burgoyne reported to his government that the army of Ticonderoga was "disbanded and totally ruined." Germain cited to General Howe this example of "rapid progress," and predicted an early junction of the two armies. Men disputed in England whether most to admire the sword or the pen of Burgoyne; and were sure of the entire conquest of the confederate provinces before Christmas.

Public opinion rose against Schuyler. Of the evacuation of Ticonderoga, Hamilton reasoned rightly: "If the post was untenable, or required a larger number of troops to defend it than could be spared for the purpose, it ought long ago to have been foreseen and given up. Instead of that, we have kept a large quantity of cannon in it, and have been heaping up very valuable magazines of stores and provisions, that in the critical moment of defence are abandoned and lost." So judged the public and congress. Schuyler had, as the condition of his reappointment to the command, taken upon himself the responsibility of the defence of Ticonderoga, and had claimed praise for having piled up ample stores within its walls. He sought to escape from condemnation by insisting that the retreat was made without the least hint from himself, and was "ill-judged and not warranted by necessity." With manly frankness Saint-Clair assumed as his own the praiseworthy act which had saved to the country many of its bravest defenders.

On the second of July the convention of Vermont reassembled at Windsor. The organic law which they adopted, blending the culture of their age with the traditions of Protestantism, assumed that all men are born free and with inalienable rights; that they may emigrate from one state to another, or form a new state in vacant countries; that "every sect should observe the Lord's day, and keep up some sort of religious worship;" that every man may choose that form of religious worship "which shall seem to him most agreeable to the revealed will of God." They provided for a school in each town, a grammar-school in each county, and a university in the state. All officers, alike executive and legislative, were to be chosen annually and by ballot; the freemen of every town and all one-year's residents were electors. Every member of the house of representatives must declare "his belief in one God, the rewarder of the good and the punisher of the wicked; in the divine inspiration of the scriptures; and in the Protestant religion." The legislative power was vested in one general assembly, subject to no veto, though an advisory power was given to a board consisting of the governor, lieutenant-governor, and twelve councillors. Slavery was forbidden and forever; and there could be no imprisonment for debt. Once in seven years an elective council of censors was to take care that freedom and the constitution were preserved in purity.

The marked similarity of this system to that of Pennsylvania is ascribed in part to the influence of Thomas Young of Philadelphia, who had published an address to the people of Vermont. After the loss of Ticonderoga, the introduction of the constitution was postponed, lest the process of change should interfere with the public defence, for which the Vermont council of safety supplicated aid from the New Hampshire committee at Exeter and from Massachusetts.

On the night of the sixth, Fraser and his party made their bivouac seventeen miles from the lake, with that of Riedesel three miles in their rear. At three in the morning of the seventh both detachments were in motion. The savages having discovered the rear-guard of Saint-Clair's army, which Warner, contrary to his instructions, had encamped for the night at Hubbardton, six miles short of Castleton, Fraser, at five, ordered his troops to advance. To their great surprise, Warner, who was nobly assisted by Colonel Eben Francis and his New Hampshire regiment, turned and began the attack. The English were like to be worsted, when Riedesel with his vanguard and company of yagers came up, their music playing, the men singing a battle-hymn. Francis for a third time charged at the head of his regiment, and held his enemies at bay till he fell. On the approach of the three German battalions, his men retreated toward the south. Fraser, taking Riedesel by the hand, thanked him for the timely rescue. Of the Americans, few were killed, and most of those engaged in the fight made good their retreat; but during the day the British took more than two hundred stragglers, wounded men, and invalids. Of the Brunswickers twenty-two were killed or wounded, of the British one hundred and fifty-five. The heavy loss stopped the pursuit; and Saint-Clair, with two thousand continental troops, marched unmolested to Fort Edward.

The British regiment which chased the fugitives from Whitehall took ground within a mile of Fort Ann. On the morning of the eighth its garrison drove them nearly three miles, took a captain and three privates, and inflicted a loss of at least fifty in killed and wounded. Reinforced by a brigade, the English returned only to find the fort burned down, and the garrison beyond reach.

Burgoyne chose to celebrate these events by a day of thanksgiving. Another disappointment awaited him. He asked Carleton to hold Ticonderoga with a part of the three thousand troops left in Canada; Carleton, pleading his instructions which confined him to his own province, refused, and left Burgoyne "to drain the life-blood of his army" for the garrison. Supplies of provisions came tardily. Of the Canadian horses contracted for, not more than one third arrived in good condition over the wild mountain roads. The wagons were made of green wood, and were deficient in number. Further, Burgoyne should have turned back from Whitehall and moved to the Hudson river by way of Lake George and the old road; but the word was: "Britons never recede;" and after the halt of a fortnight he took the short cut to Fort Edward, through a wilderness bristling with woods, broken by numerous creeks, and treacherous with morasses. He reports with complacency the construction of more than forty bridges, a "log-work" over a morass two miles in extent, and the removal of layers of fallen timber-trees. But this persistent toil in the heat of midsummer, among myriads of insects, dispirited his troops.

Early in July, Burgoyne confessed to Germain that, "were the Indians left to themselves, enormities too horrid to think of would ensue; guilty and innocent, women and infants, would be a common prey." The general, nevertheless, resolved to use them as instruments of "terror," and promised, after arriving at Albany, to send them "toward Connecticut and Boston," knowing full well that they were left to themselves by La Corne Saint-Luc, their leader, who was impatient of control in the use of the scalping-knife. Every day the savages brought in scalps as well as prisoners. On the twenty-seventh, Jane Maccrea, a young woman of twenty, betrothed to a loyalist in the British service and esteeming herself under the protection of British arms, was riding from Fort Edward to the British camp at Sandy Hill, escorted by two Indians. The Indians quarrelled about the reward promised on her safe arrival, and at a half-mile from Fort Edward one of them sunk his tomahawk in her skull. The incident was not of unusual barbarity; but this massacre of a betrothed girl on her way to her lover touched all who heard the story. Burgoyne, from fear of "the total defection of the Indians," pardoned the assassin.

Schuyler owed his place to his social position, not to military talents. Anxious, and suspected of a want of personal courage, he found everything go ill under his command. To the continental troops of Saint-Clair, who were suffering from the loss of their clothes and tents, he was unable to restore confidence; nor could he rouse the people. The choice for governor of New York fell on George Clinton; "his character," said Washington to the council of safety, "will make him peculiarly useful at the head of your state." Schuyler wrote: "His family and connections do not entitle him to so distinguished a pre-eminence." There could be no hope of a successful campaign but with the hearty co-operation of New England. Of the militia of New England the British commander-in-chief has left his testimony that, "when brought to action, they were the most persevering of any in all North America;" yet Schuyler gave leave for one half of them to go home at once, the rest to follow in three weeks, and then called upon Washington to supply their places by troops from the south of Hudson river, saying to his friends that one southern soldier was worth two from New England.

On the twenty-second, long before Burgoyne was ready to advance, Schuyler retreated to a position four miles below Fort Edward. Here again he complained of his "exposure to immediate ruin." His friends urged him to silence the growing suspicion of his want of spirit; he answered: "If there is a battle, I shall certainly expose myself more than is prudent." To the New York council of safety he wrote on the twenty-fourth: "I mean to dispute every inch of ground with Burgoyne, and retard his descent as long as possible;" and in less than a week, without disputing anything, he retreated to Saratoga, having his heart set on a position at the junction of the Mohawk and Hudson. The courage of the commander being gone, his officers and his army became spiritless. From Saratoga, Schuyler, on the first of August, wrote to the council of safety of New York: "I have been on horseback all day reconnoitring the country for a place to encamp on that will give us a chance of stopping the enemy's career. I have not yet been able to find a spot that has the least prospect of answering the purpose, and I believe you will soon learn that we are retired still farther south. I wish that I could say that the troops under my command were in good spirits. They are quite otherwise. Under these circumstances the enemy are acquiring strength and advancing."

On the fourth of August he sent word to congress that "Burgoyne is at Fort Edward. He has withdrawn his troops from Castleton and is bending his whole force this way. He will probably be here in eight days, and, unless we are well reinforced, as much farther as he chooses to go."

On the sixth, Schuyler writes to Governor Clinton of New York: "The enemy will soon move, and our strength is daily decreasing. We shall again be obliged to decamp and retreat before them." And, as his only resource, he solicited aid from Washington.

The loss of Ticonderoga alarmed the patriots of New York, gladdened the royalists, and fixed the wavering Indians as enemies. Five countries were in the possession of the enemy; three others suffered from disunion and anarchy; Tryon county implored immediate aid; the militia of Westchester were absorbed in their own defence; in the other counties scarcely men enough remained at home to secure the plentiful harvest. Menaced on its border from the Susquehannah to Lake Champlain, and on every part of the Hudson, New York became the battle-field for the life of the young republic; its council seconded Schuyler's prayers for reinforcements.

The commander-in-chief, in the plan of the campaign, had assigned to the northern department more than its share of troops and resources; and had added one brigade which was beyond the agreement and of which he stood in pressing need, for the army of Howe was twice or thrice as numerous as that from Canada. In this time of perplexity, when the country from the Hudson to Maryland required to be guarded, the entreaties from Schuyler, from the council of New York, and from Jay and Gouverneur Morris as deputies of that council, poured in upon Washington. Alarmed by Schuyler's want of fortitude, he ordered to the north Arnold, who was fearless, and Lincoln, who was acceptable to the militia of the eastern states, and, even though it weakened his own army irretrievably, still one more brigade of excellent continental troops under Glover. To hasten the rising of New England, he wrote directly to the brigadier-generals of Massachusetts and Connecticut, urging them to march for Saratoga with at least one third part of the militia under their command. At the same time he bade Schuyler "never despair," explaining that the forces which might advance under Burgoyne could not much exceed five thousand men; that they must garrison every fortified post left behind them; that their progress must be delayed by their baggage and artillery, and by the necessity of cutting new roads and clearing old ones; that a party should be stationed in Vermont to keep them in continual anxiety for their rear; that Arnold should go to the relief of Fort Stanwix; that, if the invaders continued to act in detachments, one vigorous fall upon some one of those detachments might prove fatal to the whole expedition.

In a like spirit he expressed to the council of New York "the most sensible pleasure at the exertions of the state, dismembered as it was, and under every discouragement and disadvantage;" the success of Burgoyne, he predicted, would be temporary; the southern states could not be asked to detail their force, since it was all needed to keep Howe at bay; the attachment of the eastern states to the cause insured their activity when invoked for the safety of a sister state, of themselves, of the continent; the worst effect of the loss of Ticonderoga was the panic which it produced; calmly considered, the expedition was not formidable; if New York should be seasonably seconded by its eastern neighbors, Burgoyne would find it equally difficult to advance or to retreat.

All this while Schuyler continued to despond. On the thirteenth of August he could write from Stillwater to Washington: "We are obliged to give way and retreat before a vastly superior force, daily increasing in numbers, and which will be doubled if General Burgoyne reaches Albany, which I apprehend will be very soon;" and the next day he moved his army to the first island in the mouth of the Mohawk river; and at Albany accepted applause for "the wisdom of his safe retreat." The first serious blow was struck by the husbandmen of Tyron county.

Burgoyne, on his return to London in 1776, had censured Carleton to Germain for not having sent by Lake Ontario and the Oswego and Mohawk rivers an auxiliary expedition, which he had offered to lead. Germain adopted the plan, and settled the details for its execution chiefly by savages. To Carleton, whom he accused of "avoiding to employ Indians," he announced the king's "resolution that every means should be employed that Providence had put in his majesty's hand for crushing the rebellion." The detachment which was set apart for the service under the command of Lieutenant-Colonel Saint-Leger, varying from the schedule of Germain in its constituent parts more than in its numbers, exceeded seven hundred and fifty white men. "The Six Nations inclined to the rebels" from fear of being finally abandoned by the king. The Mohawks could not rise unless they were willing to leave their old hunting-grounds; the Oneidas were friendly to the Americans; even the Senecas were hard to be roused. Butler at Irondequat assured them that there was no hindrance in the war-path; that they would have only to look on and see Fort Stanwix fall; and for seven days he lavished largesses on the fighting men and on their wives and children, till "they accepted the hatchet." "Not much short of one thousand

Indian warriors," certainly "more than eight hundred," joined the white brigade of Saint-Leger. In addition to these, Hamilton, the lieutenant-governor of Detroit, in obedience to orders from the secretary of state, sent out fifteen several parties, consisting in the aggregate of two hundred and eighty-nine braves with thirty white officers and rangers, to prowl on the frontiers of Pennsylvania and Virginia.

Collecting his forces as he advanced from Montreal by way of Oswego, Saint-Leger on the third of August came near the carrying-place, where for untold ages the natives had borne their bark canoes over the narrow plain that divides the waters of the St. Lawrence from those of the Hudson. Fort Stanwix proved to be well constructed, safe by earthworks against artillery, and garrisoned by six or seven hundred men under Lieutenant-Colonel Gansevoort. A messenger from Brant's sister brought word that General Nicholas Herkimer and the militia of Tryon county were marching to its relief. A plan was made to lay for them an ambush of savages.

During the evening the savages filled the woods with yells. The next morning, having laid aside their blankets and robes of fur, they all went out, naked, or clad only in hunting-shirts, armed with spear, tomahawk, and musket, and supported by Sir John Johnson and royal Yorkers, by Colonel Butler and rangers, by Claus and Canadians, and by Lieutenant Bird and regulars.

The freeholders of the Mohawk valley, most of them with the sons of Germans from the palatinate for officers, seven or eight hundred in number, misinformed as to the strength of the besieging party, marched carelessly through the wood. About an hour before noon, when they were within six miles of the fort, their van entered the ambuscade. They were surprised in front by Johnson and his Yorkers, while the Indians attacked their flanks with fury, and, after using their muskets, rushed in with their tomahawks. The patriots fell back without confusion to better ground, and renewed the fight against superior numbers. There was no chance for tactics in this battle of the wilderness. Small parties fought from behind trees or fallen logs; or the white man, born on the banks of the Mohawk, wrestled single-handed with the Seneca warrior, like himself the child of the soil. Herkimer was badly wounded below the knee; but he remained on the ground, giving orders to the end. Thomas Spencer died the death of a hero. The battle raged for at least an hour and a half, when the Americans repulsed their assailants, but with the loss of about one hundred and sixty, killed, wounded, or taken, of the best men of western New York. The savages fought with wild valor; three-and-thirty or more, among them the chief warriors of the Senecas, lay dead beneath the trees; about as many more were badly wounded. Of the Yorkers one captain, of the rangers two were killed. What number of privates fell is not told. The British loss, including savages and white men, was probably about one hundred.

Three men having crossed the morass into Fort Stanwix to announce the approach of Herkimer, by Gansevoort's order two hundred and fifty men, half of New York, half of Massachusetts, under Lieutenant-Colonel Marinus Willett, made a sally in the direction of Oriska. They passed through the quarters of the Yorkers, the rangers, and the savages, driving before them whites and Indians, chiefly squaws and children, capturing Sir John Johnson's papers, five British flags, the fur-robes and new blankets and kettles of the Indians, and four prisoners. Learning from them the check to Herkimer, the party of Willet returned quickly to Fort Stanwix, bearing their spoils on their shoulders. The five captured colors were displayed under the continental flag; it was the first time that a captured banner had floated under the stars and stripes of the republic. The Indians were frantic at the loss of their chiefs and warriors; they suffered in the chill nights from the loss of their clothes; and not even the torturing and killing their captives in which they were indulged could prevent their beginning to return home.

Meantime, Willet, with Lieutenant Stockwell as his companion, "both good woodsmen," made their way past the Indian quarter, at the hazard of death by torture, and at their request Schuyler charged Arnold with an expedition to relieve the garrison. Long before its approach an Indian ran into Saint-Leger's camp, reporting that a thousand men were coming against them; another followed, doubling the number; a third brought a rumor that three thousand men were close at hand; and, deaf to remonstrances and entreaties from their superintendents and from Saint-Leger, the wild warriors robbed the British officers of their clothes, plundered the boats, and made off with the booty. Saint-Leger in a panic, though Arnold was not within forty miles, hurried after them before nightfall, leaving his tents, artillery, and stores.

It was Herkimer who "first reversed the gloomy scene" of the northern campaign. The pure-minded hero of the Mohawk valley "served from love of country, not for reward. He did not want a continental command or money." Before congress had decided how to manifest their gratitude he died of his wound; and they decreed him a monument. Gansevoort was rewarded by a vote of thanks and a command; Willett, by public praise and "an elegant sword."

The employment of Indian allies had failed. The king, the ministry, and, in due time, the British parliament, were informed officially that the red men "treacherously committed ravages upon their friends;" that "they could not be controlled;" that "they killed their captives;" that "there was infinite difficulty to manage them;" that "they grew more and more unreasonable and importunate." When the Senaca warriors, returning to their lodges, told the story of the slaughter of their chiefs, their villages rung with yells of rage and the howls of mourners.

Burgoyne, who on the thirtieth of July made his head-quarters on the banks of the Hudson, had detachments from seventeen savage nations. A

Brunswick officer describes them as "tall, warlike, and enterprising, but fiendishly wicked." On the third of August they brought in twenty scalps and as many captives; and Burgoyne approved their incessant activity. To prevent desertions of soldiers, it was announced in orders to each regiment that the savages were enjoined to scalp every runaway. The Ottawas longed to go home; but, on the fifth of August, Burgoyne took from all his red warriors a pledge to stay through the campaign. On the sixth he reported himself to General Howe as "well forward," "impatient to gain the mouth of the Mohawk," but not likely to "be in possession of Albany" before "the twenty-second or the twenty-third" of the month.

To aid Saint-Leger by a diversion, and fill his camp with draught cattle, horses, and provisions from fabled magazines at Bennington, Burgoyne on the eleventh of August sent out an expedition on the left, commanded by Baum, a Brunswick lieutenant-colonel of dragoons, and composed of more than four hundred Brunswickers, Hanau artillerists with two cannon, the select corps of British marksmen, a party of French Canadians, a more numerous party of provincial royalists, and a horde of about one hundred and fifty Indians. Burgoyne in his eagerness rode after Baum, and gave him verbal orders to march directly upon Bennington. After disposing of the stores at that place, he might cross the Green Mountains, descend the Connecticut river to Brattleborough, and enter Albany with Saint-Leger and the main army. The night of the thirteenth, Baum encamped about four miles from Bennington, on a hill that rises from the Walloomscoick, just within the state of New York. When, early on the morning of the fourteenth, a reconnoitring party of Americans was seen, he wrote in high spirits for more troops, and constructed strong intrenchments. Burgoyne sent him orders to maintain his post; and, at eight o'clock on the fifteenth, Breymann, a Brunswick lieutenant-colonel, with two Brunswick battalions and two cannon, marched, in a constant rain, through thick woods, to his support.

The legislature of New Hampshire, in the middle of July, receiving the supplicatory letter from Vermont, promptly resolved to co-operate "with the troops of the new state," and ordered Stark, with a brigade of militia, "to stop the progress of the enemy on their western frontier." Uprising at the call, the men of New Hampshire flew to his standard, which he set up at Charlestown, on the Connecticut river. Schuyler ordered them to join his retreating army, and, because they chose to follow their own wise plans, Schuyler brought upon Stark the censure of congress for disobedience. But the upright hero, consulting with Seth Warner of Vermont, made his bivouac on the fourteenth of August at the distance of a mile from the post of Baum, to whom he vainly offered battle. The regiment of Warner came down from Manchester during the rain of the fifteenth; and troops arrived from the westernmost county of Massachusetts.

When the sun rose on the sixteenth, Stark concerted with his officers the plan for the day. Baum, seeing small bands of men, in shirt-sleeves and carrying fowling-pieces without bayonets, steal behind his camp, mistook them for friendly country people placing themselves where he could protect them; and so five hundred men under Nichols and Herrick united in his rear. While his attention was arrested by a feint, two hundred more posted themselves on his right; and Stark, with two or three hundred, took the front. At three o'clock Baum was attacked on every side. The Indians dashed between two detachments and fled, leaving their grand chief and other warriors lifeless on the field. New England sharpshooters ran up within eight yards of the loaded cannon, to pick off the cannoneers. When, after about two hours, the firing of the Brunswickers slackened from scarcity of powder, the Americans scaled the breastwork and fought them hand to hand. Baum ordered his infantry with the bayonet, his dragoons with their sabres, to force a way; but in the attempt he fell mortally wounded, and his veteran troops surrendered.

Just then the battalions of Breymann, having taken thirty hours to march twenty-four miles, came in sight. Warner now first brought up his regiment, of one hundred and fifty men, into action; and with their aid Stark began a new attack, using the cannon just taken. The fight raged till sunset, when Breymann, abandoning his artillery and most of his wounded men, ordered a retreat. The pursuit continued till night; those who escaped owed their safety to the darkness. During the day less than thirty of the Americans were killed, and about forty were wounded; the loss of their enemy was estimated at full twice as many, besides at least six hundred and ninety-two prisoners, of whom more than four hundred were Germans.

This victory, one of the most brilliant and eventful of the war, was achieved spontaneously by the husbandmen of New Hampshire, Vermont, and western Massachusetts. Stark only confirms the reports of Hessian officers when he writes: "Had our people been Alexanders or Charleses of Sweden, they could not have behaved better."

At the news of Breymann's retreat, Burgoyne ordered his army under arms; and at the head of the forty-seventh regiment he forded the Battenkill, to meet the worn-out fugitives. The loss of troops was irreparable. Canadians and Indians of the remoter nations began to leave in disgust. For supplies, Burgoyne was thrown back upon shipments from England, painfully forwarded from Quebec by way of Lake Champlain and Lake George to the Hudson river. Before he could move forward he must, with small means of transportation, bring together stores for thirty days, and drag nearly two hundred boats over two long carrying-places.

On the first of August congress relieved Schuyler from command by a vote to which there was no negative; and on the fourth eleven states elected Gates his successor. Before Gates assumed the command, Fort Stanwix was safe and the victory of Bennington achieved; yet congress hastened to vote him all the powers and all the aid which Schuyler in his moods of despondency had entreated. Touched by the ringing appeals of Washington, thousands of the men of Massachusetts, even from the counties of Middlesex and Essex, were in motion toward Saratoga. Congress, overriding Washington's advice, gave Schuyler's successor plenary power to make further requisitions for militia on New York, New Jersey, and Pennsylvania. Washington had culled from his troops five hundred riflemen, and formed them under Morgan into a better corps of skirmishers than had ever been attached to an army even in Europe; congress directed them to be forthwith sent to assist Gates against the Indians; and Washington obeyed so promptly that the order might seem to have been anticipated.

As for Schuyler, he proffered his services to the general by whom he was superseded, heartily wished him success, and soon learned to "justify congress for depriving him of the command, convinced that it was their duty to sacrifice the feelings of an individual to the safety of the states when the people who only could defend the country refused to serve under him."

PROGRESS OF SIR WILLIAM HOWE AND BURGOYNE

A doubt arose whether Washington retained authority over the new chief of the northern department till congress declared that "they never intended to supersede or circumscribe his power;" but, from an unwillingness to confess their own mistakes, from the pride of authority and jealousy of his superior popularity, they slighted his advice and neglected his wants. They remodelled the commissary department in the midst of the campaign on a system which no competent men would undertake to execute. Washington, striving for an army, raised and officered by the United States, "used every means in his power to destroy state distinction in it, and to have every part and parcel of it considered as continental;" congress more and more reserved to the states the recruiting of men, and the appointment of all but general officers. Political and personal considerations controlled the nomination of officers; and congress had not vigor enough to drop the incapable. "The wearisome wrangles for rank," and the numerous commissions given to foreign adventurers of extravagant pretensions, made the army "a just representation of a great chaos." A reacting "spirit of reformation" was at first equally undiscerning; Kalb and Lafayette, arriving at Philadelphia near the end of July, met with a repulse. When it was told that Lafayette desired no more than leave to risk his life in the cause of liberty without pension or allowance, congress gave him the rank of major-general, and Washington received him into his family; but at first the claim of Kalb was rejected.

On the fifth of July, General Howe, leaving more than seven regiments in Rhode Island, and about six thousand men under Sir Henry Clinton at New York, began to embark the main body of his army for a joint expedition with the naval force against Philadelphia. The troops, alike foot and cavalry, were kept waiting on shipboard till the twenty-third. The fleet of nearly three hundred sail spent seven days in beating from Sandy Hook to the capes of Delaware. Finding the Delaware river obstructed, it steered for the Chesapeake, laboring against the southerly winds of the season. August was half gone when it turned Cape Charles; and on the twenty-fifth, after a voyage of thirty-three days, it anchored in Elk river, six miles below Elktown and fifty-four miles from Philadelphia.

Expressing the strange reasoning and opinions of many of his colleagues, John Adams, the head of the board of war, could write: "We shall rake and scrape enough to do Howe's business; the continental army under Washington is more numerous by several thousands than Howe's whole force; the enemy give out that they are eighteen thousand strong, but we know better, and that they have not ten thousand. Washington is very prudent; I should put more to risk, were I in his shoes; I am sick of Fabian systems. My toast is, a short and violent war." Now at that time the army of Howe, apart from the corps of engineers, counted, at the lowest statements, seventeen thousand one hundred and sixty-seven men, with officers amounting to one fifth as many more, all soldiers by profession and perfectly equipped.

Congress gave itself the air of efficiency by calling out the militia of Maryland, Delaware, Pennsylvania, and New Jersey; but New Jersey had to watch the force on the Hudson; the slaveholders on the Maryland eastern shore and in the southern county of Delaware were disaffected; the Pennsylvania militia with Washington did not exceed twelve hundred men, and never increased beyond twenty-five hundred.

On the twenty-fourth of August, Washington led the continental army, decorated with sprays of green, through the crowded streets of Philadelphia; the next day he reached Wilmington just as the British anchored in the Elk with the purpose of marching upon Philadelphia by an easy inland route through an open country which had no difficult passes, no rivers but fordable ones, and was inhabited chiefly by royalists and Quakers. When Sullivan, who had just lost two hundred of the very best men in a senseless expedition to Staten Island, brought up his division, the American army, which advanced to the highlands beyond Wilmington, was not more than half as numerous as the British; but Howe, from the waste of horses on his long voyage, was compelled to wait till others could be provided.

On the third of September the two divisions under Cornwallis and Knyphausen began the march toward Philadelphia; Maxwell and the light troops, composed of drafts of one hundred men from each brigade, occupied Iron Hill, and, after a sharp skirmish in the woods with a body of German yagers and light infantry, withdrew slowly and in perfect order. For two days longer Howe waited, to provide for his wounded men in the hospital-ship of the fleet, and purchase still more means of transportation. Four miles from him, Washington took post behind Red Clay creek, and invited an attack. On the eighth, Howe sent a strong column in front of the Americans to feign an attack, while his main army halted at Milltown. The

British and Germans went to rest in full confidence of turning Washington's right on the morrow, and cutting him off from the road to Lancaster. But Washington had divined their purpose, and, by a masterly and really secret movement, took post on the high grounds above Chad's ford on the north side of the Brandywine, directly in Howe's path.

The baggage of the army was sent forward to Chester. A battery of cannon with a good parapet guarded the ford. The American left, resting on a thick, continuous forest along the Brandywine, which below Chad's ford becomes a rapid, encumbered by rocks and shut in by abrupt high banks, was sufficiently defended by Armstrong and the Pennsylvania militia. On the right the river was hidden by thick woods and the unevenness of the country; to Sullivan was assigned the duty of taking "every necessary precaution for the security of that flank;" and the six brigades of his command, consisting of the divisions of Stirling, of Stephen, and his own, were stationed in echelons along the river.

On the tenth the two divisions of the British, led respectively by Knyphausen and Cornwallis, formed a junction at Kennet Square. At five the next morning more than half of Howe's forces, leaving their baggage even to their knapsacks behind them, and led by trusty guides, marched under the general and Cornwallis up the Great Valley road to cross the Brandywine at its forks. About ten o'clock Knyphausen with his column, coming upon the river at Chad's ford, seven miles lower down, halted and began a long cannonade, manifesting no purpose of forcing the passage. Washington had "certain" information of the movement of Howe, and resolved to strike at once at the division in his front, which was less than half of the British army, and was encumbered with the baggage of the whole. As Washington rode up and down his lines the shouts of his men witnessed their confidence, and as he spoke to them in cheering words they clamored for battle. Sending orders to Sullivan to cross the Brandywine at a higher ford, prevent the hasty return of the body with Howe and Cornwallis, and threaten the left flank of Knyphausen, Washington put his troops in motion. Greene with the advance was at the river's edge and about to begin the attack, when a message came from Sullivan announcing that he had disobeyed his orders, that the "information on which these orders were founded must be wrong."

The information on which they rested was precisely correct; but the failure of Sullivan overthrew the design, which for success required swiftness of execution. After the loss of two hours, word was brought that the division of Cornwallis had passed the forks and was coming down with the intent to turn the American right. On the instant Sullivan was ordered to confront the advance. Lord Stirling and Stephen posted their troops in two lines on a rounded eminence south-west of Birmingham meeting-house, while Sullivan, who should have gone to their right, marched his division beyond their extreme left, leaving a gap of a half-mile between them, so that he could render no service, and was exposed to be cut off. The general officers, whom he "rode on to consult," explained to him that the right of his wing was unprotected. Upon this, he began to march his division to his proper place. The British troops, which beheld this movement as they lay at rest for a full hour after their long march in the hot day, were led to the attack before he could form his line. His division, badly conducted, fled without their artillery, and could not be rallied. Their flight exposed the flank of Stirling and Stephen. These two divisions, only half as numerous as their assailants, in spite of the "unofficerlike behavior" of Stephen, fought in good earnest, using their artillery from a distance, their muskets only when their enemy was within forty paces; but under the charge of the Hessians and British grenadiers, who vied with each other in fury as they ran forward with the bayonet, the American line continued to break from the right. Conway's brigade resisted well; Sullivan showed personal courage; Lafayette, present as a volunteer, though wounded in the leg while rallying the fugitives, bound up the wound as he could, and kept the field till the close of the battle. The third Virginia regiment, commanded by Marshall and stationed apart in a wood, held out till both its flanks were turned and half its officers and one third its men were killed or wounded.

Howe seemed likely to get in the rear of the continental army and complete its overthrow. But, at the sound of the cannon on the right, Washington, taking with him Greene and the two brigades of Muhlenburg and Weedon, which lay nearest the scene of action, moved swiftly to the support of the wing that had been confided to Sullivan, and in about forty minutes met them in full retreat. His approach checked the pursuit. Cautiously making a new arrangement of his forces, Howe again pushed forward, driving the party with Greene till they came upon a strong position, chosen by Washington, which completely commanded the road, and which a regiment of Virginians under Stevens and another of Pennsylvanians under Stewart were able to hold till nightfall.

In the heat of the engagement the division with Knyphausen crossed the Brandywine in one body at Chad's ford. The left wing of the Americans, under the command of Wayne, defended their intrenchments against an attack in front; but when, near the close of the day, a strong detachment threatened their rear, they made a well-ordered retreat, and were not pursued.

Night was falling, when two battalions of British grenadiers under Meadow and Monckton received orders to occupy a cluster of houses on a hill beyond Dilworth. They marched carelessly, the officers with sheathed swords. At fifty paces from the first house they were surprised by a deadly fire from Maxwell's corps, which lay in ambush to cover the American retreat. The British officers sent for help, but were nearly routed before General Agnew could bring relief. The Americans then withdrew, and darkness ended the contest.

At midnight, Washington from Chester seized the first moment of respite to report to congress his defeat, making no excuses, casting the blame on no one, not even alluding to the disparity of forces, but closing with cheering words. His losses, in killed, wounded, and prisoners, were about one thousand, less rather than more. Except the severely wounded, few prisoners were taken. A howitzer and ten cannon, among them two Hessian field-pieces captured at Trenton, were left on the field. Several of the French officers behaved with great gallantry: Mauduit Duplessis; Lewis de Fleury, whose horse was shot under him and whose merit congress recognised by vote; Lafayette, of whom Washington said to the surgeon: "Take care of him as though he were my son." Pulaski the Pole, who on that day showed the daring of adventure rather than the qualities of a commander, was created a brigadier of cavalry.

The loss of the British army in killed and wounded was at least five hundred and seventy-nine, of whom fifty-eight were officers. Of the Hessian officers, Ewald and Wreden received from the elector a military order. Howe showed his usual courage under fire; but nightfall, the want of cavalry, and the extreme fatigue of his army, forbade pursuit.

When congress heard of the defeat at the Brandywine, it directed Putnam to send fifteen hundred continental troops to the commander-in-chief with all possible expedition, and summoned continental troops and militia from Maryland and Virginia. The militia of New Jersey were kept at home by a triple raid of Sir Henry Clinton. The assembly of Pennsylvania, rent by faction, chose this moment to change nearly all its delegates in congress. The people along Howe's route, being largely Quakers, were friendly or passive. Negro slaves prayed for his success, hoping "that, if the British power should be victorious, all the negro slaves would become free."

Washington, who had marched from Chester to Germantown, after having supplied his men with provisions and forty rounds of cartridges, recrossed the Schuylkill to confront once more the army of Howe, who had been detained near the Brandywine till he could send his wounded to Wilmington. The two chiefs marched toward Goshen. On the sixteenth, Donop and his yagers, who pressed forward too rapidly, were encountered by Wayne; but, before the battle became general, a furious rain set in, which continued all the next night; and the American army, as, from the poor quality of their accoutrements, their cartridges were drenched, were obliged to retire to replenish their ammunition.

It was next the purpose of the British to turn Washington's right, so as to shut him up between the rivers; but he took care to hold the roads to the south as well as to the north and west. Late on the eighteenth Alexander Hamilton, who was ordered to Philadelphia to secure military stores, gave congress notice of immediate danger; and its members, few in number, fled in the night to meet at Lancaster.

When, on the nineteenth, the American army passed through the Schuylkill at Parker's ford, Wayne was left with a large body of troops to fall upon any detached party of Howe's army. On the night following the twentieth, just as he had called up his men to make a junction with another American party, Major-General Grey of the British army, with three regiments, broke in upon them by surprise, and, using the bayonet only, killed, wounded, or took at least three hundred. Darkness and Wayne's presence of mind saved his cannon and the rest of his troops.

The loss opened the way to Philadelphia. John Adams, the head of the board of war, blamed Washington without stint for having crossed to the eastern side of the Schuylkill: "If he had sent one brigade of his regular troops to have headed the militia, he might have cut to pieces Howe's army in attempting to cross any of the fords. Howe will wait for his fleet in Delaware river. Heaven grant us one great soul! One leading mind would extricate the best cause from that ruin which seems to await it."

While John Adams was writing, Howe moved down the valley and encamped along the Schuylkill from Valley Forge to French creek. There were many fords on the rapid river, which in those days flowed at its will. On the twenty-second a small party of Howe's army forced the passage at Gordon's ford. The following night and morning the main body of the British army crossed at Fatland ford near Valley Forge, and encamped with its left to the Schuylkill. Congress disguised its impotence by voting Washington power to change officers under brigadiers, and by inviting him to support his army upon the country around him. He could not by swift marches hang on his enemy's rear, for more than a thousand of his men were barefoot. Rejoined by Wayne, and strengthened by a thousand Marylanders under Smallwood, he sent a peremptory order to Putnam, who was wildly planning attacks on Staten Island, Paulus Hook, New York, and Long Island, to forward a detachment of twenty-five hundred men "with the least possible delay," and to draw his remaining forces together, so that with aid from the militia of New York and Connecticut "the passes in the Highlands might be perfectly secure." He requested Gates to return the corps of Morgan, being resolved, if he could but be seconded, to force the army of Howe to retreat or capitulate before winter.

On the twenty-fifth that army encamped at Germantown; and the next morning Cornwallis, with the grenadiers, after thirty days had been consumed in a march of fifty-four miles, entered Philadelphia. But it was too late for Howe to send aid to Burgoyne.

On the nineteenth of August, Gates assumed the command of the northern army, which lay nine miles above Albany, near the mouths of the Mohawk. After the return of the battalions with Arnold and the arrival of the corps of Morgan, his continental troops, apart from continental accessions of militia, outnumbered the British and German regulars whom he was to meet. Artillery and small arms from France arrived through Portsmouth, New Hampshire; and New York brought out its resources with exhaustive patriotism.

The war of America was a war of ideas more than of material power. On the ninth of September, Jay, the first chief justice of the new commonwealth of New York, as he opened its supreme court in Kingston, charged the grand jury in these words: "Free, mild, and equal government begins to rise. Divine Providence has made the tyranny of princes instrumental in breaking the chains of their subjects. Whoever compares our present with our former constitution will admit that all the calamities incident to this war will be amply compensated by the many blessings flowing from this glorious revolution. Thirteen colonies immediately become one people, and unanimously determine to be free. The people of this state have chosen their constitution under the guidance of reason and experience. The highest respect has been paid to those great and equal rights of human nature which should forever remain inviolate in every society. You will know no power but such as you create, no laws but such as acquire all their obligation from your consent. The rights of conscience and private judgment are by nature subject to no control but that of the Deity."

Gates, after twenty days of preparation, moved his army to Stillwater, and on the twelfth of September encamped on Behmus's Heights, a spur of hills jutting out nearly to the Hudson, which Kosciuszko had selected as the ground on which their enemy was to be waited for. The army counted nine thousand effectives, eager for action.

For the army of Burgoyne a hundred and eighty boats were hauled by relays of horses over the two portages between Lake George and the river at Saratoga, and laden with provisions for one month. Then calling in all his men, he gave up his connections, and with less than six thousand rank and file he proceeded toward Albany. On the thirteenth his army crossed the Hudson at Schuylerville by a bridge of boats, and encamped within six miles of the American army.

At once Lincoln, carrying out a plan concerted with Gates, sent from Manchester five hundred light troops without artillery, under Colonel John Brown of Massachusetts, to distress the British in their rear. In the morning twilight of the eighteenth Brown surprised the outposts of Ticonderoga, including Mount Defiance; and, with the loss of not more than nine killed and wounded, he set free one hundred American prisoners, captured four companies of regulars and others who guarded the new portage between Lake Champlain and Lake George, in all two hundred and ninety-three men with arms and five cannon, and destroyed an armed sloop, gunboats, and other boats to the number of one hundred and fifty below the falls of Lake George, and fifty above them.

The British army, stopping to rebuild bridges and repair roads, advanced scarcely four miles in as many days. The right of the well-chosen camp of the Americans touched the Hudson and could not be assailed; their left was a high ridge of hills; their lines were protected by a breastwork. To get forward, Burgoyne must dislodge them. His army moved on the nineteenth, as on former days, in three columns: the artillery, protected by Riedesel and Brunswick troops, took the road through the meadows near the river; the general led the centre across a deep ravine to a field on Freeman's farm; while Fraser, with the right, made a circuit upon the ridge to occupy heights from which the left of the Americans could be assailed. Indians, Canadians, and tories hovered on the front and flanks of the several columns.

In concurrence with the advice of Arnold, Gates ordered out Morgan's riflemen and the light infantry. They put a picket to flight at a quarter past one, but retired before the division with Burgoyne. Leading his force unobserved through the woods, and securing his right by thickets and ravines, Morgan next fell unexpectedly upon the left of the British central division. To support him, Gates, at two o'clock, sent out three New Hampshire battalions, of which that of Scammel met the enemy in front, that of Cilley took them in flank. Morgan with his riflemen captured a cannon, but could not bring it off; his horse was shot under him in the warm engagement. From half-past two there was a lull of a half-hour, during which Phillips brought more artillery against the Americans, and Gates ordered out two regiments of Connecticut militia under Cook. At three the battle became general, and it raged till after sundown. Fraser sent to the aid of Burgoyne such detachments as he could spare without endangering his own position, which was the object of the day. At four, Gates ordered out the New York regiment of Cortlandt, followed in a half-hour by that of Henry Livingston. The battle was marked by the obstinate courage of the Americans, but by no manœuvre; man fought against man, regiment against regiment. An American party would capture a cannon, and drive off the British; the British would rally and recover it with the bayonet, but only to fall back before the deadly fire from the wood. The Americans used no artillery; the British employed it with effect; but the commander of their principal battery was killed, and some of his officers and thirty-six out of forty-eight matrosses were killed or wounded. At five, all too late in the day, Brigadier Learned was ordered with his brigade and a Massachusetts regiment to the enemy's rear. Before the sun went down Burgoyne was in danger of a rout; the troops about him wavered, when Riedesel, with a single regiment and two cannon, struggling through the thickets, across a ravine, climbed the hill and charged the Americans on their right flank. Evening was at hand, and those of the Americans who had been engaged for more than three hours had nearly exhausted their ammunition; they withdrew within their lines, taking with them their wounded and a hundred captives. On the British side three major-generals came on the field; on the American side not one, nor a brigadier till near its close. The glory of the day was due to the several regiments of husbandmen, who fought with one spirit and one will, and needed only proper support and an able general to have utterly routed the army of Burgoyne. Of the Americans, praise justly fell upon Morgan of Virginia and Scammel of New Hampshire; none offered their lives more freely than Cilley's continental regiment and the Connecticut militia of Cook. The American loss, including the wounded and missing, proved less than three hundred and twenty; distinguished among the dead was Lieutenant-Colonel Andrew Colburn of New Hampshire. This battle crippled the British force irretrievably. Their loss exceeded six hundred. Of the sixty-second regiment, which left Canada five hundred strong, there remained less than sixty men and four or five officers. "Tell my uncle I died like a soldier," were the last words of Hervey, one of its lieutenants, a boy of sixteen, who was mortally wounded. A shot from a rifle, meant for Burgoyne, struck an officer at his side.

The British army passed the night in bivouac under arms; the division of Burgoyne on the field of battle. Morning revealed to them their desperate condition; to former difficulties was added the encumbrance of their wounded. Their dead were buried promiscuously, except that officers were thrown into holes by themselves, in one pit three of the twentieth regiment, of whom the oldest was not more than seventeen.

An attack upon the remains of Burgoyne's division, while it was still disconnected and without intrenchments, was urged by Arnold; but Gates waited for ammunition and more troops. The quarrel between them grew more bitter; and Arnold demanded and received a passport for Philadelphia. Repenting of his rashness, he lingered in the camp, but could not obtain access to Gates, nor a command.

During the twentieth the British general encamped his army on the heights near Freeman's house, so near the American lines that he could not make a movement unobserved. On the twenty-first he received from Sir Henry Clinton a promise of a diversion on Hudson river; and answered that he could maintain his position until the twelfth of October.

Spies of the British watched the condition of Putnam, and he had not sagacity to discover theirs. In his easy manner he suffered a large part of the New York militia to go home; so that he now had but about two thousand men. Sir Henry Clinton, with four thousand troops, feigned an attack upon Fishkill by landing troops at Verplanck's Point. Putnam was duped; and, just as the British wished, retired out of the way to the hills in the rear of Peekskill. George Clinton, the governor of New York, knew the point of danger. With such force as he could collect he hastened to Fort Clinton, while his brother James took command of Fort Montgomery. Putnam should have reinforced their garrisons; instead of it, he ordered troops away from them, and left the passes unguarded. At daybreak on the sixth of October the British and Hessians disembarked at Stony Point; Vaughan, with more than one thousand men, advanced toward Fort Clinton, while a corps of about a thousand occupied the pass of Dunderberg, and, by a difficult, circuitous march of seven miles, at five o'clock came in the rear of Fort Montgomery. Vaughan's troops were then ordered to storm Fort Clinton with the bayonet. A gallant resistance was made by the governor;

but at the close of twilight the British, by the superiority of numbers, forced the works. In like manner Fort Montgomery was carried; but the two commanders and almost all of both garrisons escaped into the forest. A heavy iron chain with a boom had been stretched across the river from Fort Montgomery to Anthony's Nose. Overruling the direction of Governor Clinton, Putnam ordered down two continental frigates for the defence of the chain; but, as they were badly manned, one of them could not be got off in time; the other grounded opposite West Point; and both were set on fire in the night. Fort Constitution, on the island opposite West Point, was abandoned, so that the river was open to Albany. Putnam, receiving large reinforcements from Connecticut, did nothing with them. On the seventh he wrote to Gates: "I cannot prevent the enemy's advancing; prepare for the worst;" and on the eighth: "The enemy can take a fair wind and go to Albany or Half Moon with great expedition and without any opposition." But Sir Henry Clinton, who ought a month sooner to have gone to Albany, garrisoned Fort Montgomery and returned to New York, leaving Vaughan with a large marauding expedition to ascend the Hudson. Vaughan did no more than plunder and burn the town of Kingston and the mansions of patriots along the river.

After the battle of the nineteenth of September the condition of Burgoyne rapidly grew more perplexing. The Americans in his rear broke down the bridges which he had built, and so swarmed in the woods that he could gain no just idea of their situation. His foraging parties and advanced posts were harassed; horses grew thin and weak; the hospital was cumbered with at least eight hundred sick and wounded men. One third part of the soldier's ration was retrenched. While the British army declined in number, Gates was constantly reinforced. On the twenty-second Lincoln arrived, and took command of the right wing; he was followed by two thousand militia. The Indians melted away from Burgoyne, and by the zeal of Schuyler, contrary to the wiser policy of Gates, a small band, chiefly of Oneidas, joined the American camp. In the evening of the fourth of October, Burgoyne called Phillips, Riedesel, and Fraser to council, and proposed to them by a roundabout march to turn the left of the Americans. To do this, it was answered, the British must, for three days, leave their boats and provisions at the mercy of the Americans. Riedesel advised a swift retreat to Fort Edward; but Burgoyne still continued to wait for a co-operating army from below. On the seventh he agreed to make a grand reconnoissance, and, if the Americans could not be attacked, he would think of a retreat. At eleven o'clock on the morning of that day seven hundred men of Fraser's command, three hundred of Breymann's, and five hundred of Riedesel's, were picked out for the service. The late hour was chosen, that in case of disaster night might intervene for their relief. They were led by Burgoyne, who took with him Phillips, Riedesel, and Fraser. The fate of the army hung on the issue, and not many more than fifteen hundred men could be spared without exposing the camp. They entered a field about half a mile from the Americans, where they formed a line, and sat down in double ranks, offering battle. Their artillery, consisting of eight brass pieces and two howitzers, was well posted; their front was open; the grenadiers under Ackland, stationed in the forests, protected the left; Fraser, with the light infantry and an English regiment, formed the right, which was skirted by a wooded hill; the Brunswickers held the centre. While Fraser sent foragers into a wheat-field, Canadians, provincials, and Indians were to get upon the American rear.

Gates, having in his camp ten or eleven thousand men eager for battle, resolved to send out a force sufficient to overwhelm the detachment. By the advice of Morgan, a simultaneous attack was ordered to be made on both flanks. A little before three o'clock the column of the American right, composed of Poor's brigade, followed by the New York militia under Ten Broeck, unmoved by the well-served grape-shot from two twelve-pounders and four sixes, marched on to engage Ackland's grenadiers; while the men of Morgan were seen making a circuit, to reach the flank and rear of the British right, upon which the American light infantry under Dearborn impetuously descended. In danger of being surrounded, Burgoyne ordered Fraser with the light infantry and part of the twenty-fourth regiment to form a second line in the rear, so as to secure the retreat of the army. While executing this order, Fraser was hit by a ball from a sharpshooter, and, fatally wounded, was led back to the camp. Just then, within twenty minutes from the beginning of the action, the British grenadiers, suffering from the sharp fire of musketry in front and flank, wavered and fled, leaving Major Ackland, their commander, severely wounded. These movements exposed the Brunswickers on both flanks, and one regiment broke, turned, and fled. It rallied, but only to retreat in less disorder, driven by the Americans. Sir Francis Clarke, Burgoyne's first aid, sent to the rescue of the artillery, was mortally wounded before he could deliver his message; and the Americans took all the eight pieces. In the face of the hot pursuit, no second line could be formed. Burgoyne exposed himself fearlessly; a shot passed through his hat, and another tore his waistcoat; but he was compelled to give the word of command for all to retreat to the camp of Fraser, which lay to the right of head-quarters. As he entered, he betrayed his sense of danger, crying out: "You must defend the post till the very last man!" The Americans pursued with fury. Arnold, who had ridden upon the field without orders, without command, without a staff, and beside himself, like one intoxicated, yet carrying some authority as the highest officer present in the action, gave orders which argued thoughtlessness rather than courage. By his command an attack was made on the strongest part of the British line, and continued for more than an hour, though in vain. Meantime, the brigade of Learned made a circuit and assaulted the quarters of the regiment of Breymann, which flanked the extreme right of the British camp, and was connected with Frazer's quarters by two stockade redoubts, defended by Canadian companies. These intermediate redoubts were stormed by a Massachusetts regiment headed by John Brooks, afterward governor of that state, and with little loss. Arnold, who had joined in this last assault, lost his horse and was himself badly wounded within the works. Time and the loss of blood restored his senses. The regiment of Breymann was now exposed in front and rear. Its colonel, fighting gallantly, was mortally wounded; some of his troops fled; and the rest, about two hundred in number, surrendered. Colonel Speth, who led a small body of Germans to his support, was taken prisoner. The position of Breymann was the key to Burgoyne's camp; but the directions for its recovery could not be executed. Night ended the battle.

During the fight, neither Gates nor Lincoln appeared on the field. In his report of the action, Gates named Arnold with Morgan and Dearborn; and congress restored Arnold to the rank which he had claimed. The action was the battle of husbandmen, in which men of the valley of Virginia, of Maryland, of Pennsylvania, of New York, and of New England fought together with one spirit for the common cause. The army of Burgoyne was greatly outnumbered, its cattle starving, its hospital cumbered with sick, wounded, and dying. At ten o'clock in the night he gave orders to retreat; but at daybreak he had only transferred his camp to the heights above the hospital. Light dawned, to show the hopelessness of his position.

Fraser questioned the surgeon eagerly as to his wound, and, when he learned that he must die, he cried out in agony: "Damned ambition!" At sunset of the eighth his body, attended by the officers of his family, was borne by soldiers of his corps to the great redoubt above the Hudson where he had asked to be buried; the three major-generals, Burgoyne, Phillips, and Riedesel, and none beside, followed as mourners; and, under the fire of the American artillery, the order for the burial of the dead was strictly observed over his grave.

In the following hours Burgoyne, abandoning the wounded and sick in his hospital, continued his retreat; but, the road being narrow and heavy from rain and the night dark, he made halt two miles short of Saratoga. In the night before the tenth the British army, finding the passage of the Hudson too strongly guarded, forded the Fishkill, and in a very bad position at Saratoga made their last encampment. On the tenth Burgoyne sent out a party to reconnoitre the road on the west of the Hudson; but Stark, who after the battle of Bennington had been received at home as a conqueror, had returned with more than two thousand men of New Hampshire and held the river at Fort Edward.

At daybreak of the eleventh an American brigade, favored by a thick fog, broke up the British posts at the mouth of the Fishkill and captured all their boats and all their provisions except a short allowance for five days. On the twelfth the British army was completely invested, and every spot in its camp was exposed to rifle shot or cannon. On the thirteenth, Burgoyne for the first time called the commanders of the corps to council, and they were unanimous for treating on honorable terms.

The American army and the freeholders of New York and New England, who had voluntarily risen up to resist the invasion from Canada, had, by their unanimity, courage, and energy, left the British no chance of escape. "The great bulk of the country," wrote Burgoyne, "is undoubtedly with the congress in principle and zeal." When the general who should have directed them remained in camp, their common zeal created a harmonious correspondence of movement, and baffled the officers and veterans opposed to them. Gates, who had never appeared in the field during the campaign, took to himself the negotiation, and proposed that they should surrender as prisoners of war. Burgoyne replied by the proposal that his army should pass from the port of Boston to Great Britain upon the condition of not serving again in North America during the present contest; and that the officers should retain their carriages, horses, and baggage free from molestation or search, Burgoyne "giving his honor that there are no public stores secreted therein." Gates, uneasy at the news of British forces on the Hudson river, closed with these "articles of convention," and on the seventeenth "the convention was signed." A body of Americans marched to the tune of Yankee Doodle into the lines of the British, who marched out and in mute astonishment laid down their arms with none of the American soldiery to witness the spectacle. Bread was then served to them, for they had none left, nor flour.

Their number, including officers, was five thousand seven hundred and ninety-one, among whom were six members of parliament. Previously there had been taken eighteen hundred and fifty-six prisoners of war, including the sick and wounded who had been abandoned. Of deserters from the British ranks there were three hundred; so that, including the killed, prisoners, and disabled at Hubbardton, Fort Ann, Bennington, Orisca, the outposts of Ticonderoga, and round Saratoga, the total loss of the British in this northern campaign was not far from ten thousand.

The Americans acquired thirty-five pieces of the best ordnance then known, beside munitions of war, and more than four thousand muskets.

Complaints reached congress that the military chest of the British army, the colors of its regiments, and arms, especially bayonets, had been kept back; and that very many of the muskets which were left behind had been purposely rendered useless.

During the resistance to Burgoyne, Daniel Morgan, from the time of his transfer to the northern army, never gave other than the wisest counsels, and stood first for conduct, effective leadership, and unsurpassable courage on the field of battle; yet Gates did not recommend him for promotion, but asked and soon obtained the rank of brigadier for James Wilkinson, an undistinguished favorite of his own.

The victory at Saratoga not only thwarted the British plan to split the states but also proved that the new nation could successfully defend its independ-ence by force of arms. This encouraged England's old enemy France to give aid and ultimately sign a treaty of alliance with the United States. Without substantial military and naval assistance from France, the Con-tinental Army could not do much more than plan an unending game of hares and hounds with the British. They could harry, skirmish and with-draw, trying always to stay a little ahead of the Redcoats. For four years after Burgoyne's surrender, the British moved at will, for the most part up and down the South, without being able decisively to defeat the Ameri-cans. Then in 1781, Lord Cornwallis began to build fortifications at Yorktown, and General Washington with his French allies, Count de Rochambeau and Admiral de Grasse, who had arrived with men and ships, planned a trap.

THE LAST CAMPAIGN OF THE AMERICAN WAR

Sir Henry Clinton persevered in the purpose of holding a station in the Chesapeake bay; and, on the second of January 1781, Arnold, with sixteen hundred men, appeared by his order in the James river. The generous com-monwealth of Virginia having sent its best troops and arms to the more southern states, Governor Jefferson promptly called the whole militia from the adjacent counties; but, in the region of planters with slaves, there were not freemen enough at hand to meet the invaders. Arnold offered to spare Richmond if he might unmolested carry off its stores of tobacco; the pro-posal being rejected with scorn, on the fifth and sixth its houses and stores, public and private, were set on fire. Washington used his knowledge of the lowlands of Virginia to form for the capture of Arnold a plan of which the success seemed to him certain. From his own army he detached about twelve hundred men of the New England and New Jersey lines under the command of Lafayette, and asked the combined aid of the whole French fleet at Newport and a detachment from the land forces under Rochambeau. But d'Estouches, the French admiral, had already sent out a sixty-four-gun ship and two frigates, and did not think it prudent to put to sea with the residue of the fleet. The ships-of-war, which arrived safely in the Chesa-peake, having no land troops, could not reach Arnold; but, on their way back to Rhode Island, they captured a British fifty-gun frigate. Washington, on the sixth of March, met Rochambeau and d'Estouches in council on board the flag-ship of the French admiral at Newport, and the plan of

Washington, for a combined expedition of the French fleet and land forces into Virginia, was adopted. But the execution of the plan was too slow; the benefit of a fair wind and of a day were lost, so that Arbuthnot, with the British fleet, overtook them off the capes of Virginia. A partial engagement ensued for an hour. On the next day the French, advised by its council of war not to renew the action, returned to Newport; while the British sailed into the Chesapeake.

On the twenty-sixth of March, General Phillips, who brought from New York a reinforcement of two thousand picked men, took the command in Virginia. All the stores of produce which its planters in five quiet years had accumulated were carried off or destroyed. Their negroes, so desired in the West Indies, formed the staple article of plunder.

By a courier from Washington Lafayette received information that Virginia was to become the centre of active operations, and was instructed to defend the state as well as his means would permit. His troops, who were chiefly from New England, dreaded the climate of lower Virginia, and, besides, were destitute of everything; yet when Lafayette, from the south side of the Susquehannah, in an order of the day, offered leave to any of them to return to the North, not one would abandon him. At Baltimore he borrowed two thousand pounds sterling, supplied his men with shoes and hats, and bought linen, which the women of Baltimore made into summer garments. Then, by a forced march of two hundred miles, he arrived at Richmond on the twenty-ninth of April, the evening before Phillips reached the opposite bank of the river. Having in the night been joined by Steuben with militia, Lafayette was able to hold in check the larger British force. The line of Pennsylvania was detained in that state week after week for needful supplies; while Clinton, stimulated by Germain's praises of the activity of Cornwallis, sent another considerable detachment to Virginia.

On the thirteenth of May, General Phillips died of malignant fever. Arnold, on whom the command devolved, though only for seven days, addressed a letter to Lafayette, who returned it, refusing to correspond with a traitor. Arnold rejoined by threatening to send to the Antilles all American prisoners, unless a cartel should be immediately concluded. On the twentieth Cornwallis arrived at Petersburg, and ordered Arnold back to New York.

Clinton detached him once more, and this time against his native state. On the sixth of September his party landed on each side of New London. The town was plundered and burnt. On the other side of the river Colonel Ledyard and about one hundred and fifty ill-armed militia-men defended Fort Griswold on Groton Hill for forty minutes with the greatest resolution. Lieutenant-Colonel Eyre, who commanded the British assailants, was wounded near the works, and Major Montgomery was killed immediately after. When Ledyard had surrendered, Major Bromfield, on whom the British command had devolved, ran him through with his sword, and refused quarter to the garrison. Seventy-three of them were killed, and more than thirty wounded; about forty were carried off as prisoners. With this expedition, Arnold disappears from history.

Cornwallis now found himself where he had so persistently desired to be —in Virginia, at the head of seven thousand effective men, with not a third of that number to oppose him by land, and with undisputed command of the water. "Wanting a rudder in the storm," said Richard Henry Lee, "the good ship must inevitably be cast away;" and he proposed to send for General Washington immediately and invest him with "dictatorial powers." But Jefferson reasoned: "The thought alone of creating a dictator is treason against mankind, giving to their oppressors a proof of the imbecility of republican government in times of pressing danger. The government, instead of being braced for greater exertions, would be thrown back." As governor of Virginia, speaking for its people and representing their distresses, he wrote to Washington: "Could you lend us your personal aid? The presence of their beloved countryman would restore full confidence, and render them equal to whatever is not impossible. Should you repair to your native state, the difficulty would then be how to keep men out of the field."

During the summer, congress, against the opinion of Samuel Adams and without aid from Massachusetts, substituted for its own executive committees a single chief in each of the most important departments. Robert Morris was placed in charge of the finances of the confederation; in conformity with the wish of the French minister, which was ably sustained by Sullivan, the conduct of foreign affairs was intrusted to Robert Livingston of New York. Washington would have gladly seen Schuyler at the head of the war department.

Outside of congress, Hamilton persevered in recommending an efficient government. His views were so identical with those of Robert Morris that it is sometimes hard to say in whose mind they first sprung up. They both laid the greatest stress on the institution of a national bank; the opinion that a national debt is a national blessing was carried by Morris to a most perilous extreme.

The conduct of the war continued to languish for the want of a central government. In the states from which the most was hoped, Hancock of Massachusetts was neglectful of business; Reed, the president of Pennsylvania, was more ready to recount what the state had done than undertake to do more; so that the army was not wholly free from the danger of being disbanded for want of subsistence. Of the armed vessels of the United States, all but two frigates had been taken or destroyed.

Madison persevered in the effort to obtain power for congress to collect a revenue, and a committee was named to examine into the changes which needed to be made in the articles of confederation. "The difficulty of continuing the war under them," so wrote Luzerne, on the twenty-seventh of

August, "proves the necessity of reforming them; they were produced at an epoch when the mere name of authority inspired terror, and by men who thought to make themselves agreeable to the people. I can scarcely persuade myself that they will come to an agreement on this matter. Some persons even believe that the existing constitution, all vicious as it is, can be changed only by some violent revolution."

The French government declined to furnish means for the siege of New York. After the arrival of its final instructions, Rochambeau, attended by Chastellux, in a meeting with Washington at Weathersfield on the twenty-first of May, settled the preliminaries of the campaign. The French land force was to march to the Hudson river, and, in conjunction with the American army, be ready to move to the southward. De Grasse was charged anew on his way to the North to enter the Chesapeake. In the direction of the war for the coming season there would be union; for congress had lodged the highest power in the northern and southern departments in the hands of Washington, and France had magnanimously placed her troops under his command.

Before his return, the American general called upon the governors of the New England states, "in earnest and pointed terms," to complete their continental battalions, to hold bodies of militia ready to march in a week after being called for, and to adopt effective modes of supply. Governor Trumbull of Connecticut cheered him with the opinion that he would obtain all that he needed.

In June the French contingent, increased by fifteen hundred men newly arrived in ships-of-war, left Newport for the Hudson river. The inhabitants crowded around them on their march, glad to recognise in them allies and defenders. The rights of private property were scrupulously respected, and the petty exigencies of local laws good-naturedly submitted to.

Cornwallis began his career on the James river in Virginia by seizing horses, which were of the best breed, and mounting five or six hundred men. He then started in pursuit of Lafayette, who, with about one thousand continental troops, was posted between Wilton and Richmond, waiting for reinforcements from Pennsylvania. "Lafayette cannot escape him," wrote Clinton to Germain. The youthful major-general warily kept to the north of his pursuer; and on the seventh of June made a junction with Wayne not far from Raccoon ford. Small as was his force, he compared the British in Virginia to the French in the German kingdom of Hanover at the time of the seven years' war, and confidently predicted analogous results. Cornwallis advanced as far as the court-house of the Virginia county of Hanover, then crossed South Anna, and, not encountering Lafayette, encamped on the James river, from the Point of Fork to a little below the mouth of Byrd creek. For the next ten days his head-quarters were at Elk Hill, on a plantation belonging to Jefferson.

Two expeditions were undertaken. With one hundred and eighty dragoons and forty mounted infantry, Tarleton, destroying public stores on the way, rode seventy miles in twenty-four hours to Charlottesville, where the Virginia assembly was then in session; but the assembly, having received warning, had adjourned to the valley beyond the Blue Ridge, and Jefferson had gone to the mountains on horseback. The dragoons overtook seven of the legislature; otherwise, the expedition was fruitless.

Simcoe, with a party of mixed troops, was sent to destroy stores over which Steuben with a few more than five hundred men kept guard. Steuben had transported his magazine across the Fluvanna, and the water was too deep to be forded.

Tarleton suffered nothing of Jefferson's at Monticello to be injured. At Elk Hill, under the eye of Cornwallis, all his barns and fences were burnt; the growing crops destroyed; the fields laid absolutely waste; the throats cut of all horses that were too young for service, and the rest carried off. He took away about thirty slaves, not to receive freedom, but to suffer from a worse form of slavery in the West Indies. The rest of the neighborhood was treated in like manner, but with less of malice.

In the march of the British army from Elk Hill down the river to Williamsburg, where it arrived on the twenty-fifth of June, all dwelling-houses were plundered. The band of Lafayette hung upon its rear, but could not prevent its depredations. The Americans of that day computed that Cornwallis, in his midsummer marchings up and down Virginia, destroyed property to the value of three million pounds sterling. He nowhere gained a foothold, and his long marches thoroughly taught him that the people were bent on independence.

At Williamsburg, to his amazement and chagrin, he received orders from his chief to send back to New York about three thousand men. Clinton's letter of the eleventh expressed his fear of being attacked in New York by more than twenty thousand; there was, he said, no possibility of re-establishing order in Virginia, so general was the disaffection to Great Britain; Cornwallis should therefore take a defensive situation in any healthy station he might choose, be it at Williamsburg or Yorktown. On the fifteenth he wrote further: "I do not think it advisable to leave more troops in that unhealthy climate at this season of the year than are absolutely wanted for a defensive and a desultory water expedition." "De Grasse," so he continued on the nineteenth, "will visit this coast in the hurricane season, and bring with him troops as well as ships. But, when he hears that your lordship has taken possession of York river before him, I think that their first efforts will be in this quarter. I am, however, under no great apprehensions, as Sir George Rodney seems to have the same suspicions of de Grasse's intention that we have, and will of course follow him hither."

From this time the hate which had long existed between the lieutenant-general and the commander-in-chief showed itself without much reserve. Cornwallis was eager to step into the chief command; Sir Henry Clinton, though he had threatened to throw up his place, clung to it tenaciously, and relates of himself that he would not be "duped" by his rival into resigning.

"To your opinions it is my duty implicitly to submit," was the answer of Cornwallis to the orders of Clinton; and on the fourth of July he began his march to Portsmouth. On that day the royal army arrived near James Island, and in the evening the advanced guard reached the opposite bank of the James river. Two or three more days were required to carry over all the stores and the troops. Lafayette with his small army followed at a distance. Beside fifteen hundred regular troops, equal to the best in the royal army, he drew to his side as volunteers gallant young men mounted on their own horses from Maryland and Virginia. Youth and generosity, courage and prudence, were his spells of persuasion. His perceptions were quick, his vigilance never failed, and in his methods of gaining information of the movements of the enemy he excelled every officer in the war except Washington and Morgan. All accounts bear testimony to his caution. Of his self-possession in danger he was soon called upon to give proof.

On the sixth, Lafayette judged correctly that the great body of the British army was still on the north side of the James river; but Wayne, without his knowledge, detached a party under Colonel Galvan to carry off a field-piece of the enemy which was said to lie exposed. The information proved false. The party with Galvan retreated in column before the advancing British line till they met Wayne with the Pennsylvania brigade. It suited the character of that officer to hazard an encounter. The British moved on with loud shouts and incessant fire. Wayne, discovering that he had engaged a greatly superior force, saw his only safety in redoubling his courage; and he kept up the fight till Lafayette, braving the hottest fire in which his horse was killed under him, brought up the light infantry and rescued the Pennsylvanians from their danger. Two of Wayne's field-pieces were left behind. In killed and wounded, each side lost about one hundred and twenty. The action took its name from the Greene Springs farm, about eight miles above Jamestown, where Lafayette encamped for the night.

After passing the river, Cornwallis, on the eighth, wrote orders to Tarleton with mounted troops to ravage Prince Edward's and Bedford counties, and to destroy all stores, whether public or private. The benefit derived from the destruction of property was not equal to the loss in skirmishes on the route and from the heats of midsummer.

From his camp on Malvern Hill, Lafayette urged Washington to march to Virginia in force; and he predicted in July that, if a French fleet should enter Hampton Roads, the English army must surrender. On the eighth of the same month Cornwallis, in reply to Clinton, reasoned earnestly against a defensive post in the Chesapeake: "It cannot have the smallest influence on the war in Carolina: it only gives us some acres of an unhealthy swamp, and is forever liable to become a prey to a foreign enemy with a temporary superiority at sea." Thoroughly disgusted with the aspect of affairs in Virginia, he asked leave to transfer the command to General Leslie, and go back to Charleston. Meantime, transport ships arrived in the Chesapeake; and, in a letter which he received on the twelfth, he was desired by his chief so to hasten the embarkation of three thousand men that they might sail for New York within forty-eight hours; for, deceived by letters which were written to be intercepted, he believed that the enemy would certainly attack that post.

But the judgment of Clinton was further confused by another cause. The expectation of a brilliant campaign in Virginia had captivated the minds of Lord George Germain and the king; and, now that Cornwallis was thoroughly cured of his own presumptuous delusions, they came back to Clinton in the shape of orders from the British secretary, who dwelt on the vast importance of the occupation of Virginia, and on the wisdom of the present plan of pushing the war in that quarter. It was a great mortification to him that Clinton should think of leaving only a sufficient force to serve for garrisons in the posts that might be established there, and he continued: "Your ideas of the importance of recovering that province appearing to be so different from mine, I thought it proper to ask the advice of his majesty's other servants upon the subject, and, their opinion concurring entirely with mine, it has been submitted to the king; and I am commanded by his majesty to acquaint you that the recovery of the southern provinces and the prosecution of the war from south to north is to be considered as the chief and principal object for the employment of all the forces under your command which can be spared from the defence of the places in his majesty's possession." On Cornwallis he heaped praises, writing to him in June: "The rapidity of your movements is justly matter of astonishment to all Europe." To Clinton he repeated in the same month: "Lord Cornwallis's opinion entirely coincides with mine." So Clinton's peremptory order by which troops in Virginia had been already embarked to sail for New York was countermanded. "As to quitting the Chesapeake entirely," wrote Clinton in a letter received by Cornwallis on the twenty-first of July, "I cannot entertain a thought of such a measure. I flatter myself you will at least hold Old Point Comfort, if it is possible to do it without York." And four days later Clinton urged again: "It ever has been, is, and ever will be, my firm and unalterable opinion that it is of the first consequence to his majesty's affairs on the continent that we take possession of the Chesapeake, and that we do not afterward relinquish it." "Remain in Chesapeake, at least until the stations I have proposed are occupied and established. It never was my intention to continue a post on Elizabeth river." Now the post of Portsmouth on Elizabeth river had, as Lafayette and Washington well understood, the special value that it offered in the last resort the chance of a retreat into the Carolinas.

The infatuation of Germain was incurable; and on the seventh of July he continued: "The detachments sent to Virginia promise more toward bringing the southern colonists to obedience than any offensive operation of the war;" a week later: "You judiciously sent ample reinforcements to the Cheasapeake;" and on the second of August: "As Sir George Rodney knows the destination of de Grasse, and the French acknowledge his ships sail better than theirs, he will get before him and be in readiness to receive him when he comes upon the coast. I see nothing to prevent the recovery of the whole country to the king's obedience."

The engineers of Cornwallis, after careful and extensive surveys, reported unanimously that a work on Point Comfort would not secure ships at anchor in Hampton Roads. To General Phillips, on his embarkation in April, Clinton's words had been: "With regard to a station for the protection of the king's ships, I know of no place so proper as Yorktown." Nothing therefore remained but, in obedience to the spirit of Clinton's orders, to sieze and fortify York and Gloucester. Cornwallis accordingly, in the first week of August, embarked his troops successively, and, evacuating Portsmouth, transferred his force to Yorktown and Gloucester. Yorktown was then but a small village on a high bank, where the long peninsula dividing the York from the James river is less than eight miles wide. The water is broad, bold, and deep; so that ships of the line may ride there in safety. On the opposite side lies Gloucester, a point of land projecting into the river and narrowing till it becomes but one mile wide. These were occupied by Cornwallis, and fortified with the utmost diligence; though, in his deliberate judgment, the measure promised no honor to himself and no advantage to Great Britain.

On the other hand, Lafayette, concentrating his forces in a strong position at a distance of about eight miles, indulged in the happiest prophecies, and on the twenty-fourth of August wrote to Maurepas: "I owe you so much gratitude, and feel for you so much attachment, that I wish sometimes to recall to your recollection the rebel commander of the little Virginia army. Your interest for me will have been alarmed at the dangerous part which has been intrusted to me in my youth. Separated by five hundred miles from every other corps and without any resources, I am to oppose the projects of the court of St. James and the fortunes of Lord Cornwallis. Thus far, we have encountered no disaster." On the same day his words to Vergennes were: "In pursuance of the immense plan of his court, Lord Cornwallis left the two Carolinas exposed, and General Greene has largely profited by it. Lord Cornwallis has left to us Portsmouth, from which place he was in communication with Carolina, and he now is at York, a very advantageous place for one who has the maritime superiority. If by chance that superiority should become ours, our little army will participate in successes which will compensate it for a long and fatiguing campaign. They say that you are about to make peace. I think that you should wait for the events of this campaign."

On the very day on which Cornwallis took possession of York and Gloucester, Washington, assured of the assistance of de Grasse, turned his whole thoughts toward moving with the French troops under Rochambeau and the best part of the American army to the Chesapeake. While hostile divisions and angry jealousies increased between the two chief British officers in the United States, on the American side all things conspired happily together. De Barras, who commanded the French squadron at Newport, wrote as to his intentions: "De Grasse is my junior; yet, as soon as he is within reach, I will go to sea to put myself under his orders." The same spirit insured unanimity in the mixed council of war. The rendezvous was given to de Grasse in Chesapeake bay; and, at the instance of Washington, he was to bring with him as many land troops as could be spared from the West Indies. Clinton was so certain in his own mind that the siege of New York was the great object of Washington that, although the force under his command, including militia, was nearly eighteen thousand, he suffered the Hudson river to be crossed on the twenty-third and twenty-fourth of August without seizing the opportunity to give annoyance. Wurmb, a Hessian colonel, who had command at King's Bridge, again and again reported that the allied armies were obviously preparing to move against Cornwallis; but the general insisted that the appearances were but a stratagem. On the second of September it first broke on his mind that Washington was moving southward.

In the allied camp all was joy. The enthusiasm for political freedom took possession not of the French officers only, but of the soldiers. Every one of them was proud of being a defender of the young republic. On the fifth of September they encamped at Chester. Never had the French seen a man penetrated with a livelier or more manifest joy than Washington when he there learned that, on the last day but one in August, the Count de Grasse, with twenty-eight ships of the line and nearly four thousand land troops, had entered the Chesapeake, where, without loss of time, he had moored most of the fleet in Lynnhaven bay, blocked up York river, and, without being in the least annoyed by Cornwallis, had disembarked at James Island three thousand men under the command of the Marquis de Saint-Simon. Here, too, prevailed unanimity. Saint Simon, though older in military service as well as in years, placed himself and his troops as auxiliaries under the orders of Lafayette, because he was a major-general in the service of the United States. The combined army in their encampment could be approached only by two passages, which were in themselves difficult and were carefully guarded, so that Cornwallis could not act on the offensive, and found himself effectually blockaded by land and by sea.

One more disappointment awaited Cornwallis. Lord Sandwich, after the retirement of Howe, gave the naval command at New York to officers without ability; and the aged Arbuthnot was succeeded by Graves, a coarse and vulgar man, of mean ability and without skill in his profession. Rodney should have followed de Grasse to the north; but he had become involved in pecuniary perils by his indiscriminate seizures at St. Eustatius and conduct during the long-continued sale of his prize-goods. Pleading ill-health, he escaped to England, and in his stead sent Sir Samuel Hood, with fourteen sail of the line, frigates, and a fire-ship, into the Chesapeake, where a junction with Graves would have given the English the supremacy. But Graves, who was of higher rank than Hood, was out of the way on a cruise before Boston, to gain wealth by picking up prizes. Meantime, de Barras, with eight ships of the line, sailed from Newport, convoying ten transports which carried ordnance for the seige of Yorktown.

There was no want of information at New York, yet the British fleet did not leave Sandy Hook until the day after de Grasse had arrived in the Chesapeake. Early on the fifth of September, Graves discovered the French fleet at anchor in the mouth of that bay. De Grasse, though eighteen hundred of his seamen and ninety officers were on duty in James river, ordered his ships to slip their cables, turn out from the anchorage ground, and form the line of battle. The action began at four o'clock in the afternoon, and continued till about sunset. The British sustained so great a loss that, after remaining five days in sight of the French, they returned to New York. On the first day of their return voyage they evacuated and burned The Terrible, a ship of the line, so much had it been damaged in the engagement. De Grasse, now undisturbed master of the Chesapeake, on his way back to his anchoring ground captured two British ships, each of thirty-two guns, and he found de Barras safely at anchor in the bay.

Leaving the allied troops to descend by water from Elk river and Baltimore, Washington, with Rochambeau and Chastellux, riding sixty miles a day, on the evening of the ninth reached his "own seat at Mount Vernon." It was the first time in more than six years that he had seen his home. From its natural terrace above the Potomac his illustrious guests commanded a noble river, a wide and most pleasing expanse of country, and forest-clad heights, which were soon to become the capital of the united republic.

Two days were given to domestic life. On the fourteenth the party arrived at Williamsburg, where Lafayette, recalling the moment when in France the poor rebels were held in light esteem, and when he nevertheless came to share with them all their perils, had the pleasure of welcoming Washington as generalissimo of the combined armies of the two nations.

The first act of Washington was to repair to the Ville de Paris to congratulate de Grasse on his victory. The system of co-operation between the land and naval forces was at the same time concerted.

At this moment Gerry wrote from Massachusetts to Jay: "You will soon have the pleasure of hearing of the capture of Lord Cornwallis and his army." "Nothing can save Cornwallis," said Greene, "but a rapid retreat through North Carolina to Charleston." On the seventeenth, Cornwallis reported to Clinton: "This place is in no state of defense. If you cannot relieve me very soon, you must be prepared to hear the worst." On that same day a council of war, held by Clinton at New York, decided that Cornwallis must be relieved; "at all events before the end of October." The next day Rear-Admiral Graves answered: "I am very happy to find that Lord Cornwallis is in no immediate danger."

One peril yet menaced Washington. Count de Grasse, hearing of a reinforcement of the fleet at New York, was bent on keeping the sea, leaving only two vessels at the mouth of the York river. Against this Washington, on the twenty-fifth, addressed the plainest and most earnest remonstrance: "I should esteem myself deficient in my duty to the common cause of France and America, if I did not persevere in entreating you to resume the plans that have been so happily arranged." The letter was taken by Lafayette, who joined to it his own explanations and reasonings; and de Grasse, though reluctant, was prevailed upon to remain within the capes. Washington wrote in acknowledgment: "A great mind knows how to make personal sacrifices to secure an important general good."

The troops from the North having been safely landed at Williamsburg, on the twenty-eighth the united armies marched for the investiture of Yorktown, drove everything on the British side before them, and lay on their arms during the night.

The fortifications of Yorktown, which were nothing but earthworks freshly thrown up, consisted on the right of redoubts and batteries, with a line of stockade in the rear, which supported a high parapet. Over a marshy ravine in front of the right a large redoubt was placed. The morass extended along the centre, which was defended by a stockade and batteries. Two small redoubts were advanced before the left. The ground in front of the left was in some parts level with the works, in others cut by ravines; altogether very convenient for the besiegers. The space within the works was exceedingly narrow, and, except under the cliff, was exposed to enfilade.

The twenty-ninth was given to reconnoitring and forming a plan of attack and approach. The French entreated Washington for orders to storm the exterior posts of the British; in the course of the night before the thirtieth, Cornwallis ordered them all to be abandoned, and thus prematurely conceded to the allied armies ground which commanded his line of works in a very near advance, and gave great advantages for opening the trenches.

At Gloucester the enemy was shut in by dragoons under the Duke de Lauzun, Virginia militia under General Weedon, and eight hundred marines. Once, and once only, Tarleton and his legion, who were stationed on the same side of the river, undertook to act offensively; but the Duke de Lauzun and his dragoons, full of gayety and joy at the sight, ran against them and trampled them down. Tarleton barely escaped; his horse was taken.

In the night before the sixth of October, everything being in readiness, trenches were opened at six hundred yards' distance from the works of

Cornwallis—on the right by the Americans, on the left by the French; and the labor was executed in friendly rivalry, with so much secrecy and dispatch that it was first revealed to the enemy by the light of morning. Within three days the first parallel was completed, the redoubts were finished, and batteries were employed in demolishing the embrasures of the enemy's works and their advanced redoubts. On the night before the eleventh the French battery on the left, using red-hot shot, set on fire the frigate Charon, of forty-four guns, and three large transport ships which were entirely consumed.

On the eleventh, at night, the second parallel was begun within three hundred yards of the lines of the besieged. This was undertaken so much sooner than the British expected, that it could be conducted with the same secrecy as before; and they had no suspicion of the working parties till daylight discovered them to their pickets.

All day on the fourteenth the American batteries were directed against the abattis and salient angles of two advanced redoubts of the British, both of which needed to be included in the second parallel; and breaches were made in them sufficient to justify an assault. That on the right near York river was garrisoned by forty-five men, that on the left by thrice as many. The storming of the former fell to the Americans under the command of Lieutenant-Colonel Alexander Hamilton; that of the latter to the French, of whom four hundred grenadiers and yagers of the regiments of Gatinois and of Deux Ponts, with a large reserve, were intrusted to Count William de Deux Ponts and to Baron de l'Estrade.

At the concerted signal of six shells consecutively discharged, the corps under Hamilton advanced in two columns without firing a gun—the right composed of his own battalion, led by Major Fish, and of another commanded by Lieutenant-Colonel Gimat; the left, of a detachment under Lieutenant-Colonel Laurens, destined to take the enemy of reverse and intercept their retreat. All the movements were executed with exactness, and the redoubt was at the same moment enveloped and carried in every part. Lieutenant Mansfield conducted the vanguard with coolness and punctuality, and was wounded with a bayonet as he entered the work. Captain Olney led the first platoon of Gimat's battalion over the abattis and palisades, and gained the parapet, receiving two bayonet wounds in the thigh and in the body, but not till he had directed his men to form. Laurens was among the foremost to climb into the redoubt, making prisoner of Major Campbell, its commanding officer. Animated by his example, the battalion of Gimat overcame every obstacle by their order and resolution. The battalion under Major Fish advanced with such celerity as to participate in the assault. Incapable of imitating precedents of barbarity, the Americans spared every man that ceased to resist; so that the killed and wounded of the enemy did not exceed eight. The conduct of the affair brought conspicuous honor to Hamilton.

Precisely as the signal was given, the French on the left, in like manner, began their march in the deepest silence. At one hundred and twenty paces from the redoubt they were challenged by a German sentry from the parapet; they pressed on at a quick time, exposed to the fire of the enemy. The abattis and palisades, at twenty-five paces from the redoubt, being strong and well preserved, stopped them for some minutes and cost them many lives. So soon as the way was cleared by the brave carpenters, the storming party threw themselves into the ditch, broke through the fraises, and mounted the parapet. Foremost was Charles de Lameth, who had volunteered for this attack, and who was wounded in both knees by two different musket-balls. The order being now given, the French leaped into the redoubt and charged the enemy with the bayonet. At this moment the Count de Deux Ponts raised the cry of "Vive le roi," which was repeated by all of his companions who were able to lift their voices. De Sireuil, a very young captain of yagers who had been wounded twice before, was now wounded for the third time and mortally. Within six minutes the redoubt was mastered and manned; but in that short time nearly one hundred of the assailants were killed or wounded.

On that night "victory twined double garlands around the banners" of France and America. Washington acknowledged the emulous courage, intrepidity, coolness, and firmness of the attacking troops, Louis XVI distinguished the regiment of Gatinois by naming it "the Royal Auvergne."

By the unwearied labor of the French and Americans, both redoubts were included in the second parallel in the night of their capture. Just before the break of day of the sixteenth the British made a sortie upon a part of the second parallel and spiked four French pieces of artillery and two of the Americans; but, on the quick advance of the guards in the trenches, they retreated precipitately. The spikes were easily extracted; and in six hours the cannon again took part in the fire which enfiladed the British works.

On the seventeenth, Cornwallis, who could neither hold his post nor escape, proposed to surrender. On the eighteenth, Colonel Laurens and the Viscount de Noailles as commissioners on the American side met two high officers of the army of Cornwallis, to draft the capitulation. The articles were the same as those which Clinton had imposed upon Lincoln at Charleston. All the troops were to be prisoners of war; all public property was to be delivered up. Runaway slaves and the plunder taken by officers and soldiers in their marches through the country might be reclaimed; with this limitation, private property was to be respected. All royalists were left to be dealt with according to the laws of their own countrymen; but Cornwallis, in the packet which took his dispatches to Sir Henry Clinton, was suffered silently to send away such persons as were most obnoxious.

Of prisoners, there were seven thousand two hundred and forty-seven regular soldiers, the flower of the British army in America, beside eight hundred and forty sailors. The British loss during the seige amounted to more than three hundred and fifty. Two hundred and forty-four pieces of cannon were taken, of which seventy-five were of brass. The land forces and stores were assigned to the Americans, the ships and mariners to the French. At four o'clock in the afternoon of the nineteenth, Cornwallis remaining in his tent, Major-General O'Hara marched the British army past the lines of the combined armies and, not without signs of repugnance, made his surrender to Washington. His troops then stepped forward decently and piled their arms on the ground.

The English soldiers affected to look at the allied army with scorn; their officers conducted themselves with decorum, yet felt most keenly how decisive was their defeat.

Nor must impartial history fail to relate that the French provided for the siege of Yorktown thirty-six ships of the line; and that while the Americans supplied nine thousand troops, the contingent of the French consisted of seven thousand.

There was no day before it or after it like that on which the elder Bourbon king, through his army and navy, assisted to seal the victory of the rights of man and to pass from nation to nation the lighted torch of freedom.

When the letters of Washington announcing the capitulation reached congress, that body, with the people streaming in their train, went in procession to the Dutch Lutheran church to return thanks to Almighty God. Every breast swelled with joy. In the evening Philadelphia was illuminated with greater splendor than ever before. Congress voted honors to Washington, to Rochambeau, and to de Grasse, with special thanks to the officers and troops. The promise was given of a marble column to be erected at Yorktown, with emblems of the alliance between the United States and his most Christian majesty.

The Duke de Lauzun, chosen to take the news across the Atlantic, arrived in twenty-two days at Brest, and reached Versailles on the nineteenth of November. The king, who had just been made happy by the birth of a dauphin, received the glad news in the queen's apartment. The very last sands of the life of the Count de Maurepas were running out; but he could still recognise de Lauzun, and the tidings threw a halo round his death-bed. No statesman of his century had a more prosperous old age or such felicity in the circumstances of his death. The joy at court penetrated the people, and the name of Lafayette was pronounced with veneration. "History," said Vergennes, "offers few examples of a success so complete." "All the world agree," wrote Franklin to Washington, "that no expedition was ever better planned or better executed. It brightens the glory that must accompany your name to the latest posterity."

The first tidings of the surrender of Cornwallis reached England from France about noon on the twenty-fifth of November. "It is all over," said Lord North many times, under the deepest agitation and distress. Fox—to whom the defeats of armies of invaders, from Xerxes' time downward, gave the greatest satisfaction—heard of the capitulation of Yorktown with triumphant delight. He hoped it might become the conviction of all mankind that power resting on armed force is invidious, detestable, weak, and tottering. The official report from Sir Henry Clinton was received the same day at midnight. When on the following Tuesday parliament came together, the speech of the king was confused, the debates in the two houses augured an impending change in the opinion of parliament, and the majority of the ministry was reduced to eighty-seven. A fortnight later the motion of Sir James Lowther to give up "all further attempts to reduce the revolted colonies" was well received by the members from the country, and the majority of the ministry, after a very long and animated debate, dwindled to forty-one. The city of London entreated the king to put an end to "this unnatural and unfortunate war." Such, too, was the wish of public meetings in Westminster, in Southwark, and in the counties of Middlesex and Surrey.

The chimes of the Christmas bells had hardly died away when the king wrote as stubbornly as ever: "No difficulties can get me to consent to the getting of peace at the expense of a separation from America." Yet Lord George Germain was compelled to retire from the cabinet. It was sought to palliate his disgrace by a peerage; but, when for the first time he repaired to the house of lords, he was met by reproof for cowardice and incapacity.

JOHN FISKE

(1842-1901)

Even after Great Britain had recognized the independence of the United States in the Treaty of Paris of 1783, the troubles of the new republic continued. The Confederation government, planned during the war, had embodied the American reaction against British control, and had vested most power in the individual states. The rivalries among the states and the impotence of the central government compounded the economic difficulties created by a postwar depression. In the 1880's, John Fiske delighted lecture audiences in Boston, St. Louis, and New York with his graceful interpretive lectures on the era, which he published in 1888. He contributed little factually new, but wove in the newly popular Social Darwinist ideology to explain how out of the weak Confederation government there in time evolved the effective Federal union. "That period was preeminently the turning-point in the development of political society in the western hemisphere," he asserted. "Though small in their mere dimensions, the events here summarized were in a remarkable degree germinal events, fraught with more tremendous alternatives of future welfare or misery for mankind than it is easy for the imagination to grasp. As we now stand upon the threshold of that mighty future, in the light of which all events of the past are clearly destined to seem dwindled in dimensions and significant only in the ratio of their potency as causes ... we are put into the proper mood for estimating the significance of the causes which determined a century ago that the continent of North America should be dominated by a single powerful and pacific federal nation instead of being parcelled out among forty or fifty small communities."

The Critical Period of American History, 1783-1789

AT THE CLOSE OF THE EIGHTEENTH CENTURY THE BARBAROUS SUPERSTI-
tions of the Middle Ages concerning trade between nations still flourished
with scarcely diminished vitality. The epoch-making work of Adam Smith
had been published in the same year in which the United States declared
their independence. The one was the great scientific event, as the other was
the great political event of the age; but of neither the one nor the other
were the scope and purport fathomed at the time. Among the foremost
statesmen, those who, like Shelburne and Gallatin, understood the principles of the "Wealth of Nations" were few indeed. The simple principle
that when two parties trade both must be gainers, or one would soon stop
trading, was generally lost sight of; and most commercial legislation proceeded upon the theory that in trade, as in gambling or betting, what the
one party gains the other must lose. Hence towns, districts, and nations
surrounded themselves with walls of legislative restrictions intended to keep
out the monster Trade, or to admit him only on strictest proof that he
could do no harm. On this barbarous theory, the use of a colony consisted
in its being a customer which you could compel to trade with yourself, while
you could prevent it from trading with anybody else; and having secured this
point, you could cunningly arrange things by legislation so as to throw all
the loss upon this enforced customer, and keep all the gain to yourself. In
the seventeenth and eighteenth centuries all the commercial legislation
of the great colonizing states was based upon this theory of the use of a
colony. For effectiveness, it shared to some extent the characteristic features
of legislation for making water run up hill. It retarded commercial development all over the world, fostered monopolies, made the rich richer and the
poor poorer, hindered the interchange of ideas and the refinement of
manners, and sacrificed millions of human lives in misdirected warfare; but
what it was intended to do it did not do. The sturdy race of smugglers—
those despised pioneers of a higher civilization—thrived in defiance of
kings and parliaments; and as it was impossible to carry out such legislation
thoroughly without stopping trade altogether, colonies and mother countries

From Fiske, *The Critical Period of American History* (1888), ch. 4.

contrived to increase their wealth in spite of it. The colonies, however, understood the animus of the theory in so far as it was directed against them, and the revolutionary sentiment in America had gained much of its strength from the protest against this one-sided justice. In one of its most important aspects, the Revolution was a deadly blow aimed at the old system of trade restrictions. It was to a certain extent a step in realization of the noble doctrines of Adam Smith. But where the scientific thinker grasped the whole principle involved in the matter, the practical statesmen saw only the special application which seemed to concern them for the moment. They all understood that the Revolution had set them free to trade with other countries than England, but very few of them understood that, whatever countries trade together, the one cannot hope to benefit by impoverishing the other.

This point is much better understood in England to-day than in the United States; but a century ago there was little to choose between the two countries in ignorance of political economy. England had gained great wealth and power through trade with her rapidly growing American colonies. One of her chief fears, in the event of American independence, had been the possible loss of that trade. English merchants feared that American commerce, when no longer confined to its old paths by legislation, would somehow find its way to France and Holland and Spain and other countries, until nothing would be left for England. The Revolution worked no such change, however. The principal trade of the United States was with England, as before, because England could best supply the goods that Americans wanted; and it is such considerations, and not acts of Parliament, that determine trade in its natural and proper channels. In 1783 Pitt introduced into Parliament a bill which would have secured mutual unconditional free trade between the two countries; and this was what such men as Franklin, Jefferson, and Madison desired. Could this bill have passed, the hard feelings occasioned by the war would soon have died out, the commercial progress of both countries would have been promoted, and the stupid measures which led to a second war within thirty years might have been prevented. But the wisdom of Pitt found less favour in Parliament than the dense stupidity of Lord Sheffield, who thought that to admit Americans to the carrying trade would undermine the naval power of Great Britain. Pitt's measure was defeated, and the regulation of commerce with America was left to the King in council. Orders were forthwith passed as if upon the theory that America poor would be a better customer than America rich.

The carrying trade to the West Indies had been one of the most important branches of American industry. The men of New England were famous for seamanship, and better and cheaper ships could be built in the seaports of Massachusetts than anywhere in Great Britain. An oak vessel could be built at Gloucester or Salem for twenty-four dollars per ton; a ship of live-oak or American cedar cost not more than thirty-eight dollars per ton. On the other hand, fir vessels built on the Baltic cost thirty-five dollars per ton, and nowhere in England, France, or Holland could a ship be made of oak for less than fifty dollars per ton. Often the cost was as high as sixty dollars. It was not strange, therefore, that before the war more than one third of the tonnage afloat under the British flag was launched from American dock-yards. The war had violently deprived England of this enormous advantage, and now she sought to make the privation perpetual, in the delusive hope of confining British trade to British keels, and in the belief that it was the height of wisdom to impoverish the nation which she regarded as her best customer. In July, 1783, an order in council proclaimed that henceforth all trade between the United States and the British West Indies must be carried on in British-built ships, owned and navigated by British subjects. A serious blow was thus dealt not only at American shipping, but also at the interchange of commodities between the states and the islands, which was greatly hampered by this restriction. During the whole of the eighteenth century the West India sugar trade with the North American colonies and with Great Britain had been of immense value to all parties, and all had been seriously damaged by the curtailment of it due to the war. Now that the artificial state of things created by the war was to be perpetuated by legislation, the prospect of repairing the loss seemed indefinitely postponed. Moreover, even in trading directly with Great Britain, American ships were only allowed to bring in articles produced in the particular states of which their owners were citizens,—an enactment which seemed to add insult to injury, inasmuch as it directed especial attention to the want of union among the thirteen states. Great indignation was aroused in America, and reprisals were talked of, but efforts were first made to obtain a commercial treaty.

In 1785 Franklin returned from France, and Jefferson was sent as minister in his stead, while John Adams became the first representative of the United States at the British court. Adams was at first very courteously received by George III, and presently set to work to convince Lord Carmarthen, the foreign secretary, of the desirableness of unrestricted intercourse between the two countries. But popular opinion in England was obstinately set against him. But for the Navigation Act and the orders in council, it was said, all ships would by and by come to be built in America, and every time a frigate was wanted for the navy the Lords of Admiralty would have to send over to Boston or Philadelphia and order one. Rather than do such a thing as this, it was thought that the British navy should content itself with vessels of inferior workmanship and higher cost, built in British dockyards. Thirty years after, England gathered an unexpected fruit of this narrow policy, when, to her intense bewilderment, she saw frigate after frigate outsailed and defeated in single combat with American antagonists. Owing to her exclusive measures, the rapid improvement in

American shipbuilding had gone on quite beyond her ken, until she was thus rudely awakened to it. With similar short-sighted jealously, it was argued that the American share in the whale-fishery and in the Newfoundland fishery should be curtailed as much as possible. Spermaceti oil was much needed in England: complaints were rife of robbery and murder in the dimly lighted streets of London and other great cities. But it was thought that if American ships could carry oil to England and salt fish to Jamaica, the supply of seamen for the British navy would be diminished; and accordingly such privileges must not be granted the Americans unless valuable privileges could be granted in return. But the government of the United States could grant no privileges because it could impose no restrictions. British manufactured goods were needed in America, and Congress, which could levy no duties, had no power to keep them out. British merchants and manufacturers, it was argued, already enjoyed all needful privileges in American ports, and accordingly they asked no favours and granted none.

Such were the arguments to which Adams was obliged to listen. The popular feeling was so strong that Pitt could not have stemmed it if he would. It was in vain that Adams threatened reprisals, and urged that the British measures would defeat their own purpose. "The end of the Navigation Act," said he, "as expressed in its own preamble, is to confine the commerce of the colonies to the mother country; but now we are become independent states, instead of confining our trade to Great Britain, it will drive it to other countries:" and he suggested that the Americans might make a navigation act in their turn, admitting to American ports none but American-built ships, owned and commanded by Americans. But under the articles of confederation such a threat was idle, and the British government knew it to be so. Thirteen separate state governments could never be made to adopt any such measure in concert. The weakness of Congress had been fatally revealed in its inability to protect the loyalists or to enforce the payment of debts, and in its failure to raise a revenue for meeting its current expenses. A government thus slighted at home was naturally despised abroad. England neglected to send a minister to Philadelphia, and while Adams was treated politely, his arguments were unheeded. Whether in this behaviour Pitt's government was influenced or not by political as well as economical reasons, it was certain that a political purpose was entertained by the king and approved by many people. There was an intention of humiliating the Americans, and it was commonly said that under a sufficient weight of commercial distress the states would break up their feeble union, and come straggling back, one after another, to their old allegiance. The fiery spirit of Adams could ill brook this contemptuous treatment of the nation which he represented. Though he favoured very liberal commercial relations with the whole world, he could see no escape from the present difficulties save in systematic retaliation. "I should be sorry," he said, "to adopt a monopoly, but, driven to the necessity of it, I would not do things by halves . . . If monopolies and exclusions are the only arms of defence against monopolies and exclusions, I would venture upon them without fear of offending Dean Tucker or the ghost of Dr. Quesnay." That is to say, certain commercial privileges must be withheld from Great Britain, in order to be offered to her in return for reciprocal privileges. It was a miserable policy to be forced to adopt, for such restrictions upon trade inevitably cut both ways. Like the non-importation agreement of 1768 and the embargo of 1808, such a policy was open to the objections familiarly urged against biting off one's own nose. It was injuring one's self in the hope of injuring somebody else. It was perpetuating in time of peace the obstacles to commerce generated by a state of war. In a certain sense, it was keeping up warfare by commercial instead of military methods, and there was danger that it might lead to a renewal of armed conflict. Nevertheless, the conduct of the British government seemed to Adams to leave no other course open. But such "means of preserving ourselves," he said, "can never be secured until Congress shall be made supreme in foreign commerce."

It was obvious enough that the separate action of the states upon such a question was only adding to the general uncertainty and confusion. In 1785 New York laid a double duty on all goods whatever imported in British ships. In the same year Pennsylvania passed the first of the long series of American tariff acts, designed to tax the whole community for the alleged benefit of a few greedy manufacturers. Massachusetts sought to establish committees of correspondence for the purpose of entering into a new non-importation agreement, and its legislature resolved that "the present powers of the Congress of the United States, as contained in the articles of confederation, are not fully adequate to the great purposes they were originally designed to effect." The Massachusetts delegates in Congress—Gerry, Holton, and King—were instructed to recommend a general convention of the states for the purpose of revising and amending the articles of confederation; but the delegates refused to comply with their instructions, and set forth their reasons in a paper which was approved by Samuel Adams, and caused the legislature to reconsider its action. It was feared that a call for a convention might seem too much like an open expression of a want of confidence in Congress, and might thereby weaken it still further without accomplishing any good result. For the present, as a temporary expedient, Massachusetts took counsel with New Hampshire, and the two states passed navigation acts, prohibiting British ships from carrying goods out of their harbours, and imposing a fourfold duty upon all such goods as they should bring in. A discriminating tonnage duty was also laid upon all foreign vessels. Rhode Island soon after adopted similar measures. In Congress a scheme for a uniform navigation act, to be concurred in and passed by all the thirteen states, was suggested by one of the Maryland delegates; but it was opposed by Richard Henry Lee and most of the delegates from the far south. The southern states, having no ships or seamen of their own, feared that the exclusion of British competition might enable northern ship-owners to charge exorbitant rates for carrying their rice and tobacco, thus subjecting them to a ruinous monopoly; but the gallant Moultrie, then governor of South Carolina, taking a broader view of the case, wrote to Bowdoin, governor of Massachusetts, asserting the paramount need of harmonious and united action. In the Virginia assembly, a hot-headed member, named Thurston, declared himself in doubt "whether it would not be better to encourage the British rather than the eastern marine;" but the remark was greeted with hisses and groans, and the speaker was speedily put down. Amid such mutual jealousies and misgivings, during the year 1785 acts were passed by ten states granting to Congress the power of regulating commerce for the ensuing thirteen years. The three states which refrained from acting were Georgia, South Carolina, and Delaware. The acts of the other ten were, as might have been expected, a jumble of incongruities. North Carolina granted all the power that was asked, but stipulated that when all the states should have done likewise their acts should be summed up in a new article of confederation. Connecticut, Pennsylvania, and Maryland had fixed the date at which the grant was to take effect, while Rhode Island provided that it should not expire until after the lapse of twenty-five years. The grant by New Hampshire allowed the power to be used only in one specified way,—by restricting the duties imposable by the several states. The grants of Massachusetts, New York, New Jersey, and Virginia were not to take effect until all the others should go into operation. The only thing which Congress could do with these acts was to refer them back to the several legislatures, with a polite request to try to reduce them to something like uniformity.

Meanwhile, the different states, with their different tariff and tonnage acts, began to make commercial war upon one another. No sooner had the other three New England states virtually closed their ports to British shipping than Connecticut threw hers wide open, an act which she followed up by laying duties upon imports from Massachusetts. Pennsylvania discriminated against Delaware, and New Jersey, pillaged at once by both her greater neighbours, was compared to a cask tapped at both ends. The conduct of New York became especially selfish and blameworthy. That rapid growth which was so soon to carry the city and the state to a position of primacy in the Union had already begun. After the departure of the British the revival of business went on with leaps and bounds. The feeling of local patriotism waxed strong, and in no one was it more completely manifested than in George Clinton, the Revolutionary general, whom the people elected governor for nine successive terms. From a humble origin, by dint of shrewdness and untiring push, Clinton had come to be for the moment the most powerful man in the state of New York. He had come to look upon the state almost as if it were his own private manor, and his life was devoted to furthering its interests as he understood them. It was his first article of faith that New York must be the greatest state in the Union. But his conceptions of statesmanship were extremely narrow. In his mind, the welfare of New York meant the pulling down and thrusting aside of all her neighbours and rivals. He was the vigorous and steadfast advocate of every illiberal and exclusive measure, and the most uncompromising enemy to a closer union of the states. His great popular strength and the commercial importance of the community in which he held sway made him at this time the most dangerous man in America. The political victories presently to be won by Hamilton, Schuyler, and Livingston, without which our grand and pacific federal union could not have been brought into being, were victories won by most desperate fighting against the dogged opposition of Clinton. Under his guidance, the history of New York, during the five years following the peace of 1783, was a shameful story of greedy monopoly and sectional hate. Of all the thirteen states, none behaved worse except Rhode Island.

A single instance, which occurred early in 1787, may serve as an illustration. The city of New York, with its population of 30,000 souls, had long been supplied with firewood from Connecticut, and with butter and cheese, chickens and garden vegetables, from the thrifty farms of New Jersey. This trade, it was observed, carried thousands of dollars out of the city and into the pockets of detested Yankees and despised Jerseymen. It was ruinous to domestic industry, said the men of New York. It must be stopped by those effective remedies of the Sangrado school of economic doctors, a navigation act and a protective tariff. Acts were accordingly passed, obliging every Yankee sloop which came down through Hell Gate, and every Jersey market boat which was rowed across from Paulus Hook to Cortlandt Street, to pay entrance fees and obtain clearances at the custom-house, just as was done by ships from London or Hamburg; and not a cart-load of Connecticut firewood could be delivered at the back-door of a country-house in Beekman Street until it should have paid a heavy duty. Great and just was the wrath of the farmers and lumbermen. The New Jersey legislature made up its mind to retaliate. The city of New York had lately bought a small patch of ground on Sandy Hook, and had built a light-house there. This light-house was the one weak spot in the heel of Achilles where a hostile arrow could strike, and New Jersey gave vent to her indignation by laying a tax of $1,800 a year on it. Connecticut was equally prompt. At a great meeting of business men, held at New London, it was unanimously agreed to suspend all commercial intercourse with New York. Every merchant signed an agreement, under penalty of $250 for the first offence, not to send any goods whatever into the hated state for a period of twelve months. By such retaliatory measures, it was hoped that New York might be compelled to rescind her odious enactment. But such meetings and such resolves bore an ominous likeness to the meetings and resolves which in the years before 1775 had heralded a state of war; and but for the good work done by the federal convention another five years would scarcely have elapsed before shots would have been fired and seeds of perennial hatred sown on the shores that look toward Manhattan Island.

To these commercial disputes there were added disputes about territory. The chronic quarrel between Connecticut and Pennsylvania over the valley of Wyoming was decided in the autumn of 1782 by a special federal court, appointed in accordance with the articles of confederation. The prize was adjudged to Pennsylvania, and the government of Connecticut submitted as gracefully as possible. But new troubles were in store for the inhabitants of that beautiful region. The traces of the massacre of 1778 had disappeared, the houses had been rebuilt, new settlers had come in, and the pretty villages had taken on their old look of contentment and thrift, when in the spring of 1784 there came an accumulation of disasters. During a very cold winter great quantities of snow had fallen, and lay piled in huge masses on the mountain sides, until in March a sudden thaw set in. The Susquehanna rose, and overflowed the valley, and great blocks of ice drifted here and there, carrying death and destruction with them. Houses, barns, and fences were swept away, the cattle were drowned, the fruit trees broken down, the stores of food destroyed, and over the whole valley there lay a stratum of gravel and pebbles. The people were starving with cold and hunger, and President Dickinson urged the legislature to send prompt relief to the sufferers. But the hearts of the members were as flint, and their talk was incredibly wicked. Not a penny would they give to help the accursed Yankees. It served them right. If they had stayed in Connecticut, where they belonged, they would have kept out of harm's way. And with a blasphemy thinly veiled in phrases of pious unction, the desolation of the valley was said to have been contrived by the Deity with the express object of punishing these trespassers. But the cruelty of the Pennsylvania legislature was not confined to words. A scheme was devised for driving out the settlers and partitioning their lands among a company of speculators. A force of militia was sent to Wyoming, commanded by a truculent creature named Patterson. The ostensible purpose was to assist in restoring order in the valley, but the behaviour of the soldiers was such as would have disgraced a horde of barbarians. They stole what they could find, dealt out blows to the men and insults to the women, until their violence was met with violence in return. Then Patterson sent a letter to President Dickinson, accusing the farmers of sedition, and hinting that extreme measures were necessary. Having thus, as he thought, prepared the way, he attacked the settlement, turned some five hundred people out-of-doors, and burned their houses to the ground. The wretched victims, many of them tender women, or infirm old men, or little children, were driven into the wilderness at the point of the bayonet, and told to find their way to Connecticut without further delay. Heart-rending scenes ensued. Many died of exhaustion, or furnished food for wolves. But this was more than the Pennsylvania legislature had intended. Patterson's zeal had carried him too far. He was recalled, and the sheriff of Northumberland County was sent, with a posse of men, to protect the settlers. Patterson disobeyed, however, and withdrawing his men to a fortified lair in the mountains, kept up a guerilla warfare. All the Connecticut men in the neighbouring country flew to arms. Men were killed on both sides, and presently Patterson was besieged. A regiment of soldiers was then sent from Philadelphia, under Colonel Armstrong, who had formerly been on Gates's staff, the author of the incendiary Newburgh address. On arriving in the valley, Armstrong held a parley with the Connecticut men, and persuaded them to lay down their arms; assuring them on his honour that they should meet with no ill treatment, and that their enemy, Patterson, should be disarmed also. Having thus fallen into this soldier's clutches, they were forthwith treated as prisoners. Seventy-six of them were handcuffed and sent under guard, some to Easton and some to Northumberland where they were thrown into jail.

Great was the indignation in New England when these deeds were heard of. The matter had become very serious. A war between Connecticut and Pennsylvania might easily grow out of it. But the danger was averted through a very singular feature in the Pennsylvania constitution. In order to hold its legislature in check, Pennsylvania had a council of censors, which was assembled once in seven years in order to inquire whether the state had been properly governed during the interval. Soon after the troubles in Wyoming the regular meeting of the censors was held, and the conduct of Armstrong and Patterson was unreservedly condemned. A hot controversy ensued between the legislature and the censors, and as the people set great store by the latter peculiar institution, public sympathy was gradually awakened for the sufferers. The wickedness of the affair began to dawn upon people's minds, and they were ashamed of what had been done. Patterson and Armstrong were frowned down, the legislature disavowed their acts, and it was ordered that full reparation should be made to the persecuted settlers of Wyoming.

In the Green Mountains and on the upper waters of the Connecticut there had been trouble for many years. In the course of the Revolutionary War, the fierce dispute between New York and New Hampshire for the possession of the Green Mountains came in from time to time to influence most curiously the course of events. It was closely connected with the intrigues against General Schuyler, and thus more remotely with the Conway cabal and the treason of Arnold. About the time of Burgoyne's invasion the association of Green Mountain Boys endeavoured to cut the Gordian knot by declaring Vermont an independent state, and applying to the Continental Congress for admission into the Union. The New York delegates in Congress succeeded in defeating this scheme, but the Vermont people went on and framed their constitution. Thomas Chittenden, a man of rough manners but very considerable ability, a farmer and innkeeper, like Israel Putman, was chosen governor, and held that position for many years. New Hampshire thus far had not actively opposed these measures, but fresh grounds of quarrel were soon at hand. Several towns on the east bank of the Connecticut River wished to escape from the jurisdiction of New Hampshire. They preferred to belong to Vermont, because it was not within the Union, and accordingly not liable to requisitions of taxes from the Continental Congress. It was conveniently remembered that by the original grant, in the reign of Charles II, New Hampshire extended only sixty miles from the coast. Vermont was at first inclined to assent, but finding the scheme unpopular in Congress, and not wishing to offend that body, she changed her mind. The towns on both banks of the river then tried to organize themselves into a middle state,—a sort of Lotharingia on the banks of this New World Rhine,—to be called New Connecticut. By this time New Hampshire was aroused, and she called attention to the fact that she still believed herself entitled to dominion over the whole of Vermont. Massachusetts now began to suspect that the upshot of the matter would be the partition of the whole disputed territory between New Hampshire and New York, and, ransacking her ancient grants and charters, she decided to set up a claim on her own part to the southernmost towns in Vermont. Thus goaded on all sides, Vermont adopted an aggressive policy. She not only annexed the towns east of the Connecticut River, but also asserted sovereignty over the towns in New York as far as the Hudson. New York sent troops to the threatened frontier, New Hampshire prepared to do likewise, and for a moment war seemed inevitable. But here, as in so many other instances, Washington appeared as peacemaker, and prevailed upon Governor Chittenden to use his influence in getting the dangerous claims withdrawn. After the spring of 1784 the outlook was less stormy in the Green Mountains. The conflicting claims were allowed to lie dormant, but the possibilities of mischief remained, and the Vermont question was not finally settled until after the adoption of the Federal Constitution. Meanwhile, on the debatable frontier between Vermont and New York the embers of hatred smouldered. Barns and houses were set on fire, and belated wayfarers were found mysteriously murdered in the depths of the forest.

Incidents like those of Wyoming and Vermont seem trivial, perhaps, when contrasted with the lurid tales of border warfare in older times between half-civilized peoples of mediaeval Europe, as we read them in the pages of Froissart and Sir Walter Scott. But their historic lesson is none the less clear. Though they lift the curtain but a little way, they show us a glimpse of the untold dangers and horrors from which the adoption of our Federal Constitution has so throughly freed us that we can only with some effort realize how narrowly we have escaped them. It is fit that they should be borne in mind, that we may duly appreciate the significance of the reign of law and order which has been established on this continent during the greater part of a century. When reported in Europe, such incidents were held to confirm the opinion that the American confederacy was going to pieces. With quarrels about trade and quarrels about boundaries, we seemed to be treading the old-fashioned paths of anarchy, even as they had been trodden in other ages and other parts of the world. It was natural that people in Europe should think so, because there was no historic precedent to help them in forming a different opinion. No one could possibly foresee that within five years a number of gentlemen at Philadelphia, containing among themselves a greater amount of political sagacity than had ever before been brought together within the walls of a single room, would amicably discuss the situation and agree upon a new system of government whereby the dangers might be once for all averted. Still less could any one foresee that these gentlemen would not only agree upon a scheme among themselves, but would actually succeed, without serious civil dissension, in making the people of thirteen states adopt, defend, and cherish it. History afforded no example of such a gigantic act of constructive statesmanship. It was, moreover, a strange and apparently fortuitous combination of circumstances that were now preparing the way for it and making its accomplishment possible. No one could forecast the future. When our ministers and agents in Europe raised the question as to making commercial treaties, they were disdainfully asked whether European powers were expected to deal with thirteen governments or with one. If it was answered that the United States constituted a single government so far as their relations with foreign powers were concerned, then we were forthwith twitted with our failure to keep our engagements with England with regard to the loyalists and the collection of private debts. Yes, we see, said the European diplomats; the United States are one nation to-day and thirteen to-morrow, according as may seem to subserve their selfish interests. Jefferson, at Paris, was told again and again that it was useless for the French government to enter into any agreement with the United States, as there was no certainty that it would be fulfilled on our part; and the same things were said all over Europe. Toward the close of the war most of the European nations had seemed ready to enter into commercial arrangements with the United States, but all save Holland speedily lost interest in the subject. John Adams had succeeded in making a treaty with Holland in 1782. Frederick the Great treated us more civilly than other sovereigns. One of the last acts of his life was to conclude a treaty for ten years with the United States; asserting the principle that free ships make free goods, taking arms and military stores out of the class of contraband, agreeing to refrain from privateering even in case of war between the two countries, and in other respects showing a liberal and enlightened spirit.

This treaty was concluded in 1786. It scarcely touched the subject of international trade in time of peace, but it was valuable as regarded the matters it covered, and in the midst of the general failure of American diplomacy in Europe it fell pleasantly upon our ears. Our diplomacy had failed because our weakness had been proclaimed to the world. We were bullied by England, insulted by France and Spain, and looked askance at in Holland. The humiliating position in which our ministers were placed by the beggarly poverty of Congress was something almost beyond credence. It was by no means unusual for the superintendent of finance, when hard pushed for money, to draw upon our foreign ministers, and then sell the drafts for cash. This was not only not unusual; it was an established custom. It was done again and again, when there was not the smallest ground for supposing that the minister upon whom the draft was made would have any funds wherewith to meet it. He must go and beg the money. That was part of his duty as envoy,—to solicit loans without security for a government that could not raise enough money by taxation to defray its current expenses. It was sickening work. Just before John Adams had been appointed minister to England, and while he was visiting in London, he suddenly learned that drafts upon him had been presented to his bankers in Amsterdam to the amount of more than a million florins. Less than half a million florins were on hand to meet these demands, and unless something were done at once the greater part of this paper would go back to America protested. Adams lost not a moment in starting for Holland. In these modern days of precision in travel, when we can translate space into time, the distance between London and Amsterdam is eleven hours. It was accomplished by Adams, after innumerable delays and vexations and no little danger, in fifty-four days. The bankers had contrived, by ingenious excuses, to keep the drafts from going to protest until the minister's arrival, but the gazettes were full of the troubles of Congress and the bickerings of the states, and everybody was suspicious. Adams applied in vain to the regency of Amsterdam. The promise of the American government was not regarded as valid security for a sum equivalent to about three hundred thousand dollars. The members of the regency were polite, but inexorable. They could not make a loan on such terms; it was unbusinesslike and contrary to precedent. Finding them immovable, Adams was forced to apply to professional usurers and Jew brokers, from whom, after three weeks of perplexity and humiliation, he obtained a loan at exorbitant interest, and succeeded in meeting the drafts. It was only too plain, as he mournfully confessed, that American credit was dead. Such were the trials of our American ministers in Europe in the dark days of the League of Friendship. It was not a solitary, but a typical, instance. John Jay's experience at the unfriendly court of Spain was perhaps even more trying.

European governments might treat us with cold disdain, and European bankers might pronounce our securities worthless, but there was one quarter of the world from which even worse measure was meted out to us. Of all the barbarous communities with which the civilized world has had to deal in modern times, perhaps none have made so much trouble as the Mussulman states on the southern shore of the Mediterranean. After the breaking up of the great Moorish kingdoms of the Middle Ages, this region had fallen under the nominal control of the Turkish sultans as lords paramount of the orthodox Mohammedan world. Its miserable population became the prey of banditti. Swarms of half-savage chieftains settled down upon the land like locusts, and out of such a pandemonium of robbery and murder as has scarcely been equalled in historic times the pirate states of Morocco and Algiers, Tunis and Tripoli, gradually emerged. Of these communities history has not one good word to say. In these fair lands, once illustrious for the genius and virtues of a Hannibal and the profound philosophy of St. Augustine, there grew up some the most terrible despotisms ever known to the world. The things done daily by the robber sovereigns were such as to make a civilized imagination recoil with horror. One of these cheerful creatures, who reigned in the middle of the eighteenth century, and was called Muley Abdallah, especially prided himself on his peculiar skill in mounting a horse. Resting his left hand upon the horse's neck as he sprang into the saddle he simultaneously swung the sharp scimiter in his right hand so deftly as to cut off the head of the groom who held the bridle. From his behaviour in these sportive moods one may judge what he was capable of on serious occasions. He was a fair sample of the Barbary monarchs. The foreign policy of these wretches was summed up in piracy and blackmail. Their corsairs swept the Mediterranean and ventured far out upon the ocean, capturing merchant vessels, and murdering or enslaving their crews. Of the rich booty, a fixed proportion was paid over to the robber sovereign, and the rest was divided among the gang. So lucrative was this business that it attracted hardy ruffians from all parts of Europe, and the misery they inflicted upon mankind during four centuries was beyond calculation. One of their favourite practices was the kidnapping of eminent or wealthy persons, in the hope of extorting ransom. Cervantes and Vincent de Paul were among the celebrated men who thus tasted the horrors of Moorish slavery; but it was a calamity that might fall to the lot of any man or woman, and it was but rarely that the victims ever regained their freedom.

Against these pirates the government of Europe contended in vain. Swift cruisers frequently captured their ships, and from the days of Joan of Arc down to the days of Napoleon their skeletons swung from long rows of gibbets on all the coasts of Europe, as a terror and a warning. But their losses were easily repaired, and sometimes they cruised in fleets of seventy or eighty sail, defying the natives of England and France. It was not until after England, in Nelson's time, had acquired supremacy in the Mediterranean that this dreadful scourge was destroyed. Americans, however, have just ground for pride in recollecting that their government was foremost in chastising these pirates in their own harbours. The exploits of our little navy in the Mediterranean at the beginning of the present century form an interesting episode in American history, but in the weak days of the Confederation our commerce was plundered with impunity, and American citizens were seized and sold into slavery in the markets of Algiers and Tripoli. One reason for the long survival of this villainy was the low state of humanity among European nations. An Englishman's sympathy was but feebly aroused by the plunder of Frenchmen, and the bigoted Spaniard looked on with approval so long as it was Protestants that were kidnapped and bastinadoed. In 1783 Lord Sheffield published a pamphlet on the commerce of the United States, in which he shamelessly declared that the Barbary pirates were really useful to the great maritime powers, because they tended to keep the weaker nations out of their share in the carrying trade. This, he thought, was a valuable offset to the Empress Catherine's device of the armed neutrality, whereby small nations were protected; and on this wicked theory, as Franklin tells us, London merchants had been heard to say that "if there were no Algiers, it would be worth England's while to build one." It was largely because of such feelings that the great states of Europe so long persisted in the craven policy of paying blackmail to the robbers, instead of joining in a crusade and destroying them.

In 1786 Congress felt it necessary to take measures for protecting the lives and liberties of American citizens. The person who called himself "Emperor" of Morocco at that time was different from most of his kind. He had a taste for reading, and had thus caught a glimmering of the enlightened liberalism which French philosophers were preaching. He wished to be thought a benevolent despot, and with Morocco, accordingly, Congress succeeded in making a treaty. But nothing could be done with the other pirate states without paying blackmail. Few scenes in our history are more amusing, or more irritating, than the interview of John Adams with an envoy from Tripoli in London. The oily-tongued barbarian, with his soft voice and his bland smile, asseverating that his only interest in life was to do good and make other people happy, stands out in fine contrast with the blunt, straight-forward, and truthful New Englander; and their conversation reminds one of the old story of Coeur-de-Lion with his curtal-axe and Saladin with the blade that cut the silken cushion. Adams felt sure that the fellow was either saint or devil, but could not quite tell which. The envoy's love for mankind was so great that he could not bear the thought of hostility between the Americans and the Barbary States, and he suggested that everything might be happily arranged for a million dollars or so. Adams thought it better to fight than to pay tribute. It would be cheaper in the end, as well as more manly. At the same time, it was better economy to pay a million dollars at once than waste many times that sum in war risks and loss of trade. But Congress could do neither one thing nor the other. It was too poor to build a navy, and too poor to buy off the pirates; and so for several years to come American ships were burned and American sailors enslaved with utter impunity. With the memory of such wrongs deeply graven in his heart, it was natural that John Adams, on becoming president of the United States, should bend his energies toward founding a strong American navy.

A government touches the lowest point of ignominy when it confesses its inability to protect the lives and property of its citizens. A government which has come to this has failed in discharging the primary function of government, and forthwith ceases to have any reason for existing. In March, 1786, Grayson wrote to Madison that several members of Congress thought seriously of recommending a general convention for remodelling the government. "I have not made up my mind," says Grayson, "whether it would not be better to bear the ills we have than fly to those we know not of. I am, however, in no doubt about the weakness of the federal government. If it remains much longer in its present state of imbecility, we shall be one of the most contemptible nations on the face of the earth." "It is clear to me as A, B, C," said Washington, "that an extension of federal powers would make us one of the most happy, wealthy, respectable, and powerful nations that ever inhabited the terrestrial globe. Without them we shall soon be everything which is the direct reverse. I predict the worst consequences from a half-starved, limping government, always moving upon crutches and tottering at every step."

There is no telling how long the wretched state of things which followed the Revolution might have continued, had not the crises been precipitated by the wild attempts of the several states to remedy the distress of the people by legislation. That financial distress was widespread and deep-seated was not to be denied. At the beginning of the war the amount of accumulated capital in the country had been very small. The great majority of the people did little more than get from the annual yield of their farms or plantations enough to meet the current expenses of the year. Outside of agriculture the chief resources were the carrying trade, the exchange of commodities with England and the West Indies, and the cod and whale fisheries; and in these occupations many people had grown rich. The war had destroyed all these sources of revenue. Imports and exports had alike been stopped, so that there was a distressing scarcity of some of the commonest household articles. The enemy's navy had kept us from the fisheries. Before the war, the dock-yards of Nantucket were ringing with the busy sound of adze and hammer, rope-walks covered the island, and two hundred keels sailed yearly in quest of spermaceti. At the return of peace, the docks were silent and grass grew in the streets. The carrying trade and the fisheries began soon to revive, but it was some years before the old prosperity was restored. The war had also wrought serious damage to agriculture, and in some parts of the country the direct destruction of property by the enemy's troops had been very great. To all these causes of poverty there was added the hopeless confusion due to an inconvertible paper currency. The worst feature of this financial device is that it not only impoverishes people, but bemuddles their brains by creating a false and fleeting show of prosperity.

By violently disturbing apparent values, it always brings on an era of wild speculation and extravagance in living, followed by sudden collapse and protracted suffering. In such crises the poorest people, those who earn their bread by the sweat of their brows and have no margin of accumulated capital, always suffer the most. Above all men, it is the labouring man who needs sound money and steady values. We have seen all these points amply illustrated since the War of Secession. After the War of Independence, when the margin of accumulated capital was so much smaller, the misery was much greater. While the paper money lasted there was marked extravagance in living, and complaints were loud against the speculators, especially those who operated in bread-stuffs. Washington said he would like to hang them all on a gallows higher than that of Haman; but they were, after all, but the inevitable products of this abnormal state of things, and the more guilty criminals were the demagogues who went about preaching the doctrine that the poor man needs cheap money. After the collapse of this continental currency in 1780, it seemed as if there were no money in the country, and at the peace the renewal of trade with England seemed at first to make matters worse. The brisk importation of sorely needed manufactured goods, which then began, would naturally have been paid for in the south by indigo, rice, and tobacco, in the middle states by exports of wheat and furs, and in New England by the profits of the fisheries, the shipping, and the West India trade. But in the southern and middle states the necessary revival of agriculture could not be effected in a moment, and British legislation against American shipping and the West India trade fell with crippling force upon New England. Consequently, we had little else but specie with which to pay for imports, and the country was soon drained of what little specie there was. In the absence of a circulating medium there was a reversion to the practice of barter, and the revival of business was thus further impeded. Whiskey in North Carolina, tobacco in Virginia, did duty as measures of value; and Isaiah Thomas, editor of the Worcester "Spy," announced that he would receive subscriptions for his paper in salt pork.

It is worth while, in this connection, to observe what this specie was, the scarcity of which created so much embarrassment. Until 1785 no national coinage was established, and none was issued until 1793. English, French, Spanish, and German coins, of various and uncertain value, passed from hand to hand. Besides the ninepences and fourpence-ha'-pennies, there were bits and half-bits, pistareens, picayunes, and fips. Of gold pieces there were the johannes, or joe, the doubloon, the moidore, and pistole, with English and French guineas, carolins, ducats, and chequins. Of coppers there were English pence and half-pence and French sous; and pennies were issued at local mints in Vermont, Massachusetts, Connecticut, New Jersey, and Pennsylvania. The English shilling had everywhere degenerated in value, but differently in different localities; and among silver pieces the Spanish dollar, from Louisiana and Cuba, had begun to supersede it as a measure of value. In New England the shilling had sunk from nearly one fourth to one sixth of a dollar; in New York to one eighth; in North Carolina to one tenth. It was partly for this reason that in devising a national coinage the more uniform dollar was adopted as the unit. At the same time the decimal system of division was adopted instead of the cumbrous English system, and the result was our present admirably simple currency, which we owe to Gouverneur Morris, aided as to some points by Thomas Jefferson. During the period of the Confederation, the chaotic state of the currency was a serious obstacle to trade, and it afforded endless opportunities for fraud and extortion. Clipping and counterfeiting were carried to such lengths that every moderately cautious person, in taking payment in hard cash, felt it necessary to keep a small pair of scales beside him and carefully weigh each coin, after narrowly scrutinizing its stamp and deciphering its legend.

In view of all these complicated impediments to business on the morrow of a long and costly war, it was not strange that the whole country was in some measure pauperized. The cost of the war, estimated in cash, had been about $170,000,000—a huge sum if we consider the circumstances of the country at that time. To meet this crushing indebtedness Mr. Hildreth reckons the total amount raised by the states, whether by means of repudiated paper or of taxes, down to 1784, as not more than $30,000,000. No wonder if the issue of such a struggle seemed quite hopeless. In many parts of the country, by the year 1786, the payment of taxes had come to be regarded as an amiable eccentricity. At one moment, early in 1782, there was not a single dollar in the treasury. That the government had in any way been able to finish the war, after the downfall of its paper money, was due to the gigantic efforts of one great man,—Robert Morris, of Pennsylvania. This statesman was born in England, but he had come to Philadelphia in his boyhood, and had amassed an enormous fortune, which he devoted without stint to the service of his adopted country. Though opposed to the Declaration of Independence as rash and premature, he had, nevertheless, signed his name to that document, and scarcely any one had contributed more to the success of the war. It was he who supplied the money which enabled Washington to complete the great campaign of Trenton and Princeton. In 1781 he was made superintendent of finance, and by dint of every imaginable device of hard-pressed ingenuity he contrived to support the brilliant work which began at the Cowpens and ended at Yorktown. He established the Bank of North America as an instrument by which government loans might be negotiated. Sometimes his methods were such as doctors call heroic, as when he made sudden drafts upon our ministers in Europe after the manner already described. In every dire emergency he was Washington's chief reliance, and in his devotion to the common weal he drew upon his private resources until he became poor; and in later years—for shame be it said—an ungrateful nation allowed one of its noblest and most disinterested champions to languish in a debtor's prison. It was of ill omen for the fortunes of the weak and disorderly Confederation that in 1784, after three years of herculean struggle with impossibilities, this stout heart and sagacious head could no longer weather the storm. The task of creating wealth out of nothing had become too arduous and too thankless to be endured. Robert Morris resigned his place, and it was taken by a congressional committee of finance, under whose management the disorders only hurried to a crisis.

By 1786, under the universal depression and want of confidence, all trade had well-nigh stopped, and political quackery, with its cheap and dirty remedies, had full control of the field. In the very face of miseries so plainly traceable to the deadly paper currency, it may seem strange that people should now have begun to clamour for a renewal of the experiment which had worked so much evil. Yet so it was. As starving men are said to dream of dainty banquets, so now a craze for fictitious wealth in the shape of paper money ran like an epidemic through the country. There was a Barmecide feast of economic vagaries; only now it was the several states that sought to apply the remedy, each in its own way. And when we have threaded the maze of this rash legislation, we shall the better understand that clause in our federal constitution which forbids the making of laws impairing the obligation of contracts. The events of 1786 impressed upon men's minds more forcibly than ever the wretched and disorderly condition of the country, and went far toward calling into existence the needful popular sentiment in favour of an overruling central government.

The disorders assumed very different forms in the different states, and brought out a great diversity of opinion as to the causes of the distress and the efficacy of the proposed remedies. Only two states out of the thirteen— Connecticut and Delaware—escaped the infection, but, on the other hand, it was only in seven states that the paper money party prevailed in the legislatures. North Carolina issued a large amount of paper, and, in order to get it into circulation as quickly as possible, the state government proceeded to buy tobacco with it, paying double the specie value of the tobacco. As a natural consequence, the paper dollar instantly fell to seventy cents, and went on declining. In South Carolina an issue was tried somewhat more cautiously, but the planters soon refused to take the paper at its face value. Coercive measures were then attempted. Planters and merchants were urged to sign a pledge not to discriminate between paper and gold, and if any one dared refuse the fanatics forthwith attempted to make it hot for him. A kind of "Kuklux" society was organized at Charleston, known as the "Hint Club." Its purpose was to hint to such people that they had better look out. If they did not mend their ways, it was unnecessary to inform them more explicitly what they might expect. Houses were combustible then as now, and the use of firearms was well understood. In Georgia the legislature itself attempted coercion. Paper money was made a legal tender in spite of strong opposition, and a law was passed prohibiting any planter or merchant from exporting any produce without taking affidavit that he had never refused to receive this script at its full face value. But somehow people found that the more it was sought to keep up the paper by dint of threats and forcing acts, the faster its value fell. Virginia had issued bills of credit during the campaign of 1781, but it was enacted at the same time that they should not be a legal tender after the next January. The influence of Washington, Madison, and Mason was effectively brought to bear in favour of sound currency, and the people of Virginia were but slightly affected by the craze of 1786. In the autumn of that year a proposition from two counties for an issue of paper was defeated in the legislature by a vote of eighty-five to seventeen, and no more was heard of the matter. In Maryland, after a very obstinate fight, a rag money bill was carried in the house of representatives, but the senate threw it out; and the measure was thus postponed until the discussion over the federal constitution superseded it in popular interst. Pennsylvania had warily begun in May, 1785, to issue a million dollars in bills of credit, which were not made a legal tender for the payment of private debts. They were mainly loaned to farmers on mortgage, and were received by the state as an equivalent for specie in the payment of taxes. By August, 1786, even this carefully guarded paper had fallen some twelve cents below par,— not a bad showing for such a year as that. New York moved somewhat less cautiously. A million dollars were issued in bills of credit receivable for the custom-house duties, which were then paid into the state treasury; and these bills were made a legal tender for all money received in lawsuits. At the same time the New Jersey legislature passed a bill for issuing half a million paper dollars, to be a legal tender in all business transactions. The bill was vetoed by the governor in council. The aged Governor Livingston was greatly respected by the people; and so the mob at Elizabethtown, which had duly planted a stake and dragged his effigy up to it, refrained from inflicting the last indignities upon the image, and burned that of one of the members of the council instead. At the next session the governor yielded, and the rag money was issued. But an unforeseen difficulty arose. Most of the dealings of New Jersey people were in the cities of New York and Philadelphia, and in both cities the merchants refused their paper, so that it speedily became worthless.

The business of exchange was thus fast getting into hopeless confusion. It has been said of Bradshaw's Railway Guide, the indispensable companion of the traveller in England, that no man can study it for an hour without qualifying himself for an insane asylum. But Bradshaw is pellucid clearness compared with the American tables of exchange in 1786, with their medley of dollars and shillings, moidores and pistareens. The addition of half a dozen different kinds of paper created such a labyrinth as no human intellect could explore. No wonder that men were counted wise who preferred to take whiskey and pork instead. Nobody who had a yard of cloth to sell could tell how much it was worth. But even worse than all this was the swift and certain renewal of bankruptcy which so many states were preparing for themselves.

Nowhere did the warning come so quickly or so sharply as in New England. Connecticut, indeed, as already observed, came off scot-free. She had issued a little paper money soon after the battle of Lexington, but had stopped it about the time of the surrender of Burgoyne. In 1780 she had wisely and summarily adjusted all relations between debtor and creditor, and the crisis of 1786 found her people poor enough, no doubt, but able to wait for better times and indisposed to adopt violent remedies. It was far otherwise in Rhode Island and Massachusetts. These were preëminently the maritime states of the Union, and upon them the blows aimed by England at American commerce had fallen most severely. It was these two maritime states that suffered most from the cutting down of the carrying trade and the restriction of intercourse with the West Indies. These things worked injury to shipbuilding, to the exports of lumber and oil and salted fish, even to the manufacture of Medford rum. Nowhere had the normal machinery of business been thrown out of gear so extensively as in these two states, and in Rhode Island there was the added disturbance due to a prolonged occupation by the enemy's troops. Nowhere, perhaps, was there a larger proportion of the population in debt, and in these preëminently commercial communities private debts were a heavier burden and involved more personal suffering than in the somewhat patriarchal system of life in Virginia or South Carolina. In the time of which we are now treating, imprisonment for debt was common. High-minded but unfortunate men were carried to jail, and herded with thieves and ruffians in loathsome dungeons, for the crime of owing a hundred dollars which they could not promptly pay. Under such circumstances, a commercial disturbance, involving widespread debt, entailed an amount of personal suffering and humiliation of which, in these kinder days, we can form no adequate conception. It tended to make the debtor an outlaw, ready to entertain schemes for the subversion of society. In the crisis of 1786, the agitation in Rhode Island and Massachusetts reached white heat, and things were done which alarmed the whole country. But the course of events was different in the two states. In Rhode Island the agitators obtained control of the government, and the result was a paroxysm of tyranny. In Massachusetts the agitators failed to secure control of the government, and the result was a paroxysm of rebellion.

The debates over paper money in the Rhode Island legislature began in 1785, but the advocates of a sound currency were victorious. These men were roundly abused in the newspapers, and in the next spring election most of them lost their seats. The legislature of 1786 showed an overwhelming majority in favor of paper money. The farmers from the inland towns were unanimous in supporting the measure. They could not see the difference between the state making a dollar out of paper and a dollar out of silver. The idea that the value did not lie in the government stamp they dismissed as an idle crotchet, a wire-drawn theory, worthy only of "literary fellows." What they could see was the glaring fact that they had no money, hard or soft; and they wanted something that would satisfy their creditors and buy new gowns for their wives, whose raiment was unquestionably the worse for wear. On the other hand, the merchants from seaports like Providence, Newport, and Bristol understood the difference between real money and the promissory notes of a bankrupt government, but they were in a hopeless minority. Half a million dollars were issued in script, to be loaned to the farmers on a mortgage of their real estate. No one could obtain the script without giving a mortgage for twice the amount, and it was thought that this security would make it as good as gold. But the depreciation began instantly. When the worthy farmers went to the store for dry goods or sugar, and found the prices rising with dreadful rapidity, they were at first astonished, and then enraged. The trouble, as they truly said, was with the wicked merchants, who would not take the paper dollars at their face value. These men were thus thwarting the government, and must be punished. An act was accordingly hurried through the legislature, commanding every one to take paper as an equivalent for gold, under penalty of five hundred dollars fine and loss of the right of suffrage. The merchants in the cities thereupon shut up their shops. During the summer of 1786 all business was at a standstill in Newport and Providence, except in the bar-rooms. There and about the market-places men spent their time angrily discussing politics, and scarcely a day passed without street-fights, which at times grew into riots. In the country, too, no less than in the cities, the goddess of discord reigned. The farmers determined to starve the city people into submission, and they entered into an agreement not to send any produce into the cities until the merchants should open their shops and begin selling their goods for paper at its face value. Not wishing to lose their pigs and butter and grain, they tried to dispose of them in Boston and New York, and in the coast towns of Connecticut. But in all these places their proceedings had awakened such lively disgust that placards were posted in the taverns warning purchasers against farm produce from Rhode Island. Disappointed in these quarters, the farmers threw away their milk, used their corn for fuel, and let their apples rot on the ground, rather than supply the detested merchants. Food grew scarce in Providence and Newport, and in the latter city a mob of sailors attempted unsuccessfully to storm the provision stores. The farmers were threatened with armed violence. Town-meetings were held all over the state, to discuss the situation, and how long they might have talked to no purpose none can say, when all at once the matter was brought into court. A cabinet-maker in Newport named Trevett went into a meat-market kept by one John Weeden, and selecting a joint of meat, offered paper in payment. Weeden refused to take the paper except at a heavy discount. Trevett went to bed supperless, and next morning informed against the obstinate butcher for disobedience to the forcing act. Should the court find him guilty, it would be a good speculation for Trevett, for half of the five hundred dollars fine was to go to the informer. Hard-money men feared lest the court might prove subservient to the legislature, since that body possessed the power of removing the five judges. The case was tried in September amid furious excitement. Huge crowds gathered about the court-house and far down the street, screaming and cheering like a crowd on the night of a presidential election. The judges were clear-headed men, not to be browbeaten. They declared the forcing act unconstitutional, and dismissed the complaint. Popular wrath then turned upon them. A special session of the legislature was convened, four of the judges were removed, and a new forcing act was prepared. This act provided that no man could vote at elections or hold any office without taking a test oath promising to receive paper money at par. But this was going too far. Many soft-money men were not wild enough to support such a measure; among the farmers there were some who had grown tired of seeing their produce spoiled on their hands; and many of the richest merchants had announced their intention of moving out of the state. The new forcing act accordingly failed to pass, and presently the old one was repealed. The paper dollar had been issued in May; in November it passed for sixteen cents.

These outrageous proceedings awakened disgust and alarm among sensible people in all the other states, and Rhode Island was everywhere reviled and made fun of. One clause of the forcing act had provided that if a debtor should offer paper to his creditor and the creditor should refuse to take it at par, the debtor might carry his rag money to court and deposit it with the judge; and the judge must thereupon issue a certificate discharging the debt. The form of certificate began with the words "Know Ye," and forthwith the unhappy little state was nicknamed Rogues' Island, the home of Know Ye men and Know Ye measures.

While the scorn of the people was thus poured out upon Rhode Island, much sympathy was felt for the government of Massachusetts, which was called upon thus early to put down armed rebellion. The pressure of debt was keenly felt in the rural districts of Massachusetts. It is estimated that the private debts in the state amounted to some $7,000,000, and the state's arrears to the federal government amounted to some $7,000,000 more. Adding to these sums the arrears of bounties due to the soldiers, and the annual cost of the state, county, and town governments, there was reached an aggregate equivalent to a tax of more than $50 on every man, woman, and child in this population of 379,000 souls. Upon every head of a family the average burden was some $200 at a time when most farmers would have thought such a sum yearly a princely income. In those days of scarcity most of them did not set eyes on so much as $50 in the course of a year, and happy was he who had tucked away two or three golden guineas or moidores in an old stocking, and sewed up the treasure in his straw mattress or hidden it behind the bricks of the chimney-piece. Under such circumstances the payment of debts and taxes was out of the question; and as the same state of things made creditors clamorous and ugly, the courts were crowded with lawsuits. The lawyers usually contrived to get their money by exacting retainers in advance, and the practice of champerty was common, whereby the lawyer did his work in consideration of a percentage on the sum which was at last forcibly collected. Homesteads were sold for the payment of foreclosed mortgages, cattle were seized in distrainer, and the farmer himself was sent to jail. The smouldering fires of wrath thus kindled found expression in curses aimed at lawyers, judges, and merchants. The wicked merchants bought foreign goods and drained the state of specie to pay for them, while they drank Madeira wine and dressed their wives in fine velvets and laces. So said the farmers; and city ladies, far kinder than these railers deemed them, formed clubs, of which the members pledged themselves to wear homespun,—a poor palliative for the deep-seated ills of the time. In such mood were many of the villagers when in the summer of 1786 they were overtaken by the craze for paper money. At the meeting of the legislature in May, a petition came in from Bristol County, praying for an issue of paper. The petitioners admitted that such money was sure to deteriorate in value, and they doubted the wisdom of trying to keep it up by forcing acts. Instead of this they would have the rate of its deterioration regulated by law, so that a dollar might be worth ninety cents to-day, and presently seventy cents, and by and by fifty cents, and so on till it should go down to zero and be thrown overboard. People would thus know what to expect, and it would be all right. The delicious *naïveté* of this argument did not prevail with the legislature of Massachusetts, and soft money was frowned down by a vote of ninety-nine to nineteen. Then a bill was brought in seeking to reëstablish in legislation the ancient practice of barter, and make horses and cows legal tender for debts; and this bill was crushed by eighty-nine votes against thirty-five. At the same time this legislature passed a bill to strengthen the federal government by a grant of supplementary funds to Congress, and thus laid a further burden of taxes upon the people.

There was an outburst of popular wrath. A convention at Hatfield in August decided that the court of common pleas ought to be abolished, that no funds should be granted to Congress, and that paper money should be issued at once. Another convention at Lenox denounced such incendiary measures, approved of supporting the federal government, and declared that no good could come from the issue of paper money. But meanwhile the angry farmers had resorted to violence. The legislature, they said, had its sittings in Boston, under the influence of wicked lawyers and merchants, and thus could not be expected to do the will of the people. A cry went up that henceforth the law-makers must sit in some small inland town, where jealous eyes might watch their proceedings. Meanwhile the lawyers must be dealt with; and at Northampton, Worcester, Great Barrington, and Concord the courts were broken up by armed mobs. At Concord one Job Shattuck brought several hundred armed men into the town and surrounded the court-house, while in a fierce harangue he declared that the time had come for wiping out all debts. "Yes," squeaked a nasal voice from the crowd,—"yes, Job, we know all about them two farms you can't never pay for!" But this repartee did not save the judges, who thought it best to flee from the town. At first the legislature deemed it wise to take a lenient view of these proceedings, and it even went so far as to promise to hold its next session out of Boston. But the agitation had reached a point where it could not be stayed. In September the supreme court was to sit at Springfield, and Governor Bowdoin sent a force of 600 militia under General Shepard to protect it. They were confronted by some 600 insurgents, under the leadership of Daniel Shays. This man had been a captain in the Continental army, and in his force were many of the penniless veterans whom Gates would fain have incited to rebellion at Newburgh. Shays seems to have done what he could to restrain his men from violence, but he was a poor creature, wanting alike in courage and good faith. On the other hand the militia were lacking in spirit. After a disorderly parley, with much cursing and swearing, they beat a retreat, and the court was prevented from sitting. Fresh riots followed at Worcester and Concord. A regiment of cavalry, sent out by the governor, scoured Middlesex County, and, after a short fight in the woods near Groton, captured Job Shattuck and dispersed his men. But this only exasperated the insurgents. They assembled in Worcester to the number of 1,200 or more, where they lived for two months at free quarters, while Shays organized and drilled them.

Meanwhile the habeas corpus act was suspended for eight months, and Governor Bowdoin called out an army of 4,400 men, who were placed under command of General Lincoln. As the state treasury was nearly empty, some wealthy gentlemen in Boston subscribed the money needed for equipping these troops, and about the middle of January, 1787, they were collected at Worcester. The rebels had behaved shamefully, burning barns and seizing all the plunder they could lay hands on. As their numbers increased they found their military stores inadequate, and accordingly they marched upon Springfield, with the intent to capture the federal arsenal there, and provide themselves with muskets and cannon. General Shephard held Springfield with 1,200 men, and on the 25th of January Shays attacked him with a force of somewhat more than 2,000, hoping to crush him and seize the arsenal before Lincoln could come to the rescue. But his plan of attack was faulty, and as soon as his men began falling under Shephard's fire a panic seized them, and they retreated in disorder to Ludlow, and then to Amherst, setting fire to houses and robbing the inhabitants. On the approach of Lincoln's army, three days later, Shays retreated to Pelham, and planted his forces on two steep hills protected at the bottom by huge snow-drifts. Lincoln advanced to Hadley and sought to open negotiations with the rebels. They were reminded that a contest with the state government was hopeless, and that they had already incurred the penalty of death; but if they would now lay down their arms and go home, a free pardon could be obtained for them. Shays seemed willing to yield, and Saturday, the 3d of February, was appointed for a conference between some of the leading rebels and some of the officers. But this was only a stratagem. During the conference Shays decamped and marched his men through Prescott and North Dana to Petersham. Toward nightfall the trick was discovered, and Lincoln set his whole force in motion over the mountain ridges of Shutesbury and New Salem. The day had been mild, but during the night the thermometer dropped below zero and an icy, cutting snow began to fall. There was great suffering during the last ten miles, and indeed the whole march of thirty miles in thirteen hours over steep and snow-covered roads was a worthy exploit for these veterans of the Revolution. Shays and his men had not looked for such a display of energy, and as they were getting their breakfast on Sunday morning at Petersham they were taken by surprise. A few minutes sufficed to scatter them in flight. A hundred and fifty, including Shays himself, were taken prisoners. The rest fled in all directions, most of them to Athol and Northfield, whence they made their way into Vermont. General Lincoln then marched his troops into the mountains of Berkshire, where disturbances still continued. On the 26th of February one Captain Hamlin, with several hundred insurgents, plundered the town of Stockbridge and carried off the leading citizens as hostages. He was pursued as far as Springfield, defeated there in a sharp skirmish, with a loss of some thirty in killed and wounded, and his troops scattered. This put an end to the insurrection in Massachusetts.

During the autumn similar disturbances had occurred in the states to the northward. At Exeter in New Hampshire and at Windsor and Rutland in Vermont the courts had been broken up by armed mobs, and at Rutland there had been bloodshed. When the Shays rebellion was put down, Governor Bowdoin requested the neighbouring states to lend their aid in bringing the insurgents to justice, and all complied with the request except Vermont and Rhode Island. The legislature of Rhode Island sympathized with the rebels, and refused to allow the governor to issue a warrant for their arrest. On the other hand, the governor of Vermont issued a proclamation out of courtesy toward Massachusetts, but he caused it to be understood that this was but an empty form, as the state of Vermont could not afford to discourage immigration! A feeling of compassion for the insurgents was widely spread in Massachusetts. In March the leaders were tried, and fourteen were convicted of treason and sentenced to death; but Governor Bowdoin, whose term was about to expire, granted a reprieve for a few weeks. At the annual election in April the candidates for the governorship were Bowdoin and Hancock, and it was generally believed that the latter would be more likely than the former to pardon the convicted men. So strong was this feeling that, although much gratitude was felt toward

Bowdoin, to whose energetic measures the prompt suppression of the rebellion was due, Hancock obtained a large majority. When the question of a pardon came up for discussion, Samuel Adams, who was then president of the senate, was strongly opposed to it, and one of his arguments was very characteristic. "In monarchies," he said, "the crime of treason and rebellion may admit of being pardoned or lightly punished; but the man who dares to rebel against the laws of a republic ought to suffer death." This was Adam's sensitive point. He wanted the whole world to realize that the rule of a republic is a rule of law and order, and that liberty does not mean license. But in spite of this view, for which there was much to be said, the clemency of the American temperament prevailed, and Governor Hancock pardoned all the prisoners.

Nothing in the history of these disturbances is more instructive than the light incidentally thrown upon the relations between Congress and the state government. Just before the news of the rout at Petersham, Samuel Adams had proposed in the senate that the governor should be requested to write to Congress and inform that body of what was going on in Massachusetts, stating that "although the legislature are firmly persuaded that . . . in all probability they will be able speedily and effectively to suppress the rebellion, yet, if any unforeseen event should take place which may frustrate the measures of government, they rely upon such support from the United States as is expressly and solemnly stipulated by the articles of confederation." A resolution to this effect was carried in the senate, but defeated in the house through the influence of western county members in sympathy with the insurgents; and incredible as it may seem, the argument was freely used that it was incompatible with the dignity of Massachusetts to allow United States troops to set foot upon her soil. When we reflect that the arsenal at Springfield, where the most considerable disturbance occurred, was itself federal property, the climax of absurdity might seem to have been reached.

It was left for Congress itself, however, to cap that climax. The progress of the insurrection in the autumn in Vermont, New Hampshire, and Massachusetts, as well as the troubles in Rhode Island, had alarmed the whole country. It was feared that the insurgents in these states might join forces, and in some way kindle a flame that would run through the land. Accordingly Congress in October called upon the states for a continental force, but did not dare to declare openly what it was to be used for. It was thought necessary to say that the troops were wanted for an expedition against the northwestern Indians! National humiliation could go no further than such a confession, on the part of our central government, that it dared not use force in defence of those very articles of confederation to which it owed its existence. Things had come to such a pass that people of all shades of opinion were beginning to agree upon one thing,—that something must be done, and done quickly.

GEORGE BANCROFT

(1800-1891)

In the final chapter of his last volume, George Bancroft, having completed a lengthy account of the Constitutional Convention, described the establishment of the new Federal government and interpreted its meaning.

Establishing the New Government

IT WAS TIME FOR AMERICA TO BE KNOWN ABROAD AS A NATION. THE statesmen of France reproached her unsparingly for failing in her pecuniary engagements. Boatmen who bore the flag of the United States on the father of rivers were fearlessly arrested by Spain, while Don Gardoqui, its agent, in private conversation tempted the men of Kentucky "to declare themselves independent" by the assurance that he was authorized to treat with them as a separate power respecting commerce and the navigation of the Mississippi.

The colonists in Nova Scotia were already absorbing a part of south-eastern Maine, and inventing false excuses for doing so. Great Britain declined to meet her own obligations with regard to the slaves whom she had carried away, and who finally formed the seed of a British colony at Sierra Leone. She did not give up her negotiations with the men of Vermont. She withheld the interior posts, belonging to the United States; in the commission for the government of Upper Canada she kept out of sight the line of boundary, in order that the commanding officer might not scruple to crowd the Americans away from access to their inland water-line, and thus debar them from their rightful share in the fur-trade. She was all the while encouraging the Indian tribes within the bounds of New York and to the south of the western lakes to assert their independence. Hearing of the discontent of the Kentuckians and the men of west North Carolina, she sought to foment the passions which might hurry them out of the union, as far as it could be done without promising them protection.

In England John Adams had, in 1786, vainly explained the expectation of congress that a British plenipotentiary minister should be sent to the United States. The bills regulating Newfoundland and intercourse with America were under the leadership of the same Jenkinson who had prepared the stamp act; and, with the acquiescence of Pitt, the men and the principles which had governed British policy toward America for most of the last twenty years still prevailed. In February 1788 the son of George Grenville, speaking for the ministry in the house of commons, said: "Great Britain, ever since the peace, has condescended to favor the United States." Moreover, the British government would take no notice of American

From Bancroft, *History of the United States of America* (Author's Last Revision, 1883), vol. 6, bk. 5, ch. 3.

remonstrances against the violations of the treaty of peace. Self-respect and patriotic pride forbade John Adams to remain.

Adams and Jefferson had exchanged with each other their portraits, as lasting memorials of friendship; and Adams, on leaving Europe, had but two regrets: one, the opportunity of research in books; the other, that immediate correspondence with Jefferson which he cherished as one of the most agreeable events in his life. "A seven months' intimacy with him here and as many weeks in London have given me opportunities of studying him closely," wrote Jefferson to Madison. "He is vain, irritable, and a bad calculator of the force and probable effect of the motives which govern men. This is all the ill which can possibly be said of him. He is disinterested, profound in his views, and accurate in his judgment, except where knowledge of the world is necessary to form a judgment. He is so amiable that you will love him, if ever you become acquainted with him."

In America the new constitution was rapidly conciliating the affections of the people. Union had been held dear ever since it was formed; and now that the constitution was its surest guarantee, no party could succeed which did not inscribe union, and with union the constitution, on its banner. In September 1788 the dissidents of Pennsylvania held a conference at Harrisburg. With the delegates from beyond the mountains came Albert Gallatin, a native of Geneva, and educated there in a republic of a purely federal form. Their proceedings bear the marks of his mind. They resolved for themselves and recommended to all others to acquiesce in the organization of the government under "the federal constitution, of which the ratification had formed a new era in the American world;" they asked, however, for its speedy revision by a general convention. All their actions were kept within the bounds of legality.

In Virginia there had been a great vibration of opinion. Its assembly, which met on the twentieth of October 1788, was the first to take into consideration the proposal for another federal convention. The enemies to the government formed a decided majority of the legislature. No one of its members was able to encounter Patrick Henry in debate, and his edicts were registered without opposition. He had only to say, "Let this be law," and it became law. Taking care to set forth that so far as it depended on Virginia the new plan of government would be carried into immediate operation, the assembly, on the thirtieth, proposed a second federal convention, and invited the concurrence of every other state. Madison was the fittest man in the union to be of the senate of the United States: Henry, on the eighth of November, after pouring forth a declamation against his federal principles, nominated Richard Henry Lee and Grayson for the two senators from Virginia, and they were chosen at his bidding. He divided the state into districts, cunningly restricting each of them to its own inhabitants in the choice of its representative, and taking care to compose the district in which Madison would be a candidate out of counties which were thought to be unfriendly to federalism. Assured by these iniquitous preparations, Monroe, without scruple, took the field against Madison.

In Connecticut, in October, the circular letter of New York had a reading among other public communications, but "no anti-federalist had hardiness enough to call it up for consideration or to speak one word of its subject."

The legislature of Massachusetts concurred with Hancock, the governor, that an immediate second federal convention might endanger the union. The legislature of Pennsylvania put the question at rest by saying: "The house do not perceive this constitution wanting in any of those fundamental principles which are calculated to ensure the liberties of their country. The happiness of America and the harmony of the union depend upon suffering it to proceed undisturbed in its operation by premature amendments. The house cannot, consistently with their duty to the good people of this state or with their affection to the citizens of the United States at large, concur with Virginia in their application to congress for a convention of the states." This vote Mifflin, the governor, early in March 1789, communicated to the governor of Virginia, and the subject was heard of no more.

Congress, as early as the second of July 1788, was notified that the constitution had received the approval of nine states; but they wasted two months in wrangling about the permanent seat of the federal government, and at last could agree only on New York as its resting-place. Not till the thirteenth of September was the first Wednesday of the following January appointed for the choice of electors of president in the several states; and the first Wednesday in March, which in that year was the fourth, for commencing proceedings under the constitution. The states, each for itself, appointed the times and places for electing senators and representatives.

The interest of the elections centred in New York, Virginia, and South Carolina. In four districts out of the six into which New York was divided the federalists elected their candidates. Having in the state legislature but a bare majority in the senate, while their opponents outnumbered them in the house, each branch made a nomination of senators; but the senate refused to go into a joint ballot. For this there was the excuse that the time for a new election was close at hand. But the senate further refused to meet the house for the choice of electors of president, and this was an act of faction.

The star of Hamilton was then in the ascendant, and he controlled the federalists; but only to make his singular incapacity to conduct a party as apparent as his swiftness and power of thought. He excluded the family of the Livingstons from influence. To defeat Clinton's re-election as governor, he stepped into the camp of his opponents, and with Aaron Burr and other anti-federalists selected for their candidate Robert Yates, who had deserted his post in the federal convention, but had since avowed the opinion which was held by every one in the state that the new constitution should be supported. New York at the moment was thoroughly federal, yet

Clinton escaped defeat through the attachment of his own county of Ulster and the insignificance of his opponent, while the federalists were left without any state organization. In the new legislature both branches were federal, and, at the behest of Hamilton, against the remonstrances of Morgan Lewis and others, Rufus King, on his transfer of residence from Massachusetts to New York, received the unexampled welcome of an immediate election with Schuyler to the senate.

In Virginia, Madison went into the counties that were relied on to defeat him, reasoned with the voters face to face, and easily won the day. Of the ten delegates from the state, seven were federalists, of whom one was from Kentucky. South Carolina elected avowed anti-federalists, except Butler, of the senate, who had conceded many points to bring about the union, and yet very soon took the alarm that "the southern interest was imperilled."

Under the constitution the house of representatives formed a quorum on the first of April 1789. The senate on the sixth chose John Langdon of New Hampshire its president. The house of representatives was immediately summoned, and in the presence of the two branches he opened and counted the votes. Every one of the sixty-nine, cast by the ten states which took part in the election, was for Washington. John Adams had thirty-four votes; and as no other obtained more than nine, he was declared to be the vice-president. The house devolved upon the senate the office of communicating the result to those who had been chosen; and proceeded to business.

"I foresee contentions," wrote Madison, "first between federal and anti-federal parties, and then between northern and southern parties, which give additional disagreeableness to the prospect." The events of the next seventy years cast their shadows before. Madison revived the bill which he had presented to congress on the eighteenth of March 1783, for duties on imports, adding to it a discriminating duty on tonnage. For an immediate public revenue, Lawrence of New York proposed a general duty *ad valorem*. England herself, by restraining and even prohibiting the domestic industry of the Americans so long as they remained in the condition of colonial dependence, had trained them to consider the establishment of home manufactures as an act of patriotic resistance to tyranny. Fitzsimons of Pennsylvania disapproved a uniform *ad valorem* duty on all imports. He said: "I have in contemplation to encourage domestic manufactures by protecting duties." Tucker of South Carolina enforced the necessity of great deliberation by calling attention to the antagonistic interests of the eastern, middle, and southern states in the article of tonnage. Boudinot of New Jersey wished glass to be taxed, for there were already several manufactures of it in the country. "We are able," said Hartley of Pennsylvania, "to furnish some domestic manufactures in sufficient quantity to answer the consumption of the whole union, and to work up our stock of materials even for exportation. In these cases I take it to be the policy of free, enlightened nations to give their manufactures that encouragement necessary to perfect them without oppressing the other parts of the community."

"We must consider the general interests of the union," said Madison, "as much as the local or state interest. My general principle is that commerce ought to be free, and labor and industry left at large to find their proper object." But he admitted that "the interests of the states which are ripe for manufactures ought to have attention, as the power of protecting and cherishing them has by the present constitution been taken from the states and its exercise thrown into other hands. Regulations in some of the states have produced establishments which ought not to be allowed to perish from the alteration which has taken place, while some manufactures being once formed can advance toward perfection without any adventitious aid. Some of the propositions may be productive of revenue and some may protect our domestic manufactures, though the latter subject ought not to be too confusedly blended with the former." "I," said Tucker, "am opposed to high duties because they will introduce and establish a system of smuggling, and because they tend to the oppression of citizens and states to promote the benefit of other states and other classes of citizens."

The election to the presidency found Washington prepared with a federal policy, which was the result of long meditation. He was resolved to preserve freedom; never to transcend the powers delegated by the constitution; even at the cost of life to uphold the union, a sentiment which in him had a tinge of anxiety from his thorough acquaintance with what Grayson called "the southern genius of America;" to restore the public finances; to establish in the foreign relations of the country a thoroughly American system; and to preserve neutrality in the impending conflict between nations in Europe.

Across the Atlantic Alfieri cried out to him: "Happy are you, who have for the sublime and permanent basis of your glory the love of country demonstrated by deeds."

On the fourteenth of April he received the official announcement of his recall to the public service, and was at ten o'clock on the morning of the sixteenth on his way. Though reluctant "in the evening of life to exchange a peaceful abode for an ocean of difficulties," he bravely said: "Be the voyage long or short, although I may be deserted by all men, integrity and firmness shall never forsake me."

But for him the country could not have achieved its independence; but for him it could not have formed its union; and but for him it could not have set the federal government in successful motion. His journey to New York was one continued march of triumph. All the way he was met with addresses from the citizens of various towns, from societies, universities, and churches.

His neighbors of Alexandria crowded round him with the strongest personal affection, saying: "Farewell, and make a grateful people happy; and may the Being who maketh and unmaketh at his will, restore to us again the best of men and the most beloved fellow-citizen."

To the citizens of Baltimore, Washington said: "I hold it of little moment if the close of my life shall be embittered, provided I shall have been instrumental in securing the liberties and promoting the happiness of the American people."

He assured the society for promoting domestic manufactures in Delaware that "the promotion of domestic manufactures may naturally be expected to flow from an energetic government;" and he promised to give "a decided preference to the produce and fabrics of America."

At Philadelphia, "almost overwhelmed with a sense of the divine munificence," he spoke words of hope: "The most gracious Being, who has hitherto watched over the interests and averted the perils fo the United States, will never suffer so fair an inheritance to become a prey to anarchy or despotism."

At Trenton he was met by a party of matrons and their daughters, dressed in white, strewing flowers before him, and singing an ode of welcome to "the mighty chief" who had rescued them from a "mercenary foe."

Embarking at Elizabeth Point in a new barge, manned by pilots dressed in white, he cleaved his course swiftly across the bay, between gayly decorated boats, filled with gazers who cheered him with instrumental music, or broke out in songs. As he touched the soil of New York he was welcomed by the two houses of congress, by the governor of the state, by the magistrates of the city, by its people; and so attended he proceeded on foot to the modest mansion lately occupied by the presiding officer of the confederate congress. On that day he dined with Clinton; in the evening the city was illuminated. The senate, under the influence of John Adams and the persistency of Richard Henry Lee, would have given him the title of "Highness;" but the house, supported by the true republican simplicity of the man whom they both wished to honor, insisted on the simple words of the constitution, and prevailed.

On the thirtieth, the day appointed for the inauguration, Washington, being fifty-seven years, two months, and eight days old, was ceremoniously received by the two houses in the hall of the senate. Stepping out to the middle compartment of a balcony, which had been raised in front of it, he found before him a dense throng extending to Broad street, and filling Wall street to Broadway. All were hushed as Livingston, the chancellor of the state, administered the oath of office; but when he cried, "Long live George Washington, President of the United States!" the air was rent with huzzas, which were repeated as Washington bowed to the multitude.

Then returning to the senate-chamber, with an aspect grave almost to sadness and a voice deep and tremulous, he addressed the two houses, confessing his distrust of his own endowments and his inexperience in civil administration. The magnitude and difficulty of the duties to which his country had called him weighed upon him so heavily that he shook as he proceeded: "It would be peculiarly improper to omit, in this first official act, my fervent supplications to that Almighty Being who presides in the councils of nations, that his benediction may consecrate to the liberties and happiness of the people of the United States a government instituted by themselves. No people can be bound to acknowledge the invisible hand which conducts the affairs of men more than the people of the United States. Every step by which they have advanced to the character of an independent nation seems to have been distinguished by some token of providential agency. There exists in the economy of nature an indissoluble union between an honest and magnanimous policy and public prosperity. Heaven can never smile on a nation that disregards the eternal rules of order and right. The preservation of liberty, and the destiny of the republican model of government, are justly considered as deeply, perhaps as finally, staked on the experiment intrusted to the American people."

At the close of the ceremony the president and both branches of congress were escorted to the church of St. Paul, where the chaplain of the senate read prayers suited to the occasion, after which they all attended the president to his mansion.

"Every one without exception," so reports the French minister to his government, "appeared penetrated with veneration for the illustrious chief of the republic. The humblest was proud of the virtues of the man who was to govern him. Tears of joy were seen to flow in the hall of the senate, at church, and even in the streets, and no sovereign ever reigned more completely in the hearts of his subjects than Washington in the hearts of his fellow-citizens. Nature, which had given him the talent to govern, distinguished him from all others by his appearance. He had at once the soul, the look, and the figure of a hero. He never appeared embarrassed at homage rendered him, and in his manners he had the advantage of joining dignity to great simplicity."

To the president's inaugural speech one branch of the legislature thus responded: "The senate will at all times cheerfully co-operate in every measure which may strengthen the union and perpetuate the liberties of this great confederated republic."

The representatives of the American people likewise addressed him: "With you we adore the invisible hand which has led the American people through so many difficulties; and we cherish a conscious responsibility for the destiny of republican liberty. We join in your fervent supplication for our country; and we add our own for the choicest blessings of heaven on the most beloved of her citizens."

In the same moments of the fifth day of May 1789, when these words were reported, the ground was trembling beneath the arbitrary governments of Europe as Louis XVI proceeded to open the states-general of France. The day of wrath, against which Leibnitz had warned the monarchs of Europe, was beginning to break, and its judgments were to be the more terrible for the long delay of its coming. The great Frederick, who alone of them all had lived and toiled for the good of his land, described the degeneracy and insignificance of his fellow-rulers with cynical scorn. Not one of them had a surmise that the only sufficient reason for the existence of a king lies in his usefulness to the people. Nor did they spare one another. The law of morality was never suffered to restrain the passion for conquest. Austria preyed upon Italy until Alfieri could only say, in his despair, that despotic power had left him no country to serve; nor did the invader permit the thought that an Italian could have a right to a country. The heir in the only line of protestant kings on the continent of Europe, too blind to see that he would one day be stripped of the chief part of his own share in the spoils, joined with two other robbers to divide the country of Kosciuszko. In Holland dynastic interests were betraying the welfare of the republic. All faith was dying out; and self, in its eagerness for pleasure or advantage, stifled the voice of justice. The atheism of the great, who lived without God in the world, concealed itself under superstitious observances which were enforced by an inquisition that sought to rend beliefs from the soul, and to suppress inquiry by torments which surpassed the worst cruelties that savages could invent. Even in Great Britain all the branches of government were controlled by the aristocracy, of which the more liberal party could in that generation have no hope of being summoned by the king to frame a cabinet. The land, of which every member of a clan had had some share of ownership, had been for the most part usurped by the nobility; and the people were starving in the midst of the liberality which their own hands extorted from nature. The monarchs, whose imbecility or excesses had brought the doom of death on arbitrary power, were not only unfit to rule, but, while their own unlimited sovereignty was stricken with death, they knew not how to raise up statesmen to take their places. Well-intentioned friends of mankind burned with indignation, and even the wise and prudent were incensed by the conscious endurance of wrong; while the lowly classes, clouded by despair, were driven sometimes to admit the terrible thought that religion, which is the poor man's consolation and defence, might be but an instrument of government in the hands of their oppressors. There was no relief for the nations but through revolution, and their masters had poisoned the weapons which revolution must use.

In America a new people had risen up without king, or princes, or nobles, knowing nothing of tithes and little of landlords, the plough being for the most part in the hands of free holders of the soil. They were more sincerely religious, better educated, of serener minds, and of purer morals than the men of any former republic. By calm meditation and friendly councils they had prepared a constitution which, in the union of freedom with strength and order, excelled every one known before; and which secured itself against violence and revolution by providing a peaceful method for every needed reform. In the happy morning of their existence as one of the powers of the world, they had chosen justice for their guide; and while they proceeded on their way with well-founded confidence and joy, all the friends of mankind invoked success on the unexampled endeavor to govern states and territories of imperial extent as one federal republic.

HENRY ADAMS

(1838-1918)

The United States grew and changed with amazing rapidity between the inauguration of Washington and that of Jefferson only a dozen years later. The raw new capital city rising on the banks of the Potomac seemed to symbolize the wilderness nation itself, facing critical problems and limitless possibilities as it crossed over the threshold of the nineteenth century. This is the America that Henry Adams portrayed with incomparable skill in the first six chapters of his History of the United States of America during the Administrations of Jefferson and Madison. *Three of these chapters appear here.*

As a scholar, J. C. Levenson, has pointed out, in some respects Adams's History *was like a reverse image of Gibbon's* The Decline and Fall of the Roman Empire: *a portrait of the American nation on the rise. When Adams as a young man of 22 visited Rome, he did not presume to dream of becoming another Gibbon, but he did sit where Gibbon had when he conceived of his great work, "in the close of the evening, among the ruins of the Capitol," posing the same question, "Why?" "Substitute the word America for the word Rome, and the question became personal."*

The United States in 1800

ACCORDING TO THE CENSUS OF 1800, THE UNITED STATES OF AMERICA contained 5,308,483 persons. In the same year the British Islands contained upwards of fifteen millions; the French Republic, more than twenty-seven millions. Nearly one fifth of the American people were negro slaves; the true political population consisted of four and a half million free whites, or less than one million able-bodied males, on whose shoulders fell the burden of a continent. Even after two centuries of struggle the land was still untamed; forest covered every portion, except here and there a strip of cultivated soil; the minerals lay undisturbed in their rocky beds, and more than two thirds of the people clung to the seaboard within fifty miles of tide-water, where alone the wants of civilized life could be supplied. The centre of population rested within eighteen miles of Baltimore, north and east of Washington. Except in political arrangement, the interior was little more civilized than in 1750, and was not much easier to penetrate than when La Salle and Hennepin found their way to the Mississippi more than a century before.

A great exception broke this rule. Two wagonroads crossed the Alleghany Mountains in Pennsylvania,—one leading from Philadelphia to Pittsburg; one from the Potomac to the Monongahela; while a third passed through Virginia southwestward to the Holston River and Knoxville in Tennessee, with a branch through the Cumberland Gap into Kentucky. By these roads and by trails less passable from North and South Carolina, or by water-ways from the lakes, between four and five hundred thousand persons had invaded the country beyond the Alleghanies. At Pittsburg and on the Monongahela existed a society, already old, numbering seventy or eighty thousand persons, while on the Ohio River the settlements had grown to an importance which threatened to force a difficult problem on the union of the older States. One hundred and eighty thousand whites, with forty thousand negro slaves, made Kentucky the largest community west of the mountains; and about ninety thousand whites and fourteen thousand slaves were scattered over Tennessee. In the territory north of the Ohio less progress had been made. A New England colony existed at Marietta; some fifteen thou-

From Adams, *History of the United States of America during the Administrations of Jefferson and Madison* (9 vols., 1889-1891), vol. 1, ch, 1, 2, 6.

sand people were gathered at Cincinnati; half-way between the two, a small
town had grown up at Chillicothe, and other villages or straggling cabins
were to be found elsewhere; but the whole Ohio territory contained only
forty-five thousand inhabitants. The entire population, both free and slave,
west of the mountains, reached not yet half a million; but already they were
partly disposed to think themselves, and the old thirteen States were not
altogether unwilling to consider them, the germ of an independent empire,
which was to find its outlet, not through the Alleghanies to the seaboard,
but by the Mississippi River to the Gulf.

   Nowhere did eastern settlements touch the western. At least one hundred
miles of mountainous country held the two regions everywhere apart. The
shore of Lake Erie, where alone contact seemed easy, was still unsettled.
The Indians had been pushed back to the Cuyahoga River, and a few cabins
were built on the site of Cleveland; but in 1800, as in 1700, this intermediate region was only a portage where emigrants and merchandise were
transferred from Lake Erie to the Muskingum and Ohio valleys. Even western New York remained a wilderness: Buffalo was not laid out; Indian titles
were not extinguished; Rochester did not exist; and the county of Onondaga
numbered a population of less than eight thousand. In 1799 Utica contained
fifty houses, mostly small and temporary. Albany was still a Dutch city,
with some five thousand inhabitants; and the tide of immigration flowed
slowly through it into the valley of the Mohawk, while another stream from
Pennsylvania, following the Susquehanna, spread toward the Genesee
country.

   The people of the old thirteen States, along the Atlantic seaboard, thus
sent westward a wedge-shaped mass of nearly half a million persons, pene-
trating by the Tennessee, Cumberland, and Ohio rivers toward the western
limit of the Union. The Indians offered sharp resistance to this invasion,
exacting life for life, and yielding only as their warriors perished. By the
close of the century the wedge of white settlements, with its apex at Nashville and its flanks covered by the Ohio and Tennessee rivers, nearly split
the Indian country in halves. The northern half—consisting of the later
States of Wisconsin, Michigan, Illinois, Indiana, and one third of Ohio—
contained Wyandottes and Shawanese, Miamis, Kickapoos, and other tribes,
able to send some five thousand warriors to hunt or fight. In the southern
half, powerful confederacies of Creeks, Cherokees, Chickasaws, and Choc-
taws lived and hunted where the States of Mississippi, Alabama, and the
western parts of Georgia, Tennessee, and Kentucky were to extend; and so
weak was the State of Georgia, which claimed the southwestern territory for
its own, that a well-concerted movement of Indians might without much
difficulty have swept back its white population of one hundred thousand
toward the ocean or across the Savannah River. The Indian power had been
broken in halves, but each half was still terrible to the colonists on the edges
of their vast domain, and was used as a political weapon by the Govern-

ments whose territory bounded the Union on the north and south. The governors-general of Canada intrigued with the northwestern Indians, that they might hold in check any aggression from Washington; while the Spanish governors of West Florida and Louisiana maintained equally close relations with the Indian confederacies of the Georgia territory.

With the exception that half a million people had crossed the Alleghanies and were struggling with difficulties all their own, in an isolation like that of Jutes or Angles in the fifth century, America, so far as concerned physical problems, had changed little in fifty years. The old landmarks remained nearly where they stood before. The same bad roads and difficult rivers, connecting the same small towns, stretched into the same forests in 1800 as when the armies of Braddock and Amherst pierced the western and northern wilderness, except that these roads extended a few miles farther from the seacoast. Nature was rather man's master than his servant, and the five million Americans struggling with the untamed continent seemed hardly more competent to their task than the beavers and buffalo which had for countless generations made bridges and roads of their own.

Even by water, along the seaboard, communication was as slow and almost as irregular as in colonial times. The wars in Europe caused a sudden and great increase in American shipping employed in foreign commerce, without yet leading to general improvement in navigation. The ordinary sea-going vessel carried a freight of about two hundred and fifty tons; the largest merchant ships hardly reached four hundred tons; the largest frigate in the United States navy, the "line-of-battle ship in disguise," had a capacity of fifteen hundred and seventy-six tons. Elaborately rigged as ships or brigs, the small merchant craft required large crews and were slow sailers; but the voyage to Europe was comparatively more comfortable and more regular than the voyage from New York to Albany, or through Long Island Sound to Providence. No regular packet plied between New York and Albany. Passengers waited till a sloop was advertised to sail; they provided their own bedding and supplies; and within the nineteenth century Captain Elias Bunker won much fame by building the sloop "Experiment," of one hundred and ten tons, to start regularly on a fixed day for Albany, for the convenience of passengers only, supplying beds, wine, and provisions for the voyage of one hundred and fifty miles. A week on the North River or on the Sound was an experience not at all unknown to travellers.

While little improvement had been made in water-travel, every increase of distance added to the difficulties of the westward journey. The settler who after buying wagon and horses hauled his family and goods across the mountains, might buy or build a broad flat-bottomed ark, to float with him and his fortunes down the Ohio, in constant peril of upsetting or of being sunk; but only light boats with strong oars could mount the stream, or boats forced against the current by laboriously poling in shallow water. If he carried his tobacco and wheat down the Mississippi to the Spanish port of

New Orleans, and sold it, he might return to his home in Kentucky or Ohio by a long and dangerous journey on horseback through the Indian country from Natchez to Nashville, or he might take ship to Philadelphia, if a ship were about to sail, and again cross the Alleghanies. Compared with river travel, the sea was commonly an easy and safe highway. Nearly all the rivers which penetrated the interior were unsure, liable to be made dangerous by freshets, and both dangerous and impassable by drought; yet such as they were, these streams made the main paths of traffic. Through the mountainous gorges of the Susquehanna the produce of western New York first found an outlet; the Cuyahoga and Muskingum were the first highway from the Lakes to the Ohio; the Ohio itself, with its great tributaries the Cumberland and the Tennessee, marked the lines of western migration; and every stream which could at high water float a boat was thought likely to become a path for commerce. As General Washington, not twenty years earlier, hoped that the brawling waters of the Cheat and Youghiogheny might become the channel of trade between Chesapeake Bay and Pittsburg, so the Americans of 1800 were prepared to risk life and property on any streamlet that fell foaming down either flank of the Alleghanies. The experience of mankind proved trade to be dependent on water communications, and as yet Americans did not dream that the experience of mankind was useless to them.

If America was to be developed along the lines of water communications alone, by such means as were known to Europe, Nature had decided that the experiment of a single republican government must meet extreme difficulties. The valley of the Ohio had no more to do with that of the Hudson, the Susquehanna, the Potomac, the Roanoke, and the Santee, than the valley of the Danube with that of the Rhone, the Po, or the Elbe. Close communication by land could alone hold the great geographical divisions together either in interest or in fear. The union of New England with New York and Pennsylvania was not an easy task even as a problem of geography, and with an ocean highway; but the union of New England with the Carolinas, and of the seacoast with the interior, promised to be a hopeless undertaking. Physical contact alone could make one country of these isolated empires, but to the patriotic American of 1800, struggling for the continual existence of an embryo nation, with machinery so inadequate, the idea of ever bringing the Mississippi River, either by land or water, into close contact with New England, must have seemed wild. By water, an Erie Canal was already foreseen; by land, centuries of labor could alone conquer those obstacles which Nature permitted to be overcome.

In the minds of practical men, the experience of Europe left few doubts on this point. After two thousand years of public labor and private savings, even despotic monarchs, who employed the resources of their subjects as they pleased, could in 1800 pass from one part of their European dominions to another little more quickly than they might have done in the age of the

Antonines. A few short canals had been made, a few bridges had been built, an excellent post-road extended from Madrid to St. Petersburg; but the heavy diligence that rumbled from Calais to Paris required three days for its journey of one hundred and fifty miles, and if travellers ventured on a trip to Marseilles they met with rough roads and hardships like those of the Middle Ages. Italy was in 1800 almost as remote from the north of Europe as when carriage-roads were first built. Neither in time nor in thought was Florence or Rome much nearer to London in Wordsworth's youth than in the youth of Milton or Gray. Indeed, such changes as had occurred were partly for the worse, owing to the violence of revolutionary wars during the last ten years of the eighteenth century. Horace Walpole at his life's close saw about him a world which in many respects was less civilized than when as a boy he made the grand tour of Europe.

While so little had been done on the great highways of European travel, these highways were themselves luxuries which furnished no sure measure of progress. The post-horses toiled as painfully as ever through the sand from Hamburg to Berlin, while the coach between York and London rolled along an excellent road at the rate of ten miles an hour; yet neither in England nor on the Continent was the post-road a great channel of commerce. No matter how good the road, it could not compete with water, nor could heavy freights in great quantities be hauled long distances without extravagant cost. Water communication was as necessary for European commerce in 1800 as it had been for the Phœnicians and Egyptians; the Rhine, the Rhone, the Danube, the Elbe, were still the true commerical highways, and except for government post-roads, Europe was as dependent on these rivers in the eighteenth century as in the thirteenth. No certainty could be offered of more rapid progress in the coming century than in the past; the chief hope seemed to lie in the construction of canals.

While Europe had thus consumed centuries in improving paths of trade, until merchandise could be brought by canal a few score miles from the Rhone to the Loire and Seine, to the Garonne and the Rhine, and while all her wealth and energy had not yet united the Danube with other river systems, America was required to construct, without delay, at least three great roads and canals, each several hundred miles long, across mountain ranges, through a country not yet inhabited, to points where no great markets existed,—and this under constant peril of losing her political union, which could not even by such connections be with certainty secured. After this should be accomplished, the Alleghanies must still remain between the eastern and western States, and at any known rate of travel Nashville could not be reached in less than a fortnight or three weeks from Philadelphia. Meanwhile the simpler problem of bringing New England nearer to Virginia and Georgia had not advanced even with the aid of a direct ocean highway. In becoming politically independent of England, the old thirteen provinces developed little more commercial intercourse with each other in proportion to their wealth and population than they had maintained in colonial days. The material ties that united them grew in strength no more rapidly than the ties which bound them to Europe. Each group of States lived a life apart.

Even the lightly equipped traveller found a short journey no slight effort. Between Boston and New York was a tolerable highway, along which, thrice a week, light stage-coaches carried passengers and the mail, in three days. From New York a stage-coach started every week-day for Philadelphia, consuming the greater part of two days in the journey; and the road between Paulus Hook, the modern Jersey City, and Hackensack, was declared by the newspapers in 1802 to be as bad as any other part of the route between Maine and Georgia. South of Philadelphia the road was tolerable as far as Baltimore, but between Baltimore and the new city of Washington it meandered through forests; the driver chose the track which seemed least dangerous, and rejoiced if in wet seasons he reached Washington without miring or upsetting his wagon. In the Northern States, four miles an hour was the average speed for any coach between Bangor and Baltimore. Beyond the Potomac the roads became steadily worse, until south of Petersburg even the mails were carried on horseback. Except for a stage-coach which plied between Charleston and Savannah, no public conveyance of any kind was mentioned in the three southernmost States.

The stage-coach was itself a rude conveyance, of a kind still familiar to experienced travellers. Twelve persons, crowded into one wagon, were jolted over rough roads, their bags and parcels, thrust inside, cramping their legs, while they were protected from the heat and dust of mid-summer and the intense cold and driving snow of winter only by leather flaps buttoned to the roof and sides. In fine, dry weather this mode of travel was not unpleasant, when compared with the heavy vehicles of Europe and the hard English turnpikes; but when spring rains drew the frost from the ground the roads became nearly impassable, and in winter, when the rivers froze, a serious peril was added, for the Susquehanna or the North River at Paulus Hook must be crossed in an open boat,—an affair of hours at best, sometimes leading to fatal accidents. Smaller annoyances of many kinds were habitual. The public, as a rule, grumbled less than might have been expected, but occasionally newspapers contained bitter complaints. An angry Philadelphian, probably a foreigner, wrote in 1796 that, "with a few exceptions, brutality, negligence, and filching are as naturally expected by people accustomed to travelling in America, as a mouth, a nose, and two eyes are looked for in a man's face." This sweeping charge, probably unjust, and certainly supported by little public evidence, was chiefly founded on the experience of an alleged journey from New York:—

"At Bordentown we went into a second boat where we met with very sorry accommodation. This was about four o'clock in the afternoon. We had about twenty miles down the Delaware to reach Philadelphia. The captain, who had a most provoking tongue, was a boy about eighteen years of age. He and a few companions despatched a dozen or eighteen bottles of porter. We ran three different times against other vessels that were coming up the stream. The women and children lay all night on the bare boards of the cabin floor. . . . We reached Arch Street wharf about eight o'clock on the Wednesday morning, having been about sixteen hours on a voyage of twenty miles."

In the Southern States the difficulties and perils of travel were so great as to form a barrier almost insuperable. Even Virginia was no exception to this rule. At each interval of a few miles the horseman found himself stopped by a river, liable to sudden freshets, and rarely bridged. Jefferson in his frequent journeys between Monticello and Washington was happy to reach the end of the hundred miles without some vexatious delay. "Of eight rivers between here and Washington," he wrote to his Attorney-General in 1801, "five have neither bridges nor boats."

Expense caused an equally serious obstacle to travel. The usual charge in the Northern States was six cents a mile, by stage. In the year 1796, according to Francis Baily, President of the Royal Astronomical Society, three or four stages ran daily from Baltimore to Philadelphia, the fare six dollars, with charges amounting to two dollars and a quarter a day at the inns on the road. Baily was three days in making the journey. From Philadelphia to New York he paid the same fare and charges, arriving in one day and a half. The entire journey of two hundred miles cost him twenty-one dollars. He remarked that travelling on the main lines of road in the settled country was about as expensive as in England, and when the roads were good, about as rapid. Congress allowed its members six dollars for every twenty miles travelled. The actual cost, including hotel expenses, could hardly have fallen below ten cents a mile.

Heavy traffic never used stage routes if it could find cheaper. Commerce between one state and another, or even between the seaboard and the interior of the same state, was scarcely possible on any large scale unless navigable water connected them. Except the great highway to Pittsburg, no road served as a channel of commerce between different regions of the country. In this respect New England east of the Connecticut was as independent of New York as both were independent of Virginia, and as Virginia in her turn was independent of Georgia and South Carolina. The chief value of inter-State communication by land rested in the postal system; but the post furnished another illustration of the difficulties which barred progress. In the year 1800 one general mail-route extended from Portland in Maine to Louisville in Georgia, the time required for the trip being twenty days. Between Portsmouth in New Hampshire and Petersburg in Virginia the contracts required a daily service, except Sundays; between Petersburg and Augusta the mail was carried thrice a week. Branching from the main line at New York, a mail went to Canandaigua in ten days; from Philadelphia another branch line went to Lexington in sixteen days, to Nashville in twenty-two days. Thus more than twenty thousand miles of post-road, with nine hundred post-offices, proved the vastness of the country and the smallness of the result; for the gross receipts for postage in the year ending Oct. 1, 1801, were only $320,000.

Throughout the land the eighteenth century ruled supreme. Only within a few years had the New Englander begun to abandon his struggle with a barren soil, among granite hills, to learn the comforts of easier existence in the valleys of the Mohawk and Ohio; yet the New England man was thought the shrewdest and most enterprising of Americans. If the Puritans and the Dutch needed a century or more to reach the Mohawk, when would they reach the Mississippi? The distance from New York to the Mississippi was about one thousand miles; from Washington to the extreme south-western military post, below Natchez, was about twelve hundred. Scarcely a portion of western Europe was three hundred miles distant from some sea, but a width of three hundred miles was hardly more than an outskirt of the United States. No civilized country had yet been required to deal with physical difficulties so serious, nor did experience warrant conviction that such difficulties could be overcome.

If the physical task which lay before the American people had advanced but a short way toward completion, little more change could be seen in the economical conditions of American life. The man who in the year 1800 ventured to hope for a new era in the coming century, could lay his hand on no statistics that silenced doubt. The machinery of production showed no radical difference from that familiar to ages long past. The Saxon farmer of the eighth century enjoyed most of the comforts known to Saxon farmers of the eighteenth. The eorls and ceorls of Offa and Ecgbert could not read or write, and did not receive a weekly newspaper with such information as newspapers in that age could supply; yet neither their houses, their clothing, their food and drink, their agricultural tools and methods, their stock, nor their habits were so greatly altered or improved by time that they would have found much difficulty in accommodating their lives to that of their descendants in the eighteenth century. In this respect America was backward. Fifty or a hundred miles inland more than half the houses were log-cabins, which might or might not enjoy the luxury of a glass window. Throughout the South and West houses showed little attempt at luxury; but even in New England the ordinary farmhouse was hardly so well built, so spacious, or so warm as that of a well-to-do contemporary of Charlemagne. The cloth which the farmer's family wore was still homespun. The hats were manufactured by the village hatter; the clothes were cut and made at home; the shirts, socks, and nearly every other article of dress were also homemade. Hence came a marked air of rusticity which distinguished country from town,—awkward shapes of hat, coat, and trousers, which gave to the Yankee caricature those typical traits that soon disappeared almost as completely as coats of mail and steel headpieces. The plough was rude and clumsy; the sickle as old as Tubal Cain, and even the cradle not in general use; the flail was unchanged since the Aryan exodus; in Virginia, grain was still commonly troden out by horses. Enterprising gentlemen-farmers introduced threshing-machines and invented scientific ploughs; but these were novelties. Stock was as a rule not only unimproved, but ill cared for. The swine ran loose; the cattle were left to feed on what pastures they could find, and even in New England were not housed until the severest frosts, on the excuse that exposure hardened them. Near half a century afterward a competent judge asserted that the general treatment of cows in New England was fair matter of presentment by a grand jury. Except among the best farmers, drainage, manures, and rotation of crops were uncommon. The ordinary cultivator planted his corn as his father had planted it, sowing as much rye to the acre, using the same number of oxen to plough, and getting in his crops on the same day. He was even known to remove his barn on account of the manure accumulated round it, although the New England soil was never so rich as to warrant neglect to enrich it. The money for which he sold his wheat and chickens was of the Old World; he reckoned in shillings or pistareens, and rarely handled an American coin more valuable than a large copper cent.

At a time when the wealth and science of London and Paris could not supply an article so necessary as a common sulphur-match, the backward-ness of remote country districts could hardly be exaggerated. Yet remote districts were not the only sufferers. Of the whole United States New England claimed to be the most civilized province, yet New England was a region in which life had yet gained few charms of sense and few advantages over its rivals. Wilson, the ornithologist, a Pennsylvania Scotchman, a confirmed grumbler, but a shrewd judge, and the most thorough of American travellers, said in 1808: "My journey through almost the whole of New England has rather lowered the Yankees in my esteem. Except a few neat academies, I found their schoolhouses equally ruinous and deserted with ours; fields covered with stones; stone fences; scrubby oaks and pine-trees; wretched orchards; scarcely one grain-field in twenty miles; the taverns along the road dirty, and filled with loungers brawling about law-suits and politics; the people snappish and extortioners, lazy, and two hundred years behind the Pennsylvanians in agricultural improvements." The description was exaggerated, for Wilson forgot to speak of the districts where fields were not covered with stones, and where wheat could be grown to advantage. Twenty years earlier, Albert Gallatin, who knew Pennsylvania well, having reached Hartford on his way to Boston, wrote: "I have seen nothing in America equal to the establishments on the Connecticut River." Yet Wilson's account described the first general effect of districts in the New England States, where agriculture was backward and the country poor. The houses were thin wooden buildings, not well suited to the climate;

the churches were unwarmed; the clothing was poor; sanitary laws were few, and a bathroom or a soil-pipe was unknown. Consumption, typhoid, scarlet fever, diphtheria, and rheumatic fevers were common; habits of drinking were still a scourge in every family, and dyspepsia destroyed more victims than were consumed by drink. Population increased slowly, as though the conditions of life were more than usually hard. A century earlier, Massachusetts was supposed to contain sixty thousand inhabitants. Governor Hutchinson complained that while the other colonies quadrupled their numbers, Massachusetts failed to double its population in fifty years. In 1790 the State contained 378,000 people, not including the province of Maine; in 1800 the number rose to 423,000, which showed that a period of more rapid growth had begun, for the emigration into other States was also large.

A better measure of the difficulties with which New England struggled was given by the progress of Boston, which was supposed to have contained about eighteen thousand inhabitants as early as 1730, and twenty thousand in 1770. For several years after the Revolution it numbered less than twenty thousand, but in 1800 the census showed twenty-five thousand inhabitants. In appearance, Boston resembled an English market-town, of a kind even then old-fashioned. The footways or sidewalks were paved, like the crooked and narrow streets, with round cobblestones, and were divided from the carriage way only by posts and a gutter. The streets were almost unlighted at night, a few oil-lamps rendering the darkness more visible and the rough pavement rougher. Police hardly existed. The system of taxation was defective. The town was managed by selectmen, the elected instruments of town-meetings whose jealousy of granting power was even greater than their objection to spending money, and whose hostility to city government was not to be overcome.

Although on all sides increase of ease and comfort was evident, and roads, canals, and new buildings, public and private, were already in course of construction on a scale before unknown, yet in spite of more than a century and a half of incessant industry, intelligent labor, and pinching economy Boston and New England were still poor. A few merchants enjoyed incomes derived from foreign trade, which allowed them to imitate in a quiet way the style of the English mercantile class, but the clergy and the lawyers, who stood at the head of society, lived with much economy. Many a country clergyman, eminent for piety and even for hospitality, brought up a family and laid aside some savings on a salary of five hundred dollars a year. President Dwight, who knew well the class to which he belonged, eulogizing the life of Abijah Weld, pastor of Attleborough, declared that on a salary of two hundred and twenty dollars a year Mr. Weld brought up eleven children, besides keeping a hospitable house and maintaining charity to the poor.

On the Exchange a few merchants had done most of the business of

Boston since the peace of 1783, but six mail-coaches a week to New York, and occasional arrivals from Europe, or the departure of a ship to China, left ample leisure for correspondence and even for gossip. The habits of the commercial class had not been greatly affected by recent prosperity. Within ten or fifteen years before 1800 three Banks had been created to supply the commercial needs of Boston. One of these was a branch Bank of the United States, which employed there whatever part of its capital it could profitably use; the two others were local Banks, with capital of $1,600,000, toward which the State subscribed $400,000. Altogether the banking capital of Boston might amount to two millions and a half. A number of small Banks, representing in all about two and a half millions more, were scattered through the smaller New England towns. The extraordinary prosperity caused by the French wars opened to Boston a new career. Wealth and population were doubling; the exports and imports of New England were surprisingly large, and the shipping was greater than that of New York and Pennsylvania combined; but Boston had already learned, and was to learn again, how fleeting were the riches that depended on foreign commerce, and conservative habits were not easily changed by a few years of accidental gain.

Of manufactures New England had many, but none on a large scale. The people could feed or clothe themselves only by household industry; their whale-oil, salt fish, lumber, and rum were mostly sent abroad; but they freighted coasters with turners' articles, home-made linens and clothes, cheese, butter, shoes, nails, and what were called Yankee Notions of all sorts, which were sent to Norfolk and the Southern ports, and often peddled from the deck, as goods of every sort were peddled on the flat-boats of the Ohio. Two or three small mills spun cotton with doubtful success; but England supplied ordinary manufactures more cheaply and better than Massachusetts could hope to do. A tri-weekly mail and a few coasting sloops provided for the business of New England with domestic ports. One packet sloop plied regularly to New York.

The State of New York was little in advance of Massachusetts and Maine. In 1800 for the first time New York gained the lead in population by the difference between 589,000 and 573,000. The valuation of New York for the direct tax in 1799 was $100,000,000; that of Massachusetts was $84,000,000. New York was still a frontier State, and although the city was European in its age and habits, travellers needed to go few miles from the Hudson in order to find a wilderness like that of Ohio and Tennessee. In most material respects the State was behind New England; outside the city was to be seen less wealth and less appearance of comfort. The first impression commonly received of any new country was from its inns, and on the whole few better tests of material condition then existed. President Dwight, though maintaining that the best old-fashioned inns of New England were in their way perfect, being in fact excellent private houses, could not wholly approve what he called the modern inns, even in Connecticut; but when he passed into New York he asserted that everything suffered an instant change for the worse. He explained that in Massachusetts the authorities were strict in refusing licenses to any but respectable and responsible persons, whereas in New York licenses were granted to any one who would pay for them,—which caused a multiplication of dram-shops, bad accommodations, and a gathering of loafers and tipplers about every tavern porch, whose rude appearance, clownish manners, drunkenness, swearing, and obscenity confirmed the chief of Federalist clergymen in his belief that democracy had an evil influence on morals.

Far more movement was to be seen, and accumulation was more rapid than in colonial days; but little had yet been done for improvement, either by Government or by individuals, beyond some provision for extending roads and clearing watercourses behind the advancing settlers. If Washington Irving was right, Rip Van Winkle, who woke from his long slumber about the year 1800, saw little that was new to him, except the head of President Washington where that of King George had once hung, and strange faces instead of familiar ones. Except in numbers, the city was relatively no farther advanced than the country. Between 1790 and 1800 its population rose from 33,000 to 60,000; and if Boston resembled an old-fashioned English market-town, New York was like a foreign seaport, badly paved, undrained, and as foul as a town surrounded by the tides could be. Although the Manhattan Company was laying wooden pipes for a water supply, no sanitary regulations were enforced, and every few years —as in 1798 and 1803—yellow fever swept away crowds of victims, and drove the rest of the population, panic stricken, into the highlands. No day-police existed; constables were still officers of the courts; the night-police consisted of two captains, two deputies, and seventy-two men. The estimate for the city's expenses in 1800 amounted to $130,000. One marked advantage New York enjoyed over Boston, in the possession of a city government able to introduce reforms. Thus, although still mediæval in regard to drainage and cleanliness, the town had taken advantage of recurring fires to rebuild some of the streets with brick sidewalks and curbstones. Travellers dwelt much on this improvement, which only New York and Philadelphia had yet adopted, and Europeans agreed that both had the air of true cities: that while Boston was the Bristol of America, New York was the Liverpool, and Philadelphia the London.

In respect to trade and capital, New York possessed growing advantages, supplying half New Jersey and Connecticut, a part of Massachusetts, and all the rapidly increasing settlements on the branches of the Hudson; but no great amount of wealth, no considerable industry or new creation of power was yet to be seen. Two Banks, besides the branch Bank of the United States, supplied the business wants of the city, and employed about the same amount of capital in loans and discounts as was required for Boston.

Besides these city institutions but two other Banks existed in the State,—at Hudson and at Albany.

The proportion of capital in private hands seemed to be no larger. The value of exports from New York in 1800 was but $14,000,000; the net revenue on imports for 1799 was $2,373,000, against $1,607,000 collected in Massachusetts. Such a foreign trade required little capital, yet these values represented a great proportion of all the exchanges. Domestic manufactures could not compete with foreign, and employed little bank credit. Speculation was slow, mostly confined to lands which required patience to exchange or sell. The most important undertakings were turnpikes, bridges such as Boston built across the Charles, or new blocks of houses; and a canal, such as Boston designed to the Merrimac, overstrained the resources of capital. The entire banking means of the United States in 1800 would not have answered the stock-jobbing purposes of one great operator of Wall Street in 1875. The nominal capital of all the Banks, including the Bank of the United States, fell short of $29,000,000. The limit of credit was quickly reached, for only the richest could borrow more than fifteen or twenty thousand dollars at a time, and the United States Government itself was gravely embarrassed whenever obliged to raise money. In 1798 the Secretary of the Treasury could obtain five million dollars only by paying eight per cent interest for a term of years; and in 1814 the Government was forced to stop payments for the want of twenty millions.

The precise value of American trade was uncertain, but in 1800 the gross exports and imports of the United States may have balanced at about seventy-five million dollars. The actual consumption of foreign merchandise amounted perhaps to the value of forty or fifty million dollars, paid in wheat, cotton, and other staples, and by the profits on the shipping employed in carrying West India produce to Europe. The amount of American capital involved in a trade of fifty millions, with credits of three, six, and nine months, must have been small, and the rates of profit large.

As a rule American capital was absorbed in shipping or agriculture, whence it could not be suddenly withdrawn. No stock-exchange existed, and no broker exclusively engaged in stock-jobbing, for there were few stocks. The national debt, of about eighty millions, was held abroad, or as a permanent investment at home. States and municipalities had not learned to borrow. Except for a few banks and insurance offices, turnpikes, bridges, canals, and land-companies, neither bonds nor stocks were known. The city of New York was so small as to make extravagance difficult; the Battery was a fashionable walk, Broadway a country drive, and Wall Street an uptown residence. Great accumulations of wealth had hardly begun. The Patroon was still the richest man in the State. John Jacob Astor was a fur-merchant living where the Astor House afterward stood, and had not yet begun those purchases of real estate which secured his fortune. Cornelius Vanderbilt was a boy six years old, playing about his father's ferry-boat at Staten Island. New York city itself was what it had been for a hundred years past,—a local market.

As a national capital New York made no claim to consideration. If Bostonians for a moment forgot their town-meetings, or if Virginians overcame their dislike for cities and pavements, they visited and admired, not New York, but Philadelphia. "Philadelphia," wrote the Duc de Liancourt, "is not only the finest city in the United States, but may be deemed one of the most beautiful cities in the world." In truth, it surpassed any of its size on either side of the Atlantic for most of the comforts and some of the elegancies of life. While Boston contained twenty-five thousand inhabitants and New York sixty thousand, the census of 1800 showed that Philadelphia was about the size of Liverpool,—a city of seventy thousand people. The repeated ravages of yellow fever roused there a regard for sanitary precautions and cleanliness; the city, well paved and partly drained, was supplied with water in wooden pipes, and was the best-lighted town in America; its market was a model, and its jail was intended also for a model,—although the first experiment proved unsuccessful, because the prisoners went mad or idiotic in solitary confinement. In and about the city flourished industries considerable for the time. The iron-works were already important; paper and gunpowder, pleasure carriages and many other manufactures, were produced on a larger scale than elsewhere in the Union. Philadelphia held the seat of government until July, 1800, and continued to hold the Bank of the United States, with its capital of ten millions, besides private banking capital to the amount of five millions more. Public spirit was more active in Pennsylvania than in New York. More roads and canals were building; a new turnpike ran from Philadelphia to Lancaster, and the great highway to Pittsburg was a more important artery of national life than was controlled by any other State. The exports of Pennsylvania amounted to $12,000,000, and the custom-house produced $1,350,000. The State contained six hundred thousand inhabitants,—a population somewhat larger than that of New York.

Of all parts of the Union, Pennsylvania seemed to have made most use of her national advantages; but her progress was not more rapid than the natural increase of population and wealth demanded, while to deal with the needs of America, man's resources and his power over Nature must be increased in a ratio far more rapid than that which governed his numbers. Nevertheless, Pennsylvania was the most encouraging spectacle in the field of vision. Baltimore, which had suddenly sprung to a population and commerce greater than those of Boston, also offered strong hope of future improvement; but farther South the people showed fewer signs of change.

The city of Washington, rising in a solitude on the banks of the Potomac, was a symbol of American nationality in the Southern States. The contrast between the immensity of the task and the paucity of means seemed to challenge suspicion that the nation itself was a magnificent scheme like the federal city, which could show only a few log-cabins and negro quarters where the plan provided for the traffic of London and the elegance of Versailles. When in the summer of 1800 the government was transferred to what was regarded by most persons as a fever-stricken morass, the half-finished White House stood in a naked field overlooking the Potomac, with two awkward Department buildings near it, a single row of brick houses and a few isolated dwellings within sight, and nothing more; until across a swamp, a mile and a half away, the shapeless, unfinished Capitol was seen, two wings without a body, ambitious enough in design to make more grotesque the nature of its surroundings. The conception proved that the United States understood the vastness of their task, and were willing to stake something on their faith in it. Never did hermit or saint condemn himself to solitude more consciously than Congress and the Executive in removing the government from Philadephia to Washington: the discontented men clustered together in eight or ten boarding-houses as near as possible to the Capitol, and there lived, like a convent of monks, with no other amusement or occupation than that of going from their lodgings to the Chambers and back again. Even private wealth could do little to improve their situation, for there was nothing which wealth could buy; there were in Washington no shops or markets, skilled labor, commerce, or people. Public efforts and lavish use of public money could alone make the place tolerable; but Congress doled out funds for this national and personal object with so sparing a hand, that their Capitol threatened to crumble in pieces and crush Senate and House under the ruins, long before the building was complete.

A government capable of sketching a magnificent plan, and willing to give only a half-hearted pledge for its fulfilment; a people eager to advertise a vast undertaking beyond their present powers, which when completed would become an object of jealousy and fear,—this was the impression made upon the traveller who visited Washington in 1800, and mused among the unraised columns of the Capitol upon the destiny of the United States. As he travelled farther south his doubts were strengthened, for across the Potomac he could detect no sign of a new spirit. Manufactures had no existence. Alexandria owned a bank with half a million of capital, but no other was to be found between Washington and Charleston, except the branch Bank of the United States at Norfolk, nor any industry to which loans and discounts could safely be made. Virginia, the most populous and powerful of all the States, had a white population of 514,000, nearly equal to that of Pennsylvania and New York, besides about 350,000 slaves. Her energies had pierced the mountains and settled the western territory before the slow-moving Northern people had torn themselves from the safer and more comfortable life by the seaboard; but the Virginia ideal was patriarchal, and an American continent on the Virginia type might reproduce the virtues of Cato, and perhaps the eloquence of Cicero, but was little likely to

produce anything more practical in the way of modern progress. The
Shenandoah Valley rivalled Pennsylvania and Connecticut in richness and
skill of husbandry; but even agriculture, the favorite industry in Virginia,
had suffered from the competition of Kentucky and Tennessee, and from
the emigration which had drawn away fully one hundred thousand people.
The land was no longer very productive. Even Jefferson, the most active-
minded and sanguine of all Virginians,—the inventor of the first scientific
plough, the importer of the first threshing-machine known in Virginia, the
experimenter with a new drilling-machine, the owner of one hundred and
fifty slaves and ten thousand acres of land, whose negroes were trained to
carpentry, cabinet-making, housebuilding, weaving, tailoring, shoe-making,
—claimed to get from his land no more than six or eight bushels of wheat
to an acre, and had been forced to abandon the more profitable cultivation
of tobacco. Except in a few favored districts like the Shenandoah Valley,
land in Virginia did not average eight bushels of wheat to an acre. The
cultivation of tobacco had been almost the sole object of land-owners, and
even where the lands were not exhausted, a bad system of agriculture and
the force of habit prevented improvement.

The great planters lavished money in vain on experiments to improve
their crops and their stock. They devoted themselves to the task with
energy and knowledge; but they needed a diversity of interests and local
markets, and except at Baltimore these were far from making their
appearance. Neither the products, the markets, the relative amount of capital, nor the machinery of production had perceptibly changed. "The Virginians are not generally rich," said the Duc de Liancourt, "especially in
net revenue. Thus one often finds a well-served table, covered with silver,
in a room where for ten years half the window panes have been missing,
and where they will be missed for ten years more. There are few houses
in a passable state of repair, and of all parts of the establishment those
best cared for are the stables." Wealth reckoned in slaves or land was
plenty; but the best Virginians, from President Washington downward, were
most outspoken in their warnings against the Virginia system both of
slavery and agriculture.

The contrast between Virginia and Pennsylvania was the subject of
incessant comment.

"In Pennsylvania," said Robert Sutcliffe, an English Friend who published
travels made in 1804-1806, "we meet great numbers of wagons drawn by four or
more fine fat horses, the carriages firm and well made, and covered with stout
good linen, bleached almost white; and it is not uncommon to see ten or fifteen
together travelling cheerfully along the road, the driver riding on one of his
horses. Many of these come more than three hundred miles to Philadelphia
from the Ohio, Pittsburg, and other places, and I have been told by a respectable
Friend, a native of Philadelphia, that more than one thousand covered carriages
frequently come to Philadelphia market. . . . The appearance of things in the
Slave States is quite the reverse of this. We sometimes meet a ragged black boy

or girl driving a team consisting of a lean cow and a mule; sometimes a lean bull or an ox and a mule; and I have seen a mule, a bull, and a cow each miserable in its appearance, composing one team, with a half-naked black slave or two riding or driving as occasion suited. The carriage or wagon, if it may be called such, appeared in as wretched a condition as the team and its driver. Sometimes a couple of horses, mules, or cows would be dragging a hogshead of tobacco, with a pivot or axle driven into each end of the hogshead, and something like a shaft attached, by which it was drawn or rolled along the road. I have seen two oxen and two slaves pretty fully employed in getting along a single hogshead; and some of these come from a great distance inland."

In the middle of these primitive sights. Sutcliffe was startled by a contrast such as Virginia could always show. Between Richmond and Fredericksburg,—

"In the afternoon, as our road lay through the woods, I was surprised to meet a family party travelling along in as elegant a coach as is usually met with in the neighborhood of London, and attended by several gayly dressed footmen."

The country south of Virginia seemed unpromising even to Virginians. In the year 1796 President Washington gave to Sir John Sinclair his opinion upon the relative value of American lands. He then thought the valley of Virginia the garden of America; but he would say nothing to induce others to settle in more southern regions.

"The uplands of North and South Carolina and Georgia are not dissimilar in soil," he wrote, "but as they approach the lower latitudes are less congenial to wheat, and are supposed to be proportionably more unhealthy. Towards the seaboard of all the Southern States, and farther south more so, the lands are low, sandy, and unhealthy; for which reason I shall say little concerning them, for as I should not choose to be an inhabitant of them myself, I ought not to say anything that would induce others to be so. . . . I understand that from thirty to forty dollars per acre may be denominated the medium price in the vicinity of the Susquehanna in the State of Pennsylvania, from twenty to thirty on the Potomac in what is called the Valley, . . . and less, as I have noticed before, as you proceed southerly."

Whatever was the cause, the State of North Carolina seemed to offer few temptations to immigrants or capital. Even in white population ranking fifth among the sixteen States, her 478,000 inhabitants were unknown to the world. The beautiful upper country attracted travellers neither for pleasure nor for gain, while the country along the sea-coast was avoided except by hardy wanderers. The grumbling Wilson, who knew every nook and corner of the United States, and who found New England so dreary, painted this part of North Carolina in colors compared with which his sketch of New England was gay. "The taverns are the most desolate and beggarly imaginable; bare, bleak, and dirty walls, one or two old broken chairs and a bench form all the furniture. The white females seldom make their appearance. At supper you sit down to a meal the very sight of which is sufficient to deaden the most eager appetite, and you are surrounded by half-a-dozen dirty, half-naked blacks, male and female, whom any man of common scent might smell a quarter of a mile off. The house itself is raised upon props four or five feet, and the space below is left open for the hogs, with whose charming vocal performance the wearied traveller is serenaded the whole night long." The landscape pleased him no better,—"immense solitary pine savannahs through which the road winds among stagnant ponds; dark, sluggish creeks of the color of brandy, over which are thrown high wooden bridges without railings," crazy and rotten.

North Carolina was relatively among the poorest States. The exports and imports were of trifling value, less than one tenth of those returned for Massachusetts, which were more than twice as great as those of North Carolina and Virginia together. That under these conditions America should receive any strong impulse from such a quarter seemed unlikely; yet perhaps for the moment more was to be expected from the Carolinas than from Virginia. Backward as these States in some respects were, they possessed one new element of wealth which promised more for them than anything Virginia could hope. The steam-engines of Watt had been applied in England to spinning, weaving, and printing cotton; an immense demand had risen for that staple, and the cotton-gin had been simultaneously invented. A sudden impetus was given to industry; land which had been worthless and estates which had become bankrupt acquired new value, and in 1800 every planter was growing cotton, buying negroes, and breaking fresh soil. North Carolina felt the strong flood of prosperity, but South Carolina, and particularly the town of Charleston, had most to hope. The exports of South Carolina were nearly equal in value to those Massachusetts or Pennsylvania; the imports were equally large. Charleston might reasonably expect to rival Boston, New York, Philadelphia, and Baltimore. In 1800 these cities still stood, as far as concerned their foreign trade, within some range of comparison; and between Boston, Baltimore, and Charleston, many plausible reasons could be given for thinking that the last might have the most brilliant future. The three towns stood abreast. If Charleston had but about eighteen thousand inhabitants, this was the number reported by Boston only ten years before, and was five thousand more than Baltimore then boasted. Neither Boston nor Baltimore saw about them a vaster region to supply, or so profitable a staple to export. A cotton crop of two hundred thousand pounds sent abroad in 1791 grew to twenty millions in 1801, and was to double again by 1803. An export of fifty thousand bales was enormous, yet was only the beginning. What use might not Charleston, the only considerable town in the entire South, make of this golden flood?

The town promised hopefully to prove equal to its task. Nowhere in the Union was intelligence, wealth, and education greater in proportion to numbers than in the little society of cotton and rice planters who ruled South Carolina; and they were in 1800 not behind—they hoped soon to outstrip—their rivals. If Boston was building a canal to the Merrimac, and

Philadelphia one along the Schuylkill to the Susquehanna, Charleston had nearly completed another which brought the Santee River to its harbor, and was planning a road to Tennessee which should draw the whole interior within reach. Nashville was nearer to Charleston than to any other seaport of the Union, and Charleston lay nearest to the rich trade of the West Indies. Not even New York seemed more clearly marked for prosperity than this solitary Southern city, which already possessed banking capital in abundance, intelligence, enterprise, the traditions of high culture and aristocratic ambition, all supported by slave-labor, which could be indefinitely increased by the African slave-trade.

If any portion of the United States might hope for a sudden and magnificent bloom, South Carolina seemed entitled to expect it. Rarely had such a situation, combined with such resources, failed to produce some wonderful result. Yet as Washington warned Sinclair, these advantages were counterbalanced by serious evils. The climate in summer was too relaxing. The sun was too hot. The sea-coast was unhealthy, and at certain seasons even deadly to the whites. Finally, if history was a guide, no permanent success could be prophesied for a society like that of the low country in South Carolina, where some thirty thousand whites were surrounded by a dense mass of nearly one hundred thousand negro slaves. Even Georgia, then only partially settled, contained sixty thousand slaves and but one hundred thousand whites. The cotton States might still argue that if slavery, malaria, or summer heat barred civilization, all the civilization that was ever known must have been blighted in its infancy; but although the future of South Carolina might be brilliant, like that of other oligarchies in which only a few thousand freemen took part, such a development seemed to diverge far from the path likely to be followed by Northern society, and bade fair to increase and complicate the social and economical difficulties with which Americans had to deal.

A probable valuation of the whole United States in 1800 was eighteen hundred million dollars, equal to $328 for each human being, including slaves; or $418 to each free white. This property was distributed with an approach to equality, except in a few of the Southern States. In New York and Philadelphia a private fortune of one hundred thousand dollars was considered handsome, and three hundred thousand was great wealth. Inequalities were frequent; but they were chiefly those of a landed aristocracy. Equality was so far the rule that every white family of five persons might be supposed to own land, stock, or utensils, a house and furniture, worth about two thousand dollars; and as the only considerable industry was agriculture, their scale of life was easy to calculate,—taxes amounting to little or nothing, and wages averaging about a dollar a day.

Not only were these slender resources, but they were also of a kind not easily converted to the ready uses required for rapid development. Among the numerous difficulties with which the Union was to struggle, and

which were to form the interest of American history, the disproportion between the physical obstacles and the material means for overcoming them
was one of the most striking.

*　*　*

The growth of character, social and national,—the formation of men's
minds,—more interesting than any territorial or industrial growth, defied
the tests of censuses and surveys. No people could be expected, least of all
when in infancy, to understand the intricacies of its own character, and
rarely has a foreigner been gifted with insight to explain what natives did
not comprehend. Only with diffidence could the best-informed Americans
venture, in 1800, to generalize on the subject of their own national habits
of life and thought. Of all American travellers President Dwight was the
most experienced; yet his four volumes of travels were remarkable for no
trait more uniform than their reticence in regard to the United States.
Clear and emphatic wherever New England was in discussion, Dwight
claimed no knowledge of other regions. Where so good a judge professed
ignorance, other observers were likely to mislead; and Frenchmen like
Liancourt, Englishmen like Weld, or Germans like Bülow, were almost
equally worthless authorities on a subject which none understood. The
newspapers of the time were little more trustworthy than the books of
travel, and hardly so well written. The literature of a higher kind was
chiefly limited to New England, New York, and Pennsylvania. From materials so poor no precision of result could be expected. A few customs,
more or less local; a few prejudices, more or less popular; a few traits of
thought, suggesting habits of mind,—must form the entire material for a
study more important than that of politics or economics.

The standard of comfort had much to do with the standard of character;
and in the United States, except among the slaves, the laboring class enjoyed an ample supply of the necessaries of life. In this respect, as in some
others, they claimed superiority over the laboring class in Europe, and the
claim would have been still stronger had they shown more skill in using
the abundance that surrounded them. The Duc de Liancourt, among foreigners the best and kindest observer, made this remark on the mode of life
he saw in Pennsylvania:—

"There is a contrast of cleanliness with its opposite which to a stranger is very
remarkable. The people of the country are as astonished that one should object
to sleeping two or three in the same bed and in dirty sheets, or to drink from
the same dirty glass after half a score of others, as to see one neglect to wash
one's hands and face of a morning. Whiskey diluted with water is the ordinary
country drink. There is no settler, however poor, whose family does not take
coffee or chocolate for breakfast, and always a little salt meat; at dinner, salt
meat, or salt fish, and eggs; at supper again salt meat and coffee. This is also
the common regime of the taverns."

An amusing, though quite untrustworthy Englishman named Ashe, who invented an American journey in 1806, described the fare of a Kentucky cabin:—

"The dinner consisted of a large piece of salt bacon, a dish of hominy, and a tureen of squirrel broth. I dined entirely on the last dish, which I found incomparably good, and the meat equal to the most delicate chicken. The Kentuckian ate nothing but bacon, which indeed is the favorite diet of all the inhabitants of the State, and drank nothing but whiskey, which soon made him more than two-thirds drunk. In this last practice he is also supported by the public habit. In a country, then, where bacon and spirits form the favorite summer repast, it cannot be just to attribute entirely the causes of infirmity to the climate. No people on earth live with less regard to regimen. They eat salt meat three times a day, seldom or never have any vegetables, and drink ardent spirits from morning till night. They have not only an aversion to fresh meat, but a vulgar prejudice that it is unwholesome. The truth is, their stomachs are depraved by burning liquors, and they have no appetite for anything but what is high-flavored and strongly impregnated by salt."

Salt pork three times a day was regarded as an essential part of American diet. In the "Chainbearer," Cooper described what he called American poverty as it existed in 1784. "As for bread," said the mother, "I count that for nothing. We always have bread and potatoes enough; but I hold a family to be in a desperate way when the mother can see the bottom of the pork-barrel. Give me the children that's raised on good sound pork afore all the game in the country. Game's good as a relish, and so's bread; but pork is the staff of life. . . . My children I calkerlate to bring up on pork."

Many years before the time to which Cooper referred, Poor Richard asked: "Maids of America, who gave you bad teeth?" and supplied the answer: "Hot soupings and frozen apples." Franklin's question and answer were repeated in a wider sense by many writers, but none was so emphatic as Volney:—

"I will venture to say," declared Volney, "that if a prize were proposed for the scheme of a regimen most calculated to injure the stomach, the teeth, and the health in general, no better could be invented than that of the Americans. In the morning at breakfast they deluge their stomach with a quart of hot water, impregnated with tea, or so slightly with coffee that it is mere colored water; and they swallow, almost without chewing, hot bread, half baked, toast soaked in butter, cheese of the fattest kind, slices of salt or hung beef, ham, etc., all which are nearly insoluble. At dinner they have boiled pastes under the name of puddings, and the fattest are esteemed the most delicious; all their sauces, even for roast beef, are melted butter; their turnips and potatoes swim in hog's lard, butter, or fat; under the name of pie or pumpkin, their pastry is nothing but a greasy paste, never sufficiently baked. To digest these viscous substances they take tea almost instantly after dinner, making it so strong that it is absolutely bitter to the taste, in which state it affects the nerves so powerfully that even the English find it brings on a more obstinate restlessness than coffee. Supper again introduces salt meats or oysters. As Chastellux says, the whole day passes in heaping indigestions on one another; and to give tone to the poor, relaxed, and wearied stomach, they drink Madeira, rum, French brandy, gin, or malt spirits, which complete the ruin of the nervous system."

An American breakfast never failed to interest foreigners, on account of the variety and abundance of its dishes. On the main lines of travel, fresh meat and vegetables were invariably served at all meals; but Indian corn was the national crop, and Indian corn was eaten three times a day in another form as salt pork. The rich alone could afford fresh meat. Ice-chests were hardly known. In the country fresh meat could not regularly be got, except in the shape of poultry or game; but the hog cost nothing to keep, and very little to kill and preserve. Thus the ordinary rural American was brought up on salt pork and Indian corn, or rye; and the effect of this diet showed itself in dyspepsia.

One of the traits to which Liancourt alluded marked more distinctly the stage of social development. By day or by night, privacy was out of the question. Not only must all men travel in the same coach, dine at the same table, at the same time, on the same fare, but even their beds were in common, without distinction of persons. Innkeepers would not understand that a different arrangement was possible. When the English traveller Weld reached Elkton, on the main road from Philadelphia to Baltimore, he asked the landlord what accommodation he had. "Don't trouble yourself about that," was the reply; "I have no less than eleven beds in one room alone." This primitive habit extended over the whole country from Massachusetts to Georgia, and no American seemed to revolt against the tyranny of inn-keepers.

"At New York I was lodged with two others, in a back room on the ground floor," wrote, in 1796, the Philadelphian whose complaints have already been mentioned. "What can be the reason for that vulgar, hoggish custom, common in America, of squeezing three, six, or eight beds into one room?"

Nevertheless, the Americans were on the whole more neat than their critics allowed. "You have not seen the Americans," was Cobbett's reply, in 1819, to such charges; "you have not seen the nice, clean, neat houses of the farmers of Long Island, in New England, in the Quaker counties of Pennsylvania; you have seen nothing but the smoke-dried ultra-montanians." Yet Cobbett drew a sharp contrast between the laborer's neat cottage familiar to him in Surrey and Hampshire, and the "shell of boards" which the American occupied, "all around him as barren as a sea-beach." He added, too, that "the example of neatness was wanting;" no one taught it by showing its charm. Felix de Beaujour, otherwise not an enthusiastic American, paid a warm compliment to the country in this single respect, although he seemed to have the cities chiefly in mind:—

"American neatness must possess some very attractive quality, since it seduces every traveller; and there is no one of them who, in returning to his own country, does not wish to meet again there that air of ease and neatness which rejoiced his sight during his stay in the United States."

Almost every traveller discussed the question whether the Americans were a temperate people, or whether they drank more than the English. Temperate they certainly were not, when judged by a modern standard. Every one acknowledged that in the South and West drinking was occasionally excessive; but even in Pennsylvania and New England the universal taste for drams proved habits by no means strict. Every grown man took his noon toddy as a matter of course; and although few were seen publicly drunk, many were habitually affected by liquor. The earliest temperance movement, ten or twelve years later, was said to have had its source in the scandal caused by the occasional intoxication of ministers at their regular meetings. Cobbett thought drinking the national disease; at all hours of the day, he said, young men, "even little boys, at or under twelve years of age, go into stores and tip off their drams." The mere comparison with England proved that the evil was great, for the English and Scotch were among the largest consumers of beer and alcohol on the globe.

In other respects besides sobriety American manners and morals were subjects of much dispute, and if judged by the diatribes of travellers like Thomas Moore and H. W. Bülow, were below the level of Europe. Of all classes of statistics, moral statistics were least apt to be preserved. Even in England, social vices could be gauged only by the records of criminal and divorce courts; in America, police was wanting and a divorce suit almost, if not quite, unknown. Apart from some coarseness, society must have been pure; and the coarseness was mostly an English inheritance. Among New Englanders, Chief-Justice Parsons was the model of judicial, social, and religious propriety; yet Parsons, in 1808, presented to a lady a copy of "Tom Jones," with a letter calling attention to the adventures of Molly Seagrim and the usefulness of describing vice. Among the social sketches in the "Portfolio" were many allusions to the coarseness of Philadelphia society, and the manners common to tea-parties. "I heard from married ladies," said a writer in February, 1803, "whose station as mothers demanded from them a guarded conduct,—from young ladies, whose age forbids the audience of such conversation, and who using it modesty must disclaim,—indecent allusions, indelicate expressions, and even at times immoral innuendoes. A loud laugh or a coarse exclamation followed each of these, and the young ladies generally went through the form of raising their fans to their faces."

Yet public and private records might be searched long, before they revealed evidence of misconduct such as filled the press and formed one of the commonest topics of conversation in the society of England and France. Almost every American family, however respectable, could show some victim to intemperance among its men, but few were mortified by a public scandal due to its women.

If the absence of positive evidence did not prove American society to be as pure as its simple and primitive condition implied, the same conclusion would be reached by observing the earnestness with which critics collected every charge that could be brought against it, and by noting the substance of the whole. Tried by this test, the society of 1800 was often coarse and sometimes brutal, but, except for intemperance, was moral. Indeed, its chief offence, in the eyes of Europeans, was dulness. The amusements of a people were commonly a fair sign of social development, and the Americans were only beginning to amuse themselves. The cities were small and few in number, and the diversions were such as cost little and required but elementary knowledge. In New England, although the theatre had gained a firm foothold in Boston, Puritan feelings still forbade the running of horses.

"The principal amusements of the inhabitants," said Dwight, "are visiting, dancing, music, conversation, walking, riding, sailing, shooting at a mark, draughts, chess, and unhappily, in some of the larger towns, cards and dramatic exhibitions. A considerable amusement is also furnished in many places by the examination and exhibitions of the superior schools; and a more considerable one by the public exhibitions of colleges. Our countrymen also fish and hunt. Journeys taken for pleasure are very numerous, and are a very favorite object. Boys and young men play at foot-ball, cricket, quoits, and at many other sports of an athletic cast, and in the winter are peculiarly fond of skating. Riding in a sleigh, or sledge, is also a favorite diversion in New England."

President Dwight was sincere in his belief that college commencements and sleigh-riding satisfied the wants of his people; he looked upon whist as an unhappy dissipation, and upon the theatre as immoral. He had no occasion to condemn horse-racing, for no race-course was to be found in New England. The horse and the dog existed only in varieties little suited for sport. In colonial days New England produced one breed of horses worth preserving and developing,—the Narragansett pacer; but, to the regret even of the clergy, this animal almost disappeared, and in 1800 New England could show nothing to take its place. The germ of the trotter and the trotting-match, the first general popular amusement, could be seen in almost any country village, where the owners of horses were in the habit of trotting what were called scratch-races, for a quarter or half a mile from the door of the tavern, along the public road. Perhaps this amusement had already a right to be called a New-England habit, showing defined tastes; but the force of the popular instinct was not fully felt in Massachusetts, or even in New York, although there it was given full play. New York possessed a race-course, and made in 1792 a great stride toward popularity by importing the famous stallion "Messenger" to become the source of endless interest for future generations; but Virginia was the region where

the American showed his true character as a lover of sport. Long before
the Revolution the race-course was commonly established in Virginia and
Maryland; English running-horses of pure blood—descendants of the Dar-
ley Arabian and the Godolphin Arabian—were imported, and racing became the chief popular entertainment. The long Revolutionary War, and
the general ruin it caused, checked the habit and deteriorated the breed;
but with returning prosperity Virginia showed that the instinct was stronger
than ever. In 1798 "Diomed," famous as the sire of racers, was imported
into the State, and future rivalry between Virginia and New York could
be foreseen. In 1800 the Virginia race-course still remained at the head of
American popular amusements.

In an age when the Prince of Wales and crowds of English gentlemen
attended every prize-fight, and patronized Tom Crib, Dutch Sam, the Jew
Mendoza, and the negro Molyneux, an Englishman could hardly have expected that a Virginia race-course should be free from vice; and perhaps
travellers showed best the general morality of the people by their practice
of dwelling on Virginia vices. They charged the Virginians with fondness
for horse-racing, cock-fighting, betting, and drinking; but the popular habit
which most shocked them, and with which books of travel filled pages of
description, was the so-called rough-and-tumble fight. The practice was
not one on which authors seemed likely to dwell; yet foreigners like Weld,
and Americans like Judge Longstreet in "Georgia Scenes," united to give
it a sort of grotesque dignity like that of a bull-fight, and under their treatment it became interesting as a popular habit. The rough-and-tumble fight
differed from the ordinary prize-fight, or boxing-match, by the absence of
rules. Neither kicking, tearing, biting, nor gouging was forbidden by the
law of the ring. Brutal as the practice was, it was neither new nor exclusively
Virginian. The English travellers who described it as American barbarism,
might have seen the same sight in Yorkshire at the same date. The rough-
and-tumble fight was English in origin, and was brought to Virginia and
the Carolinas in early days, whence it spread to the Ohio and Mississippi.
The habit attracted general notice because of its brutality in a society that
showed few brutal instincts. Friendly foreigners like Liancourt were honestly
shocked by it; others showed somewhat too plainly their pleasure at finding
a vicious habit which they could consider a natural product of democratic
society. Perhaps the description written by Thomas Ashe showed best
not only the ferocity of the fight but also the antipathies of the writer, for
Ashe had something of the artist in his touch, and he felt no love for Americans. The scene was at Wheeling. A Kentuckian and a Virginian were the
combatants.

"Bulk and bone were in favor of the Kentuckian; science and craft in that
of the Virginian. The former promised himself victory from his power; the
latter from his science. Very few rounds had taken place or fatal blows given,
before the Virginian contracted his whole form, drew up his arms to his face,

with his hands nearly closed in a concave by the fingers being bent to the full extension of the flexors, and summoning up all his energy for one act of desperation, pitched himself into the bosom of his opponent. Before the effects of this could be ascertained, the sky was rent by the shouts of the multitude; and I could learn that the Virginian had expressed as much beauty and skill in his retraction and bound, as if he had been bred in a menagerie and practised action and attitude among panthers and wolves. The shock received by the Kentuckian, and the want of breath, brought him instantly to the ground. The Virginian never lost his hold. Like those bats of the South who never quit the subject on which they fasten till they taste blood, he kept his knees in his enemy's body; fixing his claws in his hair and his thumbs on his eyes, gave them an instantaneous start from their sockets. The sufferer roared aloud, but uttered no complaint. The citizens again shouted with joy."

Ashe asked his landlord whether this habit spread down the Ohio.

"I understood that it did, on the left-hand side, and that I would do well to land there as little as possible. . . . I again demanded how a stranger was to distinguish a good from a vicious house of entertainment. 'By previous inquiry, or, if that was impracticable, a tolerable judgment could be formed from observing in the landlord a possession or an absence of ears.' "

The temper of the writer was at least as remarkable in this description as the scene he pretended to describe, for Ashe's Travels were believed to have been chiefly imaginary; but no one denied the roughness of the lower classes in the South and Southwest, nor was roughness wholly confined to them. No prominent man in Western society bore himself with more courtesy and dignity than Andrew Jackson of Tennessee, who in 1800 was candidate for the post of major-general of State militia, and had previously served as Judge on the Supreme Bench of his State; yet the fights in which he had been engaged exceeded belief.

Border society was not refined, but among its vices, as its virtues, few were permanent, and little idea could be drawn of the character that would at last emerge. The Mississippi boatman and the squatter on Indian lands were perhaps the most distinctly American type then existing, as far removed from the Old World as though Europe were a dream. Their language and imagination showed contact with Indians. A traveller on the levee at Natchez, in 1808, overheard a quarrel in a flatboat near by:—

"I am a man; I am a horse; I am a team," cried one voice; "I can whip any man in all Kentucky, by God!" "I am an alligator," cried the other; "half man, half horse; can whip any man on the Mississippi, by God!" "I am a man," shouted the first; "have the best horse, best dog, best gun, and handsomest wife in all Kentucky, by God!" "I am a Mississippi snapping-turtle," rejoined the second; "have bear's claws, alligator's teeth, and the devil's tail; can whip *any* man, by God!"

And on this usual formula of defiance the two fire-eaters began their fight, biting, gouging, and tearing. Foreigners were deeply impressed by barbarism such as this, and orderly emigrants from New England and

Pennsylvania avoided contact with Southern drinkers and fighters; but even then they knew that with a new generation such traits must disappear, and that little could be judged of popular character from the habits of frontiersmen. Perhaps such vices deserved more attention when found in the older communities, but even there they were rather survivals of English low-life than products of a new soil, and they were given too much consequence in the tales of foreign travellers.

This was not the only instance where foreigners were struck by what they considered popular traits, which natives rarely noticed. Idle curiosity was commonly represented as universal, especially in the Southern settler who knew no other form of conversation:—

"Frequently have I been stopped by one of them," said Weld, "and without further preface asked where I was from, if I was acquainted with any news, where bound to, and finally my name. 'Stop, Mister! why, I guess now you be coming from the new State?' 'No, sir.' 'Why, then, I guess as how you be coming from Kentuck?' 'No, sir.' 'Oh, why, then, pray now where might you be coming from?' 'From the low country.' 'Why, you must have heard all the news, then; pray now, Mister, what might the price of bacon be in those parts?' 'Upon my word, my friend, I can't inform you.' 'Ay, ay; I see, Mister, you be'ent one of us. Pray now, Mister, what might your name be?' "

Almost every writer spoke with annoyance of the inquisitorial habits of New England and the impertinence of American curiosity. Complaints so common could hardly have lacked foundation, yet the Americans as a people were never loquacious, but inclined to be somewhat reserved, and they could not recognize the accuracy of the description. President Dwight repeatedly expressed astonishment at the charge, and asserted that in his large experience it had no foundation. Forty years later, Charles Dickens found complaint with Americans for taciturnity. Equally strange to modern experience were the continual complaints in books of travel that loungers and loafers, idlers of every description, infested the taverns, and annoyed respectable travellers both native and foreign. Idling seemed to be considered a popular vice, and was commonly associated with tippling. So completely did the practice disappear in the course of another generation that it could scarcely be recalled as offensive; but in truth less work was done by the average man in 1800 than in aftertimes, for there was actually less work to do. "Good country this for lazy fellows," wrote Wilson from Kentucky; "they plant corn, turn their pigs into the woods, and in the autumn feed upon corn and pork. They lounge about the rest of the year." The roar of the steam-engine had never been heard in the land, and the carrier's wagon was three weeks between Philadelphia and Pittsburg. What need for haste when days counted for so little? Why not lounge about the tavern when life had no better amusement to offer? Why mind one's own business when one's business would take care of itself?

Yet however idle the American sometimes appeared, and however large the class of tavern loafers may have actually been, the true American was active and industrious. No immigrant came to America for ease or idleness. If an English farmer bought land near New York, Philadelphia, or Baltimore, and made the most of his small capital, he found that while he could earn more money than in Surrey or Devonshire, he worked harder and suffered greater discomforts. The climate was trying; fever was common; the crops ran new risks from strange insects, drought, and violent weather; the weeds were annoying; the flies and mosquitoes tormented him and his cattle; laborers were scarce and indifferent; the slow and magisterial ways of England, where everything was made easy, must be exchanged for quick and energetic action; the farmer's own eye must see to every detail, his own hand must hold the plough and the scythe. Life was more exacting, and every such man in America was required to do, and actually did, the work of two such men in Europe. Few English farmers of the conventional class took kindly to American ways, or succeeded in adapting themselves to the changed conditions. Germans were more successful and became rich; but the poorer and more adventurous class, who had no capital, and cared nothing for the comforts of civilization, went West, to find a harder lot. When, after toiling for weeks, they reached the neighborhood of the Genesee or the banks of some stream in southern Ohio or Indiana, they put up a rough cabin of logs with an earthen floor, cleared an acre or two of land, and planted Indian corn between the tree-stumps,—lucky if, like the Kentuckian, they had a pig to turn into the woods. Between April and October, Albert Gallatin used to say, Indian corn made the penniless immigrant a capitalist. New settlers suffered many of the ills that would have afflicted an army marching and fighting in a country of dense forest and swamp, with one sore misery besides,—that whatever trials the men endured, the burden bore most heavily upon the women and children. The chance of being shot or scalped by Indians was hardly worth considering when compared with the certainty of malarial fever, or the strange disease called milk-sickness, or the still more depressing home-sickness, or the misery of nervous prostration, which wore out generation after generation of women and children on the frontiers, and left a tragedy in every log-cabin. Not for love of ease did men plunge into the wilderness. Few laborers of the Old World endured a harder lot, coarser fare, or anxieties and responsibilities greater than those of the Western emigrant. Not merely because he enjoyed the luxury of salt pork, whiskey, or even coffee three times a day did the American laborer claim superiority over the European.

A standard far higher than the average was common to the cities; but the city population was so small as to be trifling. Boston, New York, Philadelphia, and Baltimore together contained one hundred and eighty thousand inhabitants; and these were the only towns containing a white population of more than ten thousand persons. In a total population of more than five millions, this number of city people, as Jefferson and his friends rightly thought, was hardly American, for the true American was supposed to be essentially rural. Their comparative luxury was outweighed by the squalor of nine hundred thousand slaves alone.

From these slight notices of national habits no other safe inference could be drawn than that the people were still simple. The path their development might take was one of the many problems with which their future was perplexed. Such few habits as might prove to be fixed, offered little clew to the habits that might be adopted in the process of growth, and speculation was useless where change alone could be considered certain.

If any prediction could be risked, an observer might have been warranted in suspecting that the popular character was likely to be conservative, for as yet this trait was most marked, at least in the older societies of New England, Pennsylvania, and Virginia. Great as were the material obstacles in the path of the United States, the greatest obstacle of all was in the human mind. Down to the close of the eighteenth century no change had occurred in the world which warranted practical men in assuming that great changes were to come. Afterward, as time passed, and as science developed man's capacity to control Nature's forces, old-fashioned conservatism vanished from society, reappearing occasionally, like the stripes on a mule, only to prove its former existence; but during the eighteenth century the progress of America, except in political paths, had been less rapid than ardent reformers wished, and the reaction which followed the French Revolution made it seem even slower than it was. In 1723 Benjamin Franklin landed at Philadelphia, and with his loaf of bread under his arm walked along Market Street toward an immortality such as no American had then conceived. He died in 1790, after witnessing great political revolutions; but the intellectual revolution was hardly as rapid as he must, in his youth, have hoped.

In 1732 Franklin induced some fifty persons to found a subscription library, and his example and energy set a fashion which was generally followed. In 1800 the library he founded was still in existence; numerous small subscription libraries on the same model, containing fifty or a hundred volumes, were scattered in country towns; but all the public libraries in the United States—collegiate, scientific, or popular, endowed or unendowed—could hardly show fifty thousand volumes, including duplicates, fully one third being still theological.

Half a century had passed since Franklin's active mind drew the lightning from heaven, and decided the nature of electricity. No one in America had yet carried further his experiments in the field which he had made American. This inactivity was commonly explained as a result of the long Revolutionary War; yet the war had not prevented population and wealth from increasing, until Philadelphia in 1800 was far in advance of the Philadelphia which had seen Franklin's kite flying among the clouds.

In the year 1753 Franklin organized the postal system of the American colonies, making it self-supporting. No record was preserved of the number of letters then carried in proportion to the population, but in 1800 the gross receipts for postage were $320,000, toward which Pennsylvania contributed most largely,—the sum of $55,000. From letters the Government received in gross $290,000. The lowest rate of letter-postage was then eight cents. The smallest charge for letters carried more than a hundred miles was twelve and a half cents. If on an average ten letters were carried for a dollar, the whole number of letters was 2,900,000,—about one a year for every grown inhabitant.

Such a rate of progress could not be called rapid even by conservatives, and more than one stanch conservative thought it unreasonably slow. Even in New York, where foreign influence was active and the rewards of scientific skill were comparatively liberal, science hardly kept pace with wealth and population.

Noah Webster, who before beginning his famous dictionary edited the "New York Commercial Advertiser," and wrote on all subjects with characteristic confidence, complained of the ignorance of his countrymen. He claimed for the New Englanders an acquaintance with theology, law, politics, and light English literature; "but as to classical learning, history (civil and ecclesiastical), mathematics, astronomy, chemistry, botany, and natural history, excepting here and there a rare instance of a man who is eminent in some one of these branches, we may be said to have no learning at all, or a mere smattering." Although defending his countrymen from the criticisms of Dr. Priestley, he admitted that "our learning is superficial in a shameful degree, . . . our colleges are disgracefully destitute of books and philosophical apparatus, . . . and I am ashamed to own that scarcely a branch of science can be fully investigated in America for want of books, especially original works. This defect of our libraries I have experienced myself in searching for materials for the History of Epidemic Diseases. . . . As to libraries, we have no such things. There are not more than three or four tolerable libraries in America, and these are extremely imperfect. Great numbers of the most valuable authors have not found their way across the Atlantic."

This complaint was made in the year 1800, and was the more significant because it showed that Webster, a man equally at home in Philadelphia, New York, and Boston, thought his country's deficiencies greater than could be excused or explained by its circumstances. George Ticknor felt at least equal difficulty in explaining the reason why, as late as 1814, even good schoolbooks were rare in Boston, and a copy of Euripides in the original could not be bought at any book-seller's shop in New England. For some reason, the American mind, except in politics, seemed to these students of literature in a condition of unnatural sluggishness; and such complaints were not confined to literature or science. If Americans agreed in any opinion, they were united in wishing for roads; but even on that point whole communities showed an indifference, or hostility, that annoyed their contemporaries. President Dwight was a somewhat extreme conservative in politics and religion, while the State of Rhode Island was radical in both respects; but Dwight complained with bitterness unusual in his mouth that Rhode Island showed no spirit of progress. The subject of his criticism was an unfinished turnpike-road across the State.

"The people of Providence expended upon this road, as we are informed, the whole sum permitted by the Legislature. This was sufficient to make only those parts which I have mentioned. The turnpike company then applied to the Legislature for leave to expend such an additional sum as would complete the work. The Legislature refused. The principal reason for the refusal, as alleged by one of the members, it is said, was the following: that turnpikes and the establishment of religious worship had their origin in Great Britain, the government of which was a monarchy and the inhabitants slaves; that the people of Massachusetts and Connecticut were obliged by law to support ministers and pay the fare of turnpikes, and were therefore slaves also; that if they chose to be slaves they undoubtedly had a right to their choice, but that free-born Rhode Islanders ought never to submit to be priest-ridden, nor to pay for the privilege of travelling on the highway. This demonstrative reasoning prevailed, and the road continued in the state which I have mentioned until the year 1805. It was then completed, and free-born Rhode Islanders bowed their necks to the slavery of travelling on a good road."

President Dwight seldom indulged in sarcasm or exaggeration such as he showed in this instance; but he repeated only matters of notoriety in charging some of the most democratic communities with unwillingness to pay for good roads. If roads were to exist, they must be the result of public or private enterprise; and if the public in certain States would neither construct roads nor permit corporations to construct them, the entire Union must suffer for want of communication. So strong was the popular prejudice against paying for the privilege of travelling on a highway that in certain States, like Rhode Island and Georgia, turnpikes were long unknown, while in Virginia and North Carolina the roads were little better than where the prejudice was universal.

In this instance the economy of a simple and somewhat rude society accounted in part for indifference; in other cases, popular prejudice took a form less easily understood. So general was the hostility to Banks as to offer a serious obstacle to enterprise. The popularity of President Washington and the usefulness of his administration were impaired by his support of a national bank and a funding system. Jefferson's hostility to all the machinery of capital was shared by a great majority of the Southern people and a large minority in the North. For seven years the New York legislature refused to charter the first banking company in the State; and when in 1791 the charter was obtained, and the Bank fell into Federalist hands, Aaron Burr succeeded in obtaining banking privileges for the Manhattan Company only by concealing them under the pretence of furnishing a supply of fresh water to the city of New York.

This conservative habit of mind was more harmful in America than in

other communities, because Americans needed more than older societies
the activity which could alone partly compensate for the relative feebleness
of their means compared with the magnitude of their task. Some instances
of sluggishness, common to Europe and America, were hardly credible. For
more than ten years in England the steam-engines of Watt had been working, in common and successful use, causing a revolution in industry that
threatened to drain the world for England's advantage; yet Europe during
a generation left England undisturbed to enjoy the monopoly of steam.
France and Germany were England's rivals in commerce and manufactures,
and required steam for self-defence; while the United States were commercial allies of England, and needed steam neither for mines nor manufactures, but their need was still extreme. Every American knew that if
steam could be successfully applied to navigation, it must produce an immediate increase of wealth, besides an ultimate settlement of the most serious
material and political difficulties of the Union. Had both the national and
State Governments devoted millions of money to this object, and had the
citizens wasted, if necessary, every dollar in their slowly filling pockets to
attain it, they would have done no more than the occasion warranted, even
had they failed; but failure was not to be feared; for they had with their
own eyes seen the experiment tried, and they did not dispute its success.
For America this question had been settled as early as 1789, when John
Fitch—a mechanic, without education or wealth, but with the energy of
genius—invented engine and paddles of his own, with so much success that
during a whole summer Philadelphians watched his ferry-boat plying daily
against the river current. No one denied that his boat was rapidly, steadily,
and regularly moved against wind and tide, with as much certainty and
convenience as could be expected in a first experiment; yet Fitch's company
failed. He could raise no more money; the public refused to use his boat
or to help him build a better; they did not want it, would not believe in it,
and broke his heart by their contempt. Fitch struggled against failure, and
invented another boat moved by a screw. The Eastern public still proving
indifferent, he wandered to Kentucky, to try his fortune on the Western
waters. Disappointed there, as in Philadelphia and New York, he made a
deliberate attempt to end his life by drink; but the process proving too
slow, he saved twelve opium pills from the physician's prescription, and
was found one morning dead.

Fitch's death took place in an obscure Kentucky inn, three years before
Jefferson, the philosopher president, entered the White House. Had Fitch
been the only inventor thus neglected, his peculiarities and the defects of
his steamboat might account for his failure; but he did not stand alone. At
the same moment Philadelphia contained another inventor, Oliver Evans, a
man so ingenious as to be often called the American Watt. He, too, invented a locomotive steam-engine which he longed to bring into common
use. The great services actually rendered by this extraordinary man were

not a tithe of those he would gladly have performed, had he found support and encouragement; but his success was not even so great as that of Fitch, and he stood aside while Livingston and Fulton, by their greater re-sources and influence, forced the steamboat on a sceptical public.

While the inventors were thus ready, and while State legislatures were offering mischievous monopolies for this invention, which required only some few thousand dollars of ready money, the Philosophical Society of Rotterdam wrote to the American Philosophical Society at Philadelphia, requesting to know what improvements had been made in the United States in the construction of steam-engines. The subject was referred to Benjamin H. Latrobe, the most eminent engineer in America, and his Report, pre-sented to the Society in May, 1803, published in the Transactions, and transmitted abroad, showed the reasoning on which conservatism rested.

"During the general lassitude of mechanical exertion which succeeded the American Revolution," said Latrobe, "the utility of steam-engines appears to have been forgotten; but the subject afterward started into very general notice in a form in which it could not possibly be attended with much success. A sort of mania began to prevail, which indeed has not yet entirely subsided, for im-pelling boats by steam-engines. . . . For a short time a passage-boat, rowed by a steam-engine, was established between Bordentown and Philadelphia, but it was soon laid aside. . . . There are indeed general objections to the use of the steam-engine for impelling boats, from which no particular mode of application can be free. These are, first, the weight of the engine and of the fuel; second, the large space it occupies; third, the tendency of its action to rack the vessel and render it leaky; fourth, the expense of maintenance; fifth, the irregularity of its motion and the motion of the water in the boiler and cistern, and of the fuel-vessel in rough water; sixth, the difficulty arising from the liability of the paddles or oars to break if light, and from the weight, if made strong. Nor have I ever heard of an instance, verified by other testimony than that of the inventor, of a speedy and agreeable voyage having been performed in a steamboat of any construction. I am well aware that there are still many very respectable and ingenious men who consider the application of the steam-engine to the purpose of navigation as highly important and as very practicable, especially on the rapid waters of the Mississippi, and who would feel themselves almost offended at the expression of an opposite opinion. And perhaps some of the objections against it may be obviated. That founded on the expense and weight of the fuel may not for some years exist in the Mississippi, where there is a redundance of wood on the banks; but the cutting and loading will be almost as great an evil."

Within four years the steamboat was running, and Latrobe was its warmest friend. The dispute was a contest of temperaments, a divergence between minds, rather than a question of science; and a few visionaries such as those to whom Latrobe alluded—men like Chancellor Livingston, Joel Barlow, John Stevens, Samuel L. Mitchill, and Robert Fulton—dragged society forward. What but scepticism could be expected among a people thus asked to adopt the steamboat, when as yet the ordinary atmospheric steam-engine, such as had been in use in Europe for a hun-dred years, was practically unknown to them, and the engines of Watt were a fable? Latrobe's Report further said that in the spring of 1803, when he wrote, five steam-engines were at work in the United States,—one lately set up by the Manhattan Water Company in New York to supply the city with water; another in New York for sawing timber; two in Philadelphia, belonging to the city, for supplying water and running a rolling and slitting mill; and one at Boston employed in some manufacture. All but one of these were probably constructed after 1800, and Latrobe neglected to say whether they belonged to the old Newcomen type, or to Watt's manufacture, or to American invention; but he added that the chief American improvement on the steam-engine had been the construction of a wooden boiler, which developed sufficient power to work the Philadelphia pump at the rate of twelve strokes, of six feet, per minute. Twelve strokes a minute, or one stroke every five seconds, though not a surprising power, might have answered its purpose, had not the wooden boiler, as Latrobe admitted, quickly decomposed, and steam-leaks appeared at every bolt-hole.

If so eminent and so intelligent a man as Latrobe, who had but recently emigrated in the prime of life from England, knew little about Watt, and nothing about Oliver Evans, whose experience would have been well worth communicating to any philosophical society in Europe, the more ignorant and unscientific public could not feel faith in a force of which they knew nothing at all. For nearly two centuries the Americans had struggled on foot or horseback over roads not much better than trails, or had floated down rushing streams in open boats momentarily in danger of sinking or upsetting. They had at length, in the Eastern and Middle States, reached the point of constructing turnpikes and canals. Into these undertakings they put sums of money relatively large, for the investment seemed safe and the profits certain. Steam as a locomotive power was still a visionary idea, beyond their experience, contrary to European precedent, and exposed to a thousand risks. They regarded it as a delusion.

About three years after Latrobe wrote his Report on the steam-engine, Robert Fulton began to build the boat which settled forever the value of steam as a locomotive power. According to Fulton's well-known account of his own experience, he suffered almost as keenly as Fitch, twenty years before, under the want of popular sympathy:—

"When I was building my first steamboat at New York," he said, according to Judge Story's report, "the project was viewed by the public either with indifference or with contempt as a visionary scheme. My friends indeed were civil, but they were shy. They listened with patience to my explanations, but with a settled cast of incredulity upon their countenances. I felt the full force of the lamentation of the poet,—

> 'Truths would you teach, or save a sinking land,
> All fear, none aid you, and few understand.'

As I had occasion to pass daily to and from the building-yard while my boat was in progress, I have often loitered unknown near the idle groups of strangers gathering in little circles, and heard various inquiries as to the object of this new vehicle. The language was uniformly that of scorn, or sneer, or ridicule. The loud laugh often rose at my expense; the dry jest; the wise calculation of losses and expenditures; the dull but endless repetition of the Fulton Folly. Never did a single encouraging remark, a bright hope, or a warm wish cross my path."

Possibly Fulton and Fitch, like other inventors, may have exaggerated the public apathy and contempt; but whatever was the precise force of the innovating spirit, conservatism possessed the world by right. Experience forced on men's minds the conviction that what had ever been must ever be. At the close of the eighteenth century nothing had occurred which warranted the belief that even the material difficulties of America could be removed. Radicals as extreme as Thomas Jefferson and Albert Gallatin were contented with avowing no higher aim than that America should reproduce the simpler forms of European republican society without European vices; and even this their opponents thought visionary. The United States had thus far made a single great step in advance of the Old World,—they had agreed to try the experiment of embracing half a continent in one republican system; but so little were they disposed to feel confidence in their success, that Jefferson himself did not look on this American idea as vital; he would not stake the future on so new an invention. "Whether we remain in one confederacy," he wrote in 1804, "or form into Atlantic and Mississippi confederations, I believe not very important to the happiness of either part." Even over his liberal mind history cast a spell so strong, that he thought the solitary American experiment of political confederation "not very important" beyond the Alleghanies.

The task of overcoming popular inertia in a democratic society was new, and seemed to offer peculiar difficulties. Without a scientific class to lead the way, and without a wealthy class to provide the means of experiment, the people of the United States were still required, by the nature of their problems, to become a speculating and scientific nation. They could do little without changing their old habit of mind, and without learning to love novelty for novelty's sake. Hitherto their timidity in using money had been proportioned to the scantiness of their means. Henceforward they were under every inducement to risk great stakes and frequent losses in order to win occasionally a thousand fold. In the colonial state they had naturally accepted old processes as the best, and European experience as final authority. As an independent people, with half a continent to civilize, they could not afford to waste time in following European examples, but must devise new processes of their own. A world which assumed that what had been must be, could not be scientific; yet in order to make the Americans a successful people, they must be roused to feel the necessity of scientific training. Until they were satisfied that knowledge was money, they would not insist upon high education; until they saw with their own eyes stones turned into gold, and vapor into cattle and corn, they would not learn the meaning of science.

* * *

Nearly every foreign traveller who visited the United States during these early years, carried away an impression sober if not sad. A thousand miles of desolate and dreary forest, broken here and there by settlements; along the sea-coast a few flourishing towns devoted to commerce; no arts, a provincial literature, a cancerous disease of negro slavery, and differences of political theory fortified within geographical lines,—what could be hoped for such a country except to repeat the story of violence and brutality which the world already knew by heart, until repetition for thousands of years had wearied and sickened mankind? Ages must probably pass before the interior could be thoroughly settled; even Jefferson, usually a sanguine man, talked of a thousand years with acquiescence, and in his first Inaugural Address, at a time when the Mississippi River formed the Western boundary, spoke of the country as having "room enough for our descendants to the hundredth and thousandth generation." No prudent person dared to act on the certainty that when settled, one government could comprehend the whole; and when the day of separation should arrive, and America should have her Prussia, Austria, and Italy, as she already had her England, France, and Spain, what else could follow but a return to the old conditions of local jealousies, wars, and corruption which had made a slaughter-house of Europe?

The mass of Americans were sanguine and self-confident, partly by temperament, but partly also by reason of ignorance; for they knew little of the difficulties which surrounded a complex society. The Duc de Liancourt, like many critics, was struck by this trait. Among other instances, he met with one in the person of a Pennsylvania miller, Thomas Lea, "a sound American patriot, persuading himself that nothing good is done, and that no one has any brains, except in America; that the wit, the imagination, the genius of Europe are already in decrepitude;" and the duke added: "This error is to be found in almost all Americans,—legislators, administrators, as well as millers, and is less innocent there." In the year 1796 the House of Representatives debated whether to insert in the Reply to the President's Speech a passing remark that the nation was "the freest and most enlightened in the world,"—a nation as yet in swaddling-clothes, which had neither literature, arts, sciences, nor history; nor even enough nationality to be sure that it was a nation. The moment was peculiarly ill-chosen for such a claim, because Europe was on the verge of an outburst of genius. Goethe and Schiller, Mozart and Haydn, Kant and Fichte, Cavendish and Herschel were making way for Walter Scott, Wordsworth, and Shelley, Heine and Balzac, Beethoven and Hegel, Oersted and Cuvier, great physicists, biologists, geologists, chemists, mathematicians, meta-physicians, and historians by the score. Turner was painting his earliest landscapes, and Watt completing his latest steam-engine; Napoleon was taking command of the French armies, and Nelson of the English fleets; investigators, reformers, scholars, and philosophers swarmed, and the influence of enlightenment, even amid universal war, was working with an energy such as the world had never before conceived. The idea that Europe was in her decrepitude proved only ignorance and want of enlightenment, if not of freedom, on the part of Americans, who could only excuse their error by pleading that notwithstanding these objections, in matters which for the moment most concerned themselves Europe was a full century behind America. If they were right in thinking that the next necessity of human progress was to lift the average man upon an intellectual and social level with the most favored, they stood at least three generations nearer than Europe to their common goal. The destinies of the United States were certainly staked, without reserve or escape, on the soundness of this doubtful and even improbable principle, ignoring or overthrowing the institutions of church, aristocracy, family, army, and political intervention, which long experience had shown to be needed for the safety of society. Europe might be right in thinking that without such safeguards society must come to an end; but even Europeans must concede that there was a chance, if no greater than one in a thousand, that America might, at least for a time, succeed. If this stake of temporal and eternal welfare stood on the winning card; if man actually should become more virtuous and enlightened, by mere process of growth, without church or paternal authority; if the average human being could accustom himself to reason with the logical processes of Descartes and Newton!—what then?

Then, no one could deny that the United States would win a stake such as defied mathematics. With all the advantages of science and capital, Europe must be slower than America to reach the common goal. American society might be both sober and sad, but except for negro slavery it was sound and healthy in every part. Stripped for the hardest work, every muscle firm and elastic, every ounce of brain ready for use, and not a trace of superfluous flesh on his nervous and supple body, the American stood in the world a new order of man. From Maine to Florida, society was in this respect the same, and was so organized as to use its human forces with more economy than could be approached by any society of the world elsewhere. Not only were artificial barriers carefully removed, but every influence that could appeal to ordinary ambition was applied. No brain or appetite active enough to be conscious of stimulants could fail to answer the intense incentive. Few human beings, however sluggish, could long resist the temptation to acquire power; and the elements of power were to be had in America almost for the asking. Reversing the old-world system, the American stimulant increased in energy as it reached the lowest and most ignorant class, dragging and whirling them upward as in the blast of a furnace. The penniless and homeless Scotch or Irish immigrant was caught and consumed by it; for every stroke of the axe and the hoe made him a capitalist, and made gentlemen of his children. Wealth was the strongest agent for moving the mass of mankind; but political power was hardly less tempting to the more intelligent and better-educated swarms of American-born citizens, and the instinct of activity, once created, seemed heritable and permanent in the race.

Compared with this lithe young figure, Europe was actually in decrepitude. Mere class distinctions, the *patois* or dialect of the peasantry, the fixity of residence, the local costumes and habits marking a history that lost itself in the renewal of identical generations, raised from birth barriers which paralyzed half the population. Upon this mass of inert matter rested the Church and the State, holding down activity of thought. Endless wars withdrew many hundred thousand men from production, and changed them into agents of waste; huge debts, the evidence of past wars and bad government, created interests to support the system and fix its burdens on the laboring class; courts, with habits of extravagance that shamed common-sense, helped to consume private economies. All this might have been borne; but behind this stood aristocracies, sucking their nourishment from industry, producing nothing themselves, employing little or no active capital or intelligent labor, but pressing on the energies and ambition of society with the weight of an incubus. Picturesque and entertaining as these social anomalies were, they were better fitted for the theatre or for a museum of historical costumes than for an active workshop preparing to compete with such machinery as America would soon command. From an economical point of view, they were as incongruous as would have been the appearance of a mediæval knight in helmet and armor, with battle-axe and shield, to run the machinery of Arkwright's cotton-mill; but besides their bad economy they also tended to prevent the rest of society from gaining a knowledge of its own capacities. In Europe, the conservative habit of mind was fortified behind power. During nearly a century Voltaire himself—the friend of kings, the wit and poet, historian and philosopher of his age— had carried on, in daily terror, in exile and excommunication, a protest against an intellectual despotism contemptible even to its own supporters. Hardly was Voltaire dead, when Priestley, as great a man if not so great a wit, trying to do for England what Voltaire tried to do for France, was mobbed by the people of Birmingham and driven to America. Where Voltaire and Priestley failed, common men could not struggle; the weight of society stifled their thought. In America the balance between conservative and liberal forces was close; but in Europe conservatism held the physical power of government. In Boston a young Buckminster might be checked for a time by his father's prayers or commands in entering the path that led toward freer thought; but youth beckoned him on, and every reward that society could offer was dangled before his eyes. In London or Paris, Rome, Madrid, or Vienna, he must have sacrificed the worldly prospects of his life.

Granting that the American people were about to risk their future on a new experiment, they naturally wished to throw aside all burdens of which they could rid themselves. Believing that in the long run interest, not violence, would rule the world, and that the United States must depend for safety and success on the interests they could create, they were tempted to look upon war and preparations for war as the worst of blunders; for they were sure that every dollar capitalized in industry was a means of overthrowing their enemies more effective than a thousand dollars spent on frigates or standing armies. The success of the American system was, from this point of view, a question of economy. If they could relieve themselves from debts, taxes, armies, and government interference with industry, they must succeed in outstripping Europe in economy of production; and Americans were even then partly aware that if their machine were not so weakened by these economies as to break down in the working, it must of necessity break down every rival. If their theory was sound, when the day of competition should arrive, Europe might choose between American and Chinese institutions, but there would be no middle path; she might become a confederated democracy, or a wreck.

Whether these ideas were sound or weak, they seemed self-evident to those Northern democrats who, like Albert Gallatin, were comparatively free from slave-owning theories, and understood the practical forces of society. If Gallatin wished to reduce the interference of government to a minimum, and cut down expenditures to nothing, he aimed not so much at saving money as at using it with the most certain effect. The revolution of 1800 was in his eyes chiefly political, because it was social; but as a revolution of society, he and his friends hoped to make it the most radical that had occurred since the downfall of the Roman empire. Their ideas were not yet cleared by experience, and were confused by many contradictory prejudices, but wanted neither breadth nor shrewdness.

Many apparent inconsistencies grew from this undeveloped form of American thought, and gave rise to great confusion in the different estimates of American character that were made both at home and abroad.

That Americans should not be liked was natural; but that they should not be understood was more significant by far. After the downfall of the French republic they had no right to expect a kind word from Europe, and during the next twenty years they rarely received one. The liberal movement of Europe was cowed, and no one dared express democratic sympathies until the Napoleonic tempest had passed. With this attitude Americans had no right to find fault, for Europe cared less to injure them than to protect herself. Nevertheless, observant readers could not but feel surprised that none of the numerous Europeans who then wrote or spoke about

America seemed to study the subject seriously. The ordinary traveller was apt to be little more reflective than a bee or an ant, but some of these critics possessed powers far from ordinary; yet Talleyrand alone showed that had he but seen America a few years later than he did, he might have suggested some sufficient reason for apparent contradictions that perplexed him in the national character. The other travellers—great and small, from the Duc de Liancourt to Basil Hall, a long and suggestive list—were equally perplexed. They agreed in observing the contradictions, but all, including Talleyrand, saw only sordid motives. Talleyrand expressed extreme astonishment at the apathy of Americans in the face of religious sectarians; but he explained it by assuming that the American ardor of the moment was absorbed in money-making. The explanation was evidently insufficient, for the Americans were capable of feeling and showing excitement, even to their great pecuniary injury, as they frequently proved; but in the foreigner's range of observation, love of money was the most conspicuous and most common trait of American character. "There is, perhaps, no civilized country in the world," wrote Félix de Beaujour, soon after 1800, "where there is less generosity in the souls, and in the heads fewer of those illusions which make the charm or the consolation of life. Man here weighs everything, calculates everything, and sacrifices everything to his interest." An Englishman named Fearon, in 1818, expressed the same idea with more distinctness: "In going to America, I would say generally, the emigrant must expect to find, not an economical or cleanly people; not a social or generous people; not a people of enlarged ideas; not a people of liberal opinions, or toward whom you can express your thoughts free as air; not a people friendly to the advocates of liberty in Europe; not a people who understand liberty from investigation and principle; not a people who comprehend the meaning of the words 'honor' and 'generosity.'" Such quotations might be multiplied almost without limit. Rapacity was the accepted explanation of American peculiarities; yet every traveller was troubled by inconsistencies that required explanations of a different kind. "It is not in order to hoard that the Americans are rapacious," observed Liancourt as early as 1796. The extravagance, or what economical Europeans thought extravagance, with which American women were allowed and encouraged to spend money, was as notorious in 1790 as a century later; the recklessness with which Americans often risked their money, and the liberality with which they used it, were marked even then, in comparison with the ordinary European habit. Europeans saw such contradictions, but made no attempt to reconcile them. No foreigner of that day— neither poet, painter, nor philosopher—could detect in American life anything higher than vulgarity; for it was something beyond the range of their experience, which education and culture had not framed a formula to express. Moore came to Washington, and found there no loftier inspiration than any Federalist rhymester of Dennie's school.

> "Take Christians, Mohawks, democrats and all,
> From the rude wigwam to the Congress hall,—
> From man the savage, whether slaved or free,
> To man the civilized, less tame than he:
> 'Tis one dull chaos, one unfertile strife
> Betwixt half-polished and half-barbarous life;
> Where every ill the ancient world can brew
> Is mixed with every grossness of the new;
> Where all corrupts, though little can entice,
> And nothing's known of luxury but vice."

Moore's two small volumes of Epistles, printed in 1807, contained much more so-called poetry of the same tone,—poetry more polished and less respectable than that of Barlow and Dwight; while, as though to prove that the Old World knew what grossness was, he embalmed in his lines the slanders which the Scotch libeller Callender invented against Jefferson:—

> "The weary statesman for repose hath fled
> From halls of council to his negro's shed;
> Where, blest, he woos some black Aspasia's grace,
> And dreams of freedom in his slave's embrace."

To leave no doubt of his meaning, he explained in a footnote that his allusion was to the President of the United States; and yet even Moore, trifler and butterfly as he was, must have seen, if he would, that between the morals of politics and society in America and those then prevailing in Europe, there was no room for comparison,—there was room only for contrast.

Moore was but an echo of fashionable England in his day. He seldom affected moral sublimity; and had he in his wanderings met a race of embodied angels, he would have sung of them or to them in the slightly erotic notes which were so well received in the society he loved to frequent and flatter. His remarks upon American character betrayed more temper than truth; but even in this respect he expressed only the common feeling of Europeans, which was echoed by the Federalist society of the United States. Englishmen especially indulged in unbounded invective against the sordid character of American society, and in shaping their national policy on this contempt they carried their theory into practice with so much energy as to produce its own refutation. To their astonishment and anger, a day came when the Americans, in defiance of self-interest and in contradiction of all the qualities ascribed to them, insisted on declaring war; and readers of this narrative will be surprised at the cry of incredulity, not unmixed with terror, with which Englishmen started to their feet when they woke from their delusion on seeing what they had been taught to call the meteor flag of England, which had burned terrific at Copenhagen and Trafalgar, suddenly waver and fall on the bloody deck of the "Guerriere." Fearon and Beaujour, with a score of other contemporary critics, could see neither generosity, economy, honor, nor ideas of any kind in the American breast;

yet the obstinate repetition of these denials itself betrayed a lurking fear
of the social forces whose strength they were candid enough to record.
What was it that, as they complained, turned the European peasant into
a new man within half an hour after landing at New York? Englishmen
were never at a loss to understand the poetry of more prosaic emotions.
Neither they nor any of their kindred failed in later times to feel the "large
excitement" of the country boy, whose "spirit leaped within him to be gone
before him," when the lights of London first flared in the distance; yet
none seemed ever to feel the larger excitement of the American immigrant.
Among the Englishmen who criticised the United States was one greater
than Moore,—one who thought himself at home only in the stern beauty
of a moral presence. Of all poets, living or dead, Wordsworth felt most
keenly what he called the still, sad music of humanity; yet the highest conception he could create of America was not more poetical than that of any
Cumberland beggar he might have met in his morning walk:—

> "Long-wished-for sight, the Western World appeared;
> And when the ship was moored, I leaped ashore
> Indignantly,—resolved to be a man,
> Who, having o'er the past no power, would live
> No longer in subjection to the past,
> With abject mind—from a tyrannic lord
> Inviting penance, fruitlessly endured.
> So, like a fugitive whose feet have cleared
> Some boundary which his followers may not cross
> In prosecution of their deadly chase,
> Respiring, I looked round. How bright the sun,
> The breeze how soft! Can anything produced
> in the Old World compare, thought I, for power
> And majesty, with this tremendous stream
> Sprung from the desert? And behold a city
> Fresh, youthful, and aspiring! . . .
>   Sooth to say,
> On nearer view, a motley spectacle
> Appeared, of high pretensions—unreproved
> But by the obstreperous voice of higher still;
> Big passions strutting on a petty stage,
> Which a detached spectator may regard
> Not unamused. But ridicule demands
> Quick change of objects; and to laugh alone,
> . . . in the very centre of the crowd
> To keep the secret of a poignant scorn,
>   . . . is least fit
> For the gross spirit of mankind."

Thus Wordsworth, although then at his prime, indulging in what sounded
like a boast that he alone had felt the sense sublime of something inter-
fused, whose dwelling is the light of setting suns, and the round ocean,
and the living air, and the blue sky, and in the mind of man,—even he, to

whose moods the heavy and the weary weight of all this unintelligible world was lightened by his deeper sympathies with nature and the soul, could do no better, when he stood in the face of American democracy, than "keep the secret of a poignant scorn."

Possibly the view of Wordsworth and Moore, of Weld, Dennie, and Dickens was right. The American democrat possessed little art of expression, and did not watch his own emotions with a view of uttering them either in prose or verse; he never told more of himself than the world might have assumed without listening to him. Only with diffidence could history attribute to such a class of men a wider range of thought or feeling than they themselves cared to proclaim. Yet the difficulty of denying or even ignoring the wider range was still greater, for no one questioned the force or the scope of an emotion which caused the poorest peasant in Europe to see what was invisible to poet and philosopher,—the dim outline of a mountain-summit across the ocean, rising high above the mist and mud of American democracy. As though to call attention to some such difficulty, European and American critics, while affirming that Americans were a race without illusions or enlarged ideas, declared in the same breath that Jefferson was a visionary whose theories would cause the heavens to fall upon them. Year after year, with endless iteration, in every accent of contempt, rage, and despair, they repeated this charge against Jefferson. Every foreigner and Federalist agreed that he was a man of illusions, dangerous to society and unbounded in power of evil; but if this view of his character was right, the same visionary qualities seemed also to be a national trait, for every one admitted that Jefferson's opinions, in one form or another, were shared by a majority of the American people.

Illustrations might be carried much further, and might be drawn from every social class and from every period in national history. Of all presidents, Abraham Lincoln has been considered the most typical representative of American society, chiefly because his mind, with all its practical qualities, also inclined, in certain directions, to idealism. Lincoln was born in 1809, the moment when American character stood in lowest esteem. Ralph Waldo Emerson, a more distinct idealist, was born in 1803. William Ellery Channing, another idealist, was born in 1780. Men like John Fitch, Oliver Evans, Robert Fulton, Joel Barlow, John Stevens, and Eli Whitney were all classed among visionaries. The whole society of Quakers belonged in the same category. The records of the popular religious sects abounded in examples of idealism and illusion to such an extent that the masses seemed hardly to find comfort or hope in any authority, however old or well established. In religion as in politics, Americans seemed to require a system which gave play to their imagination and their hopes.

Some misunderstanding must always take place when the observer is at cross-purposes with the society he describes. Wordsworth might have convinced himself by a moment's thought that no country could act on the imagination as America acted upon the instincts of the ignorant and poor, without some quality that deserved better treatment than poignant scorn; but perhaps this was only one among innumerable cases in which the unconscious poet breathed an atmosphere which the self-conscious poet could not penetrate. With equal reason he might have taken the opposite view,—that the hard, practical, money-getting American democrat, who had neither generosity nor honor nor imagination, and who inhabited cold shades where fancy sickened and where genius died, was in truth living in a world of dream, and acting a drama more instinct with poetry than all the avatars of the East, walking in gardens of emerald and rubies, in ambition already ruling the world and guiding Nature with a kinder and wiser hand than had ever yet been felt in human history. From this point his critics never approached him,—they stopped at a stone's throw; and at the moment when they declared that the man's mind had no illusions, they added that he was a knave or a lunatic. Even on his practical and sordid side, the American might easily have been represented as a victim to illusion. If the Englishman had lived as the American speculator did,—in the future,—the hyperbole of enthusiasm would have seemed less monstrous. "Look at my wealth!" cried the American to his foreign visitor. "See these solid mountains of salt and iron, of lead, copper, silver, and gold! See these magnificent cities scattered broadcast to the Pacific! See my cornfields rustling and waving in the summer breeze from ocean to ocean, so far that the sun itself is not high enough to mark where the distant mountains bound my golden seas! Look at this continent of mine, fairest of created worlds, as she lies turning up to the sun's never-failing caress her broad and exuberant breasts, overflowing with milk for her hundred million children! See how she glows with youth, health, and love!" Perhaps it was not altogether unnatural that the foreigner, on being asked to see what needed centuries to produce, should have looked about him with bewilderment and indignation. "Gold! cities! cornfields! continents! Nothing of the sort! I see nothing but tremendous wastes, where sickly men and women are dying of home-sickness or are scalped by savages! mountain-ranges a thousand miles long, with no means of getting to them, and nothing in them when you get there! swamps and forests choked with their own rotten ruins! nor hope of better for a thousand years! Your story is a fraud, and you are a liar and swindler!"

Met in this spirit, the American, half perplexed and half defiant, retaliated by calling his antagonist a fool, and by mimicking his heavy tricks of manner. For himself he cared little, but his dream was his whole existence. The men who denounced him admitted that they left him in his forest-swamp quaking with fever, but clinging in the delirium of death to the illusions of his dazzled brain. No class of men could be required to support their convictions with a steadier faith, or pay more devotedly with their persons for the mistakes of their judgment. Whether imagination or greed led them to describe more than actually existed, they still saw no more than any inventor or discoverer must have seen in order to give him the energy of success. They said to the rich as to the poor, "Come and share our limitless riches! Come and help us bring to light these unimaginable stores of wealth and power!" The poor came, and from them were seldom heard complaints of deception or delusion. Within a moment, by the mere contact of a moral atmosphere, they saw the gold and jewels, the summer cornfields and the glowing continent. The rich for a long time stood aloof,—they were timid and narrow-minded; but this was not all,—between them and the American democrat was a gulf.

The charge that Americans were too fond of money to win the confidence of Europeans was a curious inconsistency; yet this was a common belief. If the American deluded himself and led others to their death by baseless speculations; if he buried those he loved in a gloomy forest where they quaked and died while he persisted in seeing there a splendid, healthy, and well-built city,—no one could deny that he sacrificed wife and child to his greed for gain, that the dollar was his god, and a sordid avarice his demon. Yet had this been the whole truth, no European capitalist would have hesitated to make money out of his grave; for, avarice against avarice, no more sordid or meaner type existed in America than could be shown on every 'Change in Europe. With much more reason Americans might have suspected that in America Englishmen found everywhere a silent influence, which they found nowhere in Europe, and which had nothing to do with avarice or with the dollar, but, on the contrary, seemed likely at any moment to sacrifice the dollar in a cause and for an object so illusory that most Englishmen could not endure to hear it discussed. European travellers who passed through America noticed that everywhere, in the White House at Washington and in log-cabins beyond the Alleghanies, except for a few Federalists, every American, from Jefferson and Gallatin down to the poorest squatter, seemed to nourish an idea that he was doing what he could to overthrow the tyranny which the past had fastened on the human mind. Nothing was easier than to laugh at the ludicrous expressions of this simple-minded conviction, or to cry out against its coarseness, or grow angry with its prejudices; to see its nobler side, to feel the beatings of a heart underneath the sordid surface of a gross humanity, was not so easy. Europeans seemed seldom or never conscious that the sentiment could possess a noble side, but found only matter for complaint in the remark that every American democrat believed himself to be working for the overthrow of tyranny, aristocracy, hereditary privilege, and priesthood, wherever they existed. Even where the American did not openly proclaim this conviction in words, he carried so dense an atmosphere of the sentiment with him in his daily life as to give respectable Europeans an uneasy sense of remoteness.

Of all historical problems, the nature of a national character is the most difficult and the most important. Readers will be troubled, at almost every chapter of the coming narrative, by the want of some formula to explain what share the popular imagination bore in the system pursued by government. The acts of the American people during the administrations of Jefferson and Madison were judged at the time by no other test. According as bystanders believed American character to be hard, sordid, and free from illusion, they were severe and even harsh in judgment. This rule guided the governments of England and France. Federalists in the United States, knowing more of the circumstances, often attributed to the democratic instinct a visionary quality which they regarded as sentimentality, and charged with many bad consequences. If their view was correct, history could occupy itself to no better purpose than in ascertaining the nature and force of the quality which was charged with results so serious; but nothing was more elusive than the spirit of American democracy. Jefferson, the literary representative of the class, spoke chiefly for Virginians, and dreaded so greatly his own reputation as a visionary that he seldom or never uttered his whole thought. Gallatin and Madison were still more cautious. The press in no country could give shape to a mental condition so shadowy. The people themselves, although millions in number, could not have expressed their finer instincts had they tried, and might not have recognized them if expressed by others.

In the early days of colonization, every new settlement represented an idea and proclaimed a mission. Virginia was founded by a great, liberal movement aiming at the spread of English liberty and empire. The Pilgrims of Plymouth, the Puritans of Boston, the Quakers of Pennsylvania, all avowed a moral purpose, and began by making institutions that consciously reflected a moral idea. No such character belonged to the colonization of 1800. From Lake Erie to Florida, in long, unbroken line, pioneers were at work, cutting into the forests with the energy of so many beavers, and with no more express moral purpose than the beavers they drove away. The civilization they carried with them was rarely illumined by an idea; they sought room for no new truth, and aimed neither at creating, like the Puritans, a government of saints, nor, like the Quakers, one of love and peace; they left such experiments behind them, and wrestled only with the hardest problems of frontier life. No wonder that foreign observers, and even the educated, well-to-do Americans of the sea-coast, could seldom see anything to admire in the ignorance and brutality of frontiersmen, and should declare that virtue and wisdom no longer guided the United States! What they saw was not encouraging. To a new society, ignorant and semi-barbarous, a mass of demagogues insisted on applying every stimulant that could inflame its worst appetites, while at the same instant taking away every influence that had hitherto helped to restrain its passions. Greed for wealth, lust for power, yearning for the blank void of savage freedom such as Indians and wolves delighted in,—these were the fires that flamed under the caldron of American society, in which, as conservatives believed, the old, well-proven, conservative crust of religion, government, family, and even common respect for age, education, and experience was rapidly melting away, and was indeed already broken into fragments, swept about by the seething mass of scum ever rising in greater quantities to the surface.

Against this Federalist and conservative view of democratic tendencies, democrats protested in a thousand forms, but never in any mode of expression which satisfied them all, or explained their whole character. Probably Jefferson came nearest to the mark, for he represented the hopes of science as well as the prejudices of Virginia; but Jefferson's writings may be searched from beginning to end without revealing the whole measure of the man, far less of the movement. Here and there in his letters a suggestion was thrown out, as though by chance, revealing larger hopes,— as in 1815, at a moment of despondency, he wrote: "I fear from the experience of the last twenty-five years that morals do not of necessity advance hand in hand with the sciences." In 1800, in the flush of triumph, he believed that his task in the world was to establish a democratic republic, with the sciences for an intellectual field, and physical and moral advancement keeping pace with their advance. Without an excessive introduction of more recent ideas, he might be imagined to define democratic progress, in the somewhat affected precision of his French philosophy: "Progress is either physical or intellectual. If we can bring it about that men are on the average an inch taller in the next generation than in this; if they are an inch larger round the chest; if their brain is an ounce or two heavier, and their life a year or two longer,—that is progress. If fifty years hence the average man shall invariably argue from two ascertained premises where he now jumps to a conclusion from a single supposed revelation,— that is progress! I expect it to be made here, under our democratic stimulants, on a great scale, until every man is potentially an athlete in body and an Aristotle in mind." To this doctrine the New Englander replied, "What will you do for moral progress?" Every possible answer to this question opened a chasm. No doubt Jefferson held the faith that men would improve morally with their physical and intellectual growth; but he had no idea of any moral improvement other than that which came by nature. He could not tolerate a priesthood, a state church, or revealed religion. Conservatives, who could tolerate no society without such pillars of order, were, from their point of view, right in answering, "Give us rather the worst despotism of Europe,—there our souls at least may have a chance of salvation!" To their minds vice and virtue were not relative, but fixed terms. The Church was a divine institution. How could a ship hope to reach port when the crew threw overboard sails, spars, and compass, unshipped their rudder, and all the long day thought only of eating and drinking. Nay, even should the new experiment succeed in a worldly sense, what was a man profited if he gained the whole world, and lost his own soul?

The Lord God was a jealous God, and visited the sins of the parents upon the children; but what worse sin could be conceived than for a whole nation to join their chief in chanting the strange hymn with which Jefferson, a new false prophet, was deceiving and betraying his people: "It does me no injury for my neighbor to say there are twenty Gods or no God!"

On this ground conservatism took its stand, as it had hitherto done with success in every similar emergency in the world's history, and fixing its eyes on moral standards of its own, refused to deal with the subject as further open to argument. The two parties stood facing opposite ways, and could see no common ground of contact.

Yet even then one part of the American social system was proving itself to be rich in results. The average American was more intelligent than the average European, and was becoming every year still more active-minded as the new movement of society caught him up and swept him through a life of more varied experiences. On all sides the national mind responded to its stimulants. Deficient as the American was in the machinery of higher instruction; remote, poor; unable by any exertion to acquire the training, the capital, or even the elementary textbooks he needed for a fair development of his natural powers,—his native energy and ambition already responded to the spur applied to them. Some of his triumphs were famous throughout the world; for Benjamin Franklin had raised high the reputation of American printers, and the actual President of the United States, who signed with Franklin the treaty of peace with Great Britain, was the son of a small farmer, and had himself kept a school in his youth. In both these cases social recognition followed success; but the later triumphs of the American mind were becoming more and more popular. John Fitch was not only one of the poorest, but one of the least-educated Yankees who ever made a name; he could never spell with tolerable correctness, and his life ended as it began,—in the lowest social obscurity. Eli Whitney was better educated than Fitch, but had neither wealth, social influence, nor patron to back his ingenuity. In the year 1800 Eli Terry, another Connecticut Yankee of the same class, took into his employ two young men to help him make wooden clocks, and this was the capital on which the greatest clock-manufactory in the world began its operations. In 1797 Asa Whittemore, a Massachusetts Yankee, invented a machine to make cards for carding wool, which "operated as if it had a soul," and became the foundation for a hundred subsequent patents. In 1790 Jacob Perkins, of Newburyport, invented a machine capable of cutting and turning out two hundred thousand nails a day; and then invented a process for transferring engraving from a very small steel cylinder to copper, which revolutionized cotton-printing. The British traveller Weld, passing through Wilmington, stopped, as Liancourt had done before him, to see the great flour-mills on the Brandywine. "The improvements," he said, "which have been made in the machinery of the flour-mills in America are very great. The chief of these consist in a new application of the screw, and the introduction of what are called elevators, the idea of which was evidently borrowed from the chain-pump." This was the invention of Oliver Evans, a native of Delaware, whose parents were in very humble life, but who was himself, in spite of every disadvantage, an inventive genius of the first order. Robert Fulton, who in 1800 was in Paris with Joel Barlow, sprang from the same source in Pennsylvania. John Stevens, a native of New York, belonged to a more favored class, but followed the same impulses. All these men were the outcome of typical American society, and all their inventions transmuted the democratic instinct into a practical and tangible shape. Who would undertake to say that there was a limit to the fecundity of this teeming source? Who that saw only the narrow, practical, money-getting nature of these devices could venture to assert that as they wrought their end and raised the standard of millions, they would not also raise the creative power of those millions to a higher plane? If the priests and barons who set their names to Magna Charta had been told that in a few centuries every swineherd and cobbler's apprentice would write and read with an ease such as few kings could then command, and reason with better logic than any university could then practise, the priest and baron would have been more incredulous than any man who was told in 1800 that within another five centuries the ploughboy would go a-field whistling a sonata of Beethoven, and figure out in quaternions the relation of his furrows. The American democrat knew so little of art that among his popular illusions he could not then nourish artistic ambition; but leaders like Jefferson, Gallatin, and Barlow might without extravagance count upon a coming time when diffused ease and education should bring the masses into familiar contact with higher forms of human achievement, and their vast creative power, turned toward a nobler culture, might rise to the level of that democratic genius which found expression in the Parthenon; might revel in the delights of a new Buonarotti and a richer Titian; might create for five hundred million people the America of thought and art which alone could satisfy their omnivorous ambition.

Whether the illusions, so often affirmed and so often denied to the American people, took such forms or not, these were in effect the problems that lay before American society: Could it transmute its social power into the higher forms of thought? Could it provide for the moral and intellectual needs of mankind? Could it take permanent political shape? Could it give new life to religion and art? Could it create and maintain in the mass of mankind those habits of mind which had hitherto belonged to men of science alone? Could it physically develop the convolutions of the human brain? Could it produce, or was it compatible with, the differentiation of a higher variety of the human race? Nothing less than this was necessary for its complete success.

THEODORE ROOSEVELT

(1858-1919)

The United States was ill prepared to fight a second war against Great Britain in 1812. Although the Americans possessed a few superior vessels, expertly manned, with which they could win in individual duels against enemy ships, they could not prevent the overwhelmingly larger Royal Navy from sweeping the seas and harassing the coasts. Theodore Roosevelt as an undergradute at Harvard became irritated with the unfair partisanship of both British and American accounts of the naval war, and gathered materials for a book of his own. The two chapters he drafted while a student he regarded afterwards as "so dry that they would have made a dictionary seem light reading by comparison." He revised them, and within two years after graduation had finished and published the work. It appeared at a propitious time, for in 1882, American interest in building a powerful navy was just reviving. "At the time I wrote the book," Roosevelt asserted in his Autobiography, *"the navy had reached its nadir, and we were then utterly incompetent to fight Spain or any other power that had a navy at all." Although Roosevelt was only 24, the patriotic fervor and technical competence of his book attracted much attention in both the United States and England. "It was listened to by the American people," Admiral William S. Sims has written, "and it profoundly affected the attitude of the nation toward its navy."*

The Naval War of 1812

DURING THE EARLY YEARS OF THIS CENTURY ENGLAND'S NAVAL POWER stood at a height never reached before or since by that of any other nation. On every sea her navies rode, not only triumphant, but with none to dispute their sway. The island folk had long claimed the mastery of the ocean, and they had certainly succeeded in making their claim completely good during the time of bloody warfare that followed the breaking out of the French Revolution. Since the year 1792 each European nation, in turn, had learned to feel bitter dread of the weight of England's hand. In the Baltic, Sir Samuel Hood had taught the Russians that they must needs keep in port when the English cruisers were in the offing. The descendants of the Vikings had seen their whole navy destroyed at Copenhagen. No Dutch fleet ever put out after the day when, off Camperdown, Lord Duncan took possession of Van Winter's shattered ships. But a few years before 1812, the greatest sea-fighter of all time had died in Trafalgar Bay, and in dying had crumbled to pieces the navies of France and of Spain.

From that day England's task was but to keep in port such of her foes' vessels as she had not destroyed. France alone still possessed fleets that could be rendered formidable, and so, from the Scheldt to Toulon, her harbors were watched and her coasts harried by the blockading squadrons of the English. Elsewhere the latter had no fear of their power being seriously assailed; but their vast commerce and numerous colonies needed ceaseless protection. Accordingly in every sea their cruisers could be found, of all sizes, from the stately ship of the line, with her tiers of heavy cannon and her many hundreds of men, down to the little cutter carrying but a score of souls and a couple of light guns. All these cruisers, but especially those of the lesser rates, were continually brought into contact with such of the hostile vessels as had run through the blockade, or were too small to be affected by it. French and Italian frigates were often fought and captured when they were skirting their own coasts, or had started off on a plundering cruise through the Atlantic, or to the Indian Ocean; and though the Danes had lost their larger ships they kept up a spirited warfare with brigs and gunboats. So the English marine was in constant exercise, attended with almost invariable success.

From Roosevelt, *The Naval War of 1812* (1882), excerpts from throughout the book.

Such was Great Britain's naval power when the Congress of the United States declared war upon her. While she could number her thousand sail, the American navy included but half a dozen frigates, and six or eight sloops and brigs; and it is small matter for surprise that the British officers should have regarded their new foe with contemptuous indifference. Hitherto the American seamen had never been heard of except in connection with two or three engagements with French frigates, and some obscure skirmishes against the Moors of Tripoli; none of which could possibly attract attention in the years that saw Aboukir, Copenhagen, and Trafalgar. And yet these same petty wars were the school which raised our marines to the highest standard of excellence. A continuous course of victory, won mainly by seamanship, had made the English sailor over-weeningly self-confident, and caused him to pay but little regard to manoeuvring or even to gunnery. Meanwhile the American learned, by receiving hard knocks, how to give them, and belonged to a service too young to feel an overconfidence in itself. One side had let its training relax, while the other had carried it to the highest possible point. Hence our ships proved, on the whole, victorious in the apparently unequal struggle, and the men who had conquered the best seamen of Europe were now in turn obliged to succumb. Compared with the great naval battles of the preceding few years, our bloodiest conflicts were mere skirmishes, but they were skirmishes between the hitherto acknowledged kings of the ocean, and new men who yet proved to be more than their equals. For over a hundred years, or since the time when they had contended on equal terms with the great Dutch admirals, the British had shown a decided superiority to their various foes, and during the later quarter of the time this superiority, as already said, was very marked indeed; in consequence, the victories of the new enemy attracted an amount of attention altogether disproportionate to their material effects. And it is a curious fact that our little navy, in which the art of handling and fighting the old broadside, sailing frigate in single conflict was brought to the highest point of perfection ever reached, that this same navy should have contained the first representative of the modern war steamer, and also the torpedo—the two terrible engines which were to drive from the ocean the very white-winged craft that had first won honor for the starry flag. The tactical skill of Hull or Decatur is now of merely archaic interest, and has but little more bearing on the manoeuvring of a modern fleet that have the tactics of the Athenian galleys. But the war still conveys some most practical lessons as to the value of efficient ships and, above all, of efficient men in them. Had we only possessed the miserable gunboats, our men could have done nothing; had we not possessed good men, the heavy frigates would have availed us little. Poor ships and impotent artillery had lost the Dutch almost their entire navy; fine ships and heavy cannon had not saved the French and Spanish from the like fate. We owed our success to putting sailors even better than the Dutch on ships even finer than those built by the two Latin seaboard powers.

The first point to be remembered in order to write a fair account of this war is that the difference in fighting skill, which certainly existed between the two parties, was due mainly to training, and not to the nature of the men. It seems certain that the American had in the beginning somewhat the advantage, because his surroundings, partly physical and partly social and political, had forced him into habits of greater self-reliance. Therefore, on the average, he offered rather the best material to start with; but the difference was very slight, and totally disappeared under good training. The combatants were men of the same race, differing but little from one another. . . .

To understand aright the efficiency of our navy, it is necessary to take a brief look at the character and antecedents of the officers and men who served in it.

When war broke out the United States navy was but a few years old, yet it already had a far from dishonorable history. The captains and lieutenants of 1812 had been taught their duties in a very practical school, and the flag under which they fought was endeared to them already by not a few glorious traditions—though these, perhaps, like others of their kind, had lost none of their glory in the telling. A few of the older men had served in the war of the Revolution, and all still kept fresh in mind the doughty deeds of the old-time privateering war-craft. Men still talked of Biddle's daring cruises and Barney's stubborn fights, or told of Scotch Paul and the grim work they had who followed his fortunes. Besides these memories of an older generation, most of the officers had themselves taken part, when younger in years and rank, in deeds not a whit less glorious. Almost every man had had a share in some gallant feat, to which he, in part at least, owed his present position. The captain had perhaps been a midshipman under Truxton when he took the *Vengeance,* and had been sent aboard the captured French frigate with the prize-master; the lieutenant had borne a part in the various attacks on Tripoli, and had led his men in the desperate hand-to-hand fights in which the Yankee cutlass proved an overmatch for the Turkish and Moorish scimitars. Nearly every senior officer had extricated himself by his own prowess or skill from the dangers of battle or storm; he owed his rank to the fact that he had proved worthy of it. Thrown upon his own resources, he had learned self-reliance; he was a first-rate practical seaman, and prided himself on the way his vessel was handled. Having reached his rank by hard work, and knowing what real fighting meant, he was careful to see that his men were trained in the *essentials* of discipline, and that they knew how to handle the guns in battle as well as polish them in peace. Beyond almost any of his countrymen, he worshipped the "Gridiron Flag," and, having been brought up in the navy, regarded its honor as his own. It was, perhaps, the navy alone that thought itself a match, ship against ship, for Great Britain. The remainder of the nation pinned its faith to the army, or rather to that weakest of weak reeds, the militia. The officers of the navy, with their strong *esprit de corps,* their jealousy of their own name and record, and the knowledge, by actual experience, that the British ships sailed no faster and were no better handled than their own, had no desire to shirk a conflict with any foe, and having tried their bravery in actual service, they made it doubly formidable by cool, wary skill. Even the younger men, who had never been in action, had been so well trained by the tried veterans over them that the lack of experience was not sensibly felt.

The sailors comprising the crews of our ships were well worthy of their leaders. There was no better seaman in the world than the American Jack; he had been bred to his work from infancy, and had been off in a fishing dory almost as soon as he could walk. When he grew older, he shipped on a merchantman or whaler, and in those warlike times, when our large merchant marine was compelled to rely pretty much on itself for protection, each craft *had* to be well handled; all who were not were soon weeded out by a process of natural selection, of which the agents were French picaroons, Spanish buccaneers, and Malay pirates. It was a rough school, but it taught Jack to be both skilful and self-reliant; and he was all the better fitted to become a man-of-war's man, because he knew more about firearms than most of his kind in foreign lands. At home he had used his ponderous ducking gun with good effect on the flocks of canvasbacks in the reedy flats of the Chesapeake, or among the sea-coots in the rough water off the New England cliffs; and when he went on a sailing voyage the chances were even that there would be some use for the long guns before he returned, for the American merchant sailor could trust to no armed escort.

The wonderful effectiveness of our seamen at the date of which I am writing as well as long subsequently to it was largely due to the curious condition of things in Europe. For thirty years all the European nations had been in a state of continuous and very complicated warfare, during the course of which each nation in turn fought almost every other, England being usually at loggerheads with all. One effect of this was to force an enormous proportion of the carrying trade of the world into American bottoms. The old Massachusetts town of Salem was then one of the main depots of the East India trade; the Baltimore clippers carried goods into the French and German ports with small regard to the blockade; New Bedford and Sag Harbor fitted out whalers for the Arctic seas as well as for the South Pacific; the rich merchants of Philadelphia and New York sent their ships to all parts of the world; and every small port had some craft in the coasting trade. On the New England seaboard but few of the boys would reach manhood without having made at least one voyage to the Newfoundland Banks after codfish; and in the whaling towns of Long Island it used to be an old saying that no man could marry till he struck his whale. The wealthy merchants of the large cities would often send their sons on a voyage or two before they let them enter their counting-houses. Thus it came about that a large portion of our population was engaged in seafaring pursuits of a nature strongly tending to develop a resolute and hardy character in the men that followed them. The British merchantmen sailed in huge convoys, guarded by men-of-war, while, as said before, our vessels went alone, and relied for protection on themselves. If a fishing-smack went to the Banks it knew that it ran a chance of falling in with some not overscrupulous Nova Scotian privateer. The barks that sailed from Salem to the Spice Islands kept their men well trained both at great guns and musketry, so as to be able to beat off either Malay proas, or Chinese junks. The New York ships, loaded for the West Indies, were prepared to do battle with the picaroons that swarmed in the Spanish Main; while the fast craft from Baltimore could fight as well as they could run. Wherever an American seaman went, he not only had to contend with all the legitimate perils of the sea, but he had also to regard almost every stranger as a foe. Whether this foe called himself pirate or privateer mattered but little. French, Spaniards, Algerines, Malays, from all alike our commerce suffered, and against all our merchants were forced to defend themselves. The effect of such a state of things, which made commerce so remunerative that the bolder spirits could hardly keep out of it, and so hazardous that only the most skilful and daring could succeed in it, was to raise up as fine a set of seamen as ever manned a navy. The stern school in which the American was brought up forced him into habits of independent thought and action which it was impossible that the more protected Briton could possess. He worked more intelligently and less from routine, and while perfectly obed-ient and amenable to discipline, was yet able to judge for himself in an emergency. He was more easily managed than most of his kind—being shrewd, quiet, and, in fact, comparatively speaking, rather moral than other-wise; if he was a New Englander, when he retired from a sea life he was not unapt to end his days as a deacon. Altogether there could not have been better material for a fighting crew than cool, gritty American Jack. Moreover, there was a good nucleus of veterans to begin with, who were well fitted to fill the more responsible positions, such as captains of guns, etc. These were men who had cruised in the little *Enterprise* after French privateers, who had been in the *Constellation* in her two victorious fights, or who, perhaps, had followed Decatur when with only eighty men he cut out the *Philadelphia,* manned by five fold his force and surrounded by hostile batteries and war-vessels—one of the boldest expeditions of the kind on record.

It is to be noted, furthermore, in this connection, that by a singular turn of fortune, Great Britain, whose system of impressing American sailors had been one of the chief causes of the war, herself became, in consequence of that very system, in some sort a nursery for the seamen of the young Republican navy. The American sailor feared nothing more than being impressed on a British ship—dreading beyond measure the hard life and cruel discipline aboard of her; but once there, he usually did well enough, and in course of time often rose to be of some little consequence. For years before 1812, the number of these impressed sailors was in reality greater than the entire number serving in the American navy, from which it will readily be seen that they formed a good stock to draw upon. Very much to their credit, they never lost their devotion to the home of their birth, more than two thousand of them being imprisoned at the beginning of the war because they refused to serve against their country. When Commodore Decatur captured the *Macedonian,* that officer, as we learn from Marshall's "Naval Biography" (II, 1019), stated that most of the seamen of his own frigate, the *United States,* had served in British war-vessels, and that some had been with Lord Nelson in the *Victory,* and had even been bargemen to the great Admiral—a pretty sure proof that the American sailors did not show at a disadvantage when compared with others.

Good seaman as the impressed American proved to be, yet he seldom missed an opportunity to escape from the British service, by desertion or otherwise. In the first place, the life was very hard, and, in the second, the American seaman was very patriotic. He had an honest and deep affection for his own flag, while, on the contrary, he felt a curiously strong hatred for England, as distinguished from Englishmen. This hatred was partly an abstract feeling, cherished through a vague traditional respect for Bunker Hill, and partly something very real and vivid, owing to the injuries he, and others like him, had received. Whether he lived in Maryland or Massachusetts, he certainly knew men whose ships had been seized by British cruisers, their goods confiscated, and the vessels condemned. Some of his friends had fallen victims to the odious right of search, and had never been heard of afterward. He had suffered many an injury to friend, fortune, or person, and some day he hoped to repay them all; and when the war did come, he fought all the better because he knew it was his own quarrel. But, as I have said, this hatred was against England, not against Englishmen. Then, as now, sailors were scattered about over the world without any great regard for nationality; and the resulting intermingling was especially great in those of Britain and America, whose people spoke the same tongue and wore the same aspect. When chance drifted the American into Liverpool or London, he was ready enough to ship in an Indiaman or whaler, caring little for the fact that he served under the British flag; and the Briton, in turn, who found himself in New York or Philadelphia, willingly sailed in one of the clipper-built barks, whether it floated the Stars and Stripes or not. When Captain Porter wrought such havoc among the British whalers in the South Seas, he found that no inconsiderable portion of their crews consisted of Americans, some of whom enlisted on board his own vessel; and among the crews of the American whalers were many British. In fact, though the skipper of each ship might brag loudly of his nationality, yet in practical life he knew well enough that there was very little to choose between a Yankee and a Briton. Both were bold and hardy, cool and intelligent, quick with their hands, and showing at their best in an emergency. They looked alike and spoke alike; when they took the trouble to think, they thought alike; and when they got drunk, which was not an unfrequent occurrence, they quarrelled alike.

Mingled with them were a few seamen of other nationalities. The Irishman, if he came from the old Dano-Irish towns of Waterford, Dublin, and Wexford, or from the Ulster coast, was very much like the two chief combatants; the Celto-Turanian kern of the West did not often appear on shipboard. The French, Danes, and Dutch were hemmed in at home; they had enough to do on their own seaboard, and could not send men into foreign fleets. A few Norse, however, did come in, and excellent sailors and fighters they made. With the Portuguese and Italians, of whom some were to be found serving under the Union Jack and others under the Stars and Stripes, it was different; although there were many excellent exceptions they did not, as a rule, make the best kind of seamen. They were treacherous, fond of the knife, less ready with their hands, and likely to lose either their wits or their courage when in a tight place.

In the American navy, unlike the British, there was no impressment; the sailor was a volunteer, and he shipped in whatever craft his fancy selected. Throughout the war there were no "picked crews" on the American side, excepting on the last two cruises of the *Constitution*. In fact (as seen by the letters of Captains Stewart and Bainbridge to Secretary Hamilton), there was often much difficulty in getting enough men. Many sailors preferred to serve in the innumerable privateers, and the two above-mentioned officers, in urging the necessity of building line-of-battle ships, state that it was hard work to recruit men for vessels of an inferior grade, so long as the enemy had ships of the line. . . .

THE CONSTITUTION AND THE GUERRIÈRE

The United States, poorly prepared, declared war on June 18, 1812. Two months later there occurred the famous duel between the Constitution *and the* Guerrière.

On August 2d the *Constitution* made sail from Boston and stood to the eastward, in hopes of falling in with some of the British cruisers. She was unsuccessful, however, and met nothing. Then she ran down to the Bay of Fundy, steered along the coast of Nova Scotia, and thence toward Newfoundland, and finally took her station off Cape Race in the Gulf of St. Lawrence, where she took and burned two brigs of little value. On the 15th she recaptured an American brig from the British sloop-ship *Avenger,* though the latter escaped; Captain Hull manned his prize and sent her in. He then sailed southward, and on the night of the 18th spoke a Salem privateer which gave him news of a British frigate to the south; thither he stood, and at 2 P. M. on the 19th, in lat. 41° 30′ N. and 55° W., made out a large sail bearing E. S. E. and to leeward, which proved to be his old acquaintance, the frigate *Guerrière,* Captain Dacres. It was a cloudy day and the wind was blowing fresh from the northwest. The *Guerrière* was standing by the wind on the starboard tack, under easy canvas; she hauled up her courses, took in her topgallantsails, and at 4.30 backed her maintopsail. Hull then very deliberately began to shorten sail, taking in topgallantsail, staysails, and flying jib, sending down the royal yards and putting another reef in the topsails. Soon the Englishman hoisted three ensigns, when the American also set his colors, one at each masthead, and one at the mizzen peak.

The *Constitution* now ran down with the wind nearly aft. The *Guerrière* was on the starboard tack, and at 5 o'clock opened with her weather guns, the shot falling short, then wore round and fired her port broadside, of which two shots struck her opponent, the rest passing over and through her rigging. As the British frigate again wore to open with her starboard battery, the *Constitution* yawed a little and fired two or three of her port bow guns. Three or four times the *Guerrière* repeated this manoeuvre, wearing and firing alternate broadsides, but with little or no effect, while the *Constitution* yawed as often to avoid being raked, and occasionally fired one of her bow guns. This continued nearly an hour, as the vessels were very far apart when the action began, hardly any loss or damage being inflicted by either party. At 6.00 the *Guerrière* bore up and ran off under her topsails and jib, with the wind almost astern, a little on her port quarter; when the Constitution set her maintop-gallantsail and foresail, and at 6.05 closed within half pistol-shot distance on her adversary's port beam. Immediately a furious cannonade opened, each ship firing as the guns bore. By the time the ships were fairly abreast, at 6.20, the *Constitution* shot away the *Guerrière's* mizzenmast, which fell over the starboard quarter, knocking a large hole in the counter, and bringing the ship round against her helm. Hitherto she had suffered very greatly and the *Constitution* hardly at all. The latter, finding that she was ranging ahead, put her helm aport and then luffed short round her enemy's bows, delivering a heavy raking fire with the starboard guns and shooting away the *Guerrière's* main-yard. Then she wore and again passed her adversary's bows, raking with her port guns. The mizzenmast of the *Guerrière,* dragging in the water, had by this time pulled her bow round till the wind came on her starboard quarter; and so near were the two ships that the Englishman's bowsprit passed diagonally over the *Constitution's* quarter-deck, and as the latter ship fell off it got foul of her mizzen-rigging, and the vessels then lay with the *Guerrière's* starboard bow against the *Constitution's* port, or lee quarter-gallery. The Englishman's bow guns played havoc with Captain Hull's cabin, setting fire to it; but the flames were soon extinguished by Lieutenant Hoffmann. On both sides the boarders were called away; the British ran forward, but Captain

Dacres relinquished the idea of attacking when he saw the crowds of men on the American's decks. Meanwhile, on the *Constitution,* the boarders and marines gathered aft, but such a heavy sea was running that they could not get on the *Guerrière.* Both sides suffered heavily from the closeness of the musketry fire; indeed, almost the entire loss on the *Constitution* occurred at this juncture. As Lieutenant Bush, of the marines, sprang upon the taffrail to leap on the enemy's decks, a British marine shot him dead; Mr. Morris, the first lieutenant, and Mr. Alwyn, the master, had also both leaped on the taffrail, and both were at the same moment wounded by the musketry fire. On the *Guerrière* the loss was far heavier, almost all the men on the forecastle being picked off. Captain Dacres himself was shot in the back and severely wounded by one of the American mizzentopmen, while he was standing on the starboard forecastle hammocks cheering on his crew; two of the lieutenants and the master were also shot down. The ships gradually worked round till the wind was again on the port quarter, when they separated, and the *Guerrière's* foremast and mainmast at once went by the board, and fell over on the starboard side, leaving her a defenseless hulk, rolling her main-deck guns into the water. At 6.30 the *Constitution* hauled aboard her tacks, ran off a little distance to the eastward, and lay to. Her braces and standing and running rigging were much cut up and some of the spars wounded, but a few minutes sufficed to repair damages, when Captain Hull stood under his adversary's lee, and the latter at once struck, at 7.00 P. M., just two hours after she had fired the first shot. On the part of the *Constitution,* however, the actual fighting, exclusive of six or eight guns fired during the first hour, while closing, occupied less than 30 minutes.

The tonnage and metal of the combatants have already been referred to. The *Constitution* had, as already said, about 456 men aboard, while of the *Guerrière's* crew, 267 prisoners were received aboard the *Constitution;* deducting 10 who were Americans and would not fight, and adding the 15 killed outright, we get 272; 28 men were absent in prizes.

The loss of the *Constitution* included Lieutenant William S. Bush, of the marines, and six seamen killed, and her first lieutenant Charles Morris, Master John C. Alwyn, four seamen, and one marine, wounded. Total, seven killed and seven wounded. Almost all this loss occurred when the ships came foul, and was due to the *Guerrière's* musketry and the two guns in her bridle-ports.

The *Guerrière* lost 23 killed and mortally wounded, including her second lieutenant, Henry Ready, and 56 wounded severely and slightly, including Captain Dacres himself, the first lieutenant, Bartholomew Kent, Master Robert Scott, two master's mates, and one midshipman.

The third lieutenant of the *Constitution,* Mr. George Campbell Read, was sent on board the prize, and the *Constitution* remained by her during the night; but at daylight it was found that she was in danger of sinking.

Captain Hull at once began removing the prisoners, and at 3 o'clock in the afternoon set the *Guerrière* on fire, and in a quarter of an hour she blew up. He then set sail for Boston, where he arrived on August 30th. "Captain Hull and his officers," writes Captain Dacres in his official letter, "have treated us like brave and generous enemies; the greatest care has been taken that we should not lose the smallest trifle.". . . .

In 1813 there came another famous encounter between two ships, the fight between the Chesapeake *and the* Shannon—*much less to the taste of Americans.*

We left the *Chesapeake,* 38, being fitted out at Boston by Captain James Lawrence, late of the *Hornet.* Most of her crew, as already stated, their time being up, left, dissatisfied with the ship's ill luck, and angry at not having received their due share of prize-money. It was very hard to get sailors, most of the men preferring to ship in some of the numerous privateers where the discipline was less strict and the chance of prize-money much greater. In consequence of this an unusually large number of foreigners had to be taken, including about forty British and a number of Portuguese. The latter were peculiarly troublesome; one of their number, a boatswain's mate, finally almost brought about a mutiny among the crew, which was only pacified by giving the men prize-checks. A few of the *Constitution's* old crew came aboard, and these, together with some of the men who had been on the *Chesapeake* during her former voyage, made an excellent nucleus. Such men needed very little training at either guns or sails; but the new hands were unpracticed, and came on board so late that the last draft that arrived still had their hammocks and bags lying in the boats stowed over the booms when the ship was captured. The officers were largely new to the ship, though the first lieutenant, Mr. A. Ludlow, had been the third in her former cruise; the third and fourth lieutenants were not regularly commissioned as such, but were only midshipmen acting for the first time in higher positions. Captain Lawrence himself was of course new to all, both officers and crew. In other words, the *Chesapeake* possessed good material, but in an exceedingly unseasoned state.

Meanwhile the British frigate *Shannon,* 38, Captain Philip Bowes Vere Broke, was cruising off the mouth of the harbor. To give some idea of the reason why she proved herself so much more formidable than her British sister frigate it may be well to quote, slightly condensing, from James:

"There was another point in which the generality of British crews, as compared with any one American crew, was miserably deficient; that is, skill in the art of gunnery. While the American seamen were constantly firing at marks, the British seamen, except in particular cases, scarcely did so once in a year; and some ships could be named on board which not a shot had been fired in this way for upward of three years. Nor was the fault wholly the captain's. The instructions under which he was bound to act forbade him to use, during the first six months after the ship had received her armament, more shots per month than amounted to a third in number of the upper-deck guns; and, after these six months, only half the quantity. Many captains never put a shot in the guns till an enemy appeared: they employed the leisure time of the men in handling the sails and in decorating the ship." Captain Broke was not one of this kind. "From the day on which he had joined her, the 14th of September, 1806, the *Shannon* began to feel the effect of her captain's proficiency as a gunner and zeal for the service. The laying of the ship's ordnance so that it may be correctly fired in a horizontal direction is justly deemed a most important operation, as upon it depends in a great measure the true aim and destructive effect of the shot; this was attended to by Captain Broke in person. By drafts from other ships, and the usual means to which a British man-of-war is obliged to resort, the *Shannon* got together a crew; and in the course of a year or two, by the paternal care and excellent regulations of Captain Broke, the ship's company became as pleasant to command as it was dangerous to meet." The *Shannon's* guns were all carefully sighted, and, moreover, "every day, for about an hour and a half in the forenoon, when not prevented by chase or the state of the weather, the men were exercised at training the guns, and for the same time in the afternoon in the use of the broadsword, pike, musket, etc. Twice a week the crew fired at targets, both with great guns and musketry; and Captain Broke, as an additional stimulus beyond the emulation excited, gave a pound of tobacco to every man that put a shot through the bull's eye." He would frequently have a cask thrown overboard and suddenly order some one gun to be manned to sink the cask. In short, the *Shannon* was very greatly superior, thanks to her careful training, to the average British frigate of her rate, while the *Chesapeake,* owing to her having a raw and inexperienced crew, was decidedly inferior to the average American frigate of the same strength.

In force the two frigates compared pretty equally, the American being the superior in just about the same proportion that the *Wasp* was to the *Frolic,* or at a later date, the *Hornet* to the *Penguin.* The *Chesapeake* carried 50 guns (26 in broadside), 28 long 18's on the gun-deck, and on the spar-deck 2 long 12's, 1 long 18, eighteen 32-pound carronades, and one 12-pound carronade (which was not used in the fight, however). Her broadside, allowing for the short weight of metal, was 542 pounds; her complement, 379 men. The *Shannon* carried 52 guns (26 in broadside), 28 long 18's on the gun-deck, and on the spar-deck 4 long 9's, 1 long 6, sixteen 32-pound carronades, and three 12-pound carronades (two of which were not used in the fight). Her broadside was 550 pounds; her crew consisted of 330 men, 30 of whom were raw hands. Early on the morning of June 1st, Captain Broke sent in to Captain Lawrence, by an American prisoner, a letter of challenge, which for courteousness, manliness, and candor is the very model of what such an epistle should be. Before it reached Boston, however, Captain Lawrence had weighed anchor, to attack the *Shannon,* which frigate was in full sight in the offing. It has been often said that he engaged against his judgment, but this may be doubted. His experience with the *Bonne Citoyenne, Espiègle,* and *Peacock* had not tended to give him a very high idea of the navy to which he was opposed, and there is no doubt that he was confident of capturing the *Shannon.* It was most unfortunate that he did not receive Broke's letter, as the latter in it expressed himself willing to meet Lawrence in any latitude and longitude he might appoint; and there would thus have been some chance of the American crew having time enough to get into shape.

At midday of June 1, 1813, the *Chesapeake* weighed anchor, stood out of Boston Harbor, and at 1 P. M. rounded the lighthouse. The *Shannon* stood off under easy sail, and at 3.40 hauled up and reefed topsails. At 4 P. M. she again bore away with her foresail brailed up, and her maintopsail braced flat and shivering, that the *Chesapeake* might overtake her. An hour later, Boston Lighthouse bearing west distant about six leagues, she again hauled up, with her head to the southeast, and lay to under topsail, topgallantsails, jib, and spanker. Meanwhile, as the breeze freshened the *Chesapeake* took in her studdingsails, topgallantsails, and royals, got her royal yards on deck, and came down very fast under topsails and jib. At 5.30, to keep under command and be able to wear if necessary, the *Shannon* filled her maintopsail and kept a close luff, and then again let the sail shiver. At 5.25 the *Chesapeake* hauled up her foresail, and with three ensigns flying, steered straight for the *Shannon's* starboard quarter. Broke was afraid that Lawrence would pass under the *Shannon's* stern, rake her, and engage her on the quarter; but either overlooking or waiving this advantage, the American captain luffed up within 50 yards upon the *Shannon's* starboard quarter, and squared his mainyard. On board the *Shannon* the captain of the 14th gun, William Mindham, had been ordered not to fire till it bore into the second main-deck port forward; at 5.50 it was fired, and then the other guns in quick succession from aft forward, the *Chesapeake* replying with her whole broadside. At 5.53 Lawrence, finding he was forging ahead, hauled up a little. The *Chesapeake's* broadsides were doing great damage; but she herself was suffering even more than her foe; the men in the *Shannon's* tops could hardly see the deck of the American frigate through the clouds of splinters, hammocks, and other wreck that was flying across it. Man after man was killed at the wheel; the fourth lieutenant, the master, and the boatswain were slain; and at 5.56, having had her jib-sheet and foretopsail tie shot away, and her spanker brails loosened so that the sail blew out, the *Chesapeake* came up into the wind somewhat, so as to expose her quarter to her antagonist's broadside, which beat in her stern-ports and swept the men from the after-guns. One of the arm chests on the quarter-deck was blown up by a hand-grenade thrown from the *Shannon*. The *Chesapeake* was now seen to have sternway on and to be paying slowly off; so the *Shannon* put her helm astarboard and shivered her mizzen-topsail, so as to keep off the wind and delay the boarding. But at that moment her jib-stay was shot away, and, her head-sails becoming becalmed, she went off very slowly. In consequence, at 6 P. M. the two frigates fell aboard, the *Chesapeake's* quarters pressing upon the *Shannon's* side just forward the starboard main-chains, and the frigates were kept in this position by the fluke of the *Shannon's* anchor catching in the *Chesapeake's* quarter port.

The *Shannon's* crew had suffered severely, but not the least panic or disorder existed among them. Broke ran forward, and seeing his foes flinching from the quarter-deck guns, he ordered the ships to be lashed together, the great guns to cease firing, and the boarders to be called. The boatswain, who had fought in Rodney's action, set about fastening the vessels together, which the grim veteran succeeded in doing, though his right arm was literally hacked off by a blow from a cutlass. All was confusion and dismay on board the *Chesapeake*. Lieutenant Ludlow had been mortally wounded and carried below; Lawrence himself, while standing on the quarter-deck, fatally conspicuous by his full-dress uniform and commanding stature, was shot down, as the vessels closed, by Lieutenant Law of the British marines. He fell dying, and was carried below, exclaiming, "Don't give up the ship"—a phrase that has since become proverbial among his countrymen. The third lieutenant, Mr. W. S. Cox, came on deck, but utterly demoralized by the aspect of affairs, he basely ran below without staying to rally the men, and was courtmartialled afterward for so doing. At 6.02 Captain Broke stepped from the *Shannon's* gangway rail on to the muzzle of the *Chesapeake's* aftermost carronade, and thence over the bulwark on to her quarter-deck, followed by about 20 men. As they came aboard, the *Chesapeake's* foreign mercenaries and the raw natives of the crew deserted their quarters; the Portugese boatswain's mate removed the gratings of the berth-deck, and he ran below, followed by many of the crew, among them one of the midshipmen named Deforest. On the quarter-deck almost the only man that made any resistance was the Chaplain, Mr. Livermore, who advanced, firing his pistol at Broke, and in return nearly had his arm hewed off by a stroke from the latter's broad Toledo blade. On the upper deck the only men who behaved well were the marines, but of their original number of 44 men, 14, including Lieutenant James Broom and Corporal Dixon, were dead, and 20, including Sergeants Twin and Harris, wounded, so that there were left but 1 corporal and 9 men, several of whom had been knocked down and bruised, though reported unwounded. There was thus hardly any resistance, Captain Broke stopping his men for a moment till they were joined by the rest of the boarders under Lieutenants Watt and Falkiner. The *Chesapeake's* mizzentopmen began firing at the boarders, mortally wound-

ing a midshipman, Mr. Samwell, and killing Lieutenant Watt; but one of
the *Shannon's* long 9's was pointed at the top and cleared it out, being assisted by the English maintopmen, under Midshipman Coshnahan. At the
same time the men in the *Chesapeake's* maintop were driven out of it by the
fire of the *Shannon's* foretopmen, under Midshipman Smith. Lieutenant
George Budd, who was on the main-deck, now for the first time learned that
the English had boarded, as the upper-deck men came crowding down,
and at once called on his people to follow him; but the foreigners and
novices held back, and only a few of the veterans followed him up. As
soon as he reached the spar-deck, Budd, followed by only a dozen men,
attacked the British as they came along the gangways, repulsing them for a
moment, and killing the British purser, Aldham, and captain's clerk, Dunn;
but the handful of Americans were at once cut down or dispersed, Lieutenant Budd being wounded and knocked down the main hatchway. "The
enemy," writes Captain Broke, "fought desperately, but in disorder."
Lieutenant Ludlow, already mortally wounded, struggled up on deck, followed by two or three men, but was at once disabled by a sabre cut. On
the forecastle a few seamen and marines turned to bay. Captain Broke was
still leading his men with the same brilliant personal courage he had all
along shown. Attacking the first American, who was armed with a pike,
he parried a blow from it, and cut down the man; attacking another he was
himself cut down, and only saved by the seaman Mindham, already mentioned, who slew his assailant. One of the American marines, using his
clubbed musket, killed an Englishman, and so stubborn was the resistance
of the little group that for a moment the assailants gave back, having lost
several killed and wounded; but immediately afterward they closed in and
slew their foes to the last man. The British fired a volley or two down the
hatchway, in response to a couple of shots fired up; all resistance was at
an end, and at 6.05, just fifteen minutes after the first gun had been fired,
and not five after Captain Broke had come aboard, the colors of the *Chesapeake* were struck. Of her crew of 379 men, 61 were killed or mortally
wounded, including her captain, her first and fourth lieutenants, the lieutenant of marines, the master (White), boatswain (Adams), and 3 midshipmen, and 85 severely and slightly wounded, including both her other
lieutenants, 5 midshipmen, and the chaplain; total, 148; the loss falling
almost entirely upon the American portion of the crew.

Of the *Shannon's* men, 33 were killed outright or died of their wounds,
including her first lieutenant, purser, captain's clerk and 1 midshipman,
and 50 wounded, including the captain himself and the boatswain; total, 83.

The *Chesapeake* was taken to Halifax, where Captain Lawrence and
Lieutenant Ludlow were both buried with military honors. Captain Broke
was made a baronet, very deservedly, and Lieutenants Wallis and Falkiner
were both made commanders. . . .

In 1813 Perry won an important victory on Lake Erie, insuring the United States against invasion from that quarter and enshrining his name in the hearts of his countrymen.

Captain Oliver Hazard Perry had assumed command of Erie and the upper lakes, acting under Commodore Chauncy. With intense energy he at once began creating a naval force which should be able to contend successfully with the foe. As already said, the latter in the beginning had exclusive control of Lake Erie; but the Americans had captured the *Caledonia,* brig, and purchased three schooners, afterward named the *Somers, Tigress,* and *Ohio,* and a sloop, the *Trippe.* These at first were blockaded in the Niagara, but after the fall of Fort George and retreat of the British forces, Captain Perry was enabled to get them out, tracking them up against the current by the most arduous labor. They ran up to Presque Isle (now called Erie), where two 20-gun brigs were being constructed under the directions of the indefatigable captain. Three other schooners, the *Ariel, Scorpion,* and *Porcupine,* were also built.

The harbor of Erie was good and spacious, but had a bar on which there was less than 7 feet of water. Hitherto this had prevented the enemy from getting in; now it prevented the two brigs from getting out. Captain Robert Heriot Barclay had been appointed commander of the British forces on Lake Erie; and he was having built at Amherstburg a 20-gun ship. Meanwhile he blockaded Perry's force, and as the brigs could not cross the bar with their guns in, or except in smooth water, they of course could not do so in his presence. He kept a close blockade for some time; but on the 2d of August he disappeared. Perry at once hurried forward everything; and on the 4th, at 2 P. M., one brig the *Lawrence,* was towed to that point of the bar where the water was deepest. Her guns were whipped out and landed on the beach, and the brig got over the bar by a hastily improvised "camel."

"Two large scows, prepared for the purpose, were hauled alongside, and the work of lifting the brig proceeded as fast as possible. Pieces of massive timber had been run through the forward and after ports, and when the scows were sunk to the water's edge, the ends of the timbers were blocked up, supported by these floating foundations. The plugs were now put in the scows, and the water was pumped out of them. By this process the brig was lifted quite two feet, though when she was got on the bar it was found that she still drew too much water. It became necessary, in consequence, to cover up everything, sink the scows anew, and block up the timbers afresh. This duty occupied the whole night."

Just as the *Lawrence* had passed the bar, at 8 A. M. on the 5th, the enemy reappeared, but too late; Captain Barclay exchanged a few shots with the schooners and then drew off. The *Niagara* crossed without difficulty. There were still not enough men to man the vessels, but a draft arrived from Ontario, and many of the frontiersmen volunteered, while soldiers also were sent on board. The squadron sailed on the 18th in pursuit of the enemy, whose ship was now ready. After cruising about some time the *Ohio* was sent down the lake, and the other ships went into Put-in Bay. On the 9th of September Captain Barclay put out from Amherstburg, being so short of provisions that he felt compelled to risk an action with the superior force opposed. On the 10th of September his squadron was discovered from the masthead of the *Lawrence* in the northwest. The Americans were certainly very greatly superior in force. . . .

Perry at once got under way; the wind soon shifted to the N. E., giving us the weather-gauge, the breeze being very light. Barclay lay to in a close column, heading to the S. W. in the following order: *Chippeway*, Master's Mate J. Campbell; *Detroit*, Captain R. H. Barclay; *Hunter*, Lieutenant G. Bignell; *Queen Charlotte*, Captain R. Finnis; *Lady Prevost*, Lieutenant Edward Buchan; and *Little Belt*, by whom commanded is not said. Perry came down with the wind on his port beam, and made the attack in column ahead, obliquely. First in order came the *Ariel*, Lieutenant John H. Packet, and *Scorpion*, Sailing-master Stephen Champlin, both being on the weather-bow of the *Lawrence*, Captain O. H. Perry; next came the *Caledonia*, Lieutenant Daniel Turner; *Niagara*, Captain Jesse D. Elliott; *Somers*, Lieutenant A. H. M. Conklin; *Porcupine*, Acting-master George Serrat; *Tigress*, Sailing-master Thomas C. Almy, and *Trippe*, Lieutenant Thomas Holdup.

As, amid light and rather baffling winds, the American squadron approached the enemy, Perry's straggling line formed an angle of about 15° with the more compact one of his foes. At 11.45 the *Detroit* opened the action by a shot from her long 24, which fell short; at 11.50 she fired a second which went crashing through the *Lawrence*, and was replied to by the *Scorpion's* long 32. At 11.55 the *Lawrence*, having shifted her port bow-chaser, opened with both the long 12's, and at meridian began with her carronades, but the shot from the latter all fell short. At the same time the action became general on both sides, though the rearmost American vessels were almost beyond the range of their own guns, and quite out of range of the guns of their antagonists. Meanwhile the *Lawrence* was already suffering considerably as she bore down on the enemy. It was twenty minutes before she succeeded in getting within good carronade range, and during that time the action at the head of the line was between the long guns of the *Chippeway* and *Detroit*, throwing 123 pounds, and those of the *Scorpion, Ariel,* and *Lawrence,* throwing 104 pounds. As the enemy's fire was directed almost exclusively at the *Lawrence* she suffered a great deal. The *Caledonia, Niagara,* and *Somers* were meanwhile engaging, at long range, the *Hunter* and *Queen Charlotte,* opposing from their long guns 96 pounds to the 39 pounds of their antagonists, while from a distance the three other American gun-vessels engaged the *Prevost* and *Little Belt*. By

12.20 the *Lawrence* had worked down to close quarters, and at 12.30 the action was going on with great fury between her and her antagonists, within canister range. The raw and inexperienced American crews committed the same fault the British so often fell into on the ocean, and overloaded their carronades. In consequence, that of the *Scoprion* upset down the hatchway in the middle of the action, and the sides of the *Detroit* were dotted with marks from shot that did not penetrate. One of the *Ariel's* long 12's also burst. Barclay fought the *Detroit* exceedingly well, her guns being most excellently aimed, though they actually had to be discharged by flashing pistols at the touch-holes, so deficient was the ship's equipment. Meanwhile the *Caledonia* came down too, but the *Niagara* was wretchedly handled, Elliott keeping at a distance which prevented the use either of his carronades or of those of the *Queen Charlotte,* his antagonist; the latter, however, suffered greatly from the long guns of the opposing schooners, and lost her gallant commander, Captain Finnis, and first lieutenant, Mr. Stokes, who were killed early in the action; her next in command, Provincial-Lieutenant Irvine, perceiving that he could do no good, passed the *Hunter* and joined in the attack on the *Lawrence,* at close quarters. The *Niagara,* the most efficient and best manned of the American vessels, was thus almost kept out of the action by her captain's misconduct. At the end of the line the fight went on at long range between the *Somers, Tigress, Porcupine,* and *Trippe* on one side, and *Little Belt* and *Lady Prevost* on the other; the *Lady Prevost* making a very noble fight, although her 12-pound carronades rendered her almost helpless against the long guns of the Americans. She was greatly cut up, her commander, Lieutenant Buchan, was dangerously, and her acting first lieutenant, Mr. Roulette, severely, wounded, and she began falling gradually to leeward.

The fighting at the head of the line was fierce and bloody to an extraordinary degree. The *Scorpion, Ariel, Lawrence,* and *Caledonia,* all of them handled with the most determined courage, were opposed to the *Chippeway, Detroit, Queen Charlotte,* and *Hunter,* which were fought to the full as bravely. At such close quarters the two sides engaged on about equal terms, the Americans being superior in weight and metal, and inferior in number of men. But the *Lawrence* had received such damage in working down as to make the odds against Perry. On each side almost the whole fire was directed at the opposing large vessel or vessels; in consequence the *Queen Charlotte* was almost disabled, and the *Detroit* was also frightfully shattered, especially by the raking fire of the gunboats, her first lieutenant, Mr. Garland, being mortally wounded, and Captain Barclay so severely injured that he was obliged to quit the deck, leaving his ship in the command of Lieutenant George Inglis. But on board the *Lawrence* matters had gone even worse, the combined fire of her adversaries having made the grimmest carnage on her decks. Of the 103 men who were fit for duty when she began the action, 83, or over four-fifths, were killed or wounded. The vessel was shallow, and the ward-room, used as a cockpit, to which the wounded were taken, was mostly above water, and the shot came through it continually, killing and wounding many men under the hands of the surgeon.

The first lieutenant, Yarnall, was three times wounded, but kept to the deck through all; the only other lieutenant on board, Brooks, of the marines, was mortally wounded. Every brace and bowline was shot away, and the brig almost completely dismantled; her hull was shattered to pieces, many shot going completely through it, and the guns on the engaged side were by degrees all dismounted. Perry kept up the fight with splendid courage. As the crew fell one by one, the commodore called down through the skylight for one of the surgeon's assistants; and this call was repeated and obeyed till none was left; then he asked, "Can any of the wounded pull a rope?" and three or four of them crawled up on deck to lend a feeble hand in placing the last guns. Perry himself fired the last effective heavy gun, assisted only by the purser and chaplain. A man who did not possess his indomitable spirit would have then struck. Instead, however, although failing in the attack so far, Perry merely determined to win by new methods, and remodelled the line accordingly. Mr. Turner, in the *Caledonia,* when ordered to close, had put his helm up, run down on the opposing line, and engaged at very short range, though the brig was absolutely without quarters. The *Niagara* had thus become the next in line astern of the *Lawrence,* and the sloop *Trippe,* having passed the three schooners in front of her, was next ahead. The *Niagara* now, having a breeze, steered for the head of Barclay's line, passing over a quarter of a mile to windward of the Lawrence, on her port beam. She was almost uninjured, having so far taken very little part in the combat, and to her Perry shifted his flag. Leaping into a rowboat, with his brother and four seamen, he rowed to the fresh brig, where he arrived at 2.30, and at once sent Elliott astern to hurry up the three schooners. The *Trippe* was now very near the *Caledonia.* The *Lawrence* having but 14 sound men left, struck her colors, but could not be taken possession of before the action recommenced. She drifted astern, the *Caledonia* passing between her and her foes. At 2.45 the schooners having closed up, Perry in his fresh vessel, bore up to break Barclay's line.

The British ships had fought themselves to a standstill. The *Lady Prevost* was crippled and sagged to leeward, though ahead of the others. The *Detroit* and *Queen Charlotte* were so disabled that they could not effectually oppose fresh antagonists. There could thus be but little resistance to Perry, as the *Niagara* stood down, and broke the British line, firing her port guns into the *Chippeway, Little Belt,* and *Lady Prevost,* and the starboard ones into the *Detroit, Queen Charlotte,* and *Hunter,* raking on both sides. Too disabled to tack, the *Detroit* and *Charlotte* tried to wear, the latter running up to leeward of the former; and, both vessels having every brace and almost every stay shot away, they fell foul. The *Niagara* luffed athwart their bows, within half pistol-shot, keeping up a terrific discharge of great guns and musketry, while on the other side the British vessels were raked by the *Caledonia* and the schooners so closely that some of their grape-shot, passing over the foe, rattled through Perry's spars. Nothing further could be done, and Barclay's flag was struck at 3 P.M., after three and a quarter hours' most gallant and desperate fighting. The *Chippeway* and *Little Belt* tried to escape, but were overtaken and brought to respectively by the *Trippe* and *Scorpion,* the commander of the latter, Mr. Stephen Champlin, firing the last, as he had the first, shot of the battle. "Captain Perry has behaved in the most humane and attentive manner, not only to myself and officers, but to all the wounded," writes Captain Barclay.

The American squadron had suffered severely, more than two-thirds of the loss falling upon the *Lawrence,* which was reduced to the condition of a perfect wreck, her starboard bulwarks being completely beaten in. She had, as already stated, 22 men killed, including Lieutenant of Marines Brooks and Midshipman Lamb; and 61 wounded, including Lieutenant Yarnall, Midshipman (acting second lieutenant) Forrest, Sailing-master Taylor, Purser Hambleton, and Midshipmen Swartout and Claxton. The *Niagara* lost 2 killed and 25 wounded (almost a fifth of her effective), including among the latter the second lieutenant, Mr. Edwards, and Midshipman Cummings. The *Caledonia* had 3, the *Somers* 2, and *Trippe* 2, men wounded. The *Ariel* had 1 killed and 3 wounded; the *Scorpion* 2 killed, including Midshipman Lamb. The total loss was 123; 27 were killed and 96 wounded, of whom 3 died.

The British loss, falling most heavily on the *Detroit* and *Queen Charlotte,* amounted to 41 killed (including Captain S. J. Garden, R. N., and Captain R. A. Finnis), and 94 wounded (including Captain Barclay and Lieutenants Stokes, Buchan, Roulette, and Bignell): in all 145. The first and second in command on every vessel were killed or wounded, a sufficient proof of the desperate nature of the defense.

The victory of Lake Erie was most important, both in its material results and in its moral effect. It gave us complete command of all the upper lakes, prevented any fears of invasion from that quarter, increased our prestige with the foe and our confidence in ourselves, and insured the conquest of upper Canada; in all these respects its importance has not been overrated. But the "glory" acquired by it most certainly *has* been estimated at more than its worth. Most Americans, even the well educated, if asked which was the most glorious victory of the war, would point to this battle. Captain Perry's name is more widely known than that of any other commander. Every schoolboy reads about *him,* if of no other sea-captain; yet he certainly stands on a lower grade than either Hull or Macdonough, and not a bit higher than a dozen others. On Lake Erie our seamen displayed great courage and skill; but so did their antagonists. The simple truth is, that, where on both sides the officers and men were equally brave and skilful, the side which possessed the superiority in force, in the proportion of three

to two, could not well help winning. The courage with which the *Lawrence*
was defended has hardly ever been surpassed, and may fairly be called
heroic; but equal praise belongs to the men on board the *Detroit,* who had
to discharge the great guns by flashing pistols at the touch-holes, and yet
made such a terribly effective defense. Courage is only one of the many
elements which go to make up the character of a first-class commander;
something more than bravery is needed before a leader can be really
called great. . . .

*In 1814 Macdonough won fame and glory for the Americans on Lake
Champlain.*

This lake, which had hitherto played but an inconspicuous part, was now
to become the scene of the greatest naval battle of the war. A British army
of 11,000 men under Sir George Prevost undertook the invasion of New
York by advancing up the western bank of Lake Champlain. This advance
was impracticable unless there was a sufficiently strong British naval force
to drive back the American squadron at the same time. Accordingly, the
British began to construct a frigate, the *Confiance,* to be added to their
already existing force, which consisted of a brig, 2 sloops, and 12 or 14
gunboats. The Americans already possessed a heavy corvette, a schooner, a
small sloop, and 10 gunboats or row-galleys; they now began to build a
large brig, the *Eagle,* which was launched about the 16th of August. Nine
days later, on the 25th, the *Confiance* was launched. The two squadrons
were equally deficient in stores, etc.; the *Confiance* having locks to her
guns, some of which could not be used, while the American schooner
Ticonderoga had to fire her guns by means of pistols flashed at the touch-
holes (like Barclay on Lake Erie). Macdonough and Downie were hurried
into action before they had time to prepare themselves thoroughly; but it
was a disadvantage common to both, and arose from the nature of the case,
which called for immediate action. The British army advanced slowly toward
Plattsburg, which was held by General Macomb with less than 2,000 effective American troops. Captain Thomas Macdonough, the American commodore, took the lake a day or two before his antagonist, and came to
anchor in Plattsburg harbor. The British fleet, under Captain George
Downie, moved from Isle-aux-Noix, on September 8th, and on the morning of the 11th sailed into Plattsburg harbor. . . .
Macdonough saw that the British would be forced to make the attack in
order to get the control of the waters. On this long, narrow lake the winds
usually blow pretty nearly north or south, and the set of the current is of
course northward; all the vessels, being flat and shallow, could not beat to
windward well, so there was little chance of the British making the attack
when there was a southerly wind blowing. So late in the season there was
danger of sudden and furious gales, which would make it risky for Downie

to wait outside the bay till the wind suited him; and inside the bay the wind was pretty sure to be light and baffling. Young Macdonough (then but twenty-eight years of age) calculated all these chances very coolly and decided to await the attack at anchor in Plattsburg Bay, with the head of his line so far to the north that it could hardly be turned, and then proceeded to make all the other preparations with the same foresight. Not only were his vessels provided with springs, but also with anchors to be used astern in any emergency. The *Saratoga* was further prepared for a change of wind, or for the necessity of winding ship, by having a kedge planted broad off on each of her bows, with a hawser and preventer hawser (hanging in bights under water) leading from each quarter to the kedge on that side. There had not been time to train the men thoroughly at the guns; and to make these produce their full effect the constant supervision of the officers had to be exerted. The British were laboring under this same disadvantage, but neither side felt the want very much, as the smooth water, stationary position of the ships, and fair range, made the fire of both sides very destructive.

Plattsburg Bay is deep and opens to the southward; so that a wind which would enable the British to sail up the lake would force them to beat when entering the bay. The east side of the mouth of the bay is formed by Cumberland Head; the entrance is about a mile and a half across, and the other boundary, southwest from the head, is an extensive shoal, and a small, low island. This is called Crab Island, and on it was a hospital and one 6-pounder gun, which was to be manned in case of necessity by the strongest patients. Macdonough had anchored in a north-and-south line a little to the south of the outlet of the Saranac, and out of range of the shore batteries, being two miles from the western shore. The head of his line was so near Cumberland Head that an attempt to turn it would place the opponent under a very heavy fire, while to the south the shoal prevented a flank attack. The *Eagle* lay to the north, flanked on each side by a couple of gunboats; then came the *Saratoga,* with three gunboats between her and the *Ticonderoga,* the next in line; then came three gunboats and the *Preble.* The four large vessels were at anchor; the galleys being under their sweeps and forming a second line about forty yards back, some of them keeping their places and some not doing so. By this arrangement his line could not be doubled upon, there was not room to anchor on his broadside out of reach of his carronades, and the enemy was forced to attack him by standing in bows on.

The morning of September 11th opened with a light breeze from the northeast. Downie's fleet weighed anchor at daylight, and came down the lake with the wind nearly aft, the booms of the two sloops swinging out to starboard. At half past seven, the people in the ships could see their adversaries' upper sails across the narrow strip of land ending in Cumberland Head, before the British doubled the latter. Captain Downie hove to with his four large vessels when he had fairly opened the bay, and waited for his galleys to overtake him. Then his four vessels filled on the starboard tack and headed for the American line, going abreast, the *Chubb* to the north heading well to windward of the *Eagle,* for whose bows the *Linnet* was headed, while the *Confiance* was to be laid athwart the hawse of the *Saratoga;* the *Finch* was to leeward with the twelve gunboats, and was to engage the rear of the American line.

As the English squadron stood bravely in, young Macdonough, who feared his foes not at all, but his God a great deal, knelt for a moment, with his officers, on the quarter-deck; and then ensued a few minutes of perfect quiet, the men waiting with grim expectancy for the opening of the fight. The *Eagle* spoke first with her long 18's, but to no effect, for the shot fell short. Then, as the *Linnet* passed the *Saratoga,* she fired her broadside of long 12's, but her shot also fell short, except one that struck a hen-coop which happened to be aboard the *Saratoga.* There was a game-cock inside, and instead of being frightened at his sudden release, he jumped up on a gun-slide, clapped his wings, and crowed lustily. The men laughed and cheered; and immediately afterward Macdonough himself fired the first shot from one of the long guns. The 24-pound ball struck the *Confiance* near the hawse-hole and ranged the length of her deck, killing and wounding several men. All the American long guns now opened and were replied to by the British galleys.

The *Confiance* stood steadily on without replying. But she was baffled by shifting winds, and was soon so cut up, having both her port bow-anchors shot way, and suffering much loss, that she was obliged to port her helm and come to while still nearly a quarter of a mile distant from the *Saratoga.* Captain Downie came to anchor in grand style—securing everything carefully before he fired a gun, and then opening with a terribly destructive broadside. The *Chubb* and *Linnet* stood further in, and anchored forward of the *Eagle's* beam. Meanwhile the *Finch* got abreast of the *Ticonderoga,* under her sweeps, supported by the gunboats. The main fighting was thus to take place between the vans, where the *Eagle, Saratoga,* and six or seven gunboats were engaged with the *Chubb, Linnet, Confiance,* and two or three gunboats; while in the rear, the *Ticonderoga,* the *Preble,* and the other American galleys engaged the *Finch* and the remaining nine or ten English galleys. The battle at the foot of the line was fought on the part of the Americans to prevent their flank being turned, and on the part of the British to effect that object. At first the fighting was at long range, but gradually the British galleys closed up, firing very well. The American galleys at this end of the line were chiefly the small ones, armed with one 12-pounder apiece, and they by degrees drew back before the heavy fire of their opponents. About an hour after the discharge of the first gun had been fired the *Finch* closed up toward the *Ticonderoga,* and was completely crippled by a couple of broadsides from the latter. She drifted helplessly down the line and grounded near Crab Island; some of the convalescent patients manned the 6-pounder and fired a shot or two at her, when she struck, nearly half of her crew being killed or wounded. About the same time the British gunboats forced the *Preble* out of line, whereupon she cut her cable and drifted inshore out of the fight. Two or three of the British gunboats had already been sufficiently damaged by some of the shot from the *Ticonderoga's* long guns to make them wary; and the contest at this part of the line narrowed down to one between the American schooner and the remaining British gunboats, who combined to make a most determined attack upon her. So hastily had the squadron been fitted out that many of the matches for her guns were at the last moment found to be defective. The captain of one of the divisions was a midshipman, but sixteen years old, Hiram Paulding. When he found the matches to be bad he fired the guns of his section by having pistols flashed at them, and continued this through the whole fight. The *Ticonderoga's* commander, Lieutenant Cassin, fought his schooner most nobly. He kept walking the taffrail amid showers of musketry and grape, coolly watching the movement of the galleys and directing the guns to be loaded with canister and bags of bullets, when the enemy tried to board. The British galleys were handled with determined gallantry, under the command of Lieutenant Bell. Had they driven off the *Ticonderoga* they would have won the day for their side, and they pushed up till they were not a boathook's length distant, to try to carry her by boarding; but every attempt was repulsed and they were forced to draw off, some of them so crippled by the slaughter they had suffered that they could hardly man the oars.

Meanwhile the fighting at the head of the line had been even fiercer. The first broadside of the *Confiance,* fired from 16 long 24's, double shotted, coolly sighted, in smooth water, at pointblank range, produced the most terrible effect on the *Saratoga*. Her hull shivered all over with the shock, and when the crash subsided nearly half of her people were seen stretched on deck, for many had been knocked down who were not seriously hurt. Among the slain was her first lieutenant, Peter Gamble; he was kneeling down to sight the bow gun, when a shot entered the port, split the quoin, and drove a portion of it against his side, killing him without breaking the skin. The survivors carried on the fight with undiminished energy. Macdonough himself worked like a common sailor, in pointing and handling a favorite gun. While bending over to sight it a round shot cut in two the spanker-boom, which fell on his head and struck him senseless for two or three minutes; he then leaped to his feet and continued as before, when a shot took off the head of the captain of the gun and drove it in his face with such a force as to knock him to the other side of the deck. But after the first broadside not so much injury was done; the guns of the *Confiance* had been levelled to pointblank range, and as the quoins were loosened by the successive discharges they were not properly replaced, so that her broadsides kept going higher and higher and doing less and less damage.

Very shortly after the beginning of the action her gallant captain was slain. He was standing behind one of the long guns when a shot from the *Saratoga* struck it and threw it completely off the carriage against his right groin, killing him almost instantly. His skin was not broken; a black mark, about the size of a small plate, was the only visible injury. His watch was found flattened, and its hand pointing to the very second at which he received the fatal blow. As the contest went on the fire gradually decreased in weight, the guns being disabled. The inexperience of both crews partly caused this. The American sailors overloaded their carronades so as to very much destroy the effect of their fire; when the officers became disabled, the men would cram the guns with shot till the last projected from the muzzle. Of course, this lessened the execution, and also gradually crippled the guns. On board the *Confiance* the confusion was even worse; after the battle the charges of the guns were drawn; and on the side she had fought one was found with a canvas bag containing two rounds of shot rammed home and wadded without any powder; another with two cartridges and no shot; and a third with a wad below the cartridge.

At the extreme head of the line the advantage had been with the British. The *Chubb* and *Linnet* had begun a brisk engagement with the *Eagle* and American gunboats. In a short time the *Chubb* had her cable, bowsprit, and main-boom shot away, drifted within the American lines, and was taken possession of by one of the *Saratoga's* midshipmen. The *Linnet* paid no attention to the American gunboats, directing her whole fire against the *Eagle,* and the latter was, in addition, exposed to part of the fire of the *Confiance*. After keeping up a heavy fire for a long time her springs were shot away, and she came up into the wind, hanging so that she could not return a shot to the well-directed broadsides of the *Linnet*. Henly accordingly cut his cable, started home his topsails, ran down, and anchored by the stern between the inshore of the *Confiance* and *Ticonderoga,* from which position he opened on the *Confiance*. The *Linnet* now directed her attention to the American gunboats, which at this end of the line were very well fought, but she soon drove them off, and then sprung her broadside so as to rake the *Saratoga* on her bows.

Macdonough by this time had his hands full, and his fire was slackening; he was bearing the whole brunt of the action, with the frigate on his beam and the brig raking him. Twice his ship had been set on fire by the hot shot of the *Confiance;* one by one his long guns were disabled by shot, and his carronades were either treated the same way or else rendered useless by excessive overcharging. Finally but a single carronade was left in the starboard batteries, and on firing it the naval-bolt broke, the gun flew off the carriage and fell down the main-hatch, leaving the commodore without a single gun to oppose to the few the *Confiance* still presented. The battle would have been lost had not Macdonough's foresight provided the means of retrieving it. The anchor suspended astern of the *Saratoga* was let go, and the men hauled in on the hawser that led to the starboard quarter, bringing the ship's stern up over the kedge. The ship now rode by the kedge and by a line that had been bent to a bight in the stream cable, and she was raked badly by the accurate fire of the *Linnet*. By rousing on the line the ship was at length got so far round that the aftermost gun of the port broadside bore on the *Confiance*. The men had been sent forward to keep as much out of harm's way as possible, and now some were at once called back to man the piece, which then opened with effect. The next gun was treated in the same manner; but the ship now hung and would go no farther round. The hawser leading from the port quarter was then got forward under the bows and passed aft to the starboard quarter, and a minute afterward the ship's whole port battery opened with fatal effect. The *Confiance* meanwhile had also attempted to round. Her springs, like those of the *Linnet*, were on the starboard side, and so of course could not be shot away as the *Eagle's* were; but, as she had nothing but springs to rely on, her efforts did little beyond forcing her forward, and she hung with her head to the wind. She had lost over half of her crew, most of her guns on the engaged side were dismounted, and her stout masts had been splintered till they looked like bundles of matches; her sails had been torn to rags, and she was forced to strike, about two hours after she had fired the first broadside. Without pausing a minute the *Saratoga* again hauled on her starboard hawser till her broadside was sprung to bear on the *Linnet,* and the ship and brig began a brisk fight, which the *Eagle* from her position could take no part in, while the *Ticonderoga* was just finishing up the British galleys. The shattered and disabled state of the *Linnet's* masts, sails, and yards precluded the most distant hope of Captain Pring's effecting his escape by cutting his cable; but he kept up a most gallant fight with his greatly superior foe, in hopes that some of the gunboats would come and tow him off, and despatched a lieutenant to the *Confiance* to ascertain her state. The lieutenant returned with news of Captain Downie's death, while the British gunboats had been driven half a mile off; and, after having maintained the fight single-handed for fifteen minutes until, from the number of shot between wind and water, the water had risen a foot above her lower deck, the plucky little brig hauled down her colors, and the fight ended, a little over two hours and a half after the first gun had been fired. Not one of the larger vessels had a mast that would bear canvas, and the prizes were in a sinking condition. The British galleys drifted to leeward, none with their colors up; but as the *Saratoga's* boarding officer passed along the deck of the *Confiance* he accidentally ran against a lock-string of one of her starboard guns, and it went off. This was apparently understood as a signal by the galleys, and they moved slowly off, pulling but a very few sweeps, and not one of them hoisting an ensign.

On both sides the ships had been cut up in the most extraordinary manner; the *Saratoga* had 55 shot-holes in her hull, and the *Confiance* 105 in hers, and the *Eagle* and *Linnet* had suffered in proportion. The number of killed and wounded cannot be exactly stated; it was probably about 200 on the American side, and over 300 on the British.

Captain Macdonough at once returned the British officers their swords. Captain Pring writes: "I have much satisfaction in making you acquainted with the humane treatment the wounded have received from Commodore Macdonough; they were immediately removed to his own hospital on Crab Island, and furnished with every requisite. His generous and polite attention to myself, the officers, and men, will ever hereafter be gratefully remembered." The effects of the victory were immediate and of the highest importance. Sir George Prevost and his army at once fled in great haste and confusion back to Canada, leaving our northern frontier clear for the remainder of the war; while the victory had a very great effect on the negotiations for peace.

In this battle the crews on both sides behaved with equal bravery, and left nothing to be desired in this respect; but from their rawness they of course showed far less skill than the crews of most of the American and some of the British ocean cruisers, such as the *Constitution, United States,* or *Shannon,* the *Hornet, Wasp,* or *Reindeer.* Lieutenant Cassin handled the *Ticonderoga,* and Captain Pring the *Linnet,* with the utmost gallantry and skill, and, after Macdonough, they divided the honors of the day. But Macdonough in this battle won a higher fame than any other commander of the war, British or American. He had a decidedly superior force to contend against, the officers and men of the two sides being about on a par in every respect; and it was solely owing to his foresight and resource that we won the victory. He forced the British to engage at a disadvantage by his excellent choice of position; and he prepared beforehand for every possible contingency. His personal prowess had already been shown at the cost of the rovers of Tripoli, and in this action he helped fight the guns as ably as the best sailor. His skill, seamanship, quick eye, readiness of resource, and indomitable pluck are beyond all praise. Down to the time of the Civil War he is the greatest figure in our naval history. A thoroughly religious man, he was as generous and humane as he was skilful and brave; one of the greatest of our sea-captains, he has left a stainless name behind him. . . .

SUMMING UP

In summing up the results of the struggle on the ocean it is to be noticed that very little was attempted, and nothing done, by the American navy that could *materially* affect the result of the war. Commodore Rodgers's expedition after the Jamaica plate fleet failed; both the efforts to get a small squadron into the East Indian waters also miscarried; and otherwise the whole history of the struggle on the ocean is, as regards the Americans, only the record of individual cruises and fights. The material results were not very great, at least in their effect on Great Britain, whose enormous navy did not feel in the slightest degree the loss of a few frigates and sloops. But morally the result was of inestimable benefit to the United States. The victories kept up the spirits of the people, cast down by the defeats on land; practically decided in favor of the Americans the chief question in dispute—Great Britain's right of search and impressment—and gave the navy, and thereby the country, a world-wide reputation. I doubt if ever before a nation gained so much honor by a few single-ship duels. For there can be no question which side came out of the war with the greatest credit. The damage inflicted by each on the other was not very unequal in amount, but the balance was certainly in favor of the United States. . . .

In addition we lost 4 revenue-cutters, mounting 24 guns, and, in the aggregate, of 387 tons, and also 25 gunboats, with 71 guns, and, in the aggregate, of nearly 2,000 tons. This would swell our loss to 12,105 tons, and 526 guns; but the loss of the revenue-cutters and gunboats can fairly be considered to be counterbalanced by the capture or destruction of the various British Royal Packets (all armed with from 2 to 10 guns), tenders, barges, etc., which would be in the aggregate of at least as great tonnage and gun force, and with more numerous crews.

But the comparative material loss gives no idea of the comparative honor gained. The British navy, numbering at the outset a thousand cruisers, had accomplished less than the American, which numbered but a dozen. Moreover, most of the loss suffered by the former was in single fight, while this had been but twice the case with the Americans, who had generally been overwhelmed by numbers. The *President* and *Essex* were both captured by more than double their force simply because they were disabled before the fight began, otherwise they would certainly have escaped. With the exceptions of the *Chesapeake* and *Argus* (both of which were taken fairly, because their antagonists, though of only equal force, were better fighters), the remaining loss of the Americans was due to the small cruisers stumbling from time to time across the path of some one of the innumerable British heavy vessels. Had Congressional forethought been sufficiently great to have allowed a few line-of-battle ships to have been in readiness some time previous to the war, results of weight might have been accomplished. But the only activity ever exhibited by Congress in materially increasing the navy previous to the war, had been in partially carrying out President Jefferson's ideas of having an enormous force of very worthless gunboats—a scheme whose wisdom was about on a par with some of that statesman's political and military theories.

JOHN BACH McMASTER

(1852-1932)

The history of the United States in the years stretching from the War of 1812 through the Jackson administration was perhaps even more than that of other eras, one that could best be told in terms of the American people. John Bach McMaster in his rich, disorderly tapestry of historical facts, catches vivid images of life during these years marked by the election of Jackson, "a great uprising of the people, a triumph of democracy." These chapters are only a very small segment of the eight large volumes of the History of the People of the United States, *covering the years from 1783 to 1861 (and appearing between 1883 and 1913). McMaster, a civil engineer turned professor of history at the University of Pennsylvania, while still a young man fell under the spell of the popular British historian, T. B. Macaulay. On the opening page of his history, McMaster, almost in paraphrase of Macaulay, proclaimed:*

"In the course of this narrative much, indeed, must be written of wars, conspiracies, and rebellions; of presidents, of congresses, of embassies, of treaties, of the ambition of political leaders in the senate-house, and of the rise of great parties in the nation. Yet the history of the people shall be the chief theme. . . . [I]t shall be my purpose to describe the dress, the occupations, the amusements, the literary canons of the times; to note the changes of manners and morals; to trace the growth of that humane spirit which abolished punishment for debt, which reformed the discipline of prisons and of jails, and which has in our own time, destroyed slavery. . . . Nor shall it be less my aim to recount the manifold improvements which, in a thousand ways, have multiplied the conveniences of life and ministered to the happiness of our race."

Toward the Age of Jackson

STATE OF THE COUNTRY FROM 1825 TO 1829

THE SOCIAL AND ECONOMIC CONDITIONS OF THE WORKING PEOPLE IN THE cities—conditions out of which the early labor movements grew—did indeed call loudly for reform. Ten years of rapid industrial development had brought into prominence problems of urban life and municipal government familiar enough to us, but new and quite beyond solution in 1825. The influx of paupers to partake of the benefits of the many charitable societies; the overcrowded labor market; the steadily increasing number of unemployed; the housing of the poor; the rise of the tenement house; the congestion of population in limited areas, with all its attendant vice and crime; and the destitution produced by low wages and lack of constant employment, had already become matters for serious consideration. An unskilled laborer, a hod-carrier, a wood-sawyer, a wood-piler in a city was fortunate if he received seventy-five cents for twelve hours of work and found employment for three hundred days in a year. Hundreds were glad to work for thirty-seven and even twenty-five cents a day in winter who in spring and summer could earn sixty-two and a half or perhaps eighty-seven and a half cents by toiling fourteen hours. On the canals and turnpikes fifteen dollars a month and found in summer and one third that sum in winter were considered good pay. In truth, it was not uncommon during the winter for men to work for their board. Nothing but perfect health, steady work, sobriety, the strictest economy, and the help of his wife could enable a married man to live on such wages. But the earnings of women were lower yet. Many trades and occupations now open to them either had no existence or were then confined to men. They might bind shoes, sew rags, fold and stitch books, become spoolers, or make coarse shirts and duck pantaloons at eight or ten cents a piece. Shirt-making was eagerly sought after, because the garments could be made in the lodgings of the seamstress, who was commonly the mother of a little family, and often a widow. Yet the most expert could not finish more than nine shirts a week, for which she would receive seventy-two or ninety cents. Fifty cents seems to have been the average.

From McMaster, *A History of the People of the United States from the Revolution to the Civil War* (8 vols., 1883-1913), ch. 44 (in part), ch. 52 (in part).

To the desperate poverty produced by such wages many evils were attributed. Intemperance was encouraged, children were sent into the streets to beg and pilfer, and young girls were driven to lives of shame to an extent which but for the report of the Magdalene Society in New York and the action of the people elsewhere would be incredible. The cities, in short, were growing with great rapidity, and were exhibiting every phase of life.

At New York, now the metropolis of the country, the growth of the city was astonishing to its own citizens. The population numbered one hundred and sixty-two thousand, an increase of forty thousand in five years. To keep pace with such an inpouring of strangers was hardly possible. More than three thousand buildings were under way in 1825; yet such was the press that not an unoccupied dwelling house existed in the entire city, and it was quite common to see families living in houses with unfinished floors, with windows destitute of sashes, and in which the carpenters had not hung a single door. Nor was this an accident. Year after year the same thing occurred, and on one first of May—the great "moving day"—three hundred homeless people gathered in the park with their household goods and were lodged in the jail till the houses they had rented were finished and made habitable.

In the upper wards entire blocks of fine brick buildings had arisen on sites which in 1820 were covered with marshes or occupied with straggling frame huts of little value. In the neighborhood of Canal Street a new city stood on what a few years before was the shore of a stagnant pool. In Greenwich new streets had been opened, and all along the Bowery new houses had been put up. Never in the history of the city had its commerce been greater. Ten million dollars had been collected in duties in one year, a sum larger by eighty thousand than in the same time had been gathered at the custom-houses of Boston, Philadelphia, Baltimore, Norfolk, and Savannah combined. Sixteen packets plied regularly between the city and Liverpool. Four more were engaged in trade with Havre. Seven were in the Savannah line, ten in the Charleston line, and four in the New Orleans, while innumerable brigs, sloops, schooners, and steamboats made stated trips to every seaport of importance on the coast. The city, it was said boastfully, was visited by merchants of every clime and from every part of the United States, so that New York might truly be called the mart of nations. Nor was this an idle boast. Five hundred new mercantile houses were said to have been established in the city in the early months of 1825, a statement well borne out by the crowded condition of the mercantile newspapers. The Gazette in seven days contained 1,115 new advertisements, and in one issue, a week later, printed 213, and stated that 23 others were left out for want of space.

There were now twelve banks in the city, with an aggregate capital of thirteen millions of dollars, paying dividends of from five to eight per cent., and ten marine insurance companies with a capital of ten million dollars.

Yet even these were not enough to transact the volume of business, and when the Legislature met applications were made for charters for twenty-seven more banks with a combined capital of twenty-two and a half millions, and for thirty-one corporations of all sorts with a total capital of fifteen millions.

Thirteen hundred sailing vessels entered the port yearly. Such as came from Great Britain were always crowded with emigrants, of whom more than five thousand arrived annually. Since 1819 some thirty-four thousand aliens had been landed in the city. Seven eighths of these were artisans, laborers, and skilled workmen, and, while some found homes in the West or went off to other cities or to inland towns, a large proportion remained and constituted an element hard to govern, for the machinery of government was of the rudest kind. Despite its growing wealth and commercial importance, New York was in many respects but a town. Population had poured into it with such rapidity that it had become large in area before it had ceased to be small in customs, usages, and the administration of affairs. Over it presided a mayor, a recorder, the aldermen, and a few officials in charge of what have since become departments of city government, some of which now expend more money each year than in 1825 was used in governing the entire State. The mayor was elected by the aldermen, who, one from each ward, were elected by the people, and were required two at a time to serve as judges in the Court of General Sessions for the city and county. The few departments in existence were of a humble kind, and were aided in the discharge of the duties assigned them by the citizens. There was a superintendent of streets, but he had little to do with cleaning them. Every occupant of a dwelling house or other building, every owner of a vacant lot on any paved street, must twice a week, from April to December, scrape and sweep the pavement before his premises as far as the middle of the roadway, must gather the dirt in a heap, and on it must place the ashes and rubbish brought out from his house or cellar. The city was responsible for nothing but the removal of the rubbish and the sweeping of paved streets before unoccupied houses at the cost of the owner. Between December and April no street-cleaning was attempted, and the sole scavengers became the hogs, who were suffered to range at large provided they had rings in their noses.

There was a rude sort of fire department, consisting of the chief engineer and his assistants, of the firewardens, and the firemen, hosemen, hook-and-ladder men, whose duty it was to drag the engines to the burning building and attach the hose. Each firewarden was assigned to a particular engine, was responsible for the supply of water, and formed the citizens in two lines stretching from his engine to the nearest pump or well. Up one line went the full buckets; down the other came the empty ones. These buckets belonged to the citizens. Each occupant of a house was still required to have in his front hall the old-fashioned leather bucket marked with his initials, the number of his house, and the name of his street. If his house had three or less fireplaces, he must keep one bucket; three to six fireplaces, two buckets; six to nine fireplaces, four buckets; which on the alarm of fire he must put out on the sidewalk to be carried off by the first passer-by. After the fire had been extinguished the owner must seek his property at the City Hall. At night the watch cried the name of the street in which the burning building was, and every occupant of a house put a lighted candle in his window.

The peace of the city was kept in the day by the constables, and in the night by the watch. The city was marked out into four districts, over each of which presided two "captains of the night watch." One served every other night, had command of as many watchmen as the Common Council saw fit to give him, assigned the men to their "rounds," and saw that they kept sober and were diligent.

The high constable, the constables, and the marshals enforced the ordinances, some of which are curious enough to be mentioned. In the crowded part of the city—that south of Grand Street on the east side and Vestry Street on the west—no horse attached to a carriage, gig, chaise, or coach could be driven faster than "slow trot," and must turn every corner walking. No drayman or cartman could sit on his wagon unless by reason of old age a special dispensation was given him by the aldermen. He must walk beside his horse. No team driven tandem could go faster than a walk. On Sunday drivers of vehicles and horsemen must walk very slowly past churches and places of worship during divine service. If a congregation pleased, chains could be hung across the street before the place of worship during service, and all passing of horses and carriages stopped. Nobody could fish on the Lord's Day; nor drive nor wade a horse into the waters of either river; nor deliver milk between nine in the morning and five in the afternoon; nor buy nor sell; nor bring anything into nor take anything out of the city.

Restrictions of this sort were by no means peculiar. Indeed, there was little in the city government of New York that could not be paralleled in that of Philadelphia. There, too, were a mayor, a recorder, fifteen aldermen, and select and common council. The people elected councils. But the Governor of Pennsylvania appointed the recorder and the aldermen to hold office during good behavior, and the councils each year elected one of the aldermen to serve as mayor. Even in the selection of so important an officer as the constable the people had little to say. Annually the voters of each ward were required to elect two persons fit to be constables, and one of them must be appointed to the office by the mayor.

In Philadelphia, as in New York, occupants of houses must have the pavement before their premises swept to the middle of the street every Friday or pay a fine of five shillings. These sweepings the city would remove; but ashes, mud, shavings, or refuse not arising "from common housekeeping" must be removed at the cost of the housekeeper. There, too, each tenant must have fire buckets and a canvas bag hanging in his hall, and must lend a hand in the extinguishment of fires. There, too, on Sundays the streets were chained in the neighborhood of churches and houses of public worship. There, too, the constables preserved the peace during the day and the superintendent of the night watch and his men guarded the city by night.

To the watch belonged the care of the oil, wicks, lamps, and utensils used in illuminating the streets, and the duty of lighting the lamps each night at sundown and keeping them burning till dawn.

As far back as 1816 an effort was made to introduce gas, and the manufacture of what was called carbonated hydrogen was begun by a Dr. Kugler. Peale promptly put the apparatus in his museum, and informed the public that on certain nights the hall would be illuminated with "gaslights which will burn without wick or oil." The managers of the new theatre next introduced it into their building as an attraction. Finally, a citizen put one of Kugler's gas machines in his dwelling house, and invited councils to come and see the new light. A committee was accordingly sent, and, after visiting Peale's Museum, the theatre, and Mr. Henry's residence, recommended that a standing committee on gas-light should be appointed to watch the progress of the new invention and report from time to time.

The public having satisfied its curiosity, the new light shared the fate of the velocipede just then exhibited in the museum, and was forgotten. In 1820, however, attention was again drawn to gas by the Masons, who, when they built their new hall, lighted it with Kugler's carbonated hydrogen. The whole neighborhood complained of the stench, and voted the Lodge Gas Works a nuisance. But the experiment proved so successful that in 1822 the Masons applied to councils for leave to lay pipes in the streets and furnish gas to such as were willing to burn it. The petition was rejected. Councils had no desire to encourage an innovation so dangerous, so offensive, and one likely to injure the business of candle makers and oil-dealers.

In other cities the friends of the new light fared better. Gas as a means of street lighting was adopted by Boston in 1822, and by New York in 1823, when the New York Gas-Light Company was incorporated. The work of actual introduction was slow, for there was not a foundry in the country where long iron pipes were cast, and every foot of the street main was brought from England.

An exhibition of Kugler's gas at Peale's Museum in Baltimore in 1816 led to the formation of a gas-light company in that city in 1817. There also the process of pipe-laying was slow, so that 1820 came before the company began business with three customers.

Now that Philadelhpia had fallen behind her sister cities in enterprise, another attempt was made to introduce gas, and in 1825 a bill to incorporate the Philadelphia Gas-Light Company and give it power to lay pipes in the streets and furnish gas was reported in the Legislature. But again public prejudice defeated the scheme. Gas was denounced as an unsafe, unsure means of illumination; its manufacture was described as a nuisance, and its use cited as one of the follies of the age. Common lamps were good enough. Two years later, when the matter was once more before the public, the struggle waxed hotter. Some one said that if gas was used to light the streets crime would be lessened. This was scoffed at, and the public was reminded that a burglar with a spade could in a few minutes destroy a gas main and leave whole squares in darkness. A burglar, it was answered, can blow out the lamps and leave whole squares in darkness. The night watch, was the reply, can relight a lamp, but not a gas-jet when the main is cut. When gas, said another, was tested in 1820, and the Masons built works in the rear of their hall, the stench tainted provisions and sickened whole families, and drove people from Peale's Museum. Peale denied the statement, and asserted that when his museum was illuminated with gas the cost was least, the attendance greatest, and his income doubled. The application was rejected by councils, and Philadelphia was without gas till 1837.

Much the same difficulty attended the introduction of a new fuel destined in time to increase the comforts of life, facilitate the use of steam, and revolutionize manufactures. That anthracite coal abounded in Pennsylvania had been known for more than thirty years, and as early as 1792 a tract of land was purchased in Lehigh County at a place where the coal cropped out and could be quarried at the surface, and the Lehigh Coal Mine Company was formed, and the vein opened. Like scores of other enterprises called into existence by the revival of confidence and the good times that followed the establishment of Government under the Constitution, the Lehigh company was far in advance of the ideas of the people and the conditions of the day. There was no market, and no way to get to market had one existed. The company, however, built a road from its mine to a landing on the river nine miles away, and when the water was high enough sent its first shipment to Philadelphia. But to a people who had wood in plenty, and whose stoves and fireplaces were suited to its use, the new fuel seemed unnecessary, and the experiment failed completely. At last, in 1798, a navigation company was organized to clear the Lehigh of obstructions, and, as one hindrance was about to be removed, interest in the mine revived, and the Lehigh company leased its property to several men, who in their turn gave up the enterprise as hopeless till the war with Great Britain and the blockade of the coast made Virginia coal scarce, and turned the attention of a wire-making firm at the Falls of the Schuylkill to the possibility of using the stone coal of Pennsylvania. Then for the third time the attempt was made, and five ark loads were started from Mauch Chunk. Three were wrecked on the way; two reached the city in safety, and were sold at twenty-one dollars a ton to the wire-makers, who then had before them the task of discovering how the coal should be ignited. Failure attended every effort till, at the close of a whole night spent in the attempt to light a fire in the furnace, the workmen shut the door and started for home in disgust. One of them, however, left his coat, and on returning a little later to get it was astonished to find the coal burning brightly and the furnace red hot. The problem of the draught was solved, and the way opened for the development of the coal and iron industries of Pennsylvania. Thenceforth anthracite was brought down in wagons, and in 1819 was advertised for sale in Philadelphia at eight dollars and forty cents a long ton. Meantime the Lehigh Navigation Company was chartered, a new coal company was organized, and in 1820 three hundred and sixty-five tons of anthracite reached Philadelphia. Two new industries—grate-making and grate-setting—now sprang up, and so increased the use of the new fuel that by 1825 demands were made that householders must be forbidden to throw their coal ashes into streets to be blown into the eyes and mouths of pedestrians by every passing gust.

In New York the prospect of a great consumption of coal seemed so good that the New York Schuylkill Company was formed, and a small quantity offered at eight dollars and a half a ton. At first it went off slowly, as householders were loath to undergo the expense of replacing andirons with grates. The company thereupon gave grates to such consumers as were willing to be beholden to it, and then, the economy of coal having been proved, the sale was rapid, and the demand so great that at one time four thousand tons were stored in the city, and made, it was boastfully said, the largest coal heap in the United States.

To New Yorkers the new fuel was most welcome, for the price of wood was rising because of the quantity consumed by the steamboats. Thirteen that plied on the Hudson burned sixteen hundred cords a week. The ferry-boats used fourteen hundred more, making a total of three thousand cords per week, or one hundred thousand for the eight months the river was open. Each steamer on the Sound consumed sixty cords a trip, and, though all the immense quantity required for the purposes of transportation on river, bay, and Sound was not furnished by New York city, so much came from it that fuel had grown to be a heavy item in household expenses.

Now that the Supreme Court had destroyed the monopoly so long held by the Fulton-Livingston Company, and had opened the waters around New York to all vessels moved by steam no matter to whom they belonged, a sharp competition had resulted, and a fuel more economical than wood was needed by the steamboat companies. Already the effect of competition was visible. The fare to Providence had fallen to three dollars, and to Albany to a dollar, and on one line to seventy-five cents, provided no meals were furnished. The old Fulton Company met this by placing on their route a "safety barge," which was hailed as one of the remarkable improvements of the day. The Lady Clinton, as the barge was named, was a vessel of two hundred tons, with neither sails nor steam nor any means of propulsion, and was used exclusively for the transportation of passengers. Within was a spacious dining soom ninety feet long, a deck cabin for ladies, state-rooms, a reading-room, and over all a promenade deck one hundred feet long shaded by an awning and provided with comfortable settees. As the barge had no means of locomotion, it was towed by the Commerce, one of the regular steamers of the line, and made the trip to Albany twice a week in sixteen hours. Passengers, said the advertisement, on the safety barge will not be exposed in the least to any accident which may happen by reason of fire or steam on board the steamboat. The noise of the machinery, the trembling of the vessel, the heat from the boilers, the furnace, and the kitchen—in short, everything which may be considered unpleasant or dangerous on a steamboat are wholly wanting on the barge. Success attended the venture from the start, and as quickly as possible a companion, the Lady Van Rensselaer, was put on the route.

A journey northward by daylight on such a vessel was indeed a pleasure, for along no other river in all the land could be found scenery so magnificent and places of such historic interest. These—as the Commerce, pouring forth great clouds of smoke and cinders from its tall stack, crept northward at a speed which would now be thought insufferably slow, with the Lady Clinton tugging at the long hawser in the stern—some self-appointed cicerone was sure to point out to the traveller. Now it was the spot on the west bank, where Hamilton fell in the ever-memorable duel with Burr; now Harlem Heights; now Fort Lee, on the summit of the Palisades, or Fort Washington, on the east bank, places famous as the scenes of gallant fights in the war for independence; now the beauty of the Palisades, rising hundreds of feet above the river and stretching away northward for twenty miles a solid wall of rock to Tappan Bay, where near the little village of Tappan had once been the grave of Major André. As the boats sped on across Tappan Bay and Haverstraw to Stony Point and West Point, the story of Arnold and André and the great conspiracy was retold in all its detail. At Catskill village a landing was always made for the accommodation in summer of passengers bound for Pine Orchard, a "resort of fashion" on the mountain side, where the Catskill Mountain Association had built a fine hotel overlooking the valley of the Hudson for sixty miles around. Long before Catskill village was reached night had come on, and the first streaks of dawn were visible when the Lady Clinton made fast to the dock at Albany, where the travellers scattered, and took passage on some of the thirteen stage lines which ran out of the city in as many directions.

Albany was now a city of sixteen thousand inhabitants, and in commercial and industrial importance was second to no other in the State save New York. Her streets were crowded with emigrants gathered from every part of the East and bound for the growing towns of the West. Now that the Erie Canal was open and in use, the canal boats, steamboats, sloops, and schooners that clustered around her wharves made an array of water craft which in number and tonnage could not be equalled by any seaport in the Union. No event in the history of the State surpassed in lasting importance the completion of the canal. After eight years of persistent labor, "the big ditch," so constantly the subject of ridicule, was finished, and in June the gates at Black Rock were opened and the waters of Lake Erie for the first time were admitted into the western division. Later in the month the capstone of that splendid chain of locks at Lockport was laid with masonic ceremonies, but it was not till October that the canal from end to end was thrown open to the public.

The celebration of the opening began at Buffalo, where, on the twenty-sixth of the month, a procession of citizens and militia escorted the orator and the invited guests to a gayly decorated fleet lying in wait on the canal. On the Seneca Chief, which headed the line, were two painted kegs full of water from Lake Erie. Behind it were the Superior, the Commodore Perry, the Buffalo, and the Lion of the West, a veritable Noah's ark, containing a bear, two eagles, two fawns, two Indian boys, birds, and fish—all typical of the products of the West before the advent of the white man. When the address had been made the signal was given, and the Seneca Chief, drawn by four gray horses, started eastward on a most memorable journey. As the fleet moved slowly along the canal, saluted by music, musketry, and the cheers of the crowd on the bank, the news was carried to the metropolis by the reports of a continuous line of cannon placed along the canal to Albany and down the Hudson to New York. When the last gun was fired at the Battery, the forts in the harbor returned the salute, and the news that New York had heard the tidings was sent back to Buffalo by a second cannonade. The progress of the little fleet was one continuous ovation, as town after town along the route vied with each other in manifestations of delight. From Albany an escort of gayly dressed steamboats accompanied the fleet down the river to New York, where the entire population, increased by thirty thousand strangers, turned out to receive it, and whence thousands, boarding every kind of craft, went down the bay to Sandy Hook. There Governor Clinton, lifting the kegs from the deck of the Seneca Chief, poured their contents into the sea, saying as he did so: "This solemnity at this place, on the first arrival of vessels from Lake Erie, is intended to indicate and commemorate the navigable communication which has been accomplished between our Mediterranean Seas and the Atlantic Ocean, in about eight years, to the extent of more than four hundred and twenty-five miles by the public spirit and energy of the people of the State of New York, and may the God of the heavens and the earth smile propitiously on this work and render it subservient to the best interests of the human race."

This ceremony over and a grand salute fired, the boats returned to the city, where a fine industrial parade, to which each trade society furnished a float with artisans at work, closed the day. At night there were balls, parties, dinners, and illuminations.

The canal thus opened to the world, which was, in truth, little more than a large ditch, for it was but four feet deep and forty feet wide, was connected with the Hudson by a basin made by inclosing a part of the river between the shore and a pier forty-three hundred feet long. From this basin the canal passes along the west bank of the Hudson nearly to the mouth of the Mohawk, which it follows to Schenectady. This part was used solely by freight boats. No canal packet, as the passenger boats were termed, ever came east of Schenectady, because of the many locks between it and the Hudson. Travellers bound west by water were carried by stage from Albany to Givens's Hotel, which stood a few rods from the canal in Schenectady. Shortly before eight in the morning and seven in the evening two blasts on a horn would give notice that the Buffalo packet was about to start, whereupon the west-bound travellers would hurry from the hotel and board a vessel not unlike a Noah's ark. The hull was eighty feet long by eleven feet wide, and carried on its deck a long, low house with a flat roof and sloping sides, which were pierced by a continous row of windows provided with green blinds and red curtains. At the forward end was a room six feet long containing four berths, and called the "Ladies' Dressing Room." Behind it was a room thirty-six feet long, which was used as a cabin and dining-room by day and a bedroom by night. Precisely at nine o'clock the steward and his helpers would appear loaded down with adjustable berths, sheets, pillows, mattresses, curtains, and in a little time the cabin would resemble the interior of a modern sleeping car. Each berth was a narrow wooden frame with a strip of canvas nailed over it, and was held in place by two iron rods which projected from one side and fitted into two holes in the wall of the cabin, and by two ropes attached to the other side of the frame and made fast to rings in the ceiling. In this manner the berths were suspended in tiers of three, one over the other, along the two walls of the cabin, making thirty-six in all, with curtains hung before them. If more than four women were on board, and there usually were, one or two tiers in front of the "Ladies' Dressing Room" were cut off for their use by an opaque curtain. When the passengers outnumbered the berths, the men slept on the dining table or the floor.

Behind the cabin was the bar, and in the rear of this was the kitchen, always presided over by a negro cook.

When the weather was fine, the travellers gathered on the roof, reading, sewing, talking, and playing cards, till the helmsman would shout, "Bridge! bridge!" when the assembled company would rush headlong down the steps and into the cabin, to come forth once more when the bridge had been passed. To walk on the roof, if the packet was crowded, was not possible. It was the custom, therefore, to jump ashore as the boat rubbed along the bank, and walk on the towpath till a bridge was reached, and then jump on board as the boat glided from beneath.

Three horses, walking one before the other, dragged the boat four miles an hour, and by dint of relays every eight miles Utica was reached in just twenty-four hours. According to the inscription on the china plates of the packet boats, Utica, the site of which thirty years before was a wilderness, was then "inferior to none in the western section of the State in population, wealth, commercial enterprise, active industry, and civil improvements." At this thriving town other packets were taken to Lockport, whence passengers bound for Niagara went by stage to the Falls. At the end of the fourth day from Schenectady the jaded traveller reached Buffalo, three hundred and sixty-three miles by canal from Albany. The debt entailed on the State by this noble work, and by another joining Lake Champlain and the Hudson, was a trifle under eight millions of dollars, carrying an annual interest of four hundred and twenty-eight thousand, to meet which the State had pledged a duty on salt and sales at auction. But, to the astonishment of the most eager advocates of inland navigation, before the canal was finished the tolls began to exceed the interest charges. In 1825 five hundred thousand, and in 1826 seven hundred and sixty-five thousand dollars, were paid in tolls. Fifty boats starting westward from Albany day after day was no uncommon sight. During 1826 nineteen thousand boats and rafts passed West Troy on the Erie and Champlain Canals. The new business created by this immense movement of freight cannot be estimated. Before the Champlain Canal was opened there were but twenty vessels on the lake. In 1826 there were two hundred and eighteen bringing timber, staves, shingles, boards, potashes, and giving employment to thousands of men in navigation, shipbuilding, and lumbering. Rochester became a flour-milling centre, and turned out one hundred and fifty thousand barrels a year. Even Ohio felt the impetus, and boats loaded with pig-iron from Madison County were seen in the basin at Albany. Orders for cherry boards and dressed lumber were received at Buffalo from Hartford and from dealers in Rhode Island. The warehouses along the canal bank at Buffalo were filled with the products of the East and the West; with wheat, grain, lumber, posts and rails, whiskey, fur and peltry bound for the markets of the Atlantic, and with salt, furniture, and merchandise bound for the West.

To the people of the West the opening of the canal was productive of vast benefit. Said a Columbus newspaper: "It takes thirty days and costs five dollars a hundred pounds to transport goods from Philadelphia to this city; but the same articles may be brought in twenty days from New York by the Hudson and the canal at a cost of two dollars and a half a hundred. Supposing our merchants to import on an average five tons twice a year; this means a saving to each of five hundred and sixty dollars." It meant, indeed, far more: it meant lower prices, more buyers, a wider-spread market, increased comfort for the settlers in the new States, and, what was of equal importance, an impetus to internal improvements which should open up regions into which even the frontiersman would not go.

As section after section of the Erie Canal was finished and opened to travel, and the day of its completion came nearer and nearer, a mania for internal improvements swept over the commercial States, and one by one many of the long-discussed projects began to take shape. On July fourth ground was broken in Ohio for a canal to join Lake Erie and the Ohio river. A fortnight later a goodly company from the counties of Ulster, Sullivan, and Orange in New York assembled at the summit level of the Delaware and Hudson Canal, and with music, prayers, and speeches beheld the beginning of that great work. The Delaware and Chesapeake was well under way; the Chesapeake and Ohio was about to be commenced; while plans were on foot for canals to join New Haven and Northampton, Providence and Worcester, Boston with the Connecticut river, and Long Island Sound with Montreal by way of the valley of the Connecticut river, Vermont, and Lake Memphremagog. Indeed, early in 1826 a convention of delegates from the towns of New Hampshire and Vermont met at Concord to consider the expediency of such an enterprise. Massachusetts, alarmed at the prospect of a diversion of her trade to New York, had already appointed a commission to examine into the possibility of cutting a canal from Boston harbor to the Hudson, that she might tap the great western trade on its way down to New York. In a message on the subject, the Governor told the General Court that trade was passing from Boston. The cheapness of transportation from Albany to New York, and the abundant and variously supplied market at the basin of the Erie Canal, had drawn west, he said, the produce of the green hills of Berkshire and the rich valley of the Housatonic. If the navigation of the Connecticut were improved as proposed, the produce of that valley would go to enrich a seaport of Connecticut, while the Blackstone Canal, joining Worcester and Providence, would open a new way from the interior of Massachusetts to the coast of Rhode Island, and all the trade of western and central Massachuetts would be taken from Boston. Land transportation from Boston to Worcester or Providence then cost ten dollars a ton; but by the canal a ton of freight could be hauled from Worcester to Providence for three dollars and thirty-three cents.

Philadelphia was in much the same condition as Boston. Her western trade was seriously threatened. The day seemed at hand when articles of her own manufacture would be sent by sloop to Albany and by canal to the West, when she would be outstripped by cities on the shore of Lake Erie, and would find herself surpassed in trade and manufactures by Pittsburg. If the great western carrying trade—an industry to which the interior of the State owed no small part of its prosperity—was not to be taken away by New York, a short and cheap route to the Ohio river must be opened, and opened quickly.

Thus impelled by necessity, the community went seriously to work on the problem before it, and was soon engaged in discussing the relative merits of railroads and canals. As far back as 1811, John Stevens, of Hoboken, a man who richly deserves to be called the father of the American railroad, applied to the Legislature of New Jersey for a railroad charter. None was granted, and the following year he turned to New York, where the Erie Canal Commissioners had just been appointed, and by means of a memoir, with plans and estimates, endeavored to persuade the commission to build a railroad and not a canal across the State to Buffalo. Again he failed, but the events of the next few years greatly changed public opinion. War with Great Britain destroyed the coastwise commerce, and developed an enormous inland-carrying trade. The sight of thousands of wagons hurrying across New Jersey with military stores and ammunition; the sight of great fleets of "the ox-marine" scudding along between New York and Trenton; the report that two million dollars had been paid during the war for the cartage of goods, wares, and produce between the Hudson and the Delaware, convinced Jerseymen that a highway of transportation was really needed across their State. When, therefore, Stevens again applied to the Legislature, he met with no difficulty in securing, in 1815, the first railroad charter ever granted in the New World. His road was to join the Delaware and Raritan rivers, and serve to connect the steamboat lines from Philadelphia to Bordentown with those from New Brunswick to New York. But the project was far ahead of the times; the money wherewith to build it could not be secured, and Stevens was again doomed to disappointment. Nevertheless, the idea of moving vehicles by steam on a railway was taking root, and in 1819 another projector yet more advanced applied to Congress for aid with which to test the utility of his invention. He had, he said, devised in theory a way of moving wheeled carriages by steam on level railroads at the rate of a mile in three minutes, and of using vehicles so large that passengers might walk in them without stooping, and be furnished with accommodations for taking their meals and their rest during the passage, as in packets. The boldness of his aims marked him out as a dreamer on whom practical congressmen were not disposed to waste either time and money, and, with the reference of the memorial to the proper committee, Dearborn and his railway were forgotten.

Stevens meanwhile had not lost heart. After failing in New York and New Jersey, he turned to Pennsylvania, and addressed a letter on railroads to the Mayor of Philadelphia, who sent it to Councils, a body which manifested not the slightest interest in the matter. With business men, however, he fared better. To them the situation was serious. The New York canal was well under way. The appearance of the steamboat on the Mississippi put it within the power of the West to ignore the East, and trade directly with the world through New Orleans. If western trade was to be held against such competition, some cheap means of transportation to Pittsburg must be opened, and this the railroad seemed likely to furnish. It was not so costly as a turnpike; it would not freeze in winter, as did the water in the canals. Some men of means and prominence were persuaded to give the enterprise a trial, and in December, 1822, Stevens and his friends applied to the Legislature for a charter. To have attempted to build a railroad across the State of Pennsylvania from the Delaware to the Ohio would have been rash in the extreme. Half the distance was all they thought of covering, and, as there were good pikes from Philadelphia to Harrisburg and a canal almost completed from the Schuylkill to the Susquehanna, the proposed railroad was to begin at Harrisburg and end at Pittsburg. The House of Representatives, however, would not hear of this. The valuable trade of the Susquehanna valley, despite turnpikes and canals, was flowing steadily to Baltimore, and, in hope of diverting it to Philadelphia, the House insisted that the railroad should extend from Philadelphia to Columbia, a town on the Susquehanna, twenty-seven miles south of Harrisburg, and carried their point.

The preamble of the act of incorporation sets forth that John Stevens had memorialized the Legislature for authority to build a railroad; that he had made many discoveries and improvements in the manner of building such highways; and that it was because of such improvements that the privileges asked for were granted. Some of these privileges now seem curious enough. The charter was to be in force for ten years; the rails were to cross all pikes and roads on causeways; and the company might charge seven cents a ton per mile on freight moving westward and half that sum on freight bound east.

With the granting of the charter the enterprise came to a standstill. The community seemed to be ignorant of what was meant by a railroad. Indeed, when a correspondent of one of the newspapers asked, "What is a railroad?" the editor answered, "Perhaps some other correspondent can tell." Nobody did tell, and the public remained unenlightened till the Pennsylvania Society for the Promotion of Internal Improvement within the Commonwealth published such information as it could gather concerning railroads in Great Britain. A committee of the society took the pains to explain that it had purchased treatises and essays on the subject, and had consulted well-informed individuals, only to find that, while many valuable facts were obtained, no connected view could be given. The society, therefore, had determined to send an agent to Europe to inspect and report on the railroads then in use, with a view to enabling the public to understand one of the most valuable internal improvements of the day, and in the meantime to call attention to the best description that had come to hand. Accompanying the text were cuts showing plans and cross sections of the rails and road-bed.

The information thus given to the public was immediately increased. Some one in Baltimore wrote two papers on the construction of railroads, and the manner of drawing wagons along them by steam locomotives, and deposited a model of a track with locomotive and cars in the Exchange Reading Rooms. Somebody in Philadelphia published a series of essays on Railways, Roads, and Canals. The Society for the Promotion of Internal Improvements printed the report of its agent, strongly indorsing railroads— a report which the friends of canals made haste to attack and refute, only to be in turn answered. In the midst of the discussion one public meeting was held at Philadelphia to consider the expediency of building a railway from the Schuylkill to the Delaware, and another to discuss the project of joining the two rivers near the city by a canal. Each approved its own scheme, and each instructed a committee to prepare plans and estimates of cost.

Such part of the community as took any interest in the commercial and industrial welfare of the State was thus rent into two opposing factions —the friends and advocates of canals and the friends and advocates of railroads. For the time being the victory was with the friends of canals. Forced on by public feeling, the Legislature of Pennsylvania, in 1824, empowered the Governor to appoint three commissioners to explore a route from Philadelphia to the Ohio. The result of the exploration was a recommendation that the Alleghany and the Conemaugh rivers on the west side of the mountains, and the Susquehanna and the Juniata on the east side, should be opened to the foot of the mountains by canal and slack-water navigation, and that they should be joined by a canal passing through a tunnel four miles long under the Alleghanies. Lest the Legislature might not know what a tunnel was, the commissioners described it as "a passage like a well dug horizontally through a hill or mountain."

The utmost interest in the work of the commissioners was manifested all over the State. In January, 1824, a public meeting at Philadelphia called for canals from the Susquehanna to Lake Erie and to the Ohio, and petitioned the Legislature not to delay the work. In May another meeting issued a call for a Canal Convention to be held at Harrisburg in August. Fifty-six counties sent delegates, who declared that canals were needed; that the money appropriated for them would not be an expenditure, but an investment; that all local objects leading to a diffusive and unconnected use of public funds ought to give way for the present; and that public opinion would fully sustain the Legislature in all its efforts in behalf of internal improvements. The Legislature had already established a regular board of canal commissioners, and a year later ordered them to proceed at once to build "The Pennsylvania Canal" at State expense, and made a first appropriation of money. On July fourth, 1826, ground was broken at Harrisburg, and Pennsylvania, after a long struggle, began the construction of her highway to the West.

Now that the State was seriously at work, the old idea of the railroad revived, and in 1826 the charter granted to Stevens was repealed, and the Columbia, Lancaster, and Philadelphia Railroad was incorporated, only to share the fate of its predecessor. Then the State, convinced that private enterprise was not equal to the task of railroad-building on a great scale, took the work into her own hands, bade the canal commissioners make surveys for such a road and build it from Philadelphia through Lancaster to Columbia, and, if possible, finish the work in two years. By the same act they were instructed to examine a route for a railroad over the Alleghany Mountains from Huntingdon on the east to Johnstown on the west side— a route which in time became celebrated as the Portage Railroad, and was long one of the engineering wonders of America.

Two years had wrought a marvellous change in the place which railroads held in public estimation. The scheme which in 1823 and 1826 seemed too visionary to be seriously thought of, and which failed because nobody was rash enough to advance the needed money, was high in favor in 1828 all over the seaboard States. New York had chartered the Mohawk and Hudson to join Albany and Schenectady, and had given the company authority to use "the power and force of steam, of animals, or of any mechanical or other power." Massachusetts had incorporated the Granite Railway Company, whose track was to extend from Quincy to tide-water, had appointed a Board of Commissioners of Internal Improvements to survey one route for a railway from Boston to the boundary line of Rhode Island and another from the same city to the boundary line of New York near Albany, and had listened to reports urging that each road when built should be operated by horse power. In New York city a railway up the Hudson was seriously meditated. The objectors protested that it would never pay; but the projectors declared that success was certain, because rails could be used in winter when ice made transportation by water impossible. At Hoboken John Stevens built a circular railway, and demonstrated beyond dispute that a locomotive could drag a train round a curve. Pennsylvania chartered five railroads. The business men of Baltimore, fully aware that the activity of Pennsylvania threatened their western connections, called a public meeting, at which it was resolved to form a company and seek a charter for a railway to the West. The charter was obtained, and on the fourth of July, 1828, the corner-stone of what is now the Baltimore and Ohio Railroad was laid with imposing ceremonies at Baltimore.

Meanwhile the merchants of Charleston, South Carolina, became enthusiastic, called a public meeting, and sent a memorial to the Legislature praying for State aid and a charter. The State was asked to bear the cost of the survey of a route from Charleston to Hamburg—a town on the Savannah river, opposite Augusta—grant an act of incorporation, and exempt the property of the company from taxation. After a brief contest the act was passed. Almost at the same time the old idea of a railroad from Camden to some point on the rivers emptying into New York Bay was revived in earnest in New Jersey. There, too, a public meeting was held, at Mount Holly, and a memorial adopted. Situated as the State was, between two great centres of trade and commerce, and blessed with resources of her own waiting to be developed, it was a reproach to the enterprise of her citizens, the resolutions declared, that no line of interstate communication had been extended across her territory. Such a link in the chain of internal intercourse along the Atlantic coast was of the utmost importance to New Jersey. Therefore the meeting earnestly recommended the Legislature to grant a charter, and a liberal one, to a company for the construction of a railway from Camden to Amboy. Like meetings were now held at Burlington, Bordentown, Princeton, Trenton, and similar memorials sent up to the Legislature in behalf of four proposed railroads, none of which were chartered. Virginia had already surveyed a route for a railroad from the coal pits of Chesterfield County to the banks of the James river opposite Richmond, and had incorporated the Chesterfield Railroad Company. In Delaware, the people of Wilmington and vicinity met and discussed the expediency of a railroad from Elkton to Wilmington.

Though many were planned, the work of construction went slowly on. The period 1825 to 1830 was one of preparation, and closed with but thirty-six miles of railroad in the country. The mechanical difficulties were great. The supply of engineers, of instrument-makers, of iron, was out of all proportion to the demand. When the Pennsylvania commissioners began work the president of the board reported that he had "made most diligent search and anxious inquiry after an engineer," and had not succeeded. When the Baltimore and Ohio Railroad Company was about to begin the building of its road-bed, Congress was asked to grant it permission to import the strap iron for its rails free of duty, because the quantity wanted —some fifteen thousand tons—could not be had in the United States. The statement was flatly denied by the friends of American manufactures. Nevertheless, the Senate passed a bill remitting the duties.

The only roads on which the work of track-laying went steadily forward were the Hudson and Mohawk, the Philadelphia and Columbia, the Baltimore and Ohio, and the South Carolina, and about as much was built in a year as can now be laid with ease in one day. Everything was experimental. The best form of road-bed, the strongest and most durable kind of rail, the most economical sort of motive power, were problems yet to be solved. According to the ideas then prevalent, there must be no steep grades, as few curves as possible, and these of the sharpest and worst sort. At first the rails were long wooden stringers, protected on the upper surface from the wear of the wheels by strap iron nailed on. Then they were great blocks of granite, resting on granite ties, and plated on the upper inner surface with strap iron bolted or riveted on; and, finally, "edge rails" of rolled iron on stone blocks and stone sills, or edge rails on stone blocks and wooden sills. Even when the rails were laid what was the best kind of motive power had not been determined. The astonishing success of Stephenson's locomotives on the Stockton and Darlington Railroad in England, and the signal triumph of his Rocket over all other competitors in the Liverpool and Manchester contest, convinced many that steam was the proper agent to use. But every experiment with a locomotive ended in failure. The Stourbridge Lion was imported from England and tried on the rails of the Delaware and Hudson Canal and Railroad Company, only to be thrown aside. The Tom Thumb was built by Peter Cooper, and run on the Baltimore and Ohio Railroad to prove that a locomotive could pass around a sharp curve, and was soon forgotten. A locomotive built by Stephenson was exhibited in New York city, but never drew a car. The early railroad managers were quite content to use the horse. . . .

The completion of the National Pike was, in its day and time, a matter of much importance. It began at Cumberland, on the banks of the Potomac, passed through Hagerstown in Maryland, and Uniontown, Brownsville, and Washington in Pennsylvania, and across Virginia to Wheeling on the Ohio. With the pike from Baltimore to Cumberland, it made a great through line of communication between the East and the West, and was already the favorite highway with travellers bound for the Ohio Valley.

Such a journey was usually begun by taking boat at Philadelphia, going down the Delaware to New Castle, crossing by stage to Frenchtown on the Elk river, a tributary of Chesapeake Bay, and then boarding another steamboat for Baltimore. Twenty years had seen a marvellous betterment in the means and speed and cost of travel. Steamboats, turnpike, ferryboats, bridges, and, above all, competition, had accomplished wonders on the routes between the great seaboard cities. But no corresponding improvement had taken place in the comforts and conveniences of the inns and taverns at which the traveller was forced to stop. We lodged, said one traveller, at the City Hotel, which is the principal inn at New York. The house is immense, and was full of company; but what a wretched place! The floors were without carpets, the beds without curtains. There was neither glass, nor mug, nor cup, and a miserable little rag was dignified with the name of towel. At another inn the same traveller was shown to a room with nine other men. "I secured a bed to myself," said he, "the narrow dimensions of which precluded the possibility of participation, and plunged into it with all possible haste, as there was not a moment to be lost." His companions "occupied by triplets the three other beds which the room contained." When you alight at a country tavern, says another, it is ten to one that you stand holding your horse, bawling for the hostler, while the landlord looks on. Once inside the tavern, every man, woman, and child plies you with questions. To get a dinner is the work of hours. At night you are put with a dozen others into the same room, and sleep two or three in a bed between sheets which have covered twenty wayfarers since they last saw the tub. In the morning you go out-of-doors to wash your face, and then repair to the bar-room to behold your countenance in the only looking-glass the tavern contains. Much allowance must indeed be made for the tales of travellers. Yet the combined testimony of them all is that a night in a wayside inn was something to be dreaded, and to this the western highways afforded no exception. Saving the inns and such discomfort as came from rising at three o'clock in the morning and sitting for sixteen hours in a crowded coach, still made on the pattern of twenty years before, a ride from Baltimore to Wheeling was most enjoyable. The road-bed was hard, the horses were fine, and the scenery as the road crossed the mountains was magnificent.

Beyond the mountains every year wrought wonderful changes. In the river towns and on the farms bordering the Ohio and its tributaries life had become much easier. The steamboats supplied the large settlements already claiming to be cities, while smaller craft carried goods, wares, and merchandise to every farmhouse and cluster of cabins. The Ohio was now dotted with floating shops. At the sound of a horn the inhabitants of the village or the settler and his family would come to the river to find a dry-goods boat fitted with counters, seats, and shelves piled with finery of every sort making fast to the bank. Now it would be a floating lottery office, where tickets were sold for cotton or produce; now a tinner's establishment, within which tinware articles of every description were made, sold, and mended; now a smithy, where horses and oxen were shod and wagons repaired; now a factory for the manufacture and sale of axes, scythes, and edge tools.

The great river was more than ever the highway of travel. The huge barge of an earlier day, almost as large as a seagoing schooner, with its arched and outlandish-looking deck and its crew of five-and-twenty men, had fallen into disuse. But the keel-boat, still the favorite for waters too shallow for steamboats, and the broad-horn were more numerous than ever. Some of the "broads," called family boats, were twenty-five by one hundred feet, had pens for cattle, and neat cabins and rooms for the "movers" fitted with tables and chairs, beds, and a stove, and were constantly to be seen floating down the river in an almost endless procession with old and young, cattle, horses, swine, and fowls all in the same bottom.

When such an emigrant reached the town nearest his destination he would sell his broad and buy some sort of a conveyance, cover it with canvas or linen smeared on the inside with tar to make it water tight, go to the United States Land Office, enter his quarter or half-quarter section, and then set off for his farm. As he went slowly along, driving his cattle before him, he would come night after night to inns especially designed to meet the needs of men such as he. At each would be a room with an earthen floor and a huge fireplace, but no furniture, no conveniences of any sort, and in this his wife would cook the evening meal and the family would sleep.

When at last, after all manner of adventures, both serious and amusing, the site of the future home was reached, the settler would cut down a few saplings, build a "half-face camp," and begin his clearing. The "half-face camp" was a shed whose three sides were of logs laid one on another horizontally, whose roof was of saplings covered with branches or bark, and whose fourth side, in front of which was the fire hole, was open save in wet weather, when it was closed by hanging up deerskin curtains. In this camp the newcomer and his family would live while he grubbed up the bushes and cut down trees enough to make a log cabin. If he were a thrifty, painstaking man, he would smooth each log on four sides with his axe, and notch it half through at each end so that when they were placed one on the other the faces would nearly touch. Saplings would make the rafters, and on them would be fastened plank laid clapboard fashion, or possibly split shingles.

An opening, of course, was left for a door, although many a cabin was built without a window, and when the door was shut received no light save that which came down the chimney, which was always on the outside of the house. To form it, an opening eight feet long and six feet high was left at one end, and around this a sort of bay window was built of logs and lined with stones on the inside. Above the top of the opening the chimney contracted and was made of branches smeared both inside and out with clay. Generally the chimney went to the peak of the roof; but it was by no means unusual for it to stop about halfway up the end of the cabin.

If the settler was too poor to buy glass, or if glass could not be had, the window frame was covered with greased paper, which let in the light, but could not be seen through. The door was a plank with leather hinges, or with iron hinges made from an old wagon tire by the nearest blacksmith or by the settler himself. There was no knob, no lock, no bolt; but instead a wooden latch on the inside, which could be lifted by a person on the outside by a leather strip which came through a hole in the door and hung down. When this latch string was out, anybody could pull it, lift the latch, and come in. When it was drawn inside, nobody could enter without knocking. The floor was made of "puncheons," or planks split and hewn with an axe from the trunk of a tree, and laid with the round side down. The furniture was such as the settler brought with him or made on the spot.

The household utensils were of the simplest kind. Brooms and brushes were of corn husks. Corn was shelled by hand or by rubbing the ear on the rough side of a piece of tin punched full of holes, and called a "gritter," which was then used to grate the kernels into meal. More commonly the corn was carried in a bag slung over the back of a horse to a mill maybe fifteen miles away, or was pounded in a wooden hominy mortar with a wooden pestle, or ground in a hand mill made by placing one flat stone on a tree stump and hanging another over it in such wise that the upper stone could be rubbed around and around on the lower. Few implements were of more importance to the frontiersman than a sharp axe; but to sharpen it he used a grindstone consisting of a thick wooden disk into the circumference of which when green he had driven particles of fine gravel and sand.

Cooking stoves were unknown. Game was roasted by hanging it with a leather string before an open fire. All baking was done in a "Dutch oven," on the hearth, or in an "out oven," built, as its name implies, out of doors. The Dutch oven was a huge iron pot with an iron lid turned up at the rims. When in use it was buried in ashes, and hot coals were piled on the lid. To build an "out oven," chips and little sticks were heaped up near the house in an oblong mound some three feet long, two feet wide by the same in height, and covered over with a thick layer of clay, which, by setting fire to the wood, was burned hard as a brick. The oven was then ready for use. When about to be used, it was first made very hot by filling it with chips and allowing them to burn to ashes. The ashes were then swept out, the bread or the pies to be baked were put in, and something placed over the door and smoke hole to keep the oven from cooling too quickly.

The land about the cabin was cleared by grubbing the bushes and chopping down trees under a foot in diameter and burning them. Big trees were "deadened," or killed, by cutting a "girdle" around them two or three feet above the ground, deep enough to destroy the sap vessels and so prevent the growth of leaves. When the settler was a shiftless fellow, he would make no attempt to clear away the dead trunks, but would suffer them to stand till, in the course of years, they became so rotten that one by one they fell to pieces or were destroyed by the wind and storms.

In the ground thus laid open to the sun were planted corn, potatoes, or wheat, which, when harvested, was threshed with a flail and fanned and cleaned with a sheet. At first the corn and wheat raised would be scarcely sufficient for home use. But as time passed there would be some to spare, and this would be wagoned to the nearest river town and sold or exchanged for "store goods." Many an early settler made the shoes his family wore from leather of his own tanning, clothed himself and children in jeans of his own manufacture, and in linen every fibre of which had been grown on his own land, and had been pulled, rotted, broken, hackled, spun, and bleached by the members of his household.

If the site selected by the emigrant were a good one, others would soon settle themselves near by, and when a cluster of cabins had been formed some enterprising speculator would appear, take up a quarter section, cut it into town lots, and call the place after himself, as Piketown, or Leesburg, or Wilson's Grove. A storekeeper with a case or two of goods would next arrive, then a tavern would be built, and possibly a blacksmith shop, a sawmill, and a grist-mill, and Piketown or Wilson's Grove would be established. Many such ventures failed; but others succeeded, and are to-day prosperous villages.

It was in such far-away settlements that frontier life appeared in its least attractive form. Common hardships, common poverty, common ignorance, and the utter inability to get anything more out of life than coarse food, coarse clothes, and a rude shelter, reduced all to a level of absolute equality which existed nowhere else. The well-to-do and the destitute, the idle and the industrious, the judge and the criminal, the preacher, the circuit-rider, and the drunkard were all members of one common family. If any man rose to importance among his fellows, he did so because he possessed those physical and moral qualities which command respect alike in an Indian tribe, in a negro village in the heart of Africa, and in communities of civilized men. . . .

THE ELECTION OF JACKSON IN 1828

In all the vast stretch of country south of the Potomac and west of Pennsylvania not one elector was secured by Adams. More than eleven hundred and fifty-five thousand voters went to the polls, and gave Jackson a majority of one hundred and thirty-nine thousand votes. It was indeed a great uprising of the people, a triumph of democracy, another political revolution the like of which the country had not seen since 1800, and no mere driving from office of a man or class of men. To the popular mind it was the downfall of a corrupt and aristocratic Administration that had encroached on the rights of the States and the liberties of the people, and had used the Federal patronage to carry elections and the Federal treasury to reward its followers. As such the victory was hailed with the wildest joy. The people have rallied in their strength, said one journal, and put down the wealth and power of an overbearing aristocracy, the only stay of a corrupt coalition, and restored the administration of the Government to its pristine purity. The same States that voted for Jefferson in 1800 have voted for Jackson in 1828. Those which supported Adams the elder have befriended Adams the younger, with the same result. He may now retire from the strife of parties, and nib his pen for a memoir of his own time, while Mr. Clay broods over his treasonable practices against the will of the people and contrives artifices to rise from his own ruin. Jackson is the President of the people, and as such they will hail him everywhere, not as a god, but as an instrument taken to avenge their wrongs.

As the day drew near when he must set out for Washington, towns and cities vied with one another to do him honor. Nashville, Lynchburg, Philadelphia, sought visits from him. The people of Pittsburg tendered a steamboat to carry "the old hero" up the Ohio from Cincinnati. The Legislature of Pennsylvania invited him to Harrisburg, and great preparations were making all over the South and West to celebrate the eighth of January, when the death of Mrs. Jackson changed joy to mourning. The journey of the President-elect from the Hermitage to the Capitol was therefore quiet and uneventful. He reached there while the two Houses were witnessing the count of the electoral vote, and just in time to hear the booming of the guns that announced to the people that he had been declared duly elected President of the United States, and took up his residence at Gadsby's Hotel. There a host of office seekers, office holders, and admirers beset him from morn to eve. The people acted, said one who witnessed the scene, as if the country had been rescued from some great danger, and came by thousands from every quarter to behold the triumph of their deliverer. The dress, the language, the behavior of the crowd gave visible evidence of the revolution that had taken place. Never before had so many of the plain people been seen at any one time in Washington. Ere the end of February, the keepers of hotels, taverns, boarding-houses, lodgings, were turning applicants away, or finding accommodations for them on the floors of tap-rooms and hallways.

To the mass of men thus herded in Washington and waiting with impatience for the fourth of March, the question of the hour was, To whom will Jackson give seats in the Cabinet? To Van Buren, lately inaugurated Governor of New York, was assigned by common rumor the Secretaryship of State; to S. D. Ingham, of Pennsylvania, the Treasury; to John H. Eaton, of Kentucky, the War Department; to John Branch, of North Carolina, the Navy; to John McPherson Berrien, of Georgia, the Attorney-Generalship; and to John McLean, of Ohio, the Post-Office, which he then held and administered with signal success. When objection was made that such a Cabinet would be weak, that, save Van Buren, there was not a strong man in it, those close to Jackson answered that he did not intend to be advised by his secretaries, that he would pursue an independent course, and that he would have a privy council composed of Van Buren, Calhoun, and McLean. When this assurance failed to satisfy the malcontents, another rumor was set afloat, and McLean was said to have been selected for Secretary of War, in order that he might become a member of the Cabinet, which up to that time no Postmaster-General had been, and add strength to a body no political leader respected. That such a change was really considered may well be believed, for, when the list of secretaries was made public in the Telegraph, the official Jackson newspaper of Washington, it was found to agree in every respect with that announced before, save that McLean was made a member of the Cabinet, a dignity which every succeeding Postmaster-General has since held.

With the announcement of the names of the Cabinet officers the scramble for office grew fiercer and fiercer. For the first time since 1801 a great political revolution had taken place, a real change in the Administration had come about, and certain reforms long promised and demanded must be carried out. But, as Jefferson had stated a generation before, when the will of the nation called for a change in the Administration, there must be a change of administrators, and never before had the will of the nation in this respect been so clearly and emphatically expressed. At the head of the Cabinet, moreover, and in high favor with Jackson, was a man whose whole political training had been gained in the corrupt school of New York, a man who had raised himself from the humblest to the highest office in that State by a steady adherence to the maxim that the laborer is worthy of his hire, that political office is the just reward for political service, and that service must be not only partisan but personal. It would be the height of injustice, however, to attribute to Jackson, or Van Buren, or any other one man the widespread proscription which now began. The people, not the leaders, were to blame. They were proud of their country, their form of government, their political institutions. They believed firmly and sincerely that these institutions were in danger; that the election of Adams had been secured, in open defiance of their wishes, by a corrupt bargain, and that the men in power were hostile to the great principle that in our country the people shall rule. After four years of ceaseless agitation the people had triumphed; their day had come, and it is folly to suppose that they would be content to see power remain in the hands of men who had worked for the leaders they had overthrown, or had remained passive spectators of a struggle they had so earnestly carried on. He who was not with them was against them, and had Jackson been as resolutely bent on non-partisan administration as was John Quincy Adams, they would have swept him aside as they did his predecessor. In the course of events the time had come for a departure from old-time methods, and, whatever may be thought of the character of that change, it had to be made. No leader in our country can debase the people. He is exactly what the will of the people enable him to be, and the moment he ceases to execute that will he ceases to be a leader. As we look back on those days the wonder is, not that so many were turned out of office, but that so many were suffered to remain.

The first indication of what was to come was given by the Senate, which from the day the election of Jackson was assured held back the confirmation of every nomination to office made by Adams. The next was the work of the House and Senate when each took away the public printing from Gales and Seaton, proprietors of the National Intelligencer, and gave it to Duff Green, proprietor of the Telegraph. The Intelligencer was accused of having published the scandalous libel on Mrs. Jackson, and its owners were now, in the eyes of the people, justly punished. The charge was false, but it mattered not, for the place was wanted as a reward for political service. Nor was this without precedent, for we are informed by Adams that when he took his seat in the United States Senate in 1803 he was visited by Mr. Samuel Adams Otis, who had been the secretary of that body since 1789; that he was told that Otis had been notified that if he wished to remain secretary he must give the Senate printing to William Duane, editor of the Aurora, and that he was asked what was best to do. The advice given is not stated, but Otis held his office, and Duane printed the Senate documents for many years.

Well knowing what was to come, the seekers of office looked forward with high hopes to the fourth of March. The ceremonies which attended the inauguration were of the simplest kind. No parade, no music, none of the pomp and show of a military chieftain, it was proudly said, marred the day. At ten the officers and soldiers, having assembled at Brown's, marched to Gadsby's and delivered an address. At half-past eleven the President-elect, on foot, uncovered, preceded by the Central Committee of the District of Columbia, surrounded on the right hand and the left by gigs, wood wagons, vehicles of every sort crowded with women eager to be near the chief, and followed by the officers of his suite, worthies of the Revolution, and hundreds of strangers without distinction of rank, "and influenced by no other order than that which their own feelings dictated," walked to the Capitol, made his way to the Senate chamber, and at noon and on the east portico, in the presence of an immense assemblage of his fellow-citizens, was sworn into office by John Marshall, Chief-Justice of the United States. "The scene," says a spectator, "was a most beautiful and inspiring spectacle. The building, noble in its size, with its richly sculptured capitals and cornices, and the fine group in the pediment; the massy columns (one for each State in the Union); the far-spreading wings and terraces; the grounds and gates, with the crowd of carriages without; the line of soldiers in the park; the towering flight of steps, covered with members of Congress, officers of the army, foreign ministers, ladies dressed in all the varying hues of fashion; the President; the crowd of heads and the innumerable eyes bent on one spot, all taken together presented to the outward eyes an assemblage of images never to be forgotten."

The customary address occupied but a few minutes in delivery, and ranks with the briefest in our history. The new President pledged himself to keep peace and cultivate friendship with foreign nations; administer the laws with a strict regard to the limitations put on the Executive powers; respect the rights of the States, and not confound the powers they had reserved with those they had granted to the Confederacy; pursue a just and liberal policy toward the Indians; and never forget what the recent demonstration of public sentiment had inscribed on the list of Executive duties in characters too legible to be overlooked—the task of reform. He would seek to correct the abuses that had brought the patronage of the Government into conflict with freedom of elections, disturbed the rightful course of appointments, and placed power in unfaithful or unfit hands.

The speech delivered, a cable that had been stretched across the steps was torn away, and with a wild shout the crowd surged up to grasp the hand of the people's President. It was with difficulty that Jackson could make his way to a horse, mount it, and, preceded, surrounded, and followed by a dense mass of human beings, start for the White House. One who was present declares that "the President was literally pursued by a motely concourse of people, riding, running helter-skelter, striving who should first gain admittance into the Executive mansion, where it was understood that refreshments were to be distributed." Once at the White House, the President found it in the possession of a disorderly mob, which swept across the grounds and into the rooms, where all semblance of order was abandoned. To serve the people with cakes and ices was impossible, and in the unseemly scramble china and glass were broken. In the hope of lessening the crush, punch was carried out in tubs and buckets to those still in the grounds. But as those without could not get in, so those within could not get out, and Jackson, despite the efforts of his friends, was pushed through the audience room, was pressed against the wall and well-nigh crushed before those near had time to link arms and make a barrier about him. "It was then," says our witness, "that the windows were thrown open, and the living torrent found an outlet. It was the people's day, the people's President, and the people would rule."

HENRY WILSON

(1812-1875)

It was next to impossible for historians in the nineteenth century to write dispassionately about the great sectional conflict culminating in the Civil War. The acid of conflict was etched so deeply into their minds that much of the polemic spilled into their writing, and has been splashed anew across most of the pages that have been written since. As Kenneth M. Stampp, an historian of the Civil War, has pointed out, two schools of historical writing on the war have developed, one northern and the other southern. The northern has tended to perpetuate the interpretations of men like Henry Wilson, the southern that of its John C. Calhouns and Jefferson Davises.

Wilson was a vigorous participant in the anti-slavery cause about which he wrote so trenchantly. Born in 1812 into a poor family, he was indentured from the age of 10 until he was 21 to a New Hampshire farmer. Later he learned cobbling and became a successful shoe manufacturer before turning to politics. He was almost entirely self-taught. On a trip to Washington he first encountered slavery, and was so revolted that he returned to New England "with the unalterable resolution to give all that I had, and all that I hope to have, of power, to the cause of emancipation in America." When he entered the United States Senate in 1855, his maiden speech was a call for the repeal of the Fugitive Slave Act. During Reconstruction, his zeal undiminished, he wrote his History of the Rise and Fall of the Slave Power in America, *published in 1872-1877. He died while serving as Vice President of the United States during the second Grant administration.*

The Anti-Slavery Cause

NOTHING AFFORDS MORE STRIKING EVIDENCE OF THE GRAVITY AND difficulties of the anti-slavery struggle than the conflicting opinions and plans of the honest and earnest men engaged in it. It was fashionable to stigmatize them as ultra, pragmatic, and angular, and to hold up their differences and divisions as a foil and shield against their arguments and appeals. Thousands consoled and defended themselves in their inaction because antislavery men were not agreed among themselves. But the facts were that some of the ablest, most honest, practical, and sagacious men of the nation were engaged in that struggle; and their differences of views and plans arose not so much from their infirmities as from the greatness and gravity of the problem they attempted to solve, and the blind and inextricable labyrinth of difficulties into which the compromises of the Constitution, the concessions of the fathers, the persistent policy of the government, and the constant aggressions of the Slave Power, had involved the nation. Slavery had inwrought itself into every department of society, political and commercial, social and religious. It had polluted everything it touched, and poisoned the very fountains of the nation's life. Men could turn in no direction without encountering its pestiferous presence, its malignant and all-grasping power. Even in the broad light of this day of freedom, now that the whole system has been swept away, with all the revelations which have been made, he must be a bold man who presumes to say exactly what they should and should not have done. How much less could they, in the dark night of slavery, in deadly conflict with the Power itself, never more arrogant and dominating, decide with perfect accuracy what to say or what to do. To err under such circumstances was not only human, but evidently no matter of surprise.

The most radical difference was that which separated those who rejected from those who adopted the principle of political action. The former were generally styled the "old organization," or Garrisonian Abolitionists; the latter embraced the Liberty party and those antislavery men who still adhered to the Whig and Democratic parties.

Having adopted the doctrine of "no union with slaveholders" as the

From Wilson, *History of the Rise and Fall of the Slave Power in America* (2 vols., 1872-1877), ch. 9, 25, 33, 45.

fundamental idea, the corner-stone of their policy and plans, the Garri-
sonians of that period directed their teachings, their arguments and appeals, to the establishment of the necessity and the inculcation of the duty
of disunion. Believing, in the language of Edmund Quincy, the Union to be
a "confederacy of crime," that "the experiment of a great nation with
popular institutions had signally failed," that the Republic was "not a
model, but a warning to the nations," that "the hopes of the yearning
ages had been mournfully defeated" through "the disturbing element of
slavery"; believing, too, that such had become the ascendency of the
system that it compelled "the entire people to be slaveholders or slaves";
believing also that "the only exodus for the slave from his bondage, the only
redemption of ourselves from our guilty participation in it, lies over the ruin
of the American state and the American church,"—they proclaimed it to
be their "unalterable purpose and determination to live and labor for a
dissolution of the present Union by all lawful and just though bloodless and
pacific means, and for the formation of a new republic, that shall be
such not in name only, but in full, living reality and truth."

But to destroy such a system as slavery, thus completely interwoven with
everything in church and state, permeating the mass and diffusing itself
through the very atmosphere of public and private life, involved the breaking up of institutions and associations hallowed by time and the most
tender memories. In attaining the great good sought there could not but
be much incidental evil; in rooting up the tares there was manifest danger
of injury to the wheat. But these consequences and conditions this class
of reformers promptly accepted, and, with an unsparing iconoclasm, they
dashed to the ground whatever idols of popular faith interfered with the
people's acceptance of the doctrines they deemed of paramount importance.
Abjuring party organizations, coming out from the churches, and con-
demning with unsparing censure whatever in their esteem gave countenance
and encouragement to slavery, they necessarily assumed an attitude of
antagonism to those they so severely condemned, and uttered many sentiments that grated harshly on the popular ear. But, while thus obnoxious
to the charge of indifference to the passions, prejudices, and even the
principles, of the dominant classes of society, and committed, as many
thought, to theories more abstract than practical, it was always seen that
to the sigh of the individual bondman their ear was ever attent, and that
for the help of the poor and trembling fugitive their hand was ever open
and generous.

From the annexation of Texas, in 1845, to the enactment of the Fugitive
Slave Law, in 1850, they pursued with a good deal of vigor this line of
policy. Discarding religious and political organizations, the ballot, and all
the enginery of its legitimate and effective use, they denied themselves many
of the ordinary methods of reaching the popular mind, and relied mainly on
the use of the press, the popular convention, and other meetings of the

people. They not only held such convocations by special appointment at various points at the North, but they always observed the anniversaries of national independence and of West India emancipation as days specially appropriate to their mission to the American people. To the annual meetings of the American, New England, and the several State societies were added fairs, held for the twofold purpose of putting funds into their exchequer and of bringing their ideas before the people. In carrying forward this work, Garrison, Phillips, Quincy, Douglass, Wright, Foster, Burleigh, and Pillsbury were among the recognized leaders and advocates. Theodore Parker and Ralph Waldo Emerson, though not distinctively belonging to their organization, largely sympathized with their efforts, and were occasionally welcomed to their platform. In the same work they were assisted by the pens and voices of several women. Among them were Mrs. Child, Mrs. Chapman, Lucretia Mott, Mrs. Abby Kelly Foster, and Lucy Stone. During a portion of these years, too, Garrison, Douglass, Henry C. Wright, and James Buffum were in Europe, and presented the cause to the British public.

But the men who agreed in the principle of political action were not always in full accord as to the best methods of applying that principle. Exercising for themselves that freedom of thought and speech which they claimed for others, as they considered the great subject, with its really inextricable and insurmountable difficulties, involving principles at once recondite and infinitely delicate and perplexing in their application and adjustment to the fearful problems before them, they often failed to see eye to eye. They differed not only in their estimate of fundamental principles, but frequently in their proposed modes of action. Some had accepted the doctrine of the unconstitutionality of slavery, and several able arguments were prepared in defence of that position. Others held that it was a local system, that its extension was to be resisted, its power overcome, and itself extirpated, under the Constitution and through constitutional modes of action. These diversities of opinion elicited no little feeling, and led to divisions and sometimes to mutual denunciations.

In June, 1845, a State convention was held at Port Byron, in New York. An address was presented, not only setting forth the unconstitutionality of slavery, but, perhaps in deference to the very general criticism that Abolitionists were men of "one idea," stating and elaborating somewhat fully the different objects government should have in view, and some of the more prominent measures that should receive its attention and support. This address, though read and printed, was not adopted. Many, however, of the Liberty party accepted its sentiments, and held a convention in June, 1847, at Macedon, in the same State. The convention nominated Gerrit Smith for President and Elihu Burritt for the Vice-Presidency, separated from the party, took the name of Liberty League, and issued an address to the people.

In October of the same year a national convention of the Liberty party was held at Buffalo. Several members of the Liberty League attended, and sought the indorsement of the convention for the candidates they had just put in nomination, but without success; John P. Hale of New Hampshire and Leicester King of Ohio receiving the nomination. This action was not taken without opposition, though the dissatisfaction was mostly confined to the State of New York. It was regarded as an abandonment of principle to go outside for a candidate, and to select one who had never identified himself or acted with the party; and Chase, Matthews, Lewis, Leavitt, and Dr. Bailey were severely censured for their course.

But this controversy between the two wings of the Liberty party, which resulted in the formation of the Liberty League, militated in no degree against either the earnestness or the honesty of the men who took opposite sides on the questions at issue. It only indicated the different methods suggested to different minds in their endeavor to solve a most difficult, not to say an insoluble problem. Neither hit upon the plan that actually secured the desired result, or that even gave promise of at least immediate success. Nothing now appears why slavery would not to-day be lording it over the land with increasing vigor, had not the South in its madness appealed to arms, and cut with its own sword the Gordian knot which others were vainly attempting to untie.

As distinguished from the other wing, it may be said that the members of the Liberty League were less practical, more disposed to adhere to theories, and more fearful of sacrificing principle to policy. Like the members of the "old organization" and the French *doctrinaires,* they seemed to have more confidence in the power of abstract right, and less in the doctrine of expediency. They calculated largely on the power of truth, and on the belief that God is the "majority." Their watchword was: "Duty is ours, results are God's."

On the other side, the men who advised and aided in putting Mr. Hale in nomination had less faith in the policy, safety, or duty of simply adhering to the proclamation of abstract ideas, however correct or forcibly expressed. They saw that, in the presence and in spite of all the arguments, appeals, and fierce invectives of the able and eloquent writers and orators of either the "old organization" or of the Liberty League, the Slave Power was marching on, with relentless purpose and increasing audacity, from victory to victory, until it appeared that, unless it could be checked, Mr. Calhoun's theory would be reduced to practice and the Constitution would carry slavery wherever it went, and slavery would be no longer sectional, but national. Texas had been annexed, vast territory had been acquired, and the question was now upon them: "Shall this territory be free or slave?" And their past bitter experience had shown that something more than appeals to reason, conscience, and the plighted faith of the fathers was necessary to prevent the final consummation for which all these previous steps had been taken. In settling that question they saw that votes were more potent than words; that an organized and growing party would prove more efficient than any amount of protest and earnest entreaty. To strengthen this purpose, such men as Chase, Leavitt, Whittier, William Jackson, and Dr. Bailey saw that there were hundreds of thousands, in both the Whig and Democratic parties, who were deeply dissatisfied with the state of affairs and the immediate prospect before them, and were anxiously looking for some practical scheme, some common ground on which they could make a stand in resistance to these aggressions. They hoped much, too, from such men as Dix, Hale, Niles, King, and Wilmot among the Democrats; Giddings, Palfrey, Seward, Mann, and Root among the Whigs; much from the Barnburners in New York and the "conscience" Whigs in Massachusetts. They judged, and the event has proved that they judged wisely, that by narrowing the platform, even if it did not contain all that the most advanced Abolitionists desired, if such men and their followers could be drawn from the Whig and Democratic parties, and be thus arrayed in a compact and vigorous organization against the Slave Power, there would be great gain. Though they could not exactly forecast the end of such a movement, they felt that it was a step in the right direction, and that, when taken, it would disclose still further the path of duty and place them in a position to go forward therein.

But the Liberty League and dissatisfied members of the Liberty party were not idle. Meeting in convention at Auburn in January, 1848, they called a national convention to meet in Buffalo in June. John Curtis of Ohio presided, and Gerrit Smith was chairman of the Committee on the Address and Resolutions. The committee reported two addresses,—one to the colored people of the free States and one to the people of the United States. In them they censured severely the action of the Liberty party for what they denounced as recreancy to the principles of the party. The colored people were told that it was the "perfection of treachery to the slave" to vote for a slaveholder, or for one who thinks that a slaveholder is fit for civil office; that it was the religious indorsement of slavery that kept it in countenance; and that it was "better, infinitely better for your poor, lashed, bleeding, and chained brothers and sisters that you should never see the inside of a church nor the inside of a Bible, than that you should by your pro-slavery connections sanctify their enslavement."

Speeches of great earnestness and directness were made by Beriah Green, Frederick Douglass, Gerrit Smith, Henry Highland Garnett, Elizur Wright, and George Bradburn. Mr. Green maintained that when the nation indorses slavery "the most marked inconsistencies creep out of the same lips, the flattest contradictions fall from the same tongues." Civil governments, he said, should be the reflection from the throne of God. To assert the claims of justice, to define and defend rights, to cherish and express a world-embracing philanthropy, to promote the general welfare, to afford counsel and protection, are "the appropriate objects of civil government." "God gave civil government," remarked Mr. Smith, "I had wellnigh said, to be on terms of companionship with the poor. Certain it is that he gave it chiefly for the purpose of protecting the rights of those who are too poor, ignorant, and weak to protect themselves." With their definition of civil government and the purposes for which it was instituted, and with their knowledge of what slavery was, such indorsement could not but seem not only unconstitutional, but inconsistent with and subversive of government itself. Antislavery men," said Mr. Smith, "should identify themselves with the slave, and be willing to be hated and despised. They should not be ashamed to do what slaveholders call slave-stealing. It was not "vulgar," he contended, "low, or mean," to help slaves to escape from the clutches of their oppressor. "As I live and as God lives," he continued, "there is not on earth a more honorable employment. There is not in all the world a more honorable tombstone than that on which the slaveholder would inscribe, 'Here lies a slave-stealer.' "

The convention, much against his own avowed wishes, nominated Mr. Smith for the Presidency. Mr. Burritt having declined the nomination of the Liberty League for the Vice-Presidency, C. C. Foot of Michigan was selected as the candidate.

* * *

The passage of the Fugitive Slave Act was the signal for a general commotion throughout the land. It involved both a wrong and a peril that menaced, if they did not actually reach, every indviidual in the Republic. Its uplifted hand was directed first against the fugitives, of whom it was estimated that there were more than twenty thousand in the free States. Nor was the full force of the blow expended on them alone; for beside them there were large numbers of free persons with whom these fugitives had intermarried, and to whom they were joined in the various relations of social and religious life. Its arbitrary and summary provisions, in the hands of base and unscrupulous men, impelled by greed of gain and love of revenge, struck terror upon the whole colored population and their sympathizing friends. These were base and brutal men at hand, willing to become agents of slaveholders in both following those recently escaped and in ferreting out those who had for a longer time eluded the search of the pursuer. Nor were they slow to act.

Only eight days after the passage of the law, one of these agents appeared in New York, armed with the power of attorney from Mary Brown of Baltimore, and a certified copy of the act itself, cut from a common newspaper, in search of James Hamlet, a husband and father, a member of the Methodist Church, and resident in the city some three years. He was seized while at work, hurried into a retired room, tried in hot haste, delivered to the agent, handcuffed, forced into a carriage, and taken by the son of the marshal to Baltimore and lodged in the prison of the notorious Hope H. Slatter; his wife and children being denied the poor satisfaction of bidding him farewell. A few days afterward another similar scene was enacted in Philadelphia. . . .

*   *   *

On Tuesday morning, the 23d of May, 1854, intelligence was flashed over the country that the House of Representatives had passed, late in the hours of the preceding night, the bill for the repeal of the Missouri prohibition of slavery. At a time, then, when the country was profoundly agitated, and all hope of defeating that obnoxious measure had died, and the people, especially of New England, were sad and indignant, Charles F. Suttle, a Virginia slaveholder, applied to Edward G. Loring of Boston for a warrant, under the Fugitive Slave Act, for the seizure of Anthony Burns. A warrant was granted the next day by this judge of probate and United States commissioner. On the evening of that day, Burns was arrested on a false pretext, taken to the Court House, and kept by the marshal under an armed guard. On the morning of the 25th, he was brought before the commissioner. Seth J. Thomas and Edward G. Parker appeared for the claimant. Wendell Phillips and Theodore Parker, hearing of the arrest, procured admittance into the Court House with no little difficulty. Mr. Parker states that he spoke with Burns, who "sat in the dock, ironed, between two of the marshal's guards." Richard H. Dana, Jr., and Charles M. Ellis, interposed, —not as counsel, but simply as *amici curiæ,* friends of the court,—protested against the unseemly haste of the proceedings, asked that counsel might be assigned to Burns, and begged for an adjournment of the examination. After repeated protests and requests, the commissioner adjourned the hearing until the morning of the 27th.

The intelligence of this arrest created widespread and intense excitement. Application was made and readily granted for the use of Faneuil Hall, in which to give expression to the public feeling. On the afternoon of the 26th, a meeting was held in Meionaon Hall. Fiery and excited speeches and all sorts of motions were made. Many were in favor of a night attack upon the Court House, for the rescue of the alleged fugitive. Albert G. Browne, Jr., who had been one of the councillors in Governor Boutwell's administration, an earnest, honest, impulsive, and bold man, deprecated this mode of action, and proposed to be one of forty men to go, under the lead of Dr. S. G. Howe, to the marshal in broad daylight, demand the unconditional release of Burns, and, if the demand was not complied with, rescue him at all hazards; but no definite action was taken.

On the evening of the 26th, an immense meeting was held in Faneuil Hall. It was called to order by Samuel E. Sewall, and presided over by George R. Russell, who said, on taking the chair: "We have made compromises until we find that compromise is concession and concession is degradation." Samuel G. Howe presented resolutions declaring that "God wills that all men should be free, and we will as God wills," and that "no man's freedom is safe unless all men are free." Wendell Phillips was "against squatter sovereignty in Nebraska, and kidnappers' sovereignty in Boston." He said that the question was whether or not Virginia should conquer Massachusetts. "If that man leaves Boston," he said, "Massachusetts is a conquered State." Francis W. Bird saw no remedy for the wrongs and outrages perpetrated upon them but "fight"; and he bitterly denounced the tools of the Slave Power and the press of Boston. John L. Swift said that they had been called cowards and the sons of cowards, and they should prove themselves to be such if they allowed Anthony Burns to be taken back to bondage. "When we go," he said, "from this Cradle of Liberty, let us go to the Tomb of Liberty, the Court House. I hope to witness in his release the resurrection of liberty." Theodore Parker said that they were the "vassals of Virginia; she reaches her arms over the graves of our mothers, and kidnaps men in the city of the Puritans." "There was once a Boston," he said, "but now it is the Northern suburb of Alexandria." The slave law, he said, was declared to be a "finality"; but there was another law which was a finality, and that law "is in your hands and your arms." He thought that if they resolutely declared that this man should not go out of Boston "without shooting a gun, then he won't go back." He proposed that they should meet at Court Square the next morning, put the vote, and declared it carried.

But there were cries in favor of going that night to the Court House and the Revere House, and there was a report that a crowd of colored men and others had gathered in Court Square, and were making demonstrations upon the building. Mr. Swift, who had been in consultation with Mr. Higginson, Seth Webb, Jr., and others that were in favor of an immediate attempt at rescue, or were apprehensive that it could not be prevented, hastened to Faneuil Hall for help. There were cries among those near the doors that the Court House was attacked, and suggestive calls for an adjournment of the meeting to the scene of the apprehended assault. Mr. Phillips then made an impassioned appeal against the proposition to go to the Revere House, to attempt, he said, "the impossible feat of insulting a slave-hunter," or of assaulting the Court House that night. He eloquently pleaded for postponement till the morrow. The zeal, he said, which would not hold out till morning, "would never free a slave." Nevertheless, the meeting hastily adjourned, and some hastened to the Court House, and found that an assault had been made on the western door, which, though strongly guarded, had been battered in by a piece of heavy timber. Through the opening thus made, a negro gained for a few moments an entrance, though he was terribly beaten by those on guard. T. W. Higginson, Seth Webb, Jr., and Lewis Hayden, struggled to enter, but failed. James Batchelder, a Boston truckman who had been appointed one of the marshal's guard, was killed. The crowd fell back, and Higginson and others who were struggling at the entrance, finding themselves unsupported, besought that they should not be deserted. A. Bronson Alcott of Concord, the thoughtful student of Plato, the associate and friend of Emerson, entered the door of the Court House, and there stood for a few moments serenely amid the clubs, axes, pistols, and other implements of war.

In explanation of the failure of this attempt to rescue Burns, it ought to be stated that at a private meeting, that afternoon, of Howe, Parker, Higginson, Phillips, and others, it had been deliberately decided that no attempt at rescue should be made that evening. With such a decision the meeting broke up about six o'clock; its members pledged to each other to prevent the Faneuil Hall meeting from being hurried into any abortive attempt at rescue. This explains the tenor of the speeches of Phillips and Parker. But during that Faneuil Hall meeting Mr. Higginson changed his mind, and obtained the promise of a few men, in the anteroom, to aid him in a rescue. Accordingly he started for the Court House, leaving a messenger to inform his friends on the platform and ask them to bring the meeting to the scene of action. This message was never delivered. Hence, when the cries were heard round the doors, they were supposed to be mere efforts to break up the meeting. Very few obeyed them; and these few, Dr. Howe among them, though making all haste, did not reach the Court House till after Mr. Higginson's attempt had ended. Indeed, of the score who had promised him their aid, very few made their appearance.

The attempt at rescue was not only a failure in itself, but it seriously complicated subsequent efforts. "It was," wrote Edmund Quincy, "a gallant and generous attempt, but ill-advised and injudicious, under the circumstances"; for it afforded just what the slave-hunter and his obsequious servitors desired, a good excuse for summoning the military to their aid, which they at once proceeded to do, by calling the marines from the Navy Yard, soldiers from Fort Independence, and the militia of Boston. Arrests were made by the Boston police. Among those arrested was Albert G. Browne, Jr., afterward Secretary to Governor Andrew and Clerk of the Supreme Court of Massachusetts. He was attempting to rescue Mr. Higginson, who had been wounded in the assault, and was in danger of falling into the hands of the officials.

The excitement produced by these occurrences not only extended outside the limits of the city, so that large numbers flocked from the surrounding towns to witness the unwonted scenes that were transpiring in its streets, but it was largely increased by several public meetings that were held during those eventful days. The New England Anti-Slavery Society held its annual meeting; the Free Soil State Convention also met, and, it being "anniversary week," there was a large number of clergymen in the city, at whose meetings frequent mention was made of the subject. On the day preceding the rendition there was a special meeting of ministers to take into consideration the general subject thus forcibly brought to their notice. A committee was appointed to confer with others, and stirring speeches were made by Lyman and Edward Beecher, Professor Stowe, Samuel Wolcott, and others.

It was claimed that Burns, on the night of his arrest, had made fatal admissions. But he was kept closely guarded, and no one was allowed to see or speak with him. The next day, therefore, after the hearing had been postponed, Wendell Phillips went to the commissioner for an order directing the marshal to allow him to see the prisoner. After giving the order the commissioner, who had heard only one witness, said: "Mr. Phillips, the case is so clear that I do not think you will be justified in placing any obstacle in the way of this man's going, as he probably will"; and the result proved the correctness of his anticipation, premature and questionable as it may have been. At the trial, Burns was ably defended by Mr. Dana and Mr. Ellis. At the close of the trial, Mr. Dana congratulated the court, the officers of the United States, and all concerned in the case, that the strange scenes they had witnessed were about to close. Referring to the brutal and infamous character of the marshal's special guard of more than one hundred men, taken mostly from the dens of vice, and whom the Boston "Atlas" denounced as the "dregs of society," "blacklegs and thieves," he said, that while violence and outrage reigned at and near the scenes of the trial and rendition, peace prevailed in other parts of the city. "The people," he said, "have not felt it necessary to lock their doors at night, the brothels are tenanted only by women; fighting dogs and racing horses have been unemployed, and Ann St. and its alleys and cellars show signs of a coming millennium." Of course this fitting characterization gave offence, and one of the guard waylaid and assaulted Mr. Dana on his return to his home in company with Mr. Burlingame. But the ruffian was afterward detected, convicted, and imprisoned under circumstances presenting and extraordinary story of "the involutions of crime and of poetic justice." Mr. Dana, in closing his plea, reminded Commissioner Loring that he was about to do an act which was to take its place in the history of America. "May your judgment," he said, "be for liberty, and not for slavery; for happiness, and not for wretchedness; for hope, and not for despair; and may the blessing of him that is ready to perish come upon you!" But the commissioner, who in this case certainly failed to give evidence that he "possessed the instincts of freedom and humanity," surrendered the unfortunate and unprotected fugitive to his claimant and to the horrors of recapture.

When this decision was made, Phillips, Parker, Dana, Ellis, and a few other anti-slavery men, took leave of Burns, whose tears expressed both his gratitude and sorrow. As soon as the rendition had been made, John C. Park draped his office in mourning. Some other lawyers followed his example. Six flags draped in mourning were flung from the Commonwealth building, and the venerable merchant Samuel May hung out from his store the flag, union down; Joseph R. Hayes, a Boston police officer, resigned his office rather than engage in the work of rendition.

Guarded by a large armed police and military force, Burns was taken through masses of excited and indignant citizens, and placed on board the revenue cutter Morris, ordered by President Pierce to take him to Virginia. A spectacle so sad and humiliating could not but excite feelings of indignation and deepen the popular abhorrence of a law which demanded and rendered possible such a deed. There can be no doubt that the rendition of Anthony Burns, with all the attendant circumstances, the superserviceable zeal of the Boston officials, and the unseemly alacrity of the President in ordering a national vessel to bear a single friendless man, of a proscribed race, back to that servitude from which he had so bravely but vainly striven to escape, largely contributed, in New England at least, to the overthrow of the politicians and parties that upheld the Slave Power.

When the procession, after passing through a continuous storm of contemptuous outcries and hisses, reached the wharf, Burns walked forward, surrounded by his guard and its piece of artillery, and went on board the vessel in waiting to bear him back to his prison-house of woe. Just at the moment when a body of resolute anti-slavery men, who had followed him to the wharf, had taken a last and sorrowful look of one whom they had vainly tried to save from the sad fate before him, the Rev. Daniel Foster,— who volunteered early in the war, became an officer, and fell fighting for his country,—with eyes and hands upturned, said in a voice sad and solemn: "Let us pray." "Instantly, as by a common impulse," says Dr. Henry I. Bowditch, who was present, "entire silence came over us, and this stranger poured forth a prayer that sunk deep into our hearts. He called on God, as our helper and as the giver of peace, to look upon us in our distress. He prayed for the poor slave and for the recreant republic. It is impossible to give any just idea of the effect produced upon us. Under the Divine influence, as I believe it to have been, one at least gained exceeding peace, and a determination that no slave-hunter should tread quietly the soil of Massachusetts." . . .

* * *

The raid on Harper's Ferry and its failure, the capture, trial, conviction, and execution of John Brown and his followers, startled and profoundly stirred the nation. The South was excited, furious, and unanimous. The North was hardly less excited, but regretful and divided. Anti-slavery men generally deplored and condemned the invasion, though they admired the stern devotion to principle and the heroism displayed therein, sympathized with its actors in their misfortunes, and mourned over its tragic results. Many, however, who admired and pitied the heroic old man and his hardly less heroic followers, felt that such a revolutionary movement compromised legitimate reforms and put in peril rightful opposition to slavery. Nor were they mistaken; for, at once and everywhere, pro-slavery men and presses sought to fix the odium of this lawless act upon anti-slavery organizations, and especially upon the Republican party. Although they signally failed in this, they did, for a time, greatly intensify the popular feeling against anti-slavery men and anti-slavery measures.

John Brown was a Puritan, and a lineal descendant of the Pilgrims. He inherited the spirit as well as the blood of his ancestry. Born in Connecticut, in the year 1800, he was taken by his father, at the age of five years, to the Western Reserve. Living in straitened circumstances in that pioneer home, he early exhibited those marked developments of character which distinguished him in after life. He was strictly conscientious and sternly religious. The Bible and the experimental writings of such men as Baxter and Bunyan were the chosen companions of his leisure hours. Principle and a nice and exacting sense of justice were the regal elements of his character, and unselfishness the resplendent virtue of his strange career. To relieve suffering, and to vindicate the rights of the injured and oppressed, were the leading objects of his life.

Recognizing no rightful claim of the master to his slave, the Underground Railroad early and ever found in him a practical and most efficient agent. Such relief of the oppressed, however, he deemed individual and of small account, and he looked for something more nearly adequate to the work to be accomplished. Despairing of a peaceful solution of the issue, the idea entered his mind that "perhaps a forcible separation of the connection between the slave and his master was necessary to educate the blacks for self-government." But, in common with his countrymen, he underestimated the strength and tenacity of the Slave Power, and underrated the difficulties in the way of the slave's redemption. Evidently, too, his wish was father to the thought, as he interpreted the probable designs of Providence towards removing the fearful evil. His reply, to one who informed him he had been marked by the Missourians for death, that "the angel of the Lord will camp round about me," revealed the secret conviction that his destiny was linked with that of the slave, and that he was a chosen instrument of the Lord to work out his deliverance. This thought unquestionably affords a key to his life, and explains many things which might otherwise seem inexplicable.

With such convictions, it is not strange that such a man should be drawn to Kansas by the terrible scenes there enacted, and that he should have taken a prominent part in that great struggle; though the immediate cause of his going there was a request for arms from his four sons, who had gone there to make for themselves homes. He hoped, too, to aid the struggling freemen there to rescue that fair territory from the polluting touch of slavery. Not to make for himself a home, but to aid others to build for coming generations, was this courageous, self-forgetful, and future martyr willing to encounter the hardships and to brave the dangers which were involved in such a purpose.

But he felt that his work, that for which he believed he was specially called of God, that over which his soul had brooded for nearly a generation, was not thus to be accomplished. He had done something, but it was only individual and fragmentary. He would relieve an enslaved race, and destroy the system that was crushing it. Combination and conference were needed, and early in the spring of 1858 he sent out a call from Chatham, Canada, for "a very quiet convention at this place" of the "true friends of freedom." Such a meeting was held; and one of its acts was the adoption of a paper, drafted by him, entitled "Provisional Constitution and Ordinances for the People of the United States." In this paper, designed to give shape and direction to the movement, it was provided that the offices of president and commander-in-chief should be held by different persons. Brown was elected commander-in-chief, Richard Realf was chosen secretary of state, and J. H. Kagi was made secretary of war.

There is much that is strange and inexplicable in all this; and it will ever remain a mystery, whatever explanations may be made, how sane men could hope to establish such an organization, with a constitution setting forth the three departments of government, legislative, judicial, and executive, defining crimes and their penalties, including death even, and yet affirm, as it is affirmed in the forty-sixth of the forty-eight articles, that "the foregoing articles shall not be construed so as in any way to encourage the overthrow of any State government or of the general government of the United States, and we look to no dissolution of the Union, but simply to amendment and repeal; and our flag shall be the same that our fathers fought under in the Revolution."

In the autumn of 1857 Brown began to organize a small body of men. For the purpose of giving them military instruction he employed Colonel Hugh Forbes, an English adventurer, who had fought with Garibaldi. The two, however, failed to see alike. The stern Puritan, who knew far more of Gideon than of Napoleon, and who looked upon war mainly in its providential aspects, had little in common with the mere adventurer, without convictions, and who looked upon war as a matter of science and a wise use of brute forces. They disagreed and separated. Immediately Forbes wrote letters to Dr. Samuel G. Howe and Frank B. Sanborn of Massachusetts, complaining that Brown had not fulfilled his promises.

In January, 1858, Brown left Kansas and went to the home of Frederick Douglass in Rochester, New York, where he wrote his plan of government. From this place he wrote to Theodore Parker, Mr. Sanborn, George L. Stearns, and T. Wentworth Higginson, asking them to aid him by raising a small sum of money to carry out "an important measure, in which the world had a deep interest." In these and other letters he spoke of important things he was intending to do, but gave no definite explanations. He wrote also to Sanborn, Stearns, and Howe, and requested them to meet him at the home of a friend in Central New York. Sanborn was, however, the only one to respond, reaching the place on the 22d of February. Here he met Brown and his own classmate, Edwin Morton, a native of Massachusetts, then a member of Gerrit Smith's family, afterward a lawyer of Boston. To this little company Brown explained his proposed constitution, indicated his plans, and specified the middle of May as the time to commence operations. For the purposes named he desired them to aid him by furnishing a thousand dollars. Recognizing the character, magnitude, and difficulties of his scheme, and the obvious inadequacy of the means, even what was asked for, to the end proposed, they endeavored to dissuade him from his purpose, or, at least, besought him to defer his attempt; but he was inflexible.

It was manifestly a moment and a case, like many that were constantly arising during the dreary reign of the Slave Power, when the best men were in a position where there seemed at least a conflict of duties,—where, the more conscientious a man was the greater the difficulty in deciding,— and where, whatever the decision, there was at least some apparent infringement of admitted obligations. They listened late into the night and during the following day; and then, though still unconvinced by his arguments, they yielded to the potent and personal influence of the man. One well acquainted with the circumstances of that conference thus writes in the "Atlantic Monthly" of 1873: "As the sun was setting over the snowy hills of the region where they met, the Massachusetts delegate walked for an hour with the principal person in that little council of war. The elder of the two, of equal age with Brown and for many years a devoted abolitionist, said: 'You see how it is; our old friend has made up his mind to this course of action, and cannot be turned from it. We cannot give him up to die alone; we must stand by him. I will raise so many hundred dollars for him; you must lay the case before your friends in Massachusetts, and see if they will do the same.' "

This he did, and at the suggestion of Theodore Parker Brown visited Boston in March. Howe, Sanborn, Stearns, and Higginson consulted with him. To them he communicated his proposed invasion of Virginia, though he spoke of his purpose in regard to Harper's Ferry only to Mr. Sanborn. A secret committee consisting of these gentlemen was formed to raise the necessary means. This was speedily accomplished; and it was decided to strike the first blow in the latter part of May. Arriving in Chatham, Canada, on the last of April, he learned that Forbes was in Washington, threatening to disclose his plans to Republican members and the government, unless, as he insisted in letters, written in April and May, to Howe and Sanborn, that Brown should be dismissed as leader, and himself installed in his place. These letters being submitted to the secret committee, it was finally agreed, Higginson dissenting, that the attack should be deferred. But Brown had determined, notwithstanding these threats of Forbes, to go forward.

In May, Forbes communicated to Dr. Bailey of the "National Era," and to Senators Seward, Hale, and Wilson, that arms which had been furnished by the Massachusetts Kansas committee had passed into the hands of Brown, who was intending to use them for unlawful purposes. Alarmed at this information, though general and not specific, Mr. Wilson, at the request of Dr. Bailey and Mr. Seward, wrote to Dr. Howe on the 9th of May, disclosing this information, suggesting that such use of the arms would inure to the disadvantage of those who had contributed them for the defence of Kansas, and pressing upon him the importance of immediately recovering them. This letter was laid before the secret committee, and forwarded at once to Brown in Canada. "This awkward complication," says the writer in the "Atlantic," "seems to have decided Dr. Howe in favor of postponing the attack, and both he and Mr. Stearns, as members of the Kansas committee, wrote Brown that the arms must not be used for the present, except for the defence of Kansas. The latter saw that nothing could then be done, and yielded, though with reluctance, to the postponement."

A meeting of the secret committee was held at the Revere House, Boston, on the 24th of May. It was agreed that the assault should be deferred till the spring of 1859; that two or three thousand dollars should be raised for Brown's assistance; and that the rifles, which were the real property of Mr. Stearns, should be transferred to him, and thus the Kansas committee should be relieved of all responsibility. He visited Boston the following week, saw the secret committee, received the custody of the arms from Stearns and five hundred dollars. But, as nothing could be done for the furtherance of his Virginia scheme, he accepted the committee's suggestion that he should return immediately to Kansas, and he at once departed to aid the free State settlers there.

While untiring in these efforts, he was, as ever, intent on aiding the slave in his attempt to escape. Learning that a family of slaves, just beyond the border, were to be sold for Texas, he planned and effected their escape with that of five others. This occasioned great excitement, and the governor of Missouri offered a reward of three thousand dollars for his arrest, which was increased by the addition of two hundred and fifty dollars by President Buchanan. This, with the public disavowal by the free State men of all sympathy with his course, induced him to leave the Territory, though hotly pursued by his enemies. With a dusky retinue of eleven bondmen, he set forth on his long, uncertain, but finally successful journey for freedom for them and safety for himself.

In May, 1859, Brown visited Boston to confer again with the secret committee, to mature plans, and to make arrangements for future action. On the 28th he dined at the Parker House with the "Bird Club," in company with two or three members of the secret committee. While at the dinner-table he sat next to Mr. Wilson, who had never seen him before. Being in possession of the letter of the latter to Dr. Howe, which had arrested his expedition, he said: "Senator Wilson, I understand you do not approve my course." To this remark Mr. Wilson replied: "I am opposed to all violations of law, and to violence, believing that they lay a burden on the anti-slavery cause." To this he responded with some positiveness and no little emphasis: "I do not agree with you, sir." He left Boston in June, having received from the secret committee some two thousand dollars, more than half of which, says the "Atlantic" writer, was the gift of George L. Stearns, "who must have furnished the old hero, first and last, more than ten thousand dollars in money and arms." This committee furnished John Brown about four thousand dollars, and nearly twice that amount in arms; most of it given with knowledge of the real object for which it was furnished.

Soon after leaving Boston, Brown went to the Kennedy farm on the Maryland side of the Potomac, five miles from Harper's Ferry, which he had rented, and which he made his rendezvous. During the summer and early autumn recruits came first to Chambersburg, Pennsylvania, and thence to this farm. Of the fact, if not the place of this movement, the Secretary of War had been apprised in August by a letter from Cincinnati, of which, however, he did not seem to have taken much notice. After taking possession of it, he wrote to the Boston committee for three hundred dollars, which was furnished. About the same time Francis Jackson Merriam, grandson of Francis Jackson, who afterward died in the Union army, came to his house, joined the expedition, and gave him six hundred dollars. Just before the assault, Frederick Douglass, who had been made acquainted with his general plan, visited him at Chambersburg, and there first learned of Brown's purpose to attack Harper's Ferry. Vainly urging him to join the enterprise, Brown said: "Go with me, Douglass. I don't want you to fight. I will protect you with my life, but I want you to be there when the bees swarm and help put them into the hive." This remark indicated the underlying idea of the movement. He thought that the slaves were ready to rise on their masters, ready to fight for liberty, and only needed a leader and a plan. Remembering the Seminole War, its protracted history, the large amount of men and money expended for the results attained, it seemed to him that with the slaves flocking to his standard, he could, in the fastnesses of the mountains and in the recesses of swamps, hold at bay any forces the government could bring against them. But he miscalculated. He failed to forecast aright the action of either the slaves or of their masters. In the lights afforded by the history of his own attempt and of the war of the Rebellion, there never was the remotest possibility of success. Tried by the rules of ordinary warfare, it was presumption and "midsummer madness." The heart that prompted the movement was right, but the head that conceived and planned it was sadly at default.

The 24th of October had been selected as the day of the assault. Fearing, however, that they had been betrayed, the 16th was substituted therefor. On the evening of that day he assembled his little force, consisting of fourteen white and five colored men, armed and equipped for war. A little after ten o'clock they entered the town, took possession of the United States armory buildings, stopped the trains of the railroad, cut the telegraph wires, captured a number of the citizens, liberated several slaves, and held the town about thirty hours. After some fighting, in which several persons were killed and wounded, Brown retired to the engine-house, where he was finally overcome and captured by a detachment of United States marines, under the command of Colonel Robert E. Lee, afterward the Confederate commander-in-chief. Brown was wounded in several places, eight of his band, including two of his sons, were killed or mortally wounded, six were captured, and five made their escape.

Brown, while confined in the guard-house, was visited by Governor Wise, to whom he stated with great frankness and fulness the motives and purposes of his action. He deeply impressed the bold, outspoken, impulsive governor, who, in an address to the citizens of Richmond, thus bore testimony of him: "They are mistaken who take him for a madman. He is a man of clear head, courageous fortitude, and simple ingenuousness. He is cool, collected, and indomitable; and it is but just to him to say that he was humane to his prisoners; and he inspired all with great trust in his integrity and as a man of truth. He is a fanatic, vain and garrulous, but firm, truthful, and intelligent." To Senator Mason and Mr. Vallandigham, who unquestionably catechized him in the hope that others, perhaps a party, would be implicated by his replies, he avowed his pity for the poor in bondage, and said that he "came to free the slaves, and only that." He expected no reward but the satisfaction of endeavoring to do to others in distress as he himself would be done by. He reminded Virginians of both their duty and their danger. "You people at the South," he said, "had better prepare yourselves for a settlement of this question, which will come up sooner than you are prepared for it." Mr. Vallandigham spoke of his "stoic faith, patience, and firmness," and of him as at "the farthest possible remove from the ordinary ruffian, fanatic, or madman."

He was indicted "for murder and other crimes," brought to trial, convicted, and on the 2d of November was sentenced to be hung. He was defended by George H. Hoyt, a young lawyer of Boston who volunteered his services, Samuel Chilton of Washington, and Henry Griswold of Ohio. Six of his followers, Coppoc, Stevens, Cook, Hazlett, Copeland, and Green, little less noble and heroic than himself, were tried, convicted, and executed. They all, except Cook, deported themselves with great firmness and propriety, leaving, like their leader, expressions of resignation, trust, and their still deathless devotion to liberty. Copeland and Green, the colored men, and Stevens, Brown's trusted lieutenant, who had been desperately wounded, were skilfully and ably defended by George Sennot, a Democratic lawyer of Boston, who went to Charlestown at the request of Dr. Howe, accompanied by Judge Russell. After the conviction of Stevens, Mr. Sennot visited Richmond and besought the legislature to spare his life. But his efforts were as unavailing as had been those of Governor Wise before the same body to secure remission of the sentence of Coppoc.

And yet the old hero himself was the principal actor in that grim tragedy, the central figure of that startling Virginia tableau with its dark background

of Southern slavery, the pitchy blackness of the one making more resplendent the beauty and brightness of the other. His port and bearing, his interviews with Wise, Mason, Vallandigham, and others, his letters, and his
remarks before sentence was passed, produced a profound impression. His
simple and unstudied words, revealing such sublime devotion to principle,
such profound sympathy for the poor, lowly, and oppressed, such serene
trust in God, were seized upon and hoarded almost as gems from another
and better land, or as the echoes from the heroic age of confessors and
martyrs of a like precious faith. Acts of sympathy and proffers of aid were
many.

During the darkest hours of the irrepressible conflict there was ever the
consoling fact that the literature of the nation was mainly on the side of
freedom, and that the brightest names in its galaxy of authors shone
benignantly on the sacred cause. Among them one of the earliest and most
cherished was that of Lydia Maria Child. From the first, her graceful and
earnest pen was consecrated to the cause of immediate emancipation, and
in her the slave and his defenders ever found a warm-hearted and self-
sacrificing friend. While Brown lay in jail awaiting his trial, she wrote to
Governor Wise. She expressed her "regret" and "surprise" at "the step
that the old veteran has taken," but added that he needed a mother or sister
to dress his wounds and speak soothingly to him, and asked to be allowed
"to perform that mission of humanity." The governor replied in courteous
and courtly style, though perhaps a trifle curt. He avowed his want of
sympathy with her "sympathy" for "one who whetted knives of butchery
for our mothers, sisters, daughters, and babes," and his surprise at her
"surprise," saying that "his attempt was a natural consequence of your
sympathy." He however gave his permission, on the ground that he was
"bound to protect" her, and accord to her the privileges and immunities
of a citizen of Massachusetts coming into Virginia. She also wrote to Brown,
disclaiming sympathy with his "method" of advancing the "cause of freedom," but avowing the greatest admiration for him personally and a strong
desire to minister to his comfort. "In brief," she wrote, "I love you and
bless you." In his reply he expressed his gratitude for her sympathy and
kind offers, but intimated that he did not need anything more than was
afforded by Captain Avis, his jailer, "a most humane man," who, "with
his family, has rendered every possible attention I have desired, or that
could be of the least advantage." This correspondence evoked no little
interest and feeling. Among the evidences of it was a letter written to Mrs.
Child by the wife of Senator Mason, in which were exhibited the usual
slaveholding assumption, arrogance, and bitterness. Mrs. Child replied to
her, as she had already to Governor Wise, in fitting terms and just as such
a woman, on such a theme and under such circumstances, would necessarily
respond.

Many friends of the slave as well as personal friends visited the prisoner
to comfort and support. Among them was Judge Russell, afterwards col-

lector of the port of Boston, at whose house he had been concealed, while fearing arrest on a requisition from the governor of Missouri. In his conversation with him he expressed in the strongest language his confidence in the Divine disposal of events and of himself; saying that he fully recognized God's sovereignty in the affair, even in the "mistakes" and "errors" which had been committed.

On the day before the execution, Mrs. Brown, accompanied by Hector Tyndale and J. Miller McKim, visited her husband, having an order from the governor—who, considering the circumstances, deported himself very courteously and chivalrously towards John Brown and his friends—for the delivery of his body, and a letter also, expressing his "sympathy with her affliction," and containing the assurance that his "authority and personal influence" should be exerted to enable her to secure "the bones of her sons and her husband" for "decent and tender interment among their kindred." Their meeting was deeply affecting. "For some minutes," it is said, "they stood speechless, with a silence more eloquent than any utterance could have been." Speaking tenderly of their children, both living and dead, he commissioned her to tell the survivors that their "father died without a single regret for the course he had pursued," and that he was satisfied that he was "right in the eyes of God and all just men." The only thing that seemed to trouble him was his anxiety for those he was leaving destitute. For those soon to be widowed and orphaned he did plead, though his requests were coupled with the characteristic remark: "I well understand that they are not the only poor in the land." For himself he had no tears; but for the loved ones he was leaving behind his heart yearned with a solicitude he could not and probably did not care to repress.

The 2d of December, appointed for the execution, having arrived, the final act in this drama of blood was performed, amid no little of "the pomp and circumstance of war," and John Brown's name was added to the list of martyrs, and the cause of impartial freedom he had served so nobly received the baptism of his blood. He died courageously and well, and his death was a fitting close of his life, lending glory to the gallows, and receiving naught of disgrace therefrom.

Immediately after the execution his body was delivered to General Tyndale and J. Miller McKim, who, with Mrs. Brown, started immediately for the North. At New York Wendell Phillips joined the little cortege, and they proceeded rapidly towards North Elba, where the widowed mother, returning from her sad pilgrimage, met her children with "a burst of love and anguish." That was, however, soon succeeded by "a holy and pensive joy," and they seemed reconciled even to this stern trial of their faith and love. They buried him on the 8th, with services as simple and unostentatious as was the character and life of the martyr himself, as was, too, the community in which he had lived and for which he had labored. Wendell Phillips could not but speak eloquently, and with such pathetic and pointed utterances as the event would naturally suggest to one so thoroughly in sympathy with the objects, if not the methods, of the dead. But, like all the opponents of slavery at that time, he evidently had little conception of the nature of the conflict itself, or of the forces that would be found needful to root up and destroy American slavery. Though it was but one brief year before South Carolina passed her ordinance of secession, raised the banners of revolt, and led the movement which ushered in the civil war, he said: "I do not believe slavery will go down in blood."

The execution became at once the signal of discussions at home and abroad. Abroad, the utterances were generally of commendation and eulogy. John Brown, if not the canonized saint, was the proclaimed hero of the hour, while America was held guilty of his murder. "Slaughtered," wrote Victor Hugo, "by the American republic, the crime assumes the proportions of the nation which commits it." This country, from press, pulpit, and platform, resounded with conflicting discussions. Large meetings were held. Few approved. The great mass condemned,—some, to show their continued fealty to the South, affirming, as was done in some Northern assemblages, that slavery was "wise, just, and beneficent," and stigmatizing anti-slavery men as "drunken mutineers"; and others, to express their confidence in the man, and in the integrity of his purpose, admiration for his heroism, sympathy for the object he had at heart, but repudiation of his methods, saying with Whittier:—

> "Perish with him the folly
> That seeks through evil good;
> Long live the generous purpose
> Unstained with human blood!
> Not the raid of midnight terror,
> But the thought that underlies;
> Not the outlaw's pride of daring,
> But the Christian sacrifice."

But whatever diversities in judgment, or errors of estimate there may have been, Mr. Phillips did not err when, standing by the open grave of John Brown, he said that his words were stronger than his arms, and that, while the echoes of his rifles had died away among the hills of Virginia, his words were guarded by a million hearts. When, a few months later, the uprising nation sent forth its loyal sons to battle, his brave, humane, and generous utterances were kept in fresh remembrance. The "John Brown Song," extemporized in Boston harbor, and sung by the "Massachusetts Twelfth," marching up State Street, down Broadway, and in its encampment in Pleasant Valley on the banks of the Potomac, struck responsive chords that vibrated through the land. Regiment after regiment, army after army, caught up the air, and in the camp, on the march, and on the battle-field, brave men associated the body "mouldering in the ground" and the soul still "marching on" of the heroic old man with the sacred idea for which he died and for which they were fighting.

JEFFERSON DAVIS

(1808-1889)

Between 1878 and 1881, Jefferson Davis, an elderly southern gentleman in his seventies, sat in his home "Beauvoir," on the Gulf of Mexico, writing the history of events in which he had been intimately involved. He refused to apply for a pardon so that the State of Mississippi could again send him to the United States Senate; his business ventures after the war had turned out badly; his home he had been fortunate enough to acquire as a legacy from an admirer. Thus it was in relative calm and obscurity that he worked on The Rise and Fall of the Confederate Government, *but the firm constitutional positions he defended in his book were much the same as those he had expounded as a Senator from Mississippi beginning in 1847, and as President of the Confederate States of America. He had asserted when he was a Senator, "I see nothing short of conquest on the one side, or submission on the other. . . . It is no longer the clamor of a noisy fanaticism, but the steady advance of a self-sustaining power to the goal of unlimited supremacy." Davis never saw any reason to change his mind.*

The Rise of the Confederacy

WHEN, AT THE CLOSE OF THE WAR OF THE REVOLUTION, EACH OF THE thirteen colonies that had been engaged in that contest was severally acknowledged by the mother-country, Great Britain, to be a free and independent State, the confederation of those States embraced an area so extensive, with climate and products so various, that rivalries and conflicts of interest soon began to be manifested. It required all the power of wisdom and patriotism, animated by the affection engendered by common sufferings and dangers, to keep these rivalries under restraint, and to effect those compromises which it was fondly hoped would insure the harmony and mutual good offices of each for the benefit of all. It was in this spirit of patriotism and confidence in the continuance of such abiding good will as would for all time preclude hostile aggression, that Virginia ceded, for the use of the confederated States, all that vast extent of territory lying north of the Ohio River, out of which have since been formed five States and part of a sixth. The addition of these States has accrued entirely to the preponderance of the Northern section over that from which the donation proceeded, and to the disturbance of that equilibrium which existed at the close of the war of the Revolution.

It may not be out of place here to refer to the fact that the grievances which led to that war were directly inflicted upon the Northern colonies. Those of the South had no material cause of complaint; but, actuated by sympathy for their Northern brethren, and a devotion to the principles of civil liberty and community independence, which they had inherited from their Anglo-Saxon ancestry, and which were set forth in the Declaration of Independence, they made common cause with their neighbors, and may, at least, claim to have done their full share in the war that ensued.

By the exclusion of the South, in 1820, from all that part of the Louisiana purchase lying north of the parallel of thirty-six degrees thirty minutes, and not included in the State of Missouri; by the extension of that line of exclusion to embrace the territory acquired from Texas; and by the appropriation of *all* the territory obtained from Mexico under the Treaty of

From Davis, *The Rise and Fall of the Confederate Government* (2 vols., 1881), ch. 7 (in part), ch. 10, 13.

Guadalupe Hidalgo, both north and south of that line, it may be stated with approximate accuracy that the North had monopolized to herself more than three fourths of all that had been added to the domain of the United States since the Declaration of Independence. This inequality, which began, as has been shown, in the more generous than wise confidence of the South, was employed to obtain for the North the lion's share of what was afterward added at the cost of the public treasure and the blood of patriots. I do not care to estimate the relative proportion contributed by each of the two sections.

Nor was this the only cause that operated to disappoint the reasonable hopes and to blight the fair prospects under which the original compact was formed. The effects of discriminating duties upon imports have been referred to in a former chapter—favoring the manufacturing region, which was the North; burdening the exporting region, which was the South; and so imposing upon the latter a double tax: one, by the increased price of articles of consumption, which, so far as they were of home production, went into the pockets of the manufacturer; the other, by the diminished value of articles of export, which was so much withheld from the pockets of the agriculturist. In like manner the power of the majority section was employed to appropriate to itself an unequal share of the public disbursements. These combined causes—the possession of more territory, more money, and a wider field for the employment of special labor—all served to attract immigration; and, with increasing population, the greed grew by what it fed on.

This became distinctly manifest when the so-called "Republican" Convention assembled in Chicago, on May 16, 1860, to nominate a candidate for the Presidency. It was a purely sectional body. There were a few delegates present, representing an insignificant minority in the "border States," Delaware, Maryland, Virginia, Kentucky, and Missouri; but not one from any State south of the celebrated political line of thirty-six degrees thirty minutes. It had been the invariable usage with nominating conventions of all parties to select candidates for the Presidency and Vice-Presidency, one from the North and the other from the South; but this assemblage nominated Mr. Lincoln, of Illinois, for the first office, and for the second, Mr. Hamlin, of Maine—both Northerners. Mr. Lincoln, its nominee for the Presidency, had publicly announced that the Union "could not permanently endure, half slave and half free." The resolutions adopted contained some carefully worded declarations, well adapted to deceive the credulous who were opposed to hostile aggressions upon the rights of the States. In order to accomplish this purpose, they were compelled to create a fictitious issue, in denouncing what they described as "the new dogma that the Constitution, of its own force, carries slavery into any or all of the Territories of the United States"—a "dogma" which had never been held or declared by anybody, and which had no existence outside of their own assertion. There was enough in connection with the nomination to assure the most fanatical foes of the Constitution that their ideas would be the rule and guide of the party. . . .

The people of the United States now had four rival tickets presented to them by as many contending parties, whose respective position and principles on the great and absorbing question at issue may be briefly recapitulated as follows:

1. The "Constitutional-Union" party, as it was now termed, led by Messrs. Bell and Everett, which ignored the territorial controversy altogether, and contended itself, as above stated, with a simple declaration of adherence to "the Constitution, the Union, and the enforcement of the laws."

2. The party of "popular sovereignty," headed by Douglas and Johnson, who affirmed the right of the people of the Territories, in their territorial condition, to determine their own organic institutions, independently of the control of Congress; denying the power or duty of Congress to protect the persons or property of individuals or minorities in such Territories against the action of majorities.

3. The State-Rights party, supporting Breckinridge and Lane, who held that the Territories were open to citizens of all the States, with their property, without any inequality or discrimination, and that it was the duty of the General Government to protect both persons and property from aggression in the Territories subject to its control. At the same time they admitted and asserted the right of the people of a Territory, on emerging from their territorial condition to that of a State, to determine what should then be their domestic institutions, as well as all other questions of personal or proprietary right, without interference by Congress, and subject only to the limitations and restrictions prescribed by the Constitution of the United States.

4. The so-called "Republicans," presenting the names of Lincoln and Hamlin, who held, in the language of one of their leaders, that "slavery can exist only by virtue of municipal law"; that there was "no law for it in the Territories, and no power to enact one"; and that Congress was "bound to prohibit it in or exclude it from any and every Federal Territory." In other words, they asserted the right and duty of Congress to exclude the citizens of half the States of the Union from the territory belonging in common to all, unless on condition of the sacrifice or abandonment of their property recognized by the Constitution—indeed, of the *only* species of their property distinctly and specifically recognized as such by that instrument.

On the vital question underlying the whole controversy—that is, whether the Federal Government should be a Government of the whole for the benefit of all its equal members, or (if it should continue to exist at all) a sectional Government for the benefit of a part—the first three of the parties above described were in substantial accord as against the fourth. If they could or would have acted unitedly, they could certainly have carried the election, and averted the catastrophe which followed. Nor were efforts wanting to effect such a union.

Mr. Bell, the Whig candidate, was a highly respectable and experienced statesman, who had filled many important offices, both State and Federal. He was not ambitious to the extent of coveting the Presidency, and he was profoundly impressed by the danger which threatened the country. Mr. Breckinridge had not anticipated, and it may safely be said did not eagerly desire, the nomination. He was young enough to wait, and patriotic enough to be willing to do so, if the weal of the country required it. Thus much I may confidently assert of both those gentlemen; for each of them authorized me to say that he was willing to withdraw, if an arrangement could be effected by which the divided forces of the friends of the Constitution could be concentrated upon some one more generally acceptable than either of the three who had been presented to the country. When I made this announcement to Mr. Douglas—with whom my relations had always been such as to authorize the assurance that he could not consider it as made in an unfriendly spirit—he replied that the scheme proposed was impracticable, because his friends, mainly Northern Democrats, if he were withdrawn, would join in the support of Mr. Lincoln, rather than of any one that should supplant *him* (Douglas); that he was in the hands of his friends, and was sure they would not accept the proposition.

It needed little knowledge of the *status* of parties in the several States to foresee a probable defeat if the conservatives were to continue divided into three parts, and the aggressives were to be held in solid column. But angry passions, which are always bad counselors, had been aroused, and hopes were still cherished, which proved to be illusory. The result was the election, by a minority, of a President whose avowed principles were necessarily fatal to the harmony of the Union.

Of 303 *electoral* votes, Mr. Lincoln received 180, but of the *popular* suffrage of 4,676,853 votes, which the electors represented, he obtained only 1,866,352—something over a third of the votes. This discrepancy was owing to the system of voting by "general ticket"—that is, casting the States votes as a unit, whether unanimous or nearly equally divided. Thus, in New York, the total popular vote was 675,156, of which 362,646 were cast for the so-called Republican (or Lincoln) electors, and 312,510 against them. New York was entitled to 35 electoral votes. Divided on the basis of the popular vote, 19 of these would have been cast for Mr. Lincoln, and 16 against him. But under the "general ticket" system the entire 35 votes were cast for the Republican candidates, thus giving them not only the full strength of the majority in their favor, but that of the great minority against them superadded. So of other Northern States, in which the small majorities on one side operated with the weight of entire unanimity, while the virtual unanimity in the Southern States, on the other side, counted nothing more than a mere majority would have done.

The manifestations which followed this result, in the Southern States, did not proceed, as has been unjustly charged, from chagrin at their defeat in the election, or from any personal hostility to the President-elect, but from the fact that they recognized in him the representative of a party professing principles destructive to "their peace, their prosperity, and their domestic tranquillity." The long-suppressed fire burst into frequent flame, but it was still controlled by that love of the Union which the South had illustrated in every battle-field, from Boston to New Orleans. Still it was hoped, against hope, that some adjustment might be made to avert the calamities of a practical application of the theory of an "irrepressible conflict." Few, if any, then doubted the right of a State to withdraw its grants delegated to the Federal Government, or, in other words, to secede from the Union; but in the South this was generally regarded as the remedy of last resort, to be applied only when ruin or dishonor was the alternative. No rash or revolutionary action was taken by the Southern States, but the measures adopted were considerate, and executed advisedly and deliberately. The Presidential election occurred (as far as the popular vote, which determined the result, was concerned) in November, 1860. Most of the State Legislatures convened soon afterward in regular session. In some cases special sessions were convoked for the purpose of calling State Conventions —the recognized representatives of the sovereign will of the people—to be elected expressly for the purpose of taking such action as should be considered needful and proper under the existing circumstances.

These conventions, as it was always held and understood, possessed all the power of the people assembled in mass; and therefore it was conceded that they, and they only, could take action for the withdrawal of a State from the Union. The consent of the respective States to the formation of the Union had been given through such conventions, and it was only by the same authority that it could properly be revoked. The time required for this deliberate and formal process precludes the idea of hasty or passionate action, and none who admit the primary power of the people to govern themselves can consistently deny its validity and binding obligation upon every citizen of the several States. Not only was there ample time for calm consideration among the people of the South, but for due reflection by the General Government and the people of the Northern States.

President Buchanan was in the last year of his administration. His freedom from sectional asperity, his long life in the public service, and his peace-loving and conciliatory character, were all guarantees against his precipitating a conflict between the Federal Government and any of the States; but the feeble power that he possessed in the closing months of his term to mold the policy of the future was painfully evident. Like all who had intelligently and impartially studied the history of the formation of the Constitution, he held that the Federal Government had no rightful power to coerce a State. Like the sages and patriots who had preceded him in the high office that he filled, he believed that "our Union rests upon public opinion, and can never be cemented by the blood of its citizens shed in civil war. If it can not live in the affections of the people, it must one day perish. Congress may possess many means of preserving it by conciliation, but the sword was not placed in their hand to preserve it by force."—(Message of December 3, 1860.)

Ten years before, Mr. Calhoun, addressing the Senate with all the earnestness of his nature, and with that sincere desire to avert the danger of disunion which those who knew him best never doubted, had asked the emphatic question, "How can the Union be saved?" He answered his question thus:

"There is but one way by which it can be [saved] with any certainty; and that is by a full and final settlement, on the principles of justice, of all the questions at issue between the sections. The South asks for justice—simple justice—and less she ought not to take. She has no compromise to offer but the Constitution, and no concession or surrender to make. . . .

"Can this be done? Yes, easily! Not by the weaker party; for it can of itself do nothing—not even protect itself—but by the stronger. . . . But will the North agree to do this? It is for her to answer this question. But, I will say, she can not refuse if she has half the love of the Union which she professes to have, nor without exposing herself to the charge that her love of power and aggrandizement is far greater than her love of the Union."

During the ten years that intervened between the date of this speech and the message of Mr. Buchanan cited above, the progress of sectional discord and the tendency of the stronger section to unconstitutional aggression had been fearfully rapid. With very rare exceptions, there were none in 1850 who claimed the right of the Federal Government to apply coercion to a State. In 1860 men had grown to be familiar with threats of driving the South into submission to any act that the Government, in the hands of a Northern majority, might see fit to perform. During the canvass of that year, demonstrations had been made by *quasi*-military organizations in various parts of the North, which looked unmistakably to purposes widely different from those enunciated in the preamble to the Constitution, and to the employment of means not authorized by the powers which the States had delegated to the Federal Government.

Well-informed men still remembered that, in the Convention which framed the Constitution, a proposition was made to authorize the employment of force against a delinquent State, on which Mr. Madison remarked that "the use of force against a State would look more like a declaration of war than an infliction of punishment, and would probably be considered by the party attacked as a dissolution of all previous compacts by which it might have been bound." The Convention expressly refused to confer the power proposed, and the clause was lost. While, therefore, in 1860, many violent men, appealing to passion and the lust of power, were inciting the multitude, and preparing Northern opinion to support a war waged against the Southern States in the event of their secession, there were others who took a different view of the case. Notable among such was the "New York Tribune," which had been the organ of the abolitionists, and which now declared that, "if the cotton States wished to withdraw from the Union, they should be allowed to do so"; that "any attempt to compel them to remain, by force, would be contrary to the principles of the Declaration of Independence and to the fundamental ideas upon which human liberty is based"; and that, "if the Declaration of Independence justified the secession from the British Empire of three millions of subjects in 1776, it was not seen why it would not justify the secession of five millions of Southerners from the Union in 1861." Again, it was said by the same journal that, "sooner than compromise with the South and abandon the Chicago platform," they would "let the Union slide." Taunting expressions were freely used—as, for example, "If the Southern people wish to leave the Union, we will do our best to forward their views."

All this, it must be admitted, was quite consistent with the oft-repeated declaration that the Constitution was a "covenant with hell," which stood as the caption of a leading abolitionist paper of Boston. That signs of coming danger so visible, evidences of hostility so unmistakable, disregard of constitutional obligations so wanton, taunts and jeers so bitter and insulting, should serve to increase excitement in the South, was a consequence flowing as much from reason and patriotism as from sentiment. He must have been ignorant of human nature who did not expect such a tree to bear fruits of discord and division.

* * *

The reader of many of the treatises on these events, which have been put forth as historical, if dependent upon such alone for information, might naturally enough be led to the conclusion that the controversies which arose between the States, and the war in which they culminated, were caused by efforts on the one side to extend and perpetuate human slavery, and on the other to resist it and establish human liberty. The Southern States and Southern people have been sedulously represented as "propagandists" of slavery, and the Northern as the defenders and champions of universal freedom, and this view has been so arrogantly assumed, so dogmatically asserted, and so persistently reiterated, that its authors have, in many cases, perhaps, succeeded in bringing themselves to believe it, as well as in impressing it widely upon the world.

The attentive reader of the preceding chapters—especially if he has compared their statements with contemporaneous records and other original sources of information—will already have found evidence enough to enable him to discern the falsehood of these representations, and to perceive that, to whatever extent the question of slavery may have served as an *occasion,* it was far from being the *cause* of the conflict.

I have not attempted, and shall not permit myself to be drawn into any discussion of the merits or demerits of slavery as an ethical or even as a political question. It would be foreign to my purpose, irrelevant to my subject, and would only serve—as it has invariably served in the hands of its agitators—to "darken counsel" and divert attention from the genuine issues involved.

As a mere historical fact, we have seen that African servitude among us —confessedly the mildest and most humane of all institutions to which the name "slavery" has ever been applied—existed in all the original States, and that it was recognized and protected in the fourth article of the Constitution. Subsequently, for climatic, industrial, and economical—not moral or sentimental—reasons, it was abolished in the Northern, while it continued to exist in the Southern States. Men differed in their views as to the abstract question of its right or wrong, but for two generations after the Revolution there was no geographical line of demarkation for such differences. The African slave-trade was carried on almost exclusively by New England merchants and Northern ships. Mr. Jefferson—a Southern man, the founder of the Democratic party, and the vindicator of State rights—was in theory a consistent enemy to every form of slavery. The Southern States took the lead in prohibiting the slave-trade, and, as we have seen, one of them (Georgia) was the first State to incorporate such a prohibition in her organic Constitution. Eleven years after the agitation on the Missouri question, when the subject first took a sectional shape, the abolition of slavery was proposed and earnestly debated in the Virginia Legislature, and its advocates were so near the accomplishment of their purpose, that a declaration in its favor was defeated only by a small majority, and that on the ground of expediency. At a still later period, abolitionist lecturers and teachers were mobbed, assaulted, and threatened with tar and feathers in New York, Pennsylvania, Massachusetts, New Hampshire, Connecticut, and other States. One of them (Lovejoy) was actually killed by a mob in Illinois as late as 1837.

These facts prove incontestably that the sectional hostily which exhibited itself in 1820, on the application of Missouri for admission into the Union, which again broke out on the proposition for the annexation of Texas in 1844, and which reappeared after the Mexican war, never again to be suppressed until its fell results had been fully accomplished, was not the consequence of any difference on the abstract question of slavery. It was the offspring of sectional rivalry and political ambition. It would have manifested itself just as certainly if slavery had existed in all the States, or if there had not been a negro in America. No such pretension was made in 1803 or 1811, when the Louisiana purchase, and afterward the admission into the Union of the State of that name, elicited threats of disunion from the representatives of New England. The complaint was not of slavery, but of "the acquisition of more weight at the other extremity" of the Union.

It was not slavery that threatened a rupture in 1832, but the unjust and unequal operation of a protective tariff.

It happened, however, on all these occasions, that the line of demarcation of sectional interests coincided exactly or very nearly with that dividing the States in which negro servitude existed from those in which it had been abolished. It corresponded with the prediction of Mr. Pickering, in 1803, that, in the separation certainly to come, "the white and black population would mark the boundary"—a prediction made without any reference to slavery as a source of dissension.

Of course, the diversity of institutions contributed, in some minor degree, to the conflict of interests. There is an action and reaction of cause and consequence, which limits and modifies any general statement of a political truth. I am stating general principles—not defining modifications and exceptions with the precision of a mathematical proposition or a bill in chancery. The truth remains intact and incontrovertible, that the existence of African servitude was in no wise the cause of the conflict, but only an incident. In the later controversies that arose, however, its effect in operating as a lever upon the passions, prejudices, or sympathies of mankind, was so potent that it has been spread, like a thick cloud, over the whole horizon of historic truth.

As for the institution of negro servitude, it was a matter entirely subject to the control of the States. No power was ever given to the General Government to interfere with it, but an obligation was imposed to protect it. Its existence and validity were distinctly recognized by the Constitution in at least three places:

First, in that part of the second section of the first article which prescribes that "representatives and direct taxes shall be apportioned among the several States which may be included within this Union, according to their respective members, which shall be determined by adding to the whole number of free persons, including those bound to service for a term of years, and, excluding Indians not taxed, three fifths of all other persons." "*Other* persons" than "*free* persons" and those "bound to service for a term of years" must, of course, have meant those permanently bound to service.

Secondly, it was recognized by the ninth section of the same article, which provided that "the migration or importation of such persons as any of the States now existing shall think proper to admit shall not be prohibited by Congress prior to the year one thousand eight hundred and eight." This was a provision inserted for the protection of the interests of the slave-trading New England States, forbidding any prohibition of the trade by Congress for twenty years, and thus virtually giving sanction to the legitimacy of the demand which that trade was prosecuted to supply, and which was its only object.

Again, and in the third place, it was specially recognized, and an obligation imposed upon every State, not only to refrain from interfering with it in any other State, but in certain cases to aid in its enforcement, by that clause, or paragraph, of the second secton of the fourth article which provides as follows:

"No person held to service or labor in one State, under the laws thereof, escaping into another, shall, in consequence of any law or regulation therein, be discharged from such service or labor, but shall be delivered up on claim of the party to whom such service or labor may be due."

The President and Vice-President of the United States, every Senator and Representative in Congress, the members of every State Legislature, and "all executive and judicial officers, both of the United States and of the several States," were required to take an oath (or affirmation) to support the Constitution containing these provisions. It is easy to understand how those who considered them in conflict with the "higher law" of religion or morality might refuse to take such an oath or hold such an office—as the members of some religious sects refuse to take any oath at all or to bear arms in the service of their country—but it is impossible to reconcile with the obligations of honor or honesty the conduct of those who, having taken such an oath, made use of the powers and opportunities of the offices held under its sanctions to nullify its obligations and neutralize its guarantees. The halls of Congress afforded the vantage-ground from which assaults were made upon these guarantees. The Legislatures of various Northern States enacted laws to hinder the execution of the provisions made for the rendition of fugitives from service; State officials lent their aid to the work of thwarting them; and city mobs assailed the officers engaged in the duty of enforcing them.

With regard to the provision of the Constitution above quoted, for the restoration of fugitives from service or labor, my own view was, and is, that it was not a proper subject for legislation by the Federal Congress, but that its enforcement should have been left to the respective States, which, as parties to the compact of union, should have been held accountable for its fulfillment. Such was actually the case in the earlier and better days of the republic. No fugitive slave-law existed, or was required, for two years after the organization of the Federal Government, and, when one was then passed, it was merely as an incidental appendage to an act regulating the mode of rendition of fugitives from *justice*—not from service or labor.

In 1850 a more elaborate law was enacted as part of the celebrated compromise of that year. But the very fact that the Federal Government had taken the matter into its own hands, and provided for its execution by its own officers, afforded a sort of pretext to those States which had now become hostile to this provision of the Constitution, not only to stand aloof, but in some cases to adopt measures (generally known as "personal liberty laws") directly in conflict with the execution of the provisions of the Constitution.

The preamble to the Constitution declared the object of its founders to be, "to form a more perfect union, establish justice, insure domestic tranquillity, provide for the common defense, promote the general welfare, and secure the blessings of liberty to ourselves and our posterity." Now, however (in 1860), the people of a portion of the States had assumed an attitude of avowed hostility, not only to the provisions of the Constitution itself, but to the "domestic tranquillity" of the people of other States. Long before the formation of the Constitution, one of the charges preferred in the Declaration of Independence against the Government of Great Britain, as justifying the separation of the colonies from that country, was that of having "excited domestic insurrections among us." Now, the mails were burdened with incendiary publications, secret emissaries had been sent, and in one case an armed invasion of one of the States had taken place for the very purpose of exciting "domestic insurrection."

It was not the passage of the "personal liberty laws," it was not the circulation of incendiary documents, it was not the raid of John Brown, it was not the operation of unjust and unequal tariff laws, nor all combined, that constituted the intolerable grievance, but it was the systematic and persistent struggle to deprive the Southern States of equality in the Union— generally to discriminate in legislation against the interests of their people; culminating in their exclusion from the Territories, the common property of the States, as well as by the infraction of their compact to promote domestic tranquillity.

The question with regard to the Territories has been discussed in the foregoing chapters, and the argument need not be repeated. There was, however, one feature of it which has not been specially noticed, although it occupied a large share of public attention at the time, and constituted an important element in the case. This was the action of the Federal judiciary thereon, and the manner in which it was received.

In 1854 a case (the well-known "Dred Scott case") came before the Supreme Court of the United States, involving the whole question of the *status* of the African race and the rights of citizens of the Southern States to migrate to the Territories, temporarily or permanently, with their slave property, on a footing of equality with the citizens of other States with *their* property of any sort. This question, as we have seen, had already been the subject of long and energetic discussion, without any satisfactory conclusion. All parties, however, had united in declaring, that a decision by the Supreme Court of the United States—the highest judicial tribunal in the land—would be accepted as final. After long and patient consideration of the case, in 1857, the decision of the Court was pronounced in an elaborate and exhaustive opinion, delivered by Chief-Justice Taney—a man eminent as a lawyer, great as a statesman, and stainless in his moral reputation—seven of the nine judges who composed the Court, concurring in it. The salient points established by this decision were:

1. That persons of the African race were not, and could not be, acknowledged as "part of the people," or citizens, under the Constitution of the United States;

2. That Congress had no right to exclude citizens of the South from taking their negro servants, as any other property, into any part of the common territory, and that they were entitled to claim its protection therein;

3. And, finally, as a consequence of the principle just above stated, that the Missouri Compromise of 1820, in so far as it prohibited the existence of African servitude north of a designated line, was unconstitutional and void. (It will be remembered that it had already been declared "inoperative and void" by the Kansas-Nebraska Bill of 1854.)

Instead of accepting the decision of this then august tribunal—the ultimate authority in the interpretation of constitutional questions—as conclusive of a controversy that had so long disturbed the peace and was threatening the perpetuity of the Union, it was flouted, denounced, and utterly disregarded by the Northern agitators, and served only to stimulate the intensity of their sectional hostility.

What resource for justice—what assurance of tranquillity—what guarantee of safety—now remained for the South? Still forbearing, still hoping, still striving for peace and union, we waited until a sectional President, nominated by a sectional convention, elected by a sectional vote—and that the vote of a minority of the people—was about to be inducted into office, under the warning of his own distinct announcement that the Union could not permanetnly endure "half slave and half free"; meaning thereby that it could not continue to exist in the condition in which it was formed and its Constitution adopted. The leader of his party, who was to be the chief of his Cabinet, was the man who had first proclaimed an "irrepressible conflict" between the North and the South, and who had declared that abolitionism, having triumphed in the Territories, would proceed to the invasion of the States. Even then the Southern people did not finally despair until the temper of the triumphant party had been tested in Congress and found adverse to any terms of reconciliation consistent with the honor and safety of all parties.

No alternative remained except to seek the security out of the Union which they had vainly tried to obtain within it. The hope of our people may be stated in a sentence. It was to escape from injury and strife in the Union, to find prosperity and peace out of it. . . .

*   *   *

Here, in the brief hour immediately before the outburst of the long-gathering storm, although it can hardly be necessary for the reader who has carefully considered what has already been written, we may pause for a moment to contemplate the attitude of the parties to the contest and the grounds on which they respectively stand. I do not now refer to the original causes of controversy—to the comparative claims of Statehood and Union, or to the question of the right or the wrong of secession—but to the proximate and immediate causes of conflict.

The fact that South Carolina *was* a State—whatever her relations may have been to the other States—is not and can not be denied. It is equally undeniable that the ground on which Fort Sumter was built was ceded by South Carolina to the United States *in trust* for the defense of her own soil and her own chief harbor. This has been shown, by ample evidence, to have been the principle governing all cessions by the States of sites for military purposes, but it applies with special force to the case of Charleston. The streams flowing into that harbor, from source to mouth, lie entirely within the limits of the State of South Carolina. No other State or combination of States could have any distinct interest or concern in the maintenance of a fortress at that point, unless as a means of aggression against South Carolina herself. The practical view of the case was correctly stated by Mr. Douglas, when he said: "I take it for granted that whoever permanently holds Charleston and South Carolina is entitled to the possession of Fort Sumter. Whoever permanently holds Pensacola and Florida is entitled to the possession of Fort Pickens. Whoever holds the States in whose limits those forts are placed is entitled to the forts themselves, unless there is something peculiar in the location of some particular fort that makes it important for us to hold it for the general defense of the whole country, its commerce and interests, instead of being useful only for the defense of a particular city or locality."

No such necessity could be alleged with regard to Fort Sumter. The claim to hold it as "public property" of the United States was utterly untenable and unmeaning, apart from a claim of coercive control over the State. If South Carolina was a mere province, in a state of open rebellion, the Government of the United States had a right to retain its hold of any fortified place within her limits which happened to be in its possession, and it would have had an equal right to acquire possession of any other. It would have had the same right to send an army to Columbia to batter down the walls of the State Capitol. The subject may at once be stripped of the sophistry which would make a distinction between the two cases. The one was as really an act of war as the other would have been. The right or the wrong of either depended entirely upon the question of the rightful power of the Federal Government to coerce a State into submission—a power which, as we have seen, was unanimously rejected in the formation of the Federal Constitution, and which was still unrecognized by many, perhaps by a majority, even of those who denied the right of a State to secede.

If there existed any hope or desire for a peaceful settlement of the questions at issue between the States, either party had a right to demand that, pending such settlement, there should be no hostile grasp upon its throat. This grip had been held on the throat of South Carolina for almost four months from the period of her secession, and no forcible resistance to it had yet been made. Remonstrances and patient, persistent, and reiterated attempts at negotiation for its removal had been made with two successive Administrations of the Government of the United States—at first by the State of South Carolina, and by the Government of the Confederate States after its formation. These efforts had been met, not by an open avowal of coercive purposes, but by evasion, prevarication, and perfidy. The agreement of one Administration to maintain the *status quo* at the time when the question arose, was violated in December by the removal of the garrison from its original position to the occupancy of a stronger. Another attempt was made to violate it, in January, by the introduction of troops concealed below the deck of the steamer Star of the West, but this was thwarted by the vigilance of the State service. The protracted course of fraud and prevarication practiced by Mr. Lincoln's Administration in the months of March and April has been fully exhibited. It was evident that no confidence whatever could be reposed in any pledge or promise of the Federal Government as then administered. Yet, notwithstanding all this, no resistance, other than that of pacific protest and appeals for an equitable settlement, was made, until after the avowal of a purpose of coercion, and when it was known that a hostile fleet was on the way to support and enforce it. At the very moment when the Confederate commander gave the final notice to Major Anderson of his purpose to open fire upon the fort, that fleet was lying off the mouth of the harbor, and hindered from entering only by a gale of wind.

The forbearance of the Confederate Government, under the circumstances, is perhaps unexampled in history. It was carried to the extreme verge, short of a disregard of the safety of the people who had intrusted to that government the duty of their defense against their enemies. The attempt to represent us as the *aggressors* in the conflict which ensued is as unfounded as the complaint made by the wolf against the lamb in the familiar fable. He who makes the assault is not necessarily he that strikes the first blow or fires the first gun. To have awaited further strengthening of their position by land and naval forces, with hostile purpose now declared, for the sake of having them "fire the first gun," would have been as unwise as it would be to hesitate to strike down the arm of the assailant, who levels a deadly weapon at one's breast, until he has actually fired. The disingenuous rant of demagogues about "firing on the flag" might serve to rouse the passions of insensate mobs in times of general excitement, but will be impotent in impartial history to relieve the Federal Government from the responsibility of the assault made by sending a hostile fleet against the harbor of Charleston, to coöperate with the menacing garrison of Fort Sumter. After the assault was made by the hostile descent of the fleet, the reduction of Fort Sumter was a measure of defense rendered absolutely and immediately necessary.

Such clearly was the idea of the commander of the Pawnee, when he declined, as Captain Fox informs us, without orders from a superior, to make any effort to enter the harbor, "there to inaugurate civil war." The straightforward simplicity of the sailor had not been perverted by the shams of political sophistry. Even Mr. Horace Greeley, with all his extreme partisan feeling, is obliged to admit that, "whether the bombardment and reduction of Fort Sumter shall or shall not be justified by posterity, it is clear that the Confederacy had no alternative but its own dissolution."

According to the notice given by General Beauregard, fire was opened upon Fort Sumter, from the various batteries which had been erected around the harbor, at half-past four o'clock on the morning of Friday, the 12th of April, 1861. The fort soon responded. It is not the purpose of this work to give minute details of the military operation, as the events of the bombardment have been often related, and are generally well known, with no material discrepancy in matters of fact among the statements of the various participants. It is enough, therefore, to add that the bombardment continued for about thirty-three or thirty-four hours. The fort was eventually set on fire by shells, after having been partly destroyed by shot, and Major Anderson, after a resolute defense, finally surrendered on the 13th—the same terms being accorded to him which had been offered two days before. It is a remarkable fact—probably without precedent in the annals of war—that, notwithstanding the extent and magnitude of the engagement, the number and caliber of the guns, and the amount of damage done to inanimate material on both sides, especially to Fort Sumter, nobody was injured on either side by the bombardment. The only casualty attendant upon the affair was the death of one man and the wounding of several others by the explosion of a gun in the firing of a salute to their flag by the garrison on evacuating the fort the day after the surrender.

A striking incident marked the close of the bombardment. Ex-Senator Louis T. Wigfall, of Texas—a man as generous as he was recklessly brave—when he saw the fort on fire, supposing the garrison to be hopelessly struggling for the honor of its flag, voluntarily and without authority, went under fire in an open boat to the fort, and climbing through one of its embrasures asked for Major Anderson, and insisted that he should surrender a fort which it was palpably impossible that he could hold. Major Anderson agreed to surrender on the same terms and conditions that had been offered him before his works were battered in breach, and the agreement between them to that effect was promptly ratified by the Confederate commander. Thus unofficially was inaugurated the surrender and evacuation of the fort.

The President of the United States, in his message of July 4, 1861, to the Federal Congress convened in extra session, said:

"It is thus seen that the assault upon and reduction of Fort Sumter was in no sense a matter of self-defense on the part of the assailants. They well knew that the garrison in the fort could by no possibility commit aggression upon them. They knew—they were expressly notified—that the giving of bread to the few brave and hungry men of the garrison was all which would on that occasion be attempted, unless themselves, by resisting so much, should provoke more."

Mr. Lincoln well knew that, if the brave men of the garrison were hungry, they had only him and his trusted advisers to thank for it. They had been kept for months in a place where they ought not to have been, contrary to the judgment of the General-in-Chief of his army, contrary to the counsels of the wisest statesmen in his confidence, and the protests of the commander of the garrison. A word from him would have relieved them at any moment in the manner most acceptable to them and most promotive of peaceful results.

But, suppose the Confederate authorities had been disposed to yield, and to consent to the introduction of supplies for the maintenance of the garrison, what assurance would they have had that nothing further would be attempted? What reliance could be placed in any assurances of the Government of the United States after the experience of the attempted *ruse* of the Star of the West and the deceptions practiced upon the Confederate Commissioners in Washington? He says we were "expressly notified" that nothing more "would *on that occasion* be attempted"—the words in italics themselves constituting a very significant though unobtrusive and innocent-looking limitation. But we had been just as expressly notified, long before, that the garrison would be withdrawn. It would be as easy to violate the one pledge as it had been to break the other.

Moreover, the so-called notification was a mere memorandum, without date, signature, or authentication of any kind, sent to Governor Pickens, not by an accredited agent, but by a subordinate employee of the State Department. Like the oral and written pledges of Mr. Seward, given through Judge Campbell, it seemed to be carefully and purposely divested of every attribute that could make it binding and valid, in case its authors should see fit to repudiate it. It was as empty and worthless as the complaint against the Confederate Government based upon it, is disingenuous.

JAMES FORD RHODES

(1848-1927)

The firing on Fort Sumter precipitated the tragedy of the Civil War. Under-
standably, its scope, its consequences, and its drama attracted literally hun-
dreds of historians. Even while the wounds were fresh and the ruins stark,
the accounts were already pouring out of publishing houses. Some, like
The Lost Cause *by the Richmond newspaperman, E. A. Pollard, were vivid*
although controversial; most, like the New York editor, Horace Greeley's
American Conflict, *were less polemics than products of the paste pot.*
It was a full generation later, 1892, before James Ford Rhodes began pub-
lication of a classic account, the History of the United States from the
Compromise of 1850. *It was competent in style, sound in research, and,*
though northern and nationalistic in viewpoint, relatively dispassionate in
tone.

Rhodes had been a successful associate with Marcus Alonzo Hanna,
his brother-in-law, in a Cleveland coal and iron concern. Increasingly his
interest had turned toward history, and in 1885, aged 37, he retired to de-
vote himself to his writing. He had boyhood recollections of most of the
period about which he was to write:

"I cannot remember when I did not take an interest in politics. When
only a little more than four years old, I ran away from school to hear
General Scott speak, then making a stumping tour as a presidential candi-
date. When eight, I carried a torch light in a Buchanan and Breckinridge
procession. . . . My Father was a kinsman and great admirer of Stephen A.
Douglas. . . . Douglas was at my Father's house frequently and I remem-
ber well listening to his arguments and familiar conversation."

During the Civil War, Rhodes, a boy in high school, continued to sub-
scribe to his father's Democratic political views, arguing against the
Emancipation Proclamation and supporting the loyalty of the Copperhead
C. L. Vallandigham. Immediately after the war, he was taken to the White
House to see President Johnson whom he "heard . . . declaim in private
against the radicalism of Stevens and Sumner and express the opinion that
the great heart of the country was with him."

As a mature man, Rhodes changed his views, but drew from his recol-
lections and earlier emotions a vividness in depicting the stirring times he
had known. He could breath life into the documents without engaging in
distortion, as the three episodes that appear here demonstrate.

The Civil War

ANTIETAM AND THE EMANCIPATION PROCLAMATION, 1862

LET US TAKE A LOOK AT LEE, AS LONGSTREET HAS DRAWN HIS PICTURE. Instead of the well-formed, dignified soldier, mounted at the head of his troops, and exhibiting in every movement the alertness and vigor of rich manhood, we have now before us the closet student, poring over his maps and papers, with an application so intense as sometimes to cause his thoughts to run no longer straight. Often on these occasions he would send for Longstreet and say that his ideas were working in a circle and that he needed help to find a tangent. He was now at Chantilly, in the midst of one of these perplexities. He had no intention of attacking the enemy in his fortifications about Washington, for he could not invest them and could not properly supply his army. He must either fall back to a more convenient base or invade Maryland. In that State, so allied in sympathy with his own, he even hoped for a rising in his favor, but at all events deemed it likely that he could "annoy and harass the enemy." He would strike alarm to Washington and Baltimore, and would enter Pennsylvania. Perhaps in the chances of war he might win a decisive battle and conquer a peace. His soldiers were ragged, and many of them were destitute of shoes. The army lacked "much of the material of war, is feeble in transportation." "Still," Lee wrote, "we cannot afford to be idle; we shall encounter without fear the troops of McClellan and Pope, both of which we have beaten and both of which are much weakened and demoralized." He decided to cross the Potomac. Nothing occasioned him uneasiness but "supplies of ammunition and subsistence." With this project in contemplation, he talked with Longstreet. Perhaps the friendly collision with another mind would strengthen his determination. His lieutenant related how Worth's division had marched "around the city of Monterey on two days' rations of roasting-ears and green oranges," and that we could as safely trust ourselves to "the fields of Maryland laden with ripening corn and fruit."

September 3 Lee had put his troops in motion, and had reached Dranesville when he wrote Davis that he entertained the idea of invading Mary-

From Rhodes, *History of the United States from the Compromise of 1850* (7 vols., 1893-1906), vol. 4, ch. 18 (in part), ch. 20; vol. 5, ch. 25.

land. September 4, still marching on and now at Leesburg, his despatch
to his President said, "I shall proceed to make the movement at once, unless
you should signify your disapprobation;" but before this word could have
reached Richmond, the Army of Northern Virginia had crossed the
Potomac, its soldiers singing "Maryland, my Maryland," and had continued
their rollicking march to Frederick City, which was reached on the sixth
by the van led by Jackson. His riding through the streets gave an occasion
to forge the story of Barbara Frietchie which Whittier wrote into inspiring
war verse. This poem was read in the home, in the school, and from the
platform, and stirred Northern blood at the "barbarity of rebel warfare."
It is a token of the intense emotion which clouds our judgment of the
enemy in arms. Although Stonewall Jackson not long before was eager to
raise the black flag, he was incapable of giving the order to fire at the
window of a private house for the sole reason that there "the old flag met
his sight;" and it is equally impossible that a remark of old Dame Barbara,
"Spare your country's flag," could have brought "a blush of shame" over
his face. Jackson was not of the cavalier order, but he had a religious and
chivalrous respect for women. It is related, on seemingly good authority,
that in this Frederick City, which was Union to the core, a woman, not
Barbara Frietchie, waved a Union flag as Jackson's soldiers passed and that
he paid no attention to it. One of his colonels tells the story that on their
march to Harper's Ferry, as they went through Middletown, two pretty girls,
ribbons of red, white, and blue streaming from their hair, waved with a
merry defiance their small Union flags in the face of the general. "He
bowed and raised his hat, and turning with his quiet smile to his staff, said:
'We evidently have no friends in this town.' "

In conformity with his intention in crossing the Potomac to give the
people of Maryland "an opportunity of liberating themselves," Lee issued
an address to them declaring that the South had "watched with deepest
sympathy" their wrongs, and had "seen with profound indignation their
sister State deprived of every right and reduced to the condition of a
conquered province." "To aid you in throwing off this foreign yoke" is the
object of our invasion. He was soon convinced that if the people of Maryland were oppressed they kissed the rod of the oppressor. They gave no
signs of rising. Jackson's experience was the epitome of the real feeling,
which if it had formulated itself would have issued in an earnest prayer
for the departure from their borders of the Confederate host. The most
serious effect of their cold welcome was the difficulty in procuring subsistence. Lee proposed to pay for their supplies, but all that he had to pay
with was Confederate currency, or certificates of indebtedness of the Confederate States, and these the farmers, millers, and drovers would not take
for their wheat, their flour, and their cattle. The army which had defeated
McClellan and Pope could not make the farmers thresh their wheat and the
millers grind it, nor prevent the owners of cattle from driving them into

Pennsylvania. The citizens of Frederick, caring not for the custom offered them by the officers and soldiers, closed their shops.

It was Lee's intention, and in this Davis agreed with him, to have the Confederate States propose peace to the Northern government and people on the condition of the recognition of their independence. Lincoln in declining this proposal would help the Democratic party in the coming fall elections, when a new House of Representatives was to be chosen; and if the invading army could maintain its position in the territory of the North, a clamor might arise against a further attempt to conquer the South. He purposed to attack neither Washington nor Baltimore. His objective point was probably Harrisburg, and his purpose the destruction of the long bridge of the Pennsylvania Railroad across the Susquehanna River. Since he had already severed the communication by the Baltimore and Ohio Railway, the success of this undertaking would leave no land connection between the eastern and western States except the railroad line along the lakes. He would draw the Union forces away from the capital, so that, if he fought and overcame them, they would not have the intrenchments of Washington to fall back upon.

At no time during the war were Confederate prospects so bright. Kirby Smith had defeated a Union force in Kentucky, had occupied Lexington, and was now threatening Louisville and Cincinnati, having pushed a detachment of his army within a few miles of Covington, one of the Kentucky suburbs of Cincinnati. Bragg with a large army had eluded Buell, and was marching northward toward Louisville in the hope that Kentucky would give her adhesion to the Confederacy. Cincinnati and Louisville were excited and alarmed. So impressed was Davis by the importance at this juncture of a union of statecraft with military strategy that he had started from Richmond to join Lee, expecting to sign his manifesto, offering peace from the head of the victorious army; but the general, unwilling to have him undergo the hardships of the journey and the risk of capture by the enemy, sent his aide-de-camp to warn him against continuing his progress.

Lee had now found out that he could not live upon the country, and decided that he must open a line of communication through the Shenandoah Valley so that he could procure sufficient supplies of flour. But Harper's Ferry commanded the valley, and was held by a Federal garrison, although, according to the principles laid down in the military books, this post should have been abandoned when the Confederate army crossed the Potomac. Lee had expected to see it abandoned, and McClellan had advised it, but Halleck would not give it up. It was a lucky blunder, for Lee was forced on September 10 to divide his army, sending Jackson back into Virginia to capture Harper's Ferry, while he proceeded with Longstreet toward Hagerstown.

The feeling in the North approached consternaton. That Lee should **threaten** Washington and Baltimore, then Harrisburg and Philadelphia, while Bragg threatened Louisville and Cincinnati, was a piling up of menace that shook the nerves of the coolest men. Those who were in a position to receive the fullest information seemed the most gravely anxious, for the inner councils of the nation were even more disturbed than the people. The number of the Confederates was grossly exaggerated, but their mobility and their leaders were compensation so great that their power as an invading army was still rated none too high. Taking into account that over 60,000 veteran soldiers, led by Lee, Longstreet, and Jackson, marched out of Frederick with spirits high and with confidence of victory, it may not at this day be affirmed that the alarm which spread over the North was greater than men in such peril ought to feel. In Washington the anxiety was not so much for the safety of the capital, which was well fortified and garrisoned, as for the danger to the cause. Stanton's uneasiness showed itself in the fear that communication with the North might be cut off. "The President said he had felt badly all day" (September 8). Seward, an optimist by nature and by conviction, wrote to his wife: "It would seem as if a crisis in our affairs were at hand. It would be easy to predict a favorable result, but the old armies are fearfully reduced. The new regiments come in very slowly, and of course they will be quite unreliable at first." When Lee left Frederick and made directly for Pennsylvania, the farmers on the border sent away their women and children, then their cattle, and armed themselves for the protection of their homes against cavalry raids. The despatches from Governor Curtin at Harrisburg manifest concern for that capital: he called out 50,000 militia for the defence of the State. The words which came from Philadelphia were such as utter the citizens of a wealthy city in time of panic. All sorts of suggestions of little or no value were telegraphed to Halleck, to Stanton, and to the President, who had already done all they could. The peril in which Maryland and Pennsylvania lay could for the moment be averted only by McClellan and his army.

McClellan started his troops from Washington September 5, he himself following two days later. The necessity of reorganizing his depleted army and of covering Baltimore and Washington, together with his own habitual caution and his uncertainty as to the enemy's movements, caused him to proceed slowly. September 10 he ordered a general advance, and began to ask for reinforcements; the next day he repeated this request, specified what troops in particular he wanted, and argued that it would be well even to weaken the defences about Washington for the purpose of strengthening his army: he estimated the Confederate force at 120,000. The President ordered Porter's corps to join him. September 12 a portion of the Union right wing entered Frederick City amidst the joyful acclaim of its inhabitants. McClellan arrived a day later, and wrote of his "enthusiastic reception": "I was nearly overwhelmed and pulled to pieces. . . . As to flowers,—they came in crowds!" Fortune turned his way. There was brought to him an order of Lee, disclosing the division of the Confederate army and the exact scheme of their march—the whole plan of the able strategist opposed to him was revealed. The order, addressed to D. H. Hill and wrapped around three cigars, was found by Private Mitchell of the 27th Indiana on the ground which had been occupied by Hill's troops. When General John G. Walker received his copy of this order, it occurred to him that disaster might result from its loss, and he "pinned it securely in an inside pocket." Longstreet, with the same thought, took a more certain precaution; "he memorized the order and then chewed it up." The finder and his superior officers made no doubt of its importance: it was taken at once to the headquarters of the army, where the signature to it of Lee's adjutant was verified. McClellan's joy is shown in his despatch to the President written at noon of September 13: "I have the whole rebel force in front of me, but am confident, and no time shall be lost. . . . I think Lee has made a gross mistake, and that he will be severely punished for it. The army is in motion as rapidly as possible. I hope for a great success if the plans of the rebels remain unchanged. . . . I have all the plans of the rebels, and will catch them in their own trap if my men are equal to the emergency. I now feel that I can count on them as of old. . . . My respects to Mrs. Lincoln. Received most enthusiastically by the ladies." McClellan acted with energy, but not with the energy of the great Frederick or of Napoleon. He marched his army forward, and the next day (September 14) won the battle of South Mountain. Jacob Dolson Cox, who seized an unexpected opportunity, made a brave assault in the morning, with his Kanawha division and carried the crest of Fox's Gap. In the afternoon Reno's corps, to which Cox belonged, and Hooker's corps forced Turner's Gap, securing a passage for the Union army over the South Mountain range to the field of Antietam. This victory restored the morale of the Union army, and gave heart to the President and the people of the North.

Meanwhile Franklin, on his way to relieve the garrison at Harper's Ferry, had forced Crampton's Gap. But it had been put beyond the power of generals of no more enterprise than McClellan and Franklin to save this post. The military blunder of Halleck in refusing to abandon Harper's Ferry would have been an astonishing piece of good fortune had he thrown off for the occasion his habitual vacillation. As early as September 5 he suggested to Wool, who was stationed at Baltimore and had command of a department which embraced Harper's Ferry, "the propriety of withdrawing all our forces in that vicinity to Maryland Heights," on the Maryland side of the Potomac River; but Wool did not see fit to put this suggestion in shape of an order. Why Halleck himself did not issue such a command is not entirely clear. McClellan advised it as the next best thing to having the garrison reinforce his own army, and had it been done it is difficult to imagine how Lee with all his fertility of resource could have saved himself, for Franklin and the Harper's Ferry garrison would have fought Jackson while McClellan overwhelmed the other wing of the Confederate army. Perhaps the military jealousy of which Halleck had spoken in warning to Pope had risen in his own breast, and as McClellan's star was now in the ascendant and his was declining, he would not order it because the suggestion came from his rival. Nothing could have been more unwise than this division of authority. The whole campaign should have been from the first in McClellan's hands. Yet, as haggling between Halleck and McClellan seemed to be the necessary concomitant of their endeavors to co-operate, Halleck ought to have had the courage of his conviction. Wool was a man seventy-eight years old, who had been given a place on account of meritorious service in Mexico, but who seems to have been no better than a clog in these operations; and for the general-in-chief to have suggested to him a strategic move was a piece of misplaced responsibility hardly to be expected in military affairs. D. S. Miles, the commander at Harper's Ferry, placed the strange construction on his orders that they did not permit him to mass his whole force on Maryland Heights, but required him in his exigency to coop it up in the village. Jackson and other detachments of the Confederates encompassed Harper's Ferry by occupying all the hills around it, and the garrison fell without a struggle, the surrender including 12,500 men and much material of war.

The despatches of Halleck, even after he became aware of the finding of Lee's lost order, conveyed to McClellan poor and superfluous counsel. His fears for the safety of Washington, his anxious suggestions of caution showed blindness to McClellan's great fault, and no proper comprehension of the strategy needed in this campaign. Compare this division of authority among Halleck, McClellan, and Wool, accompanied undoubtedly by pressure from the President and the Secretary of War, with the management on the other side, where a single head directed all movements. Lee was supreme. Longstreet objected to the division of the army when he was asked to command the detachment for the capture of Harper's Ferry. Lee simply ordered Jackson to make the move at first intended for Longstreet, but the arrangement was made in such manner that Longstreet did not feel aggrieved. It may have been that aversion to having his movements hampered by his superior was a reason why Lee objected to Jefferson Davis joining his army.

A citizen friendly to the Confederate cause had been present when Lee's lost order was brought to McClellan; he got an inkling of its importance to the Union army, made his way through the lines, and gave the information to Stuart, who at once transmitted it to Lee. Having this knowledge before daylight of September 14, Lee, who was disappointed and concerned at the rapid advance of McClellan, left Hagerstown, retraced his steps, disputed without success, as we have seen, the passes of South Mountain, and took up a strong position behind Antietam Creek, around the village of Sharpsburg. In the lost order Jackson and the commanders of the different detachments acting with him for the capture of Harper's Ferry were asked to join the main body of the army after accomplishing their object. Lee awaited them with his small force. His Maryland campaign so far was a failure. Circumstances had beaten him, and only a decisive victory could bring back that prestige which was his when he marched out of Frederick. It was no longer Philadelphia and Harrisburg that were in danger; it was the very army which had menaced them. McClellan, say military judges, should have pressed forward vigorously, fought Lee the afternoon of September 15 before Jackson came up, since with his superior force he ought to have crushed the Confederate army. Whether indeed he could have been ready may be questioned, but it seems clear that he ought to have attacked early in the morning of the 16th, when Jackson was still three miles away on the other side of the Potomac, when John G. Walker's division was even farther off, and when McLaws, R. H. Anderson, and A. P. Hill, who had also assisted in the capture of Harper's Ferry, were in a position not to come up until the next day. Walker arrived during the morning of the 16th, and reporting to Lee found him "calm, dignified, and even cheerful," as composed as if he had had a "well-equipped army of a hundred thousand veterans at his back," confident that he could hold his own until he was joined by the other three divisions.

McClellan and the main part of his army had left South Mountain September 15, and advanced to the field of Antietam, taking up their position on the opposite side of Antietam Creek from Lee. One is pleased with the glimpses he obtains of the Union general in these days. Cox tells about a reconnaissance made by McClellan, Burnside, and himself in the afternoon of the 15th, when, standing on a hill in the midst of a large group of officers, they attracted the fire of the enemy's artillery. "I noted," adds Cox, "the cool and business-like air with which McClellan made his examination under fire."

He had certainly purposed to give battle on the 16th. At 7 A.M. he telegraphed to Halleck, "will attack as soon as situation of enemy is developed." Our general was a busy man that day, scheming, reconnoitring, changing the position of his troops. But in his desire to have everything in perfect readiness he was letting slip an advantage which fortune and his own ability had secured. He experienced apparently no trepidation at the thought of meeting face to face the antagonist who had out-manœuvred and defeated him on the Peninsula and had driven Pope from the plains of Manassas; but he had not Lee's faculty of grasping a situation, nor would he ever combine his many perceptions in a single judgment that would gain for him the end desired.

In the afternoon of the 16th McClellan commenced operations on his right by sending Hooker, who now commanded a corps, across Antietam creek. A skirmish resulted which lasted until dark, and that night Hooker's men lay so close to the Confederate left wing that the opposing pickets could hear each other's tread.

This advance of the Union troops had shown Lee where the battle would begin on the morrow. At daylight, September 17, Hooker made a vigorous onset. He encountered stern resistance, and there was stiff wrestling and awful carnage in that historic cornfield. Knowing that he was hard pressed, Joseph K. F. Mansfield's corps, who had crossed the creek the night before, on orders to support him, was hastening to his assistance. Mansfield soon met his death, and Hooker was wounded and borne from the field. "Had you not been wounded when you were," wrote McClellan to him three days afterwards, "I believe the result of the battle would have been the entire destruction of the rebel army, for I *know* that, with you at its head, your corps would have kept on until it gained the main road." Hooker's corps, badly cut up, slowly retreated from the cornfield. Mansfield's corps pressed on, drove the Confederates before them, and part of one division effected a lodgment in the woods north of the Dunker church, which was situated on the high ground that was the key to the position of the enemy's left wing; but the greater part of the corps was finally brought to a stand. These corps had fought separate battles which by nine o'clock were practically over.

Now Sumner came forward. With "ill-regulated ardor" he put in the division of Sedgwick, who advanced "in column with his flank absolutely unprotected." But Jackson, who had the advantage of numbers, hurled Early and Walker together with McLaws, who had just arrived from Harper's Ferry, upon Sedgwick. "My God," exclaims Sumner, "we must get out of this." He attempts to avert the disaster, is unsuccessful, and gives the word to retreat. It is now perhaps ten o'clock. Hooker's and Mansfield's corps and Sedgwick's division have been hurt, and are unable to resume the offensive, but reinforced by part of Franklin's corps, which has just arrived from Crampton's pass, are still strong for defence. Sedgwick himself has been wounded. These successful blows have cost the Confederates dear.

After Sedgwick had been repulsed, French's division, afterwards assisted by Richardson's division, both of Sumner's corps, made an attack on Lee's line to the right of his extreme left where the previous fighting had been done. This was a desperate encounter, especially the struggle in the sunken road which has since been known as Bloody Lane. Richardson fell, mortally wounded; but the enemy was driven before them and would have suffered a still greater defeat but for the opportune arrival from Harper's Ferry of R. H. Anderson's division. The fighting on this part of the field ended at about one.

Burnside commanded the left of McClellan's line, which was formed by his old corps, the Ninth, under Cox, the successor of Reno, who had been killed at the battle of South Mountain. At about ten o'clock Burnside received the order to carry the bridge across the Antietam, thereafter known as Burnside's bridge. Cox took charge of the operation, which was a difficult one in that he must fight his way across the creek. The creek ran in a deep and narrow valley, and the slope on the Confederate side, which was steep, was commanded by the enemy from rifle-pits and "breastworks made of rails and stones." Rodman's division and Scammon's brigade were ordered to cross by a ford one third of a mile below the bridge. Cox at the bridge met with a stubborn resistance, but his work was stiff and persistent, for the Union right had fared badly, and orders came constantly from McClellan to push the assault. Finally, the troops made a last successful charge, carried the bridge, and at one o'clock planted the banner on the opposite bank. Rodman had crossed at the ford, and at the same time had approached the rear of the enemy's position. The heights had been won and were held. Ammunition and fresh troops were now needed, and it was three o'clock before all was again made ready. Then Cox advanced and drove the Confederates before him. Sharpsburg, the centre of Lee's position, was almost in his grasp, when up came A. P. Hill's division, which had marched that day from Harper's Ferry. These men were dressed in the blue uniforms which were part of their captured spoil, and until they began to fire, Cox's soldiers thought they were a Union force. If only Couch's division, which had been left at Maryland Heights to watch Jackson, had arrived at the same time, as perhaps they might have done had everything been ordered with care, how different had been the result! As it was, the advance of Cox was checked. He withdrew his troops in good order, but still held much of the ground he had gained by forcing the passage of the creek.

The battle of Antietam was over. Lee had had 55,000 available troops, McClellan 87,000. McClellan used only about 60,000 in the battle; Lee employed every man who reached the field of action, but since the concentration of his troops at Sharpsburg had required swift marches from more than one half of his army, the men whom he took into battle fell short of the number which the field returns gave as present for duty. The Union loss was 12,410; the Confederate, 11,172. While McClellan outnumbered Lee in the ratio of about three to two, the work of attack was his, and the position of the Confederates was strong for defence. Besides the breastworks spoken of there were "occasional ridges of limestone cropping out in such shape as to give partial cover to infantry lying under them." The Confederates had, moreover, the full benefit of interior lines.

Much controversy obtains whether Antietam was a Union or Confederate victory, and the result is variously characterized in technical terms. After an analysis of the evidence and the criticisms, it will, I think, appear to the non-professional student that McClellan was justified when on the morning of the next day he wrote to his wife what he had gained a success. We read much, however, about his defective tactics. "It was," asserts General Francis A. Walker, "a day of isolated attacks and wasted efforts." In this opinion there is so general a consensus that to traverse it will be impossible. Perhaps McClellan would have severely defeated Lee had not

his overestimate of the Confederate force forbade his using Franklin's
corps to the best advantage and making any use whatever of Porter's
corps, which he held rigidly as his reserve. But to one who is biassed by
the feeling that Lee had by this time shown himself almost invincible, it
will be natural to speak well of the general who overcame him in any way
and on any terms. While Lee's strategy and in some measure his tactics
have been censured by Longstreet, the layman will be prone to agree with
Allan that the conduct of the battle of Antietam itself "by Lee and his
principal subordinates seems absolutely above criticism."

McClellan's first impulse was to renew the battle the next day, but after
"a careful and anxious survey of the condition" of his command he decided
to rest his army and get the reinforcements which were arriving into position for an attack on the morrow. He has been blamed by military critics
for not falling upon the Confederates at once, but as Lee "awaited without
apprehension the renewal of the attack," we may conclude that McClellan's
caution redounded to the benefit of the Union cause. September 19 Lee
withdrew from the field and crossed the Potomac into Virginia. The pursuit
was neither vigorous nor effectual.

Military judges criticise McClellan's lack of celerity after he found Lee's
lost order; he acted with energy, they say, but not with the utmost possible
energy. The situation demanded uncommon diligence, the straining of every
nerve, inasmuch as the destruction or capture of Lee's army in detachments
was in sight. Lincoln and Seward, believing that more might have been
accomplished, were not satisfied. In these judgments, however, there is,
consciously or unconsciously, a reflection of what Frederick the Great or
Napoleon in like case would have done. But against a Frederick, a Napoleon, or the Grant or Sherman of 1864, Lee's strategy would have been different: he would not have invaded Maryland nor divided his army. Instead
therefore of emphasizing these criticisms, let us rather contrast the conquer-
ing host of the South as they marched through the streets of Frederick, full
of pride and hope, and singing "The Girl I left behind me," with the "horde
of disordered fugitives" fleeing before an army they had a fortnight earlier
driven "to cover under its homeward ramparts"; let us note the change of
feeling at the North from depression before South Mountain to buoyancy
after Antietam; let us reflect that a signal Confederate victory in Maryland
might have caused the Northern voters at the approaching fall elections to
declare for the peace that Jefferson Davis would offer them from the head
of Lee's victorious army, and that without McClellan's victory the Emancipation Proclamation would have been postponed and might never have been
issued!

Antietam "was the bloodiest single day of fighting of the war," writes
Longstreet, and supports the statement with an array of figures. Such fighting in a border State like Maryland makes us realize the horror of civil
conflict. On this battlefield friend fought friend, and even brother fought

brother. At the ford near Burnside bridge a Northern colonel leading a charge of his regiment was killed by the Confederates under the command of his brother, the general of a division. We may say with King Henry VI, whom Shakespeare represents in a battle of the Wars of the Roses as standing by when a son, who has killed his father unawares, recognizes the face of the slain and bursts into grief,

> "O piteous spectacle! O bloody times!
> Whiles lions roar and battle for their dens,
> Poor harmless lambs abide their enmity.
> Weep, wretched man, I'll aid thee tear for tear;
> And let our hearts and eyes, like civil war,
> Be blind with tears, and break o'ercharged with grief."

The great historical significance of the battle of Antietam is that it furnished Lincoln the victory he was waiting for to issue his proclamation of emancipation. This, as we have seen, he had laid aside on July 22, until some military success should give support to the policy. The working of his mind in the two months following that day is open to us. While he had come to a resolve, he showed the true executive quality, as well as the fair mind, in not regarding the policy of striking directly at slavery as absolutely and finally determined until it had been officially promulgated. From the cabinet meeting of July 22, when he announced tentatively his purpose, to that of September 22, when he told his advisers that he should issue an irrevocable decree, he endeavored, in his correspondence and formal interviews and private conversation, to get all the light possible to aid him in deciding when the proper moment had come to proclaim freedom to the slaves. To Conservatives he argued the radical side of the question. "I shall not surrender this game leaving any available card unplayed," he wrote Reverdy Johnson. "This government cannot much longer play a game in which it stakes all and its enemies stake nothing," he said in a letter to August Belmont. "Those enemies must understand that they cannot experiment for ten years trying to destroy the government and if they fail still come back into the Union unhurt. If they expect in any contingency to ever have the Union as it was . . . now is the time." To Radicals he put forth the conservative view or laid stress on the necessity of proceeding with caution. "My paramount object . . . is to save the Union, and is not either to save or to destroy slavery," he wrote to Horace Greeley. To the committee of clergymen from the public meeting in Chicago of Christians of all denominations who presented a memorial in favor of national emancipation, he said: "I do not want to issue a document that the whole world will see must necessarily be inoperative, like the Pope's bull against the comet. Would my word free the slaves when I cannot even enforce the Constitution in the rebel States? Is there a single court, or magistrate, or individual that would be influenced by it there?"

There was pressure on the President to issue a proclamation of emancipation, and there was pressure against it. He talked with conservatives and radicals, listened to their arguments, reasoned with them, and left different impressions on different minds. Much of his talk was after his manner of thinking aloud where the stimulation of contact with sympathetic or captious men afforded him the opportunity to revolve his thoughts, and see the question on all sides. There was, indeed, much to be considered. His warrant was the war powers of the Constitution. There ought to be a reasonable probability that a proclamation would help the operations of our army in spite of the strong opposition among many officers of high rank to a war for the negro, that it would damage the Confederates by stirring up in the slaves their inherent desire for freedom, causing every one of them to be in secret a friend of the North, and that it might lead to the employment of the blacks as soldiers. Granted these considerations, Lincoln must satisfy himself that public opinion at the North would sustain him in the action. He could not doubt that the cavilling support of the radicals would for the moment turn to enthusiasm, and the zeal of these positive anti-slavery Republicans directed in the channel of raising men and money was an influence worth having. But was the sentiment of the plain people, the mass of steady Republicans and war Democrats, ripe for an edict of freedom?

Again, the possibility that the policy might alienate the border slave States which had clung to the Union was in Lincoln's mind a serious objection, "but the difficulty was as great not to act as to act." On the other hand, emancipation would help us in Europe. England and France could not recognize the Southern Confederacy when the real issue between the sections was thus unmasked. Yet there was reason to anticipate that an avowed war against slavery would revive the opposition of the Democrats and give them a "club" to use against the administration; but the President did not regard this an objection of great moment, since party opposition at the North must in any event be expected.

Turning the question over and over in his mind, he finally settled his doubts. He believed that a proclamation of freedom was a military necessity, and that the plain people of the North would see it as he did. As the days went on, he was confirmed in the conclusion which he had come to in July, and felt that public sentiment was growing in that direction. Even in the dark hours following the second defeat of Bull Run and Lee's invasion of Maryland, he did not falter. "When the rebel army was at Frederick" [September 6-10], he afterwards said, "I determined as soon as it should be driven out of Maryland to issue a proclamation of emancipation. . . . I said nothing to any one, but I made the promise to myself and to my Maker." Antietam was won. Lee had recrossed the Potomac into Virginia. Then was held that cabinet meeting of September 22, which is a point in the history of civilization. After some general talk, the President took the word and read from Artemus Ward's book a chapter, "High-Handed Outrage at Utica." He thought it very funny and enjoyed the reading of it greatly, while the members of the cabinet except Stanton laughed with him. Was ever so sublime a thing ushered in by the ridiculous? Lincoln fell into a grave tone and told of the working of his thoughts on the slavery question since the July meeting. "The rebel army is now driven out" of Maryland, he said, and I am going to fulfil the promise I made to myself and my God. "I have got you together to hear what I have written down. I do not wish your advice about the main matter; for that I have determined for myself." He read then his proclamation of freedom: "On the first day of January, in the year of our Lord one thousand eight hundred and sixty-three, all persons held as slaves within any State or designated part of a State, the people whereof shall then be in rebellion against the United States, shall be then, thenceforward, and forever free." In the case of the loyal slave States he declared again for his policy of compensated emancipation, and colonization of the freed negroes, and said that he should in due time recommend compensation also for the loss of their slaves to loyal citizens of the States in rebellion. All the members of the cabinet except Blair approved substantially the proclamation, and Blair's objection was on the ground of expediency, not of principle. On the morrow, September 23, this edict, which heralded a new epoch in the world's progress, was given to the country.

The next evening the President made a short speech to a party who serenaded him, in which he said: "What I did, I did after a very full deliberation and under a very heavy and solemn sense of responsibility. I can only trust in God I have made no mistake. . . . It is now for the country and the world to pass judgment and, maybe, take action upon it." The immediate response of the country was apparently favorable "God bless Abraham Lincoln," the New York *Tribune* said, and it spoke for the radical and fervent Republicans. Many conservatives endorsed it because it came from the mind and pen of the President. But Lincoln himself, with his delicate touch on the pulse of public opinion, detected that there was a lack of heartiness in the response of the Northen people. In his "strictly private" letter to Hamlin, the Vice-President, he manifested his keen disappointment. "While I hope something from the proclamation," he wrote, "my expectations are not as sanguine as are those of some friends. The time for its effect southward has not come; but northward the effect should be instantaneous. It is six days old, and while commendation in newspapers and by distinguished individuals is all that a vain man could wish, the stocks have declined and troops come forward more slowly than ever. This, looked soberly in the face, is not very satisfactory. . . . The North responds to the proclamation sufficiently in breath; but breath alone kills no rebels." Lincoln's despondency is revealed also in his reply to an address by a pious Quaker woman, and in his "Meditation on the Divine Will," in which his belief in a divine Providence mingled with his present disappointment to produce the doubt whether indeed God were on our side.

CHANCELLORSVILLE AND GETTYSBURG, 1863

The appointment of Hooker to the command of the Army of the Potomac was the President's own, although it was plainly prompted by the sentiment of the rank and file and of the country which had been formed by the general's record as an excellent and dashing corps commander. But Halleck was opposed to it, and a few of the higher officers of the Potomac army who had grown up with it felt that Lincoln had made an unwise choice. Curiously enough, Chase, who was the persistent friend of Hooker and had more than once urged that he be given the command in the place of McClellan, conceived an inkling of defects that might come to the surface if he held the supreme responsibility. When he lay in Washington recovering from his wound received at Antietam, Chase visited him, and the two conversed freely. The general had "less breadth of intellect" than the Secretary had expected. His surgeon and devoted friend gave to Chase this estimate of him: "Brave, energetic, full of life, skilful on the field, not comprehensive enough, perhaps, for the plan and conduct of a great compaign."

The appointment of Hooker, however, was a natural choice and deserves no criticism. The day after it was made the President wrote him a remarkable letter. "There are some things in regard to which," he said, "I am not quite satisfied with you. . . . I think that during General Burnside's command of the army you have taken counsel of your ambition and thwarted him as much as you could, in which you did a great wrong to the country and to a meritorious and honorable brother officer. I have heard in such a way as to believe it, of your recently saying that both the army and the government needed a dictator. . . . Only those generals who gain successes can set up dictators. What I now ask of you is military success and I will risk the dictatorship. . . . I much fear that the spirit which you have aided to infuse into the army of criticising their commander and withholding confidence from him will now turn upon you. I shall assist you as far as I can to put it down. . . . Beware of rashness, but with energy and sleepless vigilance go forward and give us victories."

When Hooker took command, the Army of the Potomac had through continued defeats become "quite disheartened and almost sulky." The number of absentees was enormous, and desertions were frequent. "So anxious were parents, wives, brothers, and sisters to relieve their kindred that they filled the express trains to the army with packages of citizen clothing to assist them in escaping from the service." The general went to work energetically to correct these evils. His eminent talent for organization was felt throughout the army. "I have never known men to change from a condition of the lowest depression to that of a healthy fighting state in so short a time," wrote General Couch, one of his severest critics after Chancellorsville. A feeling of confidence grew up in the camp, while the labor of the general and its results were understood by the country. The people of the North took hope again, and their temper was buoyant as they looked forward to success.

Early in April Hooker considered his army in condition to take the offensive. He was hastened in his determination by the knowledge that the term of service of 23,000 nine months' and two years' men would soon expire. Encamped on the north bank of the Rappahannock River, he had 130,000 troops to oppose Lee's 60,000, who were at Fredericksburg: the Army of Northern Virginia had been weakened by the detachment of Longstreet and part of his corps. Hooker ordered his cavalry to advance towards Richmond for the purpose of severing the communications of the Confederates, but owing to heavy rains and high water in the river, these troops were delayed and were of no assistance to him in his operations. He was not able to wait for them to perform their part. April 27 three corps were put in motion; they crossed the Rappahannock thirty miles above Fredericksburg, then forded the Rapidan and marched to Chancellorsville on the south side of these rivers. To mask the main movement, General John Sedgwick with his corps forced the passage of the Rappahannock a short distance below Fredericksburg. Meanwhile the Second Corps under Couch had crossed the river at the United States ford and had reached Chancellorsville. There on the night of April 30 four corps were assembled with General Hooker in person in command. "It had been," writes Couch, "a brilliantly conceived and executed movement. . . . All of the army lying there that night were in exuberant spirits at the success of their general in getting 'on the other side' without fighting for a position. As I rode into Chancellorsville that night, the general hilarity pervading the camps was particularly noticeable; the soldiers, while chopping wood and lighting fires, were singing merry songs and indulging in peppery camp jokes." Hooker was full of confidence which displayed itself in a boastful order. "The operations of the last three days," he declared, "have determined that our enemy must either ingloriously fly or come out from behind his defences and give us battle on our own ground, where certain destruction awaits him." That "with twice the weight of arm and as keen a blade," and in spite of the splendid initiative, the Army of the Potomac met with disaster, is easily understood. Hooker was completely out-generalled by Lee. The Confederate commander had the perfect co-operation of Jackson, while the shortcomings of the Union general were aggravated by the carelessness of Howard, the commander of the Eleventh Corps.

Lee had early information of all of Hooker's movements, and by the afternoon of April 30 divined that his object was to turn the Confederate left. He ordered an advance to meet the Union troops who had taken position at Chancellorsville. When they pushed forward from the Wilderness, May 1, the enemy, instead of flying ingloriously, resisted and took the offensive. Hooker lost nerve and issued an order to his men to fall back. He had better left the movement to his corps and division commanders, who were

at one in the opinion that they should make a vigorous attempt to hold the
ground in the open country which they had gained. "My God," exclaimed
Meade, "if we can't hold the top of a hill, we certainly cannot hold the bottom of it." Hooker's own explanation of his decision to retreat is unsatisfactory. To abandon the offensive and take up a line of defence, when he had
two men to his opponents' one and knew it, was certainly a glaring fault
of generalship. Couch heard the reason of it from his own lips, and "retired
from his presence with the belief that my commanding general was a
whipped man." All but one of the military writers with whom I am acquainted agree that the retrograde movement was unnecessary, that it was
the abandonment of the prime object of the campaign, and demoralizing to
officers and soldiers. This note of despair must have run through rank and
file: "It is no use. No matter who is given us, we can't whip Bobby Lee."

Hooker's position of defence was in the Wilderness, a tangled forest,
an almost impenetrable thicket of dwarf oak and shrubbery. He deemed it
a strong one, and so did Lee, who considered that a direct attack upon the
Union army, which Hooker was hoping for, "would be attended with great
difficulty and loss." On the night of May 1 Lee and Stonewall Jackson
might have been seen seated on two old cracker-boxes taking counsel together. The result of the deliberation evinced their supreme contempt for
the generalship of their opponent, for, in the presence of superior numbers,
they decided to divide their own forces. Early on the morning of May 2
Jackson, "the great flanker," with thirty thousand men started on a march
which took him half-way around the Union army, his design being to attack
its right, which was held by Howard and his Eleventh Corps. Hooker
was up betimes, making an inspection of his lines, which resulted in a
joint order to Howard and Slocum, written at 9.30 A. M., warning them
to be prepared against a flank attack of the enemy. Jackson's column,
marching along, was plainly seen by our men. The movement might
be interpreted in two ways,—either that the Confederates were on the
retreat southward, or that they were on their way to attack our right. Frequent reports of the progress of Jackson's column came to Hooker and
to Howard, but they could see it in one light only,—that the enemy was
retiring before the superior force which threatened him. At noon Sickles,
who had brought his corps across the river the previous day, received
orders to harass the movement; he captured some prisoners whose tale
indicated that Jackson was bent on fight, not on retreat. This certainly
should have been strongly suspected from a study of the characters and
past generalship of Jackson and Lee. Still Hooker would not be convinced.
At 4.10 P. M. he sent word to Sedgwick: "We know that the enemy is
fleeing, trying to save his trains. Two of Sickles's divisions are among them."
It was equally impossible to make Howard see the truth. Carl Schurz, who
commanded a division in his corps, urged upon him that the facts pointed
unmistakably to an attack from the west upon their right and rear, and
advised earnestly that they execute a change of front in order to be ready

for it. But Howard would issue no such command, although Schurz on his own responsibility did change in accordance with his judgment the position of two of his regiments. The Eleventh Corps had been further weakend by the detachment on an order from headquarters of a brigade to the support of Sickles.

At three o'clock in the afternoon, after a march of fifteen miles, Jackson reached the place for which he had set out. He was west of the Union army, on the side of it directly opposite the position occupied by General Lee. Losing no time in forming his troops in battle array, he was ready soon after five and gave the order to advance.

The Eleventh Corps lay quietly in position, unsuspecting danger. The opinion at headquarters and of their own commander controlled the other officers, with a few exceptions, and pervaded also the soldiers. Some of the men were getting supper ready, others were eating or resting, some were playing cards. The warning came from the wild rush of deer and rabbits driven from their lairs by the quick march of the Confederates through the Wilderness. Twenty-six thousand of Jackson's men, "the best infantry in existence, as tough, hardy, and full of spirit as they are ill-fed, ill-clothed, and ill-looking," surprised less than half their number. The officers and men of the Eleventh Corps in the main did well. But, asks Colonel Dodge, "what can be expected of new troops, taken by surprise and attacked in front, flank, and rear at once?" After a brief resistance they ran.

It was a dearly bought victory for the Confederates. Jackson, busy in the endeavor to re-form his troops who had fallen into confusion from the charge through the thick and tangled wood, and eager to discover the intentions of Hooker, rode with his escort forward beyond his line of battle. Fired upon by the Federal troops, they turned about, and as they rode back in the obscurity of the night, were mistaken for Union horsemen and shot at by their own soldiers, Jackson receiving a mortal wound. The disabilty of the general undoubtedly prevented his victory from being more complete. Sickles was in jeopardy, but the night was clear and the moon nearly full, and he fought his way back, reoccupying his breastworks.

Hooker, despondent at the rout of the Eleventh Corps, was in mind and nerve unfit for the exercise of his great responsibility. The story of Sunday the 3d of May is that of an incompetent commander in a state of nervous collapse confronted by an able and alert general. Early in the morning Jackson's corps, yelling fiercely and crying "Remember Jackson," made the attack, seconded by the troops under Lee's immediate command. The Union soldiers resisted bravely. The efforts of officers and men were praiseworthy, but there was no head, and nothing was effective that emanated from headquarters. Thirty to thirty-five thousand fresh troops, near at hand and eager to fight, were not called into action. The parting injunction of Lincoln to Hooker on his visit to the Army of the Potomac in April, "In your next battle *put in all your men*," had gone unheeded.

Shortly after nine o'clock in the morning Hooker was knocked down and rendered senseless by a cannon ball striking a pillar of the veranda of Chancellor House, against which he was leaning; but at that time the battle was practically lost. "By 10 A. M." said Lee in his report, "we were in full possession of the field."

On the evening of May 2, after the rout of Howard, Hooker sent word to Sedgwick to march toward Chancellorsville and be "in our vicinity at daylight. You will probably fall upon the rear of the forces commanded by General Lee," the despatch continued, "and between us we will use him up." The commander had given Sedgwick an impossible undertaking. He was three miles below Fredericksburg on the south side of the river, and between him and Lee lay Early, with over 9000 men occupying places strongly fortified. He received the order at eleven at night, moved promptly, skirmishing as he advanced, and at daylight was in possession of Fredericksburg. To gain the road desired, he must take Marye's Heights, whence the Confederates the previous December had overwhelmed with slaughter Burnside's troops. Two storming colums were formed, flanked by the line of battle, and, advancing on the double quick under a destructive fire, carried the works on the heights, capturing guns and many prisoners. Sedgwick then marched towards Hooker; but ere this Hooker's battle of May 3 was over, with the result that he had been driven back from his position at Chancellorsville. Lee learned with much regret of the capture of Fredericksburg and Marye's Heights, and sent a portion of his force to meet Sedgwick's corps. They joined battle at Salem Church, and the Confederates got the better of it. The next day, May 4, leaving Jackson's corps to hold Hooker in check, Lee late in the afternoon fell with 25,000 men upon Sedgwick's 20,000, who resisted the attack until nightfall. Sedgwick, considering that he was hemmed in by the enemy, took advantage of the permission contained in one of the conflicting despatches that crossed between him and his commander, and withdrew that night to the north bank of the Rappahannock. All that day Hooker had done nothing to relieve Sedgwick, although only 22,000 Confederates confronted his 80,000. After a council of war he decided to recross the river, and by the morning of May 6 this movement was accomplished safely and without molestation. The loss of the Union army in the Chancellorsville campaign was 17,287; that of the Confederates, 12,463.

While Jackson lay suffering from his wounds, pneumonia set in, and eight days after his signal victory over Howard, he died. The Confederates had better lost the battle than this commander of genius. Nothing will as well round the conception of him which we have already acquired from following his successful career as the testimony of the ablest and noblest representative of the Southern cause. On hearing that he was wounded Lee wrote to him: "Could I have directed events, I should have chosen for the good of the country to be disabled in your stead." After the war he declared, "Had I Stonewall Jackson at Gettysburg, I would have won a great victory."

With the fervent abolitionist poet, we of the North may "let a tear fall on Stonewall's bier." He was the leader and the type of the very religious Scotch-Irish of the South, who, as we found out to our cost, were redoubtable fighters. They will never again meet us in civil strife; indeed in the war with Spain of 1898 the descendants of those who with sublime devotion had followed Stonewall Jackson responded to the common country's call.

Who may pretend to explain the incongruity of man? Both the conscientious Jackson and Barère, the man without a conscience, believed in waging war like barbarians. During the wars of the Revolution the Frenchman proposed to the Convention that no English or Hanoverian prisoners be taken. "I always thought," declared Jackson, that "we ought to meet the Federal invaders on the outer verge of just right and defence, and raise at once the black flag, viz., 'No quarter to the violators of our homes and firesides.' It would in the end have proved true humanity and mercy. The Bible is full of such wars, and it is the only policy that would bring the North to its senses."

Owing to the censorship of the telegraph by the War Department, the news of the disaster at Chancellorsville reached the North slowly. When its full extent became known, discouragement ruled. Many men who were earnest in the support of the war gave up all idea that the South could be conquered. Nothing demonstrates more painfully the sense of failure of the North to find a successful general than the serious and apparently well-considered suggestion of the Chicago *Tribune* that Abraham Lincoln take the field as the actual commander of the Army of the Potomac. We sincerely believe, the writer of this article concluded, that "Old Abe" can lead our armies to victory. "If he does not, who will?"

Nevertheless, the gloom and sickness at heart so apparent after the first and second Bull Run, the defeat of McClellan before Richmond, and the battle of Fredericksburg are not discernible in anything like the same degree. It is true that the newspapers are not so accurate a reflection of public sentiment as they had been. There was unmistakably a large amount of editorial writing for the purpose of keeping up the hope of their readers; but even after the evidence of the newspapers is corrected by the recollections of contemporaries which are printed or still exist as tradition, it is impossible to resist the inference that the depression was different in kind and measure from that which had heretofore prevailed. Business, which had commenced to improve in the autumn of 1862, was now very active. An era of money-making had begun. It is seen in wild speculation on the stock exchanges, in legitimate transactions, and in the savings of the people finding an investment in the bonds of the government. Noticeable, also is the sentiment that the war has helped trade and manufactures. The government was a large purchaser of material; one activity was breeding another; men honestly, and in some cases dishonestly, were gaining profits although the State was in distress. When the news of the defeat at Chancellorsville reached New York, gold rose in price temporarily, but railroad stocks, at first unsettled, soon resumed their active advance, while government bonds remained steady and the subscriptions of the public to the five-twenties went on. That men had ceased to enlist was an indication alike of the weariness of the war and of the many opportunities of lucrative employment offered by the improvement of business. The war, so far as getting privates into the army was concerned, had become a trade. Men were induced to shoulder the musket by bounties from the national government, States, towns, and city wards.

After the battle of Chancellorsville, Lee gave his army a rest of some weeks. He employed the time in its reorganization, dividing it into three corps, each of three divisions, commanded respectively by Longstreet, Ewell, and A. P. Hill. Believing that nothing was to be gained by his army "remaining quietly on the defensive," he decided, with the approval of Davis, on the invasion of Pennsylvania. This movement would at all events, by threatening Washington and drawing Hooker in pursuit of him, relieve Virginia of the presence of a hostile army. But after such victories as Fredericksburg and Chancellorsville he would have been modest past belief had not his expectations gone far beyond so easy an achievement. He hoped to fight the Army of the Potomac on favorable conditions. With his own well-disciplined troops in high spirits and full of confidence in their leader, he could not have entertained an idea that the result would be other than a Confederate victory: perhaps even he might destroy the Union army, when Washington would be at his mercy and he could conquer a peace on Northern soil. Nothing at this time so disturbed the Southern high councils as the operations of Grant against Vicksburg. More than one project was proposed to save it from capture, but no diversion in its favor could be so effectual as the taking of the federal capital. If ever an aggressive movement with so high an object were to be made, now was the time. Not only was it to take advantage of the flush of Confederate success, but the South by delay would lose its efficiency for the offensive. "Our resources in men are constantly diminishing." wrote Lee to Davis, "and the disproportion in this respect between us and our enemies, if they continue united in their efforts to subjugate us, is steadily augmenting." We have had frequent occasion to admire the ability and decision of Lee. To those qualities were joined uncommon industry and attention to detail. He was a constant and careful reader of the Northern newspapers, and from the mass of news comment and speculation he drew many correct inferences, and hardly lost sight of any of the conditions which should be taken into account by him who would play well the game of war. He meditated on the weariness of the contest so largely felt at the North and the growing strength of the Democrats, due in the main to Fredericksburg and Chancellorsville. "We should neglect no honorable means of dividing and weakening our enemies," he wrote to Davis. We should "give all the encouragement we can, consistently with the truth, to the rising peace party of the North. Nor do I think we should, in this connection, make nice distinctions between those who declare for peace unconditionally and those who advocate it as a means of restoring the Union, however much we may prefer the former." Lee must have followed with interest the career of Vallandigham, his arrest, trial, and banishment, and he must have noted the indignant protest that went up from the party opposed to the administration and the mild censure from some of its friends, both of which grew in strength with the suppression of the Chicago *Times*.

June 3 Lee began to move his army from the vicinity of Fredericksburg, and one week later put Ewell's corps in motion for the Shenandoah valley. Ewell drove the Union troops from Winchester and Martinsburg, and on the 15th part of his corps crossed the Potomac, the rest of it soon following. Hill and Longstreet moved forward, and by June 26 their corps had passed over the river and were in Maryland.

Hooker early suspected Lee's project of invasion, and when the movement commenced thought that he ought to attack the rear of the enemy: this operation he suggested to the President. "I have but one idea which I think worth suggesting to you," Lincoln replied, "and that is, in case you find Lee coming to the north of the Rappahannock I would by no means cross to the south of it. If he should leave a rear force at Fredericksburg, tempting you to fall upon it, it would fight in intrenchments and have you at disadvantage, and so, man for man, worst you at that point, while his main force would in some way be getting an advantage of you northward. In one word, I would not take any risk of being entangled upon the river like an ox jumped half over a fence, and liable to be torn by dogs in front and rear, without a fair chance to gore one way or kick the other." When Lee's plan of operations was further disclosed, Hooker proposed to march "to Richmond at once." He felt sure that he could take it, thus "giving the rebellion a mortal blow." Lincoln's reply was prompt. "If left to me," he said, "I would not go south of the Rappahannock upon Lee's moving north of it. If you had Richmond invested to-day, you would not be able to take it in twenty days; meanwhile your communications and with them your army would be ruined. I think Lee's army and not Richmond is your sure objective point. If he comes toward the upper Potomac, follow on his flank and on his inside track, shortening your line while he lengthens his. Fight him, too, when opportunity offers. If he stays where he is, fret him and fret him."

In these despatches Lincoln exhibits common-sense. His diligent reading of military books, the acquirement of knowledge from his generals when occasion offered, the study of the field of war, the close observation of the campaigns and battles of his armies had borne fruit, making him now the best of counsellors in the relation of the civil commander-in-chief to his officers of technical training and experience. Especially at this time was such counsel necessary from a chief who possessed tact and knowledge

of men. The relations between Halleck and Hooker were strained. There
was a lack of the harmonious co-operation requisite between those holding
so responsible positions. "Almost every request I made of General Halleck
was refused," testified Hooker, while Halleck complained that Hooker
reported directly to the President. The correspondence between the two
generals is marked with acerbity. Moreover, some of the corps and division
commanders of the Army of the Potomac had lost confidence in their general. This strained situation while the Army of Northern Virginia under
its able leader was advancing into the heart of the North might well have
dismayed many a stout soul. Lincoln met the crisis without faltering.

When Lee's northward movement seemed certain, Hooker broke up his
camps on the Rappahannock. In his march to the Potomac his management and dispositions were excellent. The Confederates kept to the west
of the Blue Ridge, he to the east, covering Washington constantly. Until
this campaign the South had enjoyed the advantage of better cavalry: that
superiority had now disappeared. This is one of many indications how surely
the North was mastering the trade of war. The improvement in the Federal cavalry, which now did credit to the service, was in some degree due
to Hooker, for it was a part of his efficient reorganization of the Army of
the Potomac. During the march northward they met in combat several
times the Confederate horsemen, and in the main fought successfully. Yet
so obstinate were the contests and so skilful were the manoeuvres that each
body of horse acted as a screen to its army, and Lee and Hooker were each
kept in ignorance of the movements of the enemy. Formerly it had been too
frequently the case that the Confederate knew everything and the Union
commander little or nothing.

Ewell waited at Hagerstown, Maryland, until Longstreet and Hill should
be within supporting distance. June 22 he received orders allowing him to
move forward. "If Harrisburg comes within your means, capture it," was
one of the directions which came from Lee. Ewell, advancing into Pennsylvania to Chambersburg, reached Carlisle on the 27th, and sent Early
with one division to seize upon York. On the formal surrender of the town
by the chief burgess and a deputation of citizens, Early laid it under contribution, receiving 1000 hats, 1200 pairs of shoes, 1000 socks, three days'
rations of all kinds, and $28,600 United States money. He destroyed be-
tween Hanover Junction and York the Northern Central Railroad, which
ran from Baltimore to Harrisburg, and sent an expedition to take possession
of the Columbia bridge over the Susquehanna. He intended to march his
division across it, cut the line of the Pennsylvania Railroad, take Lancaster,
make a requisition upon the town for supplies, and attack Harrisburg in
the rear while the rest of Ewell's corps assailed it from the front. But a
regiment of Pennsylvania militia in fleeing before the Confederates set
fire to the bridge and destroyed it. Meanwhile Ewell sent forward his
cavalry with a section of artillery to make a reconnaissance. They ap-

proached within three miles of Harrisburg, engaging the pickets of the
militia forces assembled there under General Couch for its defence. June
29 Ewell had everything in readiness, and purposed moving on the defences
of Harrisburg. Two days previously Longstreet and Hill had reached
Chambersburg, and Lee was there in command. His whole army, numbering 75,000 men, was on Pennsylvania soil.

By the middle of June the movements of Lee in Virginia warned the
North of the approaching invasion. The President called for 100,000 militia
from Maryland, Pennsylvania, Ohio, and West Virginia, the States regarded
as in immediate danger. The Secretary of War asked help from the governors of thirteen of the other States. No response was so prompt, no
action so effective, as that of Horatio Seymour of New York. "I will spare
no effort to send you troops at once" was the word which came from him
over the wires. June 16 the Confederate cavalry were heard of at Chambersburg, and busy preparations were made to defend the threatened points.
At first the surmise gained ground that Pittsburg was in jeopardy. Alarm
spread through the city, business was suspended, shops were closed, factories stopped. The citizens turned out in crowds to throw up intrenchments
on the surrounding hills. One day it was reported that 14,000 were at
work with picks and shovels, and these men were ready to take up rifles or
man the batteries should the enemy appear. Mill-owners organized their
laborers into companies, and the government furnished them arms and ammunition. A number of prominent citizens, representing the committee of
public safety, requested the President to authorize Brooks, the general in
command, to declare martial law, although Brooks thought this step unnecessary and unwise. Some desired that McClellan be placed in command
of the militia for home defence; others urged the President to give them
Frémont, who would inspire confidence and enthusiasm, and bring forward many thousand volunteers.

At one time there was some anxiety for Washington and Baltimore.
Stuart in a cavalry raid passed between the Union army and these cities. It
was in the Cumberland valley of Pennsylvania, however, that the presence
of the enemy was actually and painfully felt. Yet the Confederates under
the immediate command of Lee committed little or no depredation and
mischief. Before he himself crossed the river into Maryland, he wrote to
Davis, "I shall continue to purchase all the supplies that are furnished me
while north of the Potomac, impressing only where necessary," and he
exerted himself to the utmost to have his wishes in this regard observed.
His order of June 21 enjoined scrupulous respect for private property,
and that of the 27th, after he had reached Chambersburg, manifested his
satisfaction with his troops for their general good behavior, but mentioned
that there had been "instances of forgetfulness," and warned them that such
offenders should be brought to summary punishment. Military discipline,
mercy, and the desire to do everything possible "to promote the pacific

feeling" at the North prompted him to such a course. It is true that the payment for supplies was made in Confederate money which turned out to be worthless, but in estimating his motives it must be remembered that he paid with the only currency that he had, a currency which bade fair to have a considerable value should his confident expectation of defeating the Union army on Pennsylvania soil be realized. No attestation of Lee's sincerity in issuing these orders is needed, but it is grateful to read in various Northern journals of the time words of praise of the Southern commanders for restraining their soldiers from "acts of wanton mischief and rapine."

No matter how mercifully war may be carried on, it is at the best a rude game. At first the raid of the Confederate horsemen caused excitement in the Cumberland valley. The feeling of relief when they fell back was only temporary, and gave place to alarm and distress as Ewell's corps advanced, and later the rest of Lee's army. The country was wild with rumors. Men, women, and children fled before the enemy, and care was taken to run their horses out of the way of the invader. The refugees deemed themselves and their property safe when they had crossed the broad Susquehanna. The bridge over the river, the communication of the Cumberland valley with Harrisburg, was thronged with wagons laden with household goods and furniture. Negroes fled before the advancing host, fearing that they might be dragged back to slavery. June 26 Curtin, the governor of Pennsylvania, issued a proclamation calling for 60,000 men to come forward promptly "to defend their soil, their families, and their firesides." Harrisburg, the capital of the State, was indeed in danger, as was realized by the authorities and the citizens. Thirty regiments of Pennsylvania militia, besides artillery and cavalry, and nineteen regiments from New York assembled under the command of General Couch, who disposed his forces to the best advantage, stationing a large portion of them for the defence of Harrisburg. In the city all places of business were closed, and citizens labored on the fortifications with the pick and the spade. Men were enrolled by wards and drilled in the park and on the streets. The railroad depot was a scene of excitement, caused by the arrival in large numbers of volunteers and the departure of women and frightened men. The progress of the enemy was pretty accurately known. Reports ran that he was twenty-three miles from the city, then eighteen. June 28 cannonading was heard for two hours, and every one knew that the Confederates were within four miles of the Capitol. Harrisburg would probably have been taken had not Ewell's corps been called back by Lee.

If Harrisburg were captured it was thought that the Confederates would march on Phladelphia. Men well informed believed that Lee had nearly 100,000 men and 250 pieces of artillery. A strong pressure in Philadelphia and elsewhere was brought to bear upon the President to place McClellan in command of the Army of the Potomac, or, at all events, of the militia for the defence of Pennsylvania. The Washington *National Intelligencer,* in an article entitled "A Calm Appeal," said, "After much reflection and with a full sense of the responsibility which it involves, we feel it our solemn duty at this juncture to avow the deliberate but earnest conviction that the President cannot by any one act do so much to restore the confidence of the nation as by the recall of General McClellan to the Army of the Potomac." These words were the expression of a serious and powerful sentiment at the North. The board of Councilmen of New York City passed unanimously a resolution, Republicans as well as Democrats voting for it, asking for the restoration of McClellan to the command. It was reported that certain prominent citizens of Philadelphia had requested him to come to their city and "take military charge of things generally." Governor Parker telegraphed to the President that "The people of New Jersey want McClellan at the head of the Army of the Potomac. If that cannot be done, then we ask" that he be placed in command of the militia from New Jersey, New York, and Pennsylvania "defending these Middle States from invasion. If either appointment be made the people would rise *en masse.*" A. K. McClure, a steadfast Republican and friend of the administration, urged that McClellan be given a command. The Common Council of Philadelphia asked it. When Governor Curtin made a speech in that city to rouse its citizens, he was interrupted by cries, "Give us McClellan." A rumor got abroad in New York City that he had been made general-in-chief in the place of Halleck. He chanced to come to town that day from New Jersey, and was greeted with cheers from crowds of enthusiastic people. But there was probably no thought of placing him at the head of the Army of the Potomac or of the militia in Pennsylvania. Lincoln replied kindly to Governor Parker: "I beg you to be assured that no one out of my position can know so well as if he were in it, the difficulties and involvement of replacing General McClellan in command, and this aside from any imputations upon him."

On the evening of June 28 the rumor circulated in Philadelphia that the Confederates were shelling Harrisburg. Chestnut and Market streets were thronged with thousands of men eager for news. The next day two prominent citizens telegraphed to the President that they had reliable information that the enemy in large force was marching upon Philadelphia. Other men of influence desired him to give the general in command authority to declare martial law. Business stopped. The merchants, the manufacturers of iron, the proprietors of machine shops, the coal operators held meetings, and offered inducements to their workmen to enlist for the defence of the State. The members of the Corn Exchange furnished five companies. A meeting of the soldiers of the War of 1812 and another of clergymen were held to offer their services for home defence. It was said that bankers and merchants were making preparations to remove specie and other valuables from the city. Receipts and shipments on the Pennsylvania Railroad were suspended. With all the disturbance and alarm there was no panic. The excitement was at its height from June 27 to July 1. July 1 the sale of government five-twenties for the day amounted to $1,700,000. Few trains were running on the eastern division of the Pennsylvania Railroad, and it was expected that the track would in many places be destroyed, yet the shares of this company sold in Philadelphia at 61¾ June 27, and at 60 July 1, on a par basis of 50,—a fact as worthy of report as the story of Livy that the ground on which Hannibal encamped his army three miles from Rome, happening at that very time to be sold, brought a price none the lower on account of its possession by the invader. While gold advanced in New York, there was no panic in the stock market.

When the alarm at the invasion of Pennsylvania was at its height, when every man in the North tremblingly took up his morning newspaper and with a sinking heart watched the daily bulletins, the intelligence came that there had been a change in commanders of the Army of the Potomac. Those in authority depended for the salvation of Harrisburg, Baltimore, and Washington on this army, which the public with its half-knowledge of the situation also felt to be their mainstay.

Hooker, following upon Lee's right flank and covering Washington, crossed the Potomac, and June 27 made his headquarters at Frederick, Maryland. He proposed to strike Lee's line of communications with Richmond, and desired the garrison of 10,000, holding Maryland Heights, which commanded Harper's Ferry, as a reinforcement to the corps he had ordered to march west for that purpose. "Is there any reason why Maryland Heights should not be abandoned?" he asked Halleck. "I cannot approve their abandonment," was the answer, "except in case of absolute necessity." Hooker wrote a reply proving that the troops in question were "of no earthly account at Harper's Ferry," while, if placed at his disposition, they might be used to advantage. He ended his despatch with begging that it be presented to the President and the Secretary of War. Immediately after he had sent it, his growing anger at what he considered the unwise and shackling instructions of the general-in-chief prompted him to write, apparently in a fit of petulance, a second despatch asking to be relieved of his position. Halleck received the second telegram five minutes after the first, and referred it to the President. Lincoln made up his mind quickly, and sent an officer to the Army of the Potomac with an order relieving Hooker and appointing in his place George G. Meade. It was an excellent choice. Meade looked like a student, had scholarly habits, was an officer of courage and ability, and commanded now the Fifth Corps, having served in the Potomac army with credit, even distinction. Receiving the communication from the President late on the night of June 27 or early the next morning, he answered it at 7 A. M. in a tone of genuineness which betokened confidence. "As a soldier," he said, "I obey the order placing me in command of this army, and to the utmost of my ability will execute it." The appointment was satisfactory to the officers of the army. Although the risk was great in making a change of generals at so critical a moment, Fortune attended the step and smiled on the new commander during the next five days which gave him fame.

"You are intrusted," wrote Halleck to Meade, "with all the power which the President, the Secretary of War, or the General-in-Chief can confer upon you, and you may rely upon our full support." In answer to a specific inquiry, Meade received for a second time the permission to do as he pleased with the garrison on Maryland Heights. He withdrew it, and posted the larger part of the troops at Frederick as a reserve.

He estimated Lee's force at 80,000 to 100,000; his own he placed at the larger number. His resolution was prompt. June 29 and 30 he advanced northward, and by the evening of the 30th the First Corps had crossed the Pennsylvania line, while the Third and the Eleventh were in the northern part of Maryland; these three constituting the left wing of the army under the command of General Reynolds. The Twelfth Corps lay in Pennsylvania, but at some distance east of the First. Meade established his headquarters at Taneytown, Maryland, thirteen miles south of Gettysburg, retaining the Second and Fifth Corps within easy reach. The Sixth Corps was likewise in Maryland, but lay farther to the eastward, thirty-four miles from Gettysburg. Meade had been prompt to command, his subordinates zealous to obey. The officers, sinking for the moment all their rivalries and jealousies, were careful and untiring in their efforts, while the soldiers did wonders in making long and rapid marches in the hot sun and sultry air of the last days of June. The main idea of Meade had been "to find and fight the enemy," at the same time covering Baltimore and Washington. Hearing now that Lee was falling back and concentrating his army, he announced his present design in a despatch to Halleck. "The news proves my advance has answered its purpose," he said. "I shall not advance any, but prepare to receive an attack in case Lee makes one. A battle-field is being selected to the rear on which the army can be rapidly concentrated."

The first mistake in Lee's campaign arose from the absence of Stuart's cavalry. He had no accurate and speedy knowledge of the movements of the Federals. His own and Longstreet's instructions to Stuart lacked precision, and Stuart made an unwise use of his discretion. Forgetting perhaps that the main use of horsemen in an enemy's country is to serve as the eyes of the army, the spirit of adventure led him into a raid about the Union troops which lost him all communication with the Confederate army, so that Lee was in the dark as to the progress of his adversary. On the night of June 28 a scout brought word to him that the Union army had crossed the Potomac and was advancing northward. His communications with Virginia were menaced, and he did not dare to let them be intercepted. He might indeed for a while live upon the country, but he could not in his position suffer the interruption of his supplies of ammunition. He called Ewell back from his projected attack upon Harrisburg, and ordered him as well as Longstreet and Hill to march to Gettysburg, on the east side of the South Mountain range.

July 1 Reynolds came in contact with the Confederates. Buford with his cavalry having the day before taken possession of Gettysburg and occupied Seminary Ridge west of the town was resisting their advance when Reynolds with the First Corps came to his assistance. Sending orders to Howard to advance promptly with the Eleventh, Reynolds selected the battle-field and opened the battle of Gettysburg, but he did not live to see the result of his heroic stand. Before noon he received a bullet in his brain and died instantly. "The death of this splendid officer," writes Fitzhugh Lee with grace, "was regretted by friend and foe," and borrowing the words of another, he adds, "No man died on that field with more glory than he; yet many died, and there was much glory!"

After Reynolds's death matters went badly for the First and Eleventh Corps. They were "overborne by superior numbers and forced back through Gettysburg with great slaughter." Buford's despatch of 3.20 P.M. points out an important reason for the defeat. "In my opinion," he said, "there seems to be no directing person." All was confusion and looked like disaster when Hancock arrived on the field. On hearing that Reynolds was killed, Meade, with his excellent judgment of the right man for the place, sent Hancock forward to take the command. He restored order and inspired confidence while the Union troops were placed in a strong position on Cemetery Hill east of the town. It is thought that if the Confederates had been prompt they might have carried the height, but the order to do so from Lee to Ewell was conditional, and with his force then present he did not deem the attempt practicable. Nevertheless, the first day of the battle of Gettysburg was a Confederate success.

Late in the afternoon of July 1 Slocum with the Twelfth Corps had arrived at Gettysburg. Sickles with the Third Corps marched thither with celerity and zeal. The reports of Hancock, Howard, and others decided Meade that Gettysburg was a good place to fight his battle, and he issued orders to all of his corps to concentrate at that point. He himself arrived upon the battle-field at one in the morning, pale, tired-looking, hollow-eyed, and worn out from want of sleep, anxiety, and the weight of responsibility.

By the afternoon of July 2, Lee and Meade had their whole forces on the field, the armies being about a mile apart. Lee had 70,000, Meade 93,500, less the losses of the first day, which had been much greater on the Union than on the Confederate side. The Confederates occupied Seminary Ridge in a line concave in form, the Federals Cemetery Ridge in a convex line, a position admirably adapted for defence. Meade decided to await attack, and if he had studied closely the character and history of his energetic adversary, he might have been almost certain that it would come. Longstreet, however, differed with his commander. In a conversation at the close of the first day's fight, he expressed a desire that their troops be thrown around the left of the Union army, interposing themselves between it and Washington and forcing Meade to take the offensive. The anxiety of Lee at receiving no information from his cavalry had become excitement, and, somewhat irritated at a suggestion contrary to what he had determined upon, he said, "No, the enemy is there and I am going to attack him." From the commencement of his invasion, he had shown contempt of his foe. The stretching of his line from Fredericksburg to Winchester in the face of an opponent who had greater numbers can bear no other construction. While he deemed Meade a better general than Hooker, he thought that the change of commanders at this critical moment counterbalanced the advantage in generalship; and while he was astonished at the rapid and efficient movements of the Army of the Potomac after Meade took command, he had undoubtedly become convinced from his almost unvarying success that he and his army were invincible,—a confidence shared by nearly all of his officers and men. His victories on his own soil were extraordinary, but if we compare his campaigns of invasion with those of Napoleon we shall see how far he fell short when he undertook operations in an unfriendly country, although the troops that followed him were in fighting qualities unsurpassed. "Except in equipment," writes General Alexander, "I think a better army, better nerved up to its work, never marched upon a battle-field." With such soldiers, if Lee had been as great a general as Napoleon, Gettysburg had been an Austerlitz, Washington and the Union had fallen.

Lee was up betimes on the morning of July 2, but the movements of his soldiers were slow, and he lost much of the advantage of his more speedy concentration than Meade's. The afternoon was well advanced when he began his attack, and by that time the last of the Union army, the Sixth Corps, which had marched thirty-four miles in eighteen hours, was arriving. There was tremendous fighting and heavy loss that afternoon on both wings of each army. On the Union side Warren and Humphreys distinguished themselves. Sickles was struck by a cannon ball that caused the loss of a leg and was borne from the field. The result of the day is accurately told by Lee: "We attempted to dislodge the enemy, and, though we gained some ground, we were unable to get possession of his position." The Confederate assaults had been disjointed: to that mistake is ascribed their small success.

The feeling among the officers in Meade's camp that night was one of gloom. On the first day of the battle the First and Eleventh corps had been almost annihilated. On the second day the Fifth and part of the Second had been shattered; the Third, in the words of its commander who succeeded Sickles, was "used up and not in good condition to fight." The loss of the army had been 20,000 men. Only the Sixth and Twelfth corps were fresh. But the generals had not lost spirit, and in the council of war called by Meade all voted to "stay and fight it out." The rank and file had fought as

Anglo-Saxons nearly always fight on their own soil. On the first day and the morning of the second the martial ardor of many of the men had been mingled with cheerfulness at the report that McClellan had been restored to his old command. "The boys are all jubilant over it," said a soldier to General Hunt, "for they know that if *he* takes command everything will go right." We may guess that on this gloomy night the men went over again in their minds the fate of their army when under Pope, Burnside, and Hooker it had encountered the veterans of Lee, but in spite of this doleful retrospect they must have felt in some measure "the spirit that animated general headquarters," the energy of Meade and the faithful co-operation of his generals.

Meade had no thought of taking the offensive, and was busy in improving the natural defences of his position with earthworks. The partial successes of the Confederates determined Lee to continue the attack on the 3d of July. In the early morning there was fighting on the right of the Union line. Then followed an unnatural stillness. "The whole field became as silent as a churchyard until one o'clock." Suddenly came from the Confederate side the reports of two signal guns in quick succession. A bombardment from one hundred and fifteen cannon commenced, and was replied to by eighty guns of the Union army, whose convex line, advantageous in other respects, did not admit of their bringing into action a large part of their artillery. "It was a most terrific and appalling cannonade," said Hancock. But it did little damage. The Union soldiers lay under the protection of stone walls, swells of the ground, and earthworks, and the projectiles of the enemy passed over their heads, sweeping the open ground in their rear. Everybody from the commanding general to the privates felt that this was only preliminary to an infantry charge, and all braced themselves for the tug of war. Hancock with his staff, his corps flag flying, rode deliberately along the front of his line, and by his coolness and his magnificent presence inspired his men with courage and determination. For an hour and a half this raging cannonade was kept up, when Hunt, the chief of the Union artillery, finding his ammunition running low, gave the order to cease firing. The Confederates thought that they had silenced the Federal batteries, and made preparation for their next move.

Longstreet had no sympathy with the vigorously offensive tactics of his chief; and when Lee on the morning of this July 3 directed him to be ready after the bombardment had done its work to make an attack with Pickett's fresh division reinforced from Hill's corps up to 15,000 men, he demurred, arguing that the assault could not succeed. Lee showed a little impatience, apparently made no reply, and by silence insisted on the execution of his order. Longstreet took Pickett to the crest of Seminary Ridge, pointed out to him what was to be done, and left him with a heavy heart. Alexander of the artillery was directed to note carefully the effect of his fire, and when the favorable moment came to give Pickett the order to charge. He did not like this responsibility, and asked Longstreet for specific instructions, but the reply which came lacked precision. Still the artillery must open, and when the fire of the Federal guns had ceased, as has been related, Alexander, looking anxiously through his glass at the points whence it had proceeded, and observing no sign of life in the five minutes that followed, sent word to Pickett: "For God's sake, come quick. . . . Come quick, or my ammunition won't let me support you properly." Pickett went to Longstreet. "General, shall I advance?" he asked. Longstreet could not speak, but bowed in answer. "Sir," said Pickett, with a determined voice, "I shall lead my division forward." Alexander had ceased firing. Longstreet rode to where he stood, and exclaimed: "I don't want to make this attack. I would stop it now but that General Lee ordered it and expects it to go on. I don't see how it can succeed." But as he spoke Pickett at the head of his troops rode over the crest of Seminary Ridge and began his descent down the slope. "As he passed me," writes Longstreet, "he rode gracefully, with his jaunty cap raked well over on his right ear, and his long auburn locks, nicely dressed, hanging almost to his shoulders. He seemed a holiday soldier." From the other side the Union soldiers watched the advance of Pickett and his fifteen thousand with suspense, with admiration. As they came forward steadily and in perfect order with banners flying, those who looked on might for the moment have thought it a Fourth of July parade.

The Confederates had nearly a mile to go across the valley. As they descended the slope on that clear afternoon under the July sun in full view of their foe, they received a dreadful fire from the Union batteries, which had been put in entire readiness to check such an onset. Steadily and coolly they advanced. After they had got away, the Confederate artillery reopened over their heads, in the effort to draw the deadly fire directed at them from Cemetery Ridge; but the Union guns made no change in aim, and went on mowing down Pickett's men. Half-way across there was the shelter of a ravine. They stopped for a moment to breathe, then advanced again, still in good order. A storm of canister came. The slaughter was terrible. The left staggered; but, nothing daunted, Pickett and what was left of his own division of forty-nine hundred pressed on in the lead. The other divisions followed. Now the Union infantry opened fire. Pickett halted at musket range and discharged a volley, then rushed on up the slope. Near the Federal lines he made a pause "to close ranks and mass for a final plunge." In the last assault Armistead, a brigade commander, pressed forward, leaped the stone wall, waved his sword with his hat on it, shouted, "Give them the cold steel, boys!" and laid his hands upon a gun. A hundred of his men had followed. They planted the Confederate battle-flags on Cemetery Ridge among the cannon they had captured and for the moment held. Armistead was shot down; Garnett and Kemper, Pickett's other brigadiers, fell. The wavering divisions of Hill's corps "seemed appalled, broke their ranks," and fell back. "The Federals swarmed around Pickett," writes Longstreet, "attacking on all sides, enveloped and broke up his command. They drove the fragments back upon our lines." Pickett gave the word to retreat.

The Confederates in their charge had struck the front of the Second Corps. Hancock, its commander, "the best tactician of the Potomac army," showed the same reckless courage as Armistead, and seemed to be everywhere directing and encouraging his troops. Struck by a ball, he fell from his horse; and lying on the ground, "his wound spouting blood," he raised himself on his elbow and gave the order, "Go in, Colonel, and give it to them on the flank." Not until the battle of Gettysburg was over did he resign himself to his surgeon, and shortly afterwards he dictated this despatch to Meade: "I have never seen a more formidable attack, and if the Sixth and Fifth corps have pressed up, the enemy will be destroyed. The enemy must be short of ammunition, as I was shot with a tenpenny nail. I did not leave the field till the victory was entirely secured and the enemy no longer in sight. I am badly wounded, though I trust not seriously. I had to break the line to attack the enemy in flank on my right, where the enemy was most persistent after the front attack was repelled. Not a rebel was in sight upright when I left."

Decry war as we may and ought, "breathes there the man with soul so dead" who would not thrill with emotion to claim for his countrymen the men who made that charge and the men who met it?

Longstreet, calm and self-possessed, meriting the name "bulldog" applied to him by his soldiers, expected a counter attack, and made ready for it. Lee, entirely alone, rode up to encourage and rally his broken troops. "His face did not show signs of the slightest disappointment, care, or annoyance," recorded an English officer in his diary on the day of the battle, "and he was addressing to every soldier he met a few words of encouragement, such as, 'All this will come right in the end: we'll talk it over afterwards, but in the mean time all good men must rally. We want all good and true men just now.' He spoke to all the wounded men that passed him, and the slightly wounded he exhorted 'to bind up their hurts and take up a musket' in this emergency. Very few failed to answer his appeal, and I saw many badly wounded men take off their hats and cheer him. He said to me, 'This has been a sad day for us, Colonel—a sad day; but we can't expect always to gain victories.' . . .

Notwithstanding the misfortune which had so suddenly befallen him, General Lee seemed to observe everything, however trivial. When a mounted officer began licking his horse for shying at the bursting of a shell, he called out, 'Don't whip him, Captain; don't whip him. I've got just such another foolish horse myself, and whipping does no good.' "

An officer almost angry came up to report the state of his brigade. "General Lee immediately shook hands with him and said cheerfully, 'Never mind, General, *all this has been* MY *fault*—it is *I* that have lost this fight, and you must help me out of it in the best way you can.' "

The Books are full of the discussion whether or not Meade should have made a counter-attack. Those who say he ought to have done this maintain that the Confederate army might have been destroyed. It is true that he did not appreciate the magnitude of his victory, but ought the critic to demand from him any greater military sagacity than from Lee? The Confederate general under similar circumstances did not comprehend how badly he had beaten Burnside at Fredericksburg and did not follow up his great success.

We need concern ourselves only for a moment with the controversy between Longstreet and the friends of Lee. It is clear that Longstreet did not give his commander the hearty co-operation which the occasion demanded. On the other hand, it is difficult, if not impossible, to traverse his argument that Lee should have put some officer in charge of the movement who had confidence in the plan of attack, or, as so much depended on it, that the commander himself should have given to the operations of the third day his personal attention. The champions of Lee maintain that his orders required the charge of Pickett to be made by a more powerful column than was sent across the valley under the murderous fire of the foe, and that Longstreet was at fault for neglecting to supply his remaining two divisions for the attack. Reduced to figures, it means that 23,000 instead of 15,000 should have made the assault. They would have had to contend with 70,000 men, strongly intrenched, of whom two corps were fresh, whose generals were prepared and alert. There is no reason for thinking that the result would have been different. The comparison which is frequently made between Lee's attack at Gettysburg on the third day and Burnside's storming of Marye's Heights is a reproach to the generalship of the Confederate commander, and is keenly felt by his friends, who would all regard him infallible. Had it not been for the Gettysburg campaign, the intimations in Southern literature would be more frequent than they are that he is entitled to rank with Napoleon in the class of great commanders. But the likeness in military ability will halt before it is pushed far. Nevertheless, let the comparison of the emotions of Napoleon and Lee after disaster be made, and his countrymen will perceive what reason they have to revere the memory of the American. Thus he wrote, July 9, to Pickett: "No one grieves more than I do at the loss suffered by your noble division in the recent conflict, or honors it more for its bravery and gallantry." At the end of the account, said Napoleon in 1813, what has the Russian campaign cost me? 300,000 men, and what are the lives of a million to a man like me!

On the morning of the Fourth of July the people of the North received this word: "The President announces to the country that news from the Army of the Potomac, up to 10 P.M. of the 3d, is such as to cover that army with the highest honor, to promise a great success to the cause of the Union, and to claim the condolence of all for the many gallant fallen, and that for this he especially desires that on this day He whose will, not ours, should ever be done be everywhere remembered and reverenced with profoundest gratitude." The rejoicing of the people was not boisterous; it took the character of supreme thankfulness for a great deliverance. The victory of Gettysburg demonstrated that Lee and his army were not invincible, and that the Confederates had lost in playing the card of an invasion of the North. Nothing now remained to them but a policy of stubborn defence. That this would likewise end in ruin was foreshadowed by the fateful event of the Fourth of July. Vicksburg surrendered to General Grant. Meade's sturdy and victorious resistance to attack was followed by the glorious end of the most brilliant offensive campaign of the war. Had the war been one between two nations, it would now have undoubtedly terminated in a treaty of peace, with conditions imposed largely by the more successful contestant.

The Fourth of July at Gettysburg passed in tranquillity. "Under the cover of the night and heavy rain," Lee began his retreat. Meade followed. The President comprehended the importance and moral effect of the victory better than did his general. He may not have seen the remark of Napoleon in 1809, "In war the moral element and public opinion are half the battle;" but the fact he knew well. Nevertheless, he wrote Halleck at seven in the evening of July 6 from his country residence at the Soldiers' Home: "I left the telegraph office a good deal dissatisfied. You know I did not like the phrase [Meade's] 'Drive the invaders from our soil.' " Mentioning other circumstances, he added: "These things all appear to me to be connected with a purpose to cover Baltimore and Washington, and to get the enemy across the river again without a further collision, and they do not appear connected with a purpose to prevent his crossing and to destroy him. I do fear the former purpose is acted upon and the latter rejected." The next day he sent this word to Halleck: "We have certain information that Vicksburg surrendered to General Grant on the 4th of July. Now, if General Meade can complete his work, so gloriously prosecuted thus far, by the literal or substantial destruction of Lee's army, the rebellion will be over." At the same time Halleck telegraphed Meade: "Push forward and fight Lee before he can cross the Potomac." He sent other telegrams, probably on the prompting of the President, urging Meade to attack the enemy, but forwarded two despatches inconsistent with the importunity of the others. "Do not be influenced by any despatch from here against your own judgment," he said. "Regard them as suggestions only." Again he wrote: "I think it will be best for you to postpone a general battle" until everything is ready. Perhaps all of those telegrams which urged prompt action were the President's.

By July 11 Lee in his retreat had reached the Potomac, his army covering the river from Williamsport to Falling Waters. Three days before he had written Davis: "A series of storms . . . has placed the river beyond fording stage, and the present storm will keep it so far at least a week. I shall therefore have to accept battle if the enemy offers it, whether I wish to or not. . . . I hope your Excellency will understand that I am not in the least discouraged, or that my faith in the protection of an all-merciful Providence or in the fortitude of this army is at all shaken." The condition of the army "is good, and its confidence unimpaired." July 10 he sent confidentially this word to Stuart: "We must prepare for a vigorous battle, and trust in the mercy of God and the valor of our troops." July 12, after he had taken up his very strong position on the Potomac, he wrote Davis: "But for the power the enemy possesses of accumulating troops I should be willing to await his attack, excepting that in our restricted limits the means of obtaining subsistence are becoming precarious. The river has now fallen to four feet, and a bridge, which is being constructed, I hope will be passable by to-morrow."

By July 11 Meade in his pursuit had come within striking distance of Lee. Reinforced by some fresh troops, he might have attacked on the 12th or 13th and ought to have done so. Defeat could not result in disaster. A success no greater than Antietam would be a help to the cause, and a complete victory was possible that might end the war. While proceeding with great caution, Meade had determined to make an attack July 13; but, wavering in mind and weighed down with responsibility, he called, contrary to the best military maxims, a council of war. Five out of seven of his corps commanders were opposed to the projected attack, which influenced him to delay giving the orders for it. He devoted July 13 to an examination of the enemy's position, strength, and defensive works, and the next day advanced his army for a reconnaissance in force or an assault if conditions justified it, when he ascertained that during the night previous the Confederate army had crossed the Potomac. "The escape of Lee's army without another battle has created great dissatisfaction in the mind of the President," telegraphed Halleck. Meade asked to be relieved of the command of the army: his application was refused.

During the 12th and 13th of July Lincoln was a prey to intense anxiety, and when he got the intelligence, soon after noon of the 14th, that Lee and his army were safely across the river, he could hardly restrain his irritation within bounds. "We had them within our grasp," he declared; "we had only to stretch forth our hands and they were ours, and nothing I could say or do could make the army move. I regret that I did not myself go to the army and personally issue the order for an attack." On the spur of the moment he gave vent to his feelings in a letter to Meade which on second thoughts he did not sign or send. Prefacing his censure with "I am sorry now to be the author of the slightest pain to you," he wrote: "You fought and beat the enemy at Gettysburg; and of course, to say the least, his loss was as great as yours. He retreated, and you did not, as it seemed to me, pressingly pursue him; but a flood in the river detained him, till by slow degrees you were again upon him. You had at least twenty thousand vet-

eran troops directly with you, and as many more raw ones within supporting distance, all in addition to those who fought with you at Gettysburg;
while it was not possible that he had received a single recruit; and yet you
stood and let the flood run down, bridges be built, and the enemy move
away at his leisure without attacking him. . . . Again, my dear general, I
do not believe you appreciate the magnitude of the misfortune involved in
Lee's escape. He was within your easy grasp, and to have closed upon him
would, in connection with our other late successes, have ended the war.
As it is, the war will be prolonged indefinitely. If you could not safely attack
Lee last Monday, how can you possibly do so south of the river, when you
can take with you very few more than two thirds of the force you then had
in hand? It would be unreasonable to expect, and I do not expect [that]
you can now effect much. Your golden opportunity is gone, and I am
distressed immeasurably because of it."

The disappointment of Lincoln was profound and enduring. Somewhat
later he said: "Our army held the war in the hollow of their hand and they
would not close it. We had gone through all the labor of tilling and planting
an enormous crop, and when it was ripe we did not harvest it. Still I am
very grateful to Meade for the great service he did at Gettysburg."

Nothing can so fitly close my account of the battle of Gettysburg as the
reproduction of Lincoln's two-minute address at the dedication of the
Gettysburg National Cemetery, November 19, 1863: "Fourscore and seven
years ago our fathers brought forth on this continent a new nation, conceived in liberty and dedicated to the proposition that all men are created
equal.

Now we are engaged in a great civil war, testing whether that nation or
any nation so conceived and so dedicated can long endure. We are met on a
great battle-field of that war. We have come to dedicate a portion of that
field as a final resting-place for those who here gave their lives that that nation might live. It is altogether fitting and proper that we should do this.

But, in a larger sense, we cannot dedicate—we cannot consecrate—we
cannot hallow—this ground. The brave men, living and dead, who struggled
here, have consecrated it far above our poor power to add or detract. The
world will little note nor long remember what we say here, but it can
never forget what they did here. It is for us the living, rather, to be dedicated
here to the unfinished work which they who fought here have thus far so
nobly advanced. It is rather for us to be here dedicated to the great task remaining before us,—that from these honored dead we take increased devotion to that cause for which they gave the last full measure of devotion;
that we here highly resolve that these dead shall not have died in vain; that
this nation under God shall have a new birth of freedom; and that government of the people, by the people, for the people, shall not perish from
the earth."

THE END OF THE WAR

As late as April 1, Davis apparently thought that there was no immediate necessity for the abandonment of Richmond. On the morning of the 2d, which was Sunday, he was at St. Paul's listening to the noble liturgy of the Episcopal Church, when the clergyman was reading for the last time in his ministry the prayer for the President of the Confederate States. Here Davis was apprised by a messenger from the War Department of the gravity of the military situation. He left his pew quietly and walked out of the church with dignity, learning soon the contents of Lee's despatch which gave an account of his disaster and advised that Richmond be abandoned. The news spread rapidly, and so unexpectedly had it come upon the city that the greatest confusion and excitement prevailed as functionaries and citizens made ready for flight. Davis with all the members of his cabinet except Breckinridge, a number of his staff and other officials, got away at eleven o'clock in the evening on a train of the Richmond and Danville Railroad and reached Danville the next afternoon in safety. Under a previous order of Lee Ewell who was in command of the troops in Richmond directed that the tobacco in the city should be burned and that all stores which could not be removed should be destroyed. It is probable that the fires lighted in pursuance of this order spread to shops and houses and it is certain that a mob of both sexes and colours in the early morning of April 3 set fire to buildings and "began to plunder the city." Ewell says in his report that by daylight the riot was subdued and Jones writes that at seven o'clock in the morning men went to the liquor shops in execution of an order of the city government and commanded that the spirits be poured into the streets. The gutters ran with liquor from which pitchers and buckets were filled by black and white women and boys. By seven o'clock also the evacuation of Richmond by the Confederates had been completed.

The Union troops passed cautiously the first line of Confederate works but as they met with no opposition, they went by the next lines at a double-quick, and when the spires of the city came into view, they unfurled the national banner, and, their bands striking up "Rally round the flag," they sent up cheer on cheer as they marched in triumph through the streets. But they found confusion, an extensive conflagration, and a reign of pillage and disorder. Their commander Weitzel received the surrender of Richmond at the city hall at quarter past eight, and, by two o'clock in the afternoon they had quelled the tumult and put out the fires but not before a considerable portion of the city had been destroyed.

The Union soldiers were received by the white people gratefully and by the negroes with joy. Full of meaning was the visit of President Lincoln to Richmond which was made from City Point the next day in an unostentatious and careless manner and in utter disregard of Stanton's warning.

Proper arrangements for his conveyance and escort had been made but, owing to two accidents, the President completed his river journey in a twelve-oared barge and walked about a mile and a half through the streets of Richmond accompanied by Admiral Porter and three other officers with a guard of only ten sailors armed with carbines. He was received with demonstrations of joy by the negroes and, though the city was full of drunken Confederates, he met with neither molestation nor indignity. He went to the house which Davis had occupied as a residence, now the head-quarters of Weitzel and, if we may believe some personal recollections, he looked about the house and sat in Davis's chair with boyish delight. Lincoln passed the night in Richmond and April 5 returned to City Point. Under that date Jones reported perfect order in the city and Dana tele-graphed from Richmond, "*Whig* appeared yesterday as Union paper" and the "theatre opens here to-night."

Now the Confederates had evacuated Richmond and Petersburg during the night of April 2 and the early morning of the 3d. Grant without tarrying for a visit to Richmond set after them in hot pursuit. On the 4th he sent this despatch to Stanton from Wilson's Station: "The army is push-ing forward in the hope of overtaking or dispersing the remainder of Lee's army. Sheridan with his cavalry and the Fifth Corps is between this and the Appomattox; General Meade with the Second and Sixth following; General Ord is following the line of the South Side Railroad." On the next day Sheridan reported that the "whole of Lee's army is at or near Amelia Court-House." Lee gives this account: "Upon arriving at Amelia Court-House on the morning of the 4th with the advance of the army, on the retreat from the lines in front of Richmond and Petersburg, and not finding the supplies ordered to be placed there, nearly twenty-four hours were lost in endeavoring to collect in the country subsistence for men and horses. This delay was fatal and could not be retrieved." On moving forward on the 5th, his troops, "wearied by continual fighting and march-ing" and not able to obtain rest or refreshment, found that Sheridan had possession of the Richmond and Danville Railroad which cut off their retreat to Danville, therefore they were ordered to march towards Lynch-burg. From Jetersville Sheridan telegraphed Grant on the 5th, "From present indications the retreat of the enemy is rapidly becoming a rout"; but somewhat later he said, "I wish you were here yourself. I feel con-fident of capturing the Army of Northern Virginia if we exert ourselves. I see no escape for Lee." Grant with four of his staff and a mounted escort of fourteen men started at once to ride the sixteen miles which separated him from Sheridan. Darkness had come on and, his route lying through the woods, he did not reach Sheridan's camp until about half-past ten. As he and his companions picked their way to headquarters the awakened troopers, recognizing Grant, gave vent to their astonishment at the uncommon occurrence of the General-in-Chief appearing at that late hour so near the enemy's lines. "Why there's the old man," said one. "Boys this means business." "Great Scott!" exclaimed another, "the old chief's out here himself. The rebs are going to get busted to-morrow certain." Grant, having acquired from Sheridan a thorough knowledge of the situation, made a midnight visit to Meade and ordered the movements for the next day with the design of heading off Lee.

The result of the plans laid for April 6 is told best by Sheridan. At noon his report is, "the enemy are moving to our left with their trains and whole army." They "were moving all last night and are very short of provisions and very tired indeed. . . . They are reported to have begged provisions from the people of the country all along the road as they passed. I am working around farther to our left." Later, in the same day he sent this word to Grant: "The enemy made a stand. . . . I attacked them with two divisions of the Sixth Army Corps, and routed them handsomely. . . . If the thing is pressed I think that Lee will surrender." Let Lee take up the story: "The army continued its march during the night [April 6] and every effort was made to reorganize the divisions which had been shattered by the day's operations; but the men being depressed by fatigue and hunger, many threw away their arms, while others followed the wagon trains and embarrassed their progress. On the morning of the 7th rations were issued to the troops as they passed Farmville, but the safety of the trains requiring their removal upon the approach of the enemy all could not be supplied. The army reduced to two corps under Longstreet and Gordon moved steadily on the road to Appomattox Court-House." Then Grant: "On the morning of the 7th the pursuit was renewed. . . . It was soon found that the enemy had crossed to the north side of the Appomattox; but so close was the pursuit that the Second Corps got possession of the common bridge at High Bridge before the enemy could destroy it and immediately crossed over. The Sixth Corps and a division of cavalry crossed at Farmville to its support. Feeling now that General Lee's chance of escape was utterly hopeless I addressed him the following communication from Farmville: 'April 7. General: The result of the last week must convince you of the hopelessness of further resistance on the part of the Army of Northern Virginia in this struggle. I feel that it is so, and regard it as my duty to shift from myself the responsibility of any further effusion of blood, by asking of you the surrender of that portion of the C. S. army known as the Army of Northern Virginia.'" Lee replied inquiring what terms Grant would offer. To this communication came promptly the answer: "Peace being my great desire there is but one condition I would insist upon, namely, that the men and officers surrendered shall be disqualified for taking up arms again against the Government of the United States until properly exchanged." "Early on the morning of the 8th the pursuit was resumed," continues Grant. "General Meade followed north of the Appomattox and General Sheridan with all the cavalry pushed straight for Appomattox Station followed by General Ord's command and the Fifth Corps. During the day General Meade's advance had considerable fighting with the enemy's rear guard but was unable to bring on a general engagement. Late in the evening General Sheridan struck the railroad at Appomattox Station, drove the enemy from there, and captured twenty-five pieces of artillery, a hospital train, and four trains of cars loaded with supplies for Lee's army."

Sheridan was alive to the situation; he telegraphed to Grant at twenty minutes past nine on the evening of the 8th, "we will perhaps finish the job in the morning. I do not think Lee means to surrender until compelled to do so." Lee gives this account of that day: "By great efforts the head of the column reached Appomattox Court-House on the evening of the 8th and the troops were halted for rest." Still clinging to the hope that he might yet escape, he wrote Grant in his second communication that he had not intended to propose the surrender of the Army of Northern Virginia, as in his opinion no such emergency had arisen, but that he would like to meet Grant to confer with him touching the restoration of peace. Grant was too wary to be entrapped in a fruitless negotiation which might serve for delay and replying, "I have no authority to treat on the subject of peace," pushed forward his operations. On the morning of April 9 Lee made "a desperate effort to break through" Sheridan's cavalry which had formed in his front across the road on which he must continue his march. Sheridan fell back gradually. General Ord, who with two corps had marched from daylight on the 8th until the morning of the 9th with a rest of only three hours, now deployed his men and barred the way of the Confederates. In order to learn whether or not his situation was hopeless Lee despatched one of his staff to Gordon who sent back this word: "Tell General Lee I have fought my corps to a frazzle and I fear I can do nothing unless I am heavily supported by Longstreet's corps." Longstreet was in the rear with Meade close upon him and not available for an attack in front. The Army of Northern Virginia was hemmed in and had no alternative but surrender. After receiving the message from Gordon, Lee was convinced and said: "Then there is nothing left me but to go and see General Grant and I would rather die a thousand deaths."

He ordered the white flag to be displayed, requested by letter a suspension of hostilities and an interview with Grant. The two generals met at McLean's house in the little village of Appomattox Court-House. Lee wore a new, full-dress uniform of Confederate gray "buttoned to the throat" and a handsome sword, the hilt of which was studded with jewels, while Grant had on "a blouse of dark-blue flannel unbuttoned in front" and carried no sword. "In my rough travelling suit," wrote Grant, "the uniform of a private with the straps of a lieutenant-general, I must have contrasted very strangely with a man so handsomely dressed, six feet high and of faultless form." The two generals had met while in the old army during the Mexican War, and Lee, fifteen years the senior and of higher rank, had made a distinct impression on Grant.

Twenty years later (1885) when he knew that what remained to him of life was but a span to be measured by weeks if not by days Grant wrote an account of this interview, giving us an insight into his soul which exacts our admiration and which we ought not to forget when in future pages we are contemplating another side of the man. "My own feelings," said Grant, "which had been quite jubilant on the receipt of Lee's letter were sad and depressed. I felt like anything rather than rejoicing at the downfall of a foe who had fought so long and valiantly. . . . We soon fell into a conversation about old army times. . . ." This "grew so pleasant that I almost forgot the object of our meeting." He was brought to the business in hand by Lee who suggested that he write out the terms on which he proposed to receive the surrender of the Army of Northern Virginia. Grant set down these conditions: "the officers to give their individual paroles not to take up arms against the Government of the United States until properly exchanged; and each company or regimental commander sign a like parole for the men of their commands. The arms, artillery and public property to be parked and stacked and turned over to the officers appointed by me to receive them. This will not embrace the side-arms of the officers nor their private horses or baggage. This done, each officer and man will be allowed to return to their homes, not to be disturbed by U. S. authority so long as they observe their paroles and the laws in force where they may reside." Grant tells us how he composed this letter: "When I put my pen to the paper I did not know the first word that I should make use of in writing the terms. I only knew what was in my mind and I wished to express it clearly so that there could be no mistaking it. As I wrote on the thought occurred to me that the officers had their own private horses and effects, which were important to them but of no value to us; also that it would be an unnecessary humiliation to call upon them to deliver their side-arms. . . . When General Lee read over that part . . . he remarked with some feeling, I thought, that this would have a happy effect upon his army."

I shall continue the account of this interview from the article of Horace Porter which is written largely from contemporary memoranda. Shortly after Lee had read the proposition he said: " 'There is one thing I should like to mention. The cavalrymen and artillerists own their own horses in our army. Its organization in this respect differs from that of the United States. . . . I should like to understand whether these men will be permitted to retain their horses.'

" 'You will find that the terms as written do not allow this,' General Grant replied; 'only the officers are permitted to take their private property.'

"Lee read over the second page of the letter again, and then said: 'No, I see the terms do not allow it; that is clear.' His face showed plainly that he was quite anxious to have this concession made; and Grant said very promptly, and without giving Lee time to make a direct request:

" 'Well, the subject is quite new to me. Of course I did not know that any private soldiers owned their animals; but I think we have fought the last battle of the war,—I sincerely hope so,—and that the surrender of this army will be followed soon by that of all the others; and I take it that most of the men in the ranks are small farmers, and as the country has been so raided by the two armies, it is doubtful whether they will be able to put in a crop to carry themselves and their families through the next winter without the aid of the horses they are now riding, and I will arrange it in this way. I will not change the terms as now written, but I will instruct the officers I shall appoint to receive the paroles to let all the men who claim to own a horse or mule take the animals home with them to work their little farms. . . .'

"Lee now looked greatly relieved, and though anything but a demonstrative man, he gave every evidence of his appreciation of this concession, and said: 'This will have the best possible effect upon the men. It will be very gratifying, and will do much toward conciliating our people.' "

Lee then accepted the proposition. The number of men surrendered was 26,765. The Confederates had "been living for the last few days principally upon parched corn" and were badly in need of food. Grant supplied them with rations. As soon as the Union soldiers heard of the surrender they commenced firing salutes at different points along the lines. He ordered them stopped, saying, "The war is over; the rebels are our countrymen again: and the best sign of rejoicing after the victory will be to abstain from all demonstrations in the field."

Lee rode back sorrowfully to his soldiers. "The men gathered round him," writes Cooke, "wrung his hand and in broken words called upon God to help him. . . . The tears came to his eyes and looking at the men with a glance of proud feeling, he said, in suppressed tones, which trembled slightly: 'We have fought through the war together. I have done the best I could for you. My heart is too full to say more.' " On the morrow he issued a farewell address to the Army of Northern Virginia and rode away to Richmond. The army disbanded and dispersed to their homes.

On the day after the surrender Grant had an interview with Lee and suggested that he use his great influence in advising the capitulation of the remaining Southern armies. The Union general did not enter the Confederate lines, did not go to Richmond and gave no sign of exultation. He went back to City Point and thence to Washington in order to stop further military preparations. The day of his arrival there, four days after the surrender of Lee, he and the War Department came to the determination, "to stop all drafting and recruiting, to curtail purchases for arms, ammunition," etc.; "to reduce the number of general and staff officers to the actual necessities of the service," and "to remove all military restrictions upon trade and commerce so far as may be consistent with public safety."

Having spoken freely of the mistakes of Grant in the Virginia campaign of 1864 I must in candour express the opinion that in these final operations he outgeneralled Lee. The conditions were not unequal; 49,000 men opposed 113,000 and the game was escape or surrender. Lee's force was dispersed by defeat, weakened by captures and the shattered and discouraged remnant of it was forced to capitulate. That Lee was outgeneralled in this Appomattox campaign is a judgment supported by the intimations of some Confederate writers, made with the utmost deference to their general, that if everything had been managed properly the Army of Northern Virginia might have eluded surrender and protracted the war.

The news of the surrender of Lee was received in Washington at nine o'clock Sunday evening April 9 and at a somewhat later hour in other cities of the land. While the people had exulted at the occupation of Richmond they perceived that the possession of the capital of the Confederacy did not imply the end of the war. But now, it was in everybody's mouth, "the great captain of the rebellion had surrendered": this imported that slavery was dead, the Union restored and that the nation lived. So pregnant an event ought speedily to be known to Europe and the Inman line despatched a special steamer on the Monday to carry the intelligence across the ocean. The people of the North rejoiced on the night of the 9th and during the day and evening of the 10th as they had never rejoiced before nor did they during the remainder of the century on any occasion show such an exuberance of gladness. Business was suspended and the courts adjourned. Cannons fired, bells rang, flags floated, houses and shops were gay with the red, white and blue. There were illuminations and bonfires. The streets of the cities and town were filled with men, who shook hands warmly, embraced each other, shouted, laughed and cheered and were indeed beside themselves in their great joy. There were pledges in generous wines and much common drinking in bar-rooms and liquor shops. There were fantastic processions, grotesque performances and some tomfoolery. Grave and old gentlemen forgot their age and dignity and played the pranks of schoolboys. But always above these foolish and bibulous excesses sounded the patriotic and religious note of the jubilee. "Praise God from whom all blessings flow" were the words most frequently sung in the street, the Board of Trade and on the Stock Exchange. One writer records that in the bar-room of Willard's Hotel, Washington, when the news arrived, an elderly gentleman sprang upon the bar and led the crowd in singing with unwonted fervour the well-known doxology. "Twenty thousand men in the busiest haunts of trade in one of the most thronged cities of the world," Motley wrote, uncovered their heads spontaneously and sang the psalm of thanskgiving, "Praise God." Noteworthy was the service in Trinity Church, New York, one hour after midday of the Tuesday following the surrender, when the church overflowed with worshippers, who were in the main people of distinction. The choir chanted the "Te Deum" and at the bidding of the clergyman, the congregation rose, and, inspired by the great organ and guided by the choir, sang the noble anthem "Gloria in Excelsis." These opening words, "Glory be to God on high, and on earth peace, good will towards men," had a peculiar significance to the Northern people who during these days of rejoicing were for the most part full of generous feeling for the South. Patriotism expressed itself in the songs "John Brown's Body," "My country, 'tis of thee," "Rally round the flag" and the "Star-spangled Banner." Lowell instinctively put into words what his countrymen had in their hearts: "The news, my dear Charles, is from Heaven. I felt a strange and tender exaltation. I wanted to laugh and I wanted to cry, and ended by holding my peace and feeling devoutly thankful. There is something magnificent in having a country to love."

Before I proceed to relate how this universal rejoicing was quickly followed by horror and deep mourning I shall give an account of Lincoln's attitude towards reconstruction during the last days of his life.

While the President was in Richmond (April 4, 5) he had two interviews with Judge Campbell, in the last of which he gave to this self-constituted representative of the Southern people a written memorandum, stating the three indispensable conditions to peace: the national authority must be restored throughout the States; the Executive will make no recession concerning slavery; and all forces hostile to the government must disband. On his return to City Point, as a result of his deliberation, he wrote to General Weitzel, April 6, that he might permit "the gentlemen who have acted as the legislature of Virginia . . . to assemble at Richmond and take measures to withdraw the Virginia troops and other support from resistance to the general government." Nothing came of this. The surrender of Lee and Campbell's misconstruction of Lincoln's letter to Weitzel incited the President to telegraph to his general withdrawing both his letter and memorandum. This was not done however before there had been published, in the Richmond *Whig,* with the approval of Weitzel, an address to the people of Virginia signed by many of the State senators and representatives and a number of citizens, who solicited that the governor, the members of the legislature and certain men of prominence should come together in Richmond by the 25th of April, in order that from such a conference might ensue an immediate meeting of the General Assembly and the restoration of peace to their commonwealth. The interest of this circumstance in its bearing on the after history lies in the opposition of the radical Republicans to any such mode of reconstruction. Stanton in cabinet meeting showed that he was disturbed by the President's action; and the committee on the conduct of the war, who were on a visit to Richmond at the time the address appeared, "were all thunderstruck and fully sympathized with the hot indignation and wrathful words of" their chairman Senator Wade.

One loves to linger over the last days of Lincoln. He had nothing but mercy and kindness for his bygone enemies. "Do not allow Jefferson Davis to escape the law; he must be hanged," was said to him. "Judge not that ye be not judged" came the reply. On the boat journey from City Point to Washington (April 8, 9) he and his companions, among whom was Sumner, conversed with the freedom of a "small family party" and were happy that the end of the war was in sight. On the Sunday (the 9th) he read to them from his favorite play, "Macbeth,"

> "Duncan is in his grave;
> After life's fitful fever he sleeps well;
> Treason has done his worst: nor steel, nor poison,
> Malice domestic, foreign levy, nothing
> Can touch him further."

A second time he read these words aloud.

On Tuesday evening, April 11, Lincoln made to the rejoicing people who had come to the White House to hear him his last public speech. "By these recent successes," he said, "the reinauguration of the national authority—reconstruction—which has had a large share of thought from the first, is pressed much more closely upon our attention. It is fraught with great difficulty." He then proceeded to defend his action in regard to the government of Louisiana. "As to sustaining it [the Louisiana government]," he continued, "my promise is out. But as bad promises are better broken than kept, I shall treat this as a bad promise, and break it whenever I shall be convinced that keeping it is adverse to the public interest; but I have not yet been so convinced. I have been shown a letter on this subject, supposed to be an able one, in which the writer expresses regret that my mind has not seemed to be definitely fixed on the question whether the seceded States, so called, are in the Union or out of it. It would perhaps add astonishment to his regret were he to learn that since I have found professed Union men endeavoring to make that question, I have purposely forborne any public expression upon it. As appears to me, that question has not been, nor yet is, a practically material one, and that any discussion of it, while it thus remains practically immaterial, could have no effect other than the mischievous one of dividing our friends. As yet, whatever it may hereafter become, that question is bad as the basis of a controversy, and good for nothing at all—a merely pernicious abstraction.

"We all agree that the seceded States, so called, are out of their proper practical relation with the Union, and that the sole object of the government, civil and military, in regard to those States is to again get them into that proper practical relation. I believe that it is not only possible, but in fact easier, to do this without deciding or even considering whether these States have ever been out of the Union, than with it. Finding themselves safely at home, it would be utterly immaterial whether they had ever been abroad. . . . The amount of constituency, so to speak, on which the new Louisiana government rests, would be more satisfactory to all if it contained 50,000, or 30,000, or even 20,000, instead of only about 12,000, as it does. It is also unsatisfactory to some that the elective franchise is not given to the colored man. I would myself prefer that it were now conferred on the very intelligent and on those who serve our cause as soldiers.

"Still, the question is not whether the Louisiana government, as it stands, is quite all that is desirable. The question is, will it be wiser to take it as it is and help to improve it, or to reject and disperse it? Can Louisiana be brought into proper, practical relations with the Union sooner by sustaining or by discarding her new State government? Some 12,000 voters in the heretofore slave State of Louisiana have sworn allegiance to the Union, assumed to be the rightful political power of the State, held elections, organized a State government, adopted a free-State constitution, giving the benefit of public schools equally to black and white and empowering the legislature to confer the elective franchise upon the colored man. Their legislature has already voted to ratify the constitutional amendment recently passed by Congress, abolishing slavery throughout the nation. These 12,000 persons are thus fully committed to the Union and to perpetual freedom in the State—committed to the very things, and nearly all the things, the nation wants—and they ask the nation's recognition and its assistance to make good their committal. Now, if we reject and spurn them, we do our utmost to disorganize and disperse them. We, in effect, say to the white man: You are worthless or worse; we will neither help you nor be helped by you. To the blacks we say: This cup of liberty which these, your old masters, hold to your lips we will dash from you, and leave you to the chances of gathering the spilled and scattered contents in some vague and undefined when, where and how. . . . Concede that the new government of Louisiana is only to what it should be as the egg is to the fowl, we shall sooner have the fowl by hatching the egg than by smashing it. . . . What has been said of Louisiana will apply generally to other States. . . . In the present situation, as the phrase goes, it may be my duty to make some new announcement to the people of the South. I am considering, and shall not fail to act when satisfied that action will be proper."

Of this speech Sumner wrote to Lieber: "The President's speech and other things augur confusion and uncertainty in the future, with hot controversy. Alas! alas!"

Friday, April 14 Lincoln held his last cabinet meeting. General Grant was present and said that he was anxious in his continual expectation of hearing from Sherman. The President replied: "I have no doubt that favorable news will soon come for I had last night my usual dream which has preceded nearly every important event in the war. I seemed to be in a singular and indescribable vessel, but always the same and to be moving with great rapidity toward a dark and indefinite shore." Matters of routine were disposed of and then the subject of reconstruction was taken up. After some discussion the President said: " I think it providential that this great rebellion is crushed just as Congress has adjourned and there are none of the disturbing elements of that body to hinder and embarrass us. If we are wise and discreet we shall reanimate the States and get their governments in successful operation, with order prevailing and the Union re-established before Congress comes together in December. . . . I hope there will be no persecution, no bloody work after the war is over. No one need expect me to take any part in hanging or killing those men, even the worst of them. Frighten them out of the country, open the gates, let down the bars, scare them off [throwing up his hands as if scaring sheep]. Enough lives have been sacrificed. We must extinguish our resentments if we expect harmony and union. There is too much of a desire on the part of some of our very good friends to be masters, to interfere with and dictate to those States, to treat the people not as fellow-citizens; there is too little respect for their rights. I do not sympathize in these feelings." He then spoke of the Louisiana government, joined in the discussion regarding the status of Virginia and said at the close of the meeting: Reconstruction "is the great question pending and we must now begin to act in the interest of peace." Stanton gave two accounts of this council. "At a cabinet meeting yesterday," he wrote at half-past one in the morning of April 15, "the President was very cheerful and hopeful; spoke very kindly of General Lee and others of the Confederacy and the establishment of government in Virginia." At 11.40 the same morning he said in a letter to Adams: "The President was more cheerful and happy than I had ever seen [him], rejoiced at the near prospect of firm and durable peace at home and abroad, manifested in marked degree the kindness and humanity of his disposition and the tender and forgiving spirit that so eminently distinguished him."

Rejoicing over Lee's surrender which began on Sunday night continued through the week but by Friday it had abated in the Northern cities leaving in its train a serene content. The most significant celebration took place at Charleston, South Carolina and had been arranged sometime beforehand for the purpose of hoisting the flag over Fort Sumter four years from the day on which it fell; but much was added to the joyful anniversary by the intelligence of Lee's surrender which was learned on their arrival by the distinguished visitors from the North who went there to participate in what Beecher called "a grand national event." The religious exercises at the fort were marked by a puritanical fervour; and distinct efforts were made to evoke the memories of the past. The chaplain who had thanked God at the flag-raising December 27, 1860 now offered a prayer. General Robert Anderson made a brief speech with deep feeling and raised the same United States flag over the ruins of Fort Sumter which he had lowered April 14, 1861. Sumter saluted the flag with one hundred guns and every fort and battery which had fired upon the little garrison at the commencement of the war now gave a national salute. The people sang the "Star-spangled Banner." Henry Ward Beecher delivered an impressive oration. At the banquet at the Charleston Hotel in the town one of the speakers was William Lloyd Garrison, who had been hanged and burned in effigy at Charleston thirty years before, and on whose head the South had set a price.

While the rejoicing went on in Charleston and echoes of the jubilation of the early week resounded throughout the North, Lincoln was assassinated. Walt Whitman has told the story of the exultation over the end of the war and of the death of the Captain with the peaceful haven in sight:

"O Captain! my Captain! our fearful trip is done,
The ship has weather'd every rack, the prize we sought is won,
The port is near, the bells I hear, the people all exulting,
While follow eyes the steady keel, the vessel grim and daring.
                . . . .

O Captain! my Captain! rise up and hear the bells;
Rise up—for you the flag is hung—for you the bugle trills,
For you bouquets and ribboned wreaths—for you the shores a-crowding,
For you they call, the swaying mass, their eager faces turning.
                . . . .

My Captain does not answer, his lips are pale and still,
My father does not feel my arm, he has no pulse nor will,
The ship is anchored safe and sound, its voyage closed and done,
From fearful trip the victor ship comes in with object won;

Exult O shores and ring O bells!
But I with mournful tread,
Walk the deck my Captain lies,
Fallen cold and dead."

Somewhat after two o'clock on the afternoon of April 14 General Grant bade the President good-by having declined his invitation to accompany him to the theatre that evening, the desire of seeing their children taking Mrs. Grant and himself to New Jersey. Lincoln spent an agreeable afternoon. He had an hour's chat with his son Robert (who for a short time had been a captain on Grant's staff), and then took a long drive with his wife, his happy and tender mood colouring his review of the past and anticipation of the future. Schuyler Colfax, Speaker of the last House and prospective Speaker of the next, was unable to join the theatre party but called at the White House at half-past seven in the evening in order to have a few last words before setting out on his journey to the Pacific coast. At ten minutes past eight the President rose and said to his wife, "Mother, I suppose it's time to go though I would rather stay," then grasping Colfax's hand with, "Pleasant journey to you, I'll telegraph you at San Francisco, good-by" he went with Mrs. Lincoln, Miss Harris and Major Rathbone to Ford's theatre to see Laura Keene's company play the comedy "Our American Cousin."

John Wilkes Booth, an erratic actor delighting in the gloom of "Richard III." and Schiller's "Robbers," a man of intemperate habits, and a fanatical sympathizer with the South, had organized a conspiracy for the murder of the President, Vice-President, General Grant and Secretary Seward, in which he had chosen for his part the assassination of the President. Between ten o'clock and half-past, Booth, fortified by liquor, showed a card to the servant sitting outside of the President's box, was allowed to pass, entered the box stealthily, put a pistol to Lincoln's head and shouting *Sic semper tyrannis,* fired. Dropping his pistol he struck with a knife at Rathbone, who was endeavouring to seize him, and jumped from the box to the stage. Although a high leap it would not have been difficult for an actor of Booth's training had not his spur caught in the folds of the flag with which the Presidential box was draped. He fell to the stage, breaking his leg, rose immediately, and, turning to the audience, brandished his knife, rushed out of the theatre, and, mounting a fleet horse rode away.

The ball had entered Lincoln's brain, at once rendering him insensible. He was taken to a house opposite, lay in a state of coma all night and died at twenty-two minutes past seven in the morning.

In Stanton's account of the tragedy, he said, the door of the President's private box "was unguarded." Had one of the million soldiers which Lincoln commanded been on guard with proper orders, by far the most precious life in the country, the one life absolutely necessary to the nation, would have been saved. There is but one other historic assassination fraught with such consequence to country, perhaps to civilization—that of Julius Caesar. "And when some of his friends did counsel Caesar," wrote Plutarch, "to have a guard for the safety of his person and some also did offer to serve him: he would never consent to it but said, It was better to die once than always to be afraid of death." Such was the attitude of Lincoln.

"Caesar was the entire and perfect man," wrote Mommsen. ". . . But in this very circumstance lies the difficulty, we may perhaps say the impossibility, of depicting Caesar to the life. As the artist can paint everything save only consummate beauty, so the historian, when once in a thousand years he encounters the perfect, can only be silent regarding it." This were truer of Lincoln than of Caesar, yet it is true of neither. In intellect Caesar surpassed Lincoln. Yet it remained for Washington and Lincoln to render false for the first time in history the generalization of Montesquieu: "Constant experience shows us that every man invested with power is apt to abuse it; he pushes on till he comes to something that limits him. Is it not strange though true to say that virtue itself has need of limits!"

Poet, preacher and orator have said all that can be said of Lincoln. It were too much to claim for him a world glory alongside of those men

of titanic intellects who have bestrode the Old World, and whose deeds
have amazed the New. It is enough that he is dear to Americans and en-
shrined next to Washington in their hearts. What a tribute to the worth
of the man is the love and respect of the two sections of the country that
strove against each other in a long and cruel war! Men marvel at Alexander,
Caesar and Napoleon; their intimates and their subjects feared them. No one
stood in awe of Lincoln; we respect, admire and love him. The others
were puffed up with pride until they thought themselves demi-gods; he
received suggestion and counsel that any other powerful ruler would have
spurned. Personal aggrandizement ruled the giants; abnegation of self
him who was moulded from the clay "of the unexhausted West."

A historian, who for sixteen years has studied closely Lincoln's character and actions, who has reflected upon his speeches, his public and private
letters, who has tried to know him as those did that saw him daily, feels in
recording his death a poignant regret that he should have been taken
away when his people still needed him and when his wisdom would have
had full scope. His truthfulness, honesty and self-abnegation make better
men of the students of his words and deeds and we all experience a moral
uplifting in the contemplation of his character. The uncouthness and
oddity of the man have gone with him to the grave; his speeches, state
papers, letters, records of his conversation and some of his stories remain.
We see the best, but the man we see is not untrue to life. Indeed the roughness of his manners was an incident so trivial that we forget it naturally
without making an effort to ignore it. We can see into the very soul of
Lincoln and know him as he knew himself. Let everything be told about
him and we shall never respect him less but shall always love him more.

Lincoln's love of country hardly left room for love of self. Other rulers
of great power have remorselessly crushed those who stood in their way.
He said, "I am not in favor of crushing anybody out." It is sometimes
thought that virtue in a man of action cannot coexist with great ability
and it is undeniable that much contemporary opinion of Lincoln ran:
well-meaning but weak, honest but without force. When his death came,
men recognized all the more his goodness, but then too they said he had
been wise: a judgment which a later generation has confirmed. "The new
pilot," as Emerson said, "was hurried to the helm in a tornado"; but
after he had taken his bearings what a skilful pilot he made!

HENRY ADAMS

(1838-1918)

Young Henry Adams and his brother, Charles Francis Adams, Jr., were trying to perform a public service when, early in the Grant administration, they began writing articles on corrupt relations between big business and government. They regarded the scandalous "Black Friday"—September 24, 1869, when Jay Gould and Jim Fisk tried to corner the market in gold as an unparalleled opportunity to dramatize these new relationships; the brothers jumped at it, reminisced Henry Adams, "like a salmon at a fly." Both of them interviewed the flamboyant "Jubilee Jim" Fisk at his Opera House. Then while Charles Francis Adams pursued his earlier interest in the tangled record of chicanery engulfing the Erie Railroad, Henry Adams utilized the data his friend Representative James A. Garfield gathered through a House Bank and Currency Committee investigation, to write a detailed account of the gold scandal. After two British publications rejected it as potentially libelous, the Westminster Review *finally published it. (Many of Adams's figures appear in pounds at the exchange rate of $5 per £1). Like his brother's articles on the Erie, Henry Adams's article remains a significant piece of contemporary historical writing, chronicling and suggesting the significance of an unsavory aspect of the new industrial age. It is printed here as it appeared in revised form in* Chapters of Erie and Other Essays *(1886).*

The New York Gold Conspiracy

THE CIVIL WAR IN AMERICA, WITH ITS ENORMOUS ISSUES OF DEPRECIATING currency, and its reckless waste of money and credit by the government, created a speculative mania such as the United States, with all its experience in this respect, had never before known. Not only in Broad Street, the centre of New York speculation, but far and wide throughout the Northern States, almost every man who had money at all employed a part of his capital in the purchase of stocks or of gold, of copper, of petroleum, or of domestic produce, in the hope of a rise in prices, or staked money on the expectation of a fall. To use the jargon of the street, every farmer and every shopkeeper in the country seemed to be engaged in "carrying" some favorite security "on a margin." Whoever could obtain five pounds sent it to a broker with orders to buy fifty pounds' worth of stocks, or whatever amount the broker would consent to purchase. If the stock rose, the speculator prospered; if it fell until the five pounds of deposit or margin were lost, the broker demanded a new deposit, or sold the stock to protect himself. By means of this simple and smooth machinery, which differs in no essential respect from the processes of *roulette* or *rouge-et-noir,* the whole nation flung itself into the Stock Exchange, until the "outsiders," as they were called, in opposition to the regular brokers of Broad Street, represented nothing less than the entire population of the American Republic. Every one speculated, and for a time every one speculated successfully.

The inevitable reaction began when the government, about a year after the close of the war, stopped its issues and ceased borrowing. The greenback currency had for a moment sunk to a value of only 37 cents to the dollar. It is even asserted that on the worst day of all, the 11th of July, 1864, one sale of £20,000 in gold was actually made at 310, which is equivalent to about 33 cents in the dollar. At this point, however, the depreciation stopped; and the paper which had come so near falling into entire discredit steadily rose in value, first to 50 cents, then to 60, to 70, and within the present year to more than 90 cents. So soon as the industrious part of the public felt the touch of this return to solid values, the whole fabric of fictitious wealth began to melt away under their eyes.

Thus it was not long before the so-called "outsiders," the men who

From Charles Francis and Henry Adams, *Chapters of Erie and Other Essays* (1886).

speculated on their own account, and could not act in agreement or combination, began to suffer. One by one, or in great masses, they were made
prey of the larger operators; their last margins were consumed, and they
dropped down to the solid level of slow, productive industry. Some lost
everything; many lost still more than they had, and there are few families of
ordinary connection and standing in the United States which cannot tell,
if they choose, some dark story of embezzlement, or breach of trust, committed in these days. Some men, who had courage and a sense of honor,
found life too heavy for them; others went mad. But the greater part turned
in silence to their regular pursuits, and accepted their losses as they could.
Almost every rich American could produce from some pigeon-hole a bundle
of worthless securities, and could show check-books representing the only
remaining trace of margin after margin consumed in vain attempts to satisfy
the insatiable broker. A year or two of incessant losses swept the weaker
gamblers from the street.

But even those who continued to speculate found it necessary to change
their mode of operations. Chance no longer ruled over the Stock Exchange and the gold market. The fate of a battle, the capture of a city, or the
murder of a President, had hitherto been the influences which broke through
the plans of the strongest combinations, and put all speculators, whether
great or small, on fairly even ground; but as the period of sudden and
uncontrollable disturbing elements passed away, the market fell more and
more completely into the hands of cliques which found a point of adhesion
in some great mass of incorporated capital. Three distinct railways, with
all their enormous resources, became the property of Cornelius Vanderbilt,
who, by means of their credit and capital, again and again swept millions
of dollars into his pocket by a process curiously similar to gambling with
loaded dice. But Vanderbilt was one of the most respectable of these great
operators. The Erie Railway was controlled by Daniel Drew, and while
Vanderbilt at least acted in the interests of his corporations, Drew cheated
equally his corporation and the public. Between these two men and the
immense incorporated power they swayed, smaller operators, one after
another, were crushed to pieces, until the survivors learned to seek shelter
within some clique sufficiently strong to afford protection. Speculation in this
manner began to consume itself, and the largest combination of capital
was destined to swallow every weaker combination which ventured to
show it itself in the market.

Thus, between the inevitable effect of a currency which steadily shrank
the apparent wealth of the country, and the omnipotence of capital in
the stock market, a sounder and healthier state of society began to make
itself felt. Nor could the unfortunate public, which had been robbed with
such cynical indifference by Drew and Vanderbilt, feel any sincere regret
when they saw these two cormorants reduced to tearing each other. In the
year 1867 Mr. Vanderbilt undertook to gain possession of the Erie Road, as

he had already obtained possession of the New York Central, the second
trunk line between New York and the West. Mr. Vanderbilt was supposed
to own property to the value of some £10,000,000, all of which might be
made directly available for stock operations. He bought the greater part of
the Erie stock; Drew sold him all he could take, and then issued as much
more as was required in order to defeat Vanderbilt's purpose. After a violent
struggle, which overthrew all the guaranties of social order, Drew triumphed,
and Mr. Vanderbilt abandoned the contest. The Erie corporation paid
him a large sum to reimburse his alleged losses. At the same time it was
agreed that Mr. Drew's accounts should be passed, and he obtained a release in full, and retired from the direction. And the Erie Road, almost
exhausted by such systematic plundering, was left in the undisturbed, if
not peaceful, control of Mr. Jay Gould and Mr. James Fisk, Jr., whose reign
began in the month of July, 1868.

Mr. Jay Gould was a partner in the firm of Smith, Gould, & Martin,
brokers, in Wall Street. He had been engaged before now in railway enterprises, and his operations had not been of a nature likely to encourage public
confidence in his ideas of fiduciary relations. He was a broker, and a broker
is almost by nature a gambler, perhaps the very last profession suitable for
a railway manager. In character he was strongly marked by his disposition for silent intrigue. He preferred as a rule to operate on his own
account, without admitting other persons into his confidence, and he seemed
never to be satisfied except when deceiving every one as to his intentions.
There was a reminiscence of the spider in his nature. He spun huge webs,
in corners and in the dark, which were seldom strong enough to resist a
serious strain at the critical moment. His disposition to this subtlety and
elaboration of intrigue was irresistible. It is scarcely necessary to say that
he had not a conception of a moral principle. In speaking of this class of
men it must be fairly assumed at the outset that they do not and cannot
understand how there can be a distinction between right and wrong in
matters of speculation, so long as the daily settlements are punctually
effected. In this respect Mr. Gould was probably as honest as the mass of
his fellows, according to the moral standard of the street; but without
entering upon technical questions of roguery, it is enough to say that he
was an uncommonly fine and unscrupulous intriguer, skilled in all the
processes of stock-gambling, and passably indifferent to the praise or censure of society.

James Fisk, Jr., was still more original in character. He was not yet
forty years of age, and had the instincts of fourteen. He came originally
from Vermont, probably the most respectable and correct State in the
Union, and his father had been a peddler who sold goods from town to
town in his native valley of the Connecticut. The son followed his father's
calling with boldness and success. He drove his huge wagon, made resplendent with paint and varnish, with four or six horses, through the towns of

Vermont and Western Massachusetts; and when his father remonstrated in alarm at his reckless management, the young man, with his usual bravado, took his father into his service at a fixed salary, with the warning that he was not to put on airs on the strength of his new dignity. A large Boston firm which had supplied his goods on credit, attracted by his energy, took him into the house; the war broke out; his influence drew the firm into some bold speculations which were successful; in a few years he retired with some £20,000, which he subsequently lost. He formed a connection with Daniel Drew in New York, and a new sign, ominous of future trouble, was raised in Wall Street, bearing the names of Fisk & Belden, brokers.

Personally Mr. Fisk was coarse, noisy, boastful, ignorant; the type of a young butcher in appearance and mind. Nothing could be more striking than the contrast between him and his future associate Gould. One was small and slight in person, dark, sallow, reticent, and stealthy, with a trace of Jewish origin. The other was large, florid, gross, talkative, and obstreperous. Mr. Fisk's redeeming point was his humor, which had a strong flavor of American nationality. His mind was extraordinarily fertile in ideas and expedients, while his conversation was filled with unusual images and strange forms of speech, which were caught up and made popular by the New York press. In respect to honesty as between Gould and Fisk, the latter was, perhaps, if possible, less deserving of trust than the former. A story not without a keen stroke of satirical wit is told by him, which illustrates his estimate of abstract truth. An old woman who had bought of the elder Fisk a handkerchief which cost ninepence in the New England currency, where six shillings are reckoned to the dollar, complained to Mr. Fisk, Jr., that his father had cheated her. Mr. Fisk considered the case maturely, and gave a decision based on *a priori* principles. "No!" said he, "the old man wouldn't have told a lie for ninepence"; and then, as if this assertion needed some reasonable qualification, he added, "though he would have told eight of them for a dollar!" The distinction as regards the father may have been just, since the father seems to have held old-fashioned ideas as to wholesale and retail trade; but in regard to the son even this relative degree of truth cannot be predicated with any confidence, since, if the Investigating Committee of Congress and its evidence are to be believed, Mr. Fisk seldom or never speaks truth at all.

An intrigue equally successful and disreputable brought these two men into the Erie Board of Directors, whence they speedily drove their more timid predecessor Drew. In July, 1868, Gould made himself President and Treasurer of the corporation. Fisk became Comptroller. A young lawyer, named Lane, became counsel. These three directors made a majority of the Executive Committee, and were masters of Erie. The Board of Directors held no meetings. The Executive Committee was never called together, and the three men—Fisk, Gould, and Lane—became from this time the absolute, irresponsible owners of the Erie Railway, not less than if it had been their personal property and plaything.

This property was in effect, like all the great railway corporations, an empire within a republic. It consisted of a trunk line of road 459 miles in length, with branches 314 miles in extent, or 773 miles of road in all. Its capital stock amounted to about £7,000,000. Its gross receipts exceeded £3,000,000 per annum. It employed not less than 15,000 men, and supported their families. Over all this wealth and influence, greater than that directly swayed by any private citizen, greater than is absolutely and personally controlled by most kings, and far too great for the public safety either in a democracy or in any other form of society, the vicissitudes of a troubled time placed two men in irresponsible authority; and both these men belonged to a low and degraded moral and social type. Such an elevation has been rarely seen in modern history. Even the most dramatic of modern authors, even Balzac himself, who so loved to deal with similar violent alternations of fortune, or Alexandre Dumas, with all his extravagance of imagination, never have reached a conception bolder or more melodramatic than this, nor have they ever ventured to conceive a plot so enormous, or a catastrophe so original, as was now to be developed.

One of the earliest acts of the new rulers was precisely such as Balzac or Dumas might have predicted and delighted in. They established themselves in a palace. The old offices of the Erie Railway were in the lower part of the city, among the wharves and warehouses; a situation, no doubt, convenient for business, but by no means agreeable as a residence; and the new proprietors naturally wished to reside on their property. Mr. Fisk and Mr. Gould accordingly bought a huge building of white marble, not unlike a European palace, situated about two miles from the business quarter, and containing a large theatre or opera-house. They also purchased several smaller houses adjoining it. The opera-house cost about £140,000, and a large part of the building was at once leased, by the two purchasers, to themselves as the Erie corporation, to serve as offices. This suite of apartments was then furnished by themselves, as representing the corporation, at an expense of some £60,000, and in a style which, though called vulgar, is certainly not more vulgar than that of the President's official residence, and which would be magnificent in almost any palace in Europe. The adjoining houses were connected with the main building; and in one of these Mr. Fisk had his private apartments, with a private passage to his opera-box. He also assumed direction of the theatre, of which he became manager-in-chief. To these royal arrangements he brought tastes which have been commonly charged as the worst results of royal license. The atmosphere of the Erie offices was not supposed to be disturbed with moral prejudices; and as the opera itself supplied Mr. Fisk's mind with amusement, so the opera *troupe* supplied him with a permanent harem. Whatever Mr. Fisk did was done on an extraordinary scale.

These arrangements, however, regarded only the pleasures of the American Aladdin. In the conduct of their interests the new directors showed a capacity for large conceptions, and a vigor in the execution of their schemes, such as alarmed the entire community. At the annual election in 1868, when Gould, Fisk, and Lane, having borrowed or bought proxies for the greater part of the stock, caused themselves to be elected for the ensuing year, the respectable portion of the public throughout the country was astonished and shocked to learn that the new Board of Directors contained two names peculiarly notorious and obnoxious to honest men,—the names of William M. Tweed and Peter B. Sweeney. To English ears these commonplace, not to say vulgar, titles do not seem singularly alarming; but to every honest American they conveyed a peculiar sense of terror and disgust. The State of New York in its politics is much influenced, if not controlled, by the city of New York. The city politics are so entirely in the hands of the Democratic party as to preclude even the existence of a strong minority. The party organization centres in a political club, held together by its patronage and the money it controls through a system of jobbery unequalled elsewhere in the world. And the Tammany Club, thus swaying the power of a small nation of several million souls, is itself ruled by William M. Tweed and Peter B. Sweeney, absolute masters of this terrible system of theft and fraud, and to American eyes the incarnation of political immorality.

The effect of this alliance was felt in the ensuing winter in the passage of a bill through the State legislature, and its signature by the Governor, abolishing the former system of annual elections of the entire board of Erie directors, and authorizing the board to classify itself in such a manner that only a portion should be changed each year. The principle of the bill was correct. Its practical effect, however, was to enable Gould and Fisk to make themselves directors for five years, in spite of any attempt on the part of the stockholders to remove them. The formality of annual re-election was spared them; and so far as the stockholders were concerned, there was no great injustice in the act. The Erie Road was in the peculiar position of being without an owner. There was no *cestui que trust,* unless the English stockholders could be called such. In America the stock was almost exclusively held for speculation, not for investment; and in the morals of Wall Street speculation means, or had almost come to mean, disregard of intrinsic value. In this case society at large was the injured party, and society knew its risk.

This step, however, was only a beginning. The Tammany ring, as it is called, exercised a power far beyond politics. Under the existing constitution of the State, the judges of the State courts are elected by the people. There are thirty-three such judges in New York, and each of the thirty-three is clothed with equity powers running through the whole State. Of these judges Tammany Hall elected several, and the Erie Railway controlled others in country districts. Each of these judges might forbid proceedings before any and all the other judges, or stay proceedings in suits already commenced. Thus the lives and the property of the public were in the power of the new combination; and two of the city judges, Barnard and Cardozo, had already acquired a peculiarly infamous reputation as so-called "slaves to the ring," which left no question as to the depths to which their prostitution of justice would descend.

The alliance between Tammany and Erie was thus equivalent to investing Mr. Gould and Mr. Fisk with the highest attributes of sovereignty; but in order to avail themselves to the utmost of their judicial powers, they also required the ablest legal assistance. The degradation of the bench had been rapidly followed by the degradation of the bar. Prominent and learned lawyers were already accustomed to avail themselves of social or business relations with judges to forward private purposes. One whose partner might be elevated to the bench was certain to be generally retained in cases brought before this special judge; and litigants were taught by experience that a retainer in such cases was profitably bestowed. Others found a similar advantage resulting from known social relations with the court. The debasement of tone was not confined to the lower ranks of advocates; and it was probably this steady demoralization of the bar which made it possible for the Erie ring to obtain the services of Mr. David Dudley Field as its legal adviser. Mr. Field, a gentleman of European reputation, in regard to which he is understood to be peculiarly solicitous, was an eminent law reformer, author of the New York Code, delegate of the American Social Science Association to the European International Congress, and asserted by his partner, Mr. Shearman, in evidence before a committee of the New York legislature, to be a man of quixotic sense of honor. Mr. Shearman himself, a gentleman of English parentage, had earned public gratitude by arraigning and deploring, with unsurpassed courage and point, the condition of the New York judiciary, in an admirable essay which will be found in the North American Review for July, 1867. The value of Mr. Field's services to Messrs. Fisk and Gould was not to be measured even by the enormous fees their generosity paid him. His power over certain judges became so absolute as to impress the popular imagination; and the gossip of Wall Street insists that he has a silken halter round the neck of Judge Barnard, and a hempen one round that of Cardozo. It is certain that he who had a year before threatened Barnard on his own bench with impeachment now appeared in the character of Barnard's master, and issued as a matter of course the edicts of his court.

One other combination was made by the Erie managers to extend their power, and this time it was credit that was threatened. They bought a joint-stock bank in New York City, with a capital of £200,000. The assistance thus gained was purchased at a very moderate price, since it was by no means represented by the capital. The great cliques and so-called "operators" of Wall Street and Broad Street carry on their transactions by a system of credits and clearing-houses with a very limited use of money. The banks certify their checks, and the certified checks settle all balances. Nominally and by law the banks only certify to the extent of *bona fide* deposits, but in reality the custom of disregarding the strict letter of the law is not unknown, and in regard to the bank in question, the Comptroller of the Currency, an officer of the National Treasury, testifies that on an examination of its affairs in April, 1869, out of fifteen checks deposited in its hands as security for certifications made by it, selected at hazard for inquiry, and representing a nominal value of £300,000, three only were good. The rest represented accommodation extended to brokers and speculators without security. As an actual fact it is evidence that this same bank on Thursday, September 24, 1869, certified checks to the amount of nearly £1,500,000 for Mr. Gould alone. What sound security Mr. Gould deposited against this mass of credit may be left to the imagination. His operations, however, were not confined to this bank alone, although this was the only one owned by the ring.

Thus Mr. Gould and Mr. Fisk created a combination more powerful than any that has been controlled by mere private citizens in America or in Europe since society for self-protection established the supreme authority of the judicial name. They exercised the legislative and the judicial powers of the State; they possessed almost unlimited credit, and society was at their mercy. One authority alone stood above them, beyond their control; and this was the distant but threatening figure of the National Government.

Nevertheless, powerful as they were, the Erie managers were seldom in funds. The huge marble palace in which they lived, the theatre which they supported, the reckless bribery and profusion of management by which they could alone maintain their defiance of public opinion, the enormous schemes for extending their operations into which they rushed with utter recklessness, all required greater resources than could be furnished even by the wholesale plunder of the Erie Road. They were obliged from time to time to issue from their castle and harry the industrious public or their brother freebooters. The process was different from that known to the dark ages, but the objects and the results were equally robbery. At one time Mr. Fisk is said to have ordered heavy speculative sales of stock in an express company which held a contract with the Erie Railway. The sales being effected, the contract was declared annulled. The stock naturally fell, and Mr. Fisk realized the difference. He then ordered heavy purchases, and having renewed the contract the stock rose again, and Mr. Fisk a second time swept the street. In the summer and autumn of 1869 the two managers issued and sold 235,000 new shares of Erie stock, or nearly as much as its entire capital when they assumed power in July, 1868. With the aid of the money thus obtained, they succeeded in withdrawing about £2,500,000 in currency from circulation at the very moment of the year when currency was most in demand in order to harvest the crops. For weeks the whole nation writhed and quivered under the torture of this modern rack, until the national government itself was obliged to interfere and threaten a sudden opening of the treasury. But whether the Erie speculators operated for a rise or operated for a fall, whether they bought or sold, and whether they were engaged in manipulating stocks, or locking up currency, or cornering gold, they were always a public nuisance and scandal.

In order to explain the operation of a so-called corner in gold to ordinary readers with the least possible use of slang or technical phrases, two preliminary statements are necessary. In the first place it must be understood that the supply of gold immediately available for transfers is limited within distinct bounds in America. New York and the country behind it contain an amount usually estimated at about £4,000,000. The national government commonly holds from £15,000,000 to £20,000,000, which may be thrown bodily on the market if the President orders it. To obtain gold from Europe or other sources requires time.

In the second place, gold in America is a commodity bought and sold like stocks in a special market or gold-room which is situated next the Stock Exchange in Broad Street and is practically a part of it. In gold as in stocks, the transactions are both real and speculative. The real transactions are mostly purchases or loans made by importers who require coin to pay customs on their imports. This legitimate business is supposed to require from £1,000,000 to £1,500,000 per day. The speculative transactions are mere wagers on the rise or fall of price, and neither require any actual transfer of gold, nor even imply its existence, although in times of excitement hundreds of millions nominally are bought, sold, and loaned.

Under the late administration Mr. McCulloch, the Secretary of the Treasury, had thought it his duty at least to guarantee a stable currency, although Congress forbade him to restore the gold standard. During four years gold had fluctuated little, and principally from natural causes, and the danger of attempting to create an artificial scarcity in it had prevented the operators from trying an experiment which would have been sure to irritate the government. The financial policy of the new administration was not so definitely fixed, and the success of a speculation would depend on the action of Mr. Boutwell, the new secretary, whose direction was understood to have begun by a marked censure on the course pursued by his predecessor.

Of all financial operations, cornering gold is the most brilliant and the most dangerous, and possibly the very hazard and splendor of the attempt were the reasons of its fascination to Mr. Jay Gould's fancy. He dwelt upon it for months, and played with it like a pet toy. His fertile mind even went so far as to discover that it would prove a blessing to the community, and on this ingenious theory, half honest and half fraudulent, he stretched the widely extended fabric of the web in which all mankind was to be caught. This theory was in itself partially sound. Starting from the principle that

the price of grain in New York is regulated by the price in London and is
not affected by currency fluctuations, Mr. Gould argued that if it were
possible to raise the premium on gold from thirty to forty cents at harvest-
time, the farmers' grain would be worth $1.40 instead of $1.30, and as a
consequence the farmer would hasten to send all his crop to New York for
export, over the Erie Railway, which was sorely in need of freights. With
the assistance of another gentleman, Mr. Gould calculated the exact premium at which the Western farmer would consent to dispose of his grain,
and thus distance the three hundred sail which were hastening from the
Danube to supply the English market. Gold, which was then heavy at 34,
must be raised to 45.

This clever idea, like all the other ideas of these gentlemen of Erie, seems
to have had the single fault of requiring that some one, somewhere, should
be swindled. The scheme was probably feasible; but sooner or later the reaction from such an artificial stimulant must have come, and whenever it
came some one must suffer. Nevertheless, Mr. Gould probably argued that
so long as the farmer got his money, the Erie Railway its freights, and he
himself his small profits on the gold he bought, it was of little consequence
who else might be injured; and, indeed, by the time the reaction came, and
gold was ready to fall as he expected, Mr. Gould would probably have been
ready to assist the process by speculative sales in order to enable the
Western farmer to buy his spring goods cheap as he had sold his autumn
crops dear. He himself was equally ready to buy gold cheap and sell it
dear on his private account; and as he proposed to bleed New York merchants for the benefit of the Western farmer, so he was willing to bleed
Broad Street for his own. The patriotic object was, however, the one which
for obvious reasons Mr. Gould preferred to put forward most prominently,
and on the strength of which he hoped to rest his ambitious structure of
intrigue.

In the operation of raising the price of gold from 133 to 145, there was
no great difficulty to men who controlled the resources of the Erie Railway.
Credit alone was needed, and of credit Mr. Gould had an unlimited supply.
The only serious danger lay in the possible action of the national government, which had not taken the same philanthropic view of the public good
as was peculiar to the managers of Erie. Secretary Boutwell, who should
have assisted Mr. Gould in "bulling" gold, was gravely suspected of being
a bear, and of wishing to depress the premiums to nothing. If he were
determined to stand in Mr. Gould's path, it was useless even for the combined forces of Erie and Tammany to jostle against him; and it was therefore essential that Mr. Gould should control the government itself, whether
by fair means or foul, by persuasion or by purchase. He undertook the task;
and now that his proceedings in both directions have been thoroughly
drawn into light, it is well worth while for the public to see how dramatic
and how artistically admirable a conspiracy in real life may be, when slowly

elaborated from the subtle mind of a clever intriguer, and carried into execution by a band of unshrinking scoundrels.

The first requisite for Mr. Gould's purpose was some channel of direct communication with the President; and here he was peculiarly favored by chance. Mr. Abel Rathbone Corbin, formerly lawyer, editor, speculator, lobby-agent, familiar, as he claims, with everything, had succeeded, during his varied career, in accumulating from one or another of his hazardous pursuits a comfortable fortune, and he had crowned his success, at the age of sixty-seven or thereabouts, by contracting a marriage with General Grant's sister, precisely at the moment when General Grant was on the point of reaching the highest eminence possible to an American citizen. To say that Mr. Corbin's moral dignity had passed absolutely pure through the somewhat tainted atmosphere in which his life had been spent, would be flattering him too highly; but at least he was now no longer engaged in any active occupation, and he lived quietly in New York, watching the course of public affairs, and remarkable for an eminent respectability which became the President's brother-in-law. Mr. Gould enjoyed a slight acquaintance with Mr. Corbin, and he proceeded to improve it. He assumed, and he asserts that he really felt, a respect for Mr. Corbin's shrewdness and sagacity. It is amusing to observe that Mr. Corbin claims to have first impressed the famous crop theory on Mr. Gould's mind; while Mr. Gould testifies that he himself indoctrinated Mr. Corbin with this idea, which became a sort of monomania with the President's brother-in-law, who soon began to preach it to the President himself. On the 15th of June, 1869, the President came to New York, and was there the guest of Mr. Corbin, who urged Mr. Gould to call and pay his respects to the Chief Magistrate. Mr. Gould had probably aimed at precisely this result. He called; and the President of the United States not only listened to the president of Erie, but accepted an invitation to Mr. Fisk's theatre, sat in Mr. Fisk's private box, and the next evening became the guest of these two gentlemen on their magnificent Newport steamer, while Mr. Fisk, arrayed, as the newspaper reported, "in a blue uniform, with a broad gilt cap-band, three silver stars on his coat-sleeve, lavender gloves, and a diamond breast-pin as large as a cherry, stood at the gangway, surrounded by his aids, bestarred and bestriped like himself," and welcomed his distinguished friend.

It had been already arranged that the President should on this occasion be sounded in regard to his financial policy; and when the selected guests—among whom were Mr. Gould, Mr. Fisk, and others—sat down at nine o'clock to supper, the conversation was directed to the subject of finance. "Some one," says Mr. Gould, "asked the President what his view was." The "some one" in question was, of course, Mr. Fisk, who alone had the impudence to put such an inquiry. The President bluntly replied, that there was a certain amount of fictitiousness about the prosperity of the country, and that the bubble might as well be tapped in one way as another. The remark was fatal to Mr. Gould's plans, and he felt it, in his own words, as a wet blanket.

Meanwhile the post of assistant-treasurer at New York had become vacant, and it was a matter of interest to Mr. Gould that some person friendly to himself should occupy this position, which, in its relations to the public, is second in importance only to the secretaryship of the treasury itself. Mr. Gould consulted Mr. Corbin, and Mr. Corbin suggested the name of General Butterfield,—a former officer in the volunteer army. The appointment was not a wise one; nor does it appear in evidence by what means Mr. Corbin succeeded in bringing it about. There is a suggestion that he used Mr. A. T. Stewart, the wealthy importer, as his instrument for the purpose; but whatever the influence may have been, Mr. Corbin appears to have set it in action, and General Butterfield entered upon his duties towards the 1st of July.

The elaborate preparations thus made show that some large scheme was never absent from Mr. Gould's mind, although between the months of May and August he made no attempt to act upon the markets. But between the 20th of August and the 1st of September, in company with Messrs. Woodward and Kimber, two large speculators, he made what is known as a pool, or combination, to raise the premium on gold, and some ten or fifteen millions were bought, but with very little effect on the price. The tendency of the market was downwards, and it was not easily counteracted. Perhaps under ordinary circumstances he might have now abandoned his project; but an incident suddenly occurred which seems to have drawn him headlong into the boldest operations.

Whether the appointment of General Butterfield had any share in strengthening Mr. Gould's faith in Mr. Corbin's secret powers does not appear in evidence, though it may readily be assumed as probable. At all events, an event now took place which would have seemed to authorize an unlimited faith in Mr. Corbin, as well as to justify the implicit belief of an Erie treasurer in the corruptibility of all mankind. The unsuspicious President again passed through New York, and came to breakfast at Mr. Corbin's house on the 2d of September. He saw no one but Mr. Corbin while there, and the same evening at ten o'clock departed for Saratoga. Mr. Gould declares, however, that he was told by Mr. Corbin that the President, in discussing the financial situation, had shown himself a convert to the Erie theory about marketing the crops, and had "stopped in the middle of a conversation in which he had expressed his views, and written a letter" to Secretary Boutwell. This letter is not produced; but Secretary Boutwell testifies as follows in regard to it:—

"I think on the evening of the 4th of September I received a letter from the President dated at New York, as I recollect it; I am not sure where it is dated. I have not seen the letter since the night I received it. I think it is now in my residence in Groton. In that letter he expressed an opinion that it was undesirable to force down the price of gold. He spoke of the importance to the West of being able to move their crops. His idea was that if gold should fall, the West would suffer, and the movement of the crops would be retarded. The impression made on my mind by the letter was that he had rather a strong opinion to that effect. . . . Upon the receipt of the President's letter on the evening of the 4th of September, I telegraphed to Judge Richardson [Assistant Secretary at Washington] this dispatch: 'Send no order to Butterfield as to sales of gold until you hear from me.' "

Mr. Gould had therefore succeeded in reversing the policy of the national government; but this was not all. He knew what the government would do before any officer of the government knew it. Mr. Gould was at Corbin's house on the 2d of September; and although the evidence of both these gentlemen is very confused on this point, the inference is inevitable that Gould saw Corbin privately, unknown to the President, within an hour or two after this letter to Mr. Boutwell was written, and that it was at this interview, while the President was still in the house, that Mr. Corbin gave him the information about the letter; perhaps showed him the letter itself. Then followed a transaction worthy of the French stage. Mr. Corbin's evidence gives his own account of it:—

"On the 2d of September (referring to memoranda) Mr. Gould offered to let me have some of the gold he then possessed. . . . He spoke to me as he had repeatedly done before, about taking a certain amount of gold owned by him. I finally told Mr. Gould that for the sake of a lady, my wife, I would accept $500,000 of gold for her benefit, as I shared his confidence that gold would rise. . . . He afterwards insisted that I should take a million more, and I did so on the same conditions for my wife. He then sent me this paper."

The paper in question is as follows:—

"Smith, Gould, Martin, & Co., Bankers,
11 Broad Street, New York, September 2, 1869.
"Mr.——
"Dear Sir: we have bought for your account and risk—
500,000, gold, 132, R.
1,000,000, gold, 135⅝, R.
which we will carry on demand with the right to use.
"SMITH, GOULD, MARTIN, & CO."

This memorandum meant that for every rise of one per cent in the price of gold Mr. Corbin was to receive £3,000, and his name nowhere to appear. If the inference is correct that Gould had seen Corbin in the morning and had learned from him what the President had written, it is clear that he must have made his bargain on the spot, and then going directly to the city, he must in one breath have ordered this memorandum to be made out and large quantities of gold to be purchased, before the President had allowed the letter to leave Mr. Corbin's house.

No time was lost. On this same afternoon, Mr. Gould's brokers bought large amounts in gold. One testifies to buying $1,315,000 at 134⅛. On the

3d the premium was forced up to 36; on the 4th, when Mr. Boutwell received his letter, it had risen to 37. Here, however, Mr. Gould seems to have met a check, and he describes his own position in nervous Americanisms as follows:—

"I did not want to buy so much gold. In the spring I put gold up from 32 to 38 and 40, with only about seven millions. But all these fellows went in and sold short, so that in order to keep it up I had to buy, or else to back down and show the white feather. They would sell it to you all the time. I never intended to buy more than four or five millions of gold, but these fellows kept purchasing it on, and I made up my mind that I would put it up to 40 at one time. . . . We went into it as a commercial transaction, and did not intend to buy such an amount of gold. I was forced into it by the bears selling out. They were bound to put it down. I got into the contest. All these other fellows deserted me like rats from a ship. Kimber sold out and got short. . . . He sold out at 37. He got short of it, and went up" (or, in English, he failed).

It was unfortunate that the bears would not consent to lie still and be flayed, but this was unquestionably the fact. They had the great operators for once at a disadvantage, and they were bent on revenge. Mr. Gould's position was very hazardous. When Mr. Kimber sold out at 37, which was probably on the 7th of September, the market broke; and on the 8th the price fell back to 35. Nor was this all. At the same moment, when the "pool" was ended by Mr. Kimber's desertion, Mr. Corbin, with his eminent shrewdness and respectability, told Mr. Gould "that gold had gone up to 37," and that he "should like to have this matter realized," which was equivalent to saying that he wished to be paid something on account. This was on the 6th; and Gould was obliged this same day to bring him a check for £5,000, drawn to the order of Jay Gould, and indorsed in blank by him with a touching regard for Mr. Corbin's modest desire not to have his name appear. There are few financiers in the world who will not agree that this transaction does great credit to Mr. Corbin's sagacity. It indicates at least that he was acquainted with the men he dealt with. Undoubtedly it placed Mr. Gould in a difficult position; but as Mr. Gould already held some fifteen millions of gold and needed Mr. Corbin's support, he preferred to pay £5,000 outright rather than allow Corbin to throw his gold on the market. Yet the fabric of Gould's web had now been so seriously injured that, for a whole week, from the 8th to the 15th of September, he was at a loss what to do, unable to advance and equally unable to retreat without very severe losses. He sat at his desk in the opera-house, silent as usual, and tearing little slips of paper which he threw on the floor in his abstraction, while he revolved new combinations in his mind.

Down to this moment Mr. James Fisk, Jr., has not appeared in the affair. Gould had not taken him into his confidence; and it was not until after the 10th of September that Gould appears to have decided that there was nothing else to be done. Fisk was not a safe ally in so delicate an affair, but apparently there was no choice. Gould approached him; and, as usual, his touch was like magic. Mr. Fisk's evidence begins here, and may be believed when very strongly corroborated:

"Gold having settled down to 35, and I not having cared to touch it, he was a little sensitive on the subject, feeling as if he would rather take his losses without saying anything about it. . . . One day he said to me, 'Don't you think gold has got to the bottom?' I replied that I did not see the profit in buying gold unless you have got into a position where you can command the market. He then said he had bought quite a large amount of gold, and I judged from his conversation that he wanted me to go into the movement and help strengthen the market. Upon that I went into the market and bought. I should say that was about the 15th or 16th of September. I bought at that time about seven or eight millions, I think."

The market responded slowly to these enormous purchases; and on the 16th the clique was still struggling to recover its lost ground.

Meanwhile Mr. Gould had placed another million and a half of gold to the account of General Butterfield, and notified him of the purchase. So Mr. Gould swears in spite of General Butterfield's denial. The date of this purchase is not fixed. Through Mr. Corbin a notice was also sent by Gould about the middle of September to the President's private secretary, General Porter, informing him that half a million was placed to his credit. General Porter instantly wrote to repudiate the purchase, but it does not appear that Butterfield took any notice of Gould's transaction on his account. On the 10th of September the President had again come to New York, where he remained his brother-in-law's guest till the 13th; and during this visit Mr. Gould appears again to have seen him, although Mr. Corbin avers that on this occasion the President intimated his wish to the servant that this should be the last time Mr. Gould obtained admission. "Gould was always trying to get something out of him," he said; and if he had known how much Mr. Gould had succeeded in getting out of him, he would have admired the man's genius, even while shutting the door in his face. On the morning of the 13th the President set out on a journey to the little town of Washington, situated among the mountains of Western Pennsylvania, where he was to remain a few days. Mr. Gould, who now consulted Mr. Corbin regularly every morning and evening, was still extremely nervous in regard to the President's policy; and as the crisis approached, this nervousness led him into the fatal blunder of doing too much. The bribe offered to Porter was a grave mistake, but a greater mistake yet was made by pressing Mr. Corbin's influence too far. He induced Mr. Corbin to write an official article for the New York press on the financial policy of the government, an article afterwards inserted in the New York Times through the kind offices of Mr. James McHenry, and he also persuaded or encouraged Mr. Corbin to write a letter directly to the President himself. This letter, written on the 17th under the influence of Gould's anxiety, was instantly sent away by a special messenger of Fisk's to reach the President before he returned to the capital. The messenger carried also a letter of introduction to General Porter, the private secretary, in order to secure the personal delivery of this important despatch.

We have now come to the week which was to witness the explosion of all this elaborately constructed mine. On Monday, the 20th, gold again rose. Throughout Tuesday and Wednesday Fisk continued to purchase without limit, and forced the price up to 40. At this time Gould's firm of Smith, Gould, & Martin, through which the operation was conducted, had purchased some $50,000,000; and yet the bears went on selling, although they could only continue the contest by borrowing Gould's own gold. Gould, on the other hand, could no longer sell and clear himself, for the very reason that the sale of $50,000,000 would have broken the market to nothing. The struggle had become intense. The whole country was looking on with astonishment at the battle between the bulls and the bears. All business was deranged, and all values unsettled. There were indications of a panic in the stock market; and the bears in their emergency were vehemently pressing the government to intervene. Gould now wrote to Mr. Boutwell a letter so inconceivably impudent that it indicates desperation and entire loss of his ordinary coolness. He began:—

"Sir,—There is a panic in Wall Street, engineered by a bear combination. They have withdrawn currency to such an extent that it is impossible to do ordinary business. The Erie Company requires eight hundred thousand dollars to disburse. . . . Much of it in Ohio, where an exciting political contest is going on, and where we have about ten thousand employed, and the trouble is charged on the administration. . . . Cannot you, consistently, increase your line of currency?"

From a friend such a letter would have been an outrage; but from a member of the Tammany ring, the principal object of detestation to the government, such a threat or bribe—whichever it may be called—was incredible. Mr. Gould was, in fact, at his wits' end. He dreaded a panic, and he felt that it could no longer be avoided.

The scene now shifts for a moment to the distant town of Washington, among the hills of Western Pennsylvania. On the morning of the 19th of September, President Grant and his private secretary, General Porter, were playing croquet on the grass, when Fisk's messenger, after twenty-four hours of travel by rail and carriage, arrived at the house, and sent in to ask for General Porter. When the President's game was ended, General Porter came, received his own letter from Corbin, and called the President, who entered the room and took his brother-in-law's despatch. He then left the room, and after some ten or fifteen minutes' absence returned. The messenger, tired of waiting, then asked, "Is it all right?" "All right," replied the President; and the messenger hastened to the nearest telegraph station, and sent word to Fisk, "Delivered; all right."

The messenger was, however, altogether mistaken. Not only was all not right, but all was going hopelessly wrong. The president, it appears, had at the outset supposed the man to be an ordinary post-office agent, and the letter an ordinary letter which had arrived through the post-office. Nor was it until Porter asked some curious question as to the man, that the President learned of his having been sent by Corbin merely to carry this apparently unimportant letter of advice. The President's suspicions were at once excited; and the same evening, at his request, Mrs. Grant wrote a hurried note to Mrs. Corbin, telling her how greatly the President was distressed at the rumor that Mr. Corbin was speculating in Wall Street, and how much he hoped that Mr. Corbin would "instantly disconnect himself with anything of that sort."

This letter, subsequently destroyed or said to have been destroyed by Mrs. Corbin, arrived in New York on the morning of Wednesday the 22d, the same day on which Gould and his enemies the bears were making their simultaneous appeals to Secretary Boutwell. Mrs. Corbin was greatly excited and distressed by her sister-in-law's language. She at once carried the letter to her husband, and insisted that he should instantly abandon his interest in the gold speculation. Mr. Corbin, although he considered the scruples of his wife and her family to be highly absurd, assented to her wish; and when Mr. Gould came that evening as usual, with $50,000,000 of gold on his hands, and extreme anxiety on his mind, Corbin read to him two letters: the first, written by Mrs. Grant to Mrs. Corbin; the second, written by Mr. Corbin to President Grant, assuring him that he had not a dollar of interest in gold. The assurance of this second letter was, at any sacrifice, to be made good.

Mr. Corbin proposed that Mr. Gould should give him a check for £20,000, and take his $1,500,000 off his hand. A proposition more calmly impudent than this can scarcely be imagined. Gould had already paid Corbin £5,000, and Corbin asked for £20,000 more, at the very moment when it was clear that the £5,000 he had received had been given him under a misunderstanding of his services. He even had the impudence to represent himself as doing Gould a favor by letting him have a million and a half more gold at the highest market price, at a time when Gould had fifty millions which it was clear he must sell or be ruined. What Gould might, under ordinary circumstances, have replied, may be imagined; but at this moment he could say nothing. Corbin had but to show this note to a single broker in Wall Street, and the whole fabric of Gould's speculation would have fallen to pieces. Gould asked for time and went away. He consulted no one. He gave Fisk no hint of what had happened. The next morning he returned to Corbin, and made him the following offer:—

"'Mr. Corbin, I cannot give you anything if you will go out. If you will remain in, and take the chances of the market, I will give you my check [for £20,000].' 'And then,' says Mr. Corbin, 'I did what I think it would have troubled almost any other business man to consent to do,—refuse one hundred thousand dollars on a rising market. If I had not been an old man married to a middle-aged woman, I should have done it (of course with her consent) just as sure as the offer was made. I said, 'Mr. Gould, my wife says "No!" Ulysses

thinks it wrong, and that it ought to end.' So I gave it up. . . . He looked at
me with an air of severe distrust, as if he was afraid of treachery in the camp.
He remarked, 'Mr. Corbin, I am undone if that letter gets out.' . . . He stood
there for a little while looking very thoughtful, exceedingly thoughtful. He then
left and went into Wall Street, . . . and my impression is that he it was, and
not the government, that broke that market.' "

Mr. Corbin was right; throughout all these transactions his insight into
Mr. Gould's character was marvellous.

It was the morning of Thursday, the 3d; Gould and Fisk went to Broad
Street together, but as usual Gould was silent and secret, while Fisk was
noisy and communicative. There was now a complete separation in their
movements. Gould acted entirely through his own firm of Smith, Gould, &
Martin, while Fisk operated principally through his old partner, Belden.
One of Smith's principal brokers testifies:—

" 'Fisk never could do business with Smith, Gould, & Martin very com-
fortably. They would not do business for him. It was a very uncertain thing of
course where Fisk might be. He is an erratic sort of genius. I don't think anybody would want to follow him very long. I am satisfied that Smith, Gould, &
Martin controlled their own gold, and were ready to do as they pleased with
it without consulting Fisk. I do not think there was any general agreement. . . .
None of us who knew him cared to do business with him. I would not have
taken an order from him nor had anything to do with him.' Belden was considered a very low fellow. 'I never had anything to do with him or his party,'
said one broker employed by Gould. 'They were men I had a perfect detestation
of; they were no company for me. I should not have spoken to them at all
under any ordinary circumstances.' Another says, 'Belden is a man in whom
I never had any confidence in any way. For months before that, I would not
have taken him for a gold transaction.' "

And yet Belden bought millions upon millions of gold. He himself
says he had bought twenty millions by this Thursday evening, and this
without capital or credit except that of his brokers. Meanwhile Gould,
on reaching the city, had at once given secret orders to sell. From the
moment he left Corbin, he had but one idea, which was to get rid of his
gold as quietly as possible. "I purchased merely enough to make believe
I was a bull," says Gould. This double process continued all that afternoon. Fisk's wild purchases carried the price up to 144, and the panic
in the street became more and more serious as the bears realized the extremity of their danger. No one can tell how much gold which did not
exist they had contracted to deliver or pay the difference in price. One of
the clique brokers swears that on this Thursday evening the street had sold
the clique one hundred and eighteen millions of gold, and every rise of one
per cent on this sum implied a loss of more than £200,000 to the
bears. Naturally the terror was extreme, for half Broad Street and thousands of speculators would have been ruined if compelled to settle gold
at 150 which they had sold at 140. It need scarcely be said that by this
time nothing more was heard in regard to philanthropic theories of benefit
to the Western farmer.

Mr. Gould's feelings can easily be imagined. He knew that Fisk's reckless management would bring the government upon his shoulders, and he knew that unless he could sell his gold before the order came from Washington he would be a ruined man. He knew, too, that Fisk's contracts must inevitably be repudiated. This Thursday evening he sat at his desk in the Erie offices at the opera-house, while Fisk and Fisk's brokers chattered about him.

"I was transacting my railway business. I had my own views about the market, and my own fish to fry. I was all alone, so to speak, in what I did, and I did not let any of those people know exactly how I stood. I got no ideas from anything that was said there. I had been selling gold from 35 up all the time, and I did not know till the next morning that there would probably come an order about twelve o'clock to sell gold."

He had not told Fisk a word in regard to Corbin's retreat, nor his own orders to sell.

When the next day came, Gould and Fisk went together to Broad Street, and took possession of the private back office of a principal broker, "without asking the privilege of doing so," as the broker observes in his evidence. The first news brought to Gould was a disaster. The government had sent three men from Washington to examine the bank which Gould owned, and the bank sent word to Mr. Gould that it feared to certify for him as usual, and was itself in danger of a panic, caused by the presence of officers, which created distrust of the bank. It barely managed to save itself. Gould took the information silently, and his firm redoubled sales of gold. His partner, Smith, gave the orders to one broker after another,— "Sell ten millions!" "The order was given as quick as a flash, and away he went," says one of these men. "I sold only eight millions." "Sell, sell, sell! do nothing but sell!—only don't sell to Fisk's brokers," were the orders which Smith himself acknowledges. In the gold-room Fisk's brokers were shouting their rising bids, and the packed crowd grew frantic with terror and rage as each successive rise showed their increasing losses. The wide streets outside were thronged with excited people; the telegraph offices were overwhelmed with messages ordering sales or purchases of gold or stocks; and the whole nation was watching eagerly to see what the result of this convulsion was to be. All trade was stopped, and even the President felt that it was time to raise his hand. No one who has not seen the New York gold-room can understand the spectacle it presented; now a perfect pandemonium, now silent as the grave. Fisk, in his dark back office across the street, with his coat off, swaggered up and down, "a big cane in his hand," and called himself the Napoleon of Wall Street. He really believed that he directed the movement, and while the street outside imagined that he and Gould were one family, and that his purchases were made for the clique, Gould was silently flinging away his gold at any price he could get for it.

Whether Fisk really expected to carry out his contract, and force the bears to settle, or not, is doubtful; but the evidence seems to show that he was in earnest, and felt sure of success. His orders were unlimited. "Put it up to 150," was one which he sent to the gold-room. Gold rose to 150. At length the bid was made—"160 for any part of five millions," and no one any longer dared take it. "161 for five millions,"—"162 for five millions." No answer was made, and the offer was repeated,—"162 for any part of five millions." A voice replied, "Sold one million at 62." The bubble suddenly burst, and within fifteen minutes, amid an excitement without parallel even in the wildest excitements of the war, the clique brokers were literally swept away, and left struggling by themselves, bidding still 160 for gold in millions which no one would any longer take their word for; while the premium sank rapidly to 135. A moment later the telegraph brought from Washington the government order to sell, and the result was no longer possible to dispute. Mr. Fisk had gone too far, while Mr. Gould had secretly weakened the ground under his feet.

Gould, however, was saved. His fifty millions were sold; and although no one yet knows what his gains or losses may have been, his firm was now able to meet its contracts and protect its brokers. Fisk was in a very different situation. So soon as it became evident that his brokers would be unable to carry out their contracts, every one who had sold gold to them turned in wrath to Fisk's office. Fortunately for him it was protected by armed men whom he had brought with him from his castle of Erie; but nevertheless the excitement was so great that both Mr. Fisk and Mr. Gould thought it best to retire as rapidly as possible by a back entrance leading into another street, and to seek the protection of the opera-house. There nothing but an army could disturb them; no civil mandate was likely to be served without their permission within these walls, and few men would care to face Fisk's ruffians in order to force an entrance.

The subsequent winding up of this famous conspiracy may be stated in few words. But no account could possibly be complete which failed to reproduce in full the story of Mr. Fisk's last interview with Mr. Corbin, as told by Fisk himself.

"I went down to the neighborhood of Wall Street, Friday morning, and the history of that morning you know. When I got back to our office, you can imagine I was in no enviable state of mind, and the moment I got up street that afternoon I started right round to old Corbin's to rake him out. I went into the room, and sent word that Mr. Fisk wanted to see him in the dining-room. I was too mad to say anything civil, and when he came into the room, said I, 'You damned old scoundrel, do you know what you have done here, you and your people?' He began to wring his hands, and, 'Oh!' he says, 'this is a horrible position. Are you ruined?' I said I didn't know whether I was or not; and I asked him again if he knew what had happened? He had been crying, and said he had just heard; that he had been sure everything was all right; but that something had occurred entirely different from what he had anticipated. Said I, 'That don't amount to anything; we know that gold ought not to be at 31, and that it would not be but for such performances as you have had this last week; you know damned well it would not if you had not failed.' I knew that somebody had run a saw right into us, and said I, 'This whole damned thing has turned out just as I told you it would.' I considered the whole party a pack of cowards, and I expected that when we came to clear our hands they would sock it right into us. I said to him, 'I don't know whether you have lied or not, and I don't know what ought to be done with you.' He was on the other side of the table, weeping and wailing, and I was gnashing my teeth. 'Now,' he says, 'you must quiet yourself.' I told him I didn't want to be quiet. I had no desire to ever be quiet again, and probably never should be quiet again. He says, 'But, my dear sir, you will lose your reason.' Says I, 'Speyers [a broker employed by him that day] has already lost his reason; reason has gone out of everybody but me.' I continued, 'Now what are you going to do? You have got us into this thing, and what are you going to do to get out of it?' He says, 'I don't know. I will go and get my wife.' I said, 'Get her down here!' The soft talk was all over. He went up stairs and they returned, tottling into the room, looking older than Stephen Hopkins. His wife and he both looked like death. He was tottling just like that. [Illustrated by a trembling movement of his body.] I have never seen him from that day to this."

This is sworn evidence before a committee of Congress; and its humor is perhaps the more conspicuous, because there is every reason to believe that there is not a word of truth in the story from beginning to end. No such interview ever occurred, except in the unconfined apartments of Mr. Fisk's imagination. His own previous statements make it certain that he was not at Corbin's house at all that day, and that Corbin did come to the Erie offices that evening, and again the next morning. Corbin himself denies the truth of the account without limitation; and adds, that when he entered the Erie offices the next morning Fisk was there. "I asked him how Mr. Gould felt after the great calamity of the day before." He remarked, "O, he has no courage at all. He has sunk right down. There is nothing left of him but a heap of clothes and a pair of eyes." The internal evidence of truth in this anecdote would support Mr. Corbin against the world.

In regard to Mr. Gould, Fisk's graphic description was probably again inaccurate. Undoubtedly the noise and scandal of the moment were extremely unpleasant to this silent and impenetrable intriguer. The city was in a ferment, and the whole country pointing at him with wrath. The machinery of the gold exchange had broken down, and he alone could extricate the business community from the pressing danger of a general panic. He had saved himself, it is true; but in a manner which could not have been to his taste. Yet his course from this point must have been almost self-evident to his mind, and there is no reason to suppose that he hesitated.

His own contracts were all fulfilled. Fisk's contracts, all except one, in respect to which the broker was able to compel a settlement, were repudiated. Gould probably suggested to Fisk that it was better to let Belden fail, and to settle a handsome fortune on him, than to sacrifice something more than £1,000,000 in sustaining him. Fisk therefore threw Belden over,

and swore that he had acted only under Belden's order; in support of
which statement he produced a paper to the following effect:—

"September 24.

"DEAR SIR,—I hereby authorize you to order the purchase and sale of gold
on my account during this day to the extent you may deem advisable, and to
report the same to me as early as possible. It is to be understood that the profits
of such order are to belong entirely to me, and I will, of course, bear any
losses resulting.

.   "Yours,
                                                           "WILLIAM BELDEN.
"JAMES FISK, JR."

This document was not produced in the original, and certainly never
existed. Belden himself could not be induced to acknowledge the order;
and no one would have believed him if he had done so. Meanwhile the
matter is before the national courts, and Fisk may probably be held to his
contracts: but it will be far more difficult to execute judgment upon him,
or to discover his assets.

One of the first acts of the Erie gentlemen after the crisis was to summon
their lawyers, and set in action their judicial powers. The object was to
prevent the panic-stricken brokers from using legal process to force settlements, and so render the entanglement inextricable. Messrs. Field and
Shearman came, and instantly prepared a considerable number of injunc-
tions, which were sent to their judges, signed at once, and immediately
served. Gould then was able to dictate the terms of settlement; and after a
week of complete paralysis, Broad Street began at last to show signs of
returning life. As a legal curiosity, one of these documents, issued three
months after the crisis, may be reproduced, in order to show the powers
wielded by the Erie managers:—

"SUPREME COURT.

H. N. SMITH, JAY GOULD, H. H. MARTIN, ⎫
and J. B. BACH, Plaintiffs,   ⎪
                    against   ⎬   Injunction
JOHN BONNER and ARTHUR L. SEWELL,   ⎪   by order.
Defendants,   ⎭

"It appearing satisfactorily to me by the complaint duly verified by the
plantiffs that sufficient grounds for an order of injunction exist, I do hereby
order and enjoin. . . . That the defendants, John Bonner and Arthur L. Sewell,
their agents, attorneys, and servants, refrain from pressing their pretended
claims against the plaintiffs, or either of them, before the Arbitration Committee of the New York Stock Exchange, or from taking any proceedings
thereon, or in relation thereto, except in this action.

                                                    "GEORGE G. BARNARD, J. S. C.
"NEW YORK, DECEMBER 29, 1869."

Mr. Bonner had practically been robbed with violence by Mr. Gould,
and instead of his being able to bring the robber into court as the criminal,
the robber brought him into court as criminal, and the judge forbade him

to appear in any other character. Of all Mr. Field's distinguished legal reforms and philanthropic projects, this injunction is beyond a doubt the most brilliant and the most successful.

The fate of the conspirators was not severe. Mr. Corbin went to Washington, where he was snubbed by the President, and at once disappeared from public view, only coming to light again before the Congressional Committee. General Butterfield, whose share in the transaction is least understood, was permitted to resign his office without an investigation. Speculation for the next six months was at an end. Every person involved in the affair seemed to have lost money, and dozens of brokers were swept from the street. But Mr. Jay Gould and Mr. James Fisk, Jr., continued to reign over Erie, and no one can say that their power or their credit was sensibly diminished by a shock which for the time prostrated all the interests of the country.

Nevertheless it is safe to predict that sooner or later the last traces of the disturbing influence of war and paper money will disappear in America, as they have sooner or later disappeared in every other country which has passed through the same evils. The result of this convulsion itself has been in the main good. It indicates the approaching end of a troubled time. Messrs. Gould and Fisk will at last be obliged to yield to the force of moral and economical laws. The Erie Railway will be rescued, and its history will perhaps rival that of the great speculative manias of the last century. The United States will restore a sound basis to its currency, and will learn to deal with the political reforms it requires. Yet though the regular process of development may be depended upon, in its ordinary and established course, to purge American society of the worst agents of an exceptionally corrupt time, there is in the history of this Erie corporation one matter in regard to which modern society everywhere is directly interested. For the first time since the creation of these enormous corporate bodies, one of them has shown its power for mischief, and has proved itself able to override and trample on law, custom, decency, and every restraint known to society, without scruple, and as yet without check. The belief is common in America that the day is at hand when corporations far greater than the Erie—swaying power such as has never in the world's history been trusted in the hands of mere private citizens, controlled by single men like Vanderbilt, or by combinations of men like Fisk, Gould, and Lane, after having created a system of quiet but irresistible corruption—will ultimately succeed in directing government itself. Under the American form of society, there is now no authority capable of effective resistance. The national government, in order to deal with the corporations, must assume powers refused to it by its fundamental law, and even then is always exposed to the chance of forming an absolute central government which sooner or later is likely to fall into the very hands it is struggling to escape, and thus destroy the limits of its power only in order to make corruption omnipotent. Nor is this danger confined to America alone. The corporation is in its nature a threat against the popular institutions which are spreading so rapidly over the whole world. Wherever there is a popular and limited government this difficulty will be found in its path, and unless some satisfactory solution of the problem can be reached, popular institutions may yet find their very existence endangered.

WOODROW WILSON

(1856-1924)

A leading writer on American historians, Michael Kraus, has commented, "Wilson will be remembered not as one who wrote history, but rather as one who made it." It is exactly this which makes his observations on the United States between 1876 and 1900 rewarding reading. When the five volumes of A History of the American People *first appeared in 1902, it was notable as smoothly written, broadly popular history, with thick pages and elaborate illustrations drawing attention away from the paucity of facts. When Wilson became President of the United States he once declared in a jocular vein, "At one time I tried to write history. I did not know enough to write it, but I knew from experience how hard it was to find an historian out, and I trusted I would not be found out."*

Later readers have not found Wilson out, but they have been startled to discover how conservative a Cleveland Democrat he was. They are dismayed also by his racist view of the inferiority of the new immigrants from southern and eastern Europe—ideas not much different from those of Roosevelt, Fiske, and Adams in these same years, but which Wilson had to repudiate when he ran for President in 1912. The Wilson of 1902 was a successful popular author and President of Princeton University. His writing was notable for its sympathy toward the South and the West. He was a good friend of Frederick Jackson Turner, the historian of the frontier, whose ideas made their author impress upon A History of the American People. *Also it was clear from his writing that he had matured in the South of the Reconstruction. Turner in reviewing his history noted that Wilson was "the first Southern scholar of adequate training and power to deal with American history as a whole in a continental spirit." Much of the phraseology and occasional flashes of brilliant observation give promise of the President who stood for the New Freedom and the League of Nations.*

The End of the Century

WITH THE COMING IN OF MR. HAYES THE WHOLE AIR OF POLITICS SEEMED to change. Democratic critics of the administration were inclined to dwell with a good deal of acidity upon the flagrant inconsistency of the President's course in first using the questionable governments of Louisiana and South Carolina to get his office and then forthwith repudiating them and bringing about their immediate downfall by withdrawing the federal troops upon whose presence and support they relied for their existence; and his friends could urge only that the constitution provides that presidential electors shall be "appointed" by each State "in such manner as the legislature thereof may direct," and that it might with perfect consistency be argued that the legislatures of the southern States could commit to their returning boards the right to choose presidential electors while at the same time maintaining that those boards ought not to be sustained in the virtual selection of state governors and legislatures as well. But, in any case, whether consistent or inconsistent, the President's action had brought grateful peace. Almost at once affairs wore a normal aspect again. The process of reconstruction, at least, had reached its unedifying end, and the hands of political leaders were free to take up the history of the country where it had been broken off in 1861. Instead of the quick, resistless despatch of party measures from session to session by congressional majorities which even the President's veto could not check or defeat, there had come a breathing space in which no party was supreme and the slow and moderate ways of compromise and accommodation were once again vouchsafed the country, at last quite out of breath with the pace to which it had been forced in its affairs. Not for fourteen years, from the elections of 1875 to those of 1889, were either Democrats or Republicans to control both Congress and the Executive. There was leisure from passion; men could look about them deliberately and without excitement and note how the country had changed.

It was no longer the country of 1861. Sixteen years, mixed of war which forced industry to a quick, almost abnormal development and of peace that came like a release of energies cramped, pent up, uneasy, had brought something like an industrial revolution with them. The South was of a

From Wilson, *A History of the American People* (5 vols., 1902), excerpts from throughout vol. 5.

sudden added as a modern economic force to the nation. Her old system of labor, which had shut her in to a virtual isolation, was destroyed; she was open at last to the labor of the world and was to enter with all her resources the industrial life from which she had so long held off. The great Appalachian region which stretched its mighty highlands from Pennsylvania through Maryland, the Virginias, Kentucky, Tennessee, and the Carolinas full seven hundred miles into Alabama and Georgia, and which spread its broad surfaces of mountain, valley, and plateau one hundred and fifty miles by the way upon either hand, geologists knew to be an almost unbroken coal field, it might be thirty-nine thousand square miles in area. Upon its skirts and in the broken country to the east and west of it iron also abounded, and mineral deposits which no man had looked into. The world still needed the southern cotton and tobacco, and before the first crude processes of reconstruction were over the cotton fields were once more producing almost as much as they had yielded in 1860, the year of greatest abundance ere the war came on,—so readily had free labor taken the place of slave. The industrial development of the South had been joined to that of the rest of the country, and for the first time since the modern industrial age set in capitalists turned to her for investment and the enterprises that bring wealth and power.

And what was for the South as yet but an exciting prospect and confident hope was for the North already a reality. The war had been a supreme test of economic vitality, and the States of the North and West had emerged from it stronger than they went into it. Almost every industry that yielded the necessaries of modern life and action had felt and responded to its quickening compulsion; and when peace came manufacturers but looked about them for wider markets, better and cheaper processes, a broader scope of operation. Artificial stimulation in the shape of heavy tariff duties had been added to the natural stimulation of the time and of the rapid and healthy growth of the nation. Congress had taxed almost every article of use in the country to support the war, and had added to the innumerable direct taxes which it imposed an enormously expanded system of duties on imports. It had done so in part to offset the direct taxes, to enable the manufacturers, who had to pay large sums to the government on the articles they made, to keep the market nevertheless against the importers; but it had made the duties much higher than that consideration taken alone made necessary. It had raised them to a point that made profit, very great profit, certain to accrue to the manufacturer. No considerable body of manufacturers asked for such "protection" that did not get it, and as much of it as they asked for, though it reduced the revenues of the government to grant it. Hardly a month went by while the war lasted that Congress did not add a new duty or increase an old one, and every industry was nursed to make the most of itself in the home markets, until its undisputed monopoly there as against foreign manufactures gave it wide margins of profit of which to avail itself in underselling competitors in the markets of the world.

The country got visible proof of its extraordinary material progress at its Centennial Exhibition in Philadelphia. The last year of General Grant's presidency was the centennial year of the independence of the United States, and the anniversary was celebrated by a great international industrial exposition at the city of Philadelphia, where the Congress had sat which took counsel for the young republic at its birth. All the greater commercial and industrial nations were represented in its exhibits. Foreign governments responded very promptly to the invitation to lend their aid in securing its success, among the rest the government of Great Britain, whose defeat in arms the great fair was meant to celebrate. The presence of her official commissioners made it a festival of reconciliation. America's own bitter war of civil revolution also was over, and a time of healing at hand. The thronging crowds at Philadelphia, the gay and spacious buildings, the peaceable power of the world's workmen exhibited upon every hand spoke of good will and the brotherhood of nations, where there was no rivalry but the rivalry to serve and to enrich mankind.

It was significant for America that objects of beauty marked everywhere among those exhibits the refinement and the ennobling art of the world. Throughout all the long hundred years in which they had been building a nation Americans had shown themselves children of utility, not of art. Beauty they had neglected. Everything they used showed only the plain, unstudied lines of practical serviceability. Grace was not in their thought, but efficiency. The very houses they built, whether for homes or for use in their business, showed how little thought they gave to the satisfaction of the eye. Their homes were for the most part of wood and the perishable material hardly justified costly ornament or elaborate design; and yet the men of the colonial time, keeping still some of the taste of an older world, had given even their simple frame dwellings a certain grace and dignity of line, and here and there a detail, about some doorway or the columns of a stately porch, which rewarded the eye. Builders of the later time had forgotten the elder canons of taste and built without artistic perception of form even when they built elaborately and at great cost. The same plainness, the same hard lines of mere serviceability were to be seen in almost everything the country made. The things to be seen at Philadelphia, gathered from all the world, awakened it to a new sense of form and beauty. Foreign governments had generously sent priceless works of painting and sculpture over sea to give distinction to the galleries of the Exhibition. Private citizens and local museums also had freely loaned their chief art treasures. Everywhere there was some touch of beauty, some suggested grace of form. Visitors poured by the million across the grounds and through the buildings of the Exhibition, out of every State and region of the country, and the impressions they received were never wholly obliterated. Men and

women of all sorts, common and gentle alike, had from that day a keener
sense of what was fitted to please the eye. The pride of life and of great
success that came with the vision of national wealth and boundless resources
to be got from the countless exhibits of farm and factory had in it also
some touch of corrected taste, some impulse of suitable adornment. Men
knew afterwards that that had been the dawn of an artistic renaissance
in America which was to put her architects and artists alongside the modern
masters of beauty and redeem the life of her people from its ugly severity.

That great fair might also serve to mark the shifting stress of the nation's
life. Its emphasis was henceforth, for at least a generation, to rest on
economic, not upon political or constitutional, questions. . . .

On all hands there was manifest a growing uneasiness because of the
apparent rise of monopolies and the concentration of capital in the hands
of comparatively small groups of men who seemed to be in a position to
control at their pleasure the productive industries of the country; because
of the power of the railways to determine by discriminating rates what
sections of the country, what industries, what sorts of products and of
manufactures should be accorded the easiest access to the markets; because
of the increase in the cost of the necessary tools of industry and of all manufactured goods through the operation of the tariff,—the inequitable clogs
which seemed to many to be put by the law itself upon the free and wholesome rivalries of commerce and production. The farmers of the West and
South, no less than the workingmen of the industrial East, had begun,
close upon the heels of the war, to organize themselves for the protection
and advancement of their own special interests, to which the programmes
of the political parties paid little heed. Between 1872 and 1875 the local
"granges" of a secret order known as the Patrons of Industry had multiplied
in a very significant manner, until their membership rose to quite a million
and a half and was spread over almost the entire Union. It was the purpose
of the order to promote by every proper means the interests of the farmers
of the country, though it was no part of its plan to agitate questions of
politics, put candidates for office into the field at elections, or use its gathering power to determine the fate of parties. Politicians, nevertheless, found
means to use it,—felt obliged to use it because they feared to let it act for
itself. Its discussions turned often on questions of transportation, upon the
railways and their power to make or ruin; it was but a short step in such
a field from an association for mutual protection and advice to a political
party organized for the control of legislation.

"Grangers" were not always to be held off, therefore, by their prudent
leaders from using their numbers and their ready concert of action to further
or defeat the ambitions of particular groups of politicians; and even while
their granges grew other organizations of farmers came into existence whose
aims were frankly and openly political. About the time of Mr. Hayes's
accession to the presidency independent associations began to make their
appearance in the South and in the West, under the name of the "Farmers'

Alliance," whose common object it was to oppose monopoly and the power of money in public affairs in the interest of those who had neither the use of capital nor the protection of tariffs. The first "Alliance" made its appearance in Texas, to prevent the wholesale purchase of the public lands of the State by private individuals. The organization spread into other southern States, and with its extension went also an enlargement of its programme of reform. Almost at the same time a "National Farmers' Alliance" was established in Illinois which quickly extended its organization into Wisconsin, Minnesota, Iowa, Kansas, and Dakota. Many sorts of reform commended themselves to the leaders of the movement, north and south: chief among them, government control of the means of transportation, the entire divorce of the government from the banks, and a paper currency issued directly to the people on the security of their land,—some escape from the power of the money lenders and of the great railways, and a war upon monopolies. These were vague purposes, and the means of reform proposed showed the thinking of crude and ignorant minds; but politicians felt with evident concern that new, it might be incontrollable, forces had begun to play through the matters they handled, and that it must presently be harder than ever to calculate the fortunes of parties at the polls. They perceived how difficult and delicate a task it must prove to keep the tacit pledges of the protective system to the manufacturers and give the free capital of the country the proper support of government and yet satisfy the classes now astir in these new associations of laborers and farmers, whose distress was as real as their programmes of reform were visionary.

There was a significance in these new movements which did not lie upon the surface. New questions had become national and were being uncomfortably pressed upon the attention of national party leaders because the attitude of the country towards the national government had been subtly changed by the events of war and reconstruction. The war had not merely roused the spirit of nationality, until then but half conscious, into vivid life and filled every country-side of the North and West with a new ardor for that government which was greater than the government of States, the government upon which the unity and prestige of the nation itself depended. It had also disclosed the real foundations of the Union; had shown them to be laid, not in the constitution, its mere formal structure, but upon deep beds of conviction and sentiment. It was not a theory of lawyers that had won when the southern Confederacy was crushed, but the passionate beliefs of an efficient majority of the nation, to whom the constitution was but a partial expression of the ideals which underlay their common life. While the war lasted the forms of the constitution had been with difficulty observed, had, indeed, again and again given way that the whole force of the nation might run straight and unimpeded to meet the exigencies of the portentous struggle. Mr. Lincoln had wielded an authority known to none of his predecessors. There had been moments when it

seemed almost as if all constitutional rules were suspended and law superseded by force in order that the contest for nationality might not halt or
be hindered. And when the war was over the process of reconstruction
showed the same method and temper. No scrupulous care was taken to
square what was done in the South with the law of the constitution. The
will of Congress operated there like that of an absolute parliament, even
while the lawyers of the houses who supported the measures of reconstruction were protesting that the States they were handling like provinces were
still members of the Union. The internal affairs of the humbled States were
altered at the pleasure of the congressional leaders, and yet it was said that
they had not been put forth from the pale of the constitution.

It was inevitable that the whole spirit of affairs should be profoundly
affected by such events. A revolution had been wrought in the consciousness and point of view of the nation. Parts had shifted and the air had
changed. Conceptions were radically altered with regard to Congress, with
regard to the guiding and compulsive efficacy of national legislation and
the relation of the life of the land to the supremacy of the federal law-
making body. A government which had been in its whole spirit federal
had, almost of a sudden, become national, alike in method and in point
of view. The national spirit which the war had aroused to bring this about
had long been a-making. Many a silent force which grew quite unobserved
from generation to generation, in quiet times of wholesome peace and mere
increase of nature, had been slowly breeding the thoughts which had now
sprung so vividly into consciousness. The very growth of the nation, the
very lapse of time and uninterrupted habit of united action, the mere mix-
ture and movement and distribution of populations, the mere accretions of
policy, the mere consolidation of interests, had been building and
strengthening new tissue of nationality the years through, and drawing links
stronger than links of steel about the invisible body of common thought
and purpose which is the substance of nations. When the great crisis of
secession came men knew at once how their spirits were ruled, men of the
South as well as men of the North,—in what institutions, in what conceptions of government their blood was fixed to run; and a great and instant
readjustment took place, which was for the South, the minority, practically
the readjustment of conquest and fundamental revolution, but which was
for the North nothing more than an awakening.

There had been no constitutional forms for such a business. For several
years, consequently, Congress had been permitted to do by statute what,
under the older conceptions of the federal law, could properly be done only
by constitutional amendment. The necessity for that gone by, it was suffered
to embody in the constitution what it had already enacted and put into
operation as law, not by the free will of the country at large, but by the
compulsions of mere force exercised upon a minority whose assent was
necessary to the formal completion of its policy. The result restored, prac-

tically entire, the forms of the constitution; but not before new methods and irregular, the methods of majorities but not the methods of law, had been openly learned and practised, and learned in a way not likely to be forgotten. It was not merely the economic changes of a new age, therefore, that inclined laborers and farmers to make programmes of reform which they purposed to carry out through the instrumentality of Congress; it was also this new conception of the supremacy of the federal law-making body, of the potency of all legislation enacted at Washington. The country was turning thither for all sorts of relief, for assistance in all parts of its life.

And yet other changes had come upon the government at Washington which rendered it a less serviceable instrument of use than it had once been. Nothing had become more emphasized during the reconstruction period than the virtual supremacy of the houses over the President in all matters outside the field of war and foreign affairs,—in foreign affairs even, when they chose. No President since General Jackson had been the real leader of his party until Lincoln; and Lincoln's term had made no permanent difference in the practices established since Jackson's day. It had been a time apart. In war the Executive was of course at the front of affairs; Congress but sustained it in the conduct of exigent business which, in the very nature of the case, it could not itself undertake. Parties, too, were silent; the nation had put ordinary questions of policy aside. No man could say how Mr. Lincoln might have ruled the counsels of his party in times of quiet peace. With Mr. Johnson in the presidency, Congress and the Executive had swung violently apart. General Grant had not brought them together. He was no party man and no statesman, had been bred to affairs of another kind, let constructive suggestion alone, made no pretence of political leadership. Under the strong will of Mr. Thaddeus Stevens a real primacy in affairs had been created for the men who led upon the floor of the houses, and old tendencies had been confirmed. . . .

The change was for a long time not observed by the country at large, because the two parties offset each other in the houses and neither could take entire command of affairs. For fourteen years (1876-1890) neither party during any one session controlled both the houses and the presidency, except for a brief space of two years (1881-1883) when the Republicans, with a Republican President in the chair, had, by the use of the Vice President's casting vote in the Senate, a majority of a single vote in each house. So scant a margin was not a margin of power, and the Speaker happened for the nonce to be of the older type, not cast for leadership.

That long deadlock of the houses was of much more serious consequence than the mere postponement of a full application of the new methods of party leadership and legislative management. So long as it lasted no change could be made in the laws passed in support of Republican supremacy and negro suffrage in the South. The country had turned away from the Republicans, as the elections to the House showed afresh every two years, but the majority of the nation and the majority of the States were by no means one and the same, and the Senate came only for a little while into the hands of the Democrats, while a Republican President was in the chair. Democratic majorities, accordingly, did not avail to repeal the "Force Acts" and the federal law for the supervision of elections which put the southern political leaders in danger of the federal courts and kept men of the President's appointment at the polls in the South to act in behalf of the negroes and the Republican managers. Though the white men of the South were at last in control of their state governments, federal law still held them off from excluding negroes from the exercise of the suffrage by any fair or open method which should set aside without breach of law what reconstruction had done. They were driven, if the incubus of that ignorant and hostile vote was to be lifted from their affairs, to resort to covert, tricky, fraudulent means which brought their own deep demoralization.

Every device known to politicians, every plan that could be hit upon that politicians had never before been driven to resort to, was made use of to reduce or nullify the negro vote. It was a great advantage to the men who had regained their power in the South that the whole machinery of elections, at least, was again in their hands. They had never before made such use of it. The older traditions that surrounded the use of the ballot in the South were of the most honorable sort. But the poison of the reconstruction system had done its work,—no man any longer found it hard to learn methods of mastery which were not the methods of law or honor or fair play. The new election officers found many excuses for rejecting or ignoring the negroes' voting papers. Voting places were often fixed at points so remote from the centres of population that only a small proportion of the negroes could reach them during the hours for voting; or were changed without notice so that only the white voters who had been informed could find them readily. In some cases separate ballot boxes were used for the several offices to be filled at the elections, so lettered that the illiterate negroes distinguished them with difficulty and so shifted in their order from time to time that the sequence in which they stood was constantly being changed, and no vote was counted which was not put into the right box. In districts where the negroes mustered in unusual numbers too few voting places were provided, and the voters were prevented from casting their ballots rapidly by premeditated delays of all sorts, so that the full vote of the district could not be cast.

The southern legislatures hastened to adopt the device long ago originated by Mr. Gerry, of Massachusetts, and so divided the voting districts of the States as to segregate the negroes within a few districts, whimsically drawn upon the map in such a way as to seek out and include the regions in which they were chiefly massed. The "shoe-string district" contrived by the lawmakers of Mississippi, which ran its devious way across the State for three hundred miles with a width of but twenty, became known the country over as a type of what was being done to cut the negroes off from political power in the South. Where such shifts and expedients failed of their desired result or could not be made use of actual fraud was practised. The less scrupulous partisans of the white party managers folded tissue ballots within their regular voting papers and overcame the negro majority by multiple voting. Dissuasion, too, and all the less noticeable means of intimidation, played their quiet part the while in keeping the negroes away from the polls, and the negro vote fell off by the thousand. There was presently nothing left of the one-time party organization of the Republicans in the South except that the federal office holders appointed by Republican Presidents still essayed to play an influential part among the negroes, and hold them to their party allegiance.

Slowly cases tried under the various Enforcement Acts which had been meant to secure the negroes against interference and intimidation in the exercise of their civil rights crept up, by appeal, to the Supreme Court of the United States and began one by one to be reached on its interminable docket; and in each case the court declared the powers Congress had assumed in those Acts clearly incompatible with the constitution. The right of the negroes to assemble and to bear arms, for example, which Congress had sought to protect and which southern white men had repeatedly interfered with, was a right which they enjoyed, the court declared, as citizens of the States, not as citizens of the United States, and it was not competent for Congress or the federal courts to punish individuals who interfered with it. The power conferred upon Congress by the Thirteenth, Fourteenth, and Fifteenth Amendments, to secure the negroes equality of civil rights with the whites, was, it decided, a power given to be exercised in restraint of the States, not against individuals, as the Act against the "conspiracies" of the Ku Klux had used it, and the States, not the federal government, must punish those who sought to destroy that equality. The legislation which General Grant had put so energetically into execution was unconstitutional and void. But it was 1882 before that sweeping conclusion was reached; the Acts had been executed long ago and their consequences were complete. Only the thought of constitutional lawyers and the course to be pursued by the federal government for the future were cleared by the belated decisions.

* * *

Mr. Harrison entered office amidst signs of a new age. The Republican party which had put him forward was not the Republican party of the war and of reconstruction but the Republican party of the new day of industrial revolution. Old questions had fallen out of sight or were transformed by changes in the nation itself; new questions pressed for solution which had in them no flavor of the older passion of party politics. Mr. Cleveland's four years of office had altered many things. For the mass of voters they had altered the very principles of choice between parties. That choice turned now once again upon questions of the day, not upon the issues of a war long ago fought out or of a reconstruction of southern society which politicians had touched only to mar and embarrass. A full century had gone by since the government of the nation was set up. Within that century, it now began to appear, fundamental questions of governmental structure and political authority had been settled and the country drawn together to a common life. Henceforth matters were to be in debate which concerned the interests of society everywhere, in one section as in another, questions which were without geographical boundary, questions of the modern world, touching nations no less than communities which fancied themselves to lie apart.

And yet a new sectionalism began to show itself, not political, but economic. In 1890, for the first time, the census takers found it impossible to trace upon their maps any line which marked the front of settlement between the Mississippi and the rising heights of the Rockies. Hitherto there had always been a "frontier" within the body of the continent, a line along which ran the outposts of settlement, and beyond that, between the newest settlements and the slopes of the Pacific, a well defined space as yet unpeopled. But now such regions had lost their definite outlines. Here and there were yet vacant spaces, some of them, it might be, as extensive in area as a great State: some tract of desert, some region which promised neither the fruits of the earth nor hidden wealth of minerals; but for the rest population had diffused itself so generally that frontiers had disappeared and the differences between region and region seemed little more than differences in the density of population. And yet there were lines of separation, none the less, which no census taker could draw but to which statesmen of necessity gave heed, which were as significant as anything the older maps had shown. The careful student of economic conditions might almost have made a sketch upon the map of the new divisions of the country,— divisions of interest: those most fundamental of all differences, differences in the stage of development. Any observant traveller might remark them as he moved from the teeming eastern seaports into the West or South. From the Atlantic seaboard to the Mississippi and the great lakes there stretched, north of Mason and Dixon's line, a region substantially homogeneous in all the larger interests of trade and industry, not unlike European countries in the development of its resources and the complex diversification of its life; but beyond it, to the west and south, lay regions and communities of another kind, at another stage of development, agricultural for the most part, up to the very ridges of the Rockies, or else set apart to some special interest like that of mining or of cattle raising on the great scale. Throughout all the vast continent, to the east of the Mississippi as to the west, contrasts were indeed modulated; hardly anywhere was the transition sharp from one set of social and economic conditions to another. But, taken upon the large view, they were very great, very significant, openly prophetic of differences of opinion and of interest.

Settlement had crossed the continent, but always with a thin and scattered front, its masses neither homogeneous, nor uniform, its processes hasty, imperfect, crude until the third or fourth generation. In many places settlers were yet but in the first generation. Line after line to be found on the decennial maps of the census office, to mark the frontiers of fixed settlement decade by decade, was still to be traced in differences of habit and development between community and community from east to west, nor yet effaced by the feet of those who had crossed them to make home beyond. Communities were still making and to be made. Conditions as if of a first day of settlement, conditions such as had once existed on the coast of the Atlantic in the far away days of the first colonies, conditions which had been shifted generation by generation from east to west across the whole breadth of the great continent, were still to be observed in hastily built town at the far West, upon broad cattle ranches, in rough mining villages, in new regions upon the vast western plains where the plough had but just begun to break the surface of the virgin land into fruitful furrows. The land itself, by reason of its own infinite variety of character and resource, commanded changes of life and diversity of occupation. There were broad tracts of country which were entirely without cities or centres of population or any industry which brought men together in intimate co-operative groups, tracts given over by nature to the farmer and the grazier. There were States where communities sharply contrasted in life and motive were set side by side, to the sore perplexity of those who sought to make their laws and reconcile their interests: placer mines which poured the refuse of their operations down the slopes of the western mountains upon smiling farms which they were like to ruin; towns perched high within the peaks of the towering Rockies, where precious metals were to be found, which yet lay within the same political boundaries with keepers of sheep and cattle in the plains below; centres of trade and of manufacture, lying upon some great watercourse or by the coasts of the western ocean, which seemed hardly more than huge trading posts on the routes of commerce from east to west, from west to east, so little intimate part did they have in the life of the rural people amidst whose prairie farms or broad orchards of fruit they were set.

It was these differences, this lack of homogeneity, this diversity of habit, interest, and point of view which had begun to tell upon the politics of the country with the ending of the war and of the processes of reconstruction, and which now began to be decisive in the formulation of party programmes. The South, with the passing away of slavery and of the leadership of the greater landholders, bred in an elder school of politics, had become like the newer regions of the West in motive and opinion. It, too, was predominantly agricultural. Its farmers were not the aristocratic planters of the elder society which the war had destroyed, but were for the most part men of the class from which Andrew Johnson had come: plain men who did not stand for the old traditions, who had not themselves owned slaves and who had felt none of the *esprit* of privilege that had ruled affairs in the days gone by; men as new in politics, as new in political thinking and constructive purpose, as much bound within the narrow limits of their own experience as the men of the western farms. Any one who noted how the tenets of the Farmers' Alliance and the new and radical heresies with regard to money took root there could see how the South had in fact become itself a new region in all that touched its social organization and its political thinking, a region as it were of recent settlement and late development so far as all the new order of the nation's life was concerned. Errors of opinion began to prevail there, as in the new regions of the West, like those which had swept through the crude colonies in the unquiet days which preceded and followed the War for Independence: hopes that the credit of the government itself might in some manner be placed at the disposal of the farmers in the handling and marketing of their crops, demands for a "cheap" currency, of paper or of silver, which should be easier to get and easier to pay debts with than the gold which lay so secure in the vaults of the banks and of the federal Treasury. The communities from which such demands came lay remote from the centres of trade where men could see in the transactions of every day what the real laws of credit, of value, and of exchange must always be, whether legislators would have them so or not. Moreover, they felt profoundly, though vaguely, the economic uneasiness of the time, the novel power of the railways to determine markets and prices and margins of profit, the rising influence of great aggregations of capital in the controlling industries of the country, the providential oversight of banks and of those who made the arrangements of credit and exchange. Every farmer, every rural shopkeeper and trader, every man who attempted manufacture upon a small scale felt at a cruel disadvantage, and, letting his thoughts run only upon his own experience and observation, dreamed of bettering his chances by an abundant issue of at least the cheaper of the two monetary metals by the government itself, in order that bankers and capitalists might no longer keep poor men in bondage. . . .

It was growing from year to year more and more difficult to calculate, more and more difficult to guide the movements of opinion. The new age of growth which had followed the war showed a quickened pace of change. The years 1889-1890 saw six new States added to the roster of the Union: North Dakota, South Dakota, Montana, Washington, Idaho, and Wyoming, and thoughtful men perceived how significant a thing it was that but five Territories remained in all the broad continent, with scattered Reservations here and there in the farther West, set apart for the redmen. In 1889 the government had purchased of the tribes even a part of the Indian Territory which lay within the circle of Kansas, Arkansas, and Texas, to be thrown open to white settlers,—the fairest portion of it, Oklahoma, the Beautiful Land which lay almost at its heart; and all the country had heard how mad a rush there had been across its borders to secure its coveted acres. A host of settlers fifty thousand strong had encamped upon its very boundary lines to await the signal to go in and take possession. At noon on the 22d of April, 1889, at the sound of a bugle blown to mark the hour set by the President's proclamation, the waiting multitude surged madly in, and the Territory was peopled in a single day. It was the old, familiar process of first occupation and settlement carried out as if in a play, the story of the nation's making in a brief epitome. Its suddenness, its eagerness, its resistless movement of excited men marked in dramatic fashion the end of the day of settlement. The best parts of the continent, save isolated Reservations here and there, were taken up; and the stream of population was dammed at their borders only by the barriers of law. When they were removed it would spring forward like a flood.

The census of 1890 showed the population of the country increased to 62,622,250, an addition of 12,466,467 within the decade. Immigrants poured steadily in as before, but with an alteration of stock which students of affairs marked with uneasiness. Throughout the century men of the sturdy stocks of the north of Europe had made up the main strain of foreign blood which was every year added to the vital working force of the country, or else men of the Latin-Gallic stocks of France and northern Italy; but now there came multitudes of men of the lowest class from the south of Italy and men of the meaner sort out of Hungary and Poland, men out of the ranks where there was neither skill nor energy nor any initiative of quick intelligence; and they came in numbers which increased from year to year, as if the countries of the south of Europe were disburdening themselves of the more sordid and hapless elements of the population, the men whose standards of life and of work were such as American workmen had never dreamed of hitherto. The people of the Pacific coast had clamored these many years against the admission of immigrants out of China, and in May, 1892, got at last what they wanted, a federal statute which practically excluded from the United States all Chinese who had not already acquired the right of residence; and yet the Chinese were more to be desired, as workmen if not as citizens, than most of the coarse crew that came crowding in every year at the eastern ports. They had, no doubt, many an unsavory habit, bred unwholesome squalor in the crowded quarters where they most abounded in the western seaports, and seemed separated by their very nature from the people among whom they had come to live; but it was their skill, their intelligence, their hardy power of labor, their knack at succeeding and driving duller rivals out, rather than their alien habits, that made them feared and hated and led to their exclusion at the prayer of the men they were likely to displace should they multiply. The unlikely fellows who came in at the eastern port were tolerated because they usurped no place but the very lowest in the scale of labor. . . .

After President Grover Cleveland returned to office in 1893 he had serious difficulties.

His party was in fact going to pieces and turning away from him, under the compulsion of forces over which he had no control. The business of the country had fallen dull and inactive because of the financial disquietude of the time. A great poverty and depression had come upon the western mining regions and upon the agricultural regions of the West and South. Prices had fallen; crops had failed. Drought swept the western plains clean of their golden harvests. Farmers in the districts most stricken could not so much as buy clothes for their backs, and went clad in the sacks into which they would have put their grain had they had any, their feet wrapped about with pieces of coarse sackcloth for lack of shoes. Men of the poorer sort were idle everywhere, and filled with a sort of despair. All the large cities and manufacturing towns teemed with unemployed workingmen who were with the utmost difficulty kept from starvation by the systematic efforts of organized charity. In many cities public works were undertaken upon an extensive scale to give them employment. In the spring of 1894 "armies of the unemployed" began to gather in the western country for the purpose of marching upon Washington, like mendicant hosts, to make known to the government itself, face to face, the wants of the people. The dramatic plan seems to have been originated by one Coxey, of Massillon, Ohio, who announced that he would lead an "Army of the Commonweal of Christ" to Washington to propose that the government issue $500,000,000 in greenbacks to be paid out for work upon the public roads, in order that the country might at one and the same time be supplied with serviceable highways and abundant money. On the 25th of March he actually set out, and by the 1st of May was at the capital. A hundred men began the journey with him, and their ranks had swelled to three hundred and fifty by the time they entered Washington. They made no disturbance. Most of the towns and villages on their way supplied them with food, partly out of charitable good humor, partly in order to speed them on their way and be quit of them, lest they should linger or grow ugly in temper; good natured sympathizers and men who wished to see the comedy played out subscribed funds for their most urgent needs. The painful farce was soon over. Their errand of course came to nothing. They reached Washington to find that there was nothing that they could do, and dispersed. But their example was imitated with less harmless results. Other "armies" gathered, in more sullen mood, to take their turn at marching and living upon the country as they went. Some started from the faraway coasts of the Pacific. Railway trains were seized to afford them transportation across the mountains and across the long plains where marching would be most painful, tedious, and unprofitable. Country-sides experienced a sort of panic at their approach. It began to seem as if there were no law or order in the land. Society itself seemed demoralized, upset.

It was in such an atmosphere that political opinion altered, that parties dissolved and were reconstituted with many a novel purpose of reform. And yet the President moved in all matters which it fell to him to act upon with a vigor and initiative which made the years memorable. Strikes had been added to the other disturbances of the time. From April until June, 1894, a strike of the bituminous coal miners, two hundred thousand strong, threatened to embarrass the industries of the whole country. Many manufacturing establishments were obliged to close for lack of fuel. Some of the railways seized the coal which they were carrying as freight for use in feeding the fires of their locomotives. On the 11th of May a strike of the employees of the Pullman Car Company, of Chicago, began which presently became a very formidable affair. The strikers and their sympathizers mustered in dangerous numbers and made concerted effort to prevent the use of the cars of the Pullman Company by any of the railways running out of Chicago. Their violence seemed about to stop all traffic on the western roads, and Mr. Cleveland intervened. The governor of Illinois had not asked for his aid, had not even called out the militia of the State to maintain order and protect property,—sympathized, indeed, with the strikers and resented interference. Neither had the federal courts acted or asked for assistance in the execution of their writs. Mr. Cleveland deliberately took the initiative and assumed the responsibility, on the ground that the strikers were preventing the movement of the mails and blocking the course of interstate commerce, and that the carrying of the mails and the protection of commerce between the States were indisputable duties of the federal government. He ordered federal troops to the points of greatest violence and danger, and, when their mere presence and mere action as armed police did not suffice to check the mobs that aided the strikers, he issued a proclamation which practically declared the disturbed regions in a state of insurrection and threatened merciless action against all rioters as against public enemies. Order was restored and the law prevailed again. . . .

The elections of 1896 [showed], in a fashion the country was not likely to forget, the volcanic forces which had been kept but just beneath the surface while [Cleveland] was President. The issue which had dominated all the rest was the question of the coinage. But that question did not stand alone. It seemed, indeed, but a single item in the agitated thought of the time. Opinion everywhere seemed to have broken from its old moorings. There had been real distress in the country, long continued, hopeless, as if the springs of wealth and prosperity were dried up. The distress was most marked and apparently most hopeless in the great agricultural areas of the South and West. The prices of agricultural products had fallen so low that

universal bankruptcy seemed to the farmers to be but a little way off. There
was a marked depression in all kinds of business, as if enterprise were out
of heart and money nowhere to be had except among a few great capitalists
in Wall Street. Men's minds anxiously sought the cause, and each man
reasoned upon it in the light of his own observation and experience, taking
his views of matters which lay beyond his own life from the politicians who
spoke most plausibly of public affairs. Every established relationship of
law and of society fell under question. Did not the law too much favor the
combinations of capital by which small dealers and producers were shut
out of the markets? Were the courts not on the side of those who had
privilege, and against those who had none? Were not the railways the real
masters of the producer everywhere, able to make or to unmake him by
their charges and discriminations? Was not money scarce because the government would issue none that was not kept to the standard of gold, itself
too scarce, too artificially costly to be made the universal medium and
exchange?

The money question was but one of the innumerable questions that
crowded into men's minds in that time of agitation, but it seemed the question which lay at the centre of all the rest, and it more than any other
gathered passion about it. Men do not think with cool detachment about
the financial questions which touch their very means of subsistence. They
were easily persuaded that money would be more plentiful, for the individual as for the nation, if scarce gold were abandoned as the exclusive
standard of value and abundant silver substituted, so that there should be
metal currency enough for all; and they were easily beguiled to dream what
a blessed age should come when the thing should have been done. They
were not studious of the laws of value. They knew that the resources of
the country were abundant, that its prosperity came from its own skill
and its own wealth of rich material, and that it was getting a certain pre-
dominance in the markets of the world. They could not see why it should
not be sufficient unto itself, why its standards of values should not be its
own, irrespective of the practice of other countries, why its credit should be
affected by the basis upon which the currency of other countries rested, or
why international trade should dominate its domestic transactions. All the
world had in fact become at last a single commercial community. No nation,
least of all a nation which lived by trade and manufacture, could stand
aloof and insist that an ounce of gold should not be considered more valuable than sixteen ounces of silver when mere fact was against it and the
free law of supply and demand worked its will despite the statutes of
legislatures. But very few men who did not actually handle the trade of
the world saw the inexorable laws of value as they existed in fact. It went
naturally with the vast extent of the continent that most men were shut
off from a sight of the international forces which governed their economic
interests, and a very passion of belief had got abroad that all the economic

stagnation of the times could be relieved by the free coinage of both gold and silver at the ratio of sixteen to one.

It was no ordinary political opinion such as might in any election year come forward to dominate men's votes. It set men's minds on fire, filled them with an eager ardor like that of religious conviction, impelled them to break old associations and seek new comradeships in affairs. Party lines were cut athwart. The Republicans no doubt had their chief strength in the central and eastern States of the Union, where trade and manufacture moved strongest and men were most apt to understand the wide foundations of their business; the Democrats drew their support, rather, from the South and West, where disturbing changes of opinion had long been in progress and where radical programmes of relief were most apt to be looked upon with favor; and yet it was by no means certain that these new opinions upon the money question had not touched Republican voters too deeply to make it prudent for their leaders to take high ground of opposition against them. An extraordinary campaign of propaganda had been begun before the year of the presidential election came on. The advocates of the free coinage of silver were early afoot, with the ardor and irresistible zeal of veritable crusaders, to overcome dissent in both parties alike and force the country to a common view. A great national conference of silver advocates had been convened at Washington in March, 1895, and had marked the beginning of an organized movement which was carried forward with extraordinary vigor and effect, to control the action of the party conventions. As the year of the elections lengthened towards summer State after State in the South and West declared unequivocally for free coinage, and conservative men everywhere waited with a deep uneasiness to see what the leaders of the national parties would do.

The Republican convention met first, and in it the advocates of the gold standard won. The convention declared itself "unalterably opposed to every measure calculated to debase our currency or impair the credit of our country, and therefore opposed to the free coinage of silver except by international agreement with the leading commercial nations of the world." Its choice of a candidate for the presidency was not quite so definite an evidence of its purpose with regard to the currency as the words of its platform. It nominated Mr. William McKinley, recently governor of Ohio, and known to all the country for his long service in the House of Representatives, especially as chairman of the Committee of Ways and Means which had formulated the tariff of 1890 against which the Democrats had won at the polls in 1892. Mr. McKinley had more than once spoken and voted on the silver question, and had not shown himself unwilling to consider very seriously the claims of the advocates of the cheaper metal as a standard of value. They had accounted him, if not a friend, at least no determined opponent, at any rate of some of the measures upon which they had set their hearts. But there was no doubt of his great credit with his party as a man and a leader, and his explicit acquiescence in the principles of the platform upon which he had been nominated satisfied the country of his good faith and conservative purpose. The issue was definitively made up.

Three weeks later the Democratic convention demanded "the free and unlimited coinage of both gold and silver at the present legal ratio of sixteen to one, without waiting for the aid or consent of any other nation," and nominated Mr. William Jennings Bryan, of Nebraska, for the presidency. It acted with singular excitement and swung sharply away from conservative influences. It denounced what Mr. Cleveland had done to save the gold reserve and to check the riots at Chicago as hotly as any Republican policy; spoke of the decisions of the Supreme Court of the United States against the income tax as if it advocated a change in the very character of the court, should power come to the party it represented; and uttered radical doctrines of reform which sounded like sentences taken from the platforms of the People's party. Its nomination for the presidency was significant of its temper and excitement. Mr. Bland, of Missouri, one of the older leaders of the party, and a man whose name all the country knew to stand for the advanced doctrines of free coinage, had at first led in the balloting. Mr. Bryan, though he had been a member of Congress and had spoken in the House upon the coinage question, had made no place of leadership for himself hitherto, was unkown to the country at large and even to the great mass of his fellow partisans, and had come to the convention with the delegation from Nebraska unheralded, unremarked. A single speech made from the platform of the convention had won him the nomination, a speech wrought, not of argument, but of fire, and uttered in the full tones of a voice which rang clear and passionate in the authentic key of the assembly's own mood of vehemence and revolt. It was a thing for thoughtful men to note how a mere stroke of telling declamation might make an unknown, untested man the nominee of a great party for the highest office in the land, a popular assembly being the instrument of choice.

The People's party also accepted Mr. Bryan as its candidate. It uttered in its platform some radical purposes which the new Democratic leaders had not adopted, but it did not require its candidate himself to accept them. It recognized the coinage issue as the chief question of the moment, and was willing that he should be its spokesman in that. Parties were singularly confused and broken. Two weeks after the Democratic convention a considerable body of Republicans, advocates of the free coinage of silver, rejected in the counsels of their own party, assembled in convention at St. Louis, calling themselves the National Silver party, and there in their turn endorsed the candidacy and the views of Mr. Bryan. Early in September an influential body of men out of the Democratic ranks came together in convention at Indianapolis, calling themselves the National Democratic party, and formulated once more what conservative men believed to be the true traditional doctrines of the Democratic party upon questions of taxation, revenue, and coinage. Men of strong party faith hardly knew which way to turn. The great deep seemed broken up, old landmarks swept away, parties merged, confused, dispersed. Only the Republican party preserved its full historical identity. Its opponents were united in novel, uncertain, motley assembly; it was at least compact and definite.

The money issue seemed the only issue of the campaign. Party orators spoke often of other things, but upon that they grappled in close, stubborn, impassioned argument. The country had never seen such a struggle to rule opinion. Such excitement, such a stirring of the moral and intellectual forces of the country, on the one side as if to regenerate society, on the other as if to save it from disruption, had never before marked a political campaign. The election even of 1860 had been preceded by no such fever of agitation. The Democrats and their allies had the dramatic advantage. Their candidate made a gallant figure wherever he moved, and went up and down the country, as no presidential candidate before him had ever done, to give the people his own striking version of the doctrines he preached. To the excited crowds which pressed about him he seemed a sort of knight errant going about to redress the wrongs of a nation. There could be no mistaking his earnestness or his conviction or the deep power of the motives to which he appealed. His gifts were those of the practised orator, his qualities those of the genuine man of the people. His strong, musical voice carried his message to the utmost limits of any throng, and rang in a tone which warmed men's blood. There could be no doubting the forces of conviction which lay back of him. Very likely there were many charlatans in the convention which nominated him, and men who acted upon mere expediency, but the crowding ranks in that hall had been made up for the most part of men who deeply believed every word of the radical programme they put forth; and the great throngs out-of-doors who cheered the sentences of that platform with full-throated ardor cheered because they also believed. No one could deny that the country had fallen upon evil times, that the poor man found it harder than ever to live, and that many a law needed to be looked into which put the poor at a disadvantage. The country teemed with men who found themselves handicapped in all they tried to do,—they could but conjecture why. It was no new thing that multitudes, and multitudes of sensible men at that, should think that the remedy lay in making new laws of coinage and exchange. The battle was to be won by argument, not by ridicule or terror or mere stubbornness of vested interest.

It was won by argument. The country had never seen such a flood of pamphlets, such a rush of every man who could speak to the platform, of every man who could write into the columns of the newspapers and the pages of the magazines. It was in the last analysis a contest between the radical and the conservative forces of the country, and the conservative forces won. The election day, the 3d of November, saw more than fourteen million votes cast, and of these more than six and a half million were cast

for Mr. Bryan. Mr. McKinley received 7,111,607. Every State north of the
Ohio and the Potomac and east of the Mississippi gave its electoral votes
to the Republican candidate, some of them, like New York and New Jersey,
by unprecedented majorities. West of the Mississippi the Republicans carried Minnesota, Iowa, North Dakota, Oregon, and California, and south of
the Ohio and Potomac West Virginia and Kentucky. Even in North Carolina
and Tennessee the Republican vote leaped up in significant strength. Nowhere did the tide of Democratic votes run as the tide of Republican votes
ran in the States where opinion rallied strong to maintain the established
foundations of business. Republican majorities were returned again, also,
to both houses of Congress; and no one could doubt the verdict of the
country.

It was a singular thing how the excitement subsided when the sharp contest was over and the result known. Never before, perhaps, had there been
occasion to witness so noteworthy an illustration of the peaceable fruits of
untrammelled self-government, the cheerful, immediate, hearty acquiescence of a self-governing people in the processes of its own political life.
Not a tone of revolt was to be heard. The defeated party was content to
await another election and abide by the slow processes of argument and
conviction, and affairs went forward almost as if with a sense of relief on
both sides that the fight had been fought out and settled. Business took
heart again. Whatever might be said for or against the free coinage of the
two money metals at a ratio which was not the actual ratio of their real
relative values, definite assurance as to the policy to be pursued was an
indispensable prerequisite to the confident carrying forward of business
enterprises; and the verdict of the country had at last been given so decisively
that capitalists need, it seemed, have no uneasy misgivings even with regard
to the next election, when another four years should have gone by. . . .

Obviously the business world, the whole world of industry, was in
process of revolution. America, in particular, had come to the crisis and
turning point of her development. Until now she had been struggling to
release and organize her resources, to win her true economic place in the
world. Hitherto she had been always a debtor nation, her instruments of
industry making and to be made, her means of transportation, the vast
systems of steel highways which were to connect her fields and factories
with the markets of the world, as yet only in course of construction. At the
close of the civil war there were but thirty-five thousand miles of railway
upon all the vast spaces of the continent; there were one hundred and
fifty thousand more to add before its products and manufactures could be
handled freely in the world's exchanges, and for that vast increase foreign
as well as domestic capital had to be borrowed by the hundreds of millions.
Except what her fields produced, the country had as yet but little with
which to pay the interest and the capital of her debts: her fields were in
some sense the granary of the world. As agricultural prices fell it required

more and more food stuffs to pay her balances. In those fatal years of depression, 1893-1896, when business threatened to stand still because of the state of the currency and the crops fetched little more than would pay for their carriage, it was necessary to pay huge foreign balances in coin, and $87,000,000 in gold had had to be shipped over sea to the country's creditors in a single twelvemonth (1893). It was that extraordinary drain that made Mr. Cleveland's task next to impossible, to keep the Treasury reserve unexhausted and yet sustain the currency with gold payments. Not until the very year 1897, when the new Republican administration came in, did the crisis seem to be past. The country had at last built its railway and manufacturing systems up, had at last got ready to come out of its debts, command foreign markets with something more than its food stuffs, and make for itself a place of mastery. The turning point seemed to be marked by a notable transaction which took place the very month Mr. McKinley was inaugurated. In March, 1897, a great consolidation of iron-mining properties, foundries, steel mills, railroads, and steamship lines was effected which brought the country's chief supplies of iron, its chief steel producing plants, and its chief means of transporting steel products to the markets of the continent and of the world under a single organization and management, and reduced the cost of steel to a figure which put American steel factories beyond fear of competition. Steel had become the structural stuff of the modern world. Commanding its manufacture, America might command the economic fortunes of the world.

It was this new aspect of industry that disclosed the problems Republican and Democratic statesmen were to face for the coming generation. The concentration of capital was no new thing; but the new scale upon which it now began to be effected made it seem a thing novel and unexpected. The control now of this industry and again of that by small groups of capitalists, the growth of monopolies, the union of producers in each line of manufacture for the purpose of regulating prices to their own liking and profit, had been familiar circumstances, familiar signs of the times, these twenty years. The farmers had seen them and had formed their granges, their Alliances, their People's party to protect their own interests, by combination and political agitation, against the huge corporate powers that seemed to be gathering for the conquest of fortune. The industrial workingmen had seen them and had widened their organizations to meet the threat of subjection. The great strikes which followed one another, summer by summer, with such significant regularity were but the reflex of what was taking place in Wall Street, where huge combinations of capital were being arranged; at the manufacturing centres of the country, where the interests of producers were being pooled; at railway centres, where great systems of transportation were being drawn together under a single management. Mines, factories, railways, steamships were now, it appeared, to be brought into one corporate union as a single business. It was the culmination of the process, and seemed to put a new face on all that had gone before, on all that was to follow.

No wonder thoughtful men, as well as mere labor agitators, grew uneasy and looked about them to see what control the law could exercise. No doubt there was risk of deeply serious consequence in these vast aggregations of capital, these combinations of all the processes of a great industry in the hands of a single "Trust." No doubt they did give to a few men a control over the economic life of the country which they might abuse to the undoing of millions of men, it might even be to the permanent demoralization of society itself and of the government which was the instrument of society in the conduct of its united interests. The programmes of socialists and extremists proposed a remedy which was but a completion of the process: the virtual control of all industry and of all the means of transportation by the government itself. The leaders of the People's party, though they professed no socialistic doctrine, demanded government ownership of the railway and telegraph lines of the country, and their expressed desire with regard to the control of "Trusts" smacked of the extremest purposes of experiment in the field of legislation. The Interstate Commerce Act had been a beginning, a very conservative beginning, in the carrying out of what they wished to see undertaken. Neither the leaders of the Republican party nor the leaders of the Democratic party felt that such impulses of reform, such counsels of restriction could be entirely ignored; but neither party saw as yet the prudent and practicable lines of action. It would not do to check the processes which were adding so enormously to the economy and efficiency of the nation's productive work and promising to give her now at last that first place in wealth and power in the world which every son who loved her had predicted she should some day have; and yet it would not do to leave the economic liberty of the individual or the freedom and self-respect of the workingman unprotected.

In the spring of 1898, the United States, indignant over the treatment of Cuba, declared war on Spain; by August the war was over.

When the peace commissioners met at Paris in the autumn to frame their final agreements, the United States demanded and got all that their arms had touched: Cuba for the Cubans, Porto Rico and the Philippines, and the tiny island of Guam by the way, for their own possession. While the armies of the United States still lay with their lines drawn about Santiago (July 6, 1898) a joint resolution had passed the two houses of Congress which provided for the annexation of the Hawaiian Islands to the United States and consummated the revolutionary process to which Mr. Cleveland had for a little while given pause.

Of a sudden, as it seemed, and without premeditation, the United States had turned away from their longtime, deliberate absorption in their own domestic development, from the policy professed by every generation of their statesmen from the first, of separation from the embarrassing entanglements of foreign affairs; had given themselves a colonial empire, and taken their place of power in the field of international politics. No one who justly studied the courses of their life could reasonably wonder at the thing that had happened. No doubt it had come about without premeditation. There had been no thought, when this war came, of sweeping the Spanish islands of far-away seas within the sovereignty of the United States. But Spain's empire had proved a house of cards. When the American power touched it it fell to pieces. The government of Spain's colonies had everywhere failed and gone to hopeless decay. It would have been impossible, it would have been intolerable, to set it up again where it had collapsed. A quick instinct apprised American statesmen that they had come to a turning point in the progress of the nation, which would have disclosed itself in some other way if not in this, had the war for Cuba not made it plain. It had turned from developing its own resources to make conquest of the markets of the world. The great East was the market all the world coveted now, the market for which statesmen as well as merchants must plan and play their game of competition, the market to which diplomacy, and if need be power, must make an open way. The United States could not easily have dispensed with that foothold in the East which the possession of the Philippines so unexpectedly afforded them. The dream of their own poet had been fulfilled,

> "See, vast trackless spaces,
> As in a dream they change, they swiftly fill,
> Countless masses debouch upon them,
> They are now covered with people, arts, institutions."

The spaces of their own continent were occupied and reduced to the uses of civilization; they had no frontiers wherewith "to satisfy the feet of the young men": these new frontiers in the Indies and in the far Pacific came to them as if out of the very necessity of the new career set before them. It was significant how uncritically the people accepted the unlooked for consequences of the war, with what naïve enthusiasm they hailed the conquests of their fleets and armies. It was the experience of the Mexican war repeated. . . .

As the presidential election of 1900 approached the Democratic party made as if it would stake its fortunes on an opposition to the "imperial" policy of the administration; but it found that the thoughts of the people did not run with it, and turned the force of its effort again, as four years before, to the silver question. Mr. Bryan was again made its candidate, against Mr. McKinley, whom the Republicans had renominated as of course, and it once more demanded in its platform the free coinage of gold and silver at the ratio of sixteen to one. But no one feared now that it would win upon that issue. The hopes and energies of the country were turned in another direction, and Mr. McKinley was elected without difficulty.

It was interesting to note with how changed an aspect the government stood upon the threshold of a new century. The President seemed again to be always in the foreground, as if the first days of the government were to be repeated,—that first quarter of a century in which it was making good its right to exist and to act as an independent power among the nations of the world. Now, full grown, it was to take a place of leadership. The closing year of the century (1900) witnessed a great upheaval of revolutionary forces in China. Insurgent bands filled the country, the very capital itself, in protest against the presence and the growing influence of the foreigner, and particularly the occupation of new ports of entry by Russia, England, and Germany,—the dowager empress, the real mistress of the kingdom, acting as their ally. The very legations at Peking were invested in deadly siege by the insurgents; and America, with the other nations whose representatives were threatened, sent troops to their relief. America played her new part with conspicuous success. Her voice told for peace, conciliation, justice, and yet for a firm vindication of sovereign rights, at every turn of the difficult business; her troops were among the first to withdraw, to the Philippines, when their presence became unnecessary; the world noted a calm poise of judgment, a steady confidence as if of conscious power in the utterances of the American Secretary of State; the new functions of America in the East were plain enough for all to see. The old landmarks of politics within the United States themselves seemed, meanwhile, submerged. The southern States were readjusting their elective suffrage so as to exclude the illiterate negroes and so in part undo the mischief of reconstruction; and yet the rest of the country withheld its hand from interference. Sections began to draw together with a new understanding of one another. Parties were turning to the new days to come and to the common efforts of peace. Statesmen knew that it was to be their task to release the energies of the country for the great day of trade and of manufacture which was to change the face of the world: to ease the processes of labor, govern capital in the interest of those who were its indispensable servants in pushing the great industries of the country to their final value and perfection, and make law the instrument, not of justice merely, but also of social progress.

For Further Reading

THE BOOKS: William Hickling Prescott, *History of the Conquest of Mexico and History of the Conquest of Peru* (1843 and numerous reprintings, of which the most readily available is a Modern Library edition including the *History of the Conquest of Peru*); George Bancroft, *History of the United States of America from the Discovery of the Continent* (The Author's Last Revision, 6 vols., 1883); Brooks Adams, *The Emancipation of Massachusetts* (1887); Francis Parkman, *Montcalm and Wolfe* (2 vols., 1884); *A Half-Century of Conflict* (2 vols., 1892) and numerous subsequent reprintings; Samuel Eliot Morison, ed., *The Parkman Reader* (1955); John Fiske, *The Critical Period of American History* (1888) and many reprintings; Henry Adams, *History of the United States of America during the Administrations of Jefferson and Madison* (9 vols., 1889-1891; reprinted in 4 vols., with intro. by H. S. Commager, 1930; condensed by Herbert Agar under the title, *The Formative Years,* 1947; the first six chapters reprinted as a Great Seal paperback, *The United States in 1800;* Theodore Roosevelt, *The Naval War of 1812* (1882); John Bach McMaster, *A History of the People of the United States from the Revolution to the Civil War* (8 vols., 1883-1913); Henry Wilson, *History of the Rise and Fall of the Slave Power in America* (2 vols., 1872-1877); Jefferson Davis, *The Rise and Fall of the Confederate Government* (2 vols., 1881); James Ford Rhodes, *History of the United States from the Compromise of 1850* (7 vols., 1893-1906); Charles Francis and Henry Adams, *Chapters of Erie and Other Essays* (1871; the 1886 edition has been reprinted as a Great Seal paperback); Woodrow Wilson, *A History of the American People* (5 vols., 1902).

THE HISTORIANS: Michael Kraus, *The Writing of American History* (1953) is an invaluable survey; William T. Hutchinson, ed., *The Marcus W. Jernegan Essays in American Historiography* has chapters on many of the historians; David Levin's forthcoming study of Bancroft, Prescott, Motley, and Parkman promises to be especially illuminating. On Prescott, see Howard F. Cline and others, eds., *William Hickling Prescott, A Memorial* (1959); Samuel Eliot Morison, "Prescott; The American Thucydides," *Atlantic Monthly,* November, 1957; Thomas F. McGann, "Prescott's Conquests," *American Heritage,* June, 1957; C. Harvey Gardiner, *Prescott and His Publishers,* 1959. On Parkman, see Otis A. Pease, *Parkman's History; the Historian as Literary Artist* (1953); Mason Wade, *Francis Parkman, Heroic Historian* (1942) and Wade, ed., *The Journals of Francis Parkman* (2 vols., 1947). A biography of Bancroft is Russell B. Nye, *George Bancroft: Brahmin Rebel* (1944). On Henry Adams, see William H. Jordy, *Henry Adams: Scientific Historian* (1952); J. O. Levenson, *The Mind and Art of Henry Adams* (1957); Ernest Samuels, *The Young Henry Adams* (1948) and *Henry Adams: The Middle Years* (1958); and Elizabeth Stevenson, *Henry Adams* (1955). See also Arthur F. Beringause, *Brooks Adams* (1955); Eric F. Goldman; *John Bach McMaster, American Historian* (1943) and M. A. DeWolfe Howe, *James Ford Rhodes, American Historian* (1929).